DHARMA

SOURCES OF ANCIENT INDIAN LAW

Series Editor
PATRICK OLIVELLE

•

DHARMASŪTRAS

The Law Codes of
Āpastamba, Gautama, Baudhāyana, and Vasiṣṭha
PATRICK OLIVELLE

•

DHARMASŪTRA PARALLELS

Containing the Dharmasūtras of Āpastamba, Gautama, Baudhāyana, and Vasiṣṭha
PATRICK OLIVELLE

•

THE NĀRADASMṚTI

Critical Edition and Translation
RICHARD W. LARIVIERE

•

DHARMA

Studies in its Semantic, Cultural, and Religious History
PATRICK OLIVELLE

DHARMA

Studies in its Semantic, Cultural and Religious History

Edited by

PATRICK OLIVELLE

MOTILAL BANARSIDASS PUBLISHERS
PRIVATE LIMITED • DELHI

First Enlarged Indian Edition: Delhi, 2009
Reprint from the English language edition:
Journal of Indian Philosophy Volume 32/Numbers 5-6

ISBN: 978-81-208-3338-8

MOTILAL BANARSIDASS
41 U.A. Bungalow Road, Jawahar Nagar, Delhi 110 007
8 Mahalaxmi Chamber, 22 Bhulabhai Desai Road, Mumbai 400 026
203 Royapettah High Road, Mylapore, Chennai 600 004
236, 9th Main III Block, Jayanagar, Bangalore 560 011
Sanas Plaza, 1302 Baji Rao Road, Pune 411 002
8 Camac Street, Kolkata 700 017
Ashok Rajpath, Patna 800 004
Chowk, Varanasi 221 001

PRINTED IN INDIA
BY JAINENDRA PRAKASH JAIN AT SHRI JAINENDRA PRESS,
A-45 NARAINA, PHASE-I, NEW DELHI 110 028
AND PUBLISHED BY NARENDRA PRAKASH JAIN FOR
MOTILAL BANARSIDASS PUBLISHERS PRIVATE LIMITED,
BUNGALOW ROAD, DELHI 110 007

CONTENTS

PREFACE

Most generalizations about Indian culture and religion upon close scrutiny turn out to be inaccurate. An exception undoubtedly is the term *dharma*. This term and the notions underlying it clearly constitute the most central feature of Indian civilization down the centuries, irrespective of linguistic, sectarian, or regional differences. In a special way, the centrality of *dharma* to the understanding of Indian religions has been recognized by all scholars. One has only to pick up any introduction to Hinduism of Buddhism to note the prominence given to this term by the authors. Many note the broad semantic compass of the term, often commenting that the term is "untranslatable". One is also left with the impression that, following the orientālist image of the "unchanging" India, *dharma* has always been the central concept of Indian religion and culture, that this term has not been subject to evolution and change as its was appropriated, challenged, and sometimes even rejected by different groups and traditions.

Several years ago as I was working on an edition and translation of the *Dharmaśāstras* I began to inquire why a new genre of literature should emerge at a particular point in history devoted to the notion of *dharma*. The emergence of such new genres generally point to new social, economic, and religious circumstances. Invited to present a paper at a conference on "Asceticism and Power" at the School of Oriental and African Studies in London in 2001, I began to investigate the use of *dharma* in the Vedic corpus. To my surprise I found that the term was used sparingly in the texts of the middle and late vedic period; it certainly was not the central term in the religious vocabulary of the Vedas.[1]

The idea of a volume dedicated to investigating the history of *dharma* was born from those early investigations. I want to thank Phyllis Ganoff for enthusiastically embracing this idea and for devoting a volume of the *Journal of Indian Philosophy* for this purpose.

The seventeen papers included in this collection deal with many significant historical manifestations of the term *dharma;* they do not deal with all. There are many areas that are untouched by these contributions. Some have been the subject of other studies, such as the Pāli term *dhamma* studied by the Geigers.[2] Others, such as the medieval and modern appropriations of the term, especially within the language of religious nationalism (Hindutva) in India and in the vocabularies of contemporary Indian villages, remain to be studied. The selection of the topics covered in this volume was dictated, on the one hand, by the significant areas that demanded coverage and, on the other, by the availability of scholars who were willing and able to contribute.

Nevertheless, I hope that these studies by some of the leading scholars in the respective fields will both present a more nuanced picture of the semantic history of *dharma* by putting contours onto the flat landscape we have inherited and spur further studies of this concept so central for understanding the cultural history of the Indian subcontinent.

Finally, I want to thank Mr. N.P. Jain and Motilal Banarsidass for agreeing to publish this volume as a book so that it may be made available to a wider audience. In this book, two additional studies are included, John Taber's important article "The Significance of Kumārila's Philosophy" and Paul Hacker's "Dharma in Hinduism" because it deals with *dharma* within a broader perspective of its development with the Hindu tradition.

NOTES

[1] See my contribution to this volume for a more detailed study of this topic and my forthcoming article "Power of Words: The Ascetic Appropriation and the Semantic Evolution of dharma." In Peter Fluegel and Gustaaf Houtman, eds. Asceticism and Power in the Asian Context. London: Curzon.

[2] Geiger, M. & W. 1920 *Pāli Dhamma vornehmlich in der kanonischen Literatur.* Abhandlungen der Bayerischen Akademie der Wissenschaften, Phil-philologische und historische Klasse, xxxi Band, 1. Abhandlung. Munich.

PAUL HORSCH

FROM CREATION MYTH TO WORLD LAW: THE EARLY HISTORY OF *DHARMA**

Translated by Jarrod L. Whitaker

INTRODUCTION

From early on the special importance of Indian mythology was perceived in its great antiquity and its extraordinary continuity, so that its ideas and gods can be observed *in statu nascendi* and its stages of development over millennia can be traced up to the present. We forthwith contrasted the Indo-Iranian and in some cases even the Indo-Germanic antiquity to the hypothesis of origins. Instead of understanding the Vedic pantheon in the process of becoming, now it appeared as a petrified fossil of a process, which was difficult to research and partly prehistoric. The objection, however, applies to merely a part of the mythical forms and concepts, while others were created and formed in the early Vedic period, which is often clearly demonstrable on the basis of comparative linguistics. Thus we are in a position to penetrate, as it were, into the workshop of the myth-making spirit and to observe its evolution. This should cast light on the regular stages that human thought in general, and the Indian genius in particular, has passed through. But only numerous, careful examinations of individual cases will gradually bring us closer to this goal. To this end, we choose the concept *dhárma(n)*, because firstly it is of Indo-Aryan origin; secondly it occupies a central – if not to say the most comprehensive and most fundamental – position in India's intellectual history, and thirdly it can be analyzed in the most varied phases and trends of its development.[1a]

---

* This paper was originally published as 'Vom Schöpfungsmythos zum Weltgesetz', in *Asiatische Studien: Zeitschrift der Schweizerischen Gesellschaft für Asiankunde*, vol. 21 (Francke: 1967): 31–61.

THE MYTHICAL ORIGIN OF *DHÁRMAN*

The original meaning of the term is determined etymologically: from the root *dhṛ-*, 'to hold [*halten*]', 'to support [*stützen*]', an action noun [*Nomen actionis*] *dhárman*, 'hold', 'support', is formed when it is neuter, and an agent noun [*Nomen agentis*] *dharmán*, 'supporter', when it is masculine.[1b] Although the verb is found in other Indo-Germanic languages, they lack the exact equivalent of the substantive,[2] so that the concept possesses a specific Indian character from the very beginning. The frequent use of the verb already in the Ṛgveda permits a precise analysis of its principal function and its objects. Its range of application corresponds to all the nuances of 'to hold [*halten*]', 'to keep [*behalten*]', 'to maintain [*erhalten*]', and 'to hold fast [*festhalten*]'. Since it is a question of hymns to gods, the basic sense of the root principally expresses a mythical action. Thus it is said of various gods that they supported (*dhṛ-*) and kept apart (*vidhṛ-*) the earth, the sky [*Himmel*], all worlds, and all creatures. Some examples shall illustrate this:

RV 8.41.10:

sá dhā́ma pūrvyám mame
yá skambhéna ví ródasī
ajó ná dyā́m ádhārayat ...

"He (Varuṇa) measured out the first creation, who (held) apart both worlds with a pillar and like the billy-goat supported the sky [*Himmel*]."

Similarly it is said of Indra:

8.15.2:

yásya dvibárhaso bṛhát
sáho dādhā́ra ródasī |
girī́m̐r ájrām̐ apáḥ svàr vṛṣatvanā́ ||

"The great power of he who is twice as strong holds both worlds, the mountains, plains, waters, and the sun through his bull-like force."

Before he performed this cosmogonic act, everything was in chaotic disorder – insecure, unstable, and shaky:

10.44.8:

girī́m̐r ájrān réjamānām̐ adhārayad
dyaúḥ krandad antárikṣāṇi kopayat |
samīciné dhiṣáṇe ví ṣkabhāyati

"He stabilized the quaking mountains and plains. The sky roared (and) shook the airy spaces. He forces apart the bowls which were joined together (sky and earth)."

Originally the sky and earth, as the first parents, lay firmly embracing one another, until Indra separated them and thereby created the cosmos – the world order. At the same time, a mysterious magic power aided him:

2.17.5:
ádhārayat pṛthivī́ṃ viśvádhāyasam
ástabhnān māyáyā dyā́m avasrásaḥ ||

"He held fast the all-nourishing earth. With the power of magic, he supported the sky, lest it fall from on high."[3]

These few examples already refer clearly to a fundamental myth about the creation of the world. (1) Sky and earth are separated, pressed apart. (2) The firmament, sun, and stars are 'supported', so that they do not fall down. (3) The earth, with mountains, rivers, and plains, is made firm, because it was unstable at the dawn of time. (4) This creative action, putting the world in order, is attributed to one of the higher gods – mainly Indra. (5) In this way, the cosmos first comes into being, the legitimate order, light and expanse, which are still constantly threatened by the powers of chaos, darkness, and constriction. Therefore the mythical act must constantly be re-enacted anew through hymns of praise to the gods and magical rites.

MYTHOLOGICAL PARALLELS

We encounter here a mythological motif, the meaning of which is further emphasized by manifold ethnological parallels. Among them, the Iranian [parallels] are especially important, because the same root (*dar-* = *dhṛ-*) is employed. Thus in Yasna 44.4 Zarathustra addresses the question to Ahura Mazda: "Who maintains the earth below and keeps the structure of the sky from falling down? Who preserves water and plants?"[4] In this monotheistic system, it is Ahura Mazda – related to the Indian Asura Varuṇa – who performed this act. According to Yašt 13.2.4-9, he supports the sky, the mythical river Arədvī, the broad earth and the high mountains, whereby he is assisted by the Fravartis.[5] According to Bundahišn 71.9, 72.3, the firmament and earth are supported by Ahura Mazda without a base of any kind, while on the other hand the mountain Harburz, which extends around the earth and is fixed to the sky, carries out this function.[6]

The myth can even be traced back into the older Indo-Germanic period, for which the Greeks in particular give evidence. According to the Orphic interpretation, sky and earth constitute the two halves of the world egg.[7] Or this primeval parental couple lay close together in the beginning, however through a divine offspring they were forced apart and borne up. The prototype for this was seen in Gaia and Uranos, who was castrated by the son, Kronos. Atlas also belongs here, who was already designated by the etymology as bearer or supporter.[8] The primeval giant Upelluri, who bears the ocean, sky, and earth, corresponds to him in the Hurrian-Hittite Kumarbi epic.[9]

The motif is not, however, restricted to the Indo-German language family, but rather is found in the most diverse races of the world, in advanced civilizations as well as among primitive peoples. Thus in Egypt, for example, it is the god of the air, Schu, who separates the sky goddess Nut, often represented as a cow, from the earth god Geb – a strange inversion of the sexes. A similar role was ascribed to the Babylonian Marduk, who symbolizes the rising sun, because the separation of the chaotic primordial darkness is the world-ordering act of the sun. The formula is often found among the ancient Chinese: "As sky and earth were not yet separated.[10]" The notion is no less widespread among primitive tribes, especially those of the Polynesian area, as in the Maori myth of Rangi and Papa, who were pulled apart by one of their children.[11] The explanation of the myth is very diverse: overcoming darkness, the creation of paradise, banishment of the sky, and increasing the possibilities for cultivation, just as generally the support of the sky is connected with the extension and stabilization of the earth.[12] Nevertheless in India it is essentially a question of the maintenance of the world order: the collapse of the cosmos and with that the return to chaos should be prevented. For this reason the original act is at the same time important for the creation of the world: by this act order, lawfulness, permanence were created, light and fertility were gained for humanity.

DHÁRMAN IN THE COSMIC SENSE

The term *dhárman* has caused exceptional difficulties for modern commentators and translators. While Graßmann in *Wörterbuch zum R̥gveda* identifies seven different meanings, Geldner in his translation of the R̥gveda employs for the 62 instances no fewer than 20 renderings, such as 'law', 'order', 'duty', 'custom', 'quality', 'classification', 'adjudication', 'model', etc. In comparison with these arbitrary approaches, Bergaigne attempted to trace back the concept to its original meaning and consistently rendered it by 'rule [*la loi*]', 'law', whereby he nevertheless went to the opposite extreme, because he interprets *ṛta, dhāman, vrata* by 'law' as well. In this process, as we will see shortly, the concept was comprehended far too abstractly for this period and thereby too vaguely. It will be demonstrated in the following how the root meaning survived fully and completely in the noun, thus this fundamentally expresses 'to (up) hold [*Halten*]', or 'to support [*Stützen*]'. This basic meaning is revealed most clearly precisely in the cosmological myth. In all these cases *dhárman* is to be rendered by 'support' or '(up) hold [*Halt*]', as in RV 6.70.1:

dyā́vāpṛthivī́ váruṇasya dhármaṇā
víṣkabhite ajáre bhū́riretasā ||

"Sky and earth, which do not age, and are rich in semen, were forced apart by Varuṇa's support [*Stütze*]."

This calls to mind 4.42.3d, where Varuṇa proudly proclaims that he set in motion and supported both worlds (i.e. sky and earth), and he granted support [*Halt*] to them: *sám airayaṃ ródasī dhāráyaṃ ca. Dhárman* expresses the function of the verb, whereby the suffix *-man* emphasizes the active element, which is why the term is often used in the instrumental as the means by which an action is effected. At the same time the concept already begins to detach itself from God or at least begins to become independent. It is the 'supporting, hold- [*Halt*] giving power', through which Varuṇa accomplishes his action of making the cosmos stable. We must understand *dhárman* here preferably in a dynamic functional sense, rather than as a concretely reified support.

Similarly *Atharvaveda* 12.1.17b extols "the firm, wide earth, which is borne up by the supporting power [*Stützkraft*]" (*dhruvā́m bhū́mim pṛthivī́ṃ dhármaṇā dhṛtā́m*), while nothing more is said concerning from which mythical being the 'support' [*Stützen*] emanates. Thus the sun god changes *dhármaṇā*, which means by virtue of that mysterious obscure support-bestowing force, otherwise he would fall down.[13] Or there is mention of the 'supporting hold of the sky' (*divó dhárman dharúṇe*, RV 5.15.2c), on which the gods sit.

In the realm of cosmology RV 1.22.18 (= AV 7.26.5) also indicates:

trī́ṇi padā́ vi cakrame
víṣṇur gopā́ ádābhyaḥ |
áto dhármāṇi dhāráyan ||

"He strode out, three strides; Viṣṇu, the infallible guardian, firmly holding the supports from there."

The question presents itself; from where did Viṣṇu erect the supports. The commentary refers *átaḥ* (AV: *ítaḥ*) to the three footsteps, Geldner, however, refers to the sky, the highest of them, or rather to the sun, which is identified with it, nonetheless in 20c Viṣṇu's uppermost step (*paramám padám*) is after all called 'the eye, as though spread out over the sky".[14] This calls to mind the highest sky [*Himmel*], which however was supposed to lie beyond the visible firmament, since in 4.42.4b Varuṇa boasts: "I supported the (visible) sky on the seat of Ṛta."[15] From the uppermost point, from the zenith, the ridge of the Vedic world-structure, Viṣṇu holds firmly the *dhármāṇi*, the fundamental supports, which bestow support and stability on all the parts of the universe. Support [*Stützen*] from above seems absurd to us, however it is characteristic for the mythical thinking of those seers, because the divine powers are efficacious just from the sky above, so that it is as though the cosmos has been turned upside down.[16]

Let us take a look at *ví-dharman*, literally 'support apart'. Thus Indra by the power of his *dhárman* 'held apart' the plants and rivers, spread out across the field.[17] The cosmological aspect of this separating power comes to the forefront there, where it divides sky and earth, that is to say, understood concretely as 'intermediate realm', as air-space/atmosphere, as when it is said of the god Savitṛ, who is related to the sun, that he is "in the intermediate realm of space'.[18] From that the meaning 'spreading out', 'broad expansion' can be easily explained.[19]

DHÁRMAN IN THE RITUAL SENSE

Fundamental to the Vedic worldview is the division of the entire world into two externally different, yet internally connected, even magically, identical powers: the cosmic and the ritual. The first ones are controlled by the gods, who created the world order through their mythical deeds. The second ones are controlled by the priests, who not only imitate those cosmic actions through the rituals, but re-enact them in the truest sense of the word. Corresponding to this basic position, the concept *dhárman* was likewise carried over to the cultic level.

RV 1.164.50ab is informative, in which the sacrifice itself is understood as the original creative act:

yajñéna yajñám ayajanta devā́s
tā́ni dhármāṇi prathamā́ny āsan |

"The gods made one sacrifice after another. These were the first supports."[20]

The idea is explained in the hymn about the creation of the sacrifice at 10.130.6: "The human seers, our fathers, were guided by (this sacrifice), when the sacrifice was created in the time long ago. With my mind's eye I believe I see those who first offered this sacrifice."[21] The first *dhármāṇi* were equated with the fundamental, creative powers. They are the 'ritual supports', which bring about the sacred cosmic order. Therefore the Brahmanic priests repeat the mythical divine prototype of the cosmogony in the cultic ceremonies. Hence it is said that the fire god Agni is set aflame in accordance with the first *dhármāṇi*, that is to say the primordial, world-supporting, cosmos-preserving powers.[22] Or: "You, Expert, sacrifice in accordance with (Agni's) support, and perform for us the sacrificial act with the summons of the gods."[23] "When you are set afire, O Agni, you who win thousands (of gifts), thus you aid the supports, as the praiseworthy messenger of the gods."[24]

An analogous function is assigned to the cult god Soma, the personified, holy intoxicating sacrificial drink. Soma, as the bull, erected, that is to say created, the supports,[25] because he took part in the creation of the world (9.96.5), begot the gods (9.42.4c), forced apart both worlds (*ví yás tastámbha ródasī* 9.101.15b), separated and secured the sky and earth (*dyā́vāpṛthivī ví ṣkabhāyat* 6.44.24a), supported heaven (*dhartā́ diváḥ* 9.76.1a) and sustained the earth (*viṣṭambhó divó dharúṇaḥ pṛthivyā́ḥ* 9.89.6a). Here we encounter all the basic forms of the well-known cosmogonic myth. Correspondingly Soma has his *dhárman*, which enables him to 'support' [*halten*] himself, at the various levels of the universe. Hence he rises up on the wind through the power of *dhárman*;[26] which confers on him 'support [*Halt*]' for the ascent into heaven through the vast intermediate space. The wind god Vāyu himself possesses the same force, because through his 'supporting power' he rules over the entire world.[27] Soma's cosmological function is revealed most clearly when it is said, "sky and earth (exist) through his supports" (*dyaús ca yásya pṛthivī́ ca dhármabhiḥ* 9.86.9b).

It is said of the juices of Soma that they flow along on the 'prop [*Halt*]', the 'support [*Stütze*]' of the *ṛtá*, the cosmic-cultic truth and order,[28] whereby *dhárman* stands parallel to *pathā́* = 'path', which emphasizes the concrete meaning of the former. The 'support of R̥ta' is more precisely defined as the place where Soma generates the sun, namely in the highest heaven.[29] Thus Soma is situated upon this support [*Halt*], but at the same time 'bears' R̥ta,[30] a functional ambivalence that is common in the Vedic realm. Since on the other hand specifically Varuṇa is most closely connected with R̥ta, Soma flows through the power of Varuṇa's and Mitra's *dhárman* to the great R̥ta,[31] whereby it is already to be noted here that the more recent concept of *dhárma* will take over from the older idea of *r̥tá*, which is why the latter term becomes obsolete early on.

DHÁRMAN IN THE ETHICAL-SOCIAL SENSE

The rendering 'support [*Stütze*]' or 'hold [*Halt*]' always produced an adequate sense of *dhárman* on the cosmic and ritual level. A profound change of meaning nevertheless occurs when the term is transferred to the ethical or purely human level, whereby the originally concrete, mythical notion is generalized and hence turned into an abstract expression. The supports of worlds and cultic ceremonies secure for the cosmos 'hold [*Halt*]' and stability, regularity and permanence: *dhárman* becomes the foundation of order and regularity as such, thus becomes a general 'law [*Gesetz*]', to which human beings must conform. It is precisely within the ethical realm that the German translation as 'law [*Gesetz*]' has imposed itself from the time of the R̥gveda. All the semantic shades of meaning since then can be derived from this central meaning.

This universal ethical sense of *dhárman* is evident in RV 7.89.5:

yát kíṃ cedáṃ Varuṇa daívye jáne
'bhidrohám manuṣyā́s cárāmasi |
ácittī yát táva dhármā yuyopimá
mā́ nas tásmād énaso deva rīriṣaḥ ||

"Whatever sinful act we mortals commit here against the godly people, O Varuṇa, if we have violated your laws out of ignorance, may you not bring us to harm on account of these sins, O god."[32]

5.63.7 affords us an excellent insight into the early Vedic conception of the world, which is thoroughly permeated by the cosmic, cultic and ethical levels:

dhármaṇā Mitrāvaruṇā vipaścitā
vratā́ rakṣethe ásurasya māyáyā |
r̥téna víśvam bhúvanaṃ ví rājathaḥ
sū́ryam ā́ dhattho diví cítryaṃ rátham ||

"You, eloquent Mitra and Varuṇa, protect the commandments (or: the vows) through the law, with the magical power of the Asura. By means of the (cosmic) truth you rule over the entire world. You set the sun in heaven as a radiant chariot."[32]

ṚTÁ AND MĀYĀ́

The parallelism between *dhárman* and *ṛtá* is remarkable: the gods protect the commandments with the 'law', they rule over the world with the 'truth', *ṛtá* being assigned to the cosmic territory, *dhárman*, however, to the moral social sphere. Here is not the place to consider the fundamental argument about the meaning of *ṛtá* – 'truth' or '(cosmic) order' – because on the one hand, it must first be established clearly what is actually understood by 'truth' in the mythical sense. Such an investigation, which should be undertaken elsewhere, will undoubtedly lead to a new definition and differentiation of the concept. On the other hand, we are convinced that *ṛtá* must be distinguished from *satyá* = 'truth', as this still happens particularly in the Brāhmaṇa period.[34] It is the generalization of *dhárman* into 'law', which absorbed the notion of a comprehensive order, foundation and image of eternal 'truth', and with that displaced the older term.

It might appear surprising that in Pāda b of the verse cited, *māyā́*, = 'magical power' is used in the instrumental, analogously to *dhárman* and *ṛtá,* and therefore still preserves an absolutely positive meaning according to the context, just as the *ásura* to which it is ascribed, perhaps the god Varuṇa, is in any case an exalted deity.[35] Only gradually will a total change of meaning take place: as the *ásuras* are demonized into enemies of the gods,[36] *māyā́* becomes an unpredictable force – for example, Indra's ability to transform – thus to a 'counter-law', a deception, indeed ultimately to the world-illusion, as the adversary of the world law.[37] Interestingly *māyā́* also is connected with the cosmogonic myth: *mā-* = 'to measure', 'to determine by measuring', 'to construct', 'to create', 'to form', applies to the world-creating activity of the gods[38] and indicates an architectonic basic philosophy, as do 'to bear', 'to hold' and 'to support' (*dhṛ-*). Incidentally, *ṛtá* also seems to us to derive from the cosmic sphere: *ṛtá*, 'course' is produced from *ṛ-* = 'to go', especially the regular change of meteorological and astronomical events, furthermore the regularity and periodicity of all natural phenomena, like the flow of rivers or the perpetual return of the seasons, the alternation of day and night, etc.[39]

LAW, RIGHT AND DUTY

Clearly *dhárman* is assigned to the human level in all places where the duty to reproduce is involved, thus in 6.70.3c: "In accordance with the law (*dhármaṇas pári*) he (the mortal) propagates himself through offspring."[40] Etymologically, the expression could be translated with greater precision as: "For the sake of (firm) support [*Halt*] (in the world)", since through offspring one gains on the one hand a 'support [*Stütze*]' in this life and on the other hand brings about the 'preservation' of the lineage. Here the concept already moves in the realm of the later Dharma literature. The social law becomes the 'duty' of the individual person. Later specific 'rights' are added to the 'duties' which correspond to the castes. Nevertheless, in the earliest era, from the ethical standpoint, *dhárman* always implies a 'commandment', an obligation, like the procreation of male offspring. Already AV 12.1.45 calls to the earth, "which bears people in many places, each according to its fixed domicile, with different languages and various laws (*nā́nādharmāṇam*)."[41] The universal order is already split up into a plurality of 'customs', 'duties', etc. Hence at the wedding celebration, the man in AV 14.1.51cd says to his bride: "You are the wife by virtue of the law (*dhármaṇā*), I (am) your household head."[42]

The most important innovation of the Atharvaveda consists of the transformation of the suffix *-man* to an *a*-stem: *dhármaḥ*. In AV 18.3.1c it is said of the widow that she lies beside her husband, 'obeying an ancient law (*dhármam purāṇám*)', from which the meaning 'custom', 'tradition' results at the same time. From this time on, *dhárman* is seldom used any more, mostly in compound.[43] Thus the question arises of the reason for the morphological alteration. Since the attempts to explain it in linguistic terms are not completely satisfactory,[44] a semantic interpretation may be ventured. As a matter of fact, it is remarkable that this alteration takes place parallel and simultaneously with the change in meaning. While originally the suffix *-man* emphasized just the function of the root meaning – '(to) hold [*Halten*]', '(to) support [*Stützen*]', and '(to) bear [*Tragen*]' – this active, concrete meaning already changed in the R̥gveda to the general, abstract concept 'law'. In the Atharvaveda *dhárman* was separated even more emphatically from the cosmic-ritual level, in so far as it was transferred to the juridical-ethical realm, and therefore the abstractly generalizing *a*-stem replaced the action noun [*Nomen actionis*], whereby it cannot be denied that at the same time linguistic factors could have been involved in the reformation.

DHARMÁN, DHARTŔ̥, DHARÚṆA

The agent noun [*Nomen agentis*] *dharmán* = 'bearer', 'supporter', is used in the R̥gveda only in four places,[45] then to be altogether eliminated immediately, which can be explained by the fact that the much more frequent *dhartṛ́* is used synonymously in this period. The cosmological notion also comes into the foreground here, as when Mitra and Varuṇa are described as 'the bearers of the bright and earthly realm'[46], or Soma and other gods are called 'the bearers, the supporters of heaven' (*dhartā́ diváḥ*),[47] which corresponds to the use of the verb. At the actual ethical level the term is not used.[48] It remains for the most part restricted to the oldest Vedic period, which probably is connected with the early fading away of the cosmogonic myth.

Dharúṇa constitutes an additional derivation from *dhṛ-*, literally 'that which holds, bears or supports', hence 'holding', 'bearing' as adjective, 'bearer', 'supporter' and 'prop [*Halt*]', 'support' as substantive. The synonymy of terms dealt with up to this point derives from this, except that *dharúṇa* always preserves the concrete sense, thus, unlike *dhárman*, it did not develop into the abstract concept 'law'. The fundamental philosophy is also based here on the myth of the creation of the cosmos through the 'lifting apart', 'supporting' and 'stabilizing' of its different spheres, as when Soma is called 'the supporting separator of heaven' (*viṣṭambhó dharúṇo diváḥ*) or its 'supporting pillar' (*divó yá skambhó dharúṇaḥ*).[49] 1.56.5ab expresses these ideas especially clearly:

ví yát tiró dharúṇam ácyutaṃ rájó
'tiṣṭhipo divā́ ā́tāsu barháṇā |

"When you (Indra) expanded the unshakable prop [*Halt*], with power you set the atmosphere within the framework of Heaven."[50]

The 'unshakable prop' refers probably here to the earth as the 'foundation' of the cosmos, and thereby to the mythological motif of the expansion and stabilization of the earth, which is often ascribed to Indra.[51] Related to the idea of the pillars of heaven is the notion of the *skambhá*, of the 'world pillar' as *axis mundi*, originally a purely cosmological image, which in the two Skambha hymns of the Atharvaveda was nonetheless associated with the creation of the world, and finally, as the cosmic hypostasis, was equated with the absolute world principle, *bráhman*.[52]

Dharúṇa is also represented on the ritual level,[53] nevertheless is completely absent from the ethical realm. The development of the term in the area of literary history takes its course remarkably uniformly: the 33 instances in the Ṛgveda stand in contrast with only 7 in the Atharvaveda. The remaining Saṃhitās yield an analogous picture of decline, while the voluminous mass of the Brāhmaṇas reduces the usage to 22 passages, which furthermore are almost exclusively mantra quotations. In the Upaniṣads, the word is already obsolete.

RESULTS

The basis for this development probably lies anchored in the transformation in the history of ideas: the withdrawal of the mythical-ritualistic basic notion of 'prop [*Halt*]' of the cosmos, the foundation of the earth, etc. In contrast, the concept of *dhárma*(*n*) separated itself from its original world-creation associations and thereby was elevated to world law. Before we pursue its further fate, a brief review should provide clarity about the area covered so far.

1. The cosmogonic myth occurs at the beginning, according to which one of the Vedic gods separated, pressed apart and 'supported' (*dhṛ-*) sky and earth. Through this support and provision of a prop [*Haltverleihen*] a 'cosmos', an order, was first produced out of the dark, chaotic uniformity.
2. This cosmic act was nominalized to the 'holding [*Halten*]' and 'supporting' (*dhárman*) of a god, often as his magical power, for the most part concretely as a definite 'prop [*Halt*]', for example, the firmament or the Soma strainer, at the ritual level.
3. *Dhárman* separates itself gradually from the god, changes into an independent, impersonal force, which will soon stand over the gods. *Ṛtá* experienced a similar development.[54]
4. The progressive process of abstraction is crucial for the concept of *dhárman*, which entails the gradual disappearancc of the concrete notion of a cosmic-cultic 'support [*Halt*]'. The older concept of a cosmic order and truth – *ṛtá* – was absorbed by this generalization.[55]
5. The final step consisted in the transfer of *dhárman* to the human, ethical sphere. Now the concept indicates not only what grants to the cosmos 'support [*Halt*]', stability, permanence and regularity, but rather at the same time the commandments, duties, and customs of people, that is to say the maintenance [*Halt*] of the social order as such. The world law now comprises all realms: the cosmic, ritual and ethical-juridical. In Hinduism they will still preserve their connection, which is based in the mythic.

DHARMA IN THE BRĀHMANAS

The remaining Samhitās offer no noteworthy innovations from our standpoint. Such innovations first surface in the Brāhmaṇas, among which the most important will be emphasized here. The form *dharma* is now completely accepted, even preserving traces of its cosmological origin in some cases, as when Śatapatha Brāhmaṇa 14.2.2.29 still refers to the sun as 'prop [*Halt*]', though it is longer because it supports the firmament, but rather grants to creatures 'maintenance [*Halt*]' – it 'maintains [*erhält*]': "Truly, that one, who burns yonder, is the maintenance [*Halt*], since he maintains [*erhält*] this universe (or: everything here), through him this universe is maintained."[56] Or it is said that: "The waters are indeed the maintenance [*Halt*] (or the law),"[57] which traces back to the notion that the earth rests on the primordial waters, and is borne and supported [*gehalten*] by them.[58] It is interesting now to trace how the mythical content is carried over and is reinterpreted to the more recent rational-abstract meaning. "The waters are truly Dharma, because when the waters come to this world (i.e., when it rains), everything just happens here according to the Dharma. However when it does not rain the stronger overcome the weaker, since the waters are the Dharma."[59] Obviously *dharma* (=waters) is here no longer to be understood as foundation and 'support' of the earth, but rather as 'law', as 'right', since the waters, that is to say the rain, determine prosperity and fecundity. On the other hand, it depends on it whether the law is complied with or not: In times of famine, anarchy prevails, because the 'right' of the stronger is in force.

Despite the association with natural phenomena, *dharma* is thus used in the ethical-juridical sense. Jaiminīya Brāhmaṇa 3.231, where *dharman* or *vidharman* denotes a special melody (*sāman*), expresses the still magical connection to the monarchy. "Among these there is the *dharman* (*-sāman*). With the *dharman* (*-sāman*) the gods truly appropriated for themselves the prop [*Halt*] of the Asuras. With the *vidharman* (*-sāman*) they gave them another (i.e., false) prop [*Halt*] and destroyed (them). Likewise he who knows thus seizes for himself the prop [*Halt*] of his loathing rival with the *dharman* (*-sāman*); likewise he gives him with the *vidharman* (*-sāman*) another prop [*Halt*] and destroys (him). Moreover, the prop [*Halt*] is indeed wealth – truly the prop [*Halt*] is the kingdom. Through the prop [*Halt*] (i.e., through the kingdom or sovereign authority), the king is truly a prop [*Halt*]. He becomes the prop [*Halt*] for his subjects (read: *dharmas svānām*), his subjects come to him, he supports them namely with the *dharman* (-*sāman*)."[60] The connection between 'prop [*Halt*]' and 'law' is made still more explicit in the following remark from the same excerpt: "Truly the kings have another prop [*Halt*]. They truly do not share the prop [*Halt*] with the other people (read: °*yaiḥ sadharmāṇaḥ*)",[61] which probably means that kings possess their own morality and therefore are not subject to the laws of the land.

The original meaning has completely faded in Taittirīya Brāhmaṇa 2.5.7.2: "By virtue of the law Agni (the god of fire) is the eater of food; by virtue of the law Mr̥tyu (the god of death) is the lord of food", where *dharma* probably refers to internal conformity to law – the self-nature of the deities in question – it lies after all in Agni's nature to devour the sacrificial food.

The most momentous innovation occurs at the end of this period in the Śatapatha Brāhmaṇa 11.5.7.1. According to it, whoever studies and learns the Veda, obtains ten benefits, among others a focused mind, peaceful sleep, mastery of the senses, increasing knowledge and fame. The increasing knowledge, on the other hand, "generates for the Brahman four *dharmas*, namely true Brahmanhood, appropriate way of living, fame, and maturity in the world (i.e., religious influence in the (social) environment). The maturing world rewards the Brahman with four *dharmas*; with the offering of respect, with gifts, with the protection of his property and his life."[62] In the former case, the *dharmas* refer to the moral characteristics of the Brahman. In the latter, they refer to the rights and privileges to which he is entitled in return. Here the universal abstract law is therefore split up into a plurality of concrete factors, like fame, offering respect, devout behaviour, which are all called *dharmas*. This semantic process is fundamental for an appreciation of the Buddhist use of the word.

DHARMA IN THE UPANIṢADS AND IN HINDUISM

In the Upaniṣads, the mythically cosmological ideas still reverberate, as when *vāyu-prāṇa* (wind-breath) is praised as a supporting, stabilizing power, transferred here to the micro-cosmos (BĀU 1.5.23). Correspondingly, breath is defined in BĀU 2.2.1 as a sacrificial post or world pillar. Nevertheless the idea of the permanence and universality of the law comes to the foreground, which is simultaneously valid for all the events in nature and for the individual. Thus *dharma* as 'honey of all creatures' is the absolute hypostasis (BĀU 2.5.11), center and foundation (*pratiṣṭhā*) of the whole world (*Mahānārāyaṇa* U 22.1).

BĀU 1.4.14 expresses the sociological-legal aspect of our concept, according to which the ancient original *brahman* created a still better form, the law, after the four castes. "The law (*dharma*) is the ruling power (*kṣatra*) of the ruling power. The weaker also overpowers the stronger by the law, as by means of the king." What is essential here is the acknowledgement of the law's authority in the sense of a universally binding system of laws, which no longer, as in the Brāhmaṇa, is dependent on the rain or fertility or not binding for kings at all.

With this development in the history of ideas it is not surprising that *dharma* is equated with 'truth' (*satya*). "Truly the law is the truth; that is why it is said of one who speaks the truth that he speaks in accordance with the law, and of one who speaks in accordance with the law that he speaks the truth" (BĀU 1.4.14). Hence the universal maxim holds true: "Speak the truth, conduct yourself according to the law" (*satyaṃ vada dharmaṃ cara*, TaittirīyaU 11.11). We have already indicated that *ṛtá* in the Ṛgveda and Atharvaveda exhibits an analogous relationship with the concept of truth, which, however, implies no absolute synonymy.

When complied with, the 'law' or 'right [*Recht*]' becomes a 'virtue', 'ethical merit,"[63] and when abstractly comprehended, a 'doctrine', as for example in Kaṭha Upaniṣad 1.21, where the god of death alludes to the complicated *ātman*-doctrine. Here the term was usually misunderstood by renderings in the alleged Buddhist sense of 'thing', 'object', etc. This holds true to a still greater extent for stanza 4.14, which according to some scholars ought to refer to the Buddhist Dharma theory.[64] However, the 'key word' *pṛthag-dharma* has nothing to do with the doctrine of the Sarvāstivādins, but rather refers to the multiplicity of the laws in contrast to the unity of *ātman*.[65] We have recently dealt with this problem at length in an article.[66]

The concept thereby passed through the most significant stages of its development, which remain decisive for Hinduism as a whole. Above all in the sense of the moral law, rights [*Rechte*] and duties of individual castes and life stages it provided a reason for the formation of the immense Dharmaśāstra literature.[67] In the epic and in the Purāṇas Dharma was personified as the judge of the dead, a function that is appropriately suited to the incarnation of justice [*Recht*] and law [*Gesetz*].[68] Despite this increasingly moralizing tendency, the connection with the originally cosmological notion was still preserved in later times, because in the *yuga* theory the sequence of world ages is regulated by the gradual increase of *adharma* or decrease of *dharma*, that is, morality. In other words: the development of the ethical *dharma* determines the world process.

DHARMA IN BUDDHISM

The concept of *dharma* in Buddhism constitutes the synthesis of the entire Vedic development and simultaneously produces a profound change of meaning. The meaning 'law' is preserved, often however with the specific nuance: the law of a specific teacher and his school, that is the world order that he recognizes and proclaims, which has sway over the course of nature and the fate of people. That is why the word can be interpreted by 'doctrine'. Thus it was common to inquire about the *dhamma* ('doctrine') and *vinaya* ('statues of an order') of a monk or adherent of a sect,[69] whereby the distinction between practical training and theoretical law is noteworthy. Because *dharma* (Pāli: *dhamma*) also is applied to the doctrine of heretical movements, the term itself can denote false laws – heretical doctrines – as when it is said, for example, that "previously in Magadha an impure doctrine (*dhamma*), contrived by the impure, became known."[70]

However, *dhamma* principally means the 'doctrine of the Buddha', his religion *per se*, given that during the decisive experience, during the awakening (*bodhi*), he had seen, in a vision-like intuition, the universal law of becoming and passing away – *dhamma-cakkhum udapādi.*[71] And when he decided to disseminate this knowledge, which brings liberation, among the people, he 'set in motion the wheel of the law', according to the famous title of the first sermon, *dhamma-cakka-ppavattana-sutta.* The expression 'wheel of the law' is noteworthy, because it originates in the notion of the 'twelve-spoked wheel of order' (*ṛtásya*) from RV 1.164.11ab, wherein the sun is understood as the wheel of the year with the twelve months.[72] At the same time it emphasizes the dynamic character of the *dhamma*, which in Buddhism mainly refers to the law of becoming, of dependent origination.

As Beckh has already aptly observed, *dhamma* denotes "the nature of things recognized by the Buddha in its universal cosmic conformity with law, a legitimacy into which our concepts of natural law on one hand, moral law on the other, flow together completely into one concept, the nuance of which is alien to Western thought'.[73] Understandably, in Buddhism the natural law plays a rather subordinate roll, as when the flow and perpetual growth of the rivers is compared to the law of *karman* – the determinism of retaliation for actions.[74] Likewise *rukkhadhamma*, 'the law of the tree', to produce flowers and fruits, corresponds to the wholesome fruits of monastic life,[75] or it is even illustrated how the moral law determines the natural course of things.[76]

Corresponding to the existential world-view, the Buddha's *dhamma* is applied principally to people, especially to the law of actions (*kamma*), which with inescapable necessity determine the future form of life in the wheel of existence – *saṃsāra*. The conditional sequence of developments was specified in the usually twelve-part formula of 'origination in dependence' and was considered as the prototype of the perpetual conformity to law. The law of existence is itself not subject to any change, for which Buddhists coined the expression of 'perseverance' or 'steadfastness of the law' (*dhamma-ṭṭhiti*). "Whether Tathāgatas rose up or whether no Tathāgatas rose up: this basic law is certain, the lawful process, this conditionality on a given."[77] With these insistent words, the Buddha himself emphasized the absolute nature of the world law. Even in his hour of death he says to his favorite disciple: "The law and the statutes of the order, which I have preached and marked out for you, they are your teacher after my death."[78] "Those who, Ānanda, now or after my passing, seek in themselves and in the law, but nowhere else, their island and refuge, such assiduously striving monks will be the most perfect."[79] The world-law stands above the mortal master, because it is eternal (*sanātana*), timeless (*akālika*), which corresponds to the *sanātano dharmah* of the Hindu philosophers.

Since the Buddha acknowledges no god as creator and guide of the world, nor a metaphysical source in the sense of the *ātman* or *brahman* of the Upanisads, with which he was not familiar,[80] and no absolute being exists as the supreme truth, but only the abstract world-law, which has determined the course of all phenomena since beginningless time. Whoever has understood this profoundly in its essence, the universal conditionality of all events, is released, so that the Buddha's *dharma* is simultaneously a law of salvation. The highest knowledge is, above all, intuitive and experiential in nature, because "this law is profound, difficult to behold, difficult to understand, peaceful, sublime, unattainable to thought, subtle, comprehensible only to the wise."[81] Despite the manifold mystical components, the rationalistic aspect of the Buddha's doctrine has been referred to early on, which is expressed most clearly in the idea of the world-law. The cyclical development of the cosmos is subject to a stringent determinism, but above all the cycle of rebirths is conditioned by deeds. Nevertheless it is precisely this absolute conformity with law which guarantees human freedom, man's capacity to liberate himself, because as an understanding, reasonable being, he can comprehend the *dharma* and guide his deeds in accordance with this knowledge, which through complete renunciation lead necessarily to the cessation of rebirth, to Nirvāṇa.

In addition to the abstract concept of law, the analysis of concrete phenomena was crucial for Buddhist philosophy, since Buddhists saw being neither in the 'perfected', nor in the gods, nor in permanent elements, or an absolute world-basis; even an immortal individual soul was rejected and a plurality of psycho-physiological and ethical factors was put in its place, the constantly changing interplay of which forms the transitory, composite individual.[82] It was probably because they constitute the concrete foundation, likewise the material aspect of the formal law, that they were named the *dharmas*, which in etymological respects is best rendered by 'legal factors'. This also includes the elements that constitute the body, the sense organs, intellectual functions, psychological and moral states and activities, such as thought, memory, desire, hate, delusion, etc. Since it always concerns essential conditions in the salvation process, these *dharmas* could also be referred to as "basic factors of existence".[83]

However peculiar this specific Buddhist usage of the term may appear, the semantic development is nevertheless still plausible, there are also early stages, if not quite parallels, in Brahmanism. The use of the plural is old, yet it was chiefly the various 'laws', 'rights' and 'duties' that were thereby indicated.[84] The Buddha applies it on one hand to the manifold doctrinal systems, on the other hand to different components of his law of salvation, thus for example to the four sacred truths, as when he speaks after explaining them: "Thus my eyes were opened, you monks, to these laws which were not perceived earlier (or: doctrines, *pubbe ananussutesu dhammesu*), the understanding, the insight, the knowledge, and the perception became apparent to me."[85]

We already find the transition to the meaning 'factors of law' in compounds like *deyya-dhamma* = 'that which may be given lawfully', *samudaya-* and *nirodha-dhamma* = 'subject to the law of origination and cessation', etc.[86] Nevertheless, we already found the most important preliminary stage in ŚB 11.5.7.1, where pious behavior, fame, offer of respect, offering, etc., were referred to as *dharmas*, among which expressions such as *trayo dharmaskandhāḥ* and *sādhavo dharmāḥ* should be reckoned.[87] In the law books the plural of *dharma* is common.

In Buddhist dogmatics *Dharma* assumes such an important place – comparable to ideas in Platonic philosophy – that, as we saw, they can be referred to *per se* as Dharma theory. While Theravāda still limits itself largely to the classification of *dharmas* as beneficial, non-beneficial, etc.,[88] the later, speculative schools constructed a true philosophy upon that. In the case of the Sarvāstivādins and Sautrāntikas it principally involves the question of reality or phenomenality of the *dharmas*. The Madhyamika system pronounces them to be 'empty' (*śūnya*), 'substanceless' (*niḥsvabhāva*) and thereby arrives at a pure phenomenism, while the Vijñāvāda concerns itself with its ideal nature. Thereby questions were debated from a characteristically Buddhist standpoint, which exhibit manifold parallels to the medieval disputes over universals. In certain tendencies of Mahāyāna the speculation even approaches a true ontology, as for example, when it involves the Buddha's 'body of law', *dharma-kāya*, which was regarded as a metaphysical hypostasis, analogous to the logos of classical philosophers. All schools, however, expressed the quintessence of the Buddha's *dharma* in the succinct formula:

ye dharmā hetuprabhavā hetuṃ teṣāṃ tathāgato hy avadat |
teṣaṃ ca yo nırodho evaṃvadı mahaśramaṇaḥ ||

"The perfected one taught the cause of (all) the factors of existence, which originated causally, and their cessation. The great ascetic has proclaimed how it (really) is."

SUMMARY

1. The origin of the concept of *dhárman* lies in the creation myth of the holding apart (*vi-dhṛ-*) and supporting (*dhṛ-*) of heaven and earth, whereby order and 'support' [*Halt*] was produced from the primordial uniformity of the unstable chaos.
2. The basic meaning of *dhárman* is therefore 'prop' [*Halt*], 'support' [*Stütze*]; it is suitable for all older passages, sometimes with the nuance of 'keeping' and 'maintaining'; it is employed at the cosmic, ritual and ethical-social level.

3. Early on, *dhárman*, as an autonomous power of a numinous nature, separated itself from the mythical function of the 'support' of specific gods and thereby becomes a universal principle of 'maintenance' [*Halt*], stability and permanence of the cosmos. This explains the semantic development of the concrete mythical notion into the abstract concept 'law'.
4. This shift and expansion in meaning, which principally takes place in the ethical-social realm, is accompanied by the transformation of the action noun [*Nomen actionis*] *dhárman* into the abstraction *dhármaḥ*, which first appears in the Atharvaveda.
5. Since the Brāhmana era, the world law, which includes the natural law and the ethical law, has been increasingly fragmented into a variety of 'rights' [*Rechten*] and 'duties' of the different castes and stages of life, which led to the voluminous mass of the Dharmaśāstras, the Hindu textbooks of justice [*Recht*] and morality.
6. In Buddhism, *dharma* as 'world law' is elevated to the highest principle. As according to modern science, the knowledge of the eternal laws of nature serves to master it, so the knowledge of *dharma*, of the conformity to the laws of world events and human existence, is the precondition for liberation, and therefore *dharma* includes the law of salvation.
7. The abstract world law took the place of theism (god as creator and ruler of the world) and of an absolute world foundation, and it was analyzed into a plurality of conditional concrete factors of existence. These 'factors of law', which are subject to a rigorous determinism, are transitory (*anicca*), painful (*dukkha*), and unsubstantial (*anatta*), play such a prominent role in Buddhist dogmatics, that this can be referred to as Dharma theory. Meanwhile it was successfully proved that there were fundamental Brahmanical preliminary stages and parallels for this peculiar Buddhist use of the term.

NOTES

[1a] Within this framework, we have to be satisfied with an overview, however we will return to it in detail in a book about 'The Vedic universal law'. Abbreviations: AV = Atharvaveda; BĀU = Bṛhadāraṇyaka Upaniṣad; ChU = Chāndogya Upaniṣad; RV = Ṛgveda; ŚB = Śatapatha Brāhmaṇa. At the end of a word: Ā = Āraṇyaka; B = Brāhmaṇa; D = Dharmasūtra; U = Upaniṣad; S = Saṃhitā.

[1b] Cf. Wackernagel-Debrunner, AIG II, 2, p. 754, 6 (§ 601): "*-man-* frequently serves to form abstracts, especially in the ancient language, also expressions for objects and processes developed from these."

[2] Cf. M. Mayrhofer, *Kurzgefaßtes etymologisches Wörterbuch des Altindischen*, s.v. *dhārayati*, cf. but s.v. *dharmā* (neup. *dharmān* 'medicine', arm. LW *darman* 'alimentation').

[3] A number of synonymous verbs of architectonic origin play an analogous roll in cosmogonic acts: *dṛṅh-* = 'make firm', *stabh-* and *skabh-* = 'prop', *prath-* = 'spread out', *mā-* = 'measure', *takṣ-* and *tvakṣ-* = 'fashion', 'build' (cf. Tvaṣṭṛ as divine architect), *tan-* = 'stretch', etc. Additional Vedic parallels for the division of the originally united world-halves, [see] Geldner RV 3.38.3d.

[4] *kasnā dərətā zamcā adə̄ nabåscā, avapastōiš kə̄ apō urvaråscā.* Translation by H. Humbach, *Die Gāthās des Zarathustra*, I, p. 117; cf. II, p. 54. The fear that the sky would fall down was also typical of the Celts (see Arrian, *Anabasis* 1.4.7; cf. Strabo 7.3.8); cf. further RV 1.105.3 and Geldner's note on this.

[5] Cf. Yasna 23.1: The Fravartis, "who supported heaven, who supported earth, who maintained the cow, who bore the conceived children in their mothers' wombs" (*fravašayō ... yå asmanəm vīδārayən yå āpəm vīδārayən yå zəm vīδārayən yå barə þrišva puþre vīδārayən* = Yašt 13.22). Cf. Vedic *garbhaṃ dhṛ-*, 'bearing the embryo' (RV 3.2.10; 6.67.4). Similarly in Yašt 13.28; in 13.26 the Fravartis are called "the most unshakeable among those bracing themselves, the most suitable among those who act as supports"; translated by F. Wolf, *Avesta. Die heiligen Bücher der Parsen*, pp. 232–233. Nyberg, *Die Religionen des alten Iran*, p. 63, accounts for this function of the Fravartis through their association with the air. Cf. the role of the Egyptian god of the air, Schu, and the Indian Maruts as storm gods in Indra's retinue.

[6] Cf. R. Eisler, *Weltenmantel und Himmelszelt*, pp. 626–627.

[7] Cf. Eisler, ibid. Index, s.v. Weltei. Cf. ŚB 11.1.3.2; Mahābhārata 1.1.29f.; see also F.D.K. Bosch, *The Golden Germ*, 's-Gravenhage 1960, p. 55.

[8] References to H. Hunger, *Lexikon der griechischen und römischen Mythologie*, s.v. Atlas. The myth was dealt with in detail by W. Staudacher, *Die Trennung von Himmel und Erde*, Tübingen, 1942.

[9] Cf. A. Lesky, *Hethitische Texte und griechischer Mythos*, Anzeiger Österr. Akad. Wiss. phil.-hist. Kl. 87, 1950, p. 150ff.

[10] Cf. E.B. Tylor, *The Origins of Culture*, New York, 1958, pp. 325–326

[11] Cf. Tylor, ibid. p. 325 and Anm.1; Bastian, *Allerlei aus Volks- und Menschenkunde* I, p. 314; M. Müller, *Indien in seiner weltgeschichtlichen Bedeutung*, p. 127f. Similar myths among the Melanesians. Concerning Southeast Asians, see especially K. Numazawa, *Background of Myths on the Separation of Sky and Earth from the point of view of Cultural History*, Scientia 88, Milan, 1953 (unfortunately without bibliographic details).

[12] Frequently *dhṛ-* and *prath-* are used together, cf. RV 6.17.7. For the extension of the earth, cf. J. Hertel, *Die Himmelstore im Veda und Awesta*, p. 24f.

[13] RV 1.160.1d: *devó devī́ dhármaṇā sū́ryaḥ śúciḥ*. According to 10.65.5c it is Mitra's and Varuṇa's 'lofty creation', namely the sun, which 'shines forth upon the base of the supporting power' (*yáyor dhā́ma dhármaṇā rócate bṛhát*).

[14] *divìva cákṣur ā́tatam.*

[15] *dhārā́yaṃ dívaṃ sádana ṛtásya*; cf. 5.15.2ab. Concerning the location of Ṛta in the highest heaven see Lüders, *Varuṇa* II, p. 585ff., concerning the seat of Ṛta, p. 593f., 609ff.

[16] Heaven and earth are thought of as two superimposed bowls, whereby the higher one is inverted, thus also the picture of AV 10.8.9 and BĀU 2.2.2. in the same *śloka* (see Horsch, *Die vedische Gāthā- und Śloka-Literatur*, pp. 154–155 with bibliography). The symbol of the inverted tree of RV 10.73.8d and KaṭhaU 6.1 belongs here.

[17] RV 2.13.7ab: *dhármaṇā ... vy ... ádhārayaḥ.*

[18] 6.71.1d: *rájaso vídharmaṇi*, cf. AV 7.22.1: Sun as 'light in the intermediate realm' (*jyótir vídharmaṇi*).
[19] Cf. 9.86.29bc; the broad expanse of the ocean in 9.97.40; AV 16.3.6. cf. AIG II, p. 756, 41: 'reservoir, perimeter, diffusion'; TS 3.3.5.4 and PB 15.1.2 'outermost limit'.
[20] Cf. K. Hoffman, KZ 76, 1960, p. 247, n. 22. The verse was added to the Purusasūkta 10.90.16.
[21] *cālpré téna ṛ̥sayo manuṣyā̆ yajñé jāté pitáro naḥ purāṇé | páśyan manye mánasā cákṣasā tā́n yá imám yajñám áyajanta pū́rve ||*
[22] RV 3.17.1a: *samīdhyámānaḥ prathamā́nu dhármā.*
[23] RV 3.17.5cd: *tásyā́nu dhárma prá yajā cikitvó 'thā no dhā adhvarám devávītau ||*
[24] RV 5.26.6: *samidhānáḥ sahasrajid Ágne dhármāṇi puṣyasi | devā́nām dūtá ukthyàḥ ||*
[25] RV 9.64.1c: *vṛ́ṣā dhármāṇi daddhiṣe*; cf. 1.22.18 (of Viṣṇu).
[26] RV 9.63.22c: *vāyúm ā roha dhármaṇā*; cf. 9.25.2c.
[27] RV 1.134.5ef: *víśvasmād bhúvanāt pāsi dhármaṇā*; *pā-*, possibly with ablative 'prevailing' (Graßmann, *Wörterbuch*, s.v.).
[28] RV 9.7.1ab: *ásṛgram índavaḥ pathā́ dhármann ṛtásya siśríyaḥ.*
[29] RV 9.110.4. Concerning the 'abode' and 'support' of Ṛta, cf. Lüders, *Varuṇa* II, p. 599ff.
[30] RV 9.97.24d: *ṛtám bharat.*
[31] RV 9.107.15cd: *árṣan Mitrásya Várunasya dhármaṇā ... ṛtám bṛhát.*
[32] Finally cf. to the translation P. Thieme, *Gedichte aus dem Rig-Veda*, Reclam Universal-Bibliothek Nr. 8930, p. 52.
[33] Cf. 3.60.6d: *vratā́ devā́nām mánuṣaś ca dhármabhiḥ.* "(These are) the commands (or: vows) of the gods and of men (or: Manu) by virtue of the laws"; cf. H.-P. Schmidt, *Vedisch vratá und awestisch urvāta*, p. 91; pp. 90–92. Index of places where *vratá* and *dhárman* appear together. Cf. Thieme, ibid., p. 48. According to 5.72.2a Mitra and Varuṇa bring "the people to settlement through the law" (*dhármaṇā yātayájjanā*); cf. Thieme, *Mitra und Aryaman*, New Haven, 1957, p. 41. Mitra and Varuṇa are *sátyadharmāṇā* (RV 5.63.1b; cf. AV 1.10.3 of Varuṇa): "whose law are true, that means they are effective".
[34] Cf. JaiminīyaB 2.25: *satya* = day, *ṛta* = night; 2.273: *ṛta* = speech, *satya* = *prāṇa*. Explicit identifications are certainly very frequent (cf. ŚB 7.3.1.23; 14.3.1.28), however it is a question of magical-esoteric equivalences, which are used in contrast to them in the profane spheres for effective differences. No doubt *a priori*, it is unlikely that the vedic seers employed base concepts like *satyá* and *ṛtá* as absolute synonyms.
[35] In 3d it is also stated of Mitra and Varua: "You allow heaven to rain by means of the Asura's magic power" (*dyā́m varṣayatho ásurasya māyáyā*; cf. 6cd). From this one realizes how closely the cosmic control and "support" (6.70.1cd) of these gods is bound up with their dominion over the human world.
[36] Cf. Horsch, *Die vedische Gāthā- und Śloka-Literatur*, Bern, 1966, pp. 234–242.
[37] This contrast appears particularly clearly in later Buddhism, where *māyā* is identified with illusion, which leads one to believe in a phantasmagoric world, which the 'Awakened one' has destroyed through the recognition of *dharma*, the 'law'. In the acosmic ontology of Saṅkara's Vedānta there is no more room left for the 'law', since the world of becoming is the creation of *māyā*: only there does *dharma* have validity.
[38] Cf. 1.154.1; 160.4; 2.12.2; 6.7.7; 8.2; 8.25.18; 41.10; 42.1; 10.56.5; 130.3a (*pramā́*); always in the cosmogonic context, usually in connection with verbs such as *dhṛ-*, *stabh-*, *skabh-*, etc.
[39] Cf. H. Oldenberg, *Die Religion des Veda*, Stuttgart and Berlin, 1923, p. 195: "The processes whose constant unchanging quality, or whose regular recurrence, arouses

the idea of order, obey Ṛta or their occurrence is Ṛta." H. Lüders, *Varuṇa*, Band II, Göttingen, 1959 deals with *ṛta* at length (identification of *ṛtá* and *satyá* 'truth'). The transition of meaning to *ṛté* = 'without' remains unexplained. The peculiar semantic process seems to us nevertheless explainable: *ṛtá* = 'gone', 'away from', for this reason 'without' with ablative. This would confirm at the same time our approach to the meaning of *ṛtá* = 'course'.

40 *prá prajā́bhir jāyate dhármaṇas pári* = 8.27.16c; 10.63.13b.

41 *jánam bíbhratī bahudhā́ vívācasaṃ nā́nādharmāṇam pṛthivī́ yathaukasām.*

42 *pátnī tvám asi dhármaṇā.*

43 Cf. Wackernagel, *Altindische Grammatik* II, 1, p. 94, § 40a.

44 Cf. Wackernagel/Debrunner, ibid. II, 2, p. 141, § 43a: "The transition of consonantal stems occurs in the *a*-stems: (1) through the reinterpretation of the acc. sg. from *-am* to *a-m*, (2) through transfer of the end-part forms that are extended with *-a-* to the simplex, (3) through nominalizing in neuter." This also calls to mind a loss of the final consonant, as in Prakrit, thus e.g. Pālī *kamma*, occurs from time to time, yet *kamma* remains a neuter! Or was the *a*-stem inferred from *dharma-* in the first member of a compound? Then this phenomenon would have to occur more frequently.

45 1.187.1; 9.97.23; 10.21.3; 92.2.

46 5.69.4ab: *yā́ dhartā́rā rájaso rocanásya ... pā́rthivasya.*

47 9.26.2c; 76.1a; 109.6a (Soma); 4.53.2a; 10.149.4d (Savitṛ); 3.49.4a (Indra); 10.66.10a; 65.13b; 10.2d. Cf. *divó dhárman* (5.15.2; 10.170.2). This corresponds to the use of the verb, cf. 3.32.8; 42.4; 44.3; 5.62.3.

48 At best, the word still finds a place in the sociological sphere, as when Mitra and Varuna are called 'Supporters of the people' (*dhartā́rā carṣaṇīnā́m*) (5.67.2c; cf. 1.17.2c; 5.1.6d; 9.3cd; 9.86.42cd). It always refers to a god. The phrase 'Supporter of goods' (*rāyó dhartā́*), among others, also refers to the human sphere (1.102.5b; 5.15.1d; 9.35.2c).

49 9.2.5b; 74.2a. Cf. AIG II, 2, p. 484, 35.

50 Cf. Lüders, ibid. p. 185; Renou, *Etudes sur le vocabulaire du Ṛgveda*, p. 1: "Quand par delà la terre inébranlable, tu as fixé avec force l'espace aérien sure les colonnes du ciel." This interpretation is possibly support by 1.56.6ab. Geldner also renders *ā́tāsu* with "on the pillar", which can be justified, insofar as the image of the doorpost underlies it. One expects a dual!

51 Cf. 1.56.5; 62.5; 103.2; 2.11.7; 12.1; 15.2; 17.5; 6.17.7; 72.2. cf. further J. Hertel, *Die Himmelstore im Veda und in Awesta*, Leipzig 1924, pp. 24–26.

52 AV 10.7.8; cf. especially 10.7.24, 33, 34; 8.37. *skambhá* = 'pillar' is simultaneously understood as 'framework' – in the case of *ā́tā* it behaves in the opposite way (see finally W.N. Brown, JAOS 85, 1965, p. 28).

53 Cf. 9.89.5b; 107.5c; 10.44.4ab; 83.7c. As in the case of *dhartṛ́*, there is also mention of dharúṇo, one reads *rāyáḥ/rayīṇā́m*: 1.73.4; 5.15.1, 5; 7.34.24; 10.5.1; 45.5.

54 Firstly, it is mainly a question of Varuṇa's *ṛtá* analogous to the relationship of Iranian *aša* to Ahura Mazdah – , then it is elevated over him as an impersonal, world-producing and world-supporting power. Analogies are found in the case of the Greeks' idea of destiny, the Moira of Homer or Anankē of the tragedians with regard to Zeus. The difference between both cultural spheres exists essentially in that the Moira signify a disaster, an unavoidable fate, whereas Ṛta as a cosmic 'truth' or universal world order manifests itself simultaneously on the ritual level and is therefore governed by priests: The fateful power here becomes the absolute freedom of humankind. Cf. also Oldenberg, ibid. p. 197ff.

55 Originally *ṛtá* stood was most closely related to *satyá* = 'reality', 'truth', which already follows from its opposite *ánṛta*. Later *dhárma* assumes an analogous position opposite to *satyá*; cf. Taittirīya-Āraṇyaka 4.42.5; BĀU 1.4.14; TaittirīyaU 1.11;

Manu 1.81. Besides the other semantic affinities this also speaks for absorption of *ṛtá* within the concept of *dhárma*. It behaves differently with *dhā́man* = 'seat', 'creation', a word which is often rendered in the Veda with 'precept' or 'law'. In reality the concrete sense of 'seat' and 'creation' as in the cosmogony always prevails; over the course of time it even became more contracted, from the 'sole creation' of god, to a specific 'place'. This specialization is doubtless the basis for the preservation of the word. Finally: J. Gonda, *The Meaning of the Sanskrit Term Dhāman-*. Amsterdam, N.V. Noord-Hollandsche Uitgevers Maatschappij, 1967.

[56] Note the word play with the root *dhṛ-*: *dharma, dhārayati, dhṛtam.* cf. BĀU 1.5.23: The sun rises and sets in the breath, the gods made this the *dharma*, that is, the 'support' of all of nature.

[57] ŚB 11.1.6.24: *dhármo vā́ ā́paḥ.*

[58] Cf. AitareyaB 11.6.4; ŚB 7.4.1.8; 12.5.2.14; JUB 10.9-10.

[59] ŚB 11.1.6.24.

[60] This explains the so far misunderstood passage of MaitrāyaṇīS 1.5.4, 11; Mānava-Śrautasūtra 1.6.2.14; Āpastamba-Śrautasūtra 6.19.1; cf. Caland, *Das Śrautasūtra of Apastamba*, 1–7. Book, p. 203.

[61] Translation according to information in a letter from Wilhelm Rau. The difficult text reads: *tāsu dharma; dharmaṇā vai devā dharmam ādāyāsurāṇāṃ vidharmaṇaināṇ vidharmaṇaḥ kṛtvā parābhāvayan. dharmaṇaiva dharmam ādnya dviṣato bhratṛvyasya vidharmaṇainaṃ vidharmāṇaṃ kṛtvā parābhāvayati ya evaṃ veda. tac chrīr vai dharmo, rājyaṃ vai dharmo, dharmeṇa vai rājā dharmo, dharma svānāṃ bhavaty, ainaṃ svā yanti, dharmaṇo dhārayati ... tad u vā āhur vidharmāṇo vai rājāno na vai te 'nyair manuṣyai svadharmāṇaḥ.*

[62] Cf. W. Rau, *Staat und Gesellschaft im alten Indien*, Wiesbaden 1957, p. 62, n. 17.

[63] Cf. ChU 7.2.1; BĀU 4.4.5; ŚvetāśvataraU 6.6; KaṭhaU 2.14; *dharma* and *adharma*; *adharma* first occurs in the Brāhmaṇas (TaittirīyaB 3.4.6.1; ŚB 5.2.4.13).

[64] Cf. Th. Stcherbatsky, *The central conception of Buddhism and the meaning of the world 'dharma'*, London 1923, p. 56f.; H. von Glasenapp, *Buddhism in the Kaṭhopanisad*? New Indian Antiquary I, p.139ff.; *Zur Geschichte der buddhistischen Dharma-Theorie*, ZDMG 92, 2/3, 1938, pp. 383–420.

[65] Thus Gautama-Dharmaśāstra 28.50 already mentions the *pṛthag-dharma-vidaḥ*, that is, 'experts on different laws or law books', and still earlier AV 12.1.45 calls the people *nānādharman* 'possessing various laws or customs' (*nānā* = *pṛthak*). In KaṭhaU 2.13 *dharmya* means 'what belongs to the traditional justice or law': The mystic of the Upaniṣads must overcome all these worldly differences, among others right (*dharma*) and wrong (*adharma*) (KaṭhaU 2.14).

[66] *Buddhismus und Upaniṣaden*, Im Haag/Paris, Mouton, 1967.

[67] Cf. P.V. Kane, *History of Dharmaśāstra* I-V, Poona 1930–1962; concerning *dharma* especially I, p. 2: "The privileges, duties and obligations of a man, his standard of conduct as a member of the Aryan community, as a member of one of the castes, as a person in a particular stage of life."

[68] The most important survey concerning the epic concept of *dharma* is still offered by J. Dahlmann, *Das Mahābhārata als Epos und Rechtsbuch*, Berlin 1895 (especially pp. 23–27; 47–55; 58ff.; 86ff.; 106ff.). Cf. further U.N. Ghoshal, *The relation of the Dharma concept to the social and political order in Brahmanical canonical thought*, Journal of the Bihar Research Society 38, pp. 90–202; K. Aiya, *Dharma and Life*, 2 vols; N. Raghunathan, *The Concept of Dharma in Itihāsas and Purāṇas*. Since already in the epic period, divine veneration was bestowed on dharma at certain sacred sites (cf. Mahābhārata 3.84.102; 88.24), it can in no way be surprising that there was an actual dharma cult during the Indian medieval era, especially in areas where Buddhist influence was most enduring. Concerning the dharma cult of Bengal, cf.

finally Shashibhusan Dasgupta, *Obscure Religious Cults*, Calcutta, Mukhopadhyaya, 1962, p. 181ff.: relation to Śivaism and to ancient Sūrya veneration; Śiva-Dharma-Buddha (p. 304).

69 Cf. Vinaya I, p. 8. All Pāli references according to the PTS edition.

70 Vinaya I, p. 5.

71 Dīgha I, p. 86; Vinaya I, p. 11; Majjhima I, p. 247.

72 *dvā́daśāram nahí tā́j járāya várvarti cakrám pári dyā́m ṛtásya*; cf. verses . 13 and 14. The 'wheel of law' was preserved through the centuries in Hinduism, where it adorns the modern Indian flag as emblem and simultaneously symbol of the continuity in the history of ideas. Cf. Vasudeva S. Agrawala, *The Wheel Flag of India Chakra Dhvaja*. (Being a History and Exposition of the Meaning of the Dharma-Cakra and the Sarnath Lion Capital). Benares 1964. In the Buddhist 'wheel of existence' (*bhava-cakra*) the twelve spokes symbolize the primary causes of *saṃsāra*. The stipulation of the number twelve may likewise have originated in the twelve-spoked wheel of Ṛta (see Horsch, *The Wheel: An Indian Pattern of World-Interpretation*. Sino-Indian Studies V, 3–4, 1957, pp. 69–71).

73 H. Beckh, *Buddhismus*, Sammlung Göschen 1916, I, p. 20, n. 1.

74 Cf. Saṃyutta II, p. 32; V, p. 396; Aṅguttara I, p. 243.

75 Aṅguttara III, p. 371f. (*samaṇa-dhamma*).

76 Aṅguttara II, p. 74. This problem was most recently treated by A. Bareau, *Les relations entre la causalité du monde physique et la causalité du monde spirituel*, Liebenthal-Festschrift, Sino-Indian Studies 3–4, 1957, pp. 14–20.

77 Saṃyutta II, p. 24; Translation by W. Geiger (München-Neubiberg 1925). Cf. Majjhima I, pp. 190–191: *yo paṭiccasamuppādaṃ passati so dhammaṃ passati* "Whoever perceives dependent origination, perceives the law".

78 Dīgha II, p. 154.

79 Dīgha II, p. 101. cf. III, p. 84: "The law is highest (*dhammo seṭṭho*) in this world (*diṭṭhe dhamme*) as well as in the other."

80 Cf. in detail our article about this: *Buddhism and Upaniṣads*; see above p. 53, n. 66. The Buddha employs *brahman* in the purely spiritual sense of 'sacred', 'highest good', etc., whereby the concept is synonymous with *dharma*, as parallel expressions show: *dhamma-* and *brahma-cakka*, *dhamma-* and *brahma-kāya*, *dhamma-* and *brahma-bhūta*; cf. W. Geiger, *Dhamma und Brahman*, Sonderdruck der Zeitschrift für Buddhismus II, p. 1ff.

81 Vinaya I, p. 4; cf. KathaU 1.21; Mahābhārata 1.195.29; 196.10; 3.209.4, 10; 8.69.28.

82 The basic constituents of human existence are also unsubstantial, 'non-self' (*anatta*), in accordance with the principle: *sabbe dhammā anattā* (Dhammapada 279). Further all conditional (*saṃkhāta*) *dhammas* are defined as transient (*anicca*) and painful (*dukkha*).

83 Cf. H. von Glasenapp, *Zur Geschichte der buddhistischen Dharma-Theorie*, ZDMG 92, 1938, p. 385: "Dharma bezeichnet das Gesetz und alles, in dem es Ausdruck findet, auf der einen Seite Weltgesetz, Norm, Recht, Vorschrift, Lehre, Lehrtext, anderseits aber auch das durch das Weltgesetz Bedingte, die gesetzmäßig mit Notwendigkeit eintretenden Erscheinungen, die gesetzmäßigen Gegebenheiten"; *Der Ursprung der buddhistischen Dharma-Theorie*, WZKM 46, 1939, p. 253: the *dharmas* are "every spiritual condition, elements of existence, etc., which exist in accordance with the world-law, and through their action in combination, make lawful course of the world-process take place"; cf. ibid. p. 264. E. Frauwallner, *Geschichte der indischen Philosophie*, 1. Band, Salzburg 1953, translates *dharmas* by 'conditions'. All renderings, such as 'thing', 'object' etc., can be rejected; cf. finally W. Liebenthal, *Ding und Dharma*, Asiatische Studien 14, 1961, pp. 15–32.

[84]. Cf. already in RV 1.164.50: *dhármāṇi prathamā́nī*; AV 12.1.45; GautamaD 28.50; Āpastamba 1.1.2.14; Manu 2.14.
[85] Vinaya I, p. 11.
[86] Cf. *anucchitti-dharman* in BĀU 4.5.14: *ātman* 'possesses the law of indestructibility'; KapiṣṭhalaS 1.147: *cid-dharma*; PañcaviṃśaB 6.7.10: *mṛga-dharman* = 'partaking in the law, in the order or custom of the savage'.
[87] ChU 2.1.4; ChU 2.23.1: the 'three groups of laws' are: (1) sacrifice, study of the Veda, pious gift-giving; (2) asceticism; the life of a Veda student (*brahmacārin*). It is also a question of 'duties'. Cf. cattāro *dhamma-kkhandhā*, Dīgha III, p. 229; Aṅguttara I, p. 125. This means morality (*śīla*), concentration/absorption (*samādhi*), religious merit (*puñña*), liberation (*vimutti*). Manu 2.12 mentions *caturvidham dharmasya lakṣaṇam*: Veda, tradition, conduct of the good and modesty; 6.91–92: *daśakaṃ dharmalakṣaṇam*: contentment, patience, self-control etc., a terminology, which is thoroughly in the spirit of Buddhism and is nevertheless of Brahmanical origin.
[88] Although the number of *dharmas* is unlimited, *dhamma* lists were already drawn up in the Abhidhamma-Piṭaka. The number varies according to the different schools. This shows that the concept always implies something fundamental, essential, that is why the rendering of 'base factors' of existence mar appear appropriate. For the *dharma* lists cf. Ryukan Kimura, *The original and developed doctrines of Indian Buddhism in charts*, University of Calcutta, 1920.

1314 Thaddeus cove
Austin, TX 78746
USA
E-mail: jpo@uts.cc.utexas.edu

JOEL P. BRERETON

DHÁRMAN IN THE *R̥GVEDA*

In his article on the development of *dhárma*, Paul Horsch already has given consideration to the meaning of *dhárman* and related terms in the *R̥gveda*. In this essay, I examine Horsch's conclusions about *dhárman* by approaching its analysis in a somewhat different way. Where Horsch's discussion of R̥gvedic *dhárman* is set within the broader arc of the history of *dhárma* and Indian culture, I will consider only the *R̥gveda*. Where he discussed other nominal and verbal derivatives of √*dhr̥*, I will study only *dhárman* and *dharmán*. And finally, where Horsch selected examples to illustrate the semantic range of *dhárman*, I will account, or at least try to account, for all instances of *dhárman* and *dharmán* in the *R̥gveda*. This strategy will not produce a synoptic account that even approaches the scope of Horsch's work, but it may provide an anchor for the reevaluation of the history of *dhárma*.

A study of the attestations of *dhárman* in a single article is possible because *dhárman* occurs a manageable 63 times in the *R̥gveda*, including once in a compound *dharmakŕ̥t*, six times in *satyádharman*, and once in an adjective *dhármavant*. In addition, there are another four examples of *dharmán* and two of *dhárīman*. While this is not a small number, the relatively modest frequency of *dhárman* nonetheless implies that it was not a central term in the R̥gvedic lexicon or in Indian culture of the R̥gvedic period. Nor does the word have a long history before the *R̥gveda*. There are Indo-European parallels to *dhárman* (cf. Wennerberg 1981: 95f.), but the only Iranian equivalent is Old Persian *darmān* 'remedy,' which has little bearing on Indo-Aryan *dhárman*. There is thus no evidence that IIr. **dharman* was a significant culture word during the Indo-Iranian period. In this respect, *dhárman* contrasts with other terms whose semantic sphere *dhárman* sometimes intersected and eventually subsumed, such as *r̥tá* (Av. *aša*) and *vratá* (Av. *uruuata*). Both these terms had significant roles in the old Indo-Iranian religious vocabulary, and therefore study of their meanings in the *R̥gveda* has to consider the Iranian evidence and their pre-R̥gvedic history. In contrast, the discussion of *dhárman* can reasonably begin with the *R̥gveda*.

But even if it was not a central term within the *R̥gveda*, *dhárman* is thoroughly established in the text, since the word is attested at all its chronological levels. The following chart presents the occurrences of *dhárman* (including *dhármavant*, *satyádharman*, and *dharmakŕ̥t*) through the layers of the *R̥gveda* from the old family books (2, 4–6) to book 10 and the R̥gvedic appendix in 8.49–59[1]:

Old family books (2, 4–6)	11
Young family books (3, 7)	6
1, 8.1–48, 8.60–103	14
9	13
10	18
8.49–59 (Vālakhilya)	1

The distribution of the term, especially its increasing frequency in the younger layers, confirms that it is a part of the developing terminology of the *R̥gveda*. Interestingly, 7 of the 11 attestations of *dhárman* in the oldest R̥gvedic layer occur within book 5, and therefore its increasing occurrence in later books may partly reflect the influence of the Atri poets. In addition, the large number of attestations in 9, the Soma Pavamāna book, shows that *dhárman* belongs especially to the vocabulary of Soma. Not indicated by this chart, but almost as significant, is its association with Mitra and Varuṇa. These latter attestations are distributed throughout the *R̥gveda*, although they appear especially in its older levels: 6× in the family books, 2× in book 8 (including 1× in the Vālakhilya section), 1× in 9, and 2× in 10.

Since *dhárman* is a developing term in *R̥gveda*, its meaning reflects directly its etymology and form. And, happily, the formation of *dhárman* is transparent. It is derived from √*dhr̥* 'uphold, support, give foundation to' and a *-man* suffix. Therefore, it denotes a thing which upholds or supports, or, more simply, a 'foundation.' The word *dharmán*, a noun of agent, then designates an 'upholder' or 'foundation-giver.'

Unlike *dhárma* in the later period, which becomes richly evocative, *dhárman* in the *R̥gveda* has few consistent, concrete associations. To borrow an example from Stephanie Jamison (1996: 11), 'porridge' has specific literary connotations that the neutral term 'oatmeal' does not. In its R̥gvedic attestations, *dhárman* is far more 'oatmeal' than 'porridge,' and therefore, in each of its occurrences, the best approach is to see how the basic meaning of 'foundation' applies. Of course, 'foundation' is by no means a perfect rendering of *dhárman*, as I will soon amply illustrate by so translating it, but it is a good starting place. In examining its attestations, I will try to account for the use of *dhárman* in as coherent and efficient manner as possible. By 'coherent,' I mean that the actual sense of the word in a particular passage should be evidently connected to its basic meaning, 'foundation.' By 'efficient,' I intend an analysis that avoids unnecessarily inflating its semantic sphere.

DHÁRMAN AND RITUAL

Sacrifice as the ritual foundation for the world

I begin with passages in which *dhárman* describes the ritual as the basis or 'foundation' for the world. In 5.15, *dharúṇa*, which Elizarenkova (1995: 152)[2] describes as the hymn's 'magic word,' is repeated and echoed by other derivatives of √*dhṛ* throughout the hymn. *Dhárman* itself occurs only once, in 5.15.2 *ṛténa ṛtáṃ dharúṇaṃ dhārayanta yajñásya śāké paramé vyòman / divó dhárman dharúṇe sedúṣo nṝ́ñ jātaír ájātām̐ abhí yé nanakṣúḥ* "In making powerful the sacrifice in the highest heaven, they (= the Aṅgirases) supported the truth, itself a support, by means of the truth / – they who have reached the men (= the gods) that have taken their seat upon the support, upon the foundation of heaven; they who, even though they themselves were born, (have reached) the unborn." Threading through this verse is not an easy chore. The Aṅgirases have 'supported,' or given foundation to, 'the truth.' This truth is the sacrifice itself, which is the truth because it is an expression of the nature of things (cf. Skjaervø, 2003), and as such, it is the template and ultimate basis for world. Since it is the basis for the world, the truth that is the sacrifice is 'itself a support.' Moreover, the Aṅgirases supported this truth 'by means of the truth,' that is, by means of the hymns they sang. In sum, the truth (= the hymns) is the support for the truth (= the sacrifice), which, in turn, is the support for the world. In lines cd, there is an ambiguity, undoubtedly an intentional one, as to whether the seat of the gods is their heavenly seat or their seat in an earthly sacrifice. In either case, however, the 'support,' upon which the gods take their seat, is again the sacrifice. Since this sacrifice is itself the foundation (*dhárman*) of heaven,[3] *dhárman* here signifies the ritual as the foundation for the gods and the world.

In a similar manner, the sacrifice is both the support and the foundation of heaven in 10.170.2 *vibhrā́ḍ bṛhát súbhṛtaṃ vājasā́tamaṃ dhárman divó dharúṇe satyám árpitam / amitrahā́ vṛtrahā́ dasyuhántamaṃ jyótir jajñe asurahā́ sapatnahā́* "That which blazes forth aloft, well-borne, best prize-winner – (that) real (= the sun) is embedded into the foundation, the support of heaven. Striker of enemies, striker of obstacles, best striker of barbarians, the light has been born as the striker of lords, the striker of rivals." Where and what, then, is the support and foundation in which the sun is 'embedded'? On one level, at least, this foundation is likely represented by the sacrifice, in which the fire, ritually corresponding to the sun, is installed. At the end of the hymn, the sun itself then becomes a support that sustains the living world: 4c *yénemā́ víśvā bhúvanāny ā́bhṛtā* "by whom all these living worlds are borne here." Note also that in the phrase *dhárman divó dharúṇe*, the genitive *divás*, standing between the two locatives *dhárman* and *dharúṇe*, patterns with either and with both. With *dhárman*, it replicates the phrase *divó dhárman dharúṇe* of 5.15.2, and with *dharúṇe*, it inverts it. These shifts argue for the essential equivalence of *dharúṇa* 'support' and *dhárman* 'foundation.'

Not only the sacrifice in general, but also the central constituents of the sacrifice function as foundations for the world. The fire is the heart of the sacrifice, and in 10.88.1 the god Agni creates the foundation for the living world: 10.88.1 *havíṣ pā́ntam ajáraṃ svarvídi divispṛ́śy ā́hutaṃ júṣṭam agnaú / tásya bhármaṇe bhúvanāya devā́ dhármaṇe káṃ svadháyā paprathanta* "The pleasing oblation and drink is poured here in Fire, who finds the sun and touches heaven. For him to bear the living world, and yes, to give it foundation[4] in accordance with his own will, the gods will extend themselves." The hymn is addressed to Sūrya and Agni Vaiśvānara. Here Agni, the sacrificial Fire, assumes the form of the universal fire, the sun, and thereby becomes the foundation for all things.

Like Fire, so also Soma supports heaven and earth: 9.86.9 *divó ná sā́nu stanáyann acikradad dyaúś ca yásya pṛthivī́ ca dhármabhiḥ / índrasya sakhyám pavate vivévidat sómaḥ punānáḥ kaláśeṣu sīdati* "Thundering like the back of heaven, he has cried out, by whose foundations heaven and earth (have foundation).[5] / He purifies himself, rediscovering again and again his partnership with Indra. Purifying himself, Soma sits in the vats." The verse describes Soma's pressing and purification through the woollen filter, the 'back of heaven' (Oberlies, 1999: 154). The theme of the presence of *soma* throughout the universe dominates this hymn. Just preceeding this passage, for example, we hear that 8cd *ádhy asthāt sā́nu pávamāno avyáyaṃ nā́bhā pṛthivyā́ dharúṇo mahó diváḥ* "(Soma) has mounted the woollen back as he purifies himself, as the support of great heaven on the navel of the earth." And in the verses that follow vs. 9, Soma is the 'father and progenitor of the gods' (*pitā́ devā́nāṃ janitā́* vs. 10) and the 'lord of heaven' (*pátir diváḥ* vs. 11). He moves between heaven and earth (*ródasī antarā́* vs. 13); he 'touches heaven' and, 'filling the midspace, is embedded into the living worlds' (*divispŕ̥śam antarikṣaprā́ bhúvaneṣv árpitaḥ* vs. 14). His representation in vs. 9 as the foundation of heaven and earth, therefore, accords with the context of the verse and the theme of the hymn as a whole.

The sacrifice as the ritual foundation for gods

Soma can likewise act not only as the foundation of heaven and earth, but also as the foundation of gods, especially Indra. This theme occurs several times, or I think it does, for the passages become increasingly obscure. The clearest is 1.187.1 *pitúṃ nú stoṣam mahó dharmā́ṇaṃ táviṣīm, yásya tritó vy ójasā vr̥trám víparvam ardáyat* "Now I shall praise food, that gives foundation to the great one and that is his force, / that by whose power Trita violently shook away Vr̥tra, whose joints were broken." Although this is ostensibly a hymn to 'food,' the food addressed both in this verse and throughout is the *soma*.[6] Soma, then, is the *dharmán*, the one who gives foundation to the great one. We would normally expect this 'great one' to be Indra,[7] but here Trita occupies the position of Indra as the destroyer of Vr̥tra. In any case, it is on a foundation of *soma* (or sacrificially offered food more generally) that Trita successfully is empowered to break the obstacle represented by Vr̥tra.

I interpret 10.50.6 along the same lines, although the context is so open that it can be plausibly construed quite differently: 10.50.6 *etā́ víśvā sávanā tūtumā́ kr̥ṣe svayáṃ sūno sahaso yā́ni dadhiṣé / várāya te pā́traṃ dhármaṇe tánā yajñó mántro bráhmódyataṃ vácaḥ* "You have made thick all these *soma*-pressings, which you yourself have received, o son of strength. / For your choice and for your foundation, there is offered, each in its turn, the cup, the sacrifice, the *mantra*, the formulation, and speech." Even though the epithet 'son of strength' is characteristic of Fire, the god addressed here is Indra. Here the poet invites Indra to choose this sacrifice and thereby to give himself a 'foundation' in the power and presence that the sacrifice confers on him.

In 1.55.3, we enter a realm of syntactic and interpretive uncertainly, even deeper than usual: 1.55.3 *tváṃ tám indra párvataṃ ná bhójase mahó nr̥mṇásya dhármaṇām irajyasi / prá vīryèṇa devátāti cekite viśvasmā ugráḥ kármaṇe puróhitaḥ* "To enjoy that (which is) like a mountain, Indra, you have control of the foundations of great manliness. / He appears foremost among the gods by his heroism, he who is the powerful one placed at the fore for every act." I suggest that *tám* refers to the *soma* (mentioned in vs. 2c) and that the *soma* is compared to a mountain.[8] A problem for this view is that the basis for a comparison of *soma* to a mountain is not apparent.[9] But if Indra's control results in his drinking the *soma*, then his control is reasonably over the source or the basis of the *soma*, the 'foundations of great manliness.' These foundations might refer to the ritual, or possibly to the *soma* juices themselves, which are the basis of Indra's strength. The precise sense of this verse, however, continues to elude me.

The sacrifice as the ritual foundation of Soma

In a material and religious sense, the sacrifice is the foundation for *soma*, both god and oblation, for *soma* is physically and visibly created within the ritual process. This is particularly evident in the hymns of the 9th book, which celebrate and effect the appearance of both the *soma* drink and the god Soma as *soma* drips through the filter and into the *soma* vat. The ritual is the foundation on which *soma* is created in 9.7.1 *ásr̥gram índavaḥ pathā́ dhármann r̥tásya suśríyaḥ / vidānā́ asya yójanam* "The drops of great glory have been sent surging along the path upon the foundation of truth / – they that know its trek." The basic image of this passage is that of *soma* as a race horse, and the foundation on which *soma* runs is the truth. The description of the truth as a 'foundation' is particularly apt here, since *dhárman* suggests a physical foundation which could support a horse.[10] This verse describes *soma*'s descent from heaven to earth during its ritual preparation. The truth upon which the *soma*'s path rests or course runs, then, is either the sacrifice as a whole or the hymn.

A later verse in the same hymn returns to the theme of the foundation of *soma*. Here, however, the foundation of *soma* might be either that which creates Soma or that which constitutes the god Soma's nature: 9.7.7 *sá vāyúm índram aśvínā sākám mádena gachati / ráṇā yó asya dhármabhiḥ* "He goes to Vāyu, Indra, and the Aśvins, along with the invigoration, / with the joy which is according to his foundations." Because Soma has been properly fashioned in the ritual, he becomes invested with the ability to invigorate and please the gods of the morning offering. The *dhármans* signify his ritual foundations, which may be also the foundations of *soma* itself, the nature of *soma*.

The possibility that *dhárman* refers to the nature of *soma* is strengthened because of a number of passages, considered section 4, in which *dhárman* has the sense of the foundational nature of a deity. I have not included any instances of *dhárman* with Soma among those passages, however, because in the verses in which *dhárman* might refer to the nature of *soma*, the sense of *dhárman* as the ritual foundation of *soma* is still present or still possible. In the case of 9.7, vs. 1 shows the sense of *dhárman* as ritual foundation but not that of *dhárman* as the foundational nature of a god. When *dhárman* reoccurs in vs. 7, even though the sense of 'foundational nature' is possible – Re, for example, translates *dhármabhis* here as 'dans ses comportements' – it continues also to carry the sense of a ritual foundation.

Likewise, these senses of the foundations of *soma* are combined and elaborated in 9.107.24 *sá tū́ pavasva pári pā́rthivaṃ rájo divyā́ ca soma dhármabhiḥ / tvā́ṃ víprāso matíbhir vicakṣaṇa śubhrā́ṃ hinvanti dhītíbhiḥ* "Purify yourself all around the earthly realm and the heavenly (realms), o Soma, according to your foundations. / Far-gazing, it is you, the resplendent, whom the inspired poets speed with their thoughts and their insights." Again, *soma* is purified both according to his ritual foundations and possibly according to his nature as the *soma*. In addition, the poet also evokes the image of heaven and earth as the universal foundations that support *soma*.

Similarly, *dhárman* is the ritual foundation of *soma* and the foundational character of *soma* in 9.97.12 *abhí priyā́ṇi pavate punānó, devó devā́n svéna rásena pṛñcán / índur dhármāṇy ṛtuthā́ vásāno, dáśa kṣípo avyata sā́no ávye* "As he purifies himself, he purifies himself in the direction of the things dear to him – he the god that fills the gods with his own juice. / The *soma*-drop, clothing himself with his foundations following the ritual sequence, has enwrapped himself in the ten fingers on the woollen back." I have avoided the difficult problem of the identity of 'the things dear' to Soma. On the basis of 9.75.1 *abhí priyā́ṇi pavate . . . nā́māni*, Ge suggests that the 'dear' are the 'names' of Soma, but they may just as well be the water and the milk, the vessels, and perhaps the hymns and names. That is to say, the 'dear' may be all the ritual constituents toward which *soma* flows. If Soma moves toward the ritual constituents which make *soma* become truly *soma*, then these constituents can be the foundations that create and define him. Note the parallelism of 'clothing himself in his foundation' and 'has enwrapped himself in the ten fingers.' The '10 fingers' refer to the hands of the priests who ritually prepare the *soma*, so the 'foundations' can likewise refer to things that are the bases of the *soma* offering. However, both Re and Ge understand the *dhárman* not as the ritual 'foundations' through which *soma* becomes *soma*, but as the characteristics that *soma* assumes. So Re translates line c as 'revetant ses propriétés,' and Ge as 'nimmt... seine Eigenschaften an.' Such an interpretation is possible and may well be also implied. But here, I think, it is likely to be a secondary resonance, since the liturgical context implies that Soma is putting on all the physical ritual ingredients that are his foundation.

This same hymn also describes more a specific foundation on which *soma* is produced in 9.97.22 *tákṣad yádī mánaso vénato vā́g jyéṣṭhasya vā dhármaṇi kṣór ánīke / ā́d īm āyan váram ā́ vāvaśānā́ júṣṭam pátiṃ kaláśe gā́va índum* "When the speech from the thought that is tracking him fashions (Soma) on the foundation of the foremost (thought)[11] or in the face of the herd,[12] then the cows, bellowing as they wished, came to him, their delighting husband, the *soma*-drop, in the vat." The verse is open to a variety of explanations, but cd establish a specific ritual context: this part of the verse describes the mixing of milk, the 'cattle,' with *soma*, who is the husband of the cows. Therefore, in b, *soma* 'in the face of the cow' should be the *soma* as it is about to be mixed with the milk.[13] The rest of the verse refers to a different ingredient in *soma*'s creation, namely the recitation of the hymn. It is this thought of the seer which provides the foundation for *soma*. I account for the disjunctive *vā* by a locational contrast between the 'foundation of the foremost (thought)' and the 'face of the herd.' The thought is the starting point for the fashioning of *soma* (and as such, its foundation) and the 'herd' is the point toward which *soma* goes. This movement reflects a ritual sequence from the beginning of the chant at the first flowing of *soma* into the filter up to *soma*'s pouring into the milk mix.

Dhárman and *dhárīman* appear in consecutive verses in 9.86, and neither verse lends itself to easy interpretation. *Dhárīman* is attested only twice, and so it is difficult to know whether or how it differs from *dhárman*. However, the formal contrasts between the two words in this hymn are striking: *dhárman* occurs in the instrumental plural and *dhárīman* in the locative singular. Perhaps *dhárīman* is, as Re suggests, an infinitive. But whether *dhárīman* is a noun (so Wennerberg, 1981: 94), perhaps equivalent to *dhárman*, or an infinitive, in either case, it can describe the ritual as a foundation for *soma*: 9.86.4 *prá ta ā́śvinīḥ pavamāna dhījúvo divyā́ asṛgran páyasā dhárīmaṇi / prā́ntár ṛ́ṣaya sthā́virīr asṛkṣata yé tvā mṛjánty ṛṣiṣāṇa vedhásaḥ* "Forth have your (streams?),[14] that speed insights and are Aśvin-bound, been sent surging, together with the milk and upon the foundation.[15] Forth have the seers sent surging their stalwart (insights?)[16] within (the soma streams [?])[17] – they the ritual experts, who groom you, o you that win seers." The passage is amenable to the interpretation of *dhárman* I have been urging, although I cannot claim much more than that. The verse describes the blending of the *soma* juices pouring through the filter and the hymns that accompany that process. The juices and hymns are equated (by the fact they are both 'sent surging') and mixed (if indeed the hymns enter into the *soma* streams). In that context, *dhárīmaṇi* might recall the 'foundation of truth' (9.7.1, 110.4) or the 'foundation of the foremost (thought)' (9.97.22). That is to say, an additional intersection of the *soma* juices and the hymns is that the hymns provide the ritual foundation for the creation of *soma* as it flows through the filter.

The meaning of 9.86.4 is not made much clearer by vs. 5, in which *dhárman* also occurs: 9.86.5 *víśvā dhā́māni viśvacakṣa ṛ́bhvasaḥ prabhós te satáḥ pári yanti ketávaḥ / vyānaśíḥ pavase soma dhármabhiḥ pátir víśvasya bhúvanasya rājasi* "Your beacons circle around all your domains, o inventive (Soma), whose gaze falls on all, even though you are he that comes to the fore. Reaching throughout (your domains), you purify yourself according to your foundations. You rule as lord of the whole living world." The hymn operates on a double characterization of Soma as 'going around' and as 'leading.' On the one hand, *soma* visibly goes all around the filter and symbolically goes all around his domains. And in a contrasting movement, *soma* visibly leads the way forward into the *soma* vat and symbolically leads the way into the world. This double characterization of Soma's action is then resumed by the opposition between his domains and his foundations. The former describe the area *through* which *soma* moves; the latter the basis *upon* which it moves and upon which the pressed *soma* becomes the purified *soma*.[18]

Soma – or the Sun or even Soma as the Sun – is produced on the 'foundation of truth,' that is, on the foundation of the ritual, in 9.110.4 *ájījano amṛta mártyeṣv ā́m̐ ṛtásya dhármann amṛ́tasya cā́ruṇaḥ / sádāsaro vā́jam áchā sániṣyadat* "You have given it birth, o immortal one, here among mortals, upon the foundation of the truth, (upon that) of the deathless and cherished. / You have ever raced, always flowing here toward victory's prize." The initial problem in this verse is to sort out who has done what to whom. First, who has given birth? That, surely, is Soma, who is explicitly addressed throughout the hymn. Who, then, is given birth? According to

Sāyaṇa, whom Re follows, *soma* has given birth to the sun, or rather, *soma* has given birth to itself as the sun. Elsewhere, as the *soma* passes through the filter, which represents the midspace, it becomes a symbol of the sun (cf. Oberlies, 1999: 151 n. 107, 244 n. 119), and this passage is moving along the same lines. Who is the 'deathless and cherished'? Again this must be *soma*, since these are characteristic epithets of *soma*. What, then, is the 'foundation of truth'? The central problem is the relation between the 'truth' and the 'deathless and cherished.' Ge separates them by taking *amṛ́tasya cā́ruṇaḥ* as a partitive genitive with the *soma*, which is the implied object of the verb: "Du ... hast ... (den Trunk) des angenehmen Göttertranks." But in so dividing *ā́m ṛtásya* and *amṛ́tasya*, which form a figure suggesting their connection (as Re rightly points out), this syntactic analysis is forced. It is better to construe the genitives closely, and that leaves two possibilities. First, the 'deathless and cherished' is in apposition to the 'truth,' as Re interprets it: "... dans l'observance de l'Ordre, (ce) beau (principe) immortel." If the 'deathless and cherished' is *soma*, then *soma* must be the 'truth' as well. This is possible: Soma could be the foundation for the sun and, as part of the ritual process, an expression of the truth. But a second possibility is that the 'truth' and the 'deathless and cherished' are parallel genitives to *dhárman*. If the 'truth' is again the sacrifice (or the hymn), as in 9.7, then the verse would be saying that Soma as the Sun is born on a foundation of the ritual and on a foundation of *soma* itself. Despite its convolutions, I prefer this second interpretation.

At the heart of two other passages rests a paradox. Soma's journey of purification takes it from heaven to earth through the midspace,[19] but unlike heaven and earth, which are visible foundations, the midspace across which *soma* runs provides no natural foundation. According to two verses, *soma* nonetheless finds a foundation as it rides the wind toward the earth. The first is 9.25.2 *pávamāna dhiyā́ hitò 'bhí yónim kánikradat / dhármaṇā vāyúm ā́ viśa* "Purifying yourself, sped by insight, and crying loudly toward your womb, / enter the wind through your foundation." The governing image is once again that of *soma* as a horse. Here it leaps into the wind and gallops downwards toward the *soma* vat. The question is: what is the 'foundation' that allows him to do that? Re says that it is his 'nature' and Ge, his 'ordinance, instruction' ('Bestimmung'). Both are possible, but in light of 9.7.1 and 110.4 in which *soma* is founded on the truth, the foundation of *soma* here might also be the 'insight' of the priests that speeds him on his way. The difficulty with this view is that a parallel passage, 9.63.22 (below), shows no basis for a similar interpretation. Therefore, even though this passage does not demand this interpretation, I take *dhárman* to refer to the ritual in general, which provides the foundation for *soma*'s journey from heaven to earth in the purification process. The ritual gives *soma* a foundation through space, which itself offers no foundation.

As I mentioned, the interpretation of 9.25.2 must take into account 9.63.22 *pávasva devāyuṣág índraṃ gachatu te mádaḥ / vāyúm ā́ roha dhármaṇā* "Purify yourself, god, toward life.[20] Let your invigoration go to Indra. / Mount the wind through your foundation." If anything, the paradox is more sharply stated here: the wind does not offer support, but yet *soma* finds a 'foundation' that allows it to mount the wind. Here Soma is the rider rather than the horse, but the image is otherwise similar to that in 9.25.2. Again too, Re's interpretation 'selon (ton) comportement-naturel' is inviting. Ultimately, however, I think that here also *soma*'s 'foundation' is his foundation in the ritual.

Summary

This section has considered those passages in which *dhárman* describes the ritual, or elements of the ritual, as a foundation. The ritual provides a foundation for the world (5.15.2), for heaven (10.121.9, 170.2), for living beings (10.88.1), and for heaven and earth (9.86.9). It is likewise the foundation for the gods (1.187.1), or more specifically of Indra (10.50.6) or the manliness of Indra (1.55.3). The bulk of these passages, however, concern the ritual foundations of *soma*. This theme emerges especially in the verses in which *soma* depends on a 'foundation of truth' (9.7.1, 110.4, cf. 97.22, 86.4), where the truth may be the ritual or the ritual chant. The *dhárman* or *dhárman*s of *soma* may also extend beyond the realm of the ritual and the visible purification of *soma*. *Dhárman* may imply also universal foundations (cf. 9.107.24, 86.5, 110.4), physical foundations (cf. 9.25.2, 63.22), or possibly the foundational nature of Soma (cf. 9.7.7, 107.24, 97.12, 25.2, 63.22), as well as ritual foundations. But in all of these verses, the sense of the ritual foundations of *soma* remains present and primary.

DHÁRMAN AS THE FOUNDATION FOR THE RITUAL

The first foundations

Thus far, I have tried to show that *dhárman* can signify the ritual foundation for heaven and earth or for the gods. But it is also a concern of the Ṛgvedic poets that the ritual itself have a foundation. This foundation for the ritual can be its ancient precedent or ancient prototype. Especially in the younger parts of the *Ṛgveda*, where the effort to establish the basis of the ritual already emerges, poets mention the 'first foundations' which present sacrificers carry forward. The most famous instance is in the *puruṣa sūkta*, 10.90. At the end of the hymn, the poet declares the sacrifice of the *puruṣa* (or possibly the sacrifice that is the *puruṣa*) to be the foundation for subsequent ritual performance: 10.90.16 *yajñéna yajñám ayajanta devā́s tā́ni dhármāṇi prathamā́ny āsan / té ha nā́kam mahimā́naḥ sacanta yátra pū́rve sādhyā́ḥ sánti devā́ḥ*[21] "With the sacrifice the gods sacrificed the sacrifice[22]: these were the first foundations, / and those, its greatnesses, follow to heaven's vault, where exist the ancient ones who are to be attained (*sādhya*s),[23] the gods." The 'first *dhármans*' are the model sacrifice instituted by the gods and replicated in human performance, and as such, they are the 'foundations' for ritual performance.

If its use in 10.90 establishes the sense of *dhárman* as a ritual precedent, then we can allow this sense in other, less clearly marked passages. One example is 10.56.3 *vājy àsi vā́jinenā suvenī́ḥ suvitá stómaṃ suvitó dívaṃ gāḥ / suvitó dhárma prathamā́nu satyā́ suvitó devā́n suvitó 'nu* pátma "You are the prize-winning horse with the ability to win, who tracks well (?).[24] Go, having travelled easily to the praise-song,[25] having travelled easily to heaven, / having travelled easily along the first and real foundations, having travelled easily to the gods, having travelled easily along your flight." One reason that *dhárman* appears in this verse is that its literal meaning is applicable, since, as we have seen before, a horse requires a physical 'foundation.' But the horse itself may be a metaphor[26] and its 'foundations' certainly are, for the 'foundations' on which the horse runs are the foundations of ritual precedent. The *dhárman*s are thus the first foundations of the past, which are also real and present now in the current ritual performance.

In addition to the passages in the tenth book, there are several in the third, which likewise refer to the first foundations of the ritual. Two appear in the same hymn: 3.17.1 *samidhyámānaḥ prathamā́nu dhármā sám aktúbhir ajyate viśvávāraḥ / śocíṣkeśo ghṛtánirṇik pāvakáḥ suyajñó agnír yajáthāya devā́n* "Being kindled according to the first foundations, he is anointed with unguents – he that fulfills all wishes, / the flame-haired, ghee-cloaked, purifying Fire, who makes the sacrifice good – for the sake of the sacrifice to the gods." What gives the present sacrifice legitimacy is that it is a new instantiation of the ancient form, and therefore its fire is kindled according to that ancient form. If the foundations in vs. 1 refer to the ancient prototype, then this may also be the case in vs. 5, although here there is no reference to the 'first' and *dhárma* might be either singular or plural: 3.17.5 *yás tvád dhótā pū́rvo agne yájīyān dvitā́ ca sáttā svadháyā ca śambhúḥ / tásyā́nu dhárma prá yajā cikitvó 'tha no dhā adhvarám devávītau* "The *hotar*-priest who is before, o Fire, who performs sacrifice better, who sits now, as before, and is luck-bringing by nature – / following his foundations, set forth the sacrifice, o you who are perceptive, and establish the rite for us in our pursuit of the gods." There is much that is puzzling in this verse. Most centrally, who or what is the *hótā pū́rvaḥ*? If *pū́rva* has a locational sense, then the fire, whom the poet addresses and who is not the *hótā pū́rvaḥ*, might be the *gārhapatya* or of any other fire except for the *āhavanīya*. The *āhavanīya* should be the *hotar* 'before you' or 'to the east of you.' In this case, the *dhárma* of that *hotar* are either the 'foundations' or installation of the *āhavanīya*, or they are the 'foundations' or starting point for the sacrifice provided by the *āhavanīya* fire. In either case, with its installation, Fire is then asked to carry out the sacrifice. Alternatively, the *hótā pū́rvaḥ* might be the 'ancient *hotar*,' the ancient Fire, who takes his seat again as the *āhavanīya* fire. In this case, his foundations could be Fire's ancient installation, which forms the prototype for his present installation. Of these alternatives, I think the latter the more likely. In this interpretation, *dhárma* carries the same sense in this verse as it does in the first verse of the hymn.

Another verse returns us to the realms of metaphor and problematic syntax: 3.60.6 *índra ṛbhumā́n vā́javān matsvehá no 'smín sávane śácyā puruṣṭuta / imā́ni túbhyaṃ svásarāṇi yemire vratā́ devā́nām mánuṣaś ca dhármabhiḥ* "O Indra, together with Rbhu and with Vāja, may you become invigorated here in this pressing of ours, along with your power, o you who are much praised. / These pastures (= rituals?) have offered themselves to you according to the command of the gods and according to the foundations of Manu." Again the verse can be construed and interpreted in a number of plausible ways. Ge takes *vratā́* as instrumental, as I have done. This interpretation is rejected by Ol, who suggests that it might be nom. pl. with an ellipsis of *yā́* – an interpretation, especially with its supposition of an ellipsis, that seems strained.[27] If it is instrumental, then *vratā́* parallels *dhármabhiḥ*, and the two form a complementary pair. The gods command that the 'pastures,' which I take to be a metaphor for the rites that support Indra, be given to Indra. This command is in conformity with the 'foundations,' the ancient precedent of Manu's sacrifice. Since Manu is the first sacrificer, his sacrifice can form an obvious prototype.

If this is the sense of the *dhárman* of Manu in 3.60.6, then *dhárīman* may have a similar one in 1.128.1ab *ayáṃ jāyata mánuṣo dhárīmaṇi hótā yájiṣṭha uśíjām ánu vratám agníḥ svám ánu vratám* "This one here is born on the foundation of Manu – (the one) who is the best sacrificing *hotar*-priest following the command of his acolytes and who is Fire, following his own command." Various interpreters have offered varying interpretations of *dhárīmaṇi*: both Ge 'im (Feuer)behälter des Manu' and Hoffmann (1967: 121) 'in den Händen des Menschen' take it materially, Oldenberg (1897: 137) 'in Manu's firm law' more abstractly, and Re 'pour être porté par l'Homme' as an infinitive. But if it is interpreted in accord with 3.60.6, then the 'foundation of Manu,' on which the Fire is kindled, could again be the ritual precedent established by Manu. This is essentially the view of Grassmann, who translates 'nach altem Brauch' (cf. Wennerberg, 1981: 94). Always, however, there is the possibility that *dhárīman* has a double significance and that it indicates something material as well, perhaps, as Ge surmises, the fire place.

Another complex verse also refers to another kind of ancient prototype, this time the prototypes of the sages' compositions: 3.38.2 *inótá pṛcha jánimā kavīnā́m, manodhṛ́taḥ sukṛ́tas takṣata dyā́m/imā́ u te praṇyò várdhamānā, mánovātā ádha nú dhármaṇi gman* "And ask about the forceful generations of sages. Giving foundation to their thought and performing well, they fashioned heaven. / And these are your (= Indra's) leadings forth, which grow strong and which are won by thought; therefore they go now upon (that) foundation." Although not directly relevant to the the meaning of *dhárman*, it would be helpful to know what exactly is meant by *manodhṛ́t*, since *mánovātāḥ* ... *dhármaṇi* in cd echoes it. It is typically translated in the sense of 'resolute' (Ge: 'entschlossen') or, more literally, 'holding firm the mind' (Ol: 'die Festhalter des Geistes' or Hoffmann, 1967: 225: 'den Geist festhaltend'), and such an interpretation is both justifiable and sensible. But it yields a bland translation that does not reveal much about why the sages are here called *manodhṛ́t*. If *sukṛ́t* refers to the sages' ritual performance, then *manodhṛ́t* should refer to the sages' ritual speech, which would be the means through which the sages 'give foundation' ($\sqrt{}$*dhṛ*) to their thought. More critical to the interpretation of *dhárman* are Indra's 'leadings forth' (*praṇī́*). Most likely they are the hymns or rather the 'inspired thoughts,' which 3.38.1a anounces as a theme of this hymn: *abhí táṣṭeva dīdhayā manīṣā́m* "Like a fashioner, I reflect upon my inspired thought." If the 'leadings forth' do refer to the hymns, then they might be the inspirations that Indra leads toward the present generation of sages, or they might be inspirations that lead Indra forth. In favor of the latter, the descriptions of the 'leadings forth' as 'growing strong' and even more, as 'won by thought' are appropriate to the sages' poetry and its success in making Indra manifest. In this context, then, *dhárman* is the 'foundation' on which these new hymns are composed, namely, the old hymns of the ancient sages, the old hymns which helped create the world.

Fire as the creator of ritual foundations

The sacrifice has not only a historical foundation in its ancient prototypes but also a present foundation in the various constituents on which it depends. The most fundamental constituent is the fire, which sustains the sacrifice. The clearest instances of this image are two passages in which Fire is the *dharmán*, the 'foundation-giver' of the rite. The first is 10.92.2 *imám añjaspā́m ubháye akr̥ṇvata dharmā́ṇam agníṃ vidáthasya sā́dhanam/aktúṃ ná yahvám uṣásaḥ puróhitaṃ tánūnápātam aruṣásya niṃsate* "This one, drinking straightaway,[28] have both[29] made their own – Fire, the foundation-giver and success-bringer of the ritual distribution – / him, the youth, do the dawns kiss like the night, him who is installed in front and who is the bodily descendant of the ruddy one."[30] *Dharmán* and *sā́dhana* are complementary: Fire is the beginning of the rite as its founder and also its end, as the agent of its success. The second verse is 10.21.3 *tvé dharmā́ṇa āsate juhū́bhiḥ siñcatī́r iva / kr̥ṣṇā́ rūpā́ṇy árjunā ví vo máde víśvā ádhi śríyo dhiṣe vívakṣase* "The foundation-givers sit on you, like pouring (ladles) with their tongues.[31] / Colors of black and silver: you all, have I in my invigoration – / (you) and all glories you assume – have I made to declare." The address is to the Fire's flames, which repose on fire as tongues of flame, in the same way that spouts, representing tongues, are attached to the ladles that pour the offerings. The verse does not explain why the flames are foundation-givers, but in view of the preceding verse, it is most likely that they provide the foundations upon which the ritual offerings are poured.

If the flames repose on Fire, then they have their 'foundation' in the fire. Such is the meaning of 10.20.2 *agním īḷe bhujā́ṃ yáviṣṭhaṃ śāsā́ mitrám durdhárītum / yásya dhárman svàr énīḥ saparyánti mātúr ū́dhaḥ* "I call upon Fire, the youngest of those finding satisfaction [= the gods], the ally (/Mitra)[32] difficult to hold[33] through his authority, / upon whose foundation, the mottled females wait on the sun, (as on?) their mother's udder." As the parentheses and query that decorate this translation indicate, the verse is problematic in its details. The function of *dhárman*, however, is thankfully more plain. As both Ge and Re have recognized, the 'mottled females' are the flames. Here, therefore, Fire is the foundation of the flames that reach upward to the sun in order to suckle on it.

In three other passages, 3.3.1, 8.43.24, and 5.26.6, Fire creates or oversees foundations, although the identity these foundations is unstated. Given that the verses concern the ritual fire and that Fire is the 'foundation-giver' of the rite, these foundations are likely to be either foundations that are the ritual itself or foundations for the ritual. The most intriguing of these passages is 3.3.1 *vaiśvānarā́ya pr̥thupā́jase vípo rátnā vidhanta dharúṇeṣu gā́tave / agnír hí devā́ṁ amŕ̥to duvasyáty áthā dhármāṇi sanátā ná dūduṣat* "They give inspired words as riches to do honor to Vaiśvānara of broad face, in order that he go upon supports, / for Fire as a deathless one befriends the gods, and therefore, from of old, he never ruins their foundations." The 'supports' (*dharúṇa*) are the 'inspired words' that empower Fire. The reason to give these words to Fire and thereby empower him is that the Fire never compromises the 'foundations' of the gods. In my view, the foundations are the rites that the Fire brings to success. One might understand the *dhármāṇi* as the foundational 'ordinances' of the gods rather than the ritual 'foundations' that sustain the gods. However, the point of the verse is to emphasize the service that Fire renders to the gods and not his obedience to them. Further evidence from the context is inconclusive. The root √*dūṣ*, which governs *dhárman*, is only attested in two other verbal forms. In one verse, though, the thing 'ruined' is probably a ritual recitation: 7.104.9ab *yé pākaśaṃsám viháranta évair yé vā bhadrám dūṣáyanti svadhā́bhiḥ* "Who distort an innocent recitation in their ways, or who ruin a good one willfully..." If a ritual recitation can be ruined, so then can a ritual. The other example is in the notoriously problematic Vr̥ṣākapi hymn. In her study of this hymn, Jamison (1996: 78) translates the relevant lines in this way: 10.86.5ab *priyā́ taṣṭā́ni me kapír vyàktā vy àdūduṣat* "The monkey has spoiled my dear (well-)shaped and decorated things." Indrāṇī is speaking, and her 'things' are her sexual organs. In both these verses, therefore, the things ruined are perceptible objects: words or body parts. The interpretation of the *dhármāṇi* as rites carries a comparable concreteness.

If we understand 3.3.1 in this way, then 5.51.2 might be interpreted similarly. The verse addresses all the gods: 5.51.2 *ŕ̥tadhītaya ā́ gata sátyadharmāṇo adhvarám / agnéḥ pibata jihváyā* "You whose insights are truth, come here. You whose foundations are real, (come) to the rite. Drink with the tongue of Fire." Undoubtedly, the thoughts that the gods think are true, and the foundations that they institute are real. If the verse is so interpreted, *dhárman* might have the sense of 'decree' that it has in connection with Mitra and Varuṇa in 5.63.1 (below). The reference to the *r̥tá* 'truth' does bring the verse within the sphere of those sovereign gods, but even granting the possibility of this reading, a second interpretation of the verse is also implied. The 'insights' are typically the hymns that are recited to the gods, and therefore the 'foundations' could likewise be the ritual foundations that are established for the gods. This reading is particularly appropriate here at the beginning of a hymn, which is inviting the gods to come to the real and present rite that is being offered them. Supporting this second interpretation is also 1.12.7ab *kavím agním úpa stuhi satyádharmāṇam adhvaré* "Praise the sage Fire, whose foundations are real at the rite." Here the 'real foundations' are the ritual foundations that Fire creates at the ritual performance.

The possibility that *dhárman* has both a ritual and non-ritual significance is especially strong in 8.43.24 *viśā́ṃ rā́jānam ádbhutam ádhyakṣaṃ dhármaṇām imám, agním īḷe sá u śravat* "The undeceivable king of the clans and overseer of the foundations, this one here, – / Fire, I reverently invoke: he will hear." Since Fire is the 'king of the clans,' *dhárman* might also have a political sense and therefore designate the 'decrees' of a king. Oberlies (1999: 359), for example, notes that Fire is here similar to Varuṇa and translates, "Den König der Viś, diesen untrüglichen Aufseher der Ordnungen, Agni erquicke ich." But *ádhyakṣa*, unlike *rā́jan*, is not a political term. In 10.129.7, the poet asks about the 'overseer' of the world and in 10.88.13, Agni Vaiśvānara, representing the sun, is the 'overseer' of the 'marvel' (*yakṣá*), although it is not clear what that marvel is.[34] The most suggestive parallel occurs in 10.128, which is an appeal for help in the contest of sacrifices. In the first verse, this appeal is made directly to Fire: 10.128.1 *mámāgne várco vihavéṣv astu vayáṃ tvéndhānās tanvàm puṣema / máhyaṃ namantām pradíśaś cátasras tváyā́dhyakṣeṇa pŕ̥tanā jayema* "Fire, let luster be mine amid the competing calls. Kindling you, we would thrive ourselves. / Let the four directions pay reverence to me. With you as overseer, we could win the contests." The imagery is military, but the context is ritual, and here Fire is the overseer of the rite that the poet hopes will triumph over all other rites for the attention of the gods. I would suggest we have a similar context in 8.43.24, and once again, Fire is the overseer of the rites as 'foundations.' The verse would reflect Fire's double role as the image of the priest and of the clan lord, who is the sacrificer.

The idea that Fire provides the foundations for the gods by carrying forward the sacrifice appears in 5.26.6 *samidhānáḥ sahasrajid ágne dhármāṇi puṣyasi devā́nāṃ dūtá ukthyàḥ* "Being fully kindled, o Fire who conquers thousands, you made the foundations thrive, as the praiseworthy messenger of the gods." Elsewhere, the kinds of things that are 'made to thrive' are typically goods (*vásūni*) and other things worth choosing (*vā́ryā[ṇi]*), so the 'foundations' should be a material thing that makes someone's life better. Since this an address to the Fire, those things would reasonably be the ritual offerings, and those who are supported would be the gods. This interpretation is strengthened by the description of Fire as the 'messenger of the gods,' who carries the words and offerings to the gods. But with equal plausibility, these foundations could be the rewards, the 'goods' and 'things worth choosing,' that are earned by Fire's efforts in the sacrifice, and the beings so rewarded could be humans. In the latter case, the 'foundations' would then be the possessions that are the foundations of human life or the sacrifice that produces such things.

Indra

As Fire establishes foundations, so also can Indra, although in the one example, the nature of those foundations is undefined. Tentatively, I place it together with the other passages in which the foundations are foundations for the ritual: 8.98.1 *índrāya sā́ma gāyata víprāya bṛhaté bṛhát / dharmakṛ́te vipaścíte panasyáve* "To Indra sing the chant, a lofty (chant) to the lofty inspired poet, / to him that creates the foundations, that perceives poetic inspirations, and that draws admiration." Scarlata (1999: 74) considers various possible ways of construing the passage. As he points out, it is possible that the first stem of the compound *dharmakṛ́t* is *dharmán*, rather than *dhárman*. In favor of this interpretation, √*kṛ* once (in 10.92.2) has *dharmán* as its acc. object,[35] but it never has *dhárman*. But while possible, this interpretation makes the passage even more obscure. Who would be the 'givers of foundations' that Indra makes? The priests? Or Fire?

Scarlata also cites 9.64.1 where √*dhā*, which can semantically parallel √*kr̥*, governs *dhárman*. In that passage, *dhárman* has the sense of a foundational authority, and that meaning too is possible here, although otherwise the contexts of the two passages are quite different. But the thing, and it is an admittedly slight thing, that makes me believe that *dhárman* in 8.98.1 refers to the ritual is its complement *vipaścít*, which can describe a ritual performer (cf. Scarlata, 1999: 122). Since *vipaścít* establishes a ritual context, I take *dharmakŕ̥t* as meaning either that Indra creates ritual foundations (for the world) or that Indra creates foundations for the ritual.

Summary

The best evidence for the interpretation of *dhárman* as a foundation for the ritual are the passages, such as 10.90.16, that speak of the 'first foundations' of the ritual, the ritual precedents which the present rituals follow. Later on, of course, it would be appropriate to speak of the ritual 'ordinances,' eventually formulated in the *sūtra* literature, but for the period of the *R̥gveda*, in which the ritual was varied and fluid, such reference to ritual ordinances is an anachronism. The theme of the ritual's foundations carries into Agni hymns, in which Fire is the *dharmán*, the one who gives foundation to the rites (10.21.3, 92.2). In other verses (e.g., 3.3.1, 8.43.24, and 5.26.6), however, the rites that Fire governs are themselves 'foundations,' those of the gods and of humans.

DHÁRMAN AS THE FOUNDATION OF THE WORLD

While many of the 'foundations' mentioned in the *R̥gveda* have reference to the *soma* ritual, *dhárman* also means 'foundation' in the general sense of a universal, physical foundation, a foundation for all things or living beings. The earth is the ultimate foundation, since every object and living being rests upon the earth. A good example, if not entirely unproblematic, is 1.159.3 *té sūnávaḥ svápasaḥ sudáṃsaso mahī́ jajñur mātárā pūrvácittaye / sthātúś ca satyáṃ jágataś ca dhármaṇi putrásya pāthaḥ padám ádvayāvinaḥ* "These their sons, of good deeds and very wondrous skills, have given birth to the two great parents who are to be attended to first.[36] / You two protect the real one upon the foundation of the standing and the moving, and (you protect) the track of your son who is free of deception." The hymn addresses Heaven and Earth, who are the 'two great parents.'

Two problems in this verse are the identities of their 'sons' in line a and their 'son' in line c. We can leave the first undecided. As Ge suggests, they could be the gods generally or they could be ancient seers, since either might be credited with the creation of Heaven and Earth. The identity of the 'son' is more critical to the interpretation of *dhárman*. According to one explanation of Sāyaṇa, their son is the sun. Ge notes that this interpretation is supported by 1.160.1 (below), but says that the son more likely refers to the living creature. Similarly, Re understands the son as a human son. But I think Sāyaṇa's explanation is right, since it yields a perfectly coherent image of the sun moving across the sky and because it is appropriate to the context. That still leaves the question of the identification of the 'real one' in line c. It need not be the same as the 'son' in d, but if not, it should be closely connected with him. Most likely it refers to the Fire, who is 'real' because he is actually and immediately present in front of the reciter of the hymn and other participants in the rite. Elsewhere, Fire is the 'real' (1.1.5, 5.25.2), the 'real sacrificer' (3.14.1), and the 'most real' *hotar*-priest (1.76.5, 3.4.10). If so, then line c is a reference to the fire and d to the sun: the fire is on the earth, which is the foundation of both plants and animals, that is, 'the standing and the moving,' and the sun, to which the fire corresponds, is in the heaven.

The characterization of earth as the foundation also occurs in 10.16, which is a funeral hymn: 10.16.3 *sū́ryaṃ cákṣur gachatu vā́tam ātmā́ dyā́ṃ ca gacha pṛthivī́ṃ ca dhármaṇā / apó vā gacha yádi tátra te hitám óṣadhīṣu práti tiṣṭhā śárīraiḥ* "Let your eye go to the sun, your life-breath to the wind. Go to heaven and to the earth according to your foundation, / or go to the waters, if there (a place) is fixed for you. Take your stand among the plants with your body parts." Lines bc form two alternatives for the dead man: either he finds a place in heaven and earth or in the waters. The translation of line b is awkward and uncertain, but I believe the line means that the deceased should go to heaven and to earth with the earth (or heaven and earth) as his foundation. Note the parallelism in lines b and d. In d, the plants become the body parts of the deceased, as in b, the earth (or heaven and earth) become his foundation.

Heaven and earth together function as a foundation also for the sun, which moves between them. This is one sense of 1.160.1, although the verse is complicated because it may refer both to the sun and to its earthly equivalent, the ritual fire: 1.160.1 *té hí dyā́vāpṛthivī́ viśváśambhuva ṛtā́varī rájaso dhārayátkavī / sujánmanī dhiṣáṇe antár īyate devó devī́ dhármaṇā sū́ryaḥ śúciḥ* "Because these are Heaven and

Earth, that are good luck to all, that are truth-bearing, and that give foundation to the sage of the airy space, / he goes between the two stations of strong birth, he the god (goes) between two gods, he, the blazing sun (goes) according to his foundation." According to Ge (following one suggestion of Sāyaṇa) and Re, the 'sage of the airy space' is the sun. The sun is between Heaven and Earth, who give birth and foundation to it. Another possibility is suggested by Ol, who takes the sage to be the Fire. Now, clearly these two interpretations are not exclusive, since the ritual fire can represent the sun. If the 'sage' is first the Fire in line b, then line d is reenvisioning that Fire as the Sun. This interpretation would also relocate the main action and principal reference of the verse to the sacrificial ground. The two 'stations' (*dhiṣáṇe*) could refer to places in the ritual that represent earth and heaven, that is, to the fire places at the western and eastern ends of the *vedi.* The movement of the 'sage' between heaven and earth would therefore be reflected in the movement of the sacrificial fire from the west to the east, as well as in the movement of the sun from the east to the west. The 'foundation,' therefore, would be both the installation of the fire in the fire places as well as the foundation for the sun created by heaven and earth.

In 10.149, the god Savitar, rather than Heaven and Earth, establishes the foundation for the sun. This hymn presents a short cosmogony in which the sun is born on the foundation provided by Savitar: 10.149.3 *paścédám anyád abhavad yájatram ámartyasya bhúvanasya bhūnā́ / suparṇó aṅgá savitúr garútmān pū́rvo jātáḥ sá u asyā́nu dhárma* "After this (world), the other, sacrificial (world) came to be, together with the coming to be of a world of living beings that is deathless. / Surely the strong-winged bird of Savitar was born first, following upon his (= Savitar's) foundation." As obscure as it is, this translation is clearer than the verse, and especially in ab, the translation makes several interpretive leaps. With some confidence, however, we can say that ab refers to the creation of this world, and possibly also to the creation of the world of the sacrifice and to the creation of the next world. On this cosmogonic level, Savitar's 'strong-winged bird' is the sun, which here is the first created thing after heaven and earth (cf. Oberlies, 1998: 444). But this first creation rests on a foundation provided by Savitar himself. Savitar is associated with the onset of night, but he also brings the night to a close by sending the sun on its course and all the creatures to their various daylight activities (Oberlies, 1998: 222f.). Therefore, the verse depicts the birth of the sun, a birth which Savitar compels, even as he himself disappears.

The theme of the 'foundation of the sun' also occurs in 8.6.19f., which is a complex passage because it sustains metaphor through ellipsis. The result are verses that successfully defy exegetical determination: 8.6.19 *imā́s ta indra pŕ̥śnayo ghr̥tám̐ duhata āśíram / enā́m r̥tásya pipyúṣīḥ* // 20 *yā́ indra prasvàs tvāsā́ gárbham ácakriran / pári dhármeva sū́ryam* "These dappled (cows)[37] yield ghee and the milk-mix for you, Indra, / (and also) this, (a milk-mix)[38] of truth,[39] since they are swelling (with truth), // – (they, the) fruitful (cows), that have made you their new-born by their mouth, (are) around (you?) like foundations[40] (around) the sun." With the understanding that any interpretation of this verse is a risky enterprise, I understand it in the following way. The insights embedded in the hymns are the 'dappled' and 'fruitful' cows, which bring Indra into manifestation at the sacrifice (Oberlies, 1998: 276ff.). Since they bring him to manifestation, they therefore give birth to him, who is their 'new-born' child, and they surround him, for indeed the hymns do surround Indra. 'Their mouth' is the mouth of a cow licking clean a new-born calf, and the mouth of the priest who recites the hymns. Finally, because they give birth to him, these cows and hymns are his foundations.[41] Since Indra is like the sun, therefore, the cows and hymns are like foundations for the sun. The reference to the foundations of the sun may suggest a mystery: What holds the sun up in the heavens? It must have a foundation, even if it is not a visible one.

An unnamed god gives birth and foundation to the world in 10.121.9 *mā́ no hiṃsīj janitā́ yáḥ pr̥thivyā́ yó vā dívaṃ satyádharmā jajā́na / yáś cāpáś candrā́ br̥hatī́r jajā́na kásmai devā́ya havíṣā vidhema* "Let not him, who is the birth-father of earth, do us harm, or him – the one whose foundations are real – who gave birth to heaven, / and him who gave birth to the glittering, deep waters. Who is the god to whom we should do homage with our oblation?" Since the emphasis in this verse is constantly on the unnamed god as the birth-giver of the world, *satyádharman* should refer to the foundations that this god establishes, the foundations upon which heaven and all the rest of the world depend.

There is one final passage that is intriguing because, on one level, at least, it suggests a more common sense of 'foundation.' This verse is 2.13.7 which likely refers to the 'foundation' of plants. The verse addresses Indra: 2.13.7 *yáḥ puṣpíṇīś ca prasvàś ca dhármaṇā́dhi dā́ne vy àvánīr ádhārayaḥ / yáś cā́samā ájano didyúto divá urúr ūrvā́m̐ abhítaḥ sā́sy ukthyàḥ* "You, who distributed (*vi*...*adhārayas*) the flowering and fruitful (plants)[42] according to the foundation (of each) and the streams at their division (?),[43] and you, who produced the incomparable flashings of heaven, you, the wide one surrounding the containing ones,[44] you are the praiseworthy." *Dhárman* here draws and plays on *vi*+ √*dhṛ*, and represents the basis for the plants' distribution. But a variety of interpretations are then possible. The *dhárman* could belong to Indra, and therefore be the 'ordinance' according to which he assigns them their place. In this interpretation, Indra's command is their foundation. Or the *dhárman* could belong to the plants, in which case the 'foundation' could be the place where each kind of plant belongs. I think the latter is the least freighted interpretation. The 'foundation' of the plants is therefore the place of the plants.

Summary

With the exception of 2.13.7, the above passages refer to various kinds of cosmic and physical foundations. Both the living (1.159.3) and the dead (10.16.3) find foundations on heaven or earth or both. The sun especially finds a foundation (8.6.19f.), which may be on heaven and earth (1.160.1) or through the god Savitar (10.149.3). These uses of the term illustrate the breadth of *dhárman* and suggest that the liturgical sense of the term considered earlier is a reflection of the character of the *Ṛgveda* rather than that of the word *dhárman* itself.

DHÁRMAN AS THE 'FOUNDATION' OR 'NATURE' OF A DEITY

In the passages considered thus far, the sense of *dhárman* as 'foundation' has been directly applicable. What follows are passages, in which occur more extended senses of *dhárman*. These fall into two groups. In one, *dhárman* has the sense of the foundation of a deity, or more clearly, the 'foundational nature' of a deity. In a second, *dhárman* is the social and material 'foundation' provided by the authority of a king. It is not always easy to separate these senses from the more concrete meaning of 'foundation,' nor indeed from one another – a hardly surprising circumstance in a poetic collection like the *Ṛgveda*. In fact, already in the discussion of the ritual foundations of Soma, especially with regard to 9.7.7, 86.5, and 110.4, I argued that *dhárman* might refer to the nature of *soma* that is created in the ritual, as well as to its ritual foundation. Since the boundaries that separate these different senses are permeable, the following passages are those that show the senses of 'foundational nature' or 'foundational authority' more distinctly, rather than exclusively.

Both Renou and Geldner frequently recognize *dhárman* in the sense of 'nature' in their translations, indeed more emphatically and frequently than I. But they are surely right that there are passages which refer to deities' foundations in the sense of their 'natures.' In 10.44, the poet twice speaks of the 'foundation' of Indra, the character that defines his action: 10.44.1 *ā́ yātv índraḥ svápatir mádāya yó dhármaṇā tūtujānás túviṣmān / pratvakṣāṇó áti víśvā sáhāṃsy apāréṇa mahatā́ vṛ́ṣṇyena* "As the lord of his own, let Indra journey here for his invigoration – he, the vibrant, who thrusts forward according his nature (/'foundation'), / who energetically dominates[45] over all strengths according to his boundless and great bull-likeness." The parallelism in case and construction of *dhármaṇā* in b and *vṛ́ṣṇyena* in d suggest that both belong to Indra and both define who and what he is. A few verses later, *dhárman* once again appears, although here the sense is less well defined: 10.44.5 *gámann asmé vásūny ā́ hí śáṃsiṣaṃ svāśíṣam bháram ā́ yāhi somínaḥ / tvám īśiṣe sā́smínn ā́ satsi barhíṣy anādhṛṣyā́ táva pā́trāṇi dhármaṇā* "Let good things go among us, for I hope for them. Journey here to the *soma*-bearer's stake,[46] which carries his good expectation.[47] / You are master. Take your seat here on this sacred grass. Vessels which belong to you are not to be claimed (by another) according to your nature (/'foundation')." The focus of cd is still the character of Indra: the verse states that he is master and therefore the poets invite him to sit at the sacrifice. It would be reasonable, then, if the *dhárman* is that principle according to which the *soma* cups belong to Indra and to Indra alone in his foundational nature, his very character as Indra. Alternatively, these vessels may be Indra's according to *their* foundation, that is, according to their place in the ritual.

One of the problems regarding the sense of *dhárman* as the nature of a deity is the rather limited number of deities of whom it is used. In addition to the passages in which it describes the character of Indra, those considered earlier in which it might refer to the nature of Soma, and those to be considered in which it might refer to the natures of Mitra and Varuṇa, the sense of *dhárman* as 'foundational nature' appears distinctly only in connection with Savitar. The latter especially is not a major deity of the *Ṛgveda*, and yet there are four passages in which *dhárman* is the 'nature' of Savitar. The reason for this is the transparency of Savitar, or rather, the transparency of Savitar's name. Consider, for example, 10.175.1 *prá vo grāvāṇaḥ savitā́ deváḥ suvatu dhármaṇā / dhūrṣú yujyadhvaṃ sunutá* "Let the god Savitar (Compeller) compel you forth, pressing stones, according to his nature ('foundation'). / Hitch yourselves to the chariot poles. Press the *soma*!" Renou has this verse exactly right: "selon sa disposition innée (de dieu Incitateur)." 'Compelling' is the foundational nature of the god 'Compeller,' and therefore it is according to that nature that Savitar compels the pressing stones. This verse is echoed later in the same hymn and to the same effect: 10.175.4 *grā́vāṇaḥ savitā́ nú vo deváḥ suvatu dhármaṇā / yájamānāya sunvaté* "Pressing stones, let the god Savitar compel you according to his nature ('foundation') / for the sacrificer who presses *soma*." Again, it is the character of Compeller to govern the movement of the pressing stones.

Two other verses from the core *Rgveda* show the same idea, although not as obviously as in 10.175. The first is 4.53.3 *ā́prā rájāṃsi divyā́ni pā́rthivā ślókaṃ deváḥ kṛṇute svā́ya dhármaṇe / prá bāhū́ asrāk savitā́ sávīmani niveśáyan prasuvánn aktúbhir jágat* "He has filled the heavenly and earthly realms. The god sets their rhythm to his own nature (/'foundation'). / Savitar has stretched forth his two arms to compel, as he makes the moving world settle down and compels it forth at night's darkest hours." Lines cd depict Savitar as the god that brings the world to rest during the night, and then, in the dark hours before dawn, that begins to rouse it once again. This rhythm reflects his nature as the god that compels both rest and activity, and therefore the verse says that he sets that rhythm to his own nature.

A fourth example presents the most complicated (and doubtful) case: 5.81.4 *utá yāsi savitas trī́ṇi rocanótá sū́ryasya raśmíbhiḥ sám ucyasi / utá rā́trīm ubhayátaḥ párīyasa, utá mitró bhavasi deva dhármabhiḥ* "And you travel, Savitar, through the three realms of light, and you abide with sun's rays. / And you encircle the night on both sides, and you become Mitra, o god, according to (your)[48] nature (/'foundations')." In its interpretation of *dhárman*, this translation essentially follows Ge: "und du bist nach deinen Eigenschaften der Mitra" and Re 'de par (tes) dispositions-naturelles.' The question remains, however, how the verse fits together. Why is Savitar Mitra, or, to rather, why is the god that compels also the god of alliances? Lines a-c describe Savitar as embracing the two ends of the day, the beginning and end of night. In doing so, he conjoins those times, as an alliance between them would do. Because his uniting day and night is a reflection of his nature as the god that compels, he becomes, as the compeller, also the god of alliance. Alternatively, the verse might be read: "according to his (= Mitra's) nature." This latter interpretation gives the verse a slightly difference nuance. Insofar as Savitar acts as the god of alliances by uniting the space and time, he becomes the god of alliances according to the nature of Mitra.

In addition to these passages, there is a repeated line that compares an object or being to Savitar because it and Savitar share the same foundational nature, the ability to compel or impel. The first instance is from the gambler hymn, 10.34, in a verse that compares the dice to Savitar: 10.34.8 *tripañcāśáḥ krīḷati vrā́ta eṣāṃ devá iva savitā́ satyádharmā / ugrásya cin manyáve nā́ namante rā́jā cid ebhyo náma ít kr̥ṇoti* "Three times fifty in number, the army of these (dice) plays. Like god Savitar's, its foundation is real. / They do not bow even to the battle-fury of the powerful; even the king does homage to them." Were it not so awkward, I would like to translate: "Like god Savitar's, its (Savitar-like) foundation is real" or "its (Savitar-like) nature is real" because the point is not that both Savitar and the army of dice each have a real foundation, but that they each have the *same* real foundation, the same ability to compel. As the nature of Savitar is to compel, so also the dice too have become a compulsion for the gambler. The second verse is 10.139.3 *rāyó budhnáḥ saṃgámano vásūnāṃ víśvā rūpā́bhí caṣṭe śácībhiḥ / devá iva savitā́ satyádharméndro ná tasthau samaré dhánānām* "The basis of wealth and the gathering of goods, (the sun) watches over all visible things through his powers. / Whose foundation is real like god Savitar's, he stands like Indra in the contest for the stakes." This verse anticipates the merging of the identities of Savitar and the sun, for it attributes to the sun the nature of Savitar. Like a Savitar, the sun impels those whom he wishes to win in the contest for goods that he oversees.

Summary

The sense of *dhárman* as the 'foundational nature' of a deity is a difficult one to judge. It may be more prominent than I have allowed. In the above discussion of the *dhárman* of Soma, for example, I have mentioned this possibility in connection with five passages (9.7.7, 107.24, 97.12, 25:2, 63.22) and could have done so with others. But I am inclined to restrict this sense of *dhárman* primarily to contexts in which the foundational nature of a god is manifest in the god's name. This is certainly the case for Savitar, whose character is so transparent that he is often marked as *devá savitŕ̥* 'god Compeller,' where *devá* makes it clear his identity as a god. This same transparency to a foundational nature of a god and therefore the use of *dhárman* to describe that foundational nature may also be the case for Mitra and Varuṇa, whom we will consider below. Where a god's names are less transparent or their characters more complex, I would expect this use of *dhárman* to be less frequent. It is not absent, however, since *dhárman* may describe the nature of Indra in 10.44.1, 5.

DHÁRMAN AS THE FOUNDATION CREATED BY A SOVEREIGN DEITY

The last sense in which *dhárman* is a 'foundation' is the most significant, for it is on this sense that much of the later development of *dhárman* and *dhárma* is established. A *dhárman* can be the 'foundation' through which a sovereign deity upholds the life of a community. This foundation can be the material basis for the community, or it can be prescribed behaviors and social relations which structure and sustain the community. In the latter use, it is the sovereign's ruling 'authority' or 'institute' – and in these ways it may often and best be translated – upon which the life of a community depends. This use of the term is largely confined to the spheres of two deities, or rather of one deity and one complex of deities: the first is Soma and the second, Varuṇa or Varuṇa together with Ādityas.

Soma

In the case of Soma we have some of the clearer instances of the link between *dhárman* and a ruler. In them, the 'foundation' that the rule provides is likely the material foundation for the community, the wealth which sustains it. The text is not unarguably clear on this point, but the context suggests this interpretation in two verses and permits it in a third. The first is 9.35.6 *víśvo yásya vraté jáno dādhā́ra dhármaṇas pátеḥ / punānásya prabhū́vasoḥ* "Under whose command every people finds foundation (√*dhṛ*),[49] under that of the lord of foundation, / who is purifying himself, who brings the foremost good things...." The foundation that the community finds and Soma governs might be a system of social relations, but since Soma is here invoked as *prabhū́vasu*, it is more likely material. In either case, the verse establishes the link between the authority of Soma and the basis for communal life. He is the *dhármaṇas pátiḥ* because he possesses royal 'command,' and therefore establishes the foundations for the people. A similar connection between command and foundation occurs in 9.64.1 *vṛ́ṣā soma dyumā́m̐ asi vṛ́ṣā deva vṛ́ṣavrataḥ / vṛ́ṣā dhármāṇi dadhiṣe* "A bull you are, *soma*, a brilliant one – a bull, whose command is a bull, o god. / A bull, you set the foundations." Again, Soma possesses command, and it is through that command that he establishes 'foundations,' although here the passage provides little information about the nature of these foundations. Finally, a connection between kingship and the material foundation of a community occurs in one of the attestations of *dharmán* 'foundation-giver': 9.97.23 *prá dānudó divyó dānupinvá r̥tám r̥tā́ya pavate sumedhā́ḥ / dharmā́ bhuvad vrjanyàsya rā́jā prá raśmíbhir daśábhir bhāri bhū́ma* "The divine giver of drops, sweller of drops, (goes) forth. As the truth and for the truth, the very wise one purifies himself. / He will become the foundation-giver, the king of what belongs to the community. He has been brought forward toward the world by the ten reins." It is the king who is the foundation-giver, for he governs what belongs to the community, that is, its wealth. The precise sense *vrjanyà* is not certain because it is attested only here in the *R̥gveda*, but an earlier verse in this same hymn provides an indication of its sense. Here Soma, as lord of the community, conquers the land and thereby gives the people the space to live: 9.97.10cd *hánti rákṣo bā́dhate páry árātīr várivaḥ kr̥ṇván vrjánasya rā́jā* "He strikes down the demon, and he presses away hostilities on every side – he who, as king of the community, creates expanse." Soma's kingship is connected to his ability to give his people the means to raise and pasture their cattle.

Mitra, Varuṇa, and the Ādityas

Frequently, *dhárman* occurs in close association with Varuṇa, Varuṇa and Mitra, or the Ādityas and is, therefore, characteristic of the sphere of the Ādityas. While it does not give us much information about the reason for *dhárman*'s connection to Mitra and Varuṇa, 8.35.13 does illustrate how characteristic that connection is: 8.35.13 *mitrā́váruṇavantā utá dhármavantā marútvantā jaritúr gachatho hávam / sajóṣasā uṣásā sū́ryeṇa cādityaír yātam aśvinā* "Together with Mitra and Varuṇa and together with (their) foundation, together with the Maruts, you go to the singer's call. / Along with Dawn and Sun, journey with the Ādityas, Aśvins." Here *dhárman* is something that Mitra and Varuṇa would naturally bring with them when they respond to the singer's summons. It belongs to them as closely as the dawn and sun belong to the Aśvins, gods who appear characteristically in the early morning.

For the most part, when it is linked to Mitra and Varuṇa, *dhárman* carries the sense of a foundational authority. The reason for this rests not so much in the semantic resonance that *dhárman* independently possesses, but rather in the character of the Ādityas. These are the gods most closely associated with the principles that govern the actions of humans. Varuṇa is the god of commandments and Mitra is the god of alliances.[50] The distinct characters of these gods then give color to the more neutral *dhárman* and define the kind of 'foundation' it describes, and thus, *dhárman* becomes 'the foundation of authority' that structures society.

This interpretation of *dhárman* leads to another explanation, or at least another nuance, of the relationship between *dhárman* and Mitra and Varuṇa. Since they represent the authority of alliances and commandments, their 'foundation,' that is, their nature, is to represent this authority, just as the nature of Savitar is to compel. When the poets speak of the *dhárman* of Mitra and Varuṇa, therefore, this *dhárman* can be both the foundational authority that orders the social worlds of gods and humans and the foundational nature that defines the Ādityas themselves. These two sides of *dhárman* are possible in two occurrences in 5.63: vs. 1ab *ṛ́tasya gopāv ádhi tiṣṭhatho rátham sátyadharmāṇā paramé vyòmani* "Herdsmen of the truth, you two stand upon your chariot, o you whose foundations are real, in the furthest heaven" and vs. 7 *dhármaṇā mitrāvaruṇā vipaścitā vratā́ rakṣethe ásurasya māyáyā / ṛténa víśvam bhúvanaṃ ví rājathaḥ sū́ryam ā́ dhattho diví cítryaṃ rátham* "In accordance with your foundation, o Mitra and Varuṇa, who perceive inspired words, you two guard your commands through the craft of a lord. / In accordance with truth, you rule over the whole living world. You place the sun here in heaven as your shimmering chariot." *Dhármaṇā* could be explained in two different ways. First, it could be that in accordance with the foundation they provide, Mitra and Varuṇa guard the commands which keep the world in order. This foundation is their authority, the standard they impose on the world. Note that *dhármaṇā* finds a positional, syntactic, and semantic parallel in *ṛténa*, the truth that expresses the right organization of the world. Second, *dhárman* could signify the foundations of Mitra and Varuṇa as the embodiments of the authority to govern. It would then be according to their own foundation that Mitra and Varuṇa guard their commands. Note especially the appearance of *vratá*. Etymologically, it is connected to Varuṇa, which again suggests that it is especially his nature or 'foundation' as god of commands that is manifest in the "foundation" or authority according to which Mitra and he govern the world.

Similar arguments apply also to 5.72.2ab *vraténa stho dhruvákṣemā dhármaṇā yātayájjanā* "By your command, you two are those that give peaceful dwellings that endure, assigning places to the people according to your foundation." This time *vraténa* expresses the general authority of the Mitra and Varuṇa to ensure that people can dwell in peace, and *dhármaṇā* expresses their foundational authority to organize the different peoples. Note that 'assigning places to the people' is a function particularly connected with Mitra (cf. Thieme, 1957: 40f.). The appearance of *vratá* and *yātayájjana*, terms that reflect the characters of Mitra and Varuṇa, again suggests that the *dhárman* according to which they act is both their foundation as well as the foundational authority they apply to the world.

The Ādityas are kings, and the connection between royalty and *dhárman* is a constant in verses describing the *dhárman* of the Ādityas. A complex but informative example is 10.65.5 *mitrā́ya śíkṣa váruṇāya dāśúṣe yā́ samrā́jā mánasā ná prayúchataḥ / yáyor dhā́ma dhármaṇā rócate bṛhád yáyor ubhé ródasī nā́dhasī vṛ́tau* "Strive for the sake of Mitra and of Varuṇa who acts dutifully, for them, the universal kings who, through their thought, are not far away, / whose dominion shines aloft according to their foundation, for whom the two worlds are twin need[51] and twin course." Ge rightly notes that the *dhā́man* 'dominion' of Mitra and Varuṇa is probably, in one sense at least, the sun. Therefore, *dhárman* is a 'foundation' for the sun as the symbol of their rule. Thus, *dhárman* has a double resonance. On the one hand, since Mitra and Varuṇa are kings, their foundation is their authority. On the other, the hymn recalls also the image of *dhárman* as the cosmic foundation for the sun. More generally, though, *dhā́man* might refer to the whole heavenly sphere over which Mitra and Varuṇa rule and to which they give foundation by their dutiful action as gods of alliance and commandment.

Both Soma and Varuṇa occur as kings and in connection with *dhárman* in 10.167.3 *sómasya rā́jño váruṇasya dhármaṇi bṛ́haspáter ánumatyā u śármaṇi / távāhám adyá maghavann úpastutau dhā́tar vídhātaḥ kaláśāṁ abhakṣayam* "Upon the foundation of king Soma and Varuṇa,[52] and under the protection of Bṛhaspati and Anumati, / today, at your praise, o generous one (= Indra), I consumed vats (of *soma*), o you that set in place and that set apart." Note the implicit locational imagery. On top is the 'cover' (*śárman*) provided by

Bṛhaspati and Anumati and below the 'foundation' created by Soma and Varuṇa. Their designation as kings implies that the *dhárman* of Soma and Varuṇa is their royal authority. And perhaps, their appearance together reflects the complementary sides of their *dhárman*: Soma establishes material foundation, Varuṇa social foundation.

Soma and Varuṇa appear together only rarely, but given the repeated connections between Soma and *dhárman* and between Varuṇa and *dhárman*, it is not surprising that Soma and Varuṇa, when they do appear together, do so in the context of *dhárman*: 9.107.15f. *tárat samudrám pávamāna ūrmíṇā rā́jā devá ṛtám bṛhát / árṣan mitrásya váruṇasya dhármaṇā prá hinvāná ṛtám bṛhát // nṛ́bhir yemānó haryató vicakṣaṇó rā́jā deváḥ samudríyaḥ* "He crosses the sea in a wave as he purifies himself, he that is king and god – and lofty truth. / He rushes according to the foundation of Mitra and Varuṇa, being sped forth – he, the lofty truth[53] // – he, that is controlled by fine men, the enjoyed, the far-gazing, the king and god of the sea." Here *dhárman* shows its underlying meaning as the foundation upon which Soma travels. But that foundation is also the foundation that Mitra and Varuṇa provide, their authority. The reference to *dhárman* is also conditioned by these verses' insistence on the kingship of Soma. Soma moves on a foundation of royal authority because he is himself a manifestation of kingship.

A concrete sense of *dhárman* as 'foundational authority' occurs in 7.89.5 *yát kíṃ cedáṃ varuna daívye jáne 'bhidrohám manuṣyā̀ś cárāmasi / ácittī yát táva mā́ nas tásmād énaso deva rīriṣaḥ* "Whatever this deceit that we humans practice against the race of gods, Varuṇa, / if by inattention we have erased your foundations, do not harm us because of that misdeed, o god." The foundations the poets worry about effacing, therefore, are precisely those foundations we would expect the god of commandments and the embodiment of royal authority to create – his institutes, his commands. The context of the verse speaks strongly for this interpretation. In 10.134.7a *nákir devā minīmasi nákir ā́ yopayāmasi*, √*yup*, which governs *dhárman* in 7.89, parallels √*mī* (or √*mi*). This later verb characteristically governs the *vratá* and, in that context, means 'violate' these 'commands' of the gods (cf. 1.69.7, 2.24.12, 38.7, 3.32.8, 7.31.11, 47.3, 76.5, 10.10.5, etc.). The phrase *dhármā yuyopimá*, therefore, likely reproduces the sense of *vratā́(ni)* + √*mī*, and thus *dhárman* approximates the meaning of *vratá* 'command.' The *dhármans* are commands as manifestations of royal authority.

In the passages so far considered, either Varuṇa appears alone or in conjunction with Mitra. In one example, however, Mitra appears without Varuṇa: 8.52.3 *yá ukthā́ kévalā dadhé yáḥ sómaṃ dhr̥ṣitā́pibat / yásmai víṣṇus trī́ṇi padā́ vicakramá úpa mitrásya dhármabhiḥ* "He (= Indra) who made the solemn words his own, who boldly drank the *soma*, / for whom Viṣṇu strode his three steps, according to the foundations of Mitra...." The image of ascent is one basis for the occurrence of *dhárman* here, since it implies the need for a foundation for that ascent. But the *dhárman* is only figuratively a physical foundation. The real foundation of Viṣṇu's ascent is his relationship with Indra. The 'foundations of Mitra', that is, the foundations of the god of alliances, refer here to the alliance between Indra and Viṣṇu, which is the basis of Viṣṇu's three strides.

This same combination of *dhárman* in the sense of a foundational authority with the imagery of *dhárman* as a physical foundation appears in another passage concerning Viṣṇu: 1.22.18-19ab *trī́ṇi padā́ ví cakrame víṣṇur gopā́ ádābhyaḥ / áto dhármāṇi dhāráyan // víṣṇoḥ kármāṇi paśyata yáto vratā́ni paspaśé* "Three tracks he strode out: he, Viṣṇu, the undeceivable cowherd, / who gives foundation (√*dhr̥*) to the foundations from there // – see the deeds of Viṣṇu! – from where he watches over his commands." The 'there' from which Viṣṇu 'gives foundation' is probably heaven, but this still leaves the problem of identifying the 'foundations.' The reference to Viṣṇu's *vratā́ni*, his 'commands', sets this verse within the context of royal authority and again of Varuṇa. The 'foundations' to which Viṣṇu gives foundation, therefore, are his authority. At the same time, however, again as in 8.52.3, the imagery and the context also suggest the sense of *dhárman* as a physical and universal foundation. The verse preceding this passage describes the journey of Viṣṇu through the world: vs. 17 *idáṃ víṣṇur ví cakrame tredhā́ ní dadhe padám / sámūḷham asya pāṃsuré* "Viṣṇu strode out – three times he set down his track – through this (world) here, / which is drawn together in his dusty (track)." That is to say, the world is encompassed in the footprints of Viṣṇu. In vs. 18, the scene shifts explicitly to heaven, which is the limit of Viṣṇu's journey. Viṣṇu thus makes heaven the foundation for the worlds. Thus, while the primary sense of *dhárman* is a foundational authority, the poet again evokes its sense as a physical foundation.

A similar complex deployment of *dhárman* occurs also in 6.70.1-3, where again the context requires a double sense of a foundational authority and of a physical foundation:

6.70.1 *ghṛtávatī bhúvanānām abhiśrī́yorvī́ pṛthvī́ madhudúghe supéśasā / dyā́vāpṛthivī́ váruṇasya dhármaṇā víṣkabhite ajáre bhū́riretasā* "The two rich in ghee and excelling in glory over living beings, wide and broad, giving honey as their milk, well-adorned – / Heaven and Earth are buttressed apart according to the foundation of Varuṇa as the pair that are never aging, endowed with abundant semen."
6.70.2 *ásaścantī bhū́ridhāre páyasvatī ghṛtáṃ duhāte sukṛ́te śúcivrate / rā́jantī asyá bhúvanasya rodasī asmé rétaḥ siñcataṃ yán mánurhitam* "Never dry, with abundant streams, and rich in milk, they give ghee as their milk to him that performs well – they of flame-bright commands. / You two worlds that rule over this living world, may you pour the semen for us which was established for Manu."
6.70.3 *yó vām ṛjáve krámaṇāya rodasī márto dadā́śa dhiṣaṇe sá sādhati / prá prajā́bhir jāyate dhármaṇas pári yuvóḥ siktā́ víṣurūpāṇi sávratā* "Who has acted dutifully toward you in order to stride straight ahead – o you two worlds, you two stations – that mortal attains success. / He is regenerated through his offspring from your foundation. Beings of varied form but of like command are poured out from you."

The first verse tells of the foundations of Heaven and Earth. This foundation is the authority of Varuṇa that determines their place and their distinction from one another.[54] At the same time, mention of heaven and earth and of the foundations of heaven and earth also puts the verse in the context of the physical foundations of the world. The authority of Varuṇa becomes materially sensible in the stability of the worlds. The second verse mentions the commands of Mitra and Varuṇa and the theme is carried over into the third verse, in which, in complement to the first, *dhárman* becomes a temporal as well as a spatial foundation. Earth and Heaven, paralleling their function as physical foundations for the present world, are also the foundations for future generations. Because of the worshipper's reverence, the two worlds continue the life of that mortal through his offspring by providing them a foundation, a place for them to be and to prosper.[55] At the same time, *dhárman* in vs. 3 does not only have the sense of a physical foundation for generations. Again, consider the context. The sense of *dhárman* as foundational authority is established in the first verse by its association with Varuṇa, and *vratá* occurs in both vs. 2 and in the compound *sávrata* in vs. 3. Heaven and Earth inherit the characteristic *dhárman* of Varuṇa, the authority that here ordains the continuation of the sacrificer's line.

Moreover, 6.70.3c is repeated twice more in verses which again suggest the sense of *dhárman* as 'foundational authority.' In the first of these, Mitra and Varuṇa create the foundation for future generations: 8.27.16 *prá sá kṣáyaṃ tirate ví mahī́r íṣo yó vo várāya dā́śati / prá prajā́bhir jāyate dhármaṇas páry áriṣṭaḥ sárva edhate* "He extends his dwelling forward across great refreshments – he, who dutifully acts to your wish. He is regenerated through his offspring from your foundation. Never harmed and whole, he thrives." In the second, it is the Ādityas: 10.63.13 *áriṣṭaḥ sá márto víśva edhate, prá prajā́bhir jāyate dhármaṇas pári / yám ādityāso náyathā sunītíbhir, áti víśvāni duritā́ svastáye* "Never harmed, each mortal thrives, and he is regenerated through his offspring from your foundation, / whom, Ādityas, you lead with your good leading beyond all difficult ways to well-being." The function of Varuṇa and Mitra that was assumed by Heaven and Earth in 6.70 is here reassumed by those gods in these two verses. At the same time, the foundation that their authority provides is figured as a physical foundation upon which later generations stand.

Wind

One last verse that I find difficult to interpret, let alone classify, is 1.134.5 *túbhyaṃ śukrā́sah śúcayas turaṇyávo mádeṣūgrā́ iṣaṇanta bhurváṇy apā́m iṣanta bhurváṇi / tvā́ṃ tsārī́ dásamāno bhágam īṭṭe takvavī́ye / tváṃ víśvasmād bhúvanāt pāsi dhármaṇāsuryàt pāsi dhármaṇā* "For you the glistening, gleaming rapid ones, powerful in their invigorations, send themselves swirling; they send themselves towards the swirling of waters. / The one moving stealthily [= the priest?], exhausting himself, calls upon you, his fortune, in his pursuit of the swooping (bird) [= *soma*?]. / You, because of the whole living world, protect according to your foundation; you, because of your lordliness, protect according to your foundation." Since this verse is addressing the wind, I take it as a description of the movement of the *soma* through the midspace in the process of purification.[56] Perhaps this verse again reflects the idea that the wind, which seems to have no foundation, actually does. Its foundation is both all living beings, since breath is located within them, and also its own lordliness. In the latter context, therefore, this passage again attests the connection between rule and *dhárman*.

Summary

This sense of *dhárman* as 'foundational authority' is a critical source for the later development of the concept of *dhárma*, and in considering this aspect of *dhárman* several points relevant to the history of *dhárman* and *dhárma* emerge. First, *dhárman* implies not just 'foundational authority' but more specifically 'royal authority.' This facet of its meaning is indicated either by the direct description of the gods that act in connection with *dhárman* as kings (9.97.23, 5.63.7, 10.65.5, 10.167.3, 9.107.15f., 1.134.5) or by attributing commanding authority to them (as in 9.35.6, 9.64.1, 5.72.2, 1.22.18f., 6.70.1ff., cf. 7.89.5).

It is not difficult to explain directly how *dhárman* 'foundation' could come to mean 'foundational authority' or 'institute.' If an 'authority' is the basis of relationships among different beings or for the organization of the world, then it is a 'foundation'. The fact that *dhárman* as 'authority' is persistently connected to Varuṇa and *vratá,* however, suggests that it is at least partly the character of Varuṇa that invests *dhárman* with the specific sense of authority. As we have seen, *dhárman* can mean the 'foundational nature' of a deity. This sense occurs especially in connection with Savitar, whose name transparently displays his nature as the Compeller. Varuṇa's name is etymologically related to *vratá* 'command, commandment', and the Ṛgvedic poets were aware that Varuṇa embodies *vratá* and is defined by *vratá.* As Savitar is the Compeller, so Varuṇa is the god of commands. When Varuṇa (typically together with Mitra) acts in accordance with *dhárman* (cf. 5.63.7, 72.2), or when other gods (cf. 10.65.5, 6.70.1, 9.107.15) and humans (cf. 10.167.3, 7.89.5) act by or on his *dhárman*, his 'authority', that *dhárman* also expresses *his* foundation, *his* nature, as the god of commands. Since the nature of Varuṇa is defined by *vratá*, predictably *vratá* appears in close proximity to *dhárman* (5.63.7, 72.2, 6.70.1ff., and cf. 7.89.5).

Even if *dhárman* describes a foundational authority primarily in association with Varuṇa, nonetheless, already in the younger sections of the *Ṛgveda*, it carries this sense in part independently of Varuṇa. The obvious case is that of the *dhárman*, the 'foundation' that Soma establishes for human communities. Two features of *dhárman* motivate this use. First, as we have observed, *dhárman* in other senses is frequently connected with *soma*. Second, the instances in which Soma is associated with *dhárman* are often contexts involving Varuṇa or *vratá* or are suggestive of Varuṇa. In 10.167.3, ritual consumption of *soma* occurs on the 'foundation' of kings Soma and Varuṇa. In 9.35.6, Soma's command (*vratá*) provides a foundation and in 9.64.1, he sets foundations through his command. In other instances too, Varuṇa is not far when other gods possess *dhárman* as 'foundational authority'. Normally paired with Varuṇa, Mitra alone appears with *dhárman* in 8.52.3, where the *dhárman* is foundation constituted by an alliance. Parallel to the relation between Varuṇa and command, alliance is both the foundation of Mitra and the foundation that Mitra establishes. Finally, in 1.134.5, Wind protects through a 'foundation' because of his 'lordship' (*asuryá*). Although various gods are called *ásura*, Varuṇa is characteristically such a 'lord', and therefore this term once again places the passages within a Varuṇa context.

The close connection between *vratá* and *dhárman* had consequences for the future development of both terms. To a significant degree, *dhárma* inherits the functions of Ṛgvedic *vratá* 'command', while the word *vratá* itself becomes circumscribed to a 'vow.' Why this development occurs is a difficult question, but it may reflect the changing nature of the state during the Vedic period. The *dhárman* as a physical foundation of the world and of living beings would lend concreteness and legitimacy to the *dhárman* as royal and foundational authority. Moreover, while *vratás* rest on the personal authority of kings and sovereign gods in the *Ṛgveda*, *dhárman*, and certainly later *dhárma*, have universal application. As rule was institutionalized in India, therefore, *dhárman* may have become the anchor for a broader claim of authority by rulers, an authority that ultimately reflects the very foundation of the world. This claim, therefore, could have contributed to the replacement of *vratá* by *dhárman* in the political sphere.

We might posit a similar development in case of another term of the old Indo-Iranian religious vocabulary, *ṛtá*. After the early Vedic period, *ṛtá*, 'truth' has part of its semantic space occupied by *satyá* 'real, true' and part by *dhárma*. In the *Ṛgveda*, the 'truth' defines the functions of both gods and humans, the structure of the ritual, and the general order of things. These spheres resemble those of the *dhárman*, which, as we have seen, can signify the foundations of gods, humans, ritual, and world. But *dhárman* and *dhárma* came to be more closely connected to sovereigns, while *ṛtá* was less so. To describe the order of the world through *dhárma*, therefore, linked it more specifically to rulers and ruling authority than to describe it through *ṛtá*. Thus, a growing authority of the king may have made *dhárma* a seemingly more realistic description of the governing principle of the world.

CONCLUSIONS

At the end of his article, Horsch helpfully laid out a summary of his conclusions concerning the early history of *dhárman*. In order to present the results of this study for that history, I will match the points he makes about *dhárman* with my own conclusions.

(1) The origin of the concept of *dhárman* rests in its formation. It is a Vedic, rather than an Indo-Iranian word, and a more recent coinage than many other key religious terms of the Vedic tradition. Its meaning derives directly from √*dhṛ* 'support, uphold, give foundation to' and therefore 'foundation' is a reasonable gloss in most of its attestations.

(2) *Dhárman* can mean a physical and even a universal, cosmic foundation; a foundation created by the ritual and a foundation for the ritual; and a foundation comprising royal authority which creates material or social bases for communities.

(3) There is little evidence of semantic development of *dhárman* within the *Ṛgveda*. Horsch's view of a progression from myth to law is influenced by an understanding of cultural evolution that is imported into the analysis of the *Ṛgveda* and does not derive from that analysis. Indeed, the 'mythic' sense of *dhárman* as a universal foundation occurs especially in the later parts of the *Ṛgveda*, while the 'legal' sense of *dhárman* as royal authority appears regularly in the family books, the old Ṛgvedic core collection. Rather than reflecting a historical evolution within the *Ṛgveda*, the senses of *dhárman* are better understood as different and mutually supportive aspects of the meaning 'foundation.'

NOTES

[1] This chronological analysis of the text follows the generalizations of Oldenberg and Witzel, (cf. Witzel, 1995: 308ff for a more detailed discussion of the structure of the *Ṛgveda*). It need hardly be said that this periodization only generally describes the history of the composition of *Ṛgveda* hymns, and no layer forms an absolutely discreet chronological stratum.

[2] Neither Elizarenkova nor Ge, who also notes the repetition of derivatives of √*dhṛ*, is able to explain just what the purpose of these repetitions might be. The *Anukramaṇī* implies that it is a play on the name of the poet, Dharuṇa, but there are no real grounds to believe that this was the poet's name.

[3] The sacrifices could also be *at* the foundation (*dhárman*) of heaven, in which case this verse belongs with those in which *dhárman* describes the 'foundation' of the world. But see the next verse, 10.170.2.

[4] This translation takes both *bhármaṇe* and *dhármaṇe* as quasi-infinitives with *bhúvanāya* as the object of both and *tásya* as the subject. Another possibility is that *dhármaṇe* refers to the foundation of Fire himself and therefore is the sacrificial ground: "for him to bear the living world, and yes, to give him foundation. . . . " Less likely, *dhármaṇe* might be the foundation of the gods themselves: cf. Kümmel, 2000: 320 "Durch dessen Eigenkraft sollen zum Tragen der Welt die Götter [und] für [ihren] Erhalt sich ausbreiten." Other interpreters have offered other variations: Ge takes *tásya* only with *svadháyā* and therefore allows the gods both to 'bear'and 'give foundation to the world', while Ol takes *tásya* with *bhármaṇe* and *bhúvanāya* only

with with *dhármaṇe*. In support of his view, Ol refers to 10.81.4, 1.154.4 ("one who, by triple division, has given foundation to [√*dhṛ*] the earth and heaven and all living beings"), 4.54.4.

[5] The problem here is the verbal gapping in b. In this case, it is *dhárman* that suggests a form of √*dhṛ*.

[6] Ge is more circumspect: he says that *pitú* encompasses food and drink, especially the *soma* drink. Here, though, I think *soma* represents all food, cf. vss. 9–10.

[7] Cf. 3.34.6, 6.29.1, 7.25.1, 8.68.3, 10.99.12.

[8] This interpretation makes unnecessary Ge's more convoluted proposal that *tám* is for *tát* or *tā́ni* (referring to *nṛmṇá*), masculine by attraction to *párvatam*.

[9] It is true that *soma* 'grows strong on the mountain' (e.g., 9.71.4), but this is an uncertain basis for describing *soma* as mountain.

[10] The next verse continues the image of *soma* as a horse running into a vessel containing waters: 9.7.2 *prá dhā́rā mádhvo agriyó mahī́r apó ví gāhate / havír havíṣṣu vándyaḥ* "The stream, the lead (horse) of honey, (goes) forth and sinks away into the great waters, / celebrated as the oblation among oblations."

[11] The completion of the ellipsis rests principally on the nearby *mánasas*, but also cf. 1.136.1ab *prá sú jyéṣṭhaṃ nicirā́bhyām bṛhán námo havyám matím bharatā* "Bring forth the foremost (reverence) to two attentive (gods), your lofty reverence, oblation, and thought."

[12] Like *paśú* from which it derives, *kṣú* can be a singular collective 'herd', as well as 'herding animal, cow'.

[13] Ge and Re construe *jyéṣṭhasya* with *kṣós* and take the genitives phrase with *ánike*. Therefore Re translates the line, '. . .ou (quand il s'agissait d') établir (le sacrifice) en présence du plus puissant bétail.' In this interpretation, therefore, *dhárman* remains the "foundation" of the ritual. Ge interprets the 'best cow' as the *dakṣiṇā*.

[14] Jamison (pers. com.) suggests that there is an ellipsis of *dhā́rā*, perhaps suggested by *dháriman*.

[15] Or 'to be given foundation through the milk'?

[16] I am supposing that the there is an ellipsis of *dhī́* with *sthā́virī*, on the basis of *dhī́jū* in line a.

[17] Within the *soma* streams in *pāda* a – or, if not *soma* streams, whatever other object might be implied in a.

[18] *Dhárman* also occurs in vs. 9 of this hymn, which we have already considered. According to that verse, Soma provides the foundations of heaven and earth, in contrast to vs. 5, where the *dhármans* are the foundations of *soma*.

[19] Cf. 9.46.2c 'The *soma* drops are set free to the wind' and, for a discussion of Soma's journey through the filter, which represents the midspace, see Oberlies 1999: 151ff.

[20] Ol, on 9.25.5, takes *āyuṣák* as adverbial, although he does not offer a translation. Following Ol's logic, Scarlata (1999: 590) considers 'towards life' or 'lifewards' ('dem Leben zugewendet') a possibility, although ultimately he sets it aside in favor of 'accompanying the *Āyus*'.

[21] Line b occurs also in 1.164.43d and the whole verse occurs in 1.164.50, another hymn concerned with the interpretation of the sacrifice and therefore with its foundations.

[22] That is, 'performed for themselves the sacrifice' or 'sacrificed the sacrifice (= the *púruṣa*).' But the phrase might also mean 'sacrificed to the sacrifice.' Or, according to Hoffmann *Aufs.* I, 117, performed 'sacrifice after sacrifice' ('Opfer um Opfer').

[23] Are the *sādhyás* already ancient gods in heaven whose desirable status is worth attaining, as the scholarly consensus suggests (cf. *EWA* II: 722), or, as I think more likely, are the *sādhyás* simply the gods in general? The verb *sánti* stresses that heaven is where the *sādhyás* are, and this would be appropriate for the gods.

24 With Ol and Re, I understand *suveṅ́īḥ* to be nom. sgl. masc., not acc. pl. fem. Ol takes *venī* for *veṇī* and therefore as 'well braided' with reference to the braiding of pearls in the tail of the horse. On this form, cf. *AiGr* II, 1: 239, which states that *suvená* could be a compound with an adjective as second member or a *bahuvrīhi*.
25 The praise-song sent earlier to heaven?
26 Most interpreters do take it as a literal horse, but in my view, the horse is actually the fire.
27 Against Re's attempt to defend Ol's syntactic interpretation of *vratā́* and in support of Ge, see Klein 1985 I: 97.
28 The meaning of this compound is unclear. Cf. Re 'celui qui protège à l'instant meme' from √*pā* 'protect' and Scarlata (1999: 317) 'stracks sich bewegend' from √*pā* 'move'.
29 Ge: gods and humans.
30 It is not clear who the 'ruddy one' is. Ge suggests, tentively, either the fire itself (so also Re) or heaven (citing 6.49.3). In the context of the dawns, however, it might be the morning sun. Cf. 10.55.6, 30.2, both, however, with *aruṇá* rather than *aruṣá*.
31 According to Ge, they sit with ladles like women pouring water. But according to Ol, either the streams of butter are themselves pouring, or we might supply a plural form of *upasécanī* from 2c.
32 Fire is both a *mitrá*, an ally, and Mitra, the god who protects alliances. Here the word is nuanced toward the latter because of the mention of his authority.
33 Literally, of course, but also figuratively because of the authority he possesses.
34 Cf. Ge's note for other references to the 'marvel' and a suggestion, which is unlikely, that it refers to the soul or spirit.
35 In that one instance, the *dharmán* is Fire.
36 According to Ge, they are to be attended to first in the sacrifice, but I do not see that they actually are attended to first. Re offers a more likely interpretation that the thought of men should be first on them, with reference to Ge on 1.112.1 and Ol cited there.
37 On the surface level, as the context demands, the 'dappled' are cows, but the ellipsis creates the context for a metaphor. Ge identifies the 'fruitful' in vs. 20 as the 'insights' (i.e., *dhītáyas*) of the poets, and Ol identifies the 'fruitful' in vs. 20 with the 'dappled' in vs. 19. The 'dappled cows', therefore, are also the 'insights', the hymns recited by the priests.
38 There is a long discussion by Ol on *enā́m*, which does not come to a final conclusion. Ge supplies *ā́śiram*, the 'milk-mix', which, on the narrative level, I think is right. But like the 'dappled' and the 'fruitful', 'this' or 'this (milk-mix)'refers to 'insight'(*dhī́*) or something similar. Cf. 8.95.5 where *pratnā́ṃ* (*dhíyam*) occupies the position of *enā́m*. This resolution of the ellipsis depends on the suggestion of *ṛtásya*, which points toward the hymn. If there is a difference between the 'cows' and their 'milk-mix', it may be that the cows represents the general insights that give rise to hymns and the 'milk-mix' is the insight embodied in this particular hymn.
39 Ol construes *ṛtásya* with *pipyúṣīḥ*, but Ge, rightly, argues that the position of *ṛtásya* between *enā́m* and *pipyúṣīḥ* suggests that it is to be construed with both. Cf. 8.95.5, where *ṛtásya* may also be taken with the word before and after it.
40 It is not clear here whether *dhárma* is to be interpreted as singular or plural.
41 There are, to be sure, other ways of interpreting this verse. According to Ol, they make Indra surround all *dhárman* like the sun coursing around the whole world. But the position of *iva* suggests that *dhárman* is part of the comparison. According to Ge, they surround Indra like the supports or pillars the sun. But do supports or the like 'surround'? Ge refers to 5.15.2, in which the heavens have supports.
42 Both Ge and Re suggests an ellipsis 'plants,' presumably *óṣadhīḥ*.
43 Following Roth, Re 'upon the earth'and Ge 'upon the field,' a solution that is appealing, although this interpretation of *dā́na* is unique to this verse. If one were to

take *dā́na* as 'gift',then it might refer to *soma* as the 'gift'to the Indra. Therefore, the verse would then be saying that at the giving of *soma* Indra carries out his distribution of the plants and streams. But I think it less forced to take *dā́na* from √ *dā* 'divide' and therefore in the sense of 'division'.

[44] Re, Ge 'seas' and this is surely one reference, but also perhaps the vats of *soma*?

[45] Hapax. But cf. *vitvákṣaṇa* in 5.34.6.

[46] Ge: 'Menge' with a note explaining it is the 'abundance' of *soma*. In any case, it is what the *soma* offerer has put up in his offering to Indra in the hopes of gaining something back from Indra.

[47] Perhaps both for Indra and the sacrificer, who hopes for Indra's gift in return?

[48] Or 'according to his (= Mitra's) nature' as the god of alliances.

[49] On this isolated use of the active perfect of √ *dhr̥* as intransitive, see Kümmel 2000: 261.

[50] For a discussion of the role of the Ādityas in the *R̥gveda*, see Brereton 1981. The functions of Mitra and Varuṇa are defined by their names. In the *R̥gveda*, *mitrá* means 'alliance' or 'ally'(cf. pp. 25ff.), and therefore Mitra is the god that governs in the sphere of alliance. Varuṇa's name is etymologically and semantically related to *vratá* 'command, commandment'(cf. pp. 70ff.), and therefore Varuṇa governs in the sphere of 'command'or 'authoriy.'

[51] Hapax. With Ol, the word is probably dual and refers to the two 'Hilfesuchungen', personified abstracts.

[52] As Ge notes, *rā́jñas* belongs to both Soma and Varuṇa, with reference also to *Atharvaveda* 4.27.5a.

[53] On this verse, cf. Hoffmann, 1967: 117.

[54] Cf. 5.69.1 *trī́·rocanā́ varuṇa trī́mr̥ utá dyū́n trī́ṇi mitra dhārayatho rájāṃsi/ vāvr̥dhānā́v amátiṃ kṣatríyasyā́nu vratám rákṣamāṇāv ajuryám* "The three realms of light, Varuṇa, and the three heavens, the three airy spaces do you two give foundation, Mitra, / having grown strong, protecting the emblem of the ruler, in accordance with his unaging command." Here Mitra, together with Varuṇa, 'gives foundation' to the three realms of light and the other heavenly spaces.

[55] This idea that the two worlds provide a place for the mortal's continued line is reflected in the description of them as *dhiṣáṇā*s, as those that provide a location for someone or something.

[56] Who is the creeping one and who is or are the swift that the creeping one pursues? Ge takes the language as suggesting a hunter seeking his prey, and this may be the image. But it still does not explain what in the *soma* rite represents the 'hunter' and what the 'prey.' In the above translation, I have suggested that they are the priest and the *soma*. The epithet *dásamānas* would be appropriate to a priest laboring at the ritual, and *tákvan* could describe the movement of *soma* as it rushes through the filter, but neither is certain.

REFERENCES

Brereton, J.P. (1981). *The R̥gvedic Ādityas*. American Oriental Series, Vol. 63. New Haven: American Oriental Society.

Elizarenkova, T.J. (1995). *Language and Style of the Vedic* R̥ṣis. State University of New York: Albany.

Ge = Geldner, K.F. (1951). *Der Rigveda. Aus dem Sanskrit ins Deutsche Übersetzt*. 3 Vols. Cambridge, MA: Harvard University Press.

Hoffmann, K. (1967). *Der Injunktiv im Veda*. Heidelberg: Carl Winter Universitätsverlag.

Hoffmann, K. (1975). *Aufs.* = *Aufsätze zur Indoiranistik* I. Wiesbaden: Reichert Verlag.

Jamison, S. (1996). *Sacrificed Wife/Sacrificer's Wife*. New York: Oxford University Press.

Klein, J.S. (1985). *Toward a Discourse Grammar of the Rigveda*. 2 Vol. Heidelberg: Carl Winter Universitätsverlag.

Kümmel, M.J. (2000). *Das Perfekt im Indoiranischen*. Wiesbaden: Reichert Verlag.

Mayrhofer, M. (1986–2001). *EWA* = *Etymologisches Wörterbuch des Altindoarischen*. 3 volumes Heidelberg: Carl Winter Universitätsverlag.

Oberlies, T. (1998). *Die Religion des R̥gveda. Erster Teil: Das Religiöse System des R̥gveda*. Wien: De Nobili.

Oberlies, T. (1999). *Die Religion des R̥gveda. Zeiter Teil: Kompositionsanalyse der Soma-Hymnen des R̥gveda*. Wien: De Nobili.

Ol = Oldenberg, H. (1909, 1912). *R̥gveda. Textkritische und exegetische Noten*. Berlin: Weidmannsche Buchhandlung. (*AbhGWG* 11, 13).

Oldenberg, H. (1897) [rpt. (1973)]. *Vedic Hymns II: Hymns to Agni (Mandalas I-V)*. Sacred Books of the East, Vol. XLVI. Delhi: Motilal Banarsidass.

Re = Renou, L. (1955–1969). *Études védiques et pāṇinéennes*. 17 vols. Paris: Boccard.

Scarlata, S. (1999). *Die Wurzelkomposita im R̥gveda*. Wiesbaden: Reichert Verlag.

Skjaervø, P.O. (2003). Truth and Deception in Ancient Iran. In: M. Soroushian (ed.), *The Fire Within: Jamshid Soroush Soroushian Memorial*, Vol. II. 1stBooks Library: Bloomington, IN, pp. 379–430.

Thieme, P. (1957). *Mitra and Aryaman*. Transactions of the Connecticut Academy of Arts and Sciences, 41. New Haven: Yale University Press.

Wackernagel, J. (and Albert Debrunner). (1896–1957) [rpt. (1975–1987)]. *AiGr* = *Altindische Grammatik*. 3 Vol. Göttingen: Vandenhoeck & Ruprecht.

Wennerberg, C. (1981). *Die altindischen Nominalsuffixe* -man- *und* -iman- *in historisch-komparativer Beleuchtung. I. Wortanalytischer Teil – Wörterbuch*. Göteborg: Göteborgs Universitet.

Witzel, M. (1995). Rgvedic history, poets, chieftains, and politics. In: *The Indo-Aryans of Ancient South Asia*, ed. George Erdosy, Berlin: Walter de Gruyter & Co., pp. 307–352.

University of Texas
Austin
TX 78712
USA

PATRICK OLIVELLE

THE SEMANTIC HISTORY OF DHARMA THE MIDDLE AND LATE VEDIC PERIODS

The studies of the term *dharma* in the early vedic period by Paul Horsch and Joel Brereton in this volume[1] have shown that the term is used with relative frequency in the *Ṛg Veda* (67 times) with a somewhat broad semantic range including the cosmological, ritual, and ethical spheres. The frequency drops drastically in the other text from this period, the *Atharva Veda* (13 times), although maintaining a semantic range similar to the *Ṛg Veda*. Given the centrality of *dharma* in later religious literature of India, both Brahmanical and Buddhist, one would expect that the term gradually began to assume a central role in the religious vocabulary of the middle and late vedic periods represented by the Brāhmaṇas, Āraṇyakas, the Upaniṣads, and the Śrauta- and Gṛhya-sūtras, which together constitute a vast body of literature both in extent and in the variety of their topics and concerns.

A close study of the use of *dharma* in these texts, however, demonstrates the opposite: *dharma* was at best a marginal term and concept within the vocabulary of these texts, and it did not play a central role in the religious world depicted in them. On the one hand, the frequency of its usage drops rather dramatically and, on the other, its semantic range becomes narrower, being restricted for the most part to Varuṇa and his earthly counterpart, the king. In the concluding postscript I will attempt to show how this specialized meaning of *dharma* may have contributed to its further semantic development in its adoption and adaptation by Buddhism, by Aśoka, and in the later Brahmanical literature.

THE YAJURVEDA SAṂHITĀS

The Yajurveda Saṃhitās are the oldest texts we have after the *Ṛg Veda* and the *Atharva Veda*. I have examined all four extant Saṃhitās: *Maitrāyaṇī, Kāṭhaka, Taittirīya,* and *Vājasaneyi*. The study of *dharma*[2] in these texts is complicated by two factors: first, they often cite verses from the *Ṛg Veda*; and second, because they are parallel recensions of the same ritual material, they frequently present the same passages. To determine the frequency of *dharma* in the Yajurvedic vocabulary, therefore, I have discounted citations from the *Ṛg Veda* and counted only once the passages that are repeated almost verbatim in several of these Saṃhitās.

In the four Yajurveda Saṃhitās the term *dharma* is found in 22 passages.[3] Even this may be an overestimate because several of these occurrences are in stock phrases and epithets. Many of these refer to Varuṇa or Mitra-Varuṇa. Thus we have the recurrent phrase *dhruvéṇa dhármaṇā* ("with firm/enduring *dharma*") with reference to Mitra-Varuṇa: *dyutānás tvā mārutó minotu mitrā́váruṇayor dhruvéṇa dhármaṇā* – "May Dyutāna Māruta establish you in accordance with the enduring *dharma* of Mitra and Varuṇa" (at the planting of the sacrificial post; *TS*.1.3.1.2; *MS* 1.2.11; *VS* 5.27). The same phrase is repeated in a different context: *váruṇas tvā dhṛtávrato dhū́payatu mitrā́váruṇau dhruvéṇa dhármaṇā* – "May Varuṇa, whose commandment is upheld, perfume you with incense, may Mitra and Varuṇa, in accordance with their enduring *dharma*" (at the perfuming of the pan; *MS* 4.9.1).[4] And again: *mitrā́váruṇau tvottarataḥ pári dhattā́ṃ dhruvéṇa dhármaṇā* – "May Mitra and Varuṇa lay you around in the north in accordance with their enduring *dharma*" (at the laying of the enclosing sticks [*paridhi*]; *KS* 1.11; *TS* 1.1.11.2; *VS* 2.3; *ŚB* 1.3.4.4). The use of *dharman* here closely agrees with its principal usage in the *Ṛg Veda*; *dharman* is the institute or commandment of Varuṇa, an institute that is here said to be *dhruva*, firm and enduring. The *MS* (3.8.9) provides a commentary on the phrase:

mitrā́váruṇau dhruvéṇa dhármaṇéti / mitrám evaínāṃ dādhā́ra, váruṇaḥ kalpayati, vídhṛtyai ca khálu vā́ eṣā́ṃ prajā́nāṃ kḷptyai ca mīyate, mitrā́váruṇau vaí devā́nāṃ dhármadhā́rayau, daivā́ṃ vā́ etád dhármam adīdharatāṃ /
"Mitra and Varuṇa in accordance with their enduring *dharma*. Mitra, indeed, holds it fast, and Varuṇa establishes it. For the upholding of these creatures and for their establishment, it is set up. Mitra and Varuṇa are clearly the ones who uphold *dharma* among the gods. They have upheld here the divine *dharma*".

Note that the explanation clearly connects *dharma* with its root *dhṛ*, to bear, to support, to uphold. The connection between *dhruva* and *dharma* is evident also in a passage of the *KS* (35.7): *dhruvā dyaur dhruvā pṛthivī dhruvaṃ viśvam idaṃ jagat / devā ha dharmaṇā dhruvā yajamānaḥ paśubhir dhruvaḥ* – "The sky is enduring; the earth is enduring; this whole world is enduring. The gods are enduring through *dharma*, and the sacrificer is enduring through the sacrificial animals".[5]

The close connection between *dharma* and Varuṇa within the Yajurveda Saṃhitās is most evident within the context of two rituals associated with kingship, the royal consecration (*rājasūya*) and the horse sacrifice (*aśvamedha*) performed by a king to enhance and proclaim his sovereignty.[6] At the royal consecration the king is placed in close relationship to both Varuṇa and *dharma*. Several cakes (*caru*) are offered to deities who are identified with various characteristics (*TS* 1.8.10.1): Agni is the lord of the house (*gṛhapati*), Soma is the lord of the forest (*vanaspati*), Rudra is the lord of cattle (*paśupati*), and Bṛhaspati is the lord of speech (*vācaspati*). The last two are Mitra, characterized as *satya*, and Varuṇa, who is *dharmapati*, the lord of *dharma*. In the parallel passage at *MS* 2.6.6 the wording is *mitrā́ya satyásya pátaye ... váruṇāya dhármasya pátaye* – "To Mitra the lord of truth; to Varuṇa the lord of *dharma*".[7] Within the same context we have a mantra asking Savitṛ and other gods to stimulate the new king (*savitā́ tvā ... suvatām*). Once gain the deities are given their distinctive characteristics (*TS* 1.8.10.2): *mítraḥ satyā́nāṃ váruṇo dhármapatīnām* (or in *MS dhármāṇām*).[8] After this the new king is presented with the words: *eṣa vo bharatā rājā* – "This, O Bharatas, is your king!" In the *MS* (2.6.8; 4.4.2), gods are invoked to make the new king an upholder of *dharma: sómā índro váruṇo mitró agnís té devā́ dharmadhṛ́to dhármam dhārayantu* – "Soma, Indra, Varuṇa, Mitra, Agni – may these gods, the upholders of *dharma*, uphold *dharma*". The *TS* (1.8.16.2) addresses the king, identifying him with Varuṇa: *váruṇo 'si satyadhármā* – "You are Varuṇa, whose *dharma* is true/real."Here again we have the implicit statement that the epithet of Varuṇa as *satyadharmā* is applicable to the king as well. Within the Aśvamedha rite also the same epithet is used with reference to the reins of Mitra and Varuṇa's chariot: *yó vāṃ rátha ṛjúraśmiḥ sátyadharmā mithucárantam upayā́ti dūṣáyan* – "You, whose chariot with straight reins and true/real *dharma* draws near, frustrating him who acts falsely" (*MS* 3.16.5; *KS* 22.15; *TS* 4.7.15.2). In these and in other passages we will examine in the Brāhmaṇas and the Upaniṣads, the kingly power or *kṣatra* is intimately connected with *dharma*. In the same way as Varuṇa, the heavenly sovereign, his earthly counterpart is also *dharmapati*; the two are lords and upholders of *dharma* in the cosmos and within society.

The connection of *dharma* to the royal and judicial sphere is nicely illustrated by one ritual detail. In the Puruṣamedha, the real or symbolic human sacrifice, different types of men are sacrificed to various deities. The kinds of men sacrificed to *dharma* and its opposite *adharma* are instructive: to *dharma*, a *sabhāga* (presumably, a man who participates at the royal audience hall where judicial proceedings are carried out), and to *adharma*,[9] a deaf man (*badhira*), quite the opposite of the debater in the assembly hall (*VS* 30.6, 10; *TB* 3.4.1).

THE BRĀHMAṆAS

The corpus of the Brāhmaṇas is even more vast than the Yajurveda Saṃhitās. For this study I have chosen three: *Aitareya, Taittirīya,* and *Śatapatha.* Although paralleling the *Aitareya,* the *Kauṣītaki* does not use the term *dharma* at all.[10] In the three Brāhmaṇas that are the focus of this study, the term *dharma* occurs independently a total of 11 times.[11] This is striking, especially because the Brāhmaṇas, unlike the Saṃhitās, contain a wide spectrum of material and address numerous issues, including ritual and ethical ones, pertaining to Brahmanical life. One would assume, *a priori*, that if *dharma* was a key concept that defined the Brahmanical view of the world and of human life, it would have been used more frequently and within a variety of contexts.

The term is used only once in the *Aitareya Brāhmaṇa*, and, significantly, here also it occurs within the context of the royal consecration (*rājasūya*). At *AB* 8.12–14 there is a description of the great anointing (*mahābhiṣeka*) of Indra as king by the gods, which is immediately followed at *AB* 8.15–23 by the anointing of the king. Clearly, the anointing of Indra provides the model for the anointing of the king. In both we have the following public proclamation of the sovereignty of Indra and the king, the former proclaimed by the Viśvedevas and the latter by the "king-makers". (*rājakartāraḥ*). The wording is identical in the two contexts with the exception of the audience addressed, gods (*devāḥ*) in the case of Indra and men (*janāḥ*) in the case of the king:

imaṃ janā [devā] abhyutkrośata samrājaṃ sāmrājyaṃ bhojaṃ bhojapitaraṃ svarājaṃ svārājyaṃ virājaṃ vairājyaṃ parameṣṭhinaṃ pārameṣṭhyaṃ rājānaṃ rājapitaraṃ kṣatram ajani kṣatriyo 'jani viśvasya bhūtasyādhipatir ajani viśām attājany amitrāṇāṃ hantājani brāhmaṇānāṃ goptājani dharmasya goptājanīti. (*AB* 7.12, 17)

"Do ye proclaim him, O men [O gods], as overlord and overlordship, as paramount ruler and father of paramount rulers, as self ruler and self rule, as sovereign and sovereignty, as supreme lord and supreme lordship, as king and father of kings. The *kṣatra* (royal power) has been born, the *kṣatriya* has been born, the suzerain of all creation has been born, the eater of the commoners (*viś*) has been born, the slayer of foes has been born, the guardian of *brāhmaṇas* has been born, the guardian of *dharma* has been born." (Tr. Keith with modification)

The proclamation reaches its climax with the announcement that Indra/king has been born through the right of consecration as the guardian of *dharma*. Here Indra has replaced Varuṇa, but the connection of the king to *dharma* is brought to the forefront.

In the *Taittirīya Brāhmaṇa dharma* occurs four times. In three of these *dharma* is closely associated with Varuṇa and with the overlord (*adhipati*). At *TB* 3.9.16.2, which is a commentary on *TS* 7.4.16 dealing with the horse sacrifice, the mantra of the TS *namó 'dhipataye* ("Homage to the overlord") is interpreted by the *TB* as: *dhármo vā́ ádhipatiḥ, dhármam evā́varundhe* ("The overlord is *dharma*. He does, indeed, obtain *dharma*"). The person who is here identified with *ādhipatya* and with *dharma* is the king performing the horse sacrifice. In the *TS*, significantly, the mantra commented on by the *TB* comes at the end and climax of a longer mantra: "Homage to the king! Homage to Varuṇa! Homage to Prajāpati! Homage to the overlord!" Here *dharma* as the *adhipati* is placed last as the highest.

At *TB* 3.11.4.1 we have the common designation of Varuṇa as "Lord of *dharma*". Indeed the juxtaposition of *indrapatnī* and *dharmapatnī* ("wife of Indra" and "wife of *dharma*") at *TB* 3.11.1.20 makes it likely that *dharma* here stands for Varuṇa, whose epithet is *dharmapati*.

In the voluminous *Śatapatha Brāhmaṇa*, if we exclude the last section consisting of the *Bṛhadāraṇyaka Upaniṣad*, the term *dharma* occurs in just six passages. In one of the most significant statements regarding the relation between *dharma*, Varuṇa, and the king, the *Śatapatha* (5.3.3.9), within the context of the royal consecration (*rājasūya*), states:

athá váruṇāya dhármapataye / vāruṇáṃ yavamáyaṃ caruṃ nírvapati tád enaṃ váruṇa evá dhármapatir dhármasya pátiṃ karoti paramátā vaí sá yó dhármasya pátir ásad yó há paramátāṃ gácchati tíṃ hí dhárma upayánti tásmād váruṇāya dhármapataye //
"Then to Varuṇa the lord of *dharma* he offers a cake made with barley. Thereby Varuṇa himself, the lord of *dharma*, makes him [the king] the lord of *dharma*. That, surely, is the highest state when one becomes the lord of *dharma*. For when someone attains the highest state, (people) come to him (in matters relating) to *dharma*. Therefore, to Varuṇa, the lord of *dharma*".

Here we get a clearer picture as to what the author of the *Śatapatha* means by *dharma*, certainly clearer than the texts we have examined thus far. It has to do with matters regarding which people come to the king and must refer principally to legal disputes. *Dharma* is thus placed squarely within the public realm of law and social norms that must be overseen by the king. We can now understand why the king is the *dharmapati*, in the same way as Varuṇa, the sovereign who oversees the cosmic *dharma*. Perhaps this was the meaning generally attached to *dharma* during the middle vedic period and underlies the statements on *dharma* in other texts that we have examined.

Another significant passage occurs within a creation story, a passage that throws further light on the meaning of *dharma* for the author of the *ŚB*. After Prajāpati was born, he created four gods: Agni, Indra, Soma, and Parameṣṭhin. These five deities then observe the four directions. Our passage deals with the north (*ŚB* 11.1.6.24):

áthódīcīṃ díśam apaśyan / tā́m ápo 'kurvatópainām itáḥ kurvīmahī́ti taṃ dhármam akurvata dhármo vá ā́pas tásmād yádemáṃ lokám ā́pa āgácchanti sárvam èvedáṃ yathādharmáṃ bhavaty átha yadā́vr̥ṣṭir bhávati bálīyān eva tarhy ábalīyasa ā́datte dhármo hy ā́paḥ //

"Then they saw the northern direction. They made it waters. 'Let us improve it from here,' they said. They made it *dharma*. The waters, surely, are *dharma*. Therefore, when waters come to this world, all this becomes in accordance with *dharma*. But when there is no rain, then the stronger indeed seizes the weaker ones, for the waters are *dharma*".

This passage further supports the meaning of *dharma* as social order founded on law. The argument here corresponds to the "law of the fish" (*matsyanyāya*) of later Dharmaśāstras. Here, however, there is no mention of a king or the lack of a king; it is the natural phenomena of abundance created by water and famine created by drought that bring about adherence to and deviation from *dharma*. The assurance of timely rain, however, is very much a function of kingship, and Varuṇa is closely associated with water. Indeed, as Insler has recently pointed out, the royal consecration (*rājasūya*) initially may have been an annual ritual conducted during the winter solstice to assure the timely progress of the seasons and the timely arrival of rain.[12]

At *ŚB* 13.4.3.14 it is Indra who is identified with *dharma*, but even here note the connection between *dharma* and Indra as king of the gods: *dhárma índro rā́jéty āha tásya devā́ víśah* – "Indra the king is *dharma*, he says; his people are the gods".

The *Śatapatha* also uses the negative *adharma* twice in the sense of something done contrary to law or the natural order of things. At *ŚB* 3.7.3.7 the author in refuting an opponent's view about how to bind the sacrificial animal. He says that doing it the opponent's way "would be as if he intended to do an *adharma* stealthily" (*yathā́dharmaṃ tiraścáthā cíkīrṣet*). Likewise at *ŚB* 5.2.4.13 with reference to the Dakṣiṇā cow that draws a cart (*anaḍuhī*), it says: *yát strī́ satī́ váhati ádharmeṇa tád asyai vāruṇáṃ rūpám* – "In that, while she is a female she draws contrary to *dharma*, that is her Vāruṇa form".[13] In both these instances, *adharma* appears to indicate an activity that is either against the rule, whether it is ritual or natural.

An unexpected and possibly a new connotation of *dharma* as either a specific attribute or a right/obligation is found at *ŚB* 11.5.7.1, a passage in praise of *svādhyāya*, vedic study, through which a man becomes independent and wealthy, and by which his intelligence grows (*prajñāvr̥ddhi*). Such a Brahmin is said to acquire four *dharmas* and people serve him with four other *dharmas*:

prájñā várdhamānā catúro dhármān brāhmaṇám abhiníṣpādayati brā́hmaṇyaṃ pratirūpacaryā́ṃ yáśo lokapaktíṃ, lokáḥ pácyamānaś catúrbhir dhármair brāhmaṇáṃ bhunakty arcáyā ca dā́nena cājyeyátayā cāvadhyátayā ca /
"The growing intelligence brings to the Brahmin four *dharmas*: Brahmanical stature, fitting deportment, fame, and 'cooking' the world.[14] The world, as it is being 'cooked', gratifies the Brahmin with four *dharmas* – with veneration, with gifts, with the condition of not being oppressed and of not being subject to capital punishment.

There appears to be a semantic development here from "law" or "the way things are or should be" to specific attributes that characterizes a particular entity.[15] The four *dharmas* of the world vis-à-vis the Brahmin, indeed, can be seen as legal privileges granted by society to the Brahmin class.

Except for this last passage, the Brāhmaṇas do not expand the semantic range of *dharma* in a significant way. It remains closely associated with Varuṇa and with the royal power of the king. We detect, however, more clearly that *dharma* has acquired the primary meaning of law and order within society, a law that is hypostatized into an abstract entity as *dharma* that stands above and gives legitimacy to *kṣatra*, the ruling power of the king.

THE ĀRAṆYAKAS

The term *dharma* occurs only three times in the Āraṇyakas, twice in the *Taittirīya* and once in the *Aitareya*. They do not add much to the semantics of *dharma*.

At *AĀ* 2.1.7, within a section that describes the creation of the world through the organs of the Puruṣa, we have a statement that again connects *dharma* with Varuṇa and with water: *varuṇo 'sya prajāṃ dharmeṇa dādhāra* – "Varuṇa supported his offspring through *dharma*".

The *Taittirīya* passages are brief. At *TĀ* 2.19.1 various cosmic entities or categories are homologized with various parts of a Śiśumāra (alligator or porpoise). Here *dharma* is said to be the crown of its head (*mūrdhānam*). At *TĀ* 4.42.5 we have a list of divine categories that begins with *śrī* and end with *dharma*. The incorporation of *dharma* into lists of cosmic categories becomes a common feature in late vedic texts, and in these lists *dharma* is most often placed last as the highest of the categories.

THE UPANIṢADS

The Upaniṣads are the texts where we would expect to find a sustained treatment of *dharma*, given that a central theme in these documents is human activity and knowledge leading to an ultimate state beyond death. That, however, is not the case. In the four early prose Upaniṣads[16] – *Bṛhadāraṇyaka, Chāndogya, Taittirīya,* and *Aitareya* (in which the term does not occurs at all) – the term occurs in just nine passages. Even more importantly, there is no sustained focus on the term as it applies to living a righteous life, except perhaps in *ChU* 2.23.1 and *TU* 1.11.1.

The Bṛhadāraṇyaka

In the *Bṛhadāraṇyaka*, which constitutes the last portion of the ŚB, the term occurs in four passages. Significantly, it occurs only once in the central Yājñavalkya-kāṇḍa (*BU* 3–4), which forms the oldest core of the Upaniṣad. At 4.4.5, in a passage demonstrating that the *ātman* is made up of everything, there is a long list of categories. In this list, *ātman* is said to be made up of various categories and their opposites: *tejomayo 'tejomayaḥ kāmamayo 'kāmamayaḥ krodhayamo 'krodhamayaḥ dharmamayo 'dharmamayaḥ sarvamayaḥ* – "made of light and the lightless, made of desire and the desireless, made of anger and the angerless, made of *dharma* and *adharma*, made of everything". We are not told what *dharma* means here, except that it must have been viewed as occupying the highest position within the list, because after it the author simply says *sarvamayaḥ*.

The most sustained treatment of *dharma* is found in *BU* 1.4.14 within the context of a creation myth. In the beginning this world was only *brahman*. Because it was single, the author says, it "did not become fully developed" (*na vyabhavat*). *Brahman* then goes about creating "the ruling power" (*kṣatra*), including the gods, then the

Vaiśya class, and finally the Śūdra class. After each creation, the author repeats the refrain *na vyabhavat*, "it still did not become fully developed." As the final act of creation that made *brahman* fully develop and reach its full potential, it created *dharma*:

tacchreyo rūpam atyasrjata dharmam / tad etat kṣatrasya kṣatraṃ yad dharmaḥ/ tasmād dharmāt paraṃ nāsti / atho abalīyān balīyāṃsam āśaṃsate dharmeṇa / yathā rājñaivam / yo vai sa dharmaḥ satyaṃ vai tat / tasmāt satyam vadantam āhur dharmaṃ vadatīti / dharmaṃ vā vadantaṃ satyaṃ vadatīti / etad dhy evaitad ubhayaṃ bhavati / "So it created *dharma*, a form superior to and surpassing itself. And *dharma* is here the ruling power standing above the ruling power. Hence there is nothing higher than *dharma*. Therefore, a weaker man makes demands of a stronger man by appealing to *dharma*, just as one does by appealing to a king. Now, *dharma* is nothing but the truth. Therefore, when a man speaks the truth, people say that he speaks *dharma*; and when a man speaks *dharma*, people say that he speaks the truth. They are really the same thing."

This passage echoes two other significant passages of the *ŚB* that we have examined: 5.3.3.9, which presents *dharma* as the highest, something to which people go to settle disputes, and 11.1.6.24, which speaks of the stronger seizing the weak when there is the absence of *dharma*. In the *BU* passage, however, *dharma* is made the very essence of *kṣatra*, the ruling power. A weaker man can take on even a stronger opponent by resorting to *dharma* in exactly the same way as he can by resorting to the king. I think the subtext here is litigation. A weaker man can drag a stronger man to the king's court. As in many other vedic texts, *dharma* here is not only placed side by side with *satya*, truth, but is said to be identical with it.[17] The significant point in this passage for our study is that, as in the Brāhmaṇas, here also *dharma* is associated with the legal and regal spheres.

The other occurrence of *dharma* in the first chapter (*BU* 1.5.23) is in a *śloka* cited in support of the pre-eminence of breath over other faculties:

yataś codeti sūryaḥ astaṃ yatra ca gacchati /
taṃ devāś cakrire dharmaṃ sa evādya sa u śva //
"From which the sun rises, and into which it sets; the gods make it *dharma*. It is the same today and tomorrow."

The author of the *BU* comments after the first half-verse: *prāṇād vā eṣa udeti prāṇe 'stam eti* – "From breath, indeed, does it rise, and into breath it sets". The meaning of *dharma* here is unclear and the commentarial section of the text does not deal with this term. It appears likely that for the author of the *BU dharma* was the highest principle, and he equates it with breath/wind, which is here presented as the highest faculty, breath with respect to *adhyātma* and wind with respect to *adhidaivata*. In the original setting of this verse, however, *dharma* may have been viewed as the ultimate institute/statue/commandment that is responsible for the regular rising and setting of the sun, a meaning familiar from the *Ṛg Veda*.

Finally, in the Madhukāṇḍa (*BU* 2.5.11) where all cosmic categories are said to be honey, *dharma* occurs just before *satya*. The connection between these two terms is the only thing remarkable about this occurrence; nothing is said that would permit us to understand what *dharma* meant for the author.

The Chāndogya

The *Chāndogya Upaniṣad*, in which the term occurs in three passages, does not have a single extended discussion of *dharma*. The first time the term occurs is at 2.1.4. The context is the veneration of *sāman* as *sādhu* (good). The section concludes: *sa ya etad evaṃ vidvān sādhu sāmety upāste 'bhyāśo ha yad enaṃ sādhavo dharmā ā ca gaccheyur upa ca nameyur* – "When someone knows this and venerates the Sāman chant as good, he can certainly expect that good *dharmas* will come his way and fall to his share". The meaning of *dharma* in this context is quite unclear, but it may have the meaning of qualities, attributes, or simply things, somewhat similar to its usage we examined in *ŚB* 11.5.7.1.

In an eulogy of speech (*vāc*) at 7.2.1 we have another occurrence of *dharma* in a long list of things that speech makes known from the *Ṛg Veda* down to worms, moths, and ants: *dharmaṃ cādharmaṃ ca satyaṃ cānṛtaṃ ca sādhu cāsādhu ca* – "*dharma* and *adharma*, truth and untruth, good and non-good." Here *dharma* is juxtaposed with *satya* and *sādhu*. The first pair we have seen elsewhere; and I think that for the author of the *ChU satya* and *sādhu* may be concepts that are closely related. Here again we get the negative *adharma*.

The final and the most significant occurrence of *dharma* in the *Chāndogya* is in the famous passage on *dharmaskandhas* (2.23.1):[18]

trayo dharmaskandhāḥ / yajño 'dhyayanaṃ dānam iti prathamaḥ / tapa eva dvitīyaḥ / brahmacāry ācāryakulavāsī tṛtīyaḥ /
"There are three types of persons whose torso is *dharma*.[19] The first is the one who pursues sacrifice, vedic recitation, and gift-giving. The second is the one who is devoted to austerity. Third is a celibate student of the Veda living at his teacher's house."

It is clear that in this passage *dharma* specifically refers to modes of religious life, probably to the life of a Brahmanical householder, an ascetic, and a vedic student. Here for the first time in vedic literature we have an unambiguous passage that uses *dharma* in a way very close to its usage in the later Dharmaśāstras.

The Taittirīya

In the *Taittirīya Upaniṣad dharma* occurs in a passage at the end of the first chapter (*śikṣāvallī*), a passage that appears very much like a remnant of an old Gṛhyasūtra dealing with the instruction of a vedic student and his return home after his residence at his teacher's house. In his parting words to the student (*TU* 1.11.1), the teacher tells him: *satyaṃ vada / dharmaṃ cara* ("Speak the truth. Practice *dharma*"). This is the first time in the vedic literature that the verb $\sqrt{car}$ is used with reference to *dharma*, indicating that here the term is used in its classical Dharmaśāstric meaning. Note, however, that *satya* is closely associated with *dharma*.

In the same passage (*TU* 1.11.4) authoritative Brahmins, whose behavior is presented as a model to the young student, are characterized as *dharmakāmaḥ* (devoted to or loving *dharma*).

THE ŚRAUTASŪTRAS

The dates of the numerous *Śrautasūtras* are uncertain, but at least some of them are probably from a pre-Buddhist period and overlap with some of the later vedic texts. Although they are not viewed as part of the vedic canon, they continue the tradition of the Brāhmaṇas in providing rules and explanations of the vedic rituals.

In the 10 Śrautasūtras I have examined, the term *dharma* occurs in 39 passages.[20] In all but a handful of them, however, *dharma* does not have the meaning found in either the earlier vedic texts or the later Dharmaśāstras. It appears that the expert scholastic tradition focusing on the ritual developed a very special meaning of *dharma* that was restricted to this tradition. Within this specialized meaning, *dharma* refers to the specific ritual rules or ritual details of a rite. Many of these passages deal with how *dharmas*, taken as ritual details, are extended from ritual archetypes, such as the Darśapūrṇamāsa (New- and Full-moon) sacrifice to others that are modeled after it. Thus, for example, the *BhārŚr* (1.1.9) states the general principle: *tatraiṣo 'tyantapradeśo ye kecana paurṇamāsīm amāvāsyāṃ vā dharmā anārabhyāmnāyanta ubhayatraiva te kriyante* – "In this connection, this is the general rule. The characteristics (*dharmāḥ*) which have been prescribed in connection with the full-moon day or the new-moon day without specification hold good with reference to both" (Tr. Kashikar). In a more specific case, the *BhārŚr* (6.15.5) states: *sarveṣv iṣṭipaśubandheṣu dārśapaurṇamāsikā dharmā anuyanti* – "The *dharmas* of the New-moon and the Full-moon sacrifices are carried over into the *iṣṭi* and animal sacrifices."

It is significant that this meaning of *dharma* is absent in the vocabulary of the vedic texts, including the Brāhmaṇas and the Upaniṣads. This specialized and technical meaning probably developed within the expert tradition devoted to ritual that produced both the Śrautasūtras and the later Mīmāṃsā texts.

The compound *svadharma*, interestingly, is also used with a similar meaning; here it refers to the fact that a particular rite has its own ritual details (*dharmas*) specific and limited to it and not taken over from or extended to other rites.[21] This meaning is quite similar to the use of *dharma* we saw at *ŚB* 11.5.7.1 and *ChU* 2.1.4.

The only passage where the term appears to have a Dharmaśāstric meaning is *BharŚr* 9.18.4, where the question is how to tell whether an oblation is defiled: *kathaṃ duṣṭaṃ havir vidyāt / yad āryāṇāṃ dharmajñānāṃ dharmakāmānām abhojanīyaṃ na tena devān yajeta* ("How does one know a defiled oblation? What Āryas who know *dharma* and who love *dharma* consider unfit to be eaten, with that he should not make an offering to the gods"). As in the *TU*, here also we have the term *dharmakāma* with the additional phrase *dharmajña*, compounds that become commonplace in the Dharmaśāstras.

Apart from the specialized meaning of *dharma* as ritual details or characteristics[22] that may be transferred between rites, the term does not play a central role in these ritual texts.

THE GṚHYASŪTRAS

Even though many of the Gṛhyasūtras date from a period after the rise of Buddhism, some of them may be earlier. It is in these texts devoted to the life and rituals of a Brahmin householder, however, that we would expect the term *dharma* to play a central role, as it does, for example, in the parallel texts of the Dharmasūtras. That, however, is not the case. In the Gṛhyasūtras that can claim some antiquity[23] the term occurs only six times, and two of these (*ŚāṅGṛ* 3.3.7; *PārGṛ* 3.4.18) deal with a ritual connected with the building of a house. There we have a mantra that identifies *dharma* with the main post of the house: *dharma sthūnarājaḥ*.

In another ritual context, this time the offering of the Vaiśvadeva oblation, the *Kāṭaka Gṛhyasūtra* (54.6) enjoins an offering to *dharma* and *adharma* at the door: *dharmādharmayor dvāre*. Here too positive and the negative forms are taken as deities or cosmic principles, just as in the Upaniṣads.

Only in three passages do we have a usage similar to that found in the Dharmaśāstras. At *ŚānGṛ* 2.16.2 we have the refrain *iti dharmo vidhīyate* in a verse that closely resembles *MDh* 3.110. The six ślokas in this *khaṇḍa* appear to be taken from a Dharma text. In the *BauGṛ* (3.3.31) we have the term *dhārmika* with a very classical meaning used in the instruction to the student who has completed his studentship: *vratasamāptau vedasamāptau vā gurudakṣiṇām āhared dhārmiko yathāśakti* – "At the end of the observances or at the end of (the study of) the Veda, the *dhārmika* (student) should bring a gift to the teacher according to his ability." And, finally, in *ĀśGṛ* (1.7.1) we have a passage very reminiscent of Dharmaśāstras: *atha khalūccāvacā janapadadharmā grāmadharmāś ca tān vivāhe pratīyāt* – "Now, manifold are the *dharmas* of regions and the *dharmas* of villages. One should observe these at a marriage." Here *dharma* clearly refers to customs and local norms, a meaning that is identical to the Dharmaśāstric concept of *dharma*.

CONCLUDING POSTSCRIPT

This somewhat brief though comprehensive survey of the use of *dharma* in texts roughly belonging to the middle and late vedic period (around 800–400 BCE, although some of the individual texts and passages may be from a later period), shows that in the early texts of this period, especially the Brāhmaṇas and the early Upaniṣads, the term is used most frequently with reference to Varuṇa and the king. It is likely that *dharma* was part of the specialized vocabulary associated with royalty, especially because of its frequent use within the royal consecration (*rājasūya*). In all likelihood, *dharma* referred to social order and the laws of society that the king was obligated to enforce. *Dharma* thus becomes an abstract concept and entity, a cosmic force that stands above the king; it is called *kṣatrasya kṣatram*, the power behind the royal power.[24] This hypostatization of *dharma* is carried on in other texts, when *dharma* and *adharma* are considered deities or cosmic categories.

There is no doubt that the classical meaning of *dharma* is encountered in a few passages of the Upaniṣads, Śrautasūtras, and

Gṛhyasūtras. But the rarity of these passages makes one suspect that they reflect the ideology of a later period when *dharma* had come to define the very essence of the Brahmanical way of life.

The question, then, is how did this term become transformed from a somewhat marginal and specialized context of the middle vedic texts to becoming the central concept within Brahmanical religious vocabulary, generating an entire genre of expert treatises, the Dharmaśāstras? How did the meaning of *dharma* change from its earlier limited applications to defining the proper religious life both in Brahmanism and in Buddhism?

Now, it is entirely possible that the evolution was gradual and internal to the Brahmanical tradition. Within this scenario, it was the Buddhists who borrowed the fully developed concept from the Brahmanical sources. There are several reasons why this is unlikely, the most significant of which is the fact that in texts that can be dated with some confidence to a pre-Buddhist period *dharma* does not occupy a central role within the religious vocabulary; the term does not appear still to have acquired the meaning that would enable theologians to define the good religious life as *dharma*.

I will here only summarize the conclusions I have drawn in an earlier paper on the subject (Olivelle, forthcoming). My hypothesis is that the Buddha[25] borrowed *dharma* as he did many other royal symbols to locate and articulate his new religion. Buddha's own ascribed pedigree makes him an heir to the throne. Prognosticators predicted that he will be a world-conquering (*cakravartin*) king or an enlightened being. Both the Buddha and other founders of new religions during this period are called *jina*, the conqueror. The Buddha's doctrine is compared to a wheel, a metonym for the war chariot and conquest; and his first sermon is the *dharmacakrapravartanasūtra*, "the Sūtra that set the wheel of *dharma* rolling". The Buddha's teaching is *śāsana*, the counterpart of a royal edit. These are all clearly royal symbols used, deliberately I think, to define a new ascetic group and a new religious ideology. Within this context, I think, we can see how *dharma*, which was called *kṣatrasya kṣatram*, the divine principle that gave legitimacy and meaning to a worldly ruler, the term associated with the divine sovereign Varuṇa, would be a natural choice to define the new dispensation, the new truth (*satya*) that the enlightened one had discovered. If this hypothesis is correct, then it was within early Buddhism that *dharma* changed from being a peripheral concept to becoming a central and key theological concept defining the Buddhist religion. Within this transformation, there must have been a semantic development; *dharma* becomes increasingly ethicized within the primarily ethical religion of Buddhism. It came to define the good and righteous life and the truth (*satya*) the Buddha discovered which made such a life possible.

Another factor probably influenced the term's ascendancy in the religious vocabulary of India. The use of *dharma* within a single new religion could be ignored. It's use as the central concept in defining a new imperial ideology, the ethical ideology of the Maurya empire articulated by Aśoka in his edicts, could not be ignored even by the scholastic Brahmins working within the vedic *śākhās*. In his brief edits, Aśoka uses the term about 111 times (excluding the repetitions found in the multiple versions of the same edit).[26] This number stands in sharp contrast to the numbers we have examined in the much more vast literature of the middle and late vedic periods. It is very likely that Aśoka's use of *dharma* is mediated by its use within Buddhism. Aśoka not only gives pride of place to *dharma*, he also defines it in completely ethical terms. In Rock Edict 3, for example, he instructs his ministers to teach the *dharma* in the following words: "Obedience to mother and father is good (*sādhu*). Giving (*dāna*) to friends, acquaintances, and relatives, and to Brāhmaṇas and Śramaṇas is good. Not killing is good. Spending little and possessing little is good."[27] He uses *dharma* most frequently as the first member of compounds; for him everything is *dharmic:* so he calls his edits *dharmalipi*, and his pilgrimage *dharmayātrā*. I have counted 31 such compounds used by Aśoka.[28]

How did all this affect the Brahmanical community? Clearly the Aśokan reforms displaced the Brahmin's "special relationship" with the royal power; now there are two equal religious groups worthy of honor and vying for influence and patronage: *śramaṇa-brāhmaṇa*, in the compound used and possibly coined by Aśoka. The influence of the historical memory of this period is possibly reflected in Brahmanical literature of the following centuries.[29]

The term and the concept *dharma* acquired a prominence and centrality through both Buddhism and the Aśokan imperial theology that was impossible to ignore. My hypothesis is that the emergence of the Dharmaśāstric literature, first in the form of prose *sūtras* and then in metrical treatises beginning with Manu, was a direct consequence of Buddhist and Aśokan reforms. That a *śāstra*, an expert tradition of knowledge, be devoted to *dharma* would seem improbable from its marginal use within the theologies expressed in the middle and late vedic texts. Further, as Wezler and Lariviere in their studies in this volume have demonstrated, there is a deep divide between what Wezler calls "vedic *dharma*" and "Dharmaśāstric *dharma*". The latter is based squarely on "custom", the traditional customs, usages, and practices viewed as authoritative within the Brahmanical communities. Historically, I think, this happened because the Brahmanical experts reflecting on this new *dharma* that defined one's religious, ethical, and social life had to find sources that would provide access to such a *dharma*; in other words, they had to find a *pramāṇa*, an authoritative means of knowing *dharma*.

The Buddhists had already formulated just such a *pramāṇa*, and that was the "words of the Buddha" (*buddhavacana*). Only the *ipsissima verba* of the Enlightened One could give us access to the truth, to *dharma*. The Brahmanical tradition already had such an infallible *pramāṇa*, the Veda. It was natural, therefore, for the expert tradition of Dharmaśāstra to proclaim that the Veda is the *pramāṇa* or the *mūla* (root) of *dharma*. This, however, was abstract theory and theology; it was Mīmāṃsā. In reality, however, the Veda has little to say about *dharma* in its new and expanded meaning. The "real" source of *dharma*, as Wezler and Lariviere have pointed out, was custom: the *smrti* (memory) and *ācāra* (practice) of cultured, learned, and virtuous Brahmins, who came to be designated as *śiṣṭa*.

This brings up the issue of the dates of the earliest *śāstras* on *dharma*, the Dharmasūtras. The earliest reference to such texts is in Kātyāyana's *Vārttika* 39 on Pāṇini 1.2.38, which uses the term *dharmaśāstra*. Patañjali refers to "authors of Dharmasūtras" (*dharmasūtrakārāḥ*) in the plural twice in his *Mahābhāṣya* on Pāṇini 1.1.47 (p. 115), and 5.1.119 (p. 365). This would correspond to my estimate that the earliest Dharmasūtras do not date earlier than the 3rd century BCE.

If this historical reconstruction is accepted, then we will have another tool to date early Indian texts: those that reflected a developed meaning of *dharma* and give it a central role in their theology and vocabulary must be assigned to a date at least after the development of Buddhist doctrine, if not after the proclamation of Aśokan imperial ideology. We have already seen some such passages in the *Taittirīya Upaniṣad* and the *Chāndogya Upaniṣad*, as well as some of the *Grhyasūtras*. The dates of these texts, or at least the time when these passages were incorporated into them, may have to be rethought.

The same may be said for the grammarians Yāska and Pāṇini, who also use *dharma* in ways that indicate a highly developed and expanded concept. In Yāska's *Nirukta*, for example, we have the use of the verb √*car* with reference to *dharma* in the story of Devapī and Śantanu: *adharmas tvayā caritaḥ* – "You have done an *adharma*" (2.10).[30] Then there is a verse that looks very much like a Dharmaśāstric verse asserting the right of daughters to inherit property (3.4): *aviśeṣeṇa putrāṇāṃ dāyo bhavati dharmataḥ / mithunānāṃ visargādau manuḥ svāyaṃbhuvo 'bravīt //* – "In accordance with *dharma* the partition of inheritance is done among male and female children no differently from the sons".[31] Given that Yāska has been subject to later redactoral activities, it is unclear whether these these usages are original. Pāṇini also, who is generally assigned to around 400 BCE, in several *sūtras* gives derivatives of *dharma* that show the word to have a classical meaning. Thus in *sūtra* 4.4.41 he indicates the derivative *dhārmika* in the sense of *dharmaṃ carati*. In *sūtra* 4.4.91, he shows that the affix *yat* comes after *dharma* (i.e. *dharmya*) in the sense of *dharmeṇa prāpyam* (obtainable by *dharma*) and in the very next *sūtra* shows that the same affix can be used with *dharma* to mean *dharmād anapetam* (not deviating from *dharma*).[32] These terms and usages must have been derived from or at least mediated by the spoken Sanskrit of the time (*bhāṣā*) rather than directly from the vedic vocabulary. If with von Hinüber and Falk[33] we date Pāṇini 350–300 BCE, his use of *dharma* would be quite explicable within the hypothesis I have presented.

The period we have examined was probably a watershed in the semantic development of *dharma*. Once the term became the central concept defining a civilization, this development accelerated. Other studies in this volume discuss aspects of its semantic range. It is, however, important to recognize that words do not exist in a vacuum; they are used by individuals and groups that have their own histories and interests and that change the meanings of words as they use them. Philology must not simply look at the web but at the spider also. The analysis of words thus can give significant and unique insights not just into human language but into human history. Given its centrality in Indian discourse, a close study of *dharma* has the potential to reveal interesting and hitherto unknown contours of ancient Indian history.

NOTES

1 See also Willman-Grabowska (1934).

2 In this study of the middle vedic texts, I have discounted the difference between the old neuter form *dharman* and the newer thematic stem *dharma*. In texts of

this period there does not appear to be any semantic difference between the two forms.

3 MS 1.1.8; 1, 2, 11; 1.5.4, 11; 1.11.1; 2.6.6, 8; 2.8.8; 3.16.5 (75, 77); 4.12.6; KS 1.11; 8.7; 35.7; TS 1.8.14.1; 1.8.16.2; 3.2.8.1; VS 10.29; 20.9, 17; 30.6; 38.19.

4 Other texts with parallel passages omit *dhruveṇa dharmaṇā*: TS 4.1.6.1; KS 16.5; VS 11.60; ŚB 6.5.3.10. I have adopted the translation from Brereton (1981: 55), as also his translation of *dhruveṇa dharmaṇā* in other places.

5 The first half-verse is ṚV 10.173.4. The second half-verse is not found elsewhere.

6 For an examination of kingship, see Rau 1957, 90–95.

7 See also KS 15.6–7; VS 10.4, 6–9, 16, 18; TB 1.7.6; ŚB 5.3.4.27; 5.3.5.16–37; 5.4.1.15.

8 On these passages where *dharma* is connected to the king, see Rau 1957: 90–96.

9 This is the earliest occurrence of the negative *adharma* in the vedic literature.

10 According to Vishva Bandhu's *Vedic Word-Concordance* (Hoshiarpur, 1973), *dharma* occurs in 11 passages of the *Jaiminīya Brāhmaṇa* and once in the *Gopatha Brāhmaṇa*.

11 Here also I have eliminated citations from the Saṃhitās, which are for the most part mantras for ritual recitations.

12 Stanly Insler's paper "The Function of the Varuṇa Hymns of the Ṛg veda" at the Third International Vedic Workshop, Leiden, May 29–June 2, 2002. See the story of Devāpi and Śantanu in the *Bṛhaddevatā* (8.2): when a transgression against *dharma* occurred (here the younger brother becoming king in place of the older) the realm got no rain for 12 years.

13 It is unclear why acting in an *adharmic* way makes her connected with Varuṇa; one would have expected the opposite. However, even here we have the correlation between Varuṇa and *dharma*.

14 Eggeling, following Sāyaṇa, takes this expression to mean "perfecting of the people".

15 We can see how such an extension may have influenced also the ritual meaning of *dharma* as a peculiarity or ritual detail of a particular rite and especially the later Buddhist Abhidharma meaning of *dharma* as particles of the ultimately real, that which makes something that thing (*svabhāva*), which parallels the ritual use of *svadharma* in the Śrautasūtras that we will examine below.

16 I am not including the later Upaniṣad in this study because they are probably later than the rise of Buddhism and the early Dharmasūtras. The term is found in *Kauṣītaki Upaniṣad* 2.1–2; *Kaṭha Upaniṣad* 1.21; 2.13, 14; 4.14; *Śvetāśvatara Upaniṣad* 6.6.

17 See the earlier connection of Mitra with *satya* and Varuṇa with *dharma*. The connection between *dharma* and *satya* continues into the classical period: see MDh 1.81. Their connection is also apparent within the context of judicial proceedings, especially in the context of witnesses who speak the truth: see MDh 8.14, 74, 80–8.

18 For a detailed study of this passage, see Olivelle (1996).

19 As I have explained in my previous study (Olivelle, 1996), I take the compound *dharmaskandhāḥ* as a Bahuvrīhi. Traditionally, it has been taken as a Tatpuruṣa and translated "divisions of *dharma*".

20 These exclude the occurrence of the term in citations of mantras from the Saṃhitās. Āpastamba, 19.21.4, 16; 21.3.3, 10; Āśvalāyana, 10.5.15; 10.7.9; Baudhāyana, 24.37; 27.24; Bhāradvāja, 1.1.9; 6.15.5, 7, 12; 7.6.7; 9.18.3; Hiraṇyakeśin, 3.8.24, 32, 40, 41, 44, 46, 47; 13.4.27; 16.1.23; 22.4.2, 6; Kātyāyana, 1.8.7; 4.3.19; 5.8.17; 9.5.10; Lāṭyāyana, 7.7.19; Śāṅkhāyana, 4.5.13; 7.15.16–7; 9.26.2; 16.18.5; Vādhūla, 11.6.7–8, 24; and Vārāha 1.1.1.68. 70; 1.2.4.9.

21 See ĀpŚr 19.21.16; HirŚr 3.8.40; 22.4.6; BārŚr 6.15.12.

22 This meaning did not disappear after the Śrautasūtras. We find it used with precisely the same meaning in the *Pūrva-Mīmāṃsā Sūtra* 2.1.9–10.
23 I have omitted the *Vaikhānasa* and the *Āgniveśaya*, which clearly belong to a much later date.
24 On the use of such expressions, also found in *satyasya satyam*, see H. Oertel, *Zum altindischen Ausdrucksverstärkungstypus* satyasya satyam "*das Wahre des Wahren*" = "*die Quintessenz des Wahren.*" Sitzungsberichte der Bayerischen Akademie der Wissenschaften, Philosophisch-historische Abteilung, Jahrgang 1937, Heft 3. Munich: Verlag der Bayerischen Akademie der Wissenschaften, 1937.
25 I use "Buddha" as a shorthand for the early Buddhists. What the historical Buddha actually taught is impossible to determine, because we have only one lens to view it and that is the Buddhist texts written, revised, edited over centuries.
26 Number of occurrences are given within parentheses: Rock edicts I (2); III (1); IV (10); V (10); VI (1); VIII (3); IX (5); X (2); XI (5); XII (2); XIII (11); XIV (1); XV (2); Pillar edicts I (8); II (3); IV (3); VI (3); VII (30); Minor rock edict I (4 only in Gujarra version); II (1); III (3); IV (1). The last is in the trilingual edict with Aramaic and Greek translations. The Aramaic equivalent of *dharma* given by Aśoka is "qsyt" and the Greek is "eusebia". John Huehnergard (personal communication) takes the root qst means "(be) true, truth". The form qsyt is a substantivized adjective, "what is true". This term thus corresponds to *satya* with which, as we have seen, *dharma* is often paired and sometimes identified. The Greek term may mean something like piety and reverence towards gods. According to Paul Woodruff (personal communication) there may be a connection between eusebia and kingship. Augustus is Latin for Sebastos, which is used in connection with Hellenistic kingship. In classical usage, *sebein* is used for respecting monarchs and *eusebein* for relations with the gods. As the line between kings and gods was blurred in the Hellenistic era, so was this rather soft distinction. A tantalizing possibility is that Aśoka's use of *dharma* may, in fact, have been influenced by Hellenistic or Persian royal vocabularies.
27 According to the Girnar version: *sādhu mātari ca pitari ca susrūsā mitrasaṃstutañātīnaṃ bāmhaṇasamaṇānaṃ sādhu dānaṃ prāṇānaṃ sādhu anāraṃbho appavyayatā appabhāṃḍatā sādhu.*
28 Here is the list of these compounds: *dhammakāmatā, dhaṃmaguṇa, dhaṃmaghoṣa, dhaṃmacaraṇa* (*calana*), *dhaṃmatthaṃba, dhaṃmadāna, dhammādhithāna, dhaṃmaniyama, dhaṃmānuguha, dhaṃmanupaṭīpatti, dhaṃmānusathi, dhaṃmānusāsanā, dhammanisita, dhaṃmāpadāna, dhaṃmapalipuccha, dhaṃmapaliyāyāni, dhaṃmāpekkhā, dhaṃmamaṅgala, dhaṃmamahāmātā, dhammayātā, dhaṃmayuta, dhaṃmalipi, dhaṃmavāya / sīlana, dhaṃmavijaya, dhaṃmaviḍḍhi, dhaṃmavuta, dhaṃmasaṃbaṃdha, daṃmasaṃvibhāga, dhaṃmasaṃstava, dhaṃmasāvana, dhammasusuṣā.* For further details about Aśoka's use of *dharma*, see Olivelle, (forthcoming) and Thapar (1997).
29 Historical memory is not the same as historical accuracy. The historical memory of Aśoka was different among different groups; the Buddhists generally have a very positive view of Aśoka and his work, while the press is not entirely favorable to Aśoka in the Brahmanical tradition. With regard to the possible influence of such historical memory in shaping later Brahmanical literature, see James Fitzgerald, *The Mahābhārata: 11. The Book of Women, 12. The Book of Piece*. vol. 7. Chicago: Chicago University Press, 2004; and Alf Hiltebeitel, *Rethinking the Mahābhārata: A Reader's Guide to the Education of the Dharma King*. Chicago: University of Chicago Press, 2001.
30 The story is also found in *Bṛhaddevatā*, where we find the expression *dharmavyatikrama*, "transgression of *dharma*" (8.3).
31 See also *Nirukta*, 6.19; 8.10; 12.13. In chapter 14, generally considered to be a later addition, we also have similar use of *dharma:* 14.6, 14.

[32] See also Pāṇini 4.4.47 and 6.2.65 for *dharmyam*, and 4.2.46 for *dharmavat*. See also 5.2.132; 5.4.124.
[33] Oskar von Hinüber, *Der Beginn der Schrift und frühe Schriftlichkeit in Indien* (Wiesbaden: Franz Steiner, 1989), p. 34; Harry Falk, *Schrift im alten Indien: ein Forschungsbericht mit Anmerkungen* (Tübingen: Gunter Narr Verlag, 1992), p. 304.

REFERENCES

Brereton, J. (1981). *The Ṛgvedic Adityas*. American Oriental Society, vol. 63. New Haven: American Oriental Society.

Olivelle, P. (1996). *Dharmaskandhāḥ* and *Brahmasaṃsthaḥ*: A Study of *Chāndogya Upaniṣad* 2.23.1, *Journal of the American Oriental Society* **116**, 205–19.

Olivelle, P. (1999). *Dharmasūtras*: *The Law Codes of Ancient India*. Oxford: Oxford University Press.

Olivelle, P. (forthcoming). Power of words: The ascetic appropriation and the semantic evolution of dharma. In Peter Fluegel and Gustaaf Houtman (eds.), *Asceticism and Power in the Asian Context*. London: Curzon.

Thapar, R. (1997 [1961]). *Aśoka and the Decline of the Mauryas*, 2nd ed. Delhi: Oxford University Press.

Willman-Grabowska, H. (1934). Evolution sémantique du mot 'dharma'. *Rocznik Orientalistyczny* **10**, 38–50.

ABBREVIATIONS

AĀ	*Aitareya Āraṇyaka*
AB	*Aitareya Brāhmaṇa*
ĀpŚr	*Āpastamba Śrautasūtra*
ĀśGṛ	*Āśvalāyana Gṛhyasūtra*
BauGṛ	*Baudhāyana Gṛhyasūtra*
BharŚr	*Bharadvāja Śrautasūtra*
BU	*Bṛhadāraṇyaka Upaniṣad*
ChU	*Chāndogya Upaniṣad*
HirŚr	*Hiraṇyakeśi Śrautasūtra*
KS	*Kāṭhaka Saṃhitā*
MDh	*Mānava Dharmaśāstra*
MS	*Maitrāyaṇī Samhitā*
PārGṛ	*Pāraskara Gṛhyasūtra*
RV	*Ṛg Veda*
ŚāṅGṛ	*Śāṅkhāyana Gṛhyasūtra*
ŚB	*Śatapatha Brāhmaṇa*
TĀ	*Taittirīya Āraṇyaka*
TB	*Taittirīya Brāhmaṇa*
TS	*Taittirīya Saṃhitā*

TU *Taittirīya Upaniṣad*
VS *Vājasaneyi Saṃhitā*

1314 Thaddeus Cove
Austin, TX 78746
USA
E-mail: jpo@uts.cc.utexas.edu

RUPERT GETHIN

HE WHO SEES DHAMMA SEES DHAMMAS: DHAMMA IN EARLY BUDDHISM

PRELIMINARY REMARKS: BUDDHISM AND *DHARMA*

The basic subject of the present article is the understanding of the concept of *dharma* in early Buddhist literature – in the Nikāyas/Āgamas and the early *abhidhamma/abhidharma* texts. As it is clear that early Buddhist texts were composed in some form of Middle Indic and as my main sources will be Pali texts I shall generally use the Pali Middle Indic form *dhamma*.[1] There are three basic problems that I think need to be considered in order to present a clear account of the distinctively Buddhist understanding of *dhamma*: (1) we need to establish the range of meanings found in early Buddhist literature; (2) we need to consider the relationship between those different meanings and how they evolved; (3) we need also to consider the relationship of the distinctively Buddhist usage of *dhamma* to the usage and understanding of *dharma* more generally in Indian literature and thought, and especially in early Brahmanical writings. These problems are, of course, not entirely separable. Clearly how we map out the different early Buddhist uses and their relationship will affect how we understand the Buddhist usage in relation to the non-Buddhist usage. But equally how we map out the different early Buddhist uses and their relationship in the first place, depends in part on how we understand the Buddhist usage in relation to the non-Buddhist usage. Moreover, the complexities and subtleties of the broader Brahmanical and 'Hindu' usage mean that there is hardly a scholarly consensus on how best to pick up and follow the trail of the elusive spirit of dharma beyond the field of Buddhist literature. In the present context, then, what I should like to do is devote some space first of all to a consideration of the range of meanings *dhamma* has in early Buddhist texts, and then move on to a consideration of the evolution and development of the distinctively Buddhist usage and how that might relate to Vedic and early Brahmanical usage.

MODERN SCHOLARLY ACCOUNTS OF *DHAMMA*

As one of the basic terms of Buddhist thought *dhamma/dharma* has been the subject of a number of studies and articles over the last century or so. Mostly scholars have focused on the first problem identified above – the range of meanings found in early Buddhist literature – although they have offered some observations and even theories about the development and evolution of its usage in Buddhist thought. Less, perhaps, has been said about the relationship between the distinctively Buddhist usage and the usage in Indian thought in general. Three books devoted to the subject of Buddhist *dhamma/dharma* deserve special mention as being representative not only of the information about *dhamma/dharma* that modern scholarship has presented on the basis of the study Buddhist textual sources, but also of somewhat different approaches and emphases in considering the significance of that information. The first is the pioneering study of Magdelene and Wilhelm Geiger, *Pāli Dhamma vornehmlich in der kanonischen Literatur*, published in 1920.[2] This is a comprehensive philological study divided into four main sections, each of which considers a distinctive set of meanings of the term *dhamma*. The basic method is one of cataloguing and grouping the different uses and meanings and providing illustrative quotations from the Pali canonical literature. The four sets of meanings centre around 'law' (Gesetz), 'teaching' (Lehre), 'truth' (Wahrheit) and 'thing' (Ding, Sache). This last meaning of *dhamma* refers to the use of the term *dhamma* in early Buddhist texts to characterize simple mental and physical sates and phenomena as *dhammas*. The Geigers regard this usage of *dhamma* as far removed from its original usage, and identify the issue of how *dhamma* comes to be used in this way as the principal question to be addressed in accounting for the development of the usage of the term in Buddhist texts.[3]

Three years later Stcherbatsky published his *The Central Conception of Buddhism and the Meaning of the Word 'dharma'*.[4] Referring to the Geigers' achievement in having 'drawn up a concordance of nearly every case where the word *dhamma* occurs in Pali canonical literature', and having 'established a great variety of meanings', he comments that among the various meanings, 'there is, indeed, only one that really matters, that is the specifically Buddhistic technical term *dharma*.'[5] This specifically Buddhist technical meaning of *dharma* Stcherbatsky expresses as 'element of existence', and he takes as a basis for its exposition not the literature of the Pali canon, but a fourth or fifth century CE work of Buddhist systematic thought, namely Vasubandhu's *Abhidharmakośa-bhāṣya*. Rather than seeking to consider the various meanings of *dharma/dhamma* and their relationship, Stcherbatsky focuses on just one meaning, and attempts to provide a precise philosophical account of the Buddhist conception of a *dharma* as an 'element of existence'.

Just over half a century later John Ross Carter published another book-length study: *Dhamma: Western Academic and Sinhalese Buddhist Interpretations*.[6] If the Geigers' focus was basically linguistic and philological, and Stcherbatsky's philosophical, then Carter's is more broadly religious. He begins with a survey of the account of *dharma/dhamma* given in modern scholarly studies, beginning with the work of Burnouf (1844), and taking into account writings by Spence Hardy, Childers, T.W. and C.A.F. Rhys Davids, Oldenberg, Beckh, the Geigers, Keith, Stcherbatsky, Glasenapp, Thomas, Horner, Lamotte, and Conze, among others. He then turns his attention to the understanding of *dhamma* in specifically the Theravāda Buddhist tradition, focusing not only on the Pali canonical texts, but also on the way *dhamma* has been understood in the Pali commentaries and exegetical works, as well as in later vernacular Sinhala literature. Carter states explicitly that the 'dharma-theory' and the role of *dhammas* in Buddhist systematic thought is not his main focus;[7] his book instead seeks to explore and bring out the potency of *dhamma* as a religious concept: it is the teaching of a *buddha* – a fully awakened being; it is a path of religious practice, an object of devotion worthy of reverence whose qualities are to be recollected and pondered by the practitioner in order to inspire faith and engender calm; it is a transcendent reality and 'salvific Truth'.

What I have said so far has already introduced some of the principal meanings of *dhamma/dharma* that modern scholarship has identified in the early Buddhist usage. In fact, while different scholarly authors might identify fewer or more meanings, give more or less emphasis to a particular aspect of the early Buddhist understanding of *dhamma*, or present the relationship between the different meanings in different ways, there is a basic consensus in the range of meanings identified. While no particular writer presents the usage of the term *dhamma* in precisely the following terms, I think this consensus can be summed up by way of six basic meanings:[8] (1) the 'teaching' of the Buddha; (2) 'good conduct' or 'good behaviour', in general, but also more specifically the putting into practice of the good conduct prescribed by the Buddha's teaching and constituting the Buddhist path, namely keeping ethical precepts (*sīla*), developing calm and concentration (*samatha*, *samādhi*, *jhāna*), and insight and knowledge (*vipassanā*, *paññā*, *vijjā*) through the practice of meditation; (3) the 'truth' realized by the practice of the Buddhist path; (4) any particular 'nature' or 'quality' that something possesses; (5) the underlying and objective 'natural law or order' of things which the Buddha has discerned; (6) a basic mental or physical 'state' or 'thing', a plurality of which, at least in the texts of the Abhidhamma, becomes explicitly to be conceived as in some sense constituting the 'reality' of the world or experience. While the order of presentation here is intended to be suggestive of a possible affinity between certain meanings, it is not intended to indicate a judgement about which meanings have priority, either in terms of normative usage or in terms of historical development. Having, with the help of the work of earlier scholars, identified and set out this range of basic meanings, what I should like to do now is to consider them more closely with specific reference to the Pali Nikāyas in order to illustrate and establish, at least provisionally, the extent to which they do indeed reflect the usage of the early texts.

Teaching

To say that *dhamma* in certain Nikāya contexts means the 'teaching' of the Buddha is to say that it can refer to both the content of his teaching – what he taught, the collection of instructions and doctrines taught by the Buddha – and to the 'texts' that contain and set out those teachings. In the Nikāya period the latter are, of course, oral compositions rather than written texts and are often conceived as comprising nine 'parts' (*aṅga*); but later they are referred to as consisting of the three 'baskets' (*piṭaka*) or collections of Vinaya, Sutta, and Abhidhamma. A clear example of this kind of usage would be the sentence: 'a monk learns the *teaching* – the discourses, chants, analyses, verses, utterances, sayings, birth stories, marvels, and dialogues'.[9]

Good Conduct or Behaviour

A typical usage of the term *dhamma* in the broad sense of good, right or proper behaviour and conduct is in the context of the rule of kings: kings are described as ruling 'righteously' or 'justly' (*dhammena rajjaṃ kāreti*)[10] or as practicing 'justice' or 'righteousness' (*dhammaṃ carati*).[11] More generally a person may acquire a possession 'properly' or 'lawfully' (*dhammena*), or he may acquire it 'improperly' or 'unlawfully' (*adhammena*).[12] And while *dhamma* is characteristically used to refer to good, right and proper behaviour, we should note that it can be used more neutrally of conduct and behaviour, thus people indulge in the 'practice' of sexual intercourse (*methunaṃ dhammaṃ paṭisevati*).[13]

It is in the context of this use of *dhamma* in the sense of proper conduct and behaviour that we need to understand the extension of the use of the term *dhamma* to refer to the 'practices' taught by the Buddha for the benefit of gods and men:

> So, monks, those *practices* that I have taught to you for the purpose of higher knowledge – having properly grasped them, you should practise them, develop them, make them mature so that the spiritual life might continue and endure long; this will be for the good of the many, for the happiness of the many, for the sake of compassion for the world, for the benefit, good and happiness of gods and men. And what are those *practices* ...? Just these – the four ways of establishing mindfulness, the four right endeavours, the four bases of success, the five faculties, the five powers, the seven factors of awakening, the noble eightfold path.[14]

The significant point about the use of *dhamma* in such as a passage as this, is that it is clear that at least the four ways of establishing mindfulness, the four right endeavours, the four bases of success and the noble eightfold path refer to things one does or practices; they are not 'teachings' or 'texts'. Whether the five faculties, powers and factors of awakening can be so straightforwardly characterized as 'practices' perhaps needs further consideration. I shall return to this presently.

Truth

In certain contexts meanings such as 'teaching' or 'practice' seem not to fit; a meaning closer to 'truth' – the truth about the world or reality as directly realized and taught by the Buddha – seems to be required. Thus in a number of places in the Nikāyas it is described how the Buddha by means of step by step instruction (*anupubbī kathā*) leads his listeners to a vision of the truth: he talks of giving, virtuous conduct, and heaven; he reveals the danger, vanity and impurity of sense desires, and the benefit of desirelessness; and when he sees that the hearts of his listeners are ready, open and without hindrance, are inspired and confident, then he reveals the teaching of the *truth* that is special to buddhas – suffering, its arising, its cessation, the path; and at the conclusion of such step by step instruction there arises in his listeners 'the clear and spotless vision of the *truth* (*dhamma-cakkhu*)';

the listeners are now 'ones who have seen the *truth*, gained the *truth*, known the *truth*, penetrated the *truth*, gone beyond doubt, removed their questioning, and acquired full confidence in what is taught by the Teacher without having to rely on others'.[15]

Taking *dhamma* as close to 'truth', as opposed to teaching or practice, would also seem to be appropriate in such statements as the well known 'he who sees *dhamma* sees me, he who sees me sees *dhamma*', or 'he who sees dependent arising sees *dhamma*, he who sees *dhamma* sees dependent arising'.[16] That *dhamma* in these statements means something like 'truth' is reinforced by the way in which in context they are illustrated by accounts of precisely the early Buddhist understanding of the truth about the way things are: physical form, feeling, recognition, volitions, consciousness are impermanent, suffering, and not to be taken as self; the five aggregates of attachment arise dependent on factors and conditions.

Some scholars have suggested that *dhamma* in the sense of 'truth' becomes hypostasized as the highest metaphysical principle, equivalent to the *ātman-brahman* of the Upaniṣads, almost personified.[17] Such an interpretation is, of course, controversial and certainly problematic from the point of view the interpretations of traditional Theravāda Buddhism.

Nature

In the passages referred to in the previous paragraph, the particular vision of truth that the listeners are said to have at the end of the Buddha's instruction is described in each case in the following terms: 'the *dhamma* of everything whose *dhamma* it is to arise, is to cease' (*yaṃ kiñci samudaya-dhammaṃ sabbaṃ taṃ nirodha-dhamman ti*). The term *dhamma* used at the end of a *bahuvrīhi* compound in this manner has to mean something like 'nature' or 'characteristic quality': 'the *nature* of everything whose *nature* it is to arise, is to cease'. Similarly, in the 'Discourse on Establishing Mindfulness' (Satipaṭṭhāna Sutta) a monk is instructed to practice watching the *nature* of things to arise and fall away in the case of the body, feelings, and consciousness.[18] The use of *dhamma*/*dharma* at the end of a compound in the sense of a particular nature or quality possessed by something is a common usage in both Pali and Sanskrit and is not a specifically Buddhist usage. We shall return to this usage later.

Natural Law

Given that the truth one sees when one sees *dhamma* is that 'the nature of everything whose nature it is to arise, is to cease', it might seem that the truth that is *dhamma* is understood as some kind of 'law of the universe'. A number of modern scholars and interpreters have thus suggested that *dhamma* signifies the natural law or order which the world or reality conforms to. Thus T.W. Rhys Davids and William Stede in their dictionary article speak of the *dhamma* preached by the Buddha as 'the order of the law of the universe, immanent, eternal, uncreated, not as interpreted by him only, much less invented or decreed by him, but intelligible to a mind of his range, and by him made so to mankind as bodhi: revelation, awakening'.[19] Seeing *dhamma* as some form of eternal natural order or law would appear to be a more interpretative suggestion for the meaning of *dhamma* than those that we have so far considered, in that it is harder to cite passages where the translation 'Natural Law' or 'Universal Law' is clearly required by context and to be given preference over other translations. The kinds of passage referred to in order to illustrate this kind of understanding of *dhamma* are those which speak of the way things arise in dependence upon other things, or of how the mental and physical factors that make up the world (*saṃkhāra*) are all impermanent, suffering and not self, and then refer to this fact as the *dhamma-ṭṭhitatā*, the *dhamma-niyāmatā* that endures whether or not Buddhas arise in the world. Certainly these last two expressions might be translated 'the constancy of nature', 'the law of nature'. And one could also suggest that the statement quoted above – 'he who sees dependent arising sees *dhamma*' – might be rendered as 'he who sees dependent arising sees the *law*'. Yet it does not follow from such translations that we should necessarily hypostasize *dhamma* and conceive of it as some form of 'immanent, eternal, uncreated' law of the universe.[20] Possibly these two expressions should be interpreted as the constancy and law of *dhammas*, plural, rather than *dhamma*, singular,[21] and this brings us to the sixth sense of *dhamma*.

Mental or Physical State or Thing

We come now to the use of the term *dhamma* in a manner that is at once the most distinctively Buddhist and the hardest to offer a suitable translation for. Before considering the question of the appropriateness or not of particular translations, let us consider some examples of this usage.

Completely secluded from sense desires and unwholesome *dhammas*, a monk attains and remains in the joy and happiness of the first meditation.[22]

A monk ... endeavours so that bad, unwholesome *dhammas* that have not arisen, do not arise; ... he endeavours so that bad, unwholesome *dhammas* that have arisen are abandoned; ... he endeavours so that wholesome *dhammas* that have not arisen, arise; ... he endeavours so that wholesome *dhammas* that have arisen, are constant, not lost, increase, grow, develop, are complete.[23]

A monk ... dwells watching *dhammas* as *dhammas* ...[24]

Quite clearly to understand and translate *dhammas* as teachings, truths, laws – whether of nature or otherwise – simply will not do in the above contexts; 'practices' just might work in the first passage, but to think of 'practices' as things that have 'arisen' or 'not arisen', as such a translation would demand in the second passage, must rule it out. And when we read the full exposition of what watching *dhammas* as *dhammas* involves, such a conclusion is only reinforced. A monk dwells watching *dhammas* as *dhammas* in terms of: (1) the five hindrances – sensual desire, aversion, sleepiness and tiredness, excitement and depression, doubt – knowing whether each is present in him or not, how each arises and is abandoned such that it will not arise again; (2) the five aggregates of attachment – physical form, feeling, recognition, volitional formations, consciousness – how each arises and disappears; (3) the six senses and their respective objective fields, knowing the fetters that arise dependent on the two, how these fetters arise and are abandoned such that they will not arise again; (4) the seven constituents of awakening – mindfulness, *dhamma*-investigation, vigour, joy, tranquillity, concentration, equanimity – knowing whether each is present in him or not, how each arises and is brought to full development; (5) the four noble truths, knowing what suffering is, what the arising of suffering is, what the cessation of suffering is, what the way leading to the cessation of suffering is.

Clearly if watching *dhammas* involves watching the hindrances, the aggregates, the senses and their objects, and the constituents of awakening, then *dhammas* are not teachings, practices, truths, or laws. And while it might be possible in some contexts to take the Nikāyas as presenting the 'four noble truths' as four doctrinal propositions – 'suffering is the five aggregates of attachment' – the kind of usage above challenges such a notion. Suffering, its arising, its cessation, the way leading to its cessation are here not 'truths' in the sense of doctrinal propositions, but realities that have to be understood.

So what are *dhammas*? In many ways it is the usage of *dhamma* at the end of a *bahuvrīhi* compound in the sense of a particular nature or quality possessed by something that seems the best fit in the present context, only here the particular natures or qualities are not possessed by anything, they are natural qualities in their own right, which the meditating monk watches arising and disappearing, some of which he strives to stop arising, and some of which he strives to keep arising.

We can define *dhammas* in this final sense as basic qualities, both mental and physical. When we consider this particular understanding of what a *dhamma* is alongside the defining of the world or experience in its entirety (*sabbaṃ*) in terms of the five aggregates or the twelve spheres of sense, then we can go one step further and say that *dhammas* are the basic qualities, both mental and physical, that in some sense constitute experience or reality in its entirety.[25] What I think is undeniable is that, whether or not one accepts this as something the Buddha himself taught, this sense and basic understanding of a *dhamma* is firmly established and imbedded in the Nikāyas. Indeed, I think it not unreasonable to suggest that it is the prevalent usage of the word *dhamma* in the Nikāyas. It is, of course, a usage that approximates to the one found in the Abhidhamma/Abhidharma, and the question of the relationship of this Nikāya usage to the more technically precise Abhidhamma/Abhidharma usage is something that I shall return to below. But before doing that I wish first to consider how the Pali commentaries approach the issue of the different senses of the word *dhamma* in the Nikāyas.

DHAMMA AND *DHAMMAS* IN THE PALI COMMENTARIES

Obviously the commentaries offer a rather more developed understanding of *dhamma* than that found in the Nikāyas and early Abhidhamma. Nevertheless, their understanding represents a tradition of interpretation that is still relatively close to the earlier texts, and provides us with important points of references for plotting the development of the usage of the term in early Buddhist thought. A number of scholars have paid some attention to the traditional expositions of *dhamma* presented in the Pali commentaries. The Geigers and PED, for example, both begin their accounts by citing lists of meanings for *dhamma* found in the commentaries to the *Dīgha*

Nikāya, *Dhammapada* and *Dhammasaṅgaṇī*.[26] But it is John Ross Carter's work that provides the fullest account of the understanding of *dhamma* found in the Pali commentaries.[27] Drawing on especially Carter's work, I wish to highlight what seem to me the most significant aspects of the way the early Buddhist exegetical tradition approaches the notion of *dhamma*.

Some six passages from the Pali commentaries explicitly explain that in the canonical texts the word *dhamma* can have various meanings which they then go on to list (see Table I).[28] The number of meanings listed ranges from 4 to 11, although each list is explicitly open ended; in aggregate 18 different possible meanings are suggested. Having listed the possible meanings, the commentaries proceed by citing illustrative passages from the canonical texts – mostly the Nikāyas and Abhidhamma. These 18 meanings can, I think, be grouped and understood by way of five principal meanings that broadly correspond to the six meanings identified above: (1) teaching or text, (2) good qualities or conduct more generally, (3) truth, (4) the natural condition of something, (5) a mental or physical quality in a technical Abhidhamma sense (see Table II). Let me comment briefly on these in turn.

The first meaning is straightforward: *dhamma* can mean the teaching of the Buddha and the texts that contain those teachings, defined as 'the word of the Buddha contained in the Three Baskets' (*tepiṭakaṃ buddha-vacanaṃ*).[29] I have grouped the next set of meanings together in that they all take *dhamma* in the sense either of the general good qualities and conduct (*guṇa*, *puñña*) promoted by Buddhist practice or are specific examples of those qualities and conduct (*samādhi*, *paññā*). I have also grouped with these an example of *dhamma* in a more general sense of practice: in the Vinaya dhamma is used to refer to the various categories of 'offence' (*āpatti*), as in 'four offences involving defeat' (*cattāro pārājikā dhammā*).[30] What I have listed as the third meaning of *dhamma* identified by the commentaries is again straightforward: in certain contexts *dhamma* should be taken as meaning the truth or, more specifically, the four truths, more or less in the same way that I have already outlined above. The fourth meaning of 'natural condition' is once again unproblematic in that it corresponds straightforwardly to a meaning that we have already noted: *dhamma* as the last member of a compound means the natural condition (*pakati*) possessed by something, thus to describe someone as *jāti-dhamma* or *jarā-dhamma* means that birth and old age are his 'natural condition' (*pakati*).[31] An alternative term used by the commentaries here is *vikāra* in the sense of disposition.[32]

Under the fifth heading I have grouped eight distinct meanings that all relate in various ways to the technical Abhidhamma understanding of a *dhamma* as a basic 'mental or physical quality'. These eight meanings fall into four subsets (see Table II).

As I have suggested above, the word *dhamma* is quite clearly already used in the Nikāyas in the sense of a basic quality, both mental and physical, a plurality of which in some sense constitutes experience or reality in its entirety. A *dhamma* in the sense of one of these basic qualities may be defined in the commentaries as a 'a particular nature' (*sabhāva*). The canonical passage referred to for the meaning of *dhamma* in the sense of *sabhāva* is the Abhidhamma matrix of triplets (*tika-mātikā*) that is set out at the beginning of the *Dhammasaṅgaṇī* and is used as a basis of exposition in that text, the *Vibhaṅga*, *Dhātukathā*, and *Paṭṭhāna*; it begins 'wholesome qualities, unwholesome qualities, undetermined qualities' (*kusalā dhammā akusalā dhammā avyākatā dhammā*).[33] I shall return to the Abhidhamma understanding of *sabhāva* below.

We next have three terms – having no essence (*nissattatā*), being lifeless (*nijjīvatā*), being empty (*suññatā*) – that are perhaps best understood as relating the understanding of *dhammas* as basic qualities to the notion of 'not-self' (*anattan*). As illustrative of *dhamma* in these senses, the commentaries consistently cite two passages.[34] The first is a section from the *Dhammasaṅgaṇī* explicitly called 'the section on emptiness' in the text (*suññata-vāra*), which occurs after the various mental *dhammas* or qualities that arise together constituting an instance of consciousness have been set out and defined in detail. The section states simply that 'at that time there are *dhammas*, there are aggregates, there are sense-spheres ...'[35] What the commentaries seem to be suggesting is that in stating this the *Dhammasaṅgaṇī* emphasises that these *dhammas* constituting an instance of consciousness are nothing but evanescent and insubstantial non-entities that have no real essence or life of their own. The second passage cited by the commentaries in this context is one I have already referred to above, the passage describing the fourth way of establishing mindfulness by watching *dhammas* as *dhammas*. In other words, when the meditator watches *dhammas* as *dhammas* in the manner described in the *Satipaṭṭhāna Sutta*, what the commentaries are suggesting is that what he is watching is the arising and disappearance of nothing but evanescent and insubstantial non-entities that have no real essence or life of their own. This ties in with the way Buddhaghosa later alludes to a number of images and similes from the Nikāyas in order

TABLE I

Meanings	Commentary to Dīgha Nikāya (Sv I 99)	Majjhima Nikāya (Ps I 17)	Dhammapada (Dhp-a I 22)	Paṭisambhidāmagga (Paṭis-a I 18)	Buddhavaṃsa (Bv-a 13)	Dhammasaṅgaṇī (As 38)
1 *Guṇa*						
Good quality	1		1	9		3
2 *Desanā*						
Teaching	2		2			
3 *Pariyatti*						
Text	3	1	3	5	1	1
4 *Nissatta(tā)-(nijjīva(tā))*						
Without essence/life	4		4	6		4
5 (*Catu-*)*sacca*(*-dhamma*)						
(Four) truths		2			10	
6 *Samādhi*						
Concentration		3			2	
7 *Paññā*						
Wisdom		4		2	3	
8 *Pakati*						
Natural condition		5			4	
9 *Sabhāva*						
Particular nature		6		1	5	

10	*Suññatā*			
	Emptiness	7		6
11	*Puñña*			
	Merit	8	3	7
12	*Āpatti*			
	Offence	9	6	8
13	*Ñeyya*			
	Object of knowledge	10		9
14	*Paññatti*			
	Concept		4	
15	*Vikāra*			
	Disposition		8	
16	*Paccaya*			
	Causal condition		10	
17	*Paccayuppanna*			
	Arisen from a causal condition		11	
18	*Hetu*			
	Cause			2

TABLE II

Teaching/text	(Good) conduct	Truths	Nature	Mental/physical quality
Desanā	*Guṇa*	*(Catu-)sacca*	*Pakati*	*Sabhāva*
Teaching	Good quality	(Four) truths	Natural condition	Particular nature
Pariyatti	*Puñña*		*Vikāra*	
Text	Merit		Disposition	
	Samādhi			
	Concentration			*Nissatta-nijjīvatā*
	Paññā			Without life
	Wisdom			*Suññatā*
	Āpatti			Emptiness
	Offence			
				Paccaya
				Causal condition
				Paccayuppanna
				Arisen from a causal condition
				Hetu
				Cause
				Ñeyya
				Object of knowledge
				Paññatti
				Concept

to illustrate the manner in which *dhammas* that are not lasting or solid but rather things that vanish almost as soon as they appear – like dew drops at sunrise, like a bubble on water, like a line drawn on water, like a mustard-seed placed on the point of an awl, like a flash of lightning; things that lack substance and always elude one's grasp – like a mirage, a conjuring trick, a dream, the circle formed by a whirling fire brand, a fairy city, foam, or the trunk of a banana tree.[36]

The third subset comprises three terms each of which brings out the manner in which a *dhamma* is understood as a causal condition itself (*hetu*, *paccaya*)and as something that has arisen as a result of causal conditions (*paccayuppanna*). Seeing *dhammas* in this way, while not perhaps explicit in the Nikāyas, is none the less certainly implicit. Thus again the description of how the meditator is to watch *dhammas* as *dhammas* focuses in particular on the conditions which lead to the arising and abandoning of particular *dhammas.* As the commentaries put it in the context of dependent arising: nothing arises from a single cause, and all causes have multiple effects.[37]

Finally we have two terms that focus on *dhammas* as objects of consciousness: dhammas are 'things that can be known' (*ñeyya*), and they are concepts (*paññatti*). This last meaning of *dhamma* relates to the way *dhammas* are presented in the list of the six senses – eye, ear, nose, tongue, body, mind – and their corresponding objective fields – visible forms, sounds, smells, tastes, tangible sensations, *dhammas.*

As Geiger and Carter noted, in trying to evaluate the lists of terms offered as possible meanings of *dhamma* by such commentarial passages, we should not forget that they end with an 'etc.' (*ādi*) and are thus explicitly open ended. In fact, it is clear that such lists of meanings do not exhaust the commentarial and exegetical understanding of *dhamma.* There are two particular aspects of the commentarial understanding of *dhamma* that Carter has drawn attention to and which I should like to pick up on.[38] The first concerns the understanding of *dhamma* in terms of 'nine transcendent *dhammas*' (*nava lokuttara-dhammā, navavidha-lokuttara-dhamma*), the second is the understanding in terms of a threefold division by way of texts (*pariyatti*), practice (*paṭipatti*), and realization (*paṭivedha*) or attainment (*adhigama*).

At the beginning of his discussion of the meditation practice (*kamma-ṭṭhāna*) of recollecting *dhamma* (*dhammānussati*), Buddhaghosa makes a distinction between *dhamma* as the texts (*pariyatti*) containing the teaching of the Buddha on the one hand and transcendent *dhamma* on the other.[39] The latter is ninefold and comprises the four paths of stream entry, once-return, non-return, and arahatship, the four corresponding fruits, and *nibbāna* itself. Carter notes, citing some 40 examples, that the Pali commentaries frequently suggest that *dhamma* in the Nikāyas is to be understood as referring to the nine transcendent *dhammas.*[40] In the technical understanding of the commentaries, this refers to the four kinds of consciousness (*citta*) that arise as the attainment of the four 'paths' (*magga*), the four kinds of consciousness that arise as the attainment of the 'fruits' (*phala*) of those 'paths', and lastly *nibbāna* as the 'unconditioned element' (*asaṃkhata-dhātu*), 'object' (*ārammāṇa*) of those classes of consciousness.[41] In other words transcendent *dhamma* consists of the mind that knows and sees *nibbāna* at the moment of awakening (*bodhi*), and also of what is known and seen at that moment. Such a usage, in fact corresponds more or less to the usage of a word like 'knowledge' in English, which can denote both the act of knowing as well as what is known.

In several places in early Buddhist texts a list of five mental 'waste lands' (*ceto-khila*) is itemized and explained. The second of these consists in having doubts about *dhamma*.[42] The commentaries take it that this means having doubts either about Buddhist texts (*pariyatti*) – that the word of the Buddha consists of 84,000 sections – or about realization (*paṭivedha*) – that the path is achieved by insight, the fruit by the path and that *nibbāna* represents the stilling of all volitional formations.[43] The understanding of *dhamma* as 'realization' relates closely to its understanding as knowledge of *nibbāna*. Elsewhere, in explanation of the expression 'the true/good *dhamma*' (*sad-dhamma*), this twofold understanding of *dhamma* is expanded to a threefold one: texts (*pariyatti*), practice (*paṭipatti*), attainment (*adhigama*), with 'practice' taken as referring to Buddhist practice in its entirety – ascetic practices, precepts, concentration, insight – and attainment to the nine transcendent *dhammas*.[44]

While the technical *specificity* of the commentarial explanations of *dhamma* is often out of place in a Nikāya context, nevertheless the *general* meanings suggested by the commentaries are more or less consonant with the range of meanings offered by modern scholars. One meaning, however, that is brought out by modern scholars, but is not highlighted by the commentators is that of 'natural law'. Nevertheless, as we have seen, some such meaning is certainly implicit in certain contexts.

THE DEVELOPMENT OF THE BUDDHIST UNDERSTANDING OF *DHAMMA*

I noted above that the Geigers regard the usage of *dhamma* in the sense of 'thing' (or 'basic quality') as somewhat removed from its original usage, and they identify the issue of how *dhamma* comes to be used in this way as the principal question to be addressed in accounting for the development of the usage of the term in Buddhist texts. They go on to offer some brief comments on the development of this usage. They point out that the meaning of 'thing' is associated particularly with the plural usage, and that in this plural usage *dhammas* refers to the things that constitute the world of experience as perceived by the mind. It is in these things or 'norms' that the *dhamma* – the law of the world and nature consisting in the arising and disappearance, the fleetingness and emptiness of reality – becomes manifest.[45] Thus the Geigers wish to see *dhamma* in the sense of the 'law' of the world – or, perhaps, ultimate 'truth' about reality – as basic. And the 'things' that constitute reality, eventually come to be designated 'laws' or 'truths' because seeing them, one sees *the* Law, *the* Truth. While I think this account certainly resonates with the early Buddhist understanding of *dhamma*, I do not think it adequately explains the semantic development of the word and I shall suggest an alternative model presently.

More recently Richard Gombrich has offered a somewhat different account.[46] Gombrich offers his account of the history of the way the word *dhamma* is used as a way of tracing the development of a Buddhist ontology. His starting point is that 'the Dharma' of the Buddha is both the Buddha's account *describing* his 'experience' and a message *prescribing* what to do about it. The basic Buddhist understanding of *dhamma* and the basic brahmanical understanding of *dharma* are thus alike, in so far as they at once describe the nature of reality and prescribe how to act. They thus both 'obliterate' the fact-value distinction. Turning to the usage of *dhamma* in the plural to denote 'noeta', 'phenomena' or 'things' as the objects of consciousness, Gombrich finds the key to this development in meaning in the passage from the Satipaṭṭhāna Sutta describing the practice of watching *dhammas* as *dhammas*:

> First he learns to observe physical processes in his own and other people's bodies; then he learns to be similarly aware of feelings; then of states of mind. Finally he learns to be aware of *dhammā* (plural). This has been rendered as 'his thoughts'. But the *dhammā* that the text spells out are in fact the teachings of the Buddha, such as the four noble truths. The meditator moves from thinking *about* those teachings to thinking *with* them: he learns (to use an anachronistic metaphor) to see the world through Buddhist spectacles. The Buddha's teachings come to be the same as (any) objects of thought, because anything else is (for Buddhists) unthinkable. Thus the *dhammā* are the elements of reality as understood by the Buddha.

Gombrich concludes by suggesting that it is from this specific context of meditation that the usage of *dhammas* in the plural has become generalized. If I have understood him correctly Gombrich's theory is, then, that watching (*anupassati*) *dhammas* as *dhammas* originally signified contemplating (as *anupassati* is often rendered) or thinking about the teachings of the Buddha. And because thinking about those *teachings* involves seeing the world in the Buddha's way, what you see when you think *through* (in both senses) those *teachings* are the *teachings*, which have come to represent experience in its entirety for the meditator. While, once again, I think the way this account ties together different senses of the word *dhamma* has genuine resonances with the early Buddhist understanding of *dhamma*, I do not think it works as an account of the *history* of the way the word *dhamma* is used – for two reasons. First, because I think taking *dhamma* in the sense of the *teaching* of the Buddha as the starting point for the history of its usage is problematic. Secondly, because, as we saw above, apart from the four truths the *dhammas* that the text spells out as objects of contemplation are *not* in fact the *teachings* of the Buddha as such; certainly the Buddha of the Nikāyas teaches *about* the hindrances, the aggregates, the senses and their objects, etc., but these things are not actual teachings; moreover if we were to understand *dhammas* here in the sense of teachings *about* the hindrances, etc., we would be left with the problem of explaining why the watching of body as body, feelings as feelings, and consciousness as consciousness is not also included here under the heading of watching *dhammas* as *dhammas*. In fact I think there is a much simpler way of approaching the development of the Buddhist usage of *dhamma* in the sense of 'noeta', 'phenomena' or 'things'.

In order to begin to consider the question of the relationship of the various meanings of *dhamma* in early Buddhist literature, and the question of the development of the specifically Buddhist notion of a *dhamma* as a basic mental or physical quality (the Buddhist theory of *dhammas*), we need first of all to consider what notion and understanding of *dharma* Buddhist thought inherited and thus started with. This, however, must remain a problematic and even controversial issue, both because of the problems in dating particular understandings of *dharma* in relation to Buddhist developments, and because of the problems in agreeing the contours of the 'Hindu' understanding of *dharma*.[47] Nevertheless, I think it is possible to map out some general lines of development.

The beginnings of the Indian concept of *dharma* go back to the usage of the noun *dharman* and various verb forms derived from the root *dhṛ* in the Ṛg Veda. A well known example occurs at the close of the 'Hymn of the Man' (Puruṣasūkta):

> With the sacrifice the gods sacrificed to the sacrifice. These were the first *ritual laws*.[48]

In his discussion of the Vedic usage of *dharman* Halbfass emphasises that the plural usage is the norm, commenting that 'only later did an essentially singular use as a "complex" or "totality of binding norms" gain in prominence'.[49] The precise meaning of *dharman* in the Ṛg Veda is perhaps unclear. In the verse just quoted, O'Flaherty uses 'ritual laws', explaining in a note that these are 'archetypal patterns of behaviour established during this first sacrifice to serve as the model for all future sacrifices'.[50] In his study of *dharman* in the Ṛg Veda in the present volume, Joel Brereton emphasises the sense of 'foundation' – a sense which straightforwardly reflects its etymology and form – as the meaning common to the various contexts in which it is used. He translates:

With the sacrifice the gods sacrificed the sacrifice: these were its foundations.

He goes on to comment that these first 'foundations' can thus be understood as 'the model sacrifice instituted by the gods and replicated in human performance'; or, as he puts it later, 'they are the ritual precedents which the present rituals follow'. Halbfass likewise stresses the importance of the sense of the underlying root *dhṛ*: *dharmas* are thus things that 'support', 'uphold', 'maintain'; and referring to the work of Schayer, he characterises *dharma* in the Brāhmaṇas as 'the continuous *maintaining* of the social and cosmic order and norm which is achieved by the Aryan through the performance of his Vedic rites and traditional duties'. A.K. Warder too considers the primary sense of *dharman/dhṛ* in the Ṛg Veda as closely connected with the idea of maintaining.[51] Whatever the precise connotations of *dharman* in its earliest usage it seems clear that among its earliest uses is the use in the plural to refer to certain *practices* – primarily sacrificial rites – as maintaining and supporting things – the cosmic and social order. The underlying assumption is, of course, that maintaining and supporting the cosmic and social order is a good thing; *dharmans* are therefore *prescribed* practices.

Another *dharman* or 'foundation' that the Ṛg Veda identifies is, suggests Brereton, the foundational authority especially of Varuṇa and Mitra; this authority consists in the commandments of Varuṇa and the alliances governed by Mitra. This sense of authority is one that Patrick Olivelle's contribution to the present volume shows being taken up in the Brāhmaṇas, where *dharma* is understood as the social order founded on the authority of especially the king. And if these are the sources for the Brahmanical and general 'Hindu' understanding of *dharma*, so too are they for the Buddhist. I take it then that the plural usage of *dhamma* is something that early Buddhism inherited from earlier pre-Buddhist usage, and that for early Buddhist thought *dhammas* are in the first place the practices, the kinds of behaviour, prescribed and recommended on the authority of the Buddha. That *dhamma* subsequently comes to refer to the Buddha's teaching or, in the plural, teachings is then a straightforward development, just as the English word 'prescription' can denote both the act of prescribing and what is prescribed. Indeed, 'prescription' can also denote a piece of paper handed to one by a doctor, so we have an analogous development for the way in which *dhamma* comes to mean the texts that contain the teachings of the Buddha.

In fact all this ties in precisely with the general tendency of early Buddhist thought to appropriate brahmanical terminology and reinterpret it in its own terms: the true *brāhmaṇa*, the true *ārya*, is not someone who is born as such and performs the duties and rites – the *dharmas* – laid down in the Vedas, the real *ariya-puggala* or 'noble person' is the one who takes up the practices – the *dhammas* – recommended by the Buddha and roots out greed, hatred and delusion. Though, as Patrick Olivelle points out, again in his contribution to this volume, the relationship between the Buddhist and brahmanical understanding may be more complex: while the Buddhists take over the basics of the Vedic and brahmanical understanding of *dharma*, the manner in which the notion of *dhamma* functions as a pervasive concept of religious, philosophical and ethical discourse is perhaps characteristically Buddhist; and *dharma* is developed as the central concept of Hindu thought only subsequently as a reaction to Buddhist and especially Aśokan usage.

Be that as it may, the use of *dharman*/*dharma* in Vedic literature in the senses of 'foundational rituals' and 'foundational authority' is sufficient to account for the development of early Buddhist *dhamma* in its normative and prescriptive senses, but what of its descriptive sense, what of *dhamma* as the truth about the ways things are? In the course of his discussion of *dharma* in Hinduism, Halbfass comments:

> Since ancient times *dharma* has also possessed a meaning which may be rendered as 'property', 'characteristic attribute', 'essential feature', or more generally as 'defining factor' or 'predicate'. Evidence of this is available since the time of the *Śatapatha Brāhmaṇa*. In classical Hindu philosophy, and most clearly in the Nyāya and Vaiśeṣika, *dharma* functions as 'attribute' or 'property' in the broadest sense and is used to characterize anything that is inherent in, or predicable of, an identifiable substratum (*dharmin*).[52]

In fact this usage of *dharma* in the sense of 'property' or 'characteristic attribute' would seem to derive directly from the Vedic usage of *dharman* to refer to 'the foundational *nature* of a deity', while there are also several places in the Brāhmaṇas and Upaniṣads where *dharma* appears to be used in a sense close to 'qualities', 'attributes' or even just 'things'.[53] The passage of the *Śatapatha Brāhmaṇa* that Halbfass cites (14.7.3.15) is one in which *dharman* occurs as the last member of a *bahuvrīhi* compound; the same passage is also found in the *Bṛhadāraṇyaka Upaniṣad*: 'This self, you see, is imperishable; it has an indestructible *nature*.'[54] The linking of the technical philosophical usage of *dharma* in the sense of an attribute belonging to an underlying substratum (*dharmin*) to its usage as the last member of a *bahuvrīhi* compound is crucial. We have already noted that this kind of usage is common in early Buddhist texts, and again it would seem that it is a common usage inherited from earlier usage. So, to expand on Halbfass's remarks, to describe *y* as *x-dharma*, is to say that *y* is something that possesses the *dharma* – the attribute, the quality – that is *x*; and in philosophical, as opposed to purely grammatical, terms, the 'something' that possesses an attribute (*dharmin*) is an underlying substance. As Halbfass points out, this understanding of *dharma* and *dharmin* as attribute and substance respectively involves the use of *dharma* in terms of a passive derivation: a *dharma* is what is 'supported' or 'maintained' (*dhriyate*) by the underlying substance (*dharmin*). I think we can see a precisely parallel development of the usage of *dhamma* in Buddhist thought.

In fact I have already suggested that the early Buddhist understanding of *dhammas* as the basic mental and physical qualities that constitute experience or reality is to be related to the usage of *dhamma* at the end of a *bahuvrīhi* compound in the sense of a particular nature or quality possessed by something. To this extent the basic qualities of early Buddhist thought and the attributes of Nyāya-Vaiśeṣika are the same things. The crucial difference, however, is that instead of understanding these particular natures or qualities as attributes that belong to some underlying substance, early Buddhist thought takes them as natural qualities in their own right, emphasising how they arise dependent on other qualities rather than on a substratum that is somehow more real than they are.[55]

Seeing the development of the Buddhist understanding of *dhammas* in this way also casts a somewhat different light on some of the remarks made about *dhammas* in the Pali commentaries, which are perhaps often viewed too much in the light of later controversies about the precise ontological status of *dharmas* and the Madhyamaka critique of the notion of *svabhāva* in the sense of 'inherent existence'. John Ross Carter has drawn attention to the way in which the Pali commentaries later come to gloss *dhamma* at the end of a *bahuvrīhi* compound both by *pakati* and *sabhāva*.[56] It follows from this that when the commentaries define *dhammas* as *sabhāvas* this is not a statement about their ontological status and that *sabhāva* should not be translated as 'inherent existence', but is merely a gloss stating that *dhammas* are 'particular natures' or 'particular qualities'. Moreover when the commentators say that *dhammas* are so-called 'because they maintain (*dhārenti*) their own particular natures, or because they are maintained (*dhārīyanti*) by causal conditions',[57] this should be understood, I think, as a direct and deliberate counter to the idea of *dharmas* as 'particular natures' that are 'maintained' by an underlying substance (*dharmin*) distinct from themselves; it is not intended to define *dhammas* as ontologically irreducible entities.[58]

This gives us two basic meanings of *dhamma* in early Buddhist texts: the practices recommended by the Buddha and the basic qualities that constitute reality. The first takes *dhamma* as something normative and prescriptive, the second as something descriptive and factual. Both of these meanings essentially derive from pre-Buddhist usage but are adapted to the specifics of Buddhist thought.

The question of how the prescriptive and descriptive meanings of *dharma* are related is a general one and not specific to Buddhist thought. Halbfass refers to the work of Paul Hacker, who sees the self-conscious and deliberate linking of *dharma* in its prescriptive and descriptive senses as essentially modern and a feature of Neo-Hinduism.[59] The point here appears to be that in ancient Indian thought there was no *explicit* attempt to derive *dharma* in its prescriptive sense from *dharma* in its descriptive sense: there was no explicit suggestion that it is because your nature (*dharma*) is such, your duty (*dharma*) is such. While this may be so, it is not clear to me that such an understanding is not implicit in early Indian thought. Indeed without the latent idea that there is some sort of link between nature and norm, the way things are and the way we should behave, it seems to me difficult to explain the usage of *dharma* in these two senses – unless, that is, one regards it as some sort of semantic accident or coincidence.

In this context the observations of the moral philosopher Alasdair MacIntyre seem pertinent.[60] MacIntyre argues that eighteenth century European thinking about morality involved the disappearance of a hitherto taken for granted connection between the precepts of morality and the facts of human nature, such that moral philosophers, like Hume and Kant, begin to assert for the first time that moral laws cannot be derived from factual statements, an 'ought' cannot be derived from an 'is'. MacIntyre goes on to point out that this is problematic: a statement that someone is a sea-captain suggests that he ought to do what a sea-captain ought to do. This is because a 'sea-captain' is a 'functional' concept: being a sea-captain involves functioning as a sea-captain. What MacIntyre suggests is that in the classical tradition right through to the Enlightenment the concepts used in discussions of 'morality' – how one should behave – were functional: thus for Aristotle a man's living well is precisely analogous to a harpist's playing well (*Nicomachean Ethics* 1095a 16). The relevance of this in the present context is that, if the distinction between nature and norm is not made in the first place, because a deep connection between the two is assumed, then there can be no *explicit* argument that attempts to link the two. And thus that the explicit argument that derives *dharma* as duty directly from *dharma* as nature is modern – in part a reflection, perhaps, of the conceptual framework of modern European philosophy – is hardly surprising.

In fact it seems clear that *dharman/dharma* is from the very beginning itself a functional concept: it is a foundation, and a foundation that fails to perform the functions of supporting and maintaining is not much of a foundation: for something to be a *dharma/dhamma* it must maintain and support. Thus, in the present volume, Brereton suggests that in the Ṛg Veda there is a deep connection between the foundational nature of the Ādityas and their foundational authority such that they are one and the same thing. And certainly in the case of brahmanical *dharma* it seems hard to deny a deep connection between *being* a member of a particular class (*varṇa*) at a particular stage of life (*āśrama*) and *acting* accordingly – fulfilling one's *dharma*. And when the Pali commentaries come to define the 'particular natures' that are *dhammas*, they define them by what they *do*: it is contact (*phassa*) because it contacts (*phusati*), it is will (*cetanā*) because it wills (*cetayati*), it is concentration (*samādhi*) because it places (*ādhiyati*) the mind evenly (*samaṃ*) on the object; it is trust (*saddhā*) because it trusts (*saddahati*), it is memory (*sati*) because it remembers (*sarati*).[61]

HE WHO SEES *DHAMMAS* SEES *DHAMMA*

Halbfass refers to 'a certain elusive coherence' in the various meanings and functions of *dharma* in the different traditions of Hinduism,

Buddhism, and Jainism.[62] This article has largely been an attempt to seek out that elusive coherence in the case of early Buddhist thought. I should like now to attempt to sum up by returning to the description of the practice of watching *dhammas* as *dhammas* found in the (Mahā-) Satipaṭṭhāna Sutta and by offering a paraphrase of it as a final attempt at capturing that elusive coherence. Among the *dhammas* (practices) the Buddha prescribes is this practice of watching *dhammas* (mental and physical qualities) as *dhammas*; to watch these truly as *dhammas* involves watching how they arise and disappear, how the particular qualities that one wants to abandon can be abandoned, and how the particular qualities that one wants to develop can be developed. Watching *dhammas* in this way one begins to understand how they work, and in understanding how they work one begins to understand certain truths (*sacca*) – four to be exact – about these *dhammas*: their relation to suffering, its arising, its ceasing and the way to its ceasing. And in seeing these four truths one realizes the ultimate truth – *dhamma* – about the world, the extinguishing (*nibbāna*) of the fires of greed, hatred and delusion. This reading of the (Mahā-) Satipaṭṭhāna Sutta reveals the underlying equivalence between seeing *dhammas* (that is, understanding the way mental and physical qualities arise and disappear) and seeing the *dhamma* or the truth.

In the Mahāhatthipadopama Sutta Sāriputta attributes the saying to the Buddha: 'He who sees dependent arising sees *dhamma*; he who sees *dhamma* sees dependent arising.'[63] The text goes on to explain that the five aggregates of attachment have arisen dependently (*paṭicca-samuppanna*). The commentary glosses the Buddha's saying as 'he who sees causal conditions, sees dependently arisen *dhammas*'.[64] My suggestion is that this should be read in part as a quite deliberate play on the meaning of *dhamma*, a play, moreover, that is entirely consonant with the Nikāyas. As we have seen, *dhammas* are mental and physical qualities, and seeing these *dhammas* as *dhammas* – seeing how they arise and disappear, seeing how they are dependently arisen – one sees the ultimate truth: he who sees *dhammas* sees *dhamma*.

Lest I should be misunderstood, I am not trying to impute a specific technical *abhidhamma*/*abhidharma* understanding to the Nikāyas, I am not suggesting that *dhamma* is used in early Buddhist thought in the sense of an irreducible element. The use of *dhamma* in the general sense of a mental or physical quality is quite distinct from the question of the metaphysical and ontological status of those qualities. That *dhammas* are mental and physical qualities is one thing; in what precise sense those mental and physical qualities should be said to exist is quite another. Thus the issue of what precisely *dhammas/dharmas* are is one that is debated and discussed by the later schools – the Vibhajjavāda, the Sarvāstivāda, the Madhyamaka.[65] Nevertheless, alongside the use of *dhamma* in the Nikāyas in the senses of the practices, truths and teachings that are recommended on the authority of the Buddha, there is a further usage already firmly embedded in the Nikāyas: *dhammas* are the fundamental qualities, both mental and physical, that in some sense constitute – or better, support and maintain – experience or reality in its entirety.

In many ways it might be the English word *quality* in its range of uses in both the singular and plural that provides the single best fit for *dhamma* in early Buddhism.[66] Yet while it might be capable of carrying a wider range of appropriate meanings than some other term such as 'truth', it clearly falls short of conveying the full range of meanings. Often translators have resorted to 'teaching', 'law', 'doctrine', yet in addition to the problem of conveying the semantic range of *dhamma* such translations highlight the problem of evoking its religious and emotional power. That the precise understanding and translation of *dhamma* in early Buddhist thought should remain elusive and hard to pin down is perhaps fitting. It is, after all, profound, hard to see, hard to understand, peaceful, sublime, beyond the sphere of mere reasoning, subtle, to be experienced by the wise – something that the buddhas of the past, present and future honour and to which they pay respect.[67]

NOTES

[1] I make no attempt in what follows to distinguish what the Buddha taught from what the Nikāyas/Āgamas in general teach. This does not mean that I consider that the Buddha taught everything just as the Nikāyas/Āgamas say he did. It does mean, however, that I think there are serious methodological flaws in attempting to distinguish in the Nikāyas/Āgamas two clear categories consisting of 'authentic' teachings of the Buddha on the one hand and later 'inauthentic' interpretations on the other. It follows from this that my drawing principally on the Pali sources is not to be taken as indicating that they are necessarily a more 'authentic' witness of early Buddhist thought – apart from the obvious fact that they are preserved in an ancient Indian language which must be relatively close to the kind of dialect or dialects used by the Buddha and his first disciples – than the Chinese Āgamas. In any case, it would seem that any account of early Buddhist thought based on the Chinese Āgamas would be essentially similar to an account based on the Pali Nikāyas. As

Étienne Lamotte has observed, the doctrinal basis common to the Chinese Āgamas and Pali Nikāyas is remarkably uniform; such variations as exist affect only the mode of expression or the arrangement of topics; see Lamotte (1988, p. 156).

[2] Geiger and Geiger (1920).

[3] Geiger, and Geiger (1920, p. 8)

[4] Stcherbatsky (1923).

[5] Stcherbatsky (1923, p. 1)

[6] Carter (1978).

[7] Pp. 48–49.

[8] Edward Conze, for example, has distinguished seven meanings as 'philosophically important': (1) transcendent reality, (2) the order of law of the universe, (3) a truly real event, (4) objective data of the mind, (5) quality or property, (6) right behaviour and religious practice, (7) the Buddha's teaching. These seven meanings more or less correspond to the six I have suggested, although I in effect have subsumed his (3) and (4) under my (6). See Conze (1962, pp. 92–94).

[9] *Bhikkhu dhammaṃ pariyāpuṇāti suttaṃ geyyaṃ veyyākaraṇaṃ gāthaṃ udānaṃ itivuttakaṃ jātakaṃ abbhutadhammaṃ vedallaṃ* (M I 133f; A II 103f, 108f, 178f, 185f; III 86f, 177f). The precise referent of the terms that make up the *aṅgas* or parts of Buddhist texts are problematic; see von Hinüber (1994).

[10] A IV 90.

[11] M II 78.

[12] M II 257.

[13] D II 9, 88, 95; M I 523; III 125.

[14] D II 119–120: *ye vo mayā dhammā abhiññāya desitā te vo sādhukaṃ uggahetvā āsevitabbā bhāvetabbā bahulīkātabbā yathayidaṃ brahmacariyaṃ addhaniyaṃ assa ciraṭṭhitikaṃ. tadassa bahujana-hitāya bahujana-sukhāya lokānukampāya atthāya hitāya sukhāya deva-manussānaṃ. katame ca te bhikkhave dhammā ... seyyathidam cattāro satipaṭṭhānā cattāro sammappadhānā cattāro iddhipādā pañc' indriyāni pañca balāni satta bojjhaṅgā ariyo aṭṭhaṅgiko maggo.* See also D II 127–128; M II 238, 245.

[15] E.g. D I 110: *bhagavā anupubbiṃ kathaṃ kathesi, seyyathidaṃ dāna-kathaṃ sīla-kathaṃ sagga-kathaṃ; kāmānaṃ ādīnavaṃ okāraṃ saṃkilesaṃ, nekkhamme ānisaṃsaṃ pakāsesi. yadā bhagavā aññāsi brāhmaṇaṃ Pokkharasātiṃ kalla-cittaṃ mudu-cittaṃ vinīvaraṇa-cittaṃ udagga-cittaṃ pasanna-cittaṃ, atha yā buddhānaṃ sāmukkaṃsikā dhamma-desanā, taṃ pakāsesi dukkhaṃ samudayaṃ nirodhaṃ maggaṃ ... brāhmaṇassa Pokkharasātissa tasmiññ eva āsane virajaṃ vīta-malaṃ dhamma-cakkhuṃ udapādi ... atha kho brāhmaṇo Pokkharasāti diṭṭha-dhammo patta-dhammo vidita-dhammo pariyogāḷha-dhammo tiṇṇa-vicikiccho vigata-kathaṃkatho vesārajja-ppatto aparappaccayo satthu sāsane.* See also D I 149; M I 380, 501; II 146.

[16] S III 120: *yo kho Vakkali dhammaṃ passati so maṃ passati. yo maṃ passati so dhammaṃ passati.* M I 190–191: *yo paṭiccasamuppādaṃ passati so dhammaṃ passati. yo dhammaṃ passati so paṭiccasamuppādaṃ passati.*

[17] See Carter (1978, p. 13).

[18] D II 292 = M I 56: *samudaya-dhammānupassī ... viharati, vaya-dhammānupassī ... viharati.* It is possible that we should simply translate here 'the *quality* or *nature* of arising and falling away', since it is not clear whether *samudaya-dhamma* and *vaya-dhamma* should be construed with reference to a *bahuvrīhi* usage describing the nature of the unstated 'body', etc. The commentaries, in fact, construe the phrase as 'watching the conditions for arising and falling away' with reference to a more technical *abhidhamma* understanding of *dhamma*, allowing however that 'nature' is also a possible interpretation. See Gethin (1992, p. 55) and von Rosspatt (1995, pp. 203–205, n. 433).

[19] PED s.v. Dhamma (p. 336, column 1).

[20] Cf. Rahula (1974).

21 Warder, (1971, pp. 285, 288).

22 D I 73: *so vivicceva kāmehi, vivicca akusalehi dhammehi savitakkaṃ savicāraṃ vivekajaṃ pīti-sukhaṃ paṭhamaṃ jhānaṃ upasampajja viharati.* This is a stock description of the attainment of the first *jhāna* and occurs in many other places.

23 D III 221: *bhikkhu anuppannānaṃ pāpakānaṃ akusalānaṃ dhammānaṃ anuppādāya ... padahati. uppannānaṃ pāpakānaṃ akusalānaṃ dhammānaṃ pahānāya ... padahati. anuppannānaṃ kusalānaṃ dhammānaṃ uppādāya ... padahati. uppannānaṃ kusalānaṃ dhammānaṃ ṭhitiyā asammosāya bhiyyobhāvāya vepullāya bhāvanāya pāripūriyā ... padahati.* This is the stock account of the 'four right endeavours' and again occurs in many places.

24 D II 290: *bhikkhu ... dhammesu dhammānupassī viharati.* This is the stock description of the fourth way of establishing mindfulness and once more occurs in many places.

25 See Gethin (1986). For the twelve spheres of sense as the world or experience in its entirety (*sabbaṃ*), see S IV 15.

26 Geiger and Geiger (1923, p. 4); PED s.v. Dhamma.

27 See Carter (1976); Carter (1978, pp. 58–135).

28 Five of these passages (Sv I 99, Ps I 17, Dhp-a I 22, Bv-a 13, As 38) are discussed by Carter (see previous note); a sixth passage (Paṭis-a I 18) is not noted by him.

29 Sp IV 874; Sv III 1030; Ps II 68; Mp I 87; III 325; Vibh-a 504.

30 Vin II 109.

31 Ps I 17 and Bv-a 13 cite *jāti-dhammā jarā-dhammā atho maraṇa-dhammino* as an example of *dhamma* in the sense of *pakati*; Carter (1978, p. 61) takes this as a reference to M I 161–162, which, however, reads *ekacco attanā jāti-dhammo samāno jāti-dhammaṃ yeva pariyesati, attanā jarā-dhammo ... attanā maraṇa-dhammo samāno maraṇa-dhammaṃ yeva pariyesati.* In fact, a search of CSCD gives no actual example of the text precisely as quoted by Ps and Bv-a, only the variant *vyādhi-dhammā jarā-dhamma atho maraṇa-dhammino* (A I 147; III 75).

32 Paṭis-a I 18: *jāti-dhammā jarā-dhammā maraṇa-dhammā ti ādīsu vikāre.*

33 Ps I 17: *kusalā dhammā ti ādīsu sabhāve.* Paṭis-a I 18 *ayañ hi kusalā dhammā akusalā dhammā avyākatā dhammā ti ādīsu sabhāve dissati.*

34 Sv I 99: *tasmiṃ kho pana samaye dhammā honti khandhā honti ti ādīsu nissatte.* Ps I 17: *tasmiṃ kho pana samaye dhammā honti ti ādīsu suññatāyaṃ.* Dhp-a I 22: *tasmiṃ kho pana samaye dhammā honti khandhā honti ti ayaṃ nissatta-dhammo nāma nijjīva-dhammo ti pi eso eva.* Paṭis-a I 18: *tasmiṃ kho pana samaye dhammā honti, dhammesu dhammānupassī viharatī ti ādīsu nissattatāyaṃ.* As 38: *tasmiṃ kho pana samaye dhammā honti, dhammesu dhammānupassī viharatī ti ādīsu nissatta-nijjīvatāyaṃ.*

35 Dhs 25: *tasmiṃ kho pana samaye dhammā honti, khandhā honti, āyatanāni honti.* For a brief discussion of the structure of the Dhs treatment of the arising of consciousness, see Gethin (1992, pp. 312–314).

36 Vism XX 104; cf. Gethin (1998, p. 190).

37 Vism VII 105–107, Vibh-a 147–148.

38 Carter (1978, pp. 115–129, 131–135).

39 Vism VII 68.

40 Carter (1978, p. 122).

41 See Cousins (1984).

42 M I 101: *dhamme kaṅkhati vicikicchati nādhimuccati na sampasīdati.*

43 Sv III 1030 = Ps II 68 = Mp III 325 = Vibh-a 504: *pariyatti-dhamme kaṅkhamāno tepiṭakaṃ buddha-vacanaṃ caturāsīti-dhamma-kkhandha-sahassānī ti vadanti atthi nu kho etaṃ natthī ti kaṅkhati. paṭivedha-dhamme kaṅkhamāno vipassanānissando maggo nāma magganissandaṃ phalaṃ nāma sabba-saṅkhāra-paṭinissaggo nibbānaṃ nāmā ti vadanti taṃ atthi nu kho natthī ti kaṅkhati.*

[44] Sp I 225–226 = Mp V 33: *tividho saddhammo pariyatti-saddhammo paṭipatti-saddhammo adhigama-saddhammo ti. tattha sakalam pi buddha-vacanaṃ pariyatti-saddhammo nāma. terasa dhutaguṇā cāritta-vāritta-sīla-samādhi-vipassanā ti ayaṃ paṭipatti-saddhammo nāma. navalokuttara-dhammo adhigama-saddhammo nāma.*

[45] Geiger, and Geiger (1923, pp. 8–9): Wenn *dh.* die Dingbedeutung hat, wird es auch zumeist in der Mehrzahl gebraucht. Es werden damit die Dinge der Erscheinungswelt, bezeichnet, wie sie vom *manas*, dem inneren Sinn wahrgenommen werden. In diesen Dingen oder "Normen" offenbart sich aber eben der *dh.*, d. h. das Natur- und Weltgesetz von dem ewigen Werden und Vergehen, von der Flüchtigkeit und Nichtigkeit alles Seins.

[46] Gombrich (1996, pp. 34–36).

[47] See Halbfass's two essays on *dharma* in his *India and Europe: An Essay in Understanding*: '*Dharma* in the Self-understanding of Traditional Hinduism' (pp. 311–333) and 'Reinterpretations of *Dharma* in Modern Hinduism' (pp. 334–348).

[48] RV 10.90: *yajñena yajñam ayajanta devās tāni dharmāṇi prathamāny āsan.* Translation quoted from O'Flaherty (1981 p. 31).

[49] Halbfass (1988, p. 314); he cites Chāndogya Upaniṣad 2.23.1 and Taittirīya Upaniṣad 1.11.1 for the singular usage.

[50] O'Flaherty (1981, p. 32).

[51] Warder (1971, p. 275).

[52] Halbfass (1988, p. 334).

[53] See section 4 of Joel Brereton's contribution to this volume, and Patrick Olivelle's discussion of Śatapatha Brāhamaṇa 11.5.7.1 and Chāndogya Upaniṣad 2.1.4.

[54] 4.5.14: *avināśī vā are 'yam ātmānucchittidharmā.* Text and translation quoted from Olivelle (1998, pp. 130–131).

[55] Warder (1971, p. 274) raises the question of the usage of *dharma* and *dharmin* in Indian logic and its possible connection to the Buddhist understanding of a *dharma* as an element of experience, but somewhat curiously, in my view, opts to treat them as homonyms, whose homonymity is however, 'probably not accidental'.

[56] Carter (1978, p. 61) cites Ps II 170, Spk I 159; see also Spk II 41 where *khaya-dhamma* is glossed as *khaya-sabhāva.*

[57] As 39: *attano pana sabhāvaṃ dhārentī ti dhammā. dhārīyanti vā paccayehi, dhārīyanti vā yathā-sabhāvato ti dhammā.* (cf. Nidd-a I 16; Paṭis-a I 18; Moh 6)

[58] The point that the commentarial definition of a *dhamma* as that which carries its 'own nature' should not be interpreted as implying that a *dhamma* is a substantial bearer of its qualities or 'own-nature' has been made by Nyanaponika (1998, pp. 40–41) and Karunadasa (1996, pp. 14–16).

[59] Halbfass (1988, p. 334).

[60] MacIntyre (1985, pp. 57–59, 83–84).

[61] Vism XIV 134, 135, 139, 140, 141.

[62] Halbfass (1988, p. 317).

[63] M I 190–191: *yo paṭiccasamuppādaṃ passati so dhammaṃ passati, yo dhammaṃ passati so paṭiccasamuppādaṃ passati.* The saying is also found in the Chinese equivalent of this *sutta*, see T. 26, 467a; I am grateful to Kin-Tung Yit for this reference.

[64] Ps II 230: *yo paṭiccasamuppādaṃ passatī ti yo paccaye passati. so dhammaṃ passatī ti so paṭiccasamuppanna-dhamme passati.*

[65] The issue of the development of the ontology of *dhammas* in early Buddhist thought is one that has been partially explored in Gal (2003).

[66] Cf. Warder (1971, pp. 283, 290).

[67] M I 167: *dhammo gambhīro duddaso duranubodho santo paṇīto atakkāvacaro nipuṇo paṇḍita-vedanīyo.* S I 138–140: *dhammaññeva sakkatvā garuṃ katvā.*

REFERENCES

Carter, J.R. (1976). Traditional definitions of the term *dhamma*. *Philosophy East and West* **26**, 329–327.

Carter, J.R. (1978). *Dhamma: Western Academic and Sinhalese Buddhist Interpretations: A Study of a Religious Concept*. Tokyo: Hokuseido Press.

Conze, E. (1962). *Buddhist Thought in India*. London: Allen & Unwin.

Cousins, L.S. (1984). Nibbāna and Abhidhamma. *Buddhist Studies Review* **1**, 95–109.

Gal, N. (2003). A metaphysics of experience: from the Buddha's teaching to the Abhidhamma. Unpublished DPhil, University of Oxford.

Geiger, M. & Geiger, W. (1920). *Pāli Dhamma vornehmlich in der kanonischen Literatur*. Munich: Bayerischen Akademie der Wissenschaften. Reprinted in Geiger, W. (1973). *Kleine Schriften zur Indologie und Buddhismuskunde*. Wiesbaden: Franz Steiner, pp. 102–228.

Gethin, R.M.L. (1986). The five khandhas: their treatment in the Nikāyas and early Abhidhamma. *Journal of Indian Philosophy* **14**, 35–53.

Gethin, R.M.L. (1992). *The Buddhist Path to Awakening: A Study of the Bodhi-Pakkhiyā Dhammā*. Leiden: E.J. Brill; 2nd ed. Oxford: Oneworld (2001).

Gethin, R.M.L. (1998). *The Foundations of Buddhism*. Oxford: Oxford University Press.

Gombrich, R.F. (1996). *How Buddhism Began: The Conditioned Genesis of the Early Teachings*. London: Athlone.

Halbfass, W. (1998). *India and Europe: An Essay in Understanding*. Albany: State University of New York Press.

Karunadasa, Y. (1996). *The Dhamma Theory: Philosophical Cornerstone of the Abhidhamma*, The Wheel Publication 412/413. Kandy: Buddhist Publication Society.

Lamotte, É. (1988). *History of Indian Buddhism from the Origins to the Śaka Era*. Louvain: Institut Orientaliste.

MacIntyre, A. (1985). *After Virtue: A Study in Moral Theory*. London: Duckworth.

Nyanaponika. (1998). *Abhidhamma Studies: Buddhist Explorations of Consciousness and Time*. 4th ed., revised and enlarged. Boston: Wisdom.

O'Flaherty, W.D. (1981). *The Rig Veda: An Anthology*. Harmondsworth: Penguin Books.

Olivelle, P. (1998). *The Early Upaniṣads: Annotated Text and Translation*. New York: Oxford University Press.

Rahula, W. (1974). Wrong notions of *Dhammatā* (*Dharmatā*). In L.S. Cousins et al. (eds), *Buddhist Studies in Honour of I. B. Horner* (pp. 181–191). Dordrecht: Reidel.

Stcherbatsky, Th. (1923). *The Central Conception of Buddhism and the Meaning of the Word 'dharma'*. London: Royal Asiatic Society.

von Hinüber, O. (1994). Die neun Aṅgas: Ein früher Versuch Einteilung buddhistischer Texte. *Wiener Zeitschrift für die Kunde Südasiens* **38**, 121–135.

von Rospatt, A. (1995). *The Buddhist Doctrine of Momentariness: A Survey of the Origins and the Early Phase of this Doctrine up to Vasubandhu*. Stuttgart: Franz Steiner Verlag.

Warder, A.K. (1971). Dharmas and Data. *Journal of Indian Philosophy* **1**, 272–295.

ABBREVIATIONS

Unless otherwise stated editions of Pali texts are those of the Pali Text Society, Oxford.

A	Aṅguttara Nikāya
As	Atthasālinī (= Dhammasaṅgaṇī-aṭṭhakathā)
Bv-a	Buddhavaṃsa-aṭṭhakathā
CSCD	*Chaṭṭha Saṅgāyana CD-ROM*, Version 3.0 (Igatpuri: Vipassana Research Institute, 1999).
D	Dīgha Nikāya
Dhp-a	Dhammapada-aṭṭhakathā
Dhs	Dhammasaṅgaṇī
M	Majjhima Nikāya
Moh	Mohavicchedanī
Mp	Manorathapūraṇī
Nidd-a	Niddesa-aṭṭhakathā
Paṭis-a	Paṭisambhidāmagga-aṭṭhakathā
PED	T.W. Rhys Davids and W. Stede, *Pali-English Dictionary* (London: Pali Text Society, 1921–1925).
Ps	Papañcasūdanī
S	Saṃyutta Nikāya
Sp	Samantpāsādikā
Spk	Sāratthappakāsinī
Sv	Sumaṅgalavilāsinī
Vibh-a	Sammohavinodanī
Vin	Vinaya
Vism	Visuddhimagga

Department of Theology and Religious Studies
Centre for Buddhist Studies
University of Bristol
3 Woodland Road
Bristol BS8 1TB
UK
E-mail: Rupert.Gethin@bristol.ac.uk

COLLETT COX

FROM CATEGORY TO ONTOLOGY: THE CHANGING ROLE OF *DHARMA* IN SARVĀSTIVĀDA ABHIDHARMA

From Eugène BURNOUF's simple rendering "law"[1] (*loi*) to the 16 primary meanings and dozens of secondary meanings and collocations listed by Magdalene and Wilhelm Geiger,[2] perhaps no term in Indian Buddhism has generated more extensive study or greater disagreement than *dharma*. Certainly, the term is not easily understood or translated; explicit interpretations when offered inevitably reflect both the variety of source materials and the diversity of methodological approaches employed.[3] The difficulty in finding a suitable translation or presenting a unified interpretation arises from the undeniable fact that the term *dharma* is indeed used by the Indian Buddhist sources themselves with different connotations.[4] Like all religious concepts, *dharma* is an historical construct, whose sense and function have been continuously refashioned and adjusted to fit changing needs. The most problematic of these senses, first encountered in the *sūtra*s,[5] becomes the focus of later scholastic exegesis in Abhidharma literature, where its function is expanded with meanings and connotations for which there are no *sūtra* precedents. This is *dharma* in the sense that has been variously translated or glossed by factor, thing, element, constituent, phenomenon, event, datum, property, quality, fundamental existent, reality, or not infrequently left untranslated. The divergence between *dharma* as an individual "factor" and *dharma* in the sense of "law," "truth," or "teaching" presents a contrast that scholars have found difficult to reconcile. What, if anything, do these patently different senses have in common? If law is the original *sūtra* sense, then where does this sense of *dharma* as an individual "factor" originate, and should it be considered "distinctively Buddhist?" How was the term used within Abhidharma, specifically within the Sarvāstivāda Abhidharma literature, and what is the relationship between *dharma* and other terms used to explain and elaborate it such as *bhāva*, *svabhāva*, *dravya*, and *svalakṣaṇa*?

Most scholarly treatments of *dharma* follow the lead of the Geigers in listing a variety of senses, with little consideration of how they are to be conceptually or historically related. Issues of historical interconnections among the various usages within Buddhist sources and contextual connections with the non-Buddhist milieu are most often left unexplored, and for good reason, since delineating these historical and contextual connections in the context of early Indian scholasticism, although of the utmost significance for understanding doctrinal development, presents almost insurmountable difficulties. Certainly, these early traditions were complex historical phenomena, a tapestry woven in often unexpected directions as a result of both internal dynamics and external influences and events. Yet unraveling this historical interplay is complicated by the dearth of independent and contemporaneous, external sources and by the continuous recasting and reappropriation of prior materials by each tradition in order to facilitate an authoritative and yet unacknowledged reconstitution of itself. The convoluted pattern of doctrinal development is masked both by textual emendation that effaces perceived contradictions and by the retrojection of newly formulated interpretations. Attempts to fill in gaps in the historical record by reconstructing supposedly logical patterns of doctrinal development are fraught with danger: namely, that we project our own transparent values and premises or those of later tradition back onto a process that was driven by multiple factors now largely alien and opaque. Although provisional and incomplete, we must content ourselves at this stage with recovering the terminological traces left by the paths and byways of the now obscure historical interplay, and not jump to conclusions that preclude the results of further textual investigation.

A FUNDAMENTAL SENSE OF THE TERM *DHARMA?*

Our own inquiry thus must begin with the resigned acknowledgement that the ultimate origin of the various uses of the term *dharma* is obscure and that their historical development or inter-traditional diffusion is impossible to determine. Nevertheless, we can proceed by comparing parallel terminology and arguments that highlight distinctive interpretative actions within specific texts and suggest possible routes of doctrinal exchange. Fortunately, some scholars have already undertaken such comparisons, and have considered both the nuances that unite the seemingly disparate Buddhist uses of the term as well as possible connections with similar concepts or terms in non-Buddhist sources. For example, Johannes BRONKHORST, adopting the position that *dharma* in the sense of "element" is derived from *dharma* as "teaching," observes that "efforts were made to distill the most important ideas and concepts from [the Buddha's] teaching ... [which] gave rise to lists of so-called *dharmas*."[6] BRONKHORST explains this linkage between "element" and "teaching" by noting that "[i]n their efforts to preserve the teaching of the Buddha, the early Buddhists were not content to memorise his own words. They also enumerated the elements contained in his teaching, and this led to the creation of lists of so-called *dharmas*."[7] Specifying further, BRONKHORST suggests that the later "peculiarly Buddhist" sense of *dharma* as "element" might be traced to a particular, early analytical matrix (*mātr̥kā*) or list of categories consisting of psychic characteristics or *dharmas* intended as a summary of the teaching of the Buddha. This initial list then inspired or served as the direct basis for subsequent enumerative lists, to which the term *dharma* was naturally extended.[8]

Following a related meaning, Akira HIRAKAWA espouses the view that the Buddhist sense of the term as individual "factor" is distinctive, and yet connects it to other non-Buddhist uses: namely, as "that aspect of phenomena that has the quality of truth – that is, of having an enduring quality."[9] Similarly, I.B. HORNER claims that *dhamma* refers to the "natural state or condition of beings and things, the law of their being, what it is right for them to be, the very stuff of their being, *evaṃ-dhammo*. If they are what it is right for them to be ... they are true to themselves. So dhamma also means truth, with the derived meaning of 'religious' truth, hence the Buddhist doctrine ..."[10] Wilhelm HALBFASS emphasizes the etymological sense of *dharman/dharma* as "upholding" and connects this sense with what he terms a Vedic "ontology of openness" exemplified in creative rituals of separation and maintenance and contrasted with a concurrent but separate "ontology of substance."[11] As he states, "[i]n spite of all subsequent oblivion and obscuration, the Vedic cosmogonies of separation and opening, as well as the associated idea of an 'upholding' *dharma* of such openness and the polarities and distinctions that appear within it, have had their echoes and extensions in the systematic philosophies of Buddhism and Hinduism."[12] Hence, for HALBFASS, the later scholastic use of the term to denote the discriminated constituents of experience originates in the Vedic senses of maintenance and separation.

Hajime SAKURABE adopts a related perspective, beginning from *dharma* in its etymological sense of "upholding" or "maintaining," which becomes manifest in the meanings order, norm, virtue, truth and finally the Buddha's teaching. A distinctive Buddhist sense of "thing" or "entity" or that which "exists in accordance with principle or order" can then be derived from this fundamental, etymological sense. He emphasizes that *dharmas* should not be thought of as indicating things or their essences in isolation, but rather as constituting a complex network of causal interaction that structures ordinary experience.[13] Rupert GETHIN argues for an interpretation of *dhamma* that would combine its uses in the singular as teaching with those in the plural, and suggests that the notion of *dhammas* as distinct, irreducible elements, especially as developed in Sarvāstivāda Abhidharma, cannot readily be transferred to *dhammas* in the plural within Pāli materials. *Dhammas* are preeminently mental events, specifically their capabilities and activities, and hence are dynamic, rather than static. And as GETHIN notes, "the question of the relationship between *dhamma* and *dhammas* is perhaps most easily seen with reference to *paṭicca-samuppāda* [dependent origination]. It is stated in the Nikāyas that he who sees *paṭicca-samuppāda* sees *dhamma*, and that he who sees *dhamma* sees *paṭicca-samuppāda*. This is in fact a very succinct statement of the principle involved, for what is *paṭicca-samuppāda* apart from the inter-relatedness of *dhammas*?"[14]

A similar view is offered by A.K. WARDER who traces the term *dhamma* through both Vedic sources and early Buddhist Nikāya materials in an attempt to uncover a single connotation that would unite its divergent uses. From his review of the terms *dharman*/*dharma* in Vedic sources, WARDER concludes that it is a dynamic conception referring not to a permanent state, but to a force that maintains the universe, a regularity or constancy of proper actions or events.[15] Turning to the Nikāya materials, WARDER lists a variety of specific uses of *dhamma* and proposes similarities in context and meaning that are consistent with its Vedic meanings: namely, as "regularities in the universe or as forces operating in it." Specifically, he states, "[t]he conception is still dynamic: the *dhammas* are events, or classes of event, though they may perhaps be said to be grouped or defined through their qualities." The Nikāyas refer to the "reality" of *dhammas*, but "[t]his reality is not inconsistent with the impermanence of the *dhammas*; it does not imply that they continue but only that they really occur under the proper conditions."[16] The Abhidhamma sense of the term *dhamma* is not distinctive, WARDER contends, but is anticipated in both the general description and the tentative classifications of *dhammas* offered in the Pāli Nikāyas. WARDER concludes that "regularity" is the key concept in the notion of *dhamma,* a regularity that is evident in the ordered, conditioned interaction of impermanent experienced events. The "*dhamma* hypothesis" constitutes more than a simple list of constituent elements; it seeks the '"real"' laws of nature underlying the surface appearance of things, the 'real' forces underlying the personifications of superstition, the 'real' way the universe works underlying the imaginary terrors of religion and the imaginary rule of '"gods."'[17] WARDER thus argues against any conception of *dhamma* as a static substance, and suggests instead that *dhamma*s are types or classes of properties or events and therefore constitute fundamental regularities underlying and structuring the "apparent chaos of data."

THE INTER-TRADITIONAL CONTEXT

This dynamic conception of *dharma* as the efficacy of experienced events functioning in complex patterns of conditioned, "regular" interaction is helpful in considering the later Sarvāstivāda Abhidharma uses of the term and its elaboration through a variety of different concepts such as *bhāva*, *svabhāva*, *dravya*, *prajñapti*, *svalakṣaṇa*, and *sāmānyalakṣaṇa*. What sense do these different characterizations of *dharma*s convey? And in the particular case of the Sarvāstivādins, what is the connection between their interpretation of *dharma*s and their assertion that "everything exists?" Does this assertion entail a substantialist view of *dharma*s, and if so, in what sense do they accept the fundamental Buddhist position that *dharma*s are impermanent?

To clarify the later scholastic sense of the term *dharma,* one cannot begin by assuming that Buddhist usage developed solely within a Buddhist context and by ignoring the virtual certainty of mutual influence, even in the early period, among Buddhist and non-Buddhist traditions: namely, the contemporaneous, early scholastic or analytical movements within grammar, Buddhism, Sāṃkhya, Jainism, and Vaiśeṣika. In the case of the later scholastic elaborations, inter-traditional influence is clearly indicated by the shared terminology, categories, exegetical methods, and philosophical concerns. These similarities suggest a nexus of related concepts and issues that followed a complex path of development within and among the various traditions, influenced both by a logic internal to each tradition and by exchange with other traditions engaged in similar investigations. Establishing the point of origin and the direction of diffusion is complicated, however, first and foremost by the comparatively recent date of the available classical sources and by the difficulty of determining their relative dating.[18]

Space does not permit a thorough presentation of the scholarship on this problem of early scholastic, inter-traditional influence, but several relevant issues and fruitful lines of inquiry should be mentioned. First, at the very least, the similarity in terminology is unmistakable, and the earliest classical sources present notable parallels in their interpretations of terms such as *dravya*, *guṇa*, *bhāva*, and *svabhāva*. But what clues do we have for their meaning in the initial period of their formation? For example, the term *dravya,* so significant in later Sarvāstivāda Abhidharma interpretations of *dharma*s, does not appear in its later, mature sense as "really existent entity" either within the Buddhist *sūtra*s or the earliest Sarvāstivāda Abhidharma discussions. We do, however, find suggestive usages in the early grammatical literature, although there the meaning of the term *dravya* is still variable, as the interpretations recorded in Patañjali's *Mahābhāṣya* attest.[19] Under a discussion of Pāṇini's *sūtra* 1.2.64, Patañjali (following Kātyāyana) records the contrasting views of the grammarians Vājapyāyana, who maintained that words refer to a class property (or feature) (*ākṛti*), and Vyāḍi, who maintained that words refer to an individual object (or entity) (*dravya*). Patañjali himself proposes a compromise view: namely, that a word can refer to either a class property or an individual object.[20] Elsewhere in a discussion of the relation between *dravya* and quality (*guṇa*), Patañjali expands upon the sense of the term *dravya*,[21] which he suggests can refer to an entity having a distinctive nature, as in the case of cotton and iron that are distinguished by different weights, or a sword and a piece of cloth that are distinguished in terms of their ability to cut. *Dravya* can also refer to a whole or aggregation of changing qualities, as in the case of a mango or jujube fruit that change color as green, yellow, or red as they ripen. *Dravya* in this latter sense is glossed as *guṇasaṃdrāva*, a "confluence of qualities," or as *guṇasamudāya*, "collection of qualities".

These discussions raise the all-important problem of the nature of experienced objects, specifically in terms of the relation between qualities and substratum, the part and the whole, the particular and universal, or change and stability. The two senses of *dravya* offered by Patañjali, that is, as an individual object or as an aggregation of qualities, resonate with discussions of these issues in Sāṃkhya, Vaiśeṣika, Jaina, and Buddhist sources. For example, in Sāṃkhya, a change in the concept of *dravya* can be observed from an early interpretation as a collection of qualities to a later view proposing that *dravya*s are characterized by both an unchanging substrate (*dharmin*) and properties (*dharma*) that undergo transformation (*pariṇāma*).[22] Vaiśeṣika sources describe *dravya*s as entities that serve as substratum causes (*samavāyikāraṇa*) and are possessed of separate qualities (*guṇa*) and activities (*kriyā*).[23] The early Jaina scholastic text, the *Tattvārthādhigamasūtra*, uses the concept of *dravya* to define existence (*sat*), which is possessed of arising (*utpāda*), passing away (*vyaya*), and stability (*dhrauvya*). It also adopts a distinction between substance and quality whereby substance is possessed of both defining qualities (*guṇa*) and changing modes (*paryāya*).[24] The Jaina exegete Kundakunda proposes a similar view, but adds the qualification that *dravya* is also characterized by intrinsic nature (*sahāva*), which has the nature of existence (*sabbhāva*) and is not abandoned despite the arising, passing away, and modifications that occur.[25] Thus, beyond the shared terminology we see a common complex of ontological and epistemological problems that informed reflection and debate within and among these various traditions.

THE PURPOSE OF "*DHARMIC*" ANALYSIS

The Sarvāstivāda Abhidharma analysis of the character and activity of *dharma*s must be viewed as an integral part of this complex of early scholastic inquiry. Indeed, the early, emergent scholasticism of Sāṃkhya, Vaiśeṣika, and Buddhism was all directed by a similar intention: that is, a refusal to accept the world as it presents itself to untutored, common sense and a desire to analyze experience into its salient, functional constituents. In the case of Buddhism, this analysis reveals the structure of the conditioning interconnections that underlie the gross, composite objects of ordinary experience, interconnections that are not arbitrary, but are considered to be "true" or, in Buddhist parlance, to represent the "way things really are" (*yathābhūta*).

Deconstructing analysis is the key scholastic activity, but, at least in the early period, it is an analysis that focuses on the distinguishing relationships among the constituent factors, rather than on the distinctive character or ontological status of the individual analytical products. Initially, the primary concern is immediately soteriological and is directed toward supplanting defiling or ensnaring *dharma*s with those conducive to liberation. In the case of Buddhism, this soteriologically motivated analysis is most succinctly represented by the term *dharmapravicaya*, the "discrimination" or "discernment of *dharmas*," which holds a significant place throughout the history of Indian Buddhist praxis. From the earliest period onward, the discrimination of *dharmas* is listed among the seven members of enlightenment (*bodhyaṅgadharma*), which are subsumed within the most enduring, summary presentation of Buddhist praxis – the 37 limbs of enlightenment (*bodhipakṣyadharma*).[26] The formulaic description of the discrimination of *dharmas* in the Pāli *suttas* suggests that it functions specifically through insight (P *paññā*), by which one discriminates, investigates, and reflects thoroughly upon *dhammas*.[27] And indeed, the discrimination of *dharmas* and insight (*paññā*) occur frequently in tandem within the Pāli canonical Abhidharma materials, and are explicitly equated in the commentarial literature.[28]

Sarvāstivāda Abhidharma texts also link *dharmapravicaya* with insight (*prajñā*) as well as with other soteriologically efficacious mental *dharmas* such as correct view (*samyagdṛṣṭi*).[29] Abhidharma itself is defined as insight (*prajñā*), which is then identified with *dharmapravicaya*[30] that discriminates *dharmas* according to their intrinsic nature, or according to their particular inherent (*svalakṣaṇa*) and generic characteristics (*sāmānyalakṣaṇa*).[31] The activity of discriminating *dharmas* is compared to the skill of a jeweler who can recognize and distinguish any stone,[32] and as insight it becomes the sword that cuts off defilements preventing them from ever arising again.[33] Yaśomitra explains "discrimination" (*pravicaya*) as the practice by which *dharmas* that are mixed together (*saṃkīrṇa*) are discriminated (*pravicīyante*) or "picked up" (*uccīyante*) as in the case of flowers, such that one observes: "these [*dharmas*] are tending toward contamination; these are not tending toward contamination; these are possessed of material form; these are not possessed of material form."[34] And this discrimination of *dharmas* that constitutes the essence of Abhidharma is ultimately soteriological since it provides the only method by which one can understand the processes of causal interaction among all aspects of experience and pacify defilements that result in endless rebirth and suffering.[35] As the early Sarvāstivāda Abhidharma texts make clear, the discrimination of *dharmas* acts by separating and clarifying *dharmas* of all categories, in particular by distinguishing events that are unvirtuous and result in suffering from those that are virtuous and lead to liberation; the former are to be abandoned, and the latter to be cultivated.[36] Hence, this discrimination of *dharmas* is not only cited within the context of the specific set of seven members of enlightenment, but also appears in conjunction with the cultivation of virtually all forms of correct views or knowledge as the first stage in a standard series of mental cultivations that culminate in the faculty of discerning (*vipaśyanā*).[37]

Hence, the discrimination of *dharmas* has a dual soteriological purpose involving two simultaneous processes.[38] First, "evaluative" analysis, ultimately informed by the praxis-oriented goals of purification and liberation, isolates events significant to practice and clearly distinguishes those virtuous events that are to be cultivated from the unvirtuous that are to be abandoned. And second, exhaustive, "descriptive" analysis of ordinary experience reveals its "true" implicit structure and thereby undermines the commonplace entities that become ready objects of desire and attachment. Through *dharmic* discrimination, each experienced event is analyzed to bring out its constituent and, most importantly, soteriologically efficacious components.

"*DHARMIC*" ANALYSIS AS CATEGORIZATION

This dual purpose of evaluation and of description is then expressed in a variety of different analytical matrices (*mātṛkā*) or lists of categories, which themselves constitute the *dharmas*. On the one hand, the lists of categories represent the salient experiential distinctions grounded in the observed properties or activities by which *dharmas* are defined, and on the other, they become the context within which the concept of *dharma* evolves. For example, the first purpose of praxis-oriented "evaluative" analysis is represented by such rudimentary lists of *dharmas* as the four applications of mindfulness (*smṛtyupasthāna*), the five controlling faculties of practice (*indriya*), and so on. These rudimentary lists are then combined to form grouped sets and hierarchical structures, which together yield a complex, multi-level array of interrelated categories, as, for example, in the case of the 37 limbs of enlightenment.[39] The second purpose of "descriptive" analysis is represented by the set of four fundamental material elements (*mahābhūta*), or the triadic sets of the five aggregates (*skandha*), 12 sense spheres (*āyatana*), and 18 elements (*dhātu*), which became so important in the early stages of Abhidharma exegesis.[40] Each of these three sets represents a different interpretative perspective: the five aggregates are grounded in a fundamental distinction between material form (*rūpa*) and non-material, mental events (*nāma*); the 12 sense spheres and 18 elements reflect the conditions constitutive of sensory experience or perception. These rudimentary sets of *dharmas* of both types are then further elaborated through intricate attribute matrices (*mātṛkā*) consisting of secondary properties such as realm of occurrence, time period, causes, or moral quality. The attribute matrices, arranged in dyads and triads, are then applied systematically to the basic sets of *dharmas*, yielding a secondary level of mutually exclusive categories that form an abstract web of all possible conditions and characteristics exhibited by actually occurring *dharmas*. The individual character of any particular *dharma* can then be specified in accordance with every taxonomic possibility, resulting in a complete assessment of that *dharma's* range of possible occurrences. Certain of these dyads or triads are more purely "descriptive:" for example, those specifying the realm (*dhātu*) in which a *dharma* arises, its character as internal (*ādhyātmika*) or external (*bāhya*), or as conditioned (*saṃskṛta*) or not conditioned (*asaṃskṛta*). Many, however, are "evaluative," representing categories that are soteriologically significant and relevant to praxis, such as moral quality, method of abandonment, or stage of the path: for example, the dyad of *dharmas* tending toward contamination (*sāsrava*) and not tending toward contamination (*anāsrava*), or the triad of those to be abandoned by vision (*darśanaheya*), by cultivation (*bhāvanāheya*), or not to abandoned (*aheya*).[41]

Early efforts to organize the multiplying categories of *dharmas* resulted in comprehensive taxonomic systems that combine both the "evaluative" and "descriptive" purposes.[42] For example, the early comprehensive system of the 22 controlling faculties (*indriya*) subsumes earlier standard sets, which were reordered in large part to reflect these two purposes. It begins with a "descriptive" presentation of the five externally directed, corporeal sense organs (1–5), which are followed by the three controlling faculties (6–8) – namely, femininity, masculinity, and the life-force – that further qualify the final corporeal sense organ of the body. The mental sense organ is listed next (9), and is followed by the five varieties of feelings (10–14) that determine the affective quality of mental events. Here the focus shifts to the "evaluative" or soteriological purpose represented by eight praxis-oriented controlling faculties, culminating in the controlling faculty of one possessed of complete knowledge (*ājñātāvīndriya*), which is tantamount to arhatship or enlightenment.[43]

The later Sarvāstivāda fivefold taxonomy (*pañcavastuka*) is another comprehensive taxonomic system that contains both "evaluative" and "descriptive" categories, but unlike the set of 22 controlling faculties, its arrangement is not soteriologically hierarchical.[44] Instead, it attempts to present a complete and systematic listing of all possible *dharma*s classified abstractly by distinctive intrinsic nature (*svabhāva*), without regard for the particular causal or temporal conditions of their occurrence. The previous taxonomic systems begin from specific circumstances of praxis, perception, and so forth, and present detailed descriptions of the significant activities or events (*dharma*) that interact cooperatively in those particular circumstances. The fivefold taxonomy, by contrast, takes the perspective of the *dharma*s themselves and sets out a delimited number of abstract genera that are intended to encompass every experienced event or phenomenon, or in other words every possible individual instance of a *dharma*. For example, according to the Sarvāstivāda perspective, every thought (*citta*) event arises in dependence upon a sense organ and an appropriate object-field, but thought occurs in all three realms, in different sentient beings, with differences in moral quality, and so forth, yielding an unlimited number of individual instances or occurrences of thought. Even though their specific character differs, all of these instances can be placed within a single category as "thought." The genera of the fivefold taxonomy include: material form (*rūpa*); thought (*citta*); thought concomitants (*caitta*) or the variety of mental events that occur together with the central mental event of thought; conditioned forces dissociated from thought (*cittaviprayuktasaṃskāra*) or *dharma*s that cannot be classified as either material form or thought; and the unconditioned (*asaṃskṛta*).

The historical development of this fivefold taxonomy has yet to be fully studied, but the categories themselves suggest certain general principles of organization and, more importantly, of progression in the interpretation of the term *dharma*.[45] A traditional distinction between the material and the mental, typical of the older system of the five aggregates (*skandha*), is evident in the first three categories of material form, thought, and thought concomitants. But new principles of organization can also be observed that evolved from the doctrinal elaboration and resulting controversies of the early Abhidharma period. First, the distinction within the mental sphere between the two categories of thought (*citta*) and thought concomitants (*caitta*) can be seen as a natural development from the earlier distinction within the five aggregates between perceptual consciousness (*vijñāna*), identified in the new fivefold taxonomy as thought, and the other three non-material aggregates, which are subsumed and further expanded within the single category of thought concomitants. However, this distinction between thought and thought concomitants also reflects an emphasis upon perception as the central sentient experience and a newly recognized need to isolate thought as an identifiable hub that connects the various activities constituting one sentient being and, thereby, facilitates a distinction between one sentient being and another. Second, the new category of thought concomitants (*caitta*) comprises, according to the later, standard enumeration, 46 *dharma*s that are divided into six sub-groups according to their moral character as virtuous, unvirtuous, and so forth. In this regard, the category of thought concomitants clearly incorporates an "evaluative," soteriological purpose into the otherwise "descriptive" fivefold taxonomy. Third, the category of dissociated forces (*cittaviprayuktasaṃskāra*) includes *dharma*s that were proposed to account for a varied range of experiential or doctrinally necessary events and is, therefore, a miscellany of *dharma*s not unified by any overall integrating principle other than dissociation from both material form and thought.[46] Finally, the last category of the unconditioned (*asaṃskṛta*) reflects a fundamental distinction between *dharma*s included within the first four categories that are conditioned (*saṃskṛta*), or arise and pass away through causal interaction, and *dharma*s that are not so conditioned and, therefore, neither arise nor pass away.

THE CATEGORY OF THE UNCONDITIONED

Now these final two, the completely new categories of dissociated forces and unconditioned *dharma*s, clearly signal a progression in the notion of what constitutes a *dharma* and an increasingly explicit association of *dharma* with ontology. Why were these particular categories of *dharma*s posited, and what do they reveal about the interpretation of the character of a *dharma*? The answer to the first question is different in the case of each particular *dharma*, but in general terms the new categories comprise commonly experienced events or soteriologically necessary circumstances that were excluded from the existing categories. Newly evolved doctrinal constraints rendered the traditional categories insufficient and resulted in a growing and potentially unlimited number of mutually exclusive *dharma*-categories.[47] In the new, more rigorous and comprehensive *dharma* analysis each newly acknowledged experience, phenomenon, or occurrence demanded a new and separate *dharma*-category, each of which was then identified by a distinctive function. Analysis itself became the dominant concern, acquiring an abstract, self-referential character that involved the recombination of existing categories into larger relational systems. The previous schemata were distilled and rationalized producing not only new individual categories and abstract principles of organization, but also transformed and often competing notions of the character and function of the component *dharmas*.

And what does the fivefold taxonomy reveal about the evolving Sarvāstivāda notion of what constitutes a *dharma?* As noted previously, several scholars have suggested a dynamic conception of *dharmas* within Buddhism, not as static substances, but as properties or activities that separate and distinguish, and thereby manifest and uphold the inherent regularity of all experience. From this perspective, *dharmas* are distinct, but not unrelated to one another; they represent causally significant points within the complex web of experienced activities, but points that can only be determined relationally and that can only be defined dynamically. These relational distinctions that define *dharmas* are not considered arbitrary, but rather are "true" or express "the way things really are" in the sense that they articulate the fundamental causal structures implicit within all experience.[48]

This dynamic interpretation of *dharmas* fits well with a concept of experience as a mass of impermanent, mutually conditioning events, a concept that, in one form or another, typifies virtually all of early Indian Buddhism. But the category of the unconditioned (*asaṃskṛta*) within the fivefold taxonomy asserts the possibility of permanent (*nitya*) *dharmas*, in contrast to all other *dharmas* that are impermanent (*anitya*).[49] More problematic, as the harsh and protracted criticism by Buddhist opponents readily demonstrates, is the distinctive Sarvāstivāda model that all *dharmas*, permanent and impermanent alike, are defined by a fixed, intrinsic nature (*svabhāva*) and exist as real entities (*dravyatas*), whether past, present, or future. Is the category of the unconditioned inconsistent with a conception of *dharmas* as dynamic properties, and if so, in what sense can unconditioned factors be considered *dharmas?* And does the distinctive Sarvāstivāda model of intrinsic nature and existence as real entities entail a static view of all *dharmas* as permanent substances?[50]

Characterizations of the mutually exclusive categories of conditioned and unconditioned *dharmas* in the **Mahāvibhāṣā* provide some tentative answers to these questions.[51] Specifically, conditioned *dharmas* constitute the traditional categories of the five aggregates, which, as conditioned (*saṃskṛta*) themselves, also function as conditions in the arising of other *dharma*s and are, therefore, referred to as forces (*saṃskāra*).[52] They are impermanent, abiding no longer than a moment, and can be qualified in terms of the three time periods of past, present, and future. Hence, they are subject to modification (*vipariṇāma*),[53] which the **Mahāvibhāṣā* explains not as the manifestation and disappearance of a previously hidden and permanently abiding essential character,[54] but as change consisting in arising and passing away that is applied to the *dharma* itself.[55] Conditioned *dharma*s arise through the cooperative efficacy of a specific generative cause and a collocation of other requisite causes and conditions; and once arisen, they themselves act as generative causes or as conditions assisting in the arising of other conditioned *dharma*s. In the mature Sarvāstivāda model, a *dharma*'s status as conditioned is marked by four conditioning characteristics (*saṃskṛtalakṣaṇa*) that function to enable the exertion of that *dharma*'s activity.[56] Unconditioned *dharma*s include space (*ākāśa*) and the two states of cessation resulting from consideration (*pratisaṃkhyānirodha*) and not resulting from consideration (*apratisaṃkhyānirodha*). In contrast to conditioned *dharma*s, these unconditioned *dharma*s are free from arising and passing away or modification and hence abide permanently. They lack a generative cause or dependence upon a collocation of causes and conditions, as well any activity that generates its own effect. They are excluded from both the five aggregates and the three time periods, and are exempt from the four conditioning characteristics.[57]

If, as suggested above, *dharma*s refer to events or circumstances, if *dharma*s are dynamic properties that "do" something, what then do unconditioned *dharma*s "do?" Definitions offered for each of the unconditioned *dharma*s suggest that they do indeed have a function, and, as in the case of other impermanent, conditioned *dharma*s, this function is the basis that determines their distinctive character and hence both their status as *dharma*s and their existence. The discussion of the unconditioned *dharma* space (*ākāśa*) in the **Mahāvibhāṣā* provides an excellent example of the argumentation employed.[58] First, the text contends that traditional sources do not clearly distinguish space as an unconditioned *dharma* from space as a conditioned, material element (*ākāśadhātu*). Scriptural passages using the simple term "space" (*ākāśa*) actually describe space as a material element, and the *Prakaraṇapāda* also uses the "gross" characteristics of space as a material element to indicate the "subtle" unconditioned *dharma* space.[59] The **Mahāvibhāṣā* next raises the question of how, especially given its subtlety, space can be determined to exist.[60] The text first offers the view of Vasumitra who claims that its existence can be known both through scriptural authority, namely, through references to space by the Buddha, as well as through one's direct experience of its distinctive function.[61] Several explanations of this function are given, all of which utilize the same technique of *prasaṅga*, or a *reductio*-type of reasoning whereby each function must be acknowledged in order to avoid an untoward consequence. For example, "if there were no space, objects would not have a place to occur; but since there is a place for various objects, one knows that space exists."[62] Accordingly, something that has the distinctive function of not obstructing must be inferred from the observation of the coming and going, the assemblage and dispersion, and the ready occurrence of material objects that have resistance and otherwise would obstruct one another. As Vasumitra concludes, "since one observes that there are places without obstruction, one knows that space definitely exists as a real entity (*dravyatas*), because it is precisely space that has this distinctive function of non-obstruction as its characteristic."[63] In other words, the observed occurrence of phenomena must have a causal basis, and we can, therefore, assume that its basis, in this case space, exists. Vasumitra's explanation is followed by the opposing opinion of Bhadanta who claims that space cannot be known and, therefore, exists merely as a provisional designation (*prajñaptitas*).[64] The arbiter of the **Mahāvibhāṣā* finally declares, "it is not the case that [space] is not known, that is to say, that it does not exist; [one can conclude that] space exists as a real entity on the basis of the previously cited scriptural passages and reasoned arguments".[65]

The next section in the **Mahāvibhāṣā* even more clearly links function to existence in clarifying precisely what it is that space "does." It states, "if it is so [that space exists], what activity (作用 **kāritra*) does space have? Space is unconditioned and lacks any generative activity to produce an effect. However, it does function as the sovereign condition (*adhipatipratyaya*), that is, as a non-obstructing condition with regard to the various material elements of space."[66] The **Mahāvibhāṣā* then delineates a series of sovereign conditions, beginning with this non-obstructing function of space, proceeding through the material elements of space, the four fundamental material elements, the secondary material elements, and ending with thought and thought concomitants. The text concludes, "if there were no space, this series of causes and conditions proceeding in this way would not be established. This fault must be avoided. Therefore, space actually exists with intrinsic form (體相 **svarūpa*), and one should not deny it as nonexistent."[67] Elsewhere the **Mahāvibhāṣā* specifies that unconditioned *dharma*s function not only as sovereign conditions (*adhipatipratyaya*), but also as comprehensive non-obstructing causes (*kāraṇahetu*) and as object-support conditions (*ālambanapratyaya*).[68] Their function as comprehensive non-obstructing causes is identical to their function as sovereign conditions: that is, as in the case of all *dharma*s, unconditioned *dharma*s also function not to obstruct the arising of *dharma*s other than themselves. And in this function as non-obstructing causes, unconditioned *dharma*s do not exert any generative causal efficacy: that is to say, they are not active in producing an effect. As object-support conditions, unconditioned *dharma*s function as objects of mental perceptual consciousness, but here also they do not function as the generative causes for its arising. Hence, unconditioned *dharma*s are said to have no cause, since they do not arise, and no effect, since they do not function as generative causes in producing their own effect.[69] Nevertheless, even though unconditioned *dharma*s lack generative activity, they do have a function, and this functioning, as in the case of conditioned *dharma*s, makes known their characteristic nature and mandates their existence as distinct *dharma*s.

SVABHĀVA AND THE METHOD OF INCLUSION

In the framework of the distinctive Sarvāstivāda model, a dynamic conception of *dharma*s and their exertion of a transient, generative activity appear to harmonize well with the common Buddhist notion of impermanent, conditioned *dharma*s. But what of the assertion that all conditioned *dharma*s are defined by a fixed, intrinsic nature (*svabhāva*) and exist as real entities (*dravyatas*), whether past, present, or future? Does this not contradict the prior affirmation of impermanence and entail a static view of *dharma*s as permanent substances? To answer this question, we must examine more closely how the term *dharma* was defined and what was implied by the terms *svabhāva* and *dravya* through which *dharma*s were specified.

Neither the early Sarvāstivāda, canonical Abhidharma texts nor the *vibhāṣā* compendia contain an abstract definition of *dharma* as such. A definition is found, however, in Upaśānta's and Dharmatrāta's commentaries on the **Abhidharmahṛdaya*, and is transmitted in the *Abhidharmakośabhāṣya* and subsequent texts: that is, "*dharma* means 'upholding,' [namely], upholding intrinsic nature (*svabhāva*)."[70] Although lacking an overt abstract definition, the **Mahāvibhāṣā* uses similar terminology in several passages, implying a concept of *dharma* comparable to that suggested by these definitions. For example, in explaining why one meaning of the term "root" (*mūla*) is intrinsic nature (*svabhāva*), it states "intrinsic nature is able to uphold it own identity (自體 **ātmabhāva*) and not lose it; therefore, it is considered a 'root.' As in the case of unconditioned [*dharmas*] that are able to uphold their own identity and are, therefore, considered to be "roots", [here] also there is no error."[71] And elsewhere, the **Mahāvibhāṣā* interprets a grammatical (*śābdika*) explanation of the term "element" (*dhātu*), as upholding: "[the statement,] 'it is referred to as "element" because it is upholding (*saṃdhāraṇa*),' means these various elements uphold intrinsic nature (*svabhāva*)."[72]

One final passage from the **Mahāvibhāṣā* is instructive in pointing to the primary context within which *dharma*s were interpreted in these early Abhidharma texts and from which the concept of *svabhāva* naturally developed: namely, the context of categorization, where invariable criteria are demanded as the basis for unambiguous classification. This passage discusses the topic of "inclusion" (*saṃgraha*)[73] and the process by which the inclusion of *dharma*s within a specific group or category is to be applied. Here, the text first cites a standard listing of 16 categories of defilements, ranging from the three fetters (*saṃyojana*) through the 98 contaminants (*anuśaya*),[74] and inquires which of the 98 contaminants are to be included within each of the other categories.[75] The **Mahāvibhāṣā* explains that this topic is raised in order to counter the view of the Vibhajyavādins concerning the method of inclusion: namely, that "*dharma*s are included on the basis of other nature (*parabhāva*), and not on the basis of intrinsic nature (*svabhāva*)."[76] To support their view, the Vibhajyavādins appeal to both scriptural authority and common usage in which "that which includes" and "that which is included" are clearly distinct from one another, as in the case of a householder who states "I possess land, domestic animals," and so forth. In view of such examples, the Vibhajyavādins claim that inclusion is based upon other-nature.[77] The **Mahāvibhāṣā* responds that these commonplace examples involve inclusion merely in a conventional sense, which is indeed based upon other-nature and varies in accordance with both time and circumstances. However, the categories of distinct *dharma*s as utilized in Abhidharma analysis are established through inclusion in the absolute sense (*pāramārthika*), which is applied only on the basis of intrinsic nature and is free of any such contingencies. In other words, a *dharma*'s own identity (自體 **ātmabhāva*) is not contingent upon conditions and is invariable.[78] As the **Mahāvibhāṣā* concludes, "own identity" or "intrinsic nature" serves as the basis of absolute inclusion because this intrinsic nature exists, is a real entity, and can be apprehended; it is not different, not other, not separated, not apart, and is never void; it is not the case that it has not existed, does not exist, or will not exist; it neither increases nor decreases. Inclusion by intrinsic nature does not involve one thing grasping another, as in the case of grabbing food with the hand or pinching cloth with the fingers. Instead, *dharma*s each uphold their own identity and prevent it from disintegrating; the term "inclusion" is established on the basis of this sense of "upholding."[79]

This method of inclusion, integral to any taxonomic practice, is implicit within Abhidharma categorization in all periods. However, even though the earliest canonical Sarvāstivāda Abhidharma texts classify specific *dharma*s according to a method of simple inclusion, they do not utilize the intricate matrices typical of the *vibhāṣā* compendia, nor do they explicitly consider the meaning of "inclusion," its rationale, and its implications for the nature of the *dharma*s so classified, as evident in the controversy concerning intrinsic nature and other-nature outlined above.[80] The early method of simple inclusion is expanded in the canonical texts of the middle period such as the *Prakaraṇapāda*, *Vijñānakāya*, and the *Jñānaprasthāna*, which relate entire categories rather than simply classifying individual *dharma*s, but which still do not explicitly discuss the rationale for the method of inclusion in terms of a fundamental contrast between intrinsic nature and other-nature.

The earliest extant Abhidharma text to apply the method of inclusion through exhaustive and intricate matrices of categories and to refer to its basis in the intrinsic or other-nature of *dharma*s is the **Śāriputrābhidharmaśāstra*.[81] Inclusion is treated in a separate section that begins with a description of the method of inclusion, clearly citing intrinsic nature and other-nature as the criteria by which it is determined.[82] The text then offers a matrix of over 200 attribute categories structured in contrasting, affirmative and negative dyads that reflect the fundamental distinction between intrinsic nature and other nature. Finally, it indicates in general terms the *dharma*s within each category. The next section applies the method of inclusion, relating each of the over 200 dyads of the basic matrix to the three categories of the aggregates, elements, and sense spheres by asking the same set of formulaic questions. For example, "the visual sense sphere (*cakṣurāyatana*) *dharma* is included in how many aggregates, elements, and sense spheres? About what *dharma*s is this question asked? The question is asked about the *dharma* of the visual sense sphere, excluding other *dharma*s. What other *dharma*s are excluded? [The next category, namely, those] *dharma*s that are not the visual sense sphere, [is excluded]."[83] Finally, this set of formulaic questions is posed once again, but now in terms of the negative alternative of "non-inclusion," again applied to each of the over 200 dyads in the basic matrix.

This section on inclusion in the **Śāriputrābhidharmaśāstra*, with its highly formulaic, catechetical structure, would appear to tell us very little about the specific character or existence of the individual sets of *dharma*s, but that in itself is telling, suggesting that in this early period of Abhidharma exegesis the method of inclusion and its application were at least as important as any descriptive information about *dharma*s that they might yield. And the increasing abstraction in taxonomic practice, indicated by the formulaic systematization of the method of inclusion in the **Śāriputrābhidharmaśāstra* undoubtedly also reflects a concomitant abstraction in the basic notion of what constitutes a *dharma*. In this regard, it is significant to note that the term *svabhāva* in the distinctive sense of the intrinsic nature of a category or of an individual *dharma*[84] is not used in the earliest Sarvāstivāda canonical Abhidharma texts;[85] it appears only in texts from the period of the early *vibhāṣā* compendia onward, that is, concurrent with the systematic development of the analytical method of categorization by inclusion. It is then plausible to infer that this sense of *svabhāva* as intrinsic nature, so important in later Sarvāstivāda exegesis for the interpretation of the character of *dharma*s *per se*, first emerged through its function as the criterion determining categories of *dharma*s, specifically in the context of inclusion.

The probable origin of the distinctive sense of the term *svabhāva* within the context of taxonomy, that is, within the method of inclusion, also elucidates its application to *dharma*s in mature Sarvāstivāda usage. As in the case of categories that are nothing other than the *svabhāva* that demarcates them, so also *dharma*s should not be considered to possess a separately existing intrinsic nature, but are constituted by the very *svabhāva* that defines them. In this sense, each *dharma* so defined is "determined" (*pariniṣpanna*) by its intrinsic nature.[86] The composite objects of ordinary experience are, by contrast, not determined; that is to say, as complex entities that depend for their existence upon the constituents of which they are made, their character is relative and must be assessed differently depending upon the circumstances.[87] "Determination" implies two further features of *dharma*s, both of which flow naturally from the function of *svabhāva* in the context of categorization.[88] First, just as categories in a well-structured taxonomic schema are distinct and not subject to fluctuation, so also *dharma*s, as "determined," are clearly and unalterably discriminated; they are uniquely individualized and as such are not subject to confusion with other *dharma*s.[89] This feature of *dharma*s is highlighted in the **Mahāvibhāṣā* in a lengthy discussion of the character of *nirvāṇa*. Here, the text first counters the view of the Vātsīputrīyas who claim that *nirvāṇa* in its intrinsic nature has three different characteristics depending upon its method of acquisition.[90] The **Mahāvibhāṣā* responds: "Why should *nirvāṇa* have three characteristics simply because it is acquired through three different types of possession? One *dharma* should not have a threefold intrinsic form (體相 **svarūpa*) as its [intrinsic] nature."[91] And in its final comments, the **Mahāvibhāṣā* explicitly connects intrinsic nature, determination, and the absence of confusion among *dharma*s: "If the single [*dharma* of] *nirvāṇa* were subject to modification in accordance with its method of acquisition, then no *dharma*s would be determined. If [*dharma*s] were not determined, there would be confusion [among them]. If there were confusion [among *dharma*s], one should not designate characteristics of [intrinsic] nature (性相) such as permanent or impermanent as determined.[92] . . . Because *nirvāṇa* is always of [a single nature, that is, specifically] of one neither in training nor beyond training (*naivaśaikṣanāśaikṣa*), *dharma*s are determined and are without confusion; they are always established in their intrinsic nature and do not abandon their intrinsic nature."[93]

As this passage demonstrates, to be a *dharma* is to be determined by a distinctive intrinsic nature, which is never abandoned. And, as in the case of categories, it is only through clear discrimination on the basis of intrinsic nature that confusion among *dharma*s can be avoided. This leads to the second feature of *dharma*s implied by their "determination:" that is, determination by intrinsic nature undergoes no variation or modification, and hence, *dharma*s, which are in effect types or categories of intrinsic nature, are established as stable and immutable. In this regard, Sarvāstivāda Abhidharma texts speak of *dharma*s as "always established as their intrinsic nature," with the inevitable implication that they always exist as intrinsic nature. For example, the **Mahāvibhāṣā* claims that "all *dharma*s already have intrinsic nature, because from the beginning each [*dharma*] is established in [its] own particular inherent characteristic;"[94] that is to say, "every *dharma* is established in its intrinsic nature [or identity], its own self, its own form, its own characteristic, its own part, and its own original nature."[95] Hence, *dharma*s as *svabhāva*s or as abstract categories are invariable and denote an atemporal, that is, inalterable existence.

The original taxonomic function of *svabhāva* also helps to clarify an ambiguity in the application of the term *svabhāva* to both individual *dharma*s and to categorial groups *of dharma*s as a whole. In its discussion of both individual *dharma*s and categorial groups, the **Mahāvibhāṣā* follows a regular pattern, first identifying the intrinsic nature (*svabhāva*) of the individual or group by means of a formulaic characterization. For example, in the discussion of the three time periods, it states: "What do the three time periods, [understood] in this way, take as [their] intrinsic nature? They take all conditioned *dharma*s as [their] intrinsic nature. As in the case of intrinsic nature, so also the self, form, identity, characteristic, part, and original nature [of the three time periods] should be understood. The intrinsic nature [of the three time periods] has already been explained."[96] Here the term *svabhāva* is used in reference to the three time periods, even though for the Sarvāstivādins the time periods do not constitute independent *dharma*s determined by intrinsic nature, but are nothing other than the past, present, and future forces (*saṃskāra*) of which they consist.[97] Hence, the term *svabhāva*, as in the case of the three time periods, cannot be assumed to connote the real existence of an individual *dharma*. If, however, the term *svabhāva* is understood to signify the defining property of an abstract category, it can then be applied without contradiction to either categorial groups as a whole or to their individual constituents. Now given the **Mahāvibhāṣā*'s routine application of this formulaic characterization in terms of intrinsic nature to both individual, phenomenal events recognized as discrete, independent *dharma*s and to entire categorial groups of *dharma*s,[98] it seems plausible that the original function of *svabhāva* was to identify the specific property that enables the discrimination of categorial-types, whether on the level of individuals or groupings, and not to signify that the category as a whole exists as a single, independent *dharma*.

Despite its regular use of the term *svabhāva* to refer to both categorial groups and individual *dharma*s, the **Mahāvibhāṣā* also evinces an awareness of certain contradictions to which this ambiguity in usage might lead. In a discussion of the implications of the various meanings of the term "aggregate," or *skandha*, as a heap (*rāśi*), a bundle, an assemblage, or as a collection,[99] the **Mahāvibhāṣā* notes that just as the term "army" can be applied to a collection of discrete individuals without fusing the individuals into one person, so also the single name "material form aggregate" (*rūpaskandha*), can be meaningfully applied to a collection of instances of material form in the past, present, and future without merging their intrinsic natures into one. As the text states, "even though [the various instances of material form] are distinct from one another, because they are alike [in nature], a unified material form aggregate can be established."[100] Can the name "material form aggregate" also then be applied to the individual atoms (*paramāṇu*) that come together to constitute each given instance of material form? The **Mahāvibhāṣā* offers three conflicting answers. First, since the material form aggregate can only be established as an aggregation of many atoms, one individual atom alone cannot be referred to as a "material form aggregate." Second, since each and every individual atom has the characteristic of a material form aggregate, separate atoms can indeed be established as the material form aggregate. Otherwise, it would not be possible to refer to a collection of individual atoms as a whole as the "material form aggregate." The third response, that of the Abhidharma masters, suggests that ambiguity in the application of the name "material form aggregate" results from a difference in perspective. When viewed from the perspective of a conventional aggregate or an aggregate as a provisional designation, atoms should be seen as constituting only one portion of the aggregates, sense spheres, or elements. However, when viewed from the perspective of Abhidharma analysis in which an aggregate is marked by a distinctive intrinsic nature, each atom can indeed be referred to as an aggregate, sense sphere, or element.[101] The **Mahāvibhāṣā* uses the example of a person taking one kernel from a pile of grain: when viewed from the perspective of the pile of grain, one would say "I am taking one kernel from the pile of grain," but when not viewed from the perspective of the pile, one would say "I am taking grain."[102]

Ambiguous application of the term *svabhāva* continued in the later Sarvāstivāda Abhidharma texts. An original taxonomic function is still evident in several passages, for example, in a discussion of the elements (*dhātu*), where the *Abhidharmakośabhāṣya* glosses "kinds" (*jāti*) with *svabhāva*.[103] And in its discussion of inclusion, the *Abhidharmakośabhāṣya* cites the traditional classification of the visual sense organ controlling faculty (*cakṣurindriya*) within the material form aggregate, the visual sense sphere, and the visual element, by virtue of the fact that the visual sense organ controlling faculty has the same intrinsic nature as these categories (*tatsvabhāvāt*).[104] In presenting the previously cited argument from the **Mahāvibhāṣā* concerning the application of the term "aggregate," the *Abhidharmakośabhāṣya* raises the issue of whether the aggregates exist as real entities (*dravyatas*) or as provisional designations (*prajñaptitas*).[105] This suggests that for later Abhidharma texts the ambiguous application of intrinsic nature to categorial groups or to individual *dharma*s necessarily entailed addressing the problem of how the thing so characterized exists. In other words, intrinsic nature no longer functioned merely as a demarcating property that determines identity, but had connotations of existence, specifically the real and individual existence of the thing demarcated.

In these applications of intrinsic nature to both individual *dharma*s and to categorial groups, the traditional method of inclusion results in multiple levels, each of which is distinguished by a distinct intrinsic nature. A given *dharma*, such as the visual sense organ, can then be characterized by multiple intrinsic natures depending upon the categories within which it is included.[106] Once again, this ambiguity in application would not constitute a problem so long as *svabhāva* is understood primarily as indicating the criterion by which separate categories are discriminated. But if *svabhāva* also connotes existence as a unique, individual *dharma*, two problems result: first, its application to larger categorial groups would be unjustified since clearly such large categorial groups do not exist as single, individual *dharma*s; and second, a single *dharma* characterized by multiple *svabhāva*s should, in fact, exist as multiple *dharma*s.

SVABHĀVA IN RELATION TO *BHĀVA*

Indeed, one can convincingly argue that taxonomy always rests upon ontology[107] and that connotations of existence noted in the previous characterizations of *dharma*s and arguments from the **Mahāvibhāṣā* had always been present in the term *svabhāva*. To clarify further the original connotations of *svabhāva*, one can profitably turn to an examination of the evolution and use of the term *bhāva*, with which it is etymologically and functionally related. However, at the outset it must be acknowledged that the uncertainty of the Indic equivalents of terms used in the Chinese translations of early Sarvāstivāda

Abhidharma texts makes tracing the early sense of *bhāva* in these materials extremely difficult.[108] Within Pāli Abhidhamma texts, *bhāva* is used almost exclusively in compound-final position usually with the sense of "state of being X."[109] However, in one passage in the *Kathāvatthu*, within the section on "Everything Exists" (*sabbam atthi*), its sense is uncertain. This passage begins with a question raised by the text proponent who asks whether in the case of, for example, present material form, "present" (*paccuppanna*) and "material form" (*rūpa*) are one and the same with no distinction between them.[110] The opponent, who like the Sarvāstivādins supports the existence of past, present, and future *dharma*s, assents that they are the same. The text proponent then inquires: "[Text Proponent:] Does present material form that is ceasing abandon its state of being present (*paccuppannabhāva*)? [Opponent:] Yes. [Text Proponent:] Does it abandon its state of being material form (*rūpabhāva*)? [Opponent:] That is not to be said."[111] To explain his negative response, the opponent compares "present material form" to a white cloth, which when dyed abandons its state of being white (*odātabhāva*), but not its state of being a cloth (*vatthabhāva*). Similarly, the opponent would suggest, it is possible for a present instance of material form to abandon its state as "present," without abandoning its state as "material form."

Now the specific meaning of *bhāva* in this passage is not clear, since the context could support an abstract sense as "state" or "nature," or an ontological sense as "exists as" or "mode of existence," or possibly both. The surrounding argument does not allow us to decide among these three options, nor is it even certain that the text proponent and opponent understand *bhāva* in the same way. The text proponent's initial question concerning the lack of distinction between the "present" and "material form" itself suggests an understanding of *bhāva* as denoting something more akin to "nature" or even possibly "intrinsic nature." Accordingly, it would be impossible for a given *dharma* to abandon its "nature" as present, and yet concurrently retain its "nature" as material form. As the text states: "[Text Proponent:] Is it the case that material form does not abandon its state of being material form (*rūpabhāva*)? [Opponent:] Yes. [Text Proponent:] Is material form a *dharma* that is permanent, stable, eternal, and not subject to modification? [Opponent:] That is not to be said ... [Text Proponent:] If material form is impermanent, unstable, non-eternal, and subject to modification, one should certainly not say that "material form does not abandon its state of being material form."[112] As these questions indicate, the text proponent assumes that if material form does not abandon its *bhāva* as material form, it must be permanent; hence, once again, *bhāva* for the text proponent would here also apparently convey the sense of unchanging "nature." For the opponent to disagree and to maintain that material form is not permanent, he must understand *bhāva* differently. Hence, the opponent seems to understand *bhāva*, at least when used in reference to the temporal qualifications of past, present, and future, in the sense of "mode of existence." And so in this passage, the term *bhāva* would appear to be used ambiguously: that is to say, when used in conjunction with "material form" to signify a *dharma*'s defining character, *bhāva* appears to convey a more abstract sense of "nature," but when used in conjunction with the time periods, *bhāva* appears to signify "mode of existence."

The ambiguity in the sense of the term *bhāva* apparent in this section of the *Kathāvatthu* is also encountered in early Sarvāstivāda texts. Of particular interest here are passages in the *Saṅgītiparyāya* that describe *dharma*s in relation to the three time periods. For example, in discussing the material form aggregate (*rūpaskandha*), it begins with the following definition: "What is the material form aggregate? Whatever material form, whether past, future, present, internal, external, gross, subtle, inferior, superior, distant, or close, all [varieties of material form] in this way are put together in a single group, which is referred to as the material form aggregate."[113] The phrase "whether past, future, or present" is glossed with three parallel series of adjectives, which, in the case of the past, concludes with the phrase "pastness (過去性 **atītatva*), the state of being past (過去類**atītabhāva*), and being included within the past time period (過去世攝 **atītasaṃgrahīta*)."[114] In interpreting this passage, Junshō KATŌ suggests that the term *bhāva* conveys the sense of existence, that is to say, "the existent *dharma* of past material form" or "existing as past material form," and so forth. On the basis of such uses of the term *bhāva* in the *Saṅgītiparyāya*, KATŌ proposes that early Sarvāstivāda texts viewed past, present, and future *dharma*s as distinct, attributing to each a separate existence (*bhāva*).[115] For any given *dharma* such as material form, one can then speak of three separate *bhāva*s or *dharma*s of past, present, and future, all of which, in view of their designation as *bhāvas*, exist. Thus, the perspective of the early texts in using the term *bhāva* is one of *dharma*s existing in different modes such as internal, external, gross, subtle, and so forth, and also of course as past, present and future.

This interpretation of *bhāva* in the sense of "mode of existence" is corroborated by two passages from an early (c. 1st cent. CE) Gāndhārī Abhidharma manuscript where a Sarvāstivādin opponent uses *bhāva* (Gāndhārī = G *bhava*) in the plural and asserts that one *dharma* exists through or by means of various G *bhavas*: "material form exists through G *bhava* (plural), but there are not three separate [*dharmas* of] material form."[116] Since a single *dharma* is defined by one intrinsic nature, this admission of multiple *bhāvas* and the contrast between *bhāva* and material form argues that the Sarvāstivādin opponent admitted at least some kind of distinction between *bhāva* and the *dharma* as characterized by intrinsic nature (*svabhāva*).

At the comparatively early date represented by the *Kathāvatthu*, the early canonical Sarvāstivāda Abhidharma texts, and the fragmentary Gāndhārī manuscript, the combined textual evidence indicates that *bhāva* conveyed both an abstract sense as "nature" and an ontological sense as "mode of existence."[117] The term *svabhāva*, grounded logically and etymologically in the term *bhāva*, might then also be expected to carry this dual sense. In the final stage of Sarvāstivāda doctrinal investigations, that is, in Saṅghabhadra's **Nyāyanusāra, bhāva* acquired a meaning as a *dharma*'s variable "mode of existence" clearly demarcated from that of *svabhāva*, which indicates "intrinsic nature."[118] Thus, in these early accounts, we find preserved the initial stages in Sarvāstivāda theory in which the new, more technical sense of *bhāva* was beginning to develop, but the clear distinction between *bhāva* and *svabhāva* typical of the later Sarvāstivāda materials had not yet solidified. These accounts provide us with traces of the complex process through which the two terms, *bhāva* and *svabhāva*, originally used virtually synonymously, were gradually distinguished from one another: the distinctive Sarvāstivāda sense of "intrinsic nature" became centered on the term *svabhāva*, while *bhāva* acquired a new, technical sense as a *dharma*'s changing "mode of existence."

DRAVYA AS THE MARKER OF REAL EXISTENCE

This ambiguity in the term *svabhāva* then served as the bridge for a transition in the Sarvāstivāda treatment of *dharma*, from a categorial focus directed toward demarcating experientially or soteriologically significant categories to an ontological concentration on the specific character and existence of the *dharmas* constituting each category. This transition is clearly observed in the middle period of Sarvāstivāda literature represented by the *vibhāṣā* compendia and contemporaneous texts and is, at least in part, a natural outgrowth of their function as exegetical commentaries. In the texts of this middle period, traditional categories and forms of presentation are preserved, but are radically reorganized and refined in accordance with new analytical parameters. Doctrinal issues are situated in a polemical context in which a range of alternative opinions are cited and evaluated and, where possible, an authoritative position is determined. The traditional technique of formulaically structured taxonomies, although still playing a role within these issue-oriented discussions, gives way as the primary organizational method to topically arranged investigations that exhibit a more thematically coherent structure. And as a part of this shift in exegetical focus and technique, the explicit emphasis upon categorization *per se* recedes in importance as the focus shifts to clarifying the character and eventually the ontological status of individual *dharma*s. Accordingly, the term *svabhāva* acquires the dominant sense of the "intrinsic nature" specifying individual *dharma*s, as evident in the definition of *dharma* noted above. And determining individual *dharma*s through unique intrinsic nature also entails affirming their existence, as a natural function both of the etymological sense of the term *svabhāva* and of the role of *dharma*s as the fundamental constituents of experience. This then leads to the prominence of a new term that expressed this ontological focus: namely, *dravya*.

The issue of the existence of *dharma*s is most often raised in the *vibhāṣā* compendia in polemical contexts where the ontological status of individual *dharma*s is contested, but in a few passages existence is discussed in the abstract. The **Mahāvibhāṣā* contains at least four separate abstract typologies of existence, indicating considerable variety in its analysis of existence even at this comparatively early stage.[119] More importantly, however, the very presence of these typologies demonstrates that existence was not considered to be uniform; experienced objects do not simply exist or not exist, but rather can exist in different ways. The typologies present three major types of existence: real existence (*dravya*), as in the case of the category of aggregates or individual *dharma*s that are established in intrinsic nature; provisional existence (*prajñapti*), as in the case of the composite objects of ordinary experience; and relative existence (**āpekṣika*), as in the case of the mutual dependence of long and short or contingencies of time and place. *Dharma*s that are determined by intrinsic nature (*svabhāva*) exist as real entities (*dravyatas*), in contrast to composite objects that lack such a unique, defining intrinsic nature. Such composite objects exist only provisionally (*prajñaptitas*) in dependence upon their constitutive fundamental *dharmas*. Hence, the terms *dravya* and *prajñapti* connote existence, and although they depend for their application upon the presence or absence of a unique intrinsic nature, they do not, in themselves, identify the specific character of a *dharma* or composite object. This specification of character can occur only through analytical discrimination that determines intrinsic nature (*svabhāva*) in the case of individual *dharmas*, or that identifies the individual *dharmas* upon which composite objects or relative states depend.

This new concern with the character and existence of individual *dharmas* led to a wholesale reappraisal of traditional categories of *dharmas*, eventually resulting in their refinement according to ontological criteria that coincided with the now explicit ontological meaning of *svabhāva* expressed through the term *dravya*. This process of refinement is evident in the issue of whether, in the case of any given set of categories, the number of *dharmas* is equivalent to the number of *dravyas*.[120] For example, in considering the 18 elements (*dhātu*), the **Mahāvibhāṣā* notes that even though the elements are distinct as names or *dharma*-categories, as *dravya*, there are only either 17 or 12.[121] Since the single mental sense organ (*manodhātu*) encompasses all six types of perceptual consciousness (*vijñāna*), from the standpoint of their existence as real entities (*dravyatas*), one or the other should be omitted. This would result in either 12 elements, if the six types of perceptual consciousness were omitted, or 17, if the mental organ were omitted.[122]

The changing interpretation of the term *svabhāva* in this new explicitly ontological context is even more clearly indicated in a second passage concerning the 22 controlling faculties (*indriya*).[123] The **Mahāvibhāṣā* first offers the view that the 22 traditional categories of controlling faculties should be reduced to 17 *dravyas*, but then records two other dissenting views. First, the master Dharmatrāta further reduces the 17 to 14. He identifies two more of the controlling faculties with others, and rejects a third, vitality (*jīvitendriya*), because he denies the real existence (*dravyatas*) of the entire category of *dharmas* to which it belongs: namely, the forces dissociated from thought (*cittaviprayuktasaṃskāra*). Second, the master Buddhadeva adopts an even more radical position, suggesting the reduction of the 22 categories to only one *dravya*, namely, the mental controlling faculty (*manaindriya*), since, for him, conditioned *dharma*s exhibit only two varieties of intrinsic nature: material form consisting of the fundamental material elements (*mahābhūta*), and thought (*citta*).[124]

As noted previously, both the 18 elements and the 22 controlling faculties are distinguished as separate categories by intrinsic nature (*svabhāva*), but as these passages demonstrate, not all categories are considered to exist as discrete real entities (*dravya*). If *svabhāva* were equivalent to *dravya*, such differences in the number of *svabhāva* and *dravya* would be impossible. However, such differences can be explained if we keep in mind the ambiguity especially in the early usage of the term *svabhāva* and its greater specificity after the introduction of the notion of *dravya*. In the earliest period, *svabhāva* denotes the categorial-type or nature by which groups or individual *dharma*s are classified, but as the focus of Abhidharma exegesis shifts to the character of individual *dharma*s and their existence, *svabhāva* becomes a special marker for uniquely determined, individual *dharma*s. *Dravya*, by contrast, is always associated with ontology and denotes the discrete and actual existence of recognized *dharma*s. Even when both terms are in frequent use from the *vibhāṣā* compendia onward, *svabhāva* is still used when the character or nature of *dharma*s is the issue, and *dravya*, when existence is the issue. However, despite this difference in their primary denotation as "nature" or "real existence," the terms are nonetheless closely intertwined, since those things that actually exist, namely, *dharma*s, are recognized or determined on the basis of their intrinsic nature.

And how is such existence as *dravya* established? Existence is, as we have seen, connected with functioning: a *dharma*'s intrinsic nature is defined in terms of the distinctive function that it performs, and it is through the observation of a *dharma*'s distinctive function that we know that it exists. Now such functioning, from the earliest period of Abhidharma exegesis onward, is understood preeminently as causal functioning.[125] This connection between existence and specifically causal functioning is noted repeatedly in the **Mahāvibhāṣā*, in particular, in arguments with those such as the Darṣṭāntikas, who deny that causes or conditions must exist as real entities. In the formulaic presentation of passages from its root text, the *Jñānaprasthāna*, the **Mahāvibhāṣā* often begins: "[this discussion is presented] in order to counter the deluded belief concerning *dharma*s [functioning as] causes and conditions – [namely, that *dharma*s] in the state of being causes and conditions do not exist as real entities – and to make it clear that *dharma*s [functioning as] causes and conditions exist as real entities with intrinsic nature."[126] And if causes and conditions were permitted to lack intrinsic nature and existence as real entities, the same would be true of all *dharmas*, since all possible *dharmas* are included within the groups of six causes and four conditions.[127]

Now, a given *dharma* is marked by a distinctive function in accordance with its intrinsic nature, and just as it is always determined by its intrinsic nature, whether past, present, or future, so also it is always marked by its distinctive function, even if that function is not actually being performed.[128] A *dharma* is not, however, limited to a single mode of distinctive, causal functioning, but can function in various ways, any of which implies its existence.[129] For example, all *dharmas* function as comprehensive non-obstructing causes (*kāraṇahetu*) or as sovereign conditions (*adhipatipratyaya*) in not obstructing the arising of other *dharmas*. *Dharmas* also function as homogeneous causes (*sabhāgahetu*) in the arising of *dharmas* of the same type and as the object-support condition (*ālambanapratyaya*) for appropriate varieties of perceptual consciousness. And depending upon its particular character as mental, material, unvirtuous, or *karmic*, a given *dharma* can also function as a number of other types of causes or conditions.

Moreover, for the Sarvāstivādins, a *dharma*'s possible modes of functioning are not limited to the present moment. All *dharmas* can function as non-obstructing causes, as sovereign conditions, or as object-support conditions at any time, that is, as past, present, or future. Further, by the time of the *vibhāṣā* compendia, the generative causal functioning typical of conditioned *dharmas* was understood to occur in two stages. In the first stage, a *dharma* projects (*ākṣip-*) or seizes (*pratigrah-*) its effect, and in the second, it presents (*dā-*) or delivers (*prayam-*) that same effect. The first stage occurs only when the causal *dharma* is present, and indeed it is the very projecting or seizing efficacy that determines the *dharma*'s status as present. Depending upon the type of causal functioning, the second stage of generative efficacy can occur either simultaneously with the first stage, that is, when the causal *dharma* and its effect are both present, or at some time subsequent to the first stage, that is, when the causal *dharma* is already past.[130] Hence, past, present, and future *dharmas* can each function causally in multiple ways, and, therefore, must all be said to exist.

Saṅghabhadra will later distinguish clearly between a *dharma*'s preeminent, present functioning, which he terms activity (*kāritra* 作用), and other modes of functioning, which he terms capability (*sāmarthya* 功能). As in the **Mahāvibhāṣā*, activity occurs only in the present and indeed determines a *dharma*'s status as present, but for Saṅghabhadra, this present activity is subsumed within the larger category of capability, which can occur in the past, present, or future. Saṅghabhadra further limits activity to the generative, causal efficacy that is exerted within a given *dharma*'s own stream; capability, by contrast, can be exerted toward a *dharma*'s own stream, as in the case of present or past causal functioning in the second stage of presenting or delivering the effect, or it can be exerted toward the stream of a different *dharma* through various other modes of causal functioning in the past, present, or future. In this latter function, capability becomes an assisting condition that aids a separate *dharma* in the production of its own particular effect.[131] Saṅghabhadra illustrates this distinction between activity (*kāritra*) and capability (*sāmarthya*) through an example that also appears in the **Mahāvibhāṣā*: namely, that of a visual sense organ that is obstructed and unable to see. Even though according to its intrinsic nature, a visual sense organ's distinctive function is seeing material form, sight is not identified as its activity. Instead, its activity is its preeminent, present functioning as the homogeneous cause (*sabhāgahetu*) that produces a similar visual sense organ in the next moment within its own stream. This activity as a homogeneous cause is referred to as the first stage of "seizing the effect" and determines the visual sense organ's status as present. By contrast, the visual sense organ's distinctive function of seeing becomes a condition for the arising of a *dharma* of another stream, namely, visual perceptual consciousness, and is termed capability, not activity. Hence, every present *dharma*, even if unable to perform its distinctive function, still exerts an "activity" as the generative, homogeneous cause that projects its own effect. It is this activity that determines its status as present.[132]

This array of causal relations among *dharma*s is, like their intrinsic nature, also fixed; once a *dharma*'s status as a particular type of cause or condition has been determined, there is no time at which it loses that status, whether or not it is actually so functioning.[133] Since there is no time at which a *dharma* cannot be considered a cause, and since causal functioning, or the potential for causal functioning, signifies existence, there is then no time at which a *dharma* does not exist. Hence, the Sarvāstivādins' declaration that "everything exists" also implies that past, present and future *dharma*s exist.[134] The reasoned arguments offered for the existence of past and future *dharma*s are also grounded in this basic principle that causes must exist as real entities (*dravyatas*). Different arguments are offered in different texts, but they can be grouped according to four basic reasons: (1) in the case of causes that precede their effect, such as the operation of *karman*, the past must exist in order to provide an existent cause for the arising of a present effect; (2) accompaniment (*samanvāgama*) and non-accompaniment (*asamanvāgama*), which connect *dharmas* of all time periods to one's own lifestream, require an existent object upon which to operate; (3) the existence of past causes or future effects can be inferred from the occurrence of their effects or causes in the present; and (4) perceptual consciousness, meditative states, memory, and so forth, require an existent object-support.[135]

SVALAKṢAṆA AND THE EPISTEMOLOGICAL SHIFT

All of these reasons offered for the existence of past and future *dharmas* depend upon the basic principle that causal efficacy demands an existent cause. However, the last reason, that is, the requirement of an existent object-support, points to an epistemologically grounded type of causal functioning that was to become dominant from the period of the *vibhāṣā* compendia onward.[136] This epistemological emphasis is evident both in a shift in the terminology used to describe the character of *dharmas* and in the later definitions offered for existence in the abstract. The shift in terminology is indicated by the terms "particular inherent characteristic" (*svalakṣaṇa* 自相) and "generic characteristic" (*sāmānyalakṣaṇa* 共相), which come to be used in conjunction with and, in the case of the particular inherent characteristic, often in place of intrinsic nature (*svabhāva*). These terms do not appear in the canonical Sarvāstivāda Abhidharma texts, but are used in the **Śāriputrābhidharmaśāstra* in connection with the operation of the discrimination of *dharmas* (*dharmapravicaya*),[137] and frequently in the **Āryavasumitrabodhisattvasaṅgītiśāstra*, especially in the context of the arising of perceptual consciousness and cognition.[138] *Lakṣaṇa* appears prominently also in both Dharmaśreṣṭhin's **Abhidharmahṛdaya* and in Upaśānta's commentary, as well as in Dharmatrāta's **Miśrakābhidharmahṛdayaśāstra*, where the particular inherent and generic characteristics are explicitly defined and contrasted.[139]

In the **Mahāvibhāṣā*, the two terms ordinarily occur together in the context of mental faculties such as discrimination (*pravicaya*), views (*dṛṣṭi*), and insight (*prajñā*),[140] and in particular in discussions of the arising and operation of perceptual consciousness. They refer to the various characteristics or aspects of the object that are apprehended in cognition: the particular inherent characteristic is unique to an individual *dharma*, and the generic characteristic is shared by many *dharma*s. The five externally directed varieties of perceptual consciousness such as visual perceptual consciousness, and so forth, apprehend only the particular inherent characteristics of their appropriate, present object-fields, while the sixth variety of mental perceptual consciousness cognizes *dharma*s of all types and all time periods, and hence apprehends both particular inherent and generic characteristics.[141]

The **Mahāvibhāṣā* identifies the particular inherent characteristic with intrinsic nature (*svabhāva* 自性) and the generic characteristic with a "class nature" (同類性 **samānajātīyatva*),[142] but, as in the case of intrinsic nature, there is some ambiguity in determining the scope of each. In general terms, a single *dharma* is marked by many characteristics: that is, every *dharma* is marked by (at least) one particular inherent characteristic reflecting its intrinsic nature and by multiple generic characteristics, which are shared with other *dharma*s and hence signify the larger categories to which it belongs.The distinction between the particular inherent and the generic characteristics thus discriminates levels in the apprehension or discernment of *dharma*s that serve to clarifythe ambiguity encountered in the application of the term *svabhāva* to both individual *dharma*s and to categorial groups.[143] For example, in describing the four fundamental material elements (*mahābhūta*), the **Mahāvibhāṣā* notes that they are marked by the particular inherent characteristics of solidity (*khakkhaṭalakṣaṇa*), and so forth, as well as by the generic characteristic of material form (*rūpalakṣaṇa*), that is, the generic characteristic of the larger material form aggregate in which they are included.[144] However, when the perspective shifts to the level of the aggregates themselves as the salient *dharma*-category, cognition apprehends the particular inherent characteristic of each aggregate and a generic characteristic that spans two or more.[145] This ambiguity in the use of the particular inherent characteristic to refer both to an individual *dharma* and to an aggregate is addressed elsewhere in the **Mahāvibhāṣā*, which explicitly mentions two types of particular inherent characteristics: that of the individual, given thing (事自相 **vastusvalakṣaṇa*, **dravyasvalakṣaṇa*) and that of the sense sphere (處自相 **āyatanasvalakṣaṇa*).[146] These two sets of distinctions – that between particular inherent and generic characteristics and that within the particular inherent characteristic itself – both address the ambiguity inherent in the application of intrinsic nature by formalizing two levels of embedded classification. Both the multiplicity of particular inherent and generic characteristics along with multiple levels of embedding also mirror the multiple perspectives that necessarily accompany all cognition. Thus, the two methods of analytical description either by intrinsic nature (*svabhāva*) or by characteristics (*lakṣaṇa*) are separated by one important difference: whereas intrinsic nature acquires its special significance in the context of exegetical categorization, the starting point for the characteristics lies in perspectivistic cognition. Ontology is a concern for both systems, but the shift in terminology from intrinsic nature to the characteristics reflects a concurrent shift from a category-based abstract ontology to an epistemological ontology this is experientially or cognitively determined.

And indeed, we find in the mature Sarvāstivāda exegesis of Saṅghabhadra, a definition of existence in the abstract that expresses this new epistemological emphasis. For Saṅghabhadra, as for all Sarvāstivādins, existence is causally grounded, but his definition of existence suggests that this causal efficacy is specifically cognitive: "To be an object-field that produces cognition (*buddhi*) is the true characteristic of existence."[147] Such a definition is succinct, and yet sufficiently broad as to include a variety of different modes of existence. Saṅghabhadra presents a typology of existence based upon those in the **Mahāvibhāṣā*, but refined and expanded to express his own further elaboration of the relationship between a *dharma* and its functioning.[148] As in the **Mahāvibhāṣā*, Saṅghabhadra first distinguishes between existence as a real entity (*dravyasat*), or absolute existence (*paramārthasat*), and existence as a provisional designation (*prajñaptisat*), or conventional existence (*saṃvr̥tisat*). The first category of real entities consists of *dharma*s such as material form that produce cognition without depending upon anything else. The second category of provisional designations includes things such as a pot that produce cognition through primary dependence upon *dharma*s, or things such as an army that produce cognition through a secondary dependence, that is, initially upon other provisional designations and then ultimately upon *dharma*s. Provisional designations can be said to exist as causes of cognition, but since they produce cognition only in dependence upon a real entity and are not themselves *dharma*s determined by intrinsic nature, they cannot be said to exist as real entities (*dravyatas*).

Saṅghabhadra's further analyzes real existence (*dravyatas*) in order to clarify the existence and functioning of *dharma*s and defend the real existence of *dharma*s of all three time periods.[149] In this analysis he further refines the notions of intrinsic nature (*svabhāva*) and mode (*bhāva*), and of activity (*kāritra*) and capability (*sāmarthya*), and, thereby, resolves some of the ambiguities noted previously in the discussion of *svabhāva*. That is to say, *dharma*s, which by definition are determined by intrinsic nature (*svabhāva*), are always so determined, whether in the past, present, or future. However, one must distinguish various modes of functioning and hence various modes of existence. A *dharma* can exist as intrinsic nature with activity (*kāritra*), specifically as present, or as intrinsic nature without present activity, that is, as past or future. However, present activity is a subset of a larger category of *dharmic* functioning, which Saṅghabhadra refers to as capability (*sāmarthya*); a *dharma* can exhibit capability in all three time periods. Hence, *dharma*s can exist in different causally functional modes in each of the three time periods: in the present with activity and other capabilities; or in the past or future without activity, but still with various capabilities. Saṅghabhadra refers to these differing modes of existence as *bhāva*.

This model specifying the mechanics of causal functioning and distinguishing modes of existence allows Saṅghabhadra to resolve many problems of earlier Sarvāstivāda analysis. He accepted the descriptive categorization of *dharmas* in terms of intrinsic nature, and his interpretative energies were focused instead on their manner of existence and ontological status: as abstract categories, *dharma*s remain stable in their intrinsic nature, but as existents they change in mode depending upon the various types of causal functioning that they exhibit. Specifically, Saṅghabhadra's clear distinction between activity and capability permitted at least a theoretical resolution of the apparent contradiction between invariant intrinsic nature and impermanent causal functioning as applied to a single *dharma*. A single *dharma* can be apprehended as a category or type, that is, as defined by a single particular inherent characteristic reflecting its invariable identity (*svabhāva*), and yet it can function in many different ways, only one of which, namely activity, must occur when the *dharma* is present. Activity and intrinsic nature are neither identical nor completely different; as a result, the identity of a *dharma* does not change with its transient functioning, nor does variety in functioning entail multiple *dharma*s.[150] Further, for Saṅghabhadra, unconditioned *dharma*s exhibit capability as non-obstructing conditions and as object-supports in the arising of cognition, and therefore, clearly exist. And yet they lack generative activity in producing an effect and hence cannot be described as "present". And finally, for Saṅghabhadra the term *dharma* does not denote a permanent substance, but rather a cognitive category, an objective locus identifiable through cognition. The world exists only as cognized, and the regularities of this cognized world that are evident in the given objects (*dravya*) of our experience are expressed through its constitutive *dharma*s.

Thus, throughout the course of Buddhist scholasticism, the concept of *dharma* persists as an analytical framework, stable enough to enable coherent sectarian debate and elastic enough to allow refinements and further constructions in interaction with other dominant terms and themes drawn from the larger Indian philosophical milieu. For the Sarvāstivādins, reflections about *dharma* came to be dominated by concern for constructing a thoroughgoing system of causal regularities on the basis of an implicit insight into the conditioned nature of phenomena expressed in the early *sūtra*s. And to those familiar with the later history of Buddhist logic and philosophy, it is clear how the progression of Abhidharma thinking about *dharma* from inchoate categorial analysis to the rigorous epistemological ontology of Saṅghabhadra sets the stage for later systematic attempts to dissolve the multiplicity of a causal world into the activity of cognition and consciousness.

NOTES

[1] BURNOUF ([1876]1944: 80).

[2] GEIGER ([1920]1973: 101–228).

[3] For a philological approach, see GEIGER ([1920]1973); a philosophical approach, see STCHERBATSKY ([1923]1970), CONZE (1967: 92–106); an historical approach, see HIRAKAWA (1980, 1988), WATSUJI (1962: 346–389), WARDER (1971), SAKURABE (1969: 41–75), BRONKHORST (1985). For a review of various Western studies of *dhamma*, see CARTER (1978).

[4] Various traditional sources also acknowledge different senses of the term *dharma*. For example, Buddhaghosa in D-a 1: 99; Dhs-a 39; PVVŚ *shang* p. 989c 9–14.

[5] GEIGER ([1920]1973: 80–101). For a review and evaluation of earlier scholarly debates concerning whether *dharma* theory was a part of the original teaching of the sūtras, see von GLASENAPP (1938). Note also the comments of Johannes BRONKHORST (1985: 319): "A final result of this study may be to explain the presence in the Sūtras of a '*dharma*-theory.' The explanation is not that original Buddhism was, or contained, such a '*dharma*-theory;' rather it points to the influence of Abhidharma-like activities long before the completion of the Sūtrapiṭaka."

[6] BRONKHORST (1999b: 19; 1999a: 25).

[7] BRONKHORST (1996: 111–112; 1985: 318).

[8] See *mātṛkā* list I, BRONKHORST (1985: 305–306, 318–319). See also GETHIN (1992: 150).
[9] HIRAKAWA (1990: 46; 1988: 97–101). For a review of prior scholarly interpretations, see HIRAKAWA (1968).
[10] HORNER (1948: 115–116). See also, LAMOTTE ([1958]1988: 23–26).
[11] HALBFASS (1992: 32).
[12] HALBFASS (1992: 34). For an extended discussion of *dharma* in Buddhism, see HALBFASS (1992: 53ff.). In discussing what he terms the "nature-philosophical schools," Erich FRAUWALLNER ([1956]1973: pt.2, 62) locates the origin of *dharma* as an independent entity in its sense as "merit" within the "doctrine of works" or "action as a cosmic force." For Frauwallner's view of the relationship between Buddhism and his category of "nature-philosophical schools," see FRAUWALLNER ([1956]1973: pt.2, 7).
[13] SAKURABE (1969: 45–46).
[14] GETHIN (1992: 151). See also GETHIN (1992: 147–154).
[15] WARDER (1971: 275–276).
[16] WARDER (1971: 288; 1971: 286–288).
[17] WARDER (1971: 289).
[18] See BRONKHORST (1987, 1996, 1999a, 1999b); HOUBEN (1995); FRAUWALLNER ([1956] 1973: pt.2, 79ff.); MATILAL (1985: 269ff., 378ff.).
[19] Johannes BRONKHORST (1987, 1999a, 1999b) has suggested that at least the early stages of Sarvāstivāda *dharma* analysis precede grammatical exegesis. Even though his cautions concerning the difficulty of dating the various textual sources and the complex recensional history of the Sarvāstivāda works are commendable, a final determination of the relative dating of Sarvāstivāda Abhidharma and the grammatical exegesis of Patañjali awaits further evidence.
[20] SCHARF (1996: 23–39, 87–89, 116 (P 1.2.64 vt. 35), 129 (P 1.2.64 vt. 45)); BIARDEAU (1964: 43–63); BRONKHORST (1999a: 76–77).
[21] SCHARF (1996: 23–25 (P 5.1.119, 4.1.3)); MATILAL (1985: 380–386); HALBFASS (1992: 90ff.).
[22] BRONKHORST (1994; 1997).
[23] *Vaiśeṣikasūtra* I.1.15 pp. 32–34. See HALBFASS (1992: 92ff.); MATILAL (1985: 294ff.). For the question of the influence of other traditions, in particular Buddhism, on the origin of Vaiśeṣika, see BRONKHORST (1999a: 25–26; 1996: 119); MATILAL (1985: 378ff.).
[24] *Tattvārthādhigamasūtra* V.29, 30, 38 pp. 97–100. See also HALBFASS (1992: 92ff.); MATILAL (1985: 279–280, 294ff.). The association here of *dravya* with arising, passing away, and stability is remarkably similar to the characterization of conditioned *dharmas* by the set of three conditioning characteristics (*saṃskṛtalakṣaṇa*) as mentioned in Buddhist *sūtras*: namely, arising (*utpāda*), passing away (*vyaya*), and change in continuance (*sthityanyathātva*). Within the middle period of Sarvāstivāda Abhidharma exegesis, the three conditioning characteristics are expanded to four: namely, birth (*jāti*), continuance (*sthiti*), senescence (*jarā*), and desinence (*anityatā*). See COX (1995: 146–158, 305–375); *infra* notes #56, 132, 146.
[25] *Pravacanasāra* II 3, 4 pp. 112–117. See also MATILAL (1985: 279–280).
[26] For an in-depth study of the 37 limbs of enlightenment in Pāli sources, see GETHIN (1992).
[27] S 5.111: . . . *dhammesu paññāya pavicinati pavicarati parivīmaṃsam āpajjati* . . .; cf., with no explicit reference to *prajñā*, SĀ 27 #733 p. 196b21–22. For references using the singular, *taṃ dhammam*, see S 5.331, S 5.68. Rupert GETHIN (1992: 147ff., 168ff.) discusses the difficulty of determining the referents of *dhamma* in the plural as used in the pattern of the mindfulness member of enlightenment (*satisambojjhaṅga*), in contrast to its use in the singular in what GETHIN terms the "process formula." For

passages that associate *dharmapravicaya* with *prajñā* in the context of correct view (*samyagdṛṣṭi*), see M3.72; SĀ 28 #725 p. 203a29ff., 28 #788 p. 204c26ff.
[28] Dhs 11ff.; Vbh 107ff.; Paṭis 119; Paṭis-a 1.95.
[29] SaṅgP 13 p. 423b11ff., 18 p. 440b20ff.; PP (T.1542) 1 p. 693a19, 2 p. 699c20–23; AMVŚ 141 p. 726b23. See also AMVŚ 95 p. 490b9ff., 95 p. 493b7ff. In the definition of the controlling faculty of insight (*prajñendriya*), see ŚAŚ 5 p. 560c26–561a2. In the definition of correct view (*samyagdṛṣṭi*), see ŚAŚ 4 p. 554a15–27; PP (T. 1542) 8 p. 722a9ff. In the definition of *dharmapravicaya* as a member of enlightenment, see ŚAŚ 6 p. 568b10ff., 9 p. 590c6, *passim*; NA 73 p. 735c2–3.
[30] AMVŚ 1 p. 2c23; AKBh.1. 2a p. 2.4; NA 1 p. 329a28ff.
[31] AMVŚ 1 p. 4a12ff., 2 p. 5c23ff.
[32] AMVŚ 1 p. 2c1ff.
[33] AMVŚ 94 p. 487c2–4. For the central role of insight in the Sarvāstivāda path of practice by which defilements are abandoned, see Cox (1992b: 80ff.).
[34] AKV 127.27ff., esp. 30 *ime sāsravā ime 'nāsravāḥ. ime rūpiṇaḥ ime 'rūpiṇa iti*, commenting on the definition of insight (*prajñā*) as *dharmapravicaya* in AKBh 2.24 p. 54.22. Saṅghabhadra (NA 10 p. 384b6–7) offers a slightly different explanation as "discriminating the characteristics of an object-support such as false or true." 簡擇所緣邪正等相。說名爲慧。
[35] AKBh 1.3 p. 2.20ff. Here (NA 1 p. 329c13–14), Saṅghabhadra cites a scriptural passage: "As long as even one *dharma* is not understood, is not completely comprehended, [and in this way] not abandoned, I do not speak of ending suffering." "This passage is cited in the *Abhidharmakośabhāṣya*" 1.15a–b p. 10 25–26: *nā 'ham ekadharmam api anabhijñāyā 'parijñāya duḥkhasyā 'ntakriyām vadāmī 'ti evam aprahāye 'ty uktam*. See SĀ 8 #223 p. 55b7ff.; cf. S 4.18.
[36] DhSk 8 p. 491c18ff. Here, in its comments on *dharmapravicayasambodhyaṅga*, the *Dharmaskandha* resembles an interpretation presented in the *Saṃyuktāgama* (SĀ 27 #713 p. 191b24ff.), which discusses each of the seven members of enlightenment in two aspects, and connects in particular the first three members of enlightenment as stages in a process whereby one first becomes mindful internally and externally (*smṛtisambodhyaṅga*), distinguishes virtuous from unvirtuous *dharmas* (*dharmapravicayasambodhyaṅga*), and exerts oneself to cut off unvirtuous and cultivate virtuous *dharmas* (*vīryasambodhyaṅga*). See also ĀVBSŚ 8 p. 788c7ff. Saṅghabhadra (NA 50 p. 623a15–18) suggests that understanding the distinctions among *dharmas*, such as among those that are favorable, and unfavorable, and giving rise to appropriate effort in abandonment or in cultivation gives the teaching of the Buddha (*dharma*) great utility.
[37] DhSk 5 p. 474c14–17, *passim*; SaṅgP 2 p. 372a19–22 (*samprajanya*), 2 p. 374a19–22 (*dṛṣṭi*), 3 p. 375b19–22 (*vipaśyanā*), 5 p. 387c26ff. (*prajñā*), 16 p. 435a25ff. (*dharmapravicayasambodhyaṅga*), *passim*; AMVŚ 33 p. 172b1–2.
[38] Edward Conze (1967: 97–98) describes a process of "getting *dharmas* into view," which occurs in three steps: (1) differentiation, through which everyday objects are broken up into their constituent factors; (2) depersonalization, through which all reference to "oneself" is eliminated; and (3) evaluation that the *dharmic* view is more accurate than the common sense view.
[39] The set of four trance states (*dhyāna*) is frequently added to the list of 37 in formulaic descriptions of practice. See Bronkhorst (1985: 306); Gethin (1992: 180–182).
[40] Rupert Gethin (1986: 49) suggests that even though each of these three sets is discussed to varying degrees in the *suttas*, the threefold grouping as a unified and exhaustive analytical device only became standard with early Abhidhamma exegesis.
[41] For further discussion of "attribute-*mātṛkās*," see Frauwallner (1995: 5–11).
[42] Wilhelm Halbfass (1992: 48ff.) distinguishes between methods of categorization that are "vertical" – that is, cosmological and diachronic reflecting stages in evolu-

tion, as in the case of Sāṃkhya – and "horizontal" – that is, enumerative and synchronic reflecting the classification of ultimate entities, as in the case of Vaiśeṣika.

[43] DhSk 10 p. 498b12–499c24; PP (T.1542) 8 p. 723a24–c2. For a discussion of the 22 controlling faculties and their development throughout early Sarvāstivāda Abhidharma texts, see SAITŌ (2002). SAITŌ also examines the different orders in which the controlling faculties are enumerated and explores various related doctrinal and historical questions.

[44] For an in-depth study of the development of the *pañcavastuka* and its relation to other taxonomic systems such as the set of five aggregates, see FRAUWALLNER (1995: 135–147).

[45] Tetsurō WATSUJI (1962: 366ff.) discusses the development of the fivefold taxonomy in terms of the application of several abstract distinctions: for example, between the material and the non-material; thought (as the fundamental perceiving organ) and non-thought (including thought concomitants as the object-field of thought); dissociated and not dissociated; conditioned and non-conditioned.

[46] See COX (1995).

[47] See COX (1995: 67–78). Discussing the meaning of *dharma* in the context of Buddhist Abhidharma,Wilhelm HALBFASS (1992: 53–54) states: "Our question is: What is the role of *dharma* as a category of enumeration and classification? What is it that is being enumerated, classified, and identified in the *dharma* lists? But can we determine the meaning of *dharma* as such, regardless of the fact that it is the ultimate unit of enumeration and identification? In a sense, enumeration and identification, or rather enumerability and identifiability, constitute the meaning of *dharma*."

[48] For an interpretation of *dharmas* as "patterns of interconnection," particularly in relation to cognition, see WALDRON (2002: 2–16).

[49] See AMVŚ 31 p. 162b19–20: 復次一切法中唯有涅槃是善是常 。, 73 p. 380b27–28: 復次擇滅涅槃是常是善不變不易 。 生老病死所不能壞是勝義法 。, 8 p. 39c10–12: 問此中所說。當云何通。答涅槃中有常相。若謗無涅槃。亦謗此常相。如指中有四處。若撥無指 。亦撥四處 。See also AKBh 1.48b p.37.3: "Permanent *dharmas* are unconditioned." *nityā dharmā asaṃskṛtāḥ*. AMVŚ 8 p. 38c26–27: 問何謂非常 。答諸有爲法。

[50] For a discussion of the views of permanence and impermanence, see AMVŚ 8 p. 38c25ff.; for the 62 false views presented in the *Brahmajālasutta*, see AMVŚ 199 p. 196b26ff.

[51] For a general discussion of conditioned and unconditioned *dharmas*, see AMVŚ 76 p. 392c7–393a8. See also ĀVBSŚ 1 p. 724c13–20.

[52] See, for example, AMVŚ 79 p. 407a7–8: 復問取蘊爲常非常 。答言非常一刹那後決定不住。For references to scriptural passages that assert the impermanence of conditioned *dharmas*, see AMVŚ 55 p.283c2–5: 如契經說 。苾芻當知。色是無常。諸因諸緣能生色者亦是無常。既是無常因緣所起色云何常。受想行識亦復如是 。, 105 p. 542b10: 觀有爲法變壞無常。For the equivalence of *saṃskṛtadharma* and *saṃskāra*, see AMVŚ 25 p. 127b4. 彼行聲說一切有爲法。; for a discussion of *saṃskāra* and *saṃskṛta* see HIRAKAWA (1988: 106–116).

[53] See the scriptural passages cited in AKBh 6.3 p. 331.5–7, 6.3 p. 331.16, 20–21; AKV 519.24–25; SĀ 17 #473 p. 121a10–13, 17 #474 p. 121a26–27; S 4.216, 220–21.

[54] AMVŚ 193 p. 919b17–18, 199 p. 996c10ff. See also AMVŚ 11 p. 55a22–28. For the model of "hidden" and "manifest," see also Saṅghabhadra's defense of the theory of Dharmatrāta concerning the distinction among *dharmas* of the past, present, and future as based upon a difference in nature or mode of existence (*bhāva*). See *infra* notes #111,117. The *Abhidharmakośabhāṣya* (AKBh 5.26a–b p. 297.4–5) claims that Dharmatrāta' s theory implies a type of transformation (*pariṇāma*) similar to that of the Sāṃkhyas. Saṅghabhadra explains the Sāṃkhya theory of transformation as entailing a permanent intrinsic nature or real entity (體 **svabhāva*,

dravya) that extends through the three time periods in such a way that the *dharma* is hidden and then becomes manifest. Instead, according to Saṅghabhadra, Dharmatrāta claims merely that when *dharmas* pass through the time periods, they differ in mode of existence (性類 *bhāva*), even though they are the same in intrinsic form (體相 **svarūpa*). This position, Saṅghabhadra concludes, is identical to that of Vasumitra. NA 52 p. 631b6–10: 最初執法轉變故應置在數論朋中。今謂不然。非彼尊者說有爲法其體是常。歷三世時法隱法顯。但說諸法行於世時。體相雖同而性類異。此與尊者世友分同。何容判同數論外道。For 體相 see *infra* note #67. The **Miśrakābhidharmahṛdayaśāstra* (MAHS 11 p. 962a1–5) describes Dharmatrāta's view as "transformation Sarvāstivāda" (當知此是轉變薩婆多), but does not overtly criticize it nor does he connect it with the Sāṃkhya position. For the differences in the assessment of Dharmatrāta's theory in these various sources and the possible implications of the connection of Dharmatrāta's theory with "transformation," see Kawamura (1974: 45–47).

[55] See AMVŚ 200 p. 1003c18ff.: 問諸色心等何故非常。答轉變非恒。豈是常住。問寧知轉變不由隱顯而執彼體有生滅耶。In the following section, arguments against the model of the manifestation of a hidden essential character are given by both Vasumitra and a Bhadanta. For a review of references to Bhadanta in the **Mahāvibhāṣā* and the various masters to whom the term can refer, see Yamada (1959; 84, 437–438).

[56] See Cox (1995: 146–158, 305–375). These four conditioning characteristics exist as discrete, real entities that occur together with each *dharma* and include birth (*jāti*), continuance (*sthiti*), senescence (*jarā*), and desinence (*anityatā*). They act as immediately assisting conditions that aid a *dharma* in its function as a predominant, homogeneous cause and enable the arising of a *dharma's* present activity of projecting its own effect. See NA 13 p. 409a2–c8; Cox (1995: 329–333); *supra* note #24, *infra* notes #132, 146.

[57] AMVŚ 76 p. 392c19–29 問有爲無爲是何等義。答若法有生有滅有因有果得有爲相。是有爲義。若法無生無滅無因無果。得無爲相。是無爲義。復次若法依屬因緣和合作用是有爲義。若法不依屬因緣和合作用是無爲義。復次若法爲生所起。爲老所衰。爲無常所滅。是有爲義。與此相違是無爲義。復次若法流轉於世。能取果。有作用分別所緣。是有爲義。與此相違是無爲義。復次若法墮世墮蘊與苦相續。前後變易有下中上是有爲義。與此相違是無爲義。Following this passage (AMVŚ 76 p. 392c29–393a8), four masters give explanations of the distinction between the characteristics of impermanence and permanence. See also AMVŚ 33 p. 171a2–3: 若爾涅槃隨得變易。應無常故不應正理。Yaśomitra (AKV 90.22–23), commenting on AKBh 1.48 b p. 37.3, states: "The restriction is 'only unconditioned [*dharmas*] are permanent.' [They are] permanent due to the absence of passing through the time periods." *asaṃskṛtā eva nityā ity avadhāraṇam. adhvasaṃcārābhāvāt nityāḥ*; AMVŚ 23 p. 116c1–4: 問何故作此論。答爲止他宗顯正義故謂或有執過去未來體非實有。現在雖有而是無爲。爲止彼宗顯過去未來體是實有。現在是有爲世所攝故。, 23 p. 116c8–10: 爲止彼宗顯示緣起是有爲法墮三世故。無無爲法墮在三世。, 38 p.198c12–14: 無爲法生住老無常當言無爲耶有爲耶。答應言無爲法無生住老無常。, 39 p. 203a4–8: 答無爲無有生相合義故不可生。如虛空等。無破因合故不可破。無斷因合故不可斷。無生相合故不可生應知亦爾。生相與彼未嘗合故。and for this last passage in reference to the conditioning characteristic of desinence, see AMVŚ 39 p. 203a17–21.

[58] AMVŚ 75 388b19–389a7.

[59] AMVŚ 75 p. 388c8–10: "Space exists as that non-obstruction or non-resistance within which material form moves, extends, and grows." 如品類足作如是言。云何虛空謂有虛空無障無礙色於中行周遍增長。See also PP (T. 1542) 1 p. 694a29–694b1: 虛空云何。謂體空虛。寬曠無礙。不障色行。; PP (T.1541) 1 p. 628c24–25. This definition of the unconditioned *dharma* space from the *Prakaraṇapāda* resem-

bles the definition proposed later by the **Abhidharmahṛdayaśāstra* and the *Abhidharmakośabhāṣya:* that is, as non-obstruction (*anāvṛti*) that affords room for the movement of material form characterized by resistance. See AKBh 1.5d p. 3.22–23: *tatrā 'kāśam anāvṛtiḥ. anāvaraṇasvabhāvam ākāśaṃ yatra rūpasya gatiḥ*. See also AHŚ 4 p. 831b10–11: 無罣礙之相是名曰虛空。; AHŚ-U 6 p. 866b27–28; MAHŚ 9 p.944a6–7: 無諸障閡相是說爲虛空者 。 謂不障閡種種色 。以有來去等故說虛空。 However, the **Mahāvibhāṣā*'s refusal to endorse this definition and the absence of an alternative suggests that space and very possibly all categories of unconditioned *dharma*s were still being formulated in this middle period of Sarvāstivāda exegesis. For conditioned and unconditioned varieties of space, cf. ŚAŚ 21 p. 663c9ff. For an examination of changes in the interpretation of cessation not resulting from consideration (*apratisaṃkhyānirodha*), see MIYASHITA (1994: 3–4); MIYASHITA (1989).

60 AMVŚ 75 p. 388c13–29.

61 Saṅghabhadra (NA 17 p. 430a14–16) suggests that space can be known through inference on the basis of its function. 謂如眼等。雖不現知。 而由有用 。 比知有體。如是虛空 。 亦有用故 。 比知有體 。 用如前說 。 是故虛空 。 別有實體 。

62 AMVŚ 75 p. 388c16–18:若無虛空一切有物應無容處。既有容受諸有物處知有虛空。

63 AMVŚ 75 p. 388c23–24: 既現見有無障礙處故 。 知虛空決定實有 。無障礙相是虛空故 。See also Yaśomitra's comments (AKV 15.9–12) on AKBh 1.5d p. 3.22.

64 See also MAHŚ 9 p. 944a7–9, where this view is attributed to the Dārṣṭāntikas; VŚ 6 p. 460c23ff., to Dharmatāta; and AVŚ 39 p. 291b13ff., to Buddhadeva. Saṅghabhadra (NA 3 p. 347b6ff.) attributes a similar view to Sthavira (Śrīlāta) and the Dārṣṭāntikas: namely, that space as a material element cannot be distinguished from space as an unconditioned *dharma*, neither of which then exists as a real entity (*dravyatas*). After citing a supporting scriptural passage, Saṅghabhadra suggests that space as an unconditioned *dharma* functions to provide a place for light; the cause (space), which exists as a real entity in intrinsic form, is manifested by means of this effect (the appearance of light). Similar to the arguments by Vasumitra in the **Mahāvibhāṣā* that are cited here, Saṅghabhadra continues (NA 3 p. 347b12–16): "If there were no space, there would be no light. Since there is light, distinctions in material form are grasped by visual perceptual consciousness. Therefore, space exists because it is able to provide a place for light, and so forth. It is proven that space exists as a real entity." 此經意說 。 虛空無爲 。雖無所依 。 而有所作 。謂能容受一切光明。以果顯因。有實體相。虛空無者。應無光明。既有光明。眼識所取。是色差別。故有虛空。以能容受光明等故。實有虛空理極成立。

65 AMVŚ 75 p. 388c 28–29: 評曰應作是說 。 實有虛空非彼不知即謂非有由前教理實有虛空 。See MAHŚ 9 p. 944a9–10; and various views presented in ĀVBSŚ 2 p. 732c16ff.

66 AMVŚ 75 p. 389a1–2: 問若爾虛空有何作用 。 答虛空無爲無有作用 。然此能與種種空界作近增上緣。By the time of the *vibhāṣā* compendia, the Sarvāstivādins had developed a system of six causes and four conditions. The six causes include: the associated cause (*saṃprayuktahetu*); the simultaneous cause (*sahabhūhetu*); the homogeneous cause (*sabhāgahetu*); the omnipresent cause (*sarvatragahetu*); the cause of maturation (*vipākahetu*): and the non-obstructing cause (*kāraṇahetu*). The four conditions include: the causal condition (*hetupratyaya*); the immediately contiguous condition (*samanantarapratyaya*); the object-support condition (*ālambanapratyaya*); and the sovereign condition (*adhipatipratyaya*). See AMVŚ 16 p. 79a16–21 p. 109c25.

67 AMVŚ 75 p. 389a5–7: 若無虛空 。如是展轉因果次第皆不成立 。勿有此失 。是故虛空體相實有不應撥無。 The Sanskrit equivalent of 體相 is uncertain. In the majority of the six occasions that it is used in Xuanzang's translation of the *Abhidharmakośabhāṣya*, it appears to have been added by Xuanzang, and in only two

places does it have a clear equivalent in the Sanskrit edition. The first is AKBh-Xz 2 p. 11c6 (AKBh 1.43d p. 32.14), where its equivalent is *dravya*. 體相 is also used to translate what is probably *dravya* in Saṅghabhadra's paraphrase of Dharmatrāta's theory. (NA 52 p. 631b9) In the statement of Dharmatrāta's view, the *Abhidharmakośabhāṣya* (AKBh 5.26a–b p. 296.10–11) clearly uses *dravya*, and Xuanzang's translation (AKBh-Xz 20 p. 104c3–4; cf. NA 52 p. 631a14) uses the simple term 體. The second place where 體相 has a clear Sanskrit equivalent, AKBh-Xz 4 p. 19c9–10 (AKBh 2.22d p. 53.14–15), is within a view attributed by Yaśomitra (AKV 125.5–7) to the Sautrāntikas. Here, it is equivalent to *svarūpa*, which Yaśomitra glosses with *dravya*; it is contrasted with *bīja*, or latent seed, which Yaśomitra glosses with *śakti*, power, or *sāmarthya*, capability. This sense of 體相 as intrinsic form in contrast to power or capability is also evident in many of the uses of 體相 in the **Mahāvibhāṣā*, where it appears several times in a reference to the Buddha's unique ability to discern the character and activity of *dharma*s. AMVŚ 142 p. 730c12–13: 脇尊者言。佛於諸法了達究竟。善知諸法體相勢用餘不能知。See also AMVŚ 152 p. 775b29–775c1, 129 p. 674c4–5, cf. 129 p. 674c8–10. However, even in these obviously similar passages, the Chinese terms used for "character" and "activity" are not identical indicating the difficulty in securely determining Sanskrit equivalents even in the case of Xuanzang's Chinese translations. The equivalent *svarūpa* is also suggested by several passages in Saṅghabhadra's **Nyāyānusāra*, for which there is a close analogue in the *Tattvasaṃgrahapañjikā* (TSP #1803–4 p. 620). See, for example, NA 50 p.625a20ff., 52 p. 631c25ff., 52 p. 632a4ff., 53 p. 636a29ff. For discussions of 體相 see Katō (1985: 497); Aohara (1986b: 35); Fukuda (1988: 58–61).

68 AMVŚ 21 p. 107b6, 21 p. 108c26–27, 21 p. 109a29.

69 See AMVŚ 20 p. 103c23–25, 21 p. 105c13–14, 21 p. 105c17–20. For two types of non-obstructing causes, the "predominant" (*pradhāna*) or generative, and the simple non-obstructing, see AKBh 2.50a p. 82.25ff., 2.56b p. 94.22ff.; AKV 222.2ff. For *ālambanapratyaya* as non-generative, see AKBh 5.27c p. 299.18ff.; AKV 474.10ff. For unconditioned *dharma*s as being without a cause or an effect, see AKBh 2.55d p. 91.5ff.; AKV 216.23ff.

70 AHŚ-U 1 p. 834a2–3: 法者持也。持於自性。; MAHŚ 1 p. 870c5. See also PVVŚ *shang* p. 989c13–14; Dhs-a 39. Dharmaśreṣthin's **Abhidharmahṛdaya* (AHŚ 1 p. 809a9ff, 1 p. 809a19–23) does not contain this definition, but it does begin with a discussion about the characteristics of *dharmas* (法相). These include not only characteristics such as the solidity of earth, but also the characteristics of impermanence, suffering, and non-self. The *Abhidharmakośabhāṣya* (AKBh 1.2b p. 2.10) uses *svalakṣaṇa* in place of *svabhāva* in Upaśānta's definition: "Etymologically, '*dharma*' comes from upholding a particular inherent characteristic." *nirvacanaṃ tu svalakṣaṇadhāraṇād dharmaḥ*. See also AKBh-Xz 1 p. 1b8–9; AKBh-P 1 p. 162a8. Yaśomitra's comments here (AKV 9.18–19, 9.22–23) resemble the treatment of characteristics by Dharmaśreṣthin, but Yaśomitra distinguishes between particular inherent characteristics (*svalakṣaṇa*), such as solidity in the case of earth, and generic characteristics (*sāmānyalakṣaṇa*), such as impermanence and suffering in the case of all conditioned *dharma*s: *dharmalakṣaṇam ve 'ti svasāmānyalakṣaṇam khakkhaṭalakṣaṇaḥ pṛthivīdhātur anityaṃ duḥkham ity evam ādi*. Cf. PVVŚ *shang* p. 989b17–18; MAHŚ 1 p. 870c7–10. This definition of *dharma* does not appear in either Saṅghabhadra's **Nyāyānusāra* or **Abhidharmasamayapradīpikā* (T.1563).

71 AMVŚ 112 p. 580b28–c1: 自性能持自體不失故說為根。如是無為能持自體故說為根。亦無有過。This definition of *mūla* occurs at the end of a section discussing the three unvirtuous roots (*akuśalamūla*) of lust (*rāga*), hatred (*dveṣa*), and delusion (*moha*).

[72] AMVŚ 71 p. 367c24–25, esp. p. 368a16–17: 任持故名界者 。謂此諸界任持自性。AVŚ 38 p. 279c29–280a1; VŚ 5 p. 448c21–448c26. This discussion of the meaning of *dhātu* occurs after a general introduction to a section on the 18 elements (*dhātu*).

[73] The **Abhidharmavibhāṣāśāstra* and the **Mahavibhāṣā* cite inclusion (*saṃgraha*) as one among a number of fundamental methods or topics (14 or seven), by which one can acquire correct understanding of the meaning of Abhidharma. These methods constitute a type of attribute matrix by which the nature and function of *dharma*s can be specified and, thereby, clarified. See AVŚ 12 p. 92a18–26; AMVŚ 23 p. 116b16–25; cf. VŚ 1 p. 417a15–16.

[74] See JP 3 p. 929b13ff.; AMVŚ 46 p. 236b18ff. The 16 categories are: three fetters (*saṃyojana*), three unvirtuous roots (*akuśalamūla*), three fluxes (*āsrava*), four floods (*ogha*), four connections (*yoga*), four attachments (*grahaṇa*), four ties to the body (*kāyagrantha*), five hindrances (*nivaraṇa*), five fetters (*saṃyojana*), five fetters belonging to the lower realm (*avarabhāgīyasaṃyojana*), five fetters belonging to the upper realm (*ūrdhvabhāgīyasaṃyojana*), five views (*dṛṣṭi*), the group of six desires (*kāmakāya*), seven contaminants (*anuśaya*), nine fetters (*saṃyojana*), and 98 contaminants (*anuśaya*).

[75] AMVŚ 59 p. 306b10ff.

[76] AMVŚ 59 p. 306b12–14: 答爲止他宗顯正義故。謂或有說。諸法攝他性非自性攝。如分別論者。彼依假名契經。及依世俗言論故作是說。Cf. AMVŚ 106 p. 550a7–11, 154p. 785b2–4,167 p. 841b19–22,197 p. 985b5–11. See also AHŚ 1 p. 810b6ff.; AHŚ-U 1 p. 836b11ff.; MAHŚ 1 p. 880b10ff.; AKBh 1.18 p.12.4ff.

[77] AMVŚ 59 p. 306c2–6.

[78] AMVŚ 59 p. 307a9–13.

[79] AMVŚ 59 p. 308 20–28: 問云何諸法各攝自性 。 答自性於自性是有是實是可得故說名爲攝 。 自性於自性非異非外非離非別恒不空故說名爲攝 。自性於自性非不已有非不今有非不當有故名爲攝 。自性於自性非增非減故名爲攝 。諸法自性攝自性時 。 非如以手取食指捻衣等 。 然彼各各執持自體令不散 。然彼各各執持自體令不散壞故名爲攝。於執持義立以攝名。故勝義攝唯攝自性。

[80] For the periodization of Sarvāstivāda Abhidharma texts, see Cox (1992b, 1995: 29–37).

[81] At least in its bare listing of basic categories, if not in its detailed application of the method of inclusion, the **Śāriputrābhidharmaśāstra* can be dated to the early period of northern Indian Abhidharma texts. See YAMADA (1959: 69–81); *supra* note #80.

[82] ŚAŚ 21–22 p. 661a15–671b23.

[83] ŚAŚ 21 p. 666c19–20: 眼入法幾陰界入攝 。問何等法 。問眼入法 。除餘法 。除何等法。非眼入法。

[84] In Xuanzang's translations of later Sarvāstivāda texts, the translation 自性 is frequently used for *svabhāva*, while in his translation of the early Sarvāstivāda canonical texts it usually appears with the sense of "oneself" (*ātman*). Other possible equivalents for *svabhāva* include: 自體, which in the earlier texts is usually used in a context that suggests *ātmabhāva*; 性, frequently used as an equivalent for the abstract *-tva* or *-tā* suffixes; and 體, which, when used alone, can be used as an equivalent of *bhāva*, and not *svabhāva*.

[85] For a prominent exception to this generalization, where the term 自性 is used in an early canonical text with the sense of "intrinsic nature" (*svabhāva*), see the *Jñānaprasthāna* (JP 2 p. 923b19ff., esp. p. 923c17–24): 又涅槃不應有學有無學有非學非無學。若如是者 。應成二分諸法 。不決定故 。應有雜亂 。是則不應施設諸法性相決定 。佛亦不說涅槃有學有無學性。以涅槃恒是非學非無學諸法決定。無有雜亂。恒住自性 。不捨自性。涅槃常住 。無有變易 。是故涅槃但應言非學非無學 。See the lengthy

treatment of this issue concerning the nature of *nirvāṇa* in AMVŚ 33 p. 168b23ff.; *infra* note #91.

[86] For the term *pariniṣpanna* used in connection with the intrinsic nature (*svabhāva*) or particular inherent characteristic (*svalakṣaṇa*) of a *dharma*, see YBh 122. 14ff. (YBh-Xz 6 p. 304b26–27): "The past exists, the future exists, determined by a characteristic, just like the present; [they] exist as real entities, and not as provisional designations." *asty atītaṃ. asty anāgataṃ. lakṣaṇena pariniṣpannaṃ. yathai 'va pratyutpannaṃ. dravyasat. na prajñaptisat*; and in the same section, YBh 125.4–7 (YBh-Xz 6 p. 304b24ff., esp. 6 p.304c5ff.): "That *dharma* which is established by a characteristic is determined by that [characteristic]." *yo dharmo yena lakṣaṇena vyavasthitaḥ [sa] tena pariniṣpannaḥ*. See also an early (c. 1st cent. CE) Gāndhārī Abhidharma manuscript, Cox (forthcoming a: lines 78–80); Cox (forthcoming b). For references in the **Mahāvibhāṣā*, see AMVŚ 30 p. 154b18–20: 以一切法自性定故諸有爲法皆有勝劣自體決定。, 23 p. 116c19–20: 謂五蘊等自相決定。This passage is commenting specifically on the Vibhajyavāda assertion that dependent origination (*pratītyasamutpāda*) is unconditioned, which they support through a scriptural reference (AMVŚ 23 p. 116c6–8): "Whether Tathāgatas arise or do not arise, this principle is established – the establishment of *dharma*s, the fixedness of *dharma*s, namely, the process of conditioning, and it is this [process of conditioning] that the Tathāgata awakens to and comprehends." 如來出世若不出世法住法性。佛自等覺爲他開示乃至廣說。See S 2.25: *uppādā vā tathāgatānam anuppādā vā tathāgatānaṃ, ṭhitā va sā dhātu dhammaṭṭhitatā dhammaniyāmatā idappaccayatā. taṃ tathāgato abhisambujjhati abhisameti*. See also SĀ 12 #296 p. 84b16-18, p. 84b19–21; Kv 319ff. The **Mahāvibhāṣā* responds (AMVŚ 23 p.116c11–15) that this *sūtra* passage does not state that dependent origination is unconditioned, but rather that the cause and effect relationships that it describes are determined: namely, that ignorance is determined as the cause of motivations, and so on. The **Mahāvibhāṣā* explains (AMVŚ 23 p. 116c14): "The phrase 'the establishment of *dharmas*, the fixedness of *dharmas*,' means 'determination,' and not 'unconditioned'." 法住法性是決定義。非無爲義。; and (AMVŚ 23 p. 116c19–20) "Just as the five aggregates are determined in their particular inherent characteristics, so also dependent origination is determined in the relation between cause and effect." 謂五蘊等自相決定說如是言。緣起亦依因果決定。It is probable that this passage uses 決定 to refer to *sthitatā* or to *niyāmatā* as found within the *sūtra* passage, but as suggested in the final statement concerning the determination of the five aggregates, its sense would appear to be equivalent to *pariniṣpanna*. A connection between *sthitatā* and *pariniṣpanna* is also suggested by a passage in the *Kathāvatthu* (Kv 459ff.) that discusses *ṭhitatā* in terms of *parinipphannatā*. See also AMVŚ 23 p. 118b20–22: 集異門論及法蘊論俱作是說 。 若無明生行 。 決定安住不雜亂者 。 名緣起法 。 亦名緣已生法。.

[87] AMVŚ 74 p. 381b3–6: 此我所依立爲內處 。 我所緣者立爲外處 。 然內外名非圓成實 。 謂於我是內者於他名外 。 於我是外者於他名內故 。 而且依一立內外非名非不決定 。, 113 p. 588a22–24: 若雜穢語業道增時 。 一切外物時候乖變。速疾磨滅多不成實。, *passim*; in reference to the characteristics of non-self (*anātman*) and impermanence (*anityatā*), see AMVŚ 9 p. 45a22ff.

[88] The Pāli equivalent *parinipphanna* appears in the *Kathāvatthu*, but otherwise is used only in the commentarial literature. For the text proponent of the *Kathāvatthu*, *pariniphanna* apparently has the connotation of being invariably established (Kv 511 ff.), particularly in the context of being conditioned as in the case of an actually occurring *dharma* (Kv 459ff., 626ff.). Unfortunately, the sense of the term intended by the opponents is uncertain.

[89] The need to clearly discriminate *dharmas* in order to avoid their confusion, especially in the context of inclusion, is a frequent issue in the **Āryavasumitrabo-*

dhisattvasaṅgītiśāstra. See ĀVBSŚ 1 p. 724a21–25: 尊作是說。當言無量相。設一相者。法則有壞。法則有亂。此無有定處。如此諸法而有自相。猶如此有爲法不可得作無爲法。無爲法亦不可得作有爲法。; ĀVBSŚ 3 p. 737c22ff. esp.p. 737c22f. *passim*. See also PVVŚ *shang* p. 989b28–c1: 有說此論略顯諸法體類差別不相雜亂攝一切法。故唯說五。

[90]AMVŚ 33 p. 169a9–11 彼作是說。涅槃自性有三種相。一學二無學三非學非無學。Similarly, the Vibhajyavādins contend (AMVŚ 33 p. 169a29–b1): "*Nirvāṇa* is subject to modification and is not determined; it is possible that it has three types." 答如是者是分別論者答。我說涅槃轉變不定可有三種故言如是。See also AMVŚ 33 p. 169c7ff.

[91]AMVŚ 33 p. 169a14–15: 如何涅槃三得得故便有三相。一法不應有三種體相即體故。

[92]AMVŚ 33 p. 171a22–24: 若一涅槃隨得轉變。則一切法皆應不定。若不決定應有雜亂。若有雜亂不應施設常無常等性相決定。

[93]AMVŚ 33 p. 171a29–b2: 以涅槃恒是非學非無學。諸法決定無有雜亂。恒住自性不捨自性。See also JP 2 p. 923c21–23.

[94]AMVŚ 76 p. 394b23–24: 謂一切法已有自性本來各住自體相故。See also VK 12 p. 589c27–28, *passim*; JP 2 p. 923c21–23; AHŚ 1 p. 810b8; AHŚ-U 1 p. 836b13ff.; MAHŚ 1 p. 880b12ff.

[95]AMVŚ 52 p. 272a21–22: 自體在者。謂一切法各住自體自我自物自相自分自本性中。For other references to this or similar formulaic lists, see AMVŚ 1 p. 4a10–11, 6 p. 29c23, 23 p. 117c23–24, 39 p. 200a21–22, 46 p. 237c9–10, 71 p. 367c20, 73 p. 379a10, 76 p. 393c5–6, *passim*; PVVŚ *shang* p. 990b13–14.

[96]AMVŚ 76 p. 393c4–6: 問如是三世以何爲自性。答以一切有爲法爲自性。如說自性。我物自體相分本性應知亦爾。已說自性。

[97]See AMVŚ 76 p. 393a11–15, for the view of the Dārṣṭāntikas and the Vibhajyavādins, who claim that the time periods and conditioned forces are different: "The nature of the time periods is permanent (*nitya*) and the nature of conditioned forces is impermanent (*anitya*). When conditioned forces pass through the [three] time periods, it is like fruit in containers, which come out of one container and enter another container, or like a number of people, who come out of one house and enter another house. Conditioned forces are just like this: [they] enter the present time period from the future time period and enter the past time period from the present time period." 如譬喻者分別論師。彼作是說。世體是常行體無常。行行世時如器中果。從此器出轉入彼器。亦如多人從此舍出轉入彼舍。諸行亦爾。從未來世入現在世。從現在世入過去世。

[98]For *svabhāva* as applied to the aggregates (*skandha*), see AMVŚ 74 p. 383c12–15, 75 p. 386c10–12, 112 p. 579a13–14; to the elements (*dhātu*), see AMVŚ 71 p. 367c13–15, 71 p. 367c19–21, 71 p. 368a16–17; to the sense spheres (*āyatana*), see AMVŚ 73 p. 378c29ff., esp. p. 379a9–11.

[99] AMVŚ 74 p. 383c15ff., esp p. 383c29ff. See also MAHŚ 1 p. 874a24ff.

[100] AMVŚ 74 p. 384a12–14: 雖相去遠以相同故合立色蘊乃至識蘊無量剎那雖相去遠。而相同故合立識蘊。

[101] Quoted in AKBh 1.20a–b p. 14.5–7.

[102] AMVŚ 74 p. 384a14–25.

[103] AKBh 1.20a–b p. 13.24–25.

[104] AKBh 1.18d p. 12.14–15: *cakśurindriyaṃ rūpaskandhena cakṣurāyatanadhātubhyāṃ ca duḥkhasamudayasatyābhyāṃ ca saṃgṛhītam. tatsvabhāvatvāt*. See PP (T.1542) 10 p. 732a6; AMVŚ 69 p. 358b8-11. In commenting on this passage, Yaśomitra (AKV 41.10ff.) explains that the smaller is to be included within the larger, and not the larger within the smaller. Hence, the smaller category of the visual controlling faculty, which constitutes merely one part of the material form aggregate,

is to be included within the larger category of the material form aggregate, which includes all varieties of material form. Yaśomitra explains that such inclusion based upon intrinsic nature is absolute (*pāramārthika*), and not conventional or consensual (*sāṃketika*). In the **Mahāvibhāṣā*, individual *dharma*s are frequently specified through this method of inclusion in multiple categorial groups. See, for example, AMVŚ 1 p. 2c 23–25, where inclusion by intrinsic nature is applied to Abhidharma. See also AMVŚ 15 p. 74a23–24, 109 p. 619a9–14, 173 p. 872b9ff.

105 AKBh 1.20a–b p. 13.4ff., esp. p. 13.25ff.; AKV 45. 13ff. For a discussion of the controversy in the *Abhidharmakośabhāṣya* concerning the ontological status of aggregates, sense spheres, and elements and the implications of this controversy for an epistemologically based ontology, see NISHI (1975a: 503ff.); KATŌ (1989: 173–183).

106 For further discussion of levels of intrinsic nature, see NISHI (1975b: 453ff.); TSUKINOKI (1975: 274–278); KATŌ (1989: 173–176).

107 See HALBFASS (1992: 139ff.). for a discussion of the relationship between categoriology and ontology, specifically in the case of Vaiśeṣika.

108 The most likely equivalents for *bhāva* in these early texts are 性, 類, or 體. However, 性 is frequently also used for the abstract suffixes *-tva* or *-tā*, and 類, for *jāti* or *prakāra*, etc. The term 體 most often appears in the compound 自體, regularly used to render *ātmabhāva*, but it is also occasionally used to render *-bhāva* in compound final position with other nouns.

109 For *bhāva* here, I have chosen the intentionally ambiguous translation, "state of being." For examples within the Pāli Abhidhamma texts (Dhs 143; Vbh122), see *itthattaṃ iithibhāva*, "femaleness, the state of being female," and *purisattaṃ purisabhāva*, "maleness, the state of being male." The analogous passage in the *Dharmaskandha* (DhSk 10 p. 498a22 and 26), contains the two terms 女體 and 女性, but it is not certain which is equivalent to *-bhāva* and which indicates the abstract suffix *-tva*. Cf. *supra* note #84, and *infra* notes #115, 116, 117. For a similar construction with *-ttaṃ* and *-bhāva*, see Dhs 177. Further, the compound *paguṇabhāva*, "state of being familiar with," occurs in the *Dhammasaṅgaṇī* (Dhs 15), in a triad with *paguṇatā* and *paguṇattaṃ*, all of which are used to gloss the abstract form, *pāguññatā*. For similar series, see Dhs 15, 67, 144, 153, 166; Vbh 82. In these cases, the compound-final form *-bhāva* is clearly used together with other abstract forms and hence likely carries the abstract sense of "state," but also probably connotes existence in the sense, "state of being." Aside from the frequently occurring term *attabhāva,* or "personal identity," *bhāva* appears rarely in non-Abhidhamma, Pāli cononical literature. The common set phrase, *anabhāvaṃ gamete*, "one sends to non-existence," is an exception in which *bhāva/abhāva* clearly carry the nuance of "existence," as for example in M 1.11; similarly, the compound *bhiyyobhāva*, "state of being more" or "increase," for example in D 2.313. In the Pāli commentarial literature, *bhāva* comes to be used very frequently both alone and in compound-final position.

110 Kv 119ff.

111 Kv 120: *paccuppannaṃ rūpaṃ nirujjhamānaṃ paccuppannabhāvaṃ jahatī'ti. āmantā. rūpabhāvaṃ jahatī 'ti. na h' evaṃ vattabbe*. The view of the opponent implied by this criticism resembles the theory of the master Dharmatrāta concerning the distinction among *dharma*s of the three time periods (AKBh 5.26a-b p. 296. 10–15): namely, that *dharma*s of the three time periods are distinguished "due to a difference in *bhāva* (*bhāvānyathātva*), and not due to a difference as real entities (*dravyānyathātva*) ... In this way, when *dharma*s enter the present time period from the future time period, even though they abandon [their] nature as future and attain [their] nature as present, they neither attain nor abandon [their] nature as real entities (體 *dravyabhāva*). Further, when *dharma*s enter the past time period from the present time period, even though they abandon [their] nature as present and attain [their]

nature as past, they neither attain nor abandon [their] nature as real entities." *...bhāvānyathātvaṃ bhavati na dravyānyathātvam...evam dharmo 'py' anāgatād adhvanaḥ pratyutpannam adhvānam āgacchann anāgatabhāvaṃ jahāti na dravyabhāvam. evam pratyutpannād atītam adhvānaṃ gacchan pratyutpannabhāvaṃ jahāti na dravyabhāvam iti.* See also AMVŚ 77 p. 396a13–20; AVŚ 40 p. 295c8–12; VŚ 7 p. 466b8–12.

[112] Kv 120–121: *rūpaṃ rūpabhāvaṃ na jahatī 'ti. āmantā. rūpaṃ niccaṃ dhuvaṃ sassataṃ avipariṇāmadhamman ti. na h' evaṃ vattabbe... hañci rūpaṃ aniccaṃ-pe-vipariṇāmadhammaṃ no vata re vattabbe rūpaṃ rūpabhāvaṃ na jahatī 'ti.*

[113] See SaṅgP 11 p. 412a2–4: 云何色蘊。答諸所有色。若過去若未來若現在。若內若外若麁若細。若劣若勝。若遠若近。如是一切略爲一聚說名色蘊。For analogous descriptions of the other aggregates, see SaṅgP 11 p. 412c5ff.; of the three time periods, see SaṅgP 3 p. 387c12ff.

[114] SaṅgP 11 p. 412a19–22: 云何過去色。答若色已起已等起。已生已等生。已轉已現轉。已聚集已出現。落謝過去盡滅離變。過去性過去類過去世攝。是名過去色。For an analogous passage, see PP (T.1542) 6 p. 717b20–24.

[115] Katō (1985: 501–504). To support his interpretation of *bhāva*, Katō also cites passages from the *Prakaraṇapāda* that define various *dharmas* using the term 類 (PP (T.1542) 2 p. 699c8ff., 3 p. 700a16–17, 3 p. 702a5ff.), as well as formulaic definitions of the elements, sense spheres, and perceptual consciousness in terms of three types: that is, those that have functioned, are functioning, or will function as past, present, or future. See SaṅgP 15 p. 492a6–7, 12 p. 492a11–12; DhSk 10 p. 498b27–499a22; PP (T.1542) 2 p. 699a3–699b10, 701a3–5, 8 p. 723a26–29; VK 12 p. 588c12–589a16.

[116] See Cox (forthcoming a: lines 68 and 123–127). Reconstructed Gāndhārī text, line 127: *bhavehi{*ru}poṃ asti nasti {*tra}e {*ru}poṃ di*° This Gāndhārī manuscript also provides evidence for a distinction in use between *bhāva* and *svabhāva*. In one passage explicating the meaning of the phrase "everything exists" (Gāndhārī = G *sarvam asti*) (lines 71–75), the text states that "the state of being a householder exists in the past and future" (G *adidaanagada grihibhava asti*), and so also the state of being a monastery attendant (G *aramiyabhava*), and so forth. Here, *bhāva* (G *bhava*) is used where the issue is one of the existence of these various *dharmas* as past or future. The following passage (lines 75–82) uses *svabhāva* (G *svabhava*) with *pariniṣpanna* (G *parinipana*) to clarify the process by which the various categories of *dharmas* are to be determined and makes the point that categories are discriminated from one another on the basis of intrinsic nature. See Cox (forthcoming b).

[117] The ambiguity in the term *bhāva*, even at the time of the **Mahāvibhāṣā*, is apparent in the criticism of Dharmatrāta's theory of the difference among *dharmas* of the three time periods. See *supra* notes #54, 67,111. For Dharmatrāta himself, *dharmas* in the three time periods are not different as real entities (*dravya*), but differ only in *bhāva*. The * *Mahāvibhāṣā* (AMVŚ 77 p. 396b18–22) criticizes his interpretation, noting that Dharmatrāta would have to explain "what this 'state of being' (類 *bhāva*) is apart from a *dharma's* 'intrinsic nature' (自性 *svabhāva*)." 說類異者。離法自性說何爲類故亦非理。This criticism implies first that, at least for the arbiter of the **Mahāvibhāṣā*, *dravya* is equivalent to *svabhāva*, and second that *bhāva* and *svabhāva*, are so close in meaning that it would be unreasonable to suggest that a *dharma* can be different in one, and not in the other. The assumed identity of *bhāva* and *svabhāva* is also clearly indicated by the, critical verse that Vasubandhu levies against the position that "everything exists" (AKBh 5.27c p. 298.21–22): "Intrinsic nature always exists, and yet the mode of existence is not admitted to be permanent. Further, it is not said that mode of existence is something other than intrinsic nature. [This is an] act [only of] of a god." *svabhāvaḥ sarvadā cā 'sti bhāvo nityaś ca neṣyate na ca svabhāvād bhāvo" nyo vyaktam īśvaraceṣṭitam.* See also AKV 472.25ff.; NA 52 p. 633c14ff. Despite the criticism of the

*Mahāvibhāṣā it is uncertain what Dharmatrāta himself intended through his use of the term *bhāva* and precisely how he would have distinguished *bhāva* from *dravya* or *svabhāva*. For an interpretation of the possible motivations underlying Dharmatrāta's use of the term *bhāva*, see Katō (1985: 495–497).

[118]See Aohara (1986b: 34–37); Aohara (1986a: 767–768); Fukuda (1988: 58ff.); Miyashita (1994: 7–8).

[119]AMVŚ 9 p. 42a24–42b4: "Concerning existence, there are those who claim it is of two types: existence as a real entity (實物有 *dravyasat*), as in the case of the aggregates, elements, and so forth; and existence as a provisional designation (施設有 *prajñaptisat*), as in the case of a man, or woman, and so forth. There are those who claim it is of three types: relative existence (相待有), in which a given thing exists relative to one thing and does not exist relative to another; spatially dependent (or contextual) existence (和合有), in which a given thing exists in one place and does not exist in another; and temporally dependent existence (時分有), in which a given thing exists at one time and does not exist at another. There are those who claim it is of five types: nominal existence (名有), as in the case of hair on a tortoise, a horn on a rabbit, sky–garlands, and so forth; real existence (實有), as in the case of all *dharma*s, each of which is established in its intrinsic nature; provisional existence (假有), as in the case of a pot, a cloth, and so forth; existence as a collocation (和合有), as in the case of a collocation of aggregates that is provisionally designated as a person; and relative existence (相待有), as in the case of this and that shore, long and short, and so forth." 然諸有者。有說二種。一實物有。謂蘊界等。二施設有。謂男女等。有說三種。一相待有。謂如是事。待此故有。待彼故無。二和合有。謂如是事。在此處有在彼處無。三時分有。謂如是事。此時分有彼時分無。有說五種。一名有。謂龜毛兔角空花鬘等。二實有。謂一切法各住自性。三假有。謂瓶衣車乘軍林舍等。四和合有。謂於諸蘊和合施設補特伽羅五相待有。謂此彼岸長短事等。The **Abhidharmavibhāṣāśāstra* (AVS 4 p. 30c20–28) gives only the twofold and threefold typologies of existence, and lists them together with a typology of objects of repudiation (**apavāda*) given in the **Mahāvibhāṣā* within the previous section (AMVŚ 9 p. 41c24–49a1).

[120] Such discussions occur frequently in the **Mahāvibhāṣā*, usually with the number of *dharma*–categories exceeding the number of *dravyas*. See AMVŚ 48 p. 250b13ff. (where the number of *dravyas* exceeds the number of *dharma*–categories), 63 p. 325c16ff., 79 p. 408c13ff., 80 p. 412a26ff. For the discussion of the 37 limbs of enlightenment (*bodhipakṣyadharma*), see AHŚ 4 p. 828a29ff.; AHŚ-U 5 p. 862b26ff.; MAHŚ 8 p. 938a20ff.; AMVŚ 96 496a22ff.; AKBh 6.67c–d p. 383.5ff.

[121] AMVŚ 71 p. 367a28ff. The eighteen elements (*dhātu*) include the sets of six sense organs (*indriya*), consisting of the five externally directed sense organs and the mind, their six corresponding object-fields (*viṣaya*), and the six varieties of perceptual consciousness (*vijñāna*) that the organs and object-fields produce. See AMVŚ 71 p. 366a14ff.; AKBh 1.17c–d p. 11.26ff.

[122] Despite this reduction in the number of *dharma*s to either 12 or 17 *dravyas*, the traditional set of 18 categories is explained through the application of three criteria (AMVŚ 71 p. 367b6ff.): that is, the basis (*āśraya*), which yields the six sense organs; that which is dependent upon the basis (*āśrita*), which yields the six varieties of perceptual consciousness; and the object-field (*viṣaya*), which yields the six objects. An alternative view is proposed by the master Vāmalabdha (AMVŚ 71 p. 367c13ff.) who maintains that the number 18 can be explained on the basis of four criteria: intrinsic nature; basis; that which is dependent upon the basis; and the distinction among the aggregates. For Vāmalabdha, see Kimura (1937: 221); Yamada (1959: 84).

[123] AMVŚ 142 p. 730a29–730c5.

[124] A final example is significant because it concerns categories of *dharma*s included within the fivefold taxonomy (*pañcavastuka*) of 75 *dharma*s, which came to be rec-

ognized in the later commentarial tradition as the standard listing of *dharma*-categories that exist as real entities determined by intrinsic nature. In discussing two groups of mental concomitants (*caitasika*), namely, the 10 ubiquitous (*mahābhūmika*) and 10 ubiquitous, defiled (*kleśamahābhūmika*) *dharma*s, the **Mahāvibhāṣā* (AMVŚ 42 p. 220a7ff.) observes that even though these 20 categories have separate names, as *dravya* there are only 15 because five of the ubiquitous defiled *dharma*s can be identified with five *dharma*s among the ubiquitous group. As *dharma*-categories within the fivefold taxonomy, these 20 are recognized as discrete, and yet certain *dharma*s can be identified in intrinsic nature; hence, as *dravya*, that is, as they actually occur or as real entities, there are only 15.

125 See Nishi (1975b: 439ff.).

126 AMVŚ 196 p. 982b4–6 : 問何故作此論。答爲止愚於因緣法執因緣性非實有者意。顯因緣法體性實有故作斯論。 See also AMVŚ 10 p. 47a28–47b1, 16p. 79a19–21, 107p. 555a2–4, 131 p. 680b26ff., 136 p. 702b13–15, 137 p. 709a28–709b1, 146 p. 747a7–8, 165 p. 833a23–26.

127 AMVŚ 55 p. 283a24ff. See *supra* note #66.

128 AMVŚ 71 p. 367b27ff., p. 368a20ff., esp. p. 368b16–20. The classic example that is used in arguments on this point is that of a present, partially homogeneous (*tatsabhāga*) visual sense organ whose visual functioning is for some reason obstructed, but is nonetheless able to function as a cause in producing a visual sense organ in the next moment. See *infra* note #132. For the example of fire, see NA 14 p. 410c8–11.

129 AMVŚ 21 p. 108c21ff., esp. p. 109a 18–20. See also AMVŚ 21 p. 105b23ff., esp. p. 105c9–13, 55 p.283b25ff.

130 AMVŚ 21 p. 108c6ff. See also AMVŚ 18 p. 89b9ff., 47 p. 246a24ff., 76 p. 394a4–21, 119 p. 618c24ff.

131 NA 14 p. 410a3ff., 18 p. 437c6ff., 50 p. 621c28ff., 52 p. 631c5ff.

132 AMVŚ 76 p. 393c26ff. See AKBh 5.26d p. 297.14ff.; NA 14 p. 410a1ff., 19 p. 447a10ff., 52 p. 631c8ff. This distinction between activity and capability developed by Saṅghabhadra, is less explicit though implied at certain points in the **Mahāvibhāṣā*. The **Mahāvibhāṣā* regularly uses 作用 (**kāritra*) in discussing a *dharma*'s present functioning. See AMVŚ 12 p. 57b4–8, 17 p. 87b19–25, 21 p. 105a6ff., 76 p. 393c13–16. 功能 (**sāmarthya, vyāpāra*), which is used less frequently, at times appears to be synonymous with 作用 (**kāritra*), but occasionally would appear to be distinguished from it, although the distinction is not specified as it will later be by Saṅghabhadra. See AMVŚ 21 p. 105a17, 22 p. 113a28ff., 93 p. 480a26ff. In one passage on the conditioning characteristics of conditioned *dharma*s (*saṃskṛtalakṣaṇa*), the **Mahāvibhāṣā* presents two typologies of modification (**vipariṇāma*): one distinguishes between modification in intrinsic nature and modification in activity (作用 **kāritra*), and the other between modification in intrinsic nature and modification in capability (功能 **sāmarthya*) . Whereas in both cases *dharma*s are said to lack modification in intrinsic nature, which does not change, they are subject to modification in both activity and capability, which are distinguished as follows: modification in activity means that a *dharma* does not yet have activity when it is future, attains it upon becoming present, and loses it when it becomes past; modification in capability refers to the capability of such things as the characteristic of birth (*jātilakṣaṇa*) in the future time period, the capability of such things as the characteristic of desinence (*anityatālakṣaṇa*) in the present time period, and the capability of "presenting" the effect (*phaladāna*) in the past time period. See AMVŚ 39 p. 200a14ff., esp. p. 200a29–200b11.

133 AMVŚ 196 p. 982b3ff., 17 p. 86b4ff.

[134] This position that causal functioning necessitates existence does not necessarily lead to the conclusion that "everything exists." For example, the **Mahāvibhāṣā* records a controversy with the Kāśyapīyas, who claimed that the cause of maturation (*vipākahetu*) exists only so long as its matured effect has not yet matured (*avipakvavipāka*); when the matured effect matures and arises, its cause, having performed its function, ceases to exist. This position results in the view that only a portion of the past exists, namely, those past causes of maturation that have not yet produced their matured effects. Hence, the Kāśyapīyas do associate causal functioning with existence, but do not claim that "everything exists." AMVŚ 19 p. 96b6–10, 51 p. 263c25–264a1, 144 p. 741b13–16; Kv 151ff. See also Cox (forthcoming a: lines 3ff.)
[135] All texts also offer scriptural passages in addition to reasoned arguments as support for their position. For a review of differences among the reasons cited in various texts, see NISHI (1975b: 436ff.); KATŌ (1985: 487–490). See VK 1 p. 531a23–2 p. 537a26; ĀVBSŚ 9 p. 796b13ff.; VŚ 7 p. 464b25–465a25; AVŚ 40 p. 293c28–294b5; AMVŚ 76 p. 393a20–393b27; MAHŚ 11 p. 963b9ff. The **Vibhāṣāśāstra* (VŚ 7 p. 464b25–464c3) alone among the *vibhāṣā* compendia includes the reason of the existent object-support in its discussion of the existence of *dharmas* of the three time periods.
[136] See KATŌ (1985); KATŌ (1984: 72ff.); KATŌ (1989: 174ff.); NISHI (1975b: 457ff.); HIRAKAWA (1988: 122ff.).
[137] ŚAŚ 4 p. 554a23–27, 5 p. 560c27–561a2, 6 p. 568b10–15, 9 p. 590c1–5. For 相 with the virtually certain equivalent *lakṣaṇa* in the context of the conditioning characteristics (*saṃskṛtalakṣaṇa*), see ŚAŚ 16 p. 633b6, 16 p. 636b7ff.
[138] ĀVBSŚ 1 p. 723a1ff., *passim*. For 相 as *lakṣaṇa*, again in the context of the conditioning characteristics (*saṃskṛtalakṣaṇa*), see ĀVBSŚ 1 p. 723a26ff.
[139] AHŚ 1 p. 809a9ff., *passim,* where examples are given of various characteristics that will be distinguished as either particular inherent or generic; AHŚ-U 1 p. 835b6ff., *passim*; MAHŚ 1 p. 870c7ff. See also the PVVŚ *shang* p. 990b12ff., p. 990b29–990c13.
[140] See, for example, in definitions of Abhidharma, AMVŚ 1 p. 2b21, 1 p. 3b10–13, *passim*, AMVŚ 29 p. 147a27–29, 41 p. 214a7–8, 42 p. 216c15–218c10. Particular inherent and generic characteristics are also included within a listing of seven methods or topics, cited in the *vibhāṣā* compendia, through which the Abhidharma is to be understood. See AVŚ 12 p. 92a21–26; AMVŚ 23 P. 116b20–25; *supra* note #73.
[141] AMVŚ 13 p. 65a12ff, 30 p. 154c8–9, 127 p. 665b1ff., 131 p. 681c5–6.
[142] AMVŚ 34 p. 179b3–5: 問若爾無慚自性云何 。答自體自相即彼自性 。如說諸法自性即是諸法自相。同類性是共相。This formula is applied to several *dharmas* throughout the section, AMVŚ 34 p. 179b3–38 p. 196c25. See also AMVŚ 10p. 50b10–11, 48 p. 249b23–25 (where this view is attributed to Vasumitra), 81 p. 420c8–9; AKBh 6.14c–d p. 341.11ff. For definitions of *dharma* that use *svalakṣaṇa*, see *supra* note #70.
[143] Similar ambiguity attends the term *dravya*, as indicated by the discussion in the *Abhidharmakośabhāṣya* (AKBh 2.22d p. 53. 19ff.) as to whether a molecule (*saṃghātaparamāṇu*) consists of eight *dravyas per se*, or eight *dravyas* understood as sense spheres. Yaśomitra (AKV 125.30ff.) glosses the first type of *dravya per se* as "that which has a particular inherent characteristic" (*yasya svalakṣaṇam asti*); concerning the second, he states (AKV 125.32–33): "It is possible to say that *dravya* is also the sense sphere due to its nature as the generic characteristic." (*āyatanam api hi dravyam iti śakyate vaktuṃ sāmānyaviśeṣalakṣaṇasadbhāvāt*)
[144] AMVŚ 127 p. 663b10ff., esp. 15-18. For impermanence, non-self, and suffering also as generic characteristics, see AMVŚ 7 p. 33b4; MAHŚ 1 p. 870c7–10; PVVŚ *shang* p. 989b17–18; AKV 9. 18–19, 22–23.
[145] AMVŚ 42 p. 217a14–16.

[146] AMVŚ 13 p. 65a12–16, 30 127 p. 665b1–4. See also MAHŚ 1 p. 872c22–24. This multiplicity of particular inherent characteristics is also referred to in a lengthy passage in the **Mahāvibhāṣā* (AMVŚ 39 p.200b16–c12) that examines whether the four conditioning characteristics (*saṃskṛtalakṣaṇa*) should be considered particular inherent or generic characteristics. If they were particular inherent characteristics, then one *dharma* would have four distinct characteristics, which would contradict the nature of a single *dharma* as defined by one intrinsic nature. If they were generic characteristics, it would be unreasonable to claim that every conditioned *dharma* has four separate conditioning characteristics. In the following discussion, certain opinions are cited that recognize multiple particular inherent characteristics distinguished as "host" (主自相) and "guest" (客自相) or as "fundamental" (本性自相) and "united with others" (他合自相). The arbiter concludes that the conditioning characteristics are generic characteristics through association (和合共相 **saṃyoga*, **saṃnipāta*). See *supra* note #24.

[147] NA 50 p. 621c21 : 爲境生覺是真有相. See also TSŚ 2 #19 p. 254a2–3; ADV 262.1ff., p. 268.22–24.

[148] NA 50 p. 621c21ff. See also NA 15 p. 421b26ff., 19 p. 447c22ff., 58 p. 666a7ff. Saṅghabhadra also mentions that some teachers recognize a third category of relative existence (**āpekṣika*) that he would include within the prior types. See *supra* note #119; AOHARA (1986a).

[149] NA 13 p. 409b2ff., 2 p. 636a22–24. See also LA VALLÉE POUSSIN (1936–1937); WILLIAMS (1981); AOHARA (1986a); FUKUDA(1988); FRAUWALLNER (1995: 185–208).

[150] For Saṅghabhadra's attempt to defend this position that activity and intrinsic nature are neither the same nor different, see COX (1995: 144–145); AMVŚ 76 p. 394c5ff; AKBh 5.27a p. 297.18ff.; AKV 471.28ff.; NA 52 p. 631c22ff., p. 632c7ff., p. 632c23ff.; TSP #1793ff. p. 617ff., esp. #1806 p. 621 (cf. NA 52 p. 633a24ff.).

REFERENCES

Primary Sources

ADV = *Abhidharmadīpa. Abhidharmadīpa with Vibhāṣāprabhāvṛtti.* Edited by P.S. Jaini. Tibetan Sanskrit Works Series 4. Kashi Prasad Jayaswal Research Institute, Patna 1977.

AHŚ = **Abhidhrmahṛdayaśāstra.* T.1550. Dharmaśreṣthin, translated by Saṅghadeva, Huiyuan.

AHŚ-U = **Abhidharmahṛdayaśāstra.* T.1551. Upaśānta, translated by Narendrayaśas, Fazhi.

AKBh = *Abhidharmakośabhāṣya. Abhidharmakośabhāṣyam of Vasubandhu* . Edited by P. Pradhan. 2nd ed. Tibetan Sanskrit Works Series 8. Kashi Prasad Jayaswal Research Institute, Patna 1975.

AKBh-P = *Abhidharmakośabhāṣya.* T.1559. Vasubandhu. Translated by Paramārtha.

AKBh-Xz = *Abhidharmakośabhāṣya.* T.1558. Vasubandhu. Translated by Xuanzang.

AKV = *Abhidharmakośavyākhyā. Sputārthā*
Abhidharmakośavyākhyā: The Work of Yaśomitra. Edited by Unrai Wogihara. The Publishing Association of the Abhidharmakośavyākhyā, Tokyo 1932.

AMVŚ = **Abhidharmamahāvibhāṣāśāstra.* T.1545. Translated by Xuanzang.

ĀVBSŚ = **Āryavasumitrabodhisattvasaṅgītiśāstra.* T.1549. Attributed to Vasumitra, translated by Saṅghabhadra, (or Saṅghabhūti), Dharmanandin, Saṅghadeva, Zhu Fonian.

AVŚ = **Abhidharmavibhāṣāśāstra*. T.1546. Translated by Buddhavarman, Daotai.

D = *Dīghanikāya. The Dīghanikāya*. Edited by T.W. Rhys Davids and J. Estlin Carpenter. 3 Vols. Pali Text Society, London [1889–1910]1982–1992.

D-a = Buddhaghosa: *Sumaṅgalavilāsinī. Sumaṅgala-Vilāsinī. Buddhaghosa's Commentary on the Dīgha Nikāya*. Edited by T.W. Rhys Davids and J. Estlin Carpenter. 3 Vols. Pali Text Society, London [1886]1968.

Dhs = *Dhammasaṅgaṇī. The Dhammasaṅgaṇī*. Edited by Edward Müller. Pali Text Society, London [1885]1978.

Dhs-a = Buddhaghosa: *Atthasālinī. The Atthasālinī. Buddhaghosa's Commentary on the Dhammasaṅgaṇī*. Edited by Edward Müller. Pali Text Society, London [1897]1979.

DhSk = *Dharmaskandha*. T.1537. Attributed to Śāriputra (Skt.), Mahāmaudgalyāyana (Ch.), translated by Xuanzang.

JP = *Jñānaprasthāna*. T.I544. Attributed to Kātyāyanīputra, translated by Xuanzang.

Kv = *Kathāvatthu. Kathāvatthu*. Edited by A.C. Taylor. 2 Vols. Pali Text Society, London [1894, 1897]1979.

M = *Majjhimanikāya. The Majjhima-Nikāya*. Edited by V. Trenckner, R. Chalmers, and C.A.F. Rhys Davids. 4 Vols. Pali Text Society, London [1888–1925]1977–1993.

MAHŚ = **Miśrakābhidharmahṛdayaśāstra*. T.1552. Dharmatrāta, translated by Saṅghavarman, Baoyun, Huiguan.

NA = **Nyāyānusārasastra*. T.I562. Saṅghabhadra, translated by Xuanzang.

Paṭis = *Paṭisambhidāmagga. The Paṭisambhidā-magga*. Edited by A.C. Taylor. 2 Vols. Pali Text Society, London [1905,1907]1979.

Paṭis-a = *Saddhammappakāsinī, Saddhammappakāsinī. Commentary on the Paṭisambhidāmagga*. Edited by C.V. Joshi. 3 Vols. Pali Text Society, London [1933]1979.

PP(T.1541) = *Prakaraṇapāda*. T.1541. Attributed to Vasumitra, translated by Guṇabhadra, Bodhiyaśas.

PP(T.1542) = *Prakaraṇapāda*. T.1542. Attributed to Vasumitra, translated by Xuanzang.

Pravacanasāra = Kundakunda: *Pravacanasāra* (*Pavayaṇasāra*). Edited by A.N. Upadhye. Shrimad Rajachandra Ashrama, 1964.

PVVŚ = **Pañcavastukavibhāṣāśāstra*. T.1555. Attributed to Dharmatrāta, translated by Xuanzang.

S = *Saṃyuttanikāya. The Saṃyutta-Nikāya*. Edited by L. Feer. 6 Vols. Pali Text Society, London [1884–1904]1975–1991.

SĀ = *Saṃyuktāgama*. T.99. Translated by Guṇabhadra.

SaṅgP = *Saṅgītiparyāya*. T.1536. Attributed to Mahākauṣṭhila (Skt.), Śāriputra (Ch.), translated by Xuanzang.

ŚAŚ = **Śāriputrābhidharmaśāstra*. T.1548. Translated by Dharmayaśas, Dharmagupta.

T. = *Taishō shinshū Daizōkyō*. Edited by Junjirō Takakusu, Kaigyoku Watanabe. Taishō Issaikyō Kankōkai, Tokyo 1924–1932.

Tattvārthādhigamasūtra = *Tattvartha Sutram*. Edited by J.L. Jaini. Barrister Champat Rai Jain Trust, Delhi [1920]1956.

TSP = Śāntarakṣita: *Tattvasaṅgraha*. Kamalaśīla: *Tattvasaṅgrahapañjikā. Tattvasaṅgraha of Ācārya Shāntarakṣita with the Commentary "Pañjikā" of Shri Kamalashīla*. Edited by Swami Dwarikadas Shastri. 2 Vols. With continuous pagination. Bauddha Bharati Series 2. Bauddha Bharati, Varanasi 1982.

Vaiśeṣikasūtra = Kaṇāda: *Vaiśeṣikasūtra. Vaisheshika Darshana*. Edited by Mahadeva Gangadhara Bakre. Vyasa Prakashan, Varanasi [1913]1991.

Vbh = *Vibhaṅga. The Vibhaṅga*. Edited by C.A.F. Rhys Davids. Pali Text Society, London [1904]1978.

VK = *Vijñānakāya*. T.1539. Attributed to Devaśarman, translated by Xuanzang.

VŚ = **Vibhāṣāśāstra*. T.1547. Translated by Saṅghabhūti (or Saṅghabhadra), Dharmanandin, Buddharakṣa, Minzhi.

YBh-Xz = *Yogācārabhūmiśāstra*. T.1579. Attributed to Maitreya, translated by Xuanzang.

YBh = *Yogācārabhūmiśāstra. The Yogācārabhūmi of Ācārya Asaṅga*. Edited by Vidhushekhara Bhattacharya. Part 1. University of Calcutta, Calcutta 1957.

Secondary Sources

AOHARA (1986a) = Aohara, N. (1986a). "Junshōriron ni okeru u no taikei," *Indogaku Bukkyōgaku kenkyū* **34**, 765–768.

AOHARA (1986b) = Aohara, N. (1986b) "Sayū to kunō: Shugen setsu ni okeru jitsuu kōzō," *Bukkyōgaku kenkyū* **42**, 21–42.

BIARDEAU (1964) = Biardeau, M. (1964). *Théorie de la connaissance et philosophie de la parole dans le brahmanisme classique*. Mouton, Paris.

BRONKHORST (1985) = Bronkhorst, J. (1985). "Dharma and Abhidharma," *Bulletin of the School of Oriental and African Studies* **48**, 305–320.

BRONKHORST (1987) = Bronkhorst, J. (1987). "The Mahābhāṣya and the Development of Indian Philosophy," In *Three Problems Pertaining to the Mahābhāṣya* (pp. 43–71). Post-graduate and Research Department Series no. 30. Poona: Bhandarkar Oriental Research Institute.

BRONKHORST (1994) = Bronkhorst, J. (1994). "The Qualities of Sāṅkhya," *Wiener Zeitschrift für die Kunde Südasiens und Archiv für Indische Philosophie* **38**, 309–322.

BRONKHORST (1996) = Bronkhorst, J. (1996). "Sanskrit and reality: the Buddhist contribution," In J.E.M. Houben (ed.), *Ideology and Status of Sanskrit. Contributions to the History of the Sanskrit Language* (pp. 109–135). E.J. Brill, Leiden: Brill's Indological Library 13.

BRONKHORST (1997) = Bronkhorst, J. (1997). "Sāṃkhya in the Abhidharmakośa Bhāṣya," *Journal of Indian Philosophy* **25**, 393–400.

BRONKHORST (1999a) = Bronkhorst, J. (1999a). *Langage et réalité: sur un episode de la pensée indienne*. Bibliothèque de l'École des Hautes Études, Sciences Religieuses 105. Brepols, Turnhout.

BRONKHORST (1999b) = Bronkhorst, J. (1999b). *Why is there philosophy in India?* Amsterdam: Royal Netherlands Academy of Arts and Sciences.

BURNOUF ([1876]1944) = Burnouf, E. (1944). *Introduction à l' historie du buddhisme indien*. Paris: Imprimerie Royale.

CARTER (1978) = Carter, J.R. (1978). *Dhamma. Western Academic and Sinhalese Buddhist Interpretations. A Study of a Religious Concept*. Tokyo: Hokuseido Press.

CONZE (1967) = Conze, E. (1967). *Buddhist Thought in India*. Ann Arbor: Ann Arbor Paperbacks.

COX (1992a) = Cox, C. (1992a). "Attainment through Abandonment: The Sarvāstivādin Path of Removing Defilements," In R.E. Buswell, Jr. and R. Gimello (eds.), *Paths to Liberation: The Mārga and its Transformations in Buddhist Thought* (pp. 63–105). Kuroda Institute. Studies in East Asian Buddhism 7. Honolulu: University of Hawaii Press.

COX (1992b) = Cox, C. (1992b). "The Unbroken Treatise: Scripture and Argument in Early Buddhist Scholasticism," In M. Williams C. Cox and M. Jaffee (eds.), *Innovation in Religious Traditions* (pp. 143–189). Religion and Society 31. Berlin, New York: Mouton de Gruyter.

Cox (1995) = Cox, C. (1995). *Disputed Dharmas. Early Buddhist Theories on Existence*. Studia Philologica Buddhica 9. Tokyo: International Institute for Buddhist Studies.

Cox (forthcoming a) = Cox, C. (forthcoming a) *A Gāndhārī Abhidharma Text: The British Library Kharoṣṭhī Fragment 28*. Gandhāran Buddhist Texts 4. Seattle and London: University of Washington Press.

Cox (forthcoming b) = Cox, C. (forthcoming b). "Yogācāra Prehistory: The Interpretation of *Bhāva, Svabhāva, Abhiniṣpanna* and *Pariniṣpanna* in a Gāndhārī Abhidharma Manuscript."

Frauwallner ([1956]1973) = Frauwallner, E. (1973). *History of Indian Philosophy*, 2 pts., translated by V.M. Bedekar. Delhi: Motilal Banarsidass.

Frauwallner (1995) = Frauwallner, E. (1995). *Studies in Abhidharma Literature and the Origins of Buddhist Philosophical Systems*, translated by Sophie Francis Kidd. Albany: State University of New York Press.

Fukuda (1988) = Fukuda, T. (1988). "Junshōriron ne sanzejitsuu setsu," *Bukkyōgaku seminā* **48**, 48–68.

Geiger ([1920]1973) = Geiger,W. and Magdalene, Geiger. (1973). *Pāli Dhamma vornehmlich in der kanonischen Literatur* [1920], In H. Bechert (ed.), *(Wilhelm Geiger) Kleine Schriften zur Indologie und Buddhismuskunde,* (pp. 101–228). Glasenap-Stiftung 6. Wiesbaden: Franz Steiner.

Gethin (1986) = Gethin, R. (1986). "The Five Khandhas: Their Treatment in the Nikāyas and Early Abhidhamma," *Journal of Indian Philosophy* **14**, 35–53.

Gethin (1992) = Gethin, R.M.L. (1992). *The Buddhist Path to Awakening. A Study of the Bodhi-Pakkiyā Dhammā*. Leiden: E.J. Brill. Brill's Indological Library 7.

Glasenapp (1938) = Glasenapp, H. von (1938). "Zur Geschichte der buddhistischen Dharma-Theorie," *Zeitschift der Deutschen Morgenländischen Gesellschaft* **92**, 383–420.

Halbfass (1992) = Halbfass, W. (1992). *On Being and What There Is: Classical Vaiśeṣika and the History of Indian Ontology*. Albany: State University of New York Press.

Hirakawa (1968) = Hirakawa, A. (1968). "Shohō muga no 'hō,'" *Indogaku Bukkyōgaku kenkyū* **16**, 870–885.

Hirakawa (1980) = Hirakawa, A. (1980). "The Meaning of 'Dharma' and 'Abhidharma," In *Indianisme et bouddhisme: mélanges offerts à Mgr. Étienne Lamotte* (pp. 159–175). Publications de l'Institute orientaliste de Louvain 23. Louvain: Institute orientaliste de Université catholique de Louvain.

Hirakawa (1988) = Hirakawa, A. (1998). *Hō to engi.* Tokyo: Shunjūsha.

Hirakawa (1990) = Hirakawa, A. (1990). *A History of Indian Buddhism. From Śākyamuni to Early Mahāyānā*, translated and edited by Paul Groner. Asian Studies at Hawaii 36. Honolulu: University of Hawaii Press.

Horner (1948) = Horner, I.B. (1948). "Early Buddhist Dhamma," *Artibus Asiae* **11**, 115–123.

Houben (1995) = Houben, J.E.M. (1995). "Liberation and Natural Philosophy in Early Vaiśeṣika: Some Methodological Problems," *Asiatische Studien/Études Asiatiques* **48**, 711–748.

Katō (1984) = Katō, J. (1984). "Abidaruma," In *Bukkyō kenkyū nyūmon* (pp. 60–74). Tokyo: Daizō Shuppan.

Katō (1985) = Katō J. (1985). "Jishō to jisō–sanzejitsuu setsu no tenkai," In *Bukkyō shisō no shomondai. Hirakawa Akira Hakushi koki kinen ronshū* (pp. 487–509). Tokyo: Shunjūsha.

Katō (1989) = Katō J. (1989). *Kyōryōbu no kenkyū.* Tokyo: Shunjūsha.

Kawamura (1974) = Kawamura, K. (1974). *Abidatsuma ronsho no shiryō teki kenkyū.* Tokyo: Nihon Gakujitsu Shinkōkai.

KIMURA (1937) = Kimura, T. (1937). *Abidatsuma ron no kenkyū. Kimura Taiken zenshū*, Vol. 6. Tokyo: Meiji Shoin.

LA VALLÉE Poussin (1936–1937) = La Vallée Poussin, L. (1936–1937). "Documents d'Abhidharma: la controverse du temps," *Mélanges chinois et bouddhiques* **5**, 7–158.

LAMOTTE ([1958]1988) = Lamotte, É. (1988). *History of Indian Buddhism. From the Origins to the Śaka Era*, translated by Sara Webb- Boin. Publications de l'Institute Orientaliste de Louvain 36. Louvain: Peeters.

MATILAL (1985) = Matilal, B.K. (1985). *Logic, Language and Reality. Indian Philosophy and Contemporary Issues*. Delhi: Motilal Banarsidass.

MIYASHITA (1987) Miyashita, S. (1987). "Dōbun tadōbun ni tsuite," *Indogaku Bukkyōgaku kenkyū*, **35**, 96–99.

MIYASHITA (1989) = Miyashita, S. (1989). "Hichakumetsumui," *Bukkyōgaku seminā* **49**, 45–62.

MIYASHITA (1994) = Miyashita, S. (1994). "Abidaruma ni okeru jishō no imi: sanzejitsuu setsu no saikentō," *Bukkyōgaku seminā* **59**, 1–29.

NISHI (1975a) = Nishi, G. (1975a). "Kusharon jō ni okeru Seshin no taidō," In *Abidatsuma Bukkyō no kenkyū* (pp. 497–514). Tokyo: Kokusho Kankōkai.

NISHI (1975b) = Nishi, G. (1975b). "Setsuissaiubushū no konpon hōuron no kenkyū," In *Abidatsuma Bukkyō no kenkyū* (pp. 399–462). Tokyo: Kokusho Kankōkai.

SAITŌ (2002) = Saitō S. (2002). *Setsuissaiubu shisō no tenkai—kon (indriya) no kōsatsu o tōshite*. Ph.D. dissertation, University of Nagoya.

SAKURABE (1969) = Sakurabe, H. and Ueyama, S. (1969). *Sonzai to bunseki. Bukkyō shisō* 2 . Tokyo: Kadokawa Shoten.

SCHARF (1996) = Scharf, P.M. (1996). *The Denotation of Generic Terms in Ancient Indian Philosophy: Grammar, Nyāya, and Mīmāṃsa*. Transactions of the American Philosophical Society Held at Philadelphia for Promoting Useful Knowledge. Vol. 86, pt.3. Philadelphia: American Philosophical Society.

STCHERBATSKY ([1923]1970) = Stcherbatsky, Th. (1970). *The Central Conception of Buddhism and the Meaning of the Word "Dharma."* Delhi: Motilal Banarsidass.

TSUKINOKI (1975) = Tsukinoki, Y. (1975). "Jishō' to Setsuissaiubu no sonzairon," In *Bukkyō kenkyū ronshū. Hashimoto Hakushi taikan kinen Bukkyō kenkyū ronshū kankōkai hen* (pp. 273–287). Osaka: Seibundō.

WALDRON (2002) = Waldron, W. (2002). "Buddhist Steps to an Ecology of Mind: Thinking About 'Thoughts without a Thinker'," *The Eastern Buddhist* n.s. **34**, 1–52.

WARDER (1971) = Warder, A.K. (1971). "Dharmas and Data," *Journal of Indian Philosophy* **1**, 272–295.

WATSUJI (1962) = Watsuji, T. (1962). "Bukkyō tetsugaku no saishō no tenkai," In *Watsuji Tetsujō zenshū* (Vol. 5, pp.295–568). Kyoto: Iwanami Shoten.

WILLIAMS (1981) = Williams P. (1981). "On the Abhidharma Ontology," *Journal of Indian Philosophy* **9**, 227–257.

YAMADA (1959) = Yamada , R. (1959). *Daijō Bukkyō seiritsuron josetsu*. Kyoto: Heirakuji Shoten.

Asian Languages and Literature
Box 353521
University of Washington
Seattle, WA 98195
USA
E-mail: collett@u.washington.edu

OLLE QVARNSTRÖM

DHARMA IN JAINISM – A PRELIMINARY SURVEY

INTRODUCTION

Throughout the history of Jain religious and philosophic thought, the vital concept of *dharma* has been subject to extensive elaboration and taken on a plurality of meanings. These include its pan-Indian simplification into something approximating the imported Western concept of 'religion'.[1] Within the Jain tradition, serious discussion regarding the broader issue of *dharma* began in earnest during the first centuries of the common era. It was around this time that Jain writers began creating Sanskrit treatises to communicate their views to geographically wide-spread and doctrinally separated congregations, as well as to ideological opponents.

From the earliest Sanskrit texts onward, the word *dharma* has been used to indicate the Jain teaching in general. This, in fact, appears to be the most frequent use of the term. Another early denotation, as affirmed in the writings of the late canonical period (200–300 CE), is the uniquely Jain ontological category of *dharma* as 'motion', with its opposite, *adharma*, signifying 'rest'.

This article concentrates on the explication of three related denotations of the word *dharma*, parts of which were gradually synthesized into one more or less integrated theological view. Since these various notions of *dharma* appear to have played a major historical role in shaping Jain belief and practice, understanding them should enhance our overall understanding of the general development of the Jain tradition.

The first of these denotations identifies *dharma* with an ethics related to the religious and social behaviour of the lay person, on one hand, and the mendicant, on the other. The second identifies the conception of *dharma* as being somehow linked with the conception of the eternal self (*jīva*), thus locating *dharma* squarely in the transcendental sphere. Over the course of the medieval period (400–1200 CE), these two denotations were synthesized to form a definition of correct conduct as behaviour in keeping with one's intrinsic nature or essential self (*svabhāva*). On the basis of this definition, *dharma* was understood as 'twofold', incorporating both the idea of behaviour that accords with moral rules and virtues (*pravṛttidharma*) and the idea of behaviour that accords with one's intrinsic nature (*nivṛttidharma*). Towards the end of this period, *dharma* obtained yet an additional meaning: that of a universal order governing all activity in the cosmos.

The occurrence of these conceptual developments can be properly appreciated only in light of the continuous encounter between the Jain tradition and the surrounding religious environments that existed in India at the time. For example, the notion of *dharma* as virtuous behaviour is known to have been influenced by elements of Brāhmaṇical social ideology, as expressed in the *Dharmaśāstras*. And the conceptions of *dharma* as behaviour in accord with one's intrinsic nature, *dharma* as 'twofold', and *dharma* as cosmic order were influenced by Jainism's interaction with Brāhmaṇical philosophy.[2] It should be remembered, however, that Jain pundits were careful to incorporate new materials – terminologies, ideas, organizing principles, etc. – in a manner that preserved the fundamental elements of Jain teachings.[3]

Despite the obvious influence of these conceptions of *dharma* on the development of Jain thought, one rarely finds more than a passing reference to '*dharma*' in the scholarly literature on Jainism. This striking omission is likely due to the fact that the term's semantic development is somewhat difficult to trace and contextualize. The following brief remarks may be regarded as a beginning exploration of this important topic. Hopefully, however, they will serve as a source of inspiration for more comprehensive studies in the future.

DHARMA AS VIRTUOUS BEHAVIOUR

From the beginning of the early canonical period, as evidenced in the *Ācārāṅgasūtra* and *Sūtrakṛtāṅgasūtra*, the term *dharma* has been employed as a designation for the Jain teaching as a whole.[4] Gradually, a more specific understanding of *dharma* emerged during the first centuries of the common era in treatises such as the *Tattvārthasūtra* of Umāsvāti[5] and the *Pravacanasāra* of Kundakunda (150–350 CE).[6]

In the *Tattvārthasūtra*, the first Jain text penned in Sanskrit and the earliest systematization of the canonical teachings, *dharma* was defined as 'the highest forbearance, modesty, uprightness, purity, truthfulness, restraint, austerity, renunciation, non-attachment, and continence'.[7] The word *dharma* was thus employed to designate ten constituents of righteous character which closely paralleled the five vows (*mahāvrata*)[8] that have formed the basis of Jain ethics since early canonical times: non-harm (*ahiṃsā*), truthfulness (*satya*), honesty (*asteya*), continence (*brahmacarya*) and propertylessness (*aparigraha*).[9]

Both the *Tattvārthasūtra* and the *Pravacanasāra*[10] emphasize the necessity of adopting a particular state of mind as a basis for moral conduct. This tenfold *dharma* or morality, in which meditation on Jain doctrine (*dharmadhyāna*)[11] features as an item of austere practice (*tapas*), was considered instrumental in the cultivation of virtuous behaviour (*samyakcāritra*), one of three facets said to form the path of liberation (*mokṣamārga*).[12]

During the following centuries, *dharma*, conceived as *virtuous behaviour*, acquired additional meanings which were decisive for the future of the Jain tradition. These new meanings arose primarily as result of the transformation of Jainism into a full fledged religious community with a 'four-fold congregation' of monks, nuns, laymen and laywomen; and, a complex ritual structure that included a lay-oriented temple cult.[13] However, as mentioned above, one must not underestimate the significant influence of Brāhmaṇical culture on the development and application of dharmic principles in Jain society. The remainder of this section mentions but a few important outcomes of this influence.

The first and perhaps the most profound outcome of the processes of 'Brahmanization' and communal transformation was the creation in Jain society of two separate *dharmas* or moral prescriptions: one for the lay person (*śrāvakadharma*), and one for the mendicant (*yatidharma*).

The regulations governing the daily lives of lay persons, for example, were systematized in a number of treatises written during the medieval period. These texts, termed *śrāvakācāra*[14] by the Śvetāmbara tradition and *upāsakādhyāyana* by the Digambara tradition, clearly evinced a strong influence of Brāhmaṇical social ideology as expressed in the *Dharmaśāstras*. Reaching the Digambara tradition first,[15] the effect was to extend the lay person's *dharma* to include 'local customs' (*deśācāra*) in the form of central Hindu doctrines and ritual practices. Thus the primary characteristic of the process of Brahmanization involved the imposition of an increasingly detailed body of regulations over the lay person's life. These included ritual and social duties respecting gender, age, occupation, hygiene, diet, religious vows, etc.

Among the Digambaras, integration with Brāhmaṇical society found early expression in the 9th century *Ādipurāṇa* of Jinasena. This text contains, among other things, Jain renderings of the *varṇāśrama* system as well as rites (*kriyā*) modelled on, and to some extent corresponding with, the Hindu *saṃskāras*.[16] In addition, both the Digambara and Śvetāmbara traditions adopted the concept of *puruṣārtha*,[17] as well as a Tantric meditative practice, most likely stemming from Trika Śaivism.[18]

DHARMA AS BEHAVIOUR IN ACCORDANCE WITH INTRINSIC NATURE

The conception of material existence as being comprised of five or six fundamental substances or *dravyas* – the eternal self (*jīva*), principles of motion (*dharma*) and rest (*adharma*),[19] atoms (*pudgala*), space (*ākāśa*) and time (*kāla*) – developed over a period of time beginning with the *Ācārāṅgasūtra*.[20] Contributing to this development, philosophers such as Kundakunda introduced as a systematic doctrine the idea that an intrinsic nature adhered to each of these ontological categories, which together were instrumental in forming the Jain cosmos via their infinite modes.

In the *Pravacanasāra*, *dravya* is defined as:

> That which, whilst it does not forsake its innate nature, is connected with creation, maintenance and destruction and which possesses qualities and modifications, they call a substance.[21]

Among these basic substances, the substance known as self or *jīva* was obviously of prime significance when it came to defining and legitimizing correct behaviour. Commenting on Kundakunda's definition of *dharma* as conduct (*carittaṃ khalu dhammo*),[22] Amṛtacandra states:

> Conduct is behaving according to one's nature; activity obeying one's (innate) laws. And this from being the nature of things is *dharma* (duty); it means the manifestation of pure intelligence.[23]

Human performance in harmony with one's innate nature constitutes, according to Amṛtacandra, the supreme *dharma* (*paramadharma*),[24] because it consists in activity grounded in the self (*jīva*) and thus leads to liberation (*mokṣa*).[25] Amṛtacandra's analysis presupposes a conception of *dharma* as being an internal reality closely related to the self and, in some contexts, completely identified with it.[26] This understanding of *dharma*, as expressed by Kundakunda and Amṛtacandra (1964), was also emphasized by other Jain thinkers and featured prominently in the Jain confrontation with *Mīmāṃsā* philosophy on the possibility of obtaining a direct perception of *dharma*.

In the *Śāstravārtāsamuccaya*, for example, the 8th century Jain philosopher Haribhadra claimed that man could obtain a direct experience of *dharma* purely by means of the self. Here *dharma*, while conceived as residing beyond the range of the senses (*atīndriya*), was simultaneously conceived as being accessible through the attainment of an omniscient state (*sarvajñatva*).[27] Haribhadra thus argued that an action – moral, ritual or social – need not be legitimized solely on the grounds that it accords with the teaching revealed by an omniscient Tīrthaṅkara. In Jain teachings, the grounds for an action may be justified rationally by reference to one's innate nature as well.

DHARMA AS TWOFOLD

In the same *Śāstravārtāsamuccaya*, Haribhadra describes appropriate behaviour or *dharma* in terms of two antithetical yet interconnected formulations: (1) behaviour characterized by activity (*pravṛtti*), resulting in merit (*puṇya*) and enjoyment (*bhoga*); and, (2) behaviour characterized by non-activity (*nivṛtti*), resulting in liberation (*mukti*).[28]

> *Dharma* characterized by activity leads to enjoyment; characterized by its opposite, it leads to liberation.[29]

This conception of *dharma* exemplifies the historically significant tendency to incorporate the notions of 'renunciation' and 'liberation' to broaden the definition of *dharma* so as to enable the regulation and legitimization of detachment from more social and goal-oriented norms and rules.[30]

In Haribhadra's synthesis, *dharma* viewed as behaviour that accords with moral rules and virtues, and *dharma* viewed as behaviour that accords with one's intrinsic nature were conceived as two aspects of one *dharma* – *pravṛtti* and *nivṛtti*. In other words, rather than regarding these two paths as separate and distinct, they were treated as coexisting phases of religious life – one involving the path of mundane morality (*karma*) and the other involving the cultivation of higher knowledge (*jñāna*). These coexisting phases were conceived hierarchically according to degrees of purity (*aśubha–śubha–viśuddha*).

In terms of *pravṛttidharma* one was enjoined to cultivate *puṇya* or *śubha* (e.g., non-violence, tolerance and kindness) and refrain from *pāpa* or *aśubha* (e.g., anger, pride and greed). The aim was to maintain oneself in an auspicious state (*śubha*) in order to attain an elevated birth in the next life. *Nivṛttidharma*, on the other hand, involved, among other things, the practice of austerity and the cultivation of higher knowledge leading to detachment. Here the aim was to enter a state of perfect purity (*viśuddha*), transcending both good and bad activity, in order to attain ultimate liberation from the world of birth and death (*vimukti*).[31]

DHARMA AS COSMIC ORDER

At the close of the medieval period, Jainism came to embrace the notion of *dharma* as a universal or cosmic order. This universal order was said to consist of uncreated, eternal and impersonal laws – laws that constituted the intrinsic nature of each phenomenon, and which determined the activity of all that existed. In this view, everything was subject to this cosmic order as well as the laws that governed its functioning.

One of the most conspicuous differences between the Jain notion of a cosmic order and that of the surrounding Brāhmaṇical tradition, was that the Jain cosmic order rested upon an ontological plurality (the *dravyas* mentioned above) whereas the Brāhmaṇical cosmic order rested upon a single underlying principle (e.g., the universal self, *Brahman*, and so forth). As to why this was the case, little is known since research has yet to be conducted on this fascinating topic. The fact remains that the Jain cosmos was comprised of *jīva*, *dharma*, *adharma*, *pudgala*, *ākāśa* and *kāla*, with each substance having its own distinct *svabhāva* and its own specific governing rules. There was no *one principle* that served as the governing factor for them all.

The following quotation is from the fourth chapter of the 12th century Jain classic, *Yogaśāstra*. In this rare Sanskrit rendering, Hemacandra portrays a universal cosmic order using many of the meanings of *dharma* discussed above:[32]

'The eminent Jinas, who are venerable, have convincingly proclaimed a teaching (dharma) which, if understood correctly, saves one from drowning in the ocean of transmigration [and thereby from the fear of

being thrown into hell]. (92) This [dharma] is tenfold, [consisting of] restraint, truthfulness, purity, continence, non-attachment, austerity, forbearance, modesty, uprightness and renunciation. (93) Due to the impact of dharma, which is similar to a wish-fulfilling tree, all desires are fulfilled. For those who are established in the condition of adharma [this fulfilling of desires] does not occur. (94)

'The fact that the ocean does not submerge the earth, [and the fact that] the [rain] clouds give life to the earth, that is unquestionably [due to] the absolute power of dharma. (96) The fact that fire does not burn horizontally and that the wind does not blow vertically, this is the incomprehensible grandeur [of the nature of things and] dharma alone is the cause [of it]. (97) The earth has neither a support [nor] a supporter, [such as Śeṣa, Kūrma, Varāha or the dikkuñjaras], [and yet] it is the foundation of everything [moving and unmoving]. Furthermore, the fact that it [still] remains [shows that] there is no other reason [for it] than dharma. (98) The sun and the moon, which are for the benefit of mankind, definitely arise in this world by command of dharma. (99)

'Dharma [alone] protects the Self from falling into the pits of hell. Dharma alone bestows the incomparable wealth of omniscience. (102)'[33]

ACKNOWLEDGEMENTS

I would like to sincerely thank John Cort, Paul Dundas, Martin Gansten, P.S. Jaini, William Johnson, and Kristi Wiley for their kind-hearted support and assistance, and my friend and student Sven Ekelin who read and commented on the drafts of this article. I would also like to thank Alan J. Anderson, my English editor, for his significant help in rendering this article in the English language.

NOTES

[1] On conceptual changes in Indic religions during the 19th century, including the employment of *dharma* as a synonym for 'religion' (see Halbfass, 1988: chs. 17–18; Brekke, 2002: 28–32).

[2] On the paradigmatic roles of Mīmāṃsā and Dharmaśāstra (see Halbfass, 1988: 325–333).

[3] See Qvarnström (1998).

[4] For canonical references, see Yamasaki & Ousaka (1995: 120–121, 1999: 74–75).

[5] For a review of the evidence surrounding the question of Umāsvāti's identity, authorship, affiliation, etc., see Bronkhorst (1985).

[6] See Kundakunda's *Pravacanasāra* I.7, 8, 11, 91, 92, II.24. On the date of Kundakunda (see Dhaky, 1991; Dundas, 2002: 107f; Johnson 1995: 91–98; Soni 2001: 136, n.2 (with references)).

[7] *Tattvārthasūtra* IX.6: *uttamakṣamāmārdavārjavaśaucasatyasaṃyamatapastyāgākiñcanyabrahmacaryāṇi dharmaḥ* (cf. Nāgārjuna's *Ratnāvalī* I.6–9; *Manusmṛti* XII.3–7). This tenfold morality was intended for the mendicant, but was made applicable to the lay person in the form of almsgiving (*dāna*), virtue (*śīla*), ascetic practice (*tapas*) and spiritual attitude (*bhāva*), or alternatively, *dāna, śīla, upavāsa* (*tapas* as fasting), and *pūjā*. See Williams 1963: 35.

[8] See *Tattvārthasūtra* IX.2, 6 with the commentaries of Umāsvāti (*Svopajñabhāṣya*) and Pūjyapāda (*Sarvārthasiddhi*).

[9] *Ācārāṅgasūtra* II.15; *Tattvārthasūtra* VII.

[10] *Pravacansāra* I.7; Johnson (1995: 118).

[11] The account of *dharmadhyāna* in *Tattvārthasūtra* (IX.29, 37) follows the *Bhagavatīsūtra* (1953) and *Aupapātikasūtra*. It deviates, however, from the earliest account of *dharmadhyāna*, found in the *Sthānāṅgasūtra* IV.1.61–72, in the sense that it regards the shapes (*saṃsthāna*) of different beings, rather than the structure of the universe, as an object of meditation. See Schubring (1978: 313–316). For a digest of this kind of *dharmadhyāna*, (see Jaini, 1979: 252–253, 272; Tatia, 1951: 283–291).

[12] *Tattvārthasūtra* I.1. Cf. *Uttarādhyayanasūtra* XXVIII; *Sūtrakṛtāṅgasūtra* I.6.

[13] See Williams (1963: xi–xxv).

[14] In contrast, early Buddhism possessed only one Theravāda text on lay conduct, the *Upāsakajanālaṃkāra* (12th cent.); and, only one Mahāyāna text, a small portion of Śāntideva's *Śikṣāsamuccaya* (9th cent.). See Jaini (1979: 160, 1994: xxxviii). Some of the *śrāvakācāra* and *upāsakādhyāyana* texts discussed in Williams' excellent study from 1963 also include descriptions of *yatidharma*.

[15] Williams (1963: xxiii).

[16] See Jaini (2000: 232–235), Williams (1963: 274–287) and Brekke (2002: 122–125).

[17] The conception of *dharma* as part of the fourfold classification (*caturvarga*) is described in the *Yogaśāstra* of Hemacandra (I.15, 52) and the *Jñānārṇava* of Śubhacandra III.4–5. On the *puruṣārthas* in general, see Davis (forthcoming).

[18] See Śubhacandra's *Jñānārṇava* (XXXIV–XXXVII), Hemacandra's *Yogaśāstra* (VII.8–X.6), Qvarnström 1998: 40–43, 2002: 7 (with references), 146, 2003.

[19] During the late canonical period, a conception of the word *dharma* apparently unique to Jainism is confirmed in, e.g., *Uttarādhyayanasūtra* (XXVIII.7–9, 14, XXXVI.5) and *Tattvārthasūtra* (V.1, 7, 13, 17). The word *dharma* and its opposite *adharma* were equated, in these texts, with two of the five or six ontological categories (*dravyas*) – medium of movement (*dharma-dravya*) and medium of rest (*adharma-dravya*). These two *dravyas* were said to create the conditions and support for activity and non-activity respectively. For various interpretations of these two concepts, see Dundas (2002: 93), Jacobi (1906: 514, n.1), Schubring (1978: 15) and especially, Fujinaga (forthcoming) whose original treatment of these two concepts has contributed valuable insights as to their historical development as well as the philosophical rationale used to uphold their division into separate ontological categories.

[20] Dundas (2002: 93) and Malvania (1981).

[21] *Pravacanasāra* II.3: *apariccattasahāveṇuppadavvayadhuvattasaṃbaddham* / *guṇavaṃ ca sapajjāyaṃ jaṃ taṃ davvaṃ ti vuccaṃti* //. Tr. by Faddegon 1935: 64.

[22] *Pravacanasāra* I.7.

[23] Amṛtacandra *Tattvadīpikā* I.7: *svarūpe caraṇaṃ cāritraṃ svasamayapravṛttir ity arthaḥ* / *tadeva vastusvabhāvatvād dharmaḥ* / *śuddhacaitanyaprakāśanam ity arthaḥ* / Tr. by Faddegon (1935: 5).

[24] Amṛtacandra's *Tattvadīpikā* II.24.

[25] Amṛtacandra's *Tattvadīpikā* I.91 according to the Digambara tradition, the possibility of liberation was open only to male mendicants. In contrast, the Śvetāmbara tradition allowed the possibility of liberation for both males and females, as long as the candidate was a genuine mendicant and inherently capable (*bhavya*) of realizing his or her intrinsic nature (self), and/or in possession of 'the seed of *dharma* (*dharmabīja*)'. See *Tattvārthasūtra* II.7 and Haribhadra's *Yogadṛṣṭisamuccaya* 83, respectively. On the concept of *bhavya* (see Jaini, 1977; Dundas, forthcoming).

[26] *Pravacanasāra* I.7–8, 91 with Amṛtacandra's *Tattvadīpikā*. On *dharma* understood as an inherent property of the self (see *Yogaśāstra*, IV.1; Halbfass, 1988: 325).

[27] The first major Śvetāmbara response to Kumārila's criticism of an omniscient being (*sarvajña*) can be found in the *Śāstravārtāsamuccaya* and *Sarvajñasiddhi* of the 8th century Jain philosopher Haribhadra. On the *Śāstravārtāsamuccaya* and the Jain-Mīmāṃsā debate regarding omniscience, see Qvarnström forthcoming. Within the Digambara tradition, the *Siddhiviniścaya* of Akalaṅka (8th century) appears to be the first Jain text denouncing Kumārila and his denial of human omniscience.

[28] See *Śāstravārtāsamuccaya* 1–29, cf. *Dharmabindu* 2: *dhanado dhanārthināṃ proktaḥ kāmināṃ sarvakāmadaḥ / dharma evāpavargasya pāraṃparyena sādhakaḥ //* '*Dharma* is said to bestow wealth on those who desire wealth, and the fulfilment of all desires on those who have desires. It also gradually brings about liberation.' The notion of a twofold *dharma* is also found in, e.g., *Vaiśeṣikasūtra* I.1.2; Nāgārjuna's *Ratnāvalī* I.21, 24–25; Śaṅkara's introduction to *Bhagavadgītā* (1986). See Qvarnström (1999, 2002: 8, n.2). On *pravṛtti* and *nivṛtti* in Indic religions (except Jainism), see Bailey (1985).

[29] *Śāstravārtāsamuccaya* I.23ab: *bhogamuktiphalo dharmaḥ sa pravṛttītarātmakaḥ /*.

[30] Halbfass (1988: 325–326).

[31] *Śāstravārtāsamuccaya* 8, 11, 17, 25. On the concept of purity and auspiciousness, see Cort (2001: 191–192) and Jaini (2000).

[32] This description is part of the contemplation (*bhāvanā*) on 'the correctly expounded law' (*dharmasvākhyātatā*), which is also found in the *Tattvārthasūtra* (IX.7) (along with its commentaries), the *Svopajñabhāṣya* of Umāsvāti, and in the *Sarvārthasiddhi* of Pūjyapāda (1971), but with a different doctrinal content.

[33] *Yogaśāstra* IV 92–102 (tr. by Qvarnström, 2002: 92–94): *svākhyātaḥ khalu dharmo 'yaṃ bhagavadbhir jinottamaiḥ / yaṃ samālambamāno hi na majjed bhavasāgare //92// saṃyamaḥ sānṛtaṃ śaucaṃ brahmākiñcanatā tapaḥ / kṣāntir mārdavam ṛjutā muktiś ca daśadhā sa tu //93// dharmaprabhāvataḥ kalpadrumādyā dadatīpsitam / gocare 'pi na te yat syur adharmādhiṣṭhitātmanām //94// āplāvayati nāmbhodhir āśvāsayati cāmbudaḥ / yan mahīṃ sa prabhāvo 'yaṃ dhruvaṃ dharmasya kevalaḥ //96// na jvalaty analas tiryag yad ūrdhvaṃ vāti nānilaḥ / acintyamahimā tatra dharma eva nibandhanam //97// nirālambā nirādhārā viśvādhāro vasundharā / yac cāvatiṣṭhate tatra dharmād anyad na kāraṇam //98// sūryācandramasāv etau viśvopakṛtihetave / udayete jagaty asmin nūnaṃ dharmasya śāsanāt //99// dharmo narakapātālapātād avati dehinaḥ / dharmo nirupamaṃ yacchaty api sarvajñavaibhavam //102//.*

REFERENCES

Ācārāṅgasūtra (Āyāraṅga Sutta) (1984). Translated by Hermann Jacobi. *Sacred Books of the East* **XXII**: 1–213. Oxford: Clarendon Press.

Aupapātikasūtra (Uvavāi Sutta) (1882). Edited by Ernst Leumann. Leipzig: F.A. Brockhaus.

Bailey, Greg (1985). *Materials for the Study of Ancient Indian Ideologies; Pravṛtti and Nivṛtti*. Torino.

Bhagavadgītā (1896). Edited with Śaṅkara's commentary: *Śrīmadbhagavadgītā-[bhāṣya]*. Poona: Ānandāśrama Sanskrit Series 34.

Bhagavatīsūtra (*Viyāhapaṃṇatti*) (1953). In Pupphabhikkhū (ed.), *Suttāgame*, vol. I. Gurgaon.

Brekke, Torkel (2002). *Makers of Modern Indian Religion in the Late Nineteenth Century*. Oxford Oriental Monographs. Oxford: Oxford University Press.

Bronkhorst, Johannes (1985). On the Chronology of the Tattvārtha Sūtra and Some Early Commentaries. *Wiener Zeitschrift für die Kunde Südasiens* **XXIX**: 155–184.

Cort, John (2001). *Jains in the World. Religious Values and Ideology in India*. Oxford: Oxford University Press.

Davis, Don (forthcoming). *Being Hindu or Being Human: A Reappraisal of the Puruṣārthas*.

Dhaky, M.A (1991). The date of Kundakundacarya. In M.A. Dhaky & S. Jain (eds), *Aspects of Jainology*. Vol. III, *Pt. Dalsukhbhai Malvania Felicitation Volume I* (pp. 187–206). Varanasi.

Dundas, Paul (2002). *The Jains*. 2nd ed. London and New York: Routledge.

Dundas, Paul (forthcoming). Conversion to Jainism: Historical Perspectives. In R. Robinson (ed.), *Religious Conversion in South Asia*.

Fujinaga, Sin (forthcoming). Dharma and Adharma in Jaina Ontology. In P. Flügel (ed.), *Disputes and Dialogues: Studies in Jaina History and Culture*. London: RoutledgeCurzon.

Halbfass, Wilhelm (1988). *India and Europe*. Albany: State University of New York Press.

Haribhadra (1911). *Aṣṭakaprakaraṇa*. With Abhayadeva's *vṛtti* and Jineśvara's *vivṛtti*. Text publ. by M. Bhagubhai. Ahmedabad.

Haribhadra (1908). *Dharmabindu*. Ed. and translated by L. Suali. *Giornale della Societa Asiaticà Italiana* **XXI**: 224–290.

Haribhadra (1924). *Sarvajñasiddhi*. Text along with the *Hiṃsāṣṭaka*, its *Svopajña Avacūri* and *Aindrastuti*, by R.K. Saṃsthā. Rutlam.

Haribhadra (1969). *Śāstravārtāsamuccaya*. Edited by K.K. Dixit. Ahmedabad: L.D. Institute of Indology.

Haribhadra (1929). *Śāstravārtāsamuccaya by Śrī-Haribhadra-Sūri with his own Commentary named Dikpradā*. Bombay: Nirnaya-Sagar Press.

Haribhadra (1970). *Yogadṛṣṭisamuccaya* and *Yogaviṃśikā*. Text and translation by K.K. Dixit. Lalbhai Dalpatbhai Series 27. Ahmedabad.

Hemacandra (1977, 1981, 1986). *Yogaśāstraṃ Svopajñavṛttivibhūṣitam*. Edited by Muni Jambūvijaya. Vols. I–III. Bombay: Jaina Sāhitya Vikāsa Maṇḍala.

Hemacandra (2002). *Yogaśāstra*. Translated by Olle Qvarnström, *The Yogaśāstra of Hemacandra. A Twelfth Century Handbook on Jainism*. Harvard Oriental Series, vol. 60. Cambridge: Harvard University Press.

Jacobi, Hermann (1906). See Umāsvāti. *Tattvārthasūtra*.

Jaini, Padmanabh S. (1977). Bhavyatva and abhavyatva: A Jaina Doctrine of Predestination. In A.N. Upadhye (ed.), *Mahāvīra and His Teachings (2.500 Nirvāṇa Anniversary Volume)* (pp. 95–111) Bombay.

Jaini, Padmanabh S. (1979). *The Jaina Path of Purification*. Berkeley: University of California Press.

Jaini, Padmanabh S. (1994). The Jaina Faith and its History. In N. Tatia (ed.), *Tattvārtha Sūtra. That Which Is* (pp. xxv–xxxxiv). London/New York: Harper Collins Publishers.

Jaini, Padmanabh S. (2000). The Pure and the Auspicious in the Jaina Tradition. In P.S. Jaini (ed.), *Collected Papers on Jaina Studies* (pp. 229–241). Delhi: Motilal Banarsidass.

Johnson, William J. (1995). *Harmless Souls. Karmic Bondage and Religious Change in Early Jainism with Special Reference to Umāsvāti and Kundakunda.* Delhi: Motilal Banarsidass.

Kundakunda (1935). *Pravacanasāra.* Translated with Amṛtacandra's commentary, *Tattvadīpikā*, by Barend Faddegon. Cambridge: Cambridge University Press.

Kundakunda and Amṛtacandra (1964). *Pravacanasāra* and *Tattvadīpikā. Pravacanasāra* (*Pavayanasara*). Ed. with the Sanskrit Commentary of Amṛtacandra by A.N. Upadhye. Agas: Śrīmad Rājacandra Jaina Śāstramālā.

Kundakunda (1930). *Samayasāra.* Text and translated by J.L. Jaini. *Sacred Books of the East*, vol. VIII. Lucknow.

Malvania, Pt. Dalsukh (1981). Beginnings of Jaina Philosophy in the Ācārāṅgasūtra. In K. Bruhn & A. Wezler (eds.), *Studium zum Jainismus and Buddhismus: Gedenkschrift für Ludwig Alsdorf* (pp. 151–153) Wiesbaden.

Manusmṛti (1887). *Mānava Dharma-Śāstra.* The Code of Manu. Edited by J. Jolly. London.

Nāgārjuna (1982). *Ratnāvalī.* Edited by Michael Hahn. Indica et Tibetica, vol. I. Bonn.

Pūjyapāda (1971). *Sarvārthasiddhi.* Edited by Pt. Phoolchandra Siddhant Shastry. Delhi/Varanasi: Bhāratīya Jñānapīṭha.

Qvarnström, Olle (1998). Stability and Adaptability. A Jain Strategy for Survival and Growth. *Indo-Iranian Journal* **41**, 33–55.

Qvarnström, Olle (1999). Haribhadra and the Beginnings of Doxography in India. In O. Qvarnström & N.K. Wagle (eds.), *Approaches to Jaina Studies: Philosophy, Logic, Rituals and Symbols* (pp. 169–210). Toronto: University of Toronto.

Qvarnström, Olle (2002). See Hemacandra. *Yogaśāstra.*

Qvarnström, Olle (2003). Losing One's Mind and Becoming Enlightened. Some Remarks on the Concept of Yoga in Śvetāmbara Jainism and its relation to the Nāth siddha Tradition. In D. Carpenter & I. Whicher (eds), *Yoga: The Indian Tradition* (pp. 130–142). London and New York: RoutledgeCurzon.

Qvarnström, Olle (forthcoming). The Jain-Mīmāṃsā Debate on Omniscience. In P. Flügel (ed.), *Disputes and Dialogues: Studies in Jaina History and Culture.* London: RoutledgeCurzon.

Schubring, Walther (1934, 1978). *The Doctrine of the Jainas.* Delhi: Motilal Banarsidass (translated from the German by W. Beurlen).

Soni, Jayandra (2000). Basic Jaina Epistemology. *Philosophy East & West* **50**(3), 367–377.

Soni, Jayandra (2001). A Note on the Jaina tattva/padārtha. In J. Soni (ed.), *Vasantagauravam. Essays in Jainism* (pp. 135–140). Mumbai: Vakils, Feffer & Simons Ltd.

Soni, Jayandra (2003). Kundakunda and Umāsvāti on Anekāntavāda. In P. Balcerowicz (ed.), *Essays in Jaina Philosophy and Religion* (pp. 25–35). Delhi: Motilal Banarsidass.

Sthānāṅga Sūtra (*Ṭhāṇaṅga Sutta*). Edited with Abhayadeva Sūri's commentary by Muni Jambūvijaya. Delhi, 1985.

Śubhacandra (1977a) *Jñānārṇava.* Edited by H.L. Jain, K.Ch. Siddhantacharya & A.N. Upadhye. Sholapur.

Śubhacandra (1977b) *Jñānārṇava.* Edited by B. Shastri. Sholapur: Jaina Samskriti Samrakshaka Sangha.

Sūtrakṛtāṅga Sūtra (*Sūyagadāṅga Sutta*) (1895). Translated by Hermann Jacobi. *Sacred Books of the East* **XLV**: 235–435. Oxford: Clarendon Press.

Tatia, Nathmal (1951). *Studies in Jaina Philosophy.* Varanasi.

Umāsvāti (1906). *Tattvārthasūtra.* Edited and translated by Hermann Jacobi. Leipzig.

Umāsvāti (1994). *Tattvārthasūtra*. Translated by Nathmal Tatia [based on the commentaries of Umāsvāti (*Svopajñabhāṣya*), Pūjyapāda (*Sarvārthasiddhi*) and Siddhasenagaṇi (*Svopajñabhāṣyaṭīkā*)] as *That Which Is*. New York: Harper Collins Publishers.

Uttarādhyayanasūtra (1922). Edited by Jarl Charpentier. *Archives D'Études Orientales* 21–22. Upsala.

Uttarādhyayanasūtra (1895). Translated by Hermann Jacobi. *Sacred Books of the East* **XLV**: 1–232. Oxford: Clarendon Press.

Vaiśeṣikasūtra (1918). Translated by Barend Faddegon as *The Vaiśeṣika-System, Described with the Help of the Oldest Texts*. Amsterdam.

Williams, R (1963). *Jaina Yoga. A Survey of the Mediaeval Śrāvakācāras*. Oxford: Oxford University Press.

Yamazaki, Moriichi & Ousaka, Yumi (1995). *A Pāda Index and Reverse Pāda Index to Early Jain Canons*. Tokyo: Kosei Publishing Co.

Yamazaki, Moriichi & Ousaka, Yumi (1999). *A Word Index and Reverse Word Index to Early Jain Canonical Texts*. Tokyo: The Chūō Academic Research Institute.

Department of History of Religions
Lund University
Allhelgona Kyrkogata 8
SE-223 62 Lund
Sweden
E-mail: olle.qvarnstrom@teol.lu.se

RICHARD W. LARIVIERE

DHARMAŚĀSTRA, CUSTOM, 'REAL LAW' AND 'APOCRYPHAL' SMṚTIS*

One of the questions that we must confront in attempting to examine the relationship between law and the state in ancient India is that of the general nature *dharmaśāstra*.[1] What is its relationship to 'law'? Does it represent the law of the land? What is its value for the history of Indian society? What does this literature tell us about how people actually lived? I am not the first to ask these questions, obviously. These are questions which underlay much of the scholarship related to *dharmaśāstra*, and one might expect that 200 years of European and Indian scholarship on this question would have settled the issue. This is not the case. The answers to these questions given by various scholars over the years have been contradictory to say the least. The following examples are representative of views held by theoreticians of Hindu Law. The standard textbook on Hindu Law, *Mayne's* Treatise on Hindu Law and Usage states: '*there can be no doubt that these rules were concerned with the practical administration of Law.*'[2]

Govinda Das had a very different opinion: '*It is a profound error to regard these texts as complete codes of law or as getting all their 'rules' rigidly enforced by the political authorities of their time.*[3] [...] *Hindu law was in the main [n]ever more than a pious wish of its metaphysically-minded, ceremonial ridden, priestly promulgators and but seldom a stern reality.*'[4] *Ludo Rocher* has said very recently: '*I am convinced that, during the time of the commentaries and digests, these texts did not represent the law of the land. They were purely panditic, learned commentaries on ancient authoritative texts. The fact that they display differences does not mean, as some have proposed, that the commentators adapted the ancient sacred texts to local customs. That would have been pure sacrilege on their part.*'[5]

Thus on the basis of these examples, the *dharmaśāstra* literature is:

1. undoubtedly concerned with real law
2. merely pious wishes with no political sanction
3. purely panditic commentaries with no relation to custom.

What are we to make of this? Is one view correct and the others not? Are these views mutually exclusive? Are there other alternative views possible? Before I answer any of these questions, it is necessary to remind the reader of the complexity of the *dharma* literature, and to

* This article is reprinted by permission. It first appeared in *Recht, Staat und Verwaltung im klassischen Indien* edited by Bernhard Kölver, Oldenbourg, Munich, 1997.

provide myself with a convenient escape. The hundreds of surviving texts that comprise the *dharma* literature extend from the 6th century B.C. to the 18th century A.D. Any generalizations about it are fraught with danger. Yet, the very length, size, and continuity of the tradition means that it must have a cultural import that can be generally described.

Let me begin by giving my view of the nature of the *dharmaśāstra* literature. I believe that the *dharmaśāstra* literature represents a peculiarly Indian record of local social norms and traditional standards of behavior. It represents in very definite terms the law of the land. This is different than the view held by my teacher, Ludo Rocher. It is different than the view of Govinda Das, and in an important way it is different from what *Mayne* understood. What I mean is that the whole of the *dharma* corpus can be viewed as a record of custom. It is not always a clear record because of the idiom and the fictions which came to be the mode of expression of the *dharma* literature. That the *dharma* literature is a record of custom is obfuscated by the fact that the idiom of all the *dharma* literature is one of eternality and timelessness. This means that there are no contemporaneous references which can help us to establish the chronology of these ideas, nor is there admission that custom and practice changed and evolved over time.[6] It is further obfuscated by the fact that the *dharma* literature clings to the claim that all of its provisions can be traced directly or indirectly to the Veda, the very root of dharma.

How can I justify my view that *dharmaśāstra* is a record of custom by examining the theoretical statements made in the *dharmaśāstras* and in the *Mīmāṃsā* literature, and by examining the nature of particular rules preserved in the *dharmaśāstra* texts.

J.D.M. Derrett has made the claim that the *dharmaśāstra* was always only of 'suasive' authority and that the British misunderstood the literature and treated it as positive law.[7] First of all, to say that *dharmaśāstra* is not positive law raises the question of what we mean by positive law. If by positive law we mean law enacted by a properly constituted authority for the government of society, then it is my view that the provisions of *dharmaśāstra* qualify as positive law. That they are based on normative values or find expression in the exemplary behavior of specific groups does not diminish the positive character of the laws. *All* legal systems are based on norms and beliefs which, if pressed as to their sources, are ultimately normative and in some sense, therefore, 'natural' law.[8]

If we pause for a moment to consider what a properly constituted authority might have been in classical India, we come face to face with one of the most nettlesome problems in the history of *dharmaśāstra*: we do not know by whom or when our texts were composed. The texts themselves – concerned to preserve the fiction of Vedic timelessness – tell us nothing about their own histories. We are left to extrapolate how these texts may have come into being. What we do know – as certainly as we can know anything in *dharmaśāstra* – is that a significant portion of the laws administered in royal courts were those which had been authored by representative bodies of regions, guilds, trade groups, castes, etc. We know from Kātyāyana, Bṛhaspati, Manu, and Pitāmaha that the king was obliged to sanction and enforce those regional conventions which were the consensus of local leaders. These *vyavasthās* were to be the basis for the king's decision in his own courts, not just in the local courts[9]. Nārada (10.2–3) tells us that the king is obliged to enforce even the customs of heretics:

pāṣaṇḍanaigamaśreṇipugavratagaṇādiṣu |
saṃrakṣet samayaṃ rājā durge janapade tathā ||
yo dharmaḥ karma yac caiṣam upasthānavidhiś ca yaḥ |
yac caiṣām vṛttyutpādānam anumanyeta tat tathā ||

'The king must protect the conventions of heretics, corporate bodies, guilds, councils, troops, groups, and the like in towns and in the countryside. Whatever their laws, duties, rules for worship, or mode of livelihood, he must permit them.'

Lingat objects that these laws – which he prefers to call statutes (French *statuts*) – are not 'legislation' since they were regulations that applied to 'restricted circles in the population and had not the general application which is required by our definition of 'legislation.''[10] What is more, he does not consider the findings of the court real law because 'It is *dharma* only for the two parties in the case. It cannot leave any trace in the sphere of the law itself.' *Lingat* further objects to describing the findings of the king's court as law because the *rājaśāsana* which results from the king's court is 'merely an expression of the royal policies, which could be inspired by considerations of convenience, opportunism, or equity, of which the king is and must remain the sole judge.'[11] This seems to me to be a parochial view of the phenomena of law. To claim, as *Lingat* does, that 'law is understood to express the will of all' is naïve insofar as there is not, nor has there ever been, a society in which the 'will of all' is anything more than a fiction. To require that every law apply uniformly to every person is to establish a standard for ancient India that is ludicrous. There is *no* system where laws apply equally to all whom they govern. Quite aside from the fact that specific laws are never applied to certain individuals (for example, laws restricting the activities of physicians have no applicability to plumbers or professors unless they are also physicians), there is inherent in every society relationships which mitigate the application of laws. Whether it is the policeman who winks at the excesses of his colleagues or the rich man who hires enough legal talent to intimidate and exhaust his opponent,[12] the fact is that using universal applicability as a standard is not helpful. *Lingat's* judgment on the nature of the *dharma* literature is clouded by his definition of positive law. As to the objection that a decision by the king is motivated by convenience, opportunism, or equity, this seems a peculiar view in light of the contemporary judicial history in France, Great Britain, and the United States. Surely *Lingat* does not mean to suggest that there is a single, brilliantly apparent set of immutable legal norms obvious to and uniformly applied by every judge.

Blackstone and *Cicero* provide us with definitions of law which are more useful for Indian society. *Cicero* said, 'Law (*lex*) is the highest reason, implanted in nature, which commands what ought to be done and forbids the opposite.'[13] *Blackstone* stated that law is 'a rule of civil conduct prescribed by the supreme power in a state, commanding what is right and prohibiting what is wrong.'[14] In the light of these definitions, the pronouncements of the king's court are most assuredly law. They are law because they command what is right and prohibit what is wrong.

Lingat's objection that the decisions of a king's court are not law because they are *dharma* only for the litigants is not a sound objection, because we must consider that nearly all *dharma* is *svadharma*. That is, questions of right and wrong – questions of dharma – are unique to each individual. We know from anthropological literature that dispute settlement in India is never done by weighing a set of facts in abstraction (except in government courts), rather the total history and relationship of the individuals involved is taken into account either overtly or implicitly.[15] The reason for this is that in the Indian view each set of facts is unique and each dispute is therefore unique. To be bound by precedent is to be bound to give a wrong verdict since no previous decision can be anything more than the most general guidepost.[16]

I think that too much has been made of the difference between *dharmaśāstra* and positive law. From our outsiders', western perspective we see huge gaps between an articulated theory of the law and the society we know from other sources such as inscriptions, literature, and anthropology. We conclude that this system must be a priestly fabrication or at least something other than law. Since it is not like Gaius or Justinian or the U.S. Constitution it must not be positive law. This is wrong. The Indian tradition is simply more overt and bold about the theological underpinnings of its legal system.[17] There is a sophistication and wisdom about the nature of law and legal literature that we have only begun to approach in the Common Law tradition.

We in the west have deluded and deceived ourselves into thinking that law – especially written law – has a reality, a fixed and certain character which it does not. There is implicit in the notion of positive law a constancy, a permanence and a certainty which is not justified. The notion of positive law arises from a European tradition which only knows law as recorded in texts. By texts, here, I mean written and eventually printed texts: black letter law. These texts have often given scholars and legal theorists a sense of certainty and confidence that may not be fully justified by the nature of the printed text.[18] My colleague *Sanford Levinson* has said of a written source of law, 'To view it as a genuine source of guidance is naïve, however heartbreaking this realization might be.'[19] India's tradition treated texts differently than we do. I believe that the ancient Indians intuitively held the view that no legal writing was ever intended to be valid in and of itself, but only as it was understood by those members of society who were trustworthy. The trustworthiness of these individuals was determined by their intimacy with the Veda. These were the arbiters of custom and, hence, of law.

These worthies knew that dharma – like justice – is context sensitive. The application of all law is context sensitive. It is a delusion to think that the law can be proclaimed for all time and in every circumstance. The authors of the *dharma* literature understood this context sensitivity of *dharma*. It was never their intention to exhaustively record and codify all law applicable for all time.[20] It was their intention to provide a means whereby law could be 'discovered' in each specific context. In an Indian context there was never the idea that any two crimes or civil wrongs were identical, so there was nor reason to be concerned with precedent. Each dispute was unique and what was needed was a general set of guidelines for procedure and for classification of the dispute. This is what the *dharmaśāstra* provided for dispute settlers of ancient India.

What was the source for the guidelines and classifications provided by these texts? The fiction was that it was the Veda, but a closer examination indicates that the tradition itself recognized that the ultimate source of *dharma* in a legal sense was custom. There are frequent acknowledgements of this in the *dharma* literature. Āpastambadharmasūtra (1.7.20.6–7) has said: *Na dharmādharmau carata āvam sva iti na devagandharvā na pitara ity ācakṣate 'yam dharmo 'yam adharma iti. Yat tv āryāḥ kriyamāṇam praśaṃsanti sa dharmo yad garhante so 'dharmaḥ* 'Dharma and *Adharma* do not go about saying, 'Here we are.' Nor do gods, gandharvas, or pitṛs say, 'This is *dharma*. This is *adharma*.' [So there is nothing for it but to define] *dharma* [as] 'That which honorable men praise, [and] *adharma* [as] that which they condemn.'

Then there is the well-known concept of the four feet of legal procedure articulated in Nārada (1.10–11): dharma, legal procedure, custom, and the king's decree are the four bases of legal procedure. According to the understandings of this verse recorded by commentators, custom is the overriding source of rules of conduct which the king must enforce.[21]

This is not to say that custom did not accommodate itself to the texts – it certainly must have – Sanskritization cannot be a wholly modern phenomenon.[22] Nor do I mean to state that there is no distortion or sanitizing in the brāhmaṇas' recording of custom – there certainly was. The utter absence of any temporal reference and the fog of the fictional Vedic source are clear indicators that they are doctoring the record. In general, however, the brāhmaṇa *dharmaśāstra* writers were constrained by the burden placed on them as recorders and synthesizers of customary practice. They were obliged by the interested constituencies, by the king, and by considerations of social and political harmony to record the practice as they found it. They were also obliged to explain how these customs fit with the tradition, and it is in these 'explanations' that we may find the most outré flights of brāhmaṇa imagination. In the notion of mixed castes, for example, we are told that the plethora of castes came from admixture of the original four castes recorded in the eternal Veda.[23] This sort of explanation is where brāhmaṇa authors become inventive and paint the data with their unique perspective. Still, this very brahminical explanation affirms the existence of the many castes and their relative autonomy, and the deference with which the king is obliged to treat the customs of these castes establishes their customs as legally binding.

Similarly, the response of the commentators and digest writers to the Nāradasmṛti's provision for the remarriage of widows and other women who have entered into unsuitable marriages is an example of how the brāhmaṇa authors explained rather than dictated custom. Nāradasmṛti 12.97 says:

naṣṭe mṛte pravrajite klībe ca patite patau |
pañcasv āpatsu narīnām patir anyo vidhīyate[24] ||

'There are five catastrophes in which women are required to take another husband: if the husband disappears, dies, or becomes a world-renouncer, a eunuch, or an outcaste.' Commentators such as Medhātithi are not very comfortable with this provision. Their explanations reflect a definite disagreement with this blanket admonition to remarry. Medhātithi in commenting on Manu 9.76 flatly rejects this view altogether and says it is wrong. Mādhavācārya commenting on Parāśaradharmasaṃhitā 4.30 says that this is a rule applicable only in previous yugas (*yugāntaraviṣaya*). Bhavasvāmin limits the applicability of this rule only to virgin women (*akṣaṭayoni*), and even then the rules of *niyoga* apply. Bālambhaṭṭa (p. 685) on Yājñavalkya 2.127 says that this only applies in those cases where there has been a verbal commitment of marriage but the actual *saṃskāra* itself has not been completed. Māskarin commenting on Gautama 18.4 intimates that the verse quoted above is to be understood as advocating *niyoga* – the sole motive for the remarriage should be the birth of offspring.[25]

In spite of the fact that this Nāradasmṛtivacana is unambiguous in its admonition to remarry, the commentators don't like it.[26] They struggle with it and use their considerable hermeneutical skills to interpret it in such a way as to minimize its applicability. Yet, the verse survives. Why? If the provision really applies to a previous *yuga*, why should it be preserved and passed on to contemporary students? The tradition knows well the idea of 'editing' texts for use in different eras of human development, [27] so why not do a little editing here? The reasons are no doubt many and complex, but have to do with the fundamentally conservative nature of the *smṛti* tradition.[28] Nevertheless, I believe that in many cases the compilers of *smṛti* texts were confronted with practices that they did not approve of, but that were commonly accepted either in other sectors of society or in other villages or regions.[29] Sometimes these practices were dismissed as the practice of depraved classes,[30] and at other times they registered their uncertainty by attributing rules to 'others' or by introducing them with 'some say'.[31]

The point here is that the *smṛti* texts were the record of actual customs and practices found in classical India. These customs were recorded whether the compilers of *smṛtis* agreed with them or not because it was the purpose of these texts – on one level – to record the norms of those communities which accepted *dharma* as the standard of behavior. In addition, it was the object of the recorders of these customs to integrate these practices into the brahminical/vedic *weltanschauung* the promotion of which was the basic motive for their recording the customs in the first place.[32] It is in their explanations of these customs that we find the 'pious wish[es]' and 'metaphysically minded, ceremonial ridden priestly promulga[tion]' that Govinda *Das* decried. The brāhmaṇas' peculiar understandings and strained explanations do not diminish the fact that custom is the source of dharma. There is much made of the Vedic source, but ultimately, the immediate source is custom.

The legal texts themselves tell us this in very clear terms. All custom is binding. The commentators, the *nibandhakāras*, and the *Mīmāṃsakas* went to great lengths to establish that *śiṣṭācāra* (the practices of learned brāhmaṇas) was binding as was established custom for all others. The elevation of *śiṣṭācāra* in the hierarchy of sources of *dharma* is theologically possible because these practices are based on some lost or forgotten Vedic passage. As for the inclusion of the established customs of others as 'legally' binding, this also has a theological motive, namely to include those communities which are not under the immediate sway of the brahminical influence within the vedic world – to Sanskritize them in reverse.

This has the effect of sanctifying custom and generously granting the status of *dharma* to local practice. A reading of the *holakādhikāraṇa* of the Mīmāṃsāsūtras (1.3.15–18) and the commentaries and subcommentaries thereon reveals the liberality with which custom is treated – anything goes as long as it is the practice of those persons the community holds to be virtuous. This principle is carried to the most extreme lengths by Mitramiśra who says that the customs of Śūdras are *dharma* for Śūdras[33] even though they obviously cannot be based on any Śūdra elders' familiarity with the Veda. There is clearly a greater value and esteem placed on the practices of the ideal brāhmaṇa, but his practices are *dharma* for the brāhmaṇa, not for anyone else. The *dharmaśāstra* writers would like for all readers to come away with the notion that brāhmaṇas are the best, most worthy, most important elements of society, and that their lives are exemplary and at the very peak of the normative heap. This may have been true in some settings, and that the brāhmaṇas wished this to be so is almost certain. Whether it was the universal norm is doubtful, and one piece of evidence is the persistence with which unpopular provisions in the *dharmaśāstras* survive: there must have been large segments of classical Indian society, just as there are large segments of modern Indian society, for whom brāhmaṇas are of little social or political consequence.

From the standpoint of a scholar outside of the tradition, what we are seeing in this liberal acceptance of local practice is a device which assures the inclusion of dominant local custom within the mainstream of Hindu orthodoxy. This means that the local consensus concerning norms of behavior is the real source of dharma, and that the validation of that local practice by tying it to some long forgotten Vedic text is a fiction which serves to provide an umbrella of orthodoxy for all of Bhāratavarṣa. It is the acceptance of this fiction which is the real test of Hindu orthodoxy – not any particular practice or theology.[34]

This has consequences, of course, for how we, as scholars, approach these texts in our attempts to reconstruct the social and legal history of classical India. *J.D.M. Derrett's 'Dharmaśāstra* and Juridical Literature' is a case in point. This important, laconic, and sometimes brilliant little book introduces an interpretive category to the world of *dharmaśāstra* scholarship. In his discussion of the *dharma* literature he divides texts into two categories: those which are 'genuine' and those which are not. Now, the notion of a genuine *dharma* text is not a difficult one. However, the idea that some of these texts were 'apocryphal,'[35] or 'bogus,'[36] or 'supposititious'[37] requires some explanation. Unfortunately, he does not provide us with any explanation of his criteria for categorizing such texts. He uses these terms in a general manner and rarely gives specific textual examples. Even when he refers to specific texts[38] he does not explain why these texts are spurious or apocryphal. His style is to simply toss out these words without elaboration: 'In the end an apocryphal *smṛti* says that ancestral customs are more important than any rule in the śāstras'[39]...The *Paraśarasmṛti*...is an ancient *smṛti*,...not to be confused with the supposititious *smṛtis* which arose during the period of the commentators.[40] ...The wave of 'bogus' *smṛti* writing, which may have extended into the 17th century, was not juridical in inspiration.'[41]

In only one instance does he give any explanation for the use of these adjectives: 'Texts appearing once only and attributed to named authors may in fact be apocryphal.'[42] This general statement is unsupported by any further argumentation. What he seems to mean from the context is that when a verse is only cited once in the tradition then it should be suspect. By this he does not mean if a verse is found cited once and in only one manuscript then it should be rejected. He means to say that if a verse is found in only one place in the commentaries and *nibandhas* then it is apocryphal.

This standard for judging a verse to be 'bogus' is unacceptable. First, it is not the place of scholars to make this judgment. We can identify texts as chronologically recent, theologically innovative, more or less effective in articulating a position, but if a writer puts forth an opinion it is not within a scholar's province to label it apocryphal. This is a judgment that can only be made by the tradition itself, and even then a text's apocryphal status is only one group's opinion. No Gnostic ever called the Book of John 'The Apocryphon of John,' [43] but if a Christian theologian views it in this way, then we may adopt his category as a descriptive one, but we may not adopt the evaluative, normative judgment implicit in that Christian theologian's usage. In *Derrett's* usage of the terms apocryphal, etc. one has the clear impression that the verses so described have been judged by him to be wrong or incorrect in some way. This is not historical scholarship.

Second, to characterize a text on this basis is to ignore the role of custom and the manner in which texts are transmitted. There is no ecclesiastical body in the Hindu tradition which is empowered to adjudicate on the canonicity of verses or even whole texts. The ultimate test of the verity of a text is whether or not it is acceptable to successive generations of *śiṣṭas*. These are the vectors for the transmission of any text. If the *śiṣṭas* determined that a verse or whole text was bogus, apocryphal, etc. then they would not have bothered to transmit it. The methods of transmission – by teaching a text to students and by having a manuscript copied – ensured that there was an informed, vigilant, and conservative audience which would be able to detect a fraud quickly.

The very notion of a fraudulent passage in a *smṛti* text requires some explanation. What can it mean? Why would anyone invent a verse in the first place? There can only be two general reasons for doing so: (1) for venal reasons a verse might be created in order to help one party or another in a dispute; and (2) to adapt the tradition to new social circumstances – when local custom has presented practices or circumstances which were not provided for in earlier texts. The venality of the first reason is guarded against by the presence of a large, informed community of experts in *dharma* who would be able to immediately detect a fraudulent verse created for the express purpose of promoting individual interests.[44]

The second reason for the creation of a verse – to adapt the tradition to new circumstances – was not fraud. This was the ongoing process that gave the tradition vitality and the ability to endure. Not only was the adaptation of the textual tradition to the changing needs of society implicit in the development of the *dharmaśāstra*, it was explicitly recognized within the tradition. *Derrett* opposes 'bogus' *smṛtis* with the category of 'genuine' *smṛtis* by 'known' authors (an interesting term in itself since we know almost nothing about these authors). By this he means those authors found in lists of authors of *smṛti* works within the textual tradition: thus Manu, Yājñavalkya, Nārada, etc. There can be no doubt that these texts have a universal appeal to all of the Hindu tradition. We are told very explicitly, for example, that Manu is the most authoritative of these authoritative texts.[45] Kumārila Bhaṭṭa in his commentary on the above mentioned *holakādhikāraṇa* of the Mīmāṃsāsūtras also mentions the Manusmṛti (along with the *purāṇas* and *itihāsa*) as uniquely universal in their acceptance throughout the region of Bhāratavarṣa. But universal authority is not to be confused with genuineness.

Kumārila goes on to state that *all smṛti* texts, however limited in their geographical or social applicability, are authoritative for those people who recognize them as such. That is, as long as a practice is

1. time-honored,
2. not opposed to the express provisions of the Veda or of *smṛti*,
3. regarded as obligatory by the *śiṣṭas*,
4. not immoral, and
5. *adṛṣṭārtha*,

it is considered to be authoritative. Custom, therefore, – even for the tradition itself – is the productive and vital source of rules found in the *dharmaśāstra*.

What *Derrett* seems to imply is that older texts are more authoritative than newer ones. Texts written for specific purposes which can be located in a specific region or time are 'bogus' or 'apocryphal.' But this is not acceptable criterion. Let us look at one of the texts which he dismisses as 'apocryphal.' The *Devalasmṛti*, according to *Derrett*, is a text which was written to cope with the problem of Hindu women who were abducted into marriage or raped by invading Muslims in Sind. This makes it a very late text and one written for very specific purposes, therefore apocryphal, i.e., of dubious authenticity.

The *Devalasmṛti* does contain enough geographical information that it is safe to conclude that it was composed in northwestern India and at a relatively late date. The *mlecchas* mentioned were probably invading Muslims. The penances mentioned are for forcible abduction. *Derrett* is correct in his assessment of the purpose and intention of the *Devalasmṛti*, but by what criterion could we possibly call this text apocryphal. It is attempting to provide specific remedies for a situation which that society had not previously encountered – wholesale abduction of its women by members of a hostile and heterodox religious tradition. The *prayaścittas* mentioned are intended to expunge the taint inherent in this situation. The mere fact that the text has been passed on for generations through the work of copyists is enough to validate its claim to authoritativeness within the tradition. These penances meet all of the criteria mentioned above for acceptance within the tradition:

1. time-honored,
2. not opposed to the express provisions of the Veda or of *smṛti*,
3. regarded as obligatory by the *śiṣṭas*,
4. not immoral, and
5. *adṛṣṭārtha*.

The mere fact that these provisions have not been formulated in exactly this way in earlier *smṛtis*, or that these penances have not before been mentioned as being applicable to women who have suffered the specific insults described in this text is not enough to render them apocryphal or bogus. This is just an example of the tradition continuing to adapt itself to the changing needs of society.

The categories of apocryphal and supposititious have no place in the discussion of the surviving Sanskrit *dharma* literature. The works which we have may be of limited geographical or chronological applicability. They may represent various strata in the evolution of the *dharmaśāstra*, but every provision found in every text can and must be viewed as a codification of practice or of norms accepted by some part of the society. They are not fraudulent or venal attempts at deception. To characterize them as such is to distort the tradition and to misunderstand the nature of the corpus of *dharma* literature.

To return to the three representative views of the nature of *dharmaśāstra* with which we began this essay, I distinguish my view from that found in *Mayne's* Treatise in that we must understand that the *dharmaśāstras* were not composed as literary templates to be applied *in toto* to every situation and every dispute without differentiation. They were collections of aphorisms, guidelines, and advice which could be drawn upon when required to inform and validate a judge's, or a guru's, or a king's opinion. In this way they are indeed concerned with the practical administration of law, but they are not in a modern, western sense 'codes.' Thus Govinda *Das* was right to point out the error of treating them as codes of law.[46] The contents of the *dharmaśāstra* were, however, much more than 'pious wishes' and represent a definite 'reality' that must have been rigidly enforced by contemporary political authorities. *Rocher's* view that the commentaries and digests did not represent the law of the land must be modified to some extent.[47] The rationalizations, the explanations, and the justifications for certain views must fall in the category of 'panditic' reasoning, but the 'authoritative texts' were just that, and the laws found in these texts remained of importance, and, if very late *jayapattras* are valid testimony, remained applicable.[48] It seems reasonable to conclude, then, that *dharmaśāstra* does represent 'law' in a very real sense; that the practices recorded in *dharmaśāstra* did represent the law of the land and are of very real value in constructing the history of Indian society since these texts tell us how – alas, not where and when – people actually lived.

NOTES

[1] The remarks in this paper are concerned with the *vyavahāra* (legal procedure) portions of dharmaśāstra. Although I believe that the general notion of the ascendancy of custom and the efforts to include rather than exclude local practice within the realm of *dharma* apply equally as well to *ācāra* and *prayaścitta*, I am not addressing those portions of the *dharmaśāstra* literature here.

[2] [*John D.*] *Mayne's* Treatise on Hindu Law and Usage, 12th edition, revised by Justice Alladi *Kuppuswami*, Delhi 1986, p. 2. It must be pointed out that this view does not seem to have been first included in the eleventh edition revised by *N. Chandrasekhara Aiyar* in 1950.

[3] 'The Real Character of Hindu Law,' the introduction to the Vyavahāra-bāla mbhaṭṭī of Bālambhaṭṭa Pāyagunde, edited by *Nityanand Pant Parvatiya*, Chowkhamba Sanskrit Series 41, Benares, 1914, p. 8.

[4] Ibid, p. 16.

[5] *Ludo Rocher*, 'Changing Patterns of Diversification in Hindu Law,' in: Identity and Diversification in Cults and Sects in South Asia, Philadelphia, 1984, pp. 31–44 at 41.

[6] The *kalivarjyas* are the only explicit recognition of the possibility of change in custom and its instantiation in rules. The formal theory of *kalivarjyas* is a very late one and its primary purpose seems to have been to explain inconsistencies in the texts whose origins were then lost in the mists of the past. For dates, see *Baṭuknāth Bhattacharya*, The 'Kalivarjyas' or Prohibitions in the 'Kali' Age, Calcutta, 1943, pp. 176–177. While the formal theory is late, the notion that the parameters of *dharmic* behavior changed over time is an old one, see, for example, Nirukta 1.20 and Gautamadharmasūtra 1.3–5.
[7] Dharmaśāstra and Juridical Literature, Wiesbaden, 1973, p. 9.
[8] For an analysis of the Indian case, one cannot do better than that of *Wilhelm Halbfass* in India and Europe, Albany, 1988, pp. 330–333.
[9] 48–50 says: *deśasyānumatenaiva vyavasthā yā nirupitā |*
likhitā tu sadā dhāryā mudritā rājamudrayā || 48 || *śāstravad yatnato rakṣyā tam nirīkṣya virnirṇayet* ||
naigamasthais tu yat kāryam likhitaṃ yad vyavasthitam || 49 || *tasmāt tat sampravarteta nānyathaiva pravartayet* || 50 ||
'A written convention determined by the consensus of regional inhabitants is to be kept and sealed with the royal seal. It should be strictly enforced just like the *śāstra* and considered when rendering a decision. A regulation which is written down by traders is justiciable and should therefore be adhered to. He (the king?) should not conduct himself otherwise.' For similar passages in Bṛhaspati see Vīramitrodaya Vyavahāraprakāśa p. 22, for Pitāmaha see Smṛticandrikā Vyavahārakāṇḍa p. 58, and Manu 8.41.
[10] *Robert Lingat*, The Classical Law of India (translated from the French with additions by *J. Duncan M. Derrett*), Berkeley 1973, p. 228 and note 53.
[11] Ibid. p. 256.
[12] See, for example, *Marc Galanter*, 'Why the 'haves' come out ahead: speculations on the limits of legal change,' in: Law and Society Review 9 (1974), pp. 95–160.
[13] *De Legibus*, Book I vi (Loeb Classical Library ed. Translated By *C.W. Keyes*), Cambridge, MA, 1928, p. 317.
[14] *Sir William Blackstone*, Commentaries on the laws of England, 4 vols., Buntingford (England) 1966 (reprint of 1st ed. 1765–1769), vol. 1, p. 44.
[15] See *Bernard S. Cohn*, 'Some Notes on Law and Change in North India,' in: Economic Development and Cultural Chang 8 (1959–1960) pp. 79–93, and 'Anthropological Notes on Disputes and Law in India,' in: American Anthropologist 67 (1965) pp. 82–122. 'A Caste Dispute Among Washermen of Mysore,' in: Eastern Anthropologist 6–7 (1952–1954) pp. 148–168. Also *Robert M. Hayden*, 'Excommunication as Everyday Event and Ultimate Sanction: The Nature of Suspension from an Indian Caste,' in: The Journal of Asian Studies 42 (1983) pp. 291–308, and *David G. Mandelbaum*, Society in India, vol. 1, Berkeley, 1972, pp. 310–311.
[16] Uniform application of the law is a fiction in any society claiming such application. One need only look at the legal escapades of Richard Nixon, Edward Kennedy, and Ronald Reagan, and the grotesque disproportion of African-Americans sentenced to death for capital crimes to see sad but eloquent testimony to the lack of uniform applicability of laws in the United States.
[17] For an eloquent articulation of the religion of the U.S. Constitution and of the American state, see *Sidney E. Mead*, The Lively Experiment, New York, 1963, especially chapter 5, 'Abraham Lincoln's 'Last, Best Hope of Earth': The American Dream of Destiny and Democracy.'
[18] There is a plethora of literature assailing the certainty of texts. See, for example, *Stanley Fish*: Is there a Text in This Class?, Cambridge (MA) 1980 and Doing what comes naturally: change, rhetoric, and the practice of theory in literary and legal studies, Durham (North Carolina), 1989.

[19] *Sanford Levinson*, 'Law as Literature' in: The Texas Law Review 60 (1982) p. 378.

[20] Gautamadharmśāstra ends (28.49) with the statement that in cases where no specific rule has been given, then the matter should be decided by a properly constituted assembly. *Derrett* recognizes this as well, 'Law thus did not depend on texts, but upon how texts were used.' (*Derrett, Sontheimer, Smith,* Beiträge zum Indischen Rechtsdenken, Weisbaden, 1979, p. 108.)

[21] See *Robert Lingat*, Les 'quatres pieds du procès' in: Journal Asiatique 250 (1962) pp. 489–503.

[22] It is a concept that extends back to Śivāji, certainly, inasmuch as he worked diligently to expunge the Persian influence from the language and government of his empire. See *Benoy Kumar Sarkar*, The Positive Background of Hindu Sociology, Delhi 1985 (reprint of 1937), pp. 507–508. That *Sarkar* was actually the first to use the term Sanskritization (15 years before *M.N. Srinivas* in his Religion and Society Among the Coorgs) has been pointed out by *Pabitrakumar Gupta* in 'Acharya Benoykumar Sarkar on Sanskritization' in: Acarya Binaykumar Sarkar, edited by *Pradyot Ghosh*, Maldah 1988, pp. A–E. I am grateful to my colleague, Dr. *Rahul Peter Das*, for bringing this article to my attention. *Derrett* (Beiträge, p. 108) holds a similar view of the mutual influence of custom and *śāstra*, although he denies that was law 'it became evident that *śāstra* was not law, but one of the means whereby law occurred. The *śāstra* in fact reflected selected customs, some of which it systemized in an intellectual sense and in the direction of righteousness; and in due course customs began to move in time with the *śāstra*, but unevenly and unpredictably.'

[23] For a thorough discussion of the various mixed caste systems and the explanations thereof, see *Horst Brinkhaus*, Die altindischen Mischkastensysteme, Wiesbaden, 1978.

[24] This verse is also found in Parāśaradharmasaṃhitā 4.30 and attributed to Bṛhaspati by the Maskaribhāṣya on Gautamadharmasūtra 18.4.

[25] There are many such 'problems' that confront the interpreters of the *smṛti* tradition including the explanation of such well known institutions as the *āśrama* system, and *niyoga*, the levirate marriage which is first praised and then condemned all within five verses of the same chapter of Manu (9.59 and 9.64). For a first rate, comprehensive account of how the *āśrama* system – which we take so much for granted – evolved, and how the textual accounts differ from the 'standard' understanding of the institutions, see *Patrick Olivelle's* The āśrama System: the History and Hermeneutics of a Religious Institution, Oxford University Press, New York, 1993.

[26] For a more complete discussion of the implications of and reactions to this verse see *R.W. Lariviere*, 'Matrimonial Remedies for Women in Classical Indian Law: Alternatives to Divorce,' in: Rules and Remedies in Classical Indian Law, ed. *Julia Leslie*, Leiden, 1991, pp. 37–45; and *Paul Thieme*, 'Jungfrauengatte' in: Kleine Schriften, Wiesbaden, 1984, pp. 426–513.

[27] See, for example, the account of the transmission of the Manusmṛti found in the beginning of Mātrkā 1 of the Nāradasmṛti.

[28] See the Introduction to my translation of the Nāradasmṛti, pp. xii–xiv.

[29] Another interesting example is the apparent acknowledgement of the existence of testamentary disposition of paternal property – a will – in classical Hindu Law. Nāradasmṛti 13.15 says

pitraiva tu vibhaktā ye hīnādhikasamair dhanaih
tesāṃ sa eva dharmaḥ syāt sarvasya hi pitā prabhuḥ ||

'The partition done by the father is legally binding on the coparceners whether the shares are equal or not, because the father is the master of everything.' This flies in the face of the normal rules of inheritance, and the commentators are uneasy about it. The Dayabhaga 53 and the Smṛticandrikā Vyavahārakāṇḍa 609–610, both stipulate that this can only apply to property acquired by the testator – not to ancestral property. The Parāśaramādhavīya 414 says that this disposition is sanctioned by *smṛti*, but since it violates common practice (*lokaviruddha*) and scripture (*śrutiviruddha*) it is better to divide the property equally. In opposition to this view Bhavasvāmin 153 in his commentary on the Nāradīyamanusaṃhitā says that whatever the father wishes in such a case is what must be done. The Vyavahāramayukha 99 flatly states that this provision of Nārada's applies to a different *yuga*. There is an apparent reference to a will in the Gilgit manuscripts (*patrābhilekhya* and *patrābhilikhita*), see: Giglit Manuscripts vol. III part 2 edited by *Nalinaksha Dutt*, Bibliotheca Indo-Buddhica 17, Srinagar 1942, p. 140. I am grateful to *Gregory Schopen* for this reference, who discusses it in an unpublished article, 'The Monks' Obligation to Make Merit for Deceased Donors: A Buddhist Parallel to Monastic Practice in the Medieval West.'

30 As in the discussion of a husband's liability for a woman's debt at Nāradasmṛti 1.16.

31 See *Olivelle, loc.cit.*, section 3.1.1 and 3.2.1.1.

32 Ibid., *passim*, makes clear that much of the history of what we have come to call the *āśrama* system can rightly be seen as attempting to theologically synthesize a wide range of practices.

33 *Vīramitrodaya-paribhāṣaprakāśa* p. 9.

34 It is possible that social change – perhaps the effects of the urbanization of the mid-1st millennium B.C. – diminished the capacity of a brāhmaṇa class to influence the practices.

35 *Derrett, Dharmaśāstra*, p. 41.

36 Ibid., p. 40.

37 Ibid., p. 39.

38 For example, ibid., p. 36 note 184 where he simply cites 'Katy. 37–51, 225, 884a.'

39 Ibid., p. 39, Sumantu quoted in the *Smṛticandrika, Sanskārakāṇnda*, p. 9.

40 Ibid., p. 39.

41 Ibid., p. 40.

42 Ibid., pp. 40–41.

43 See *Hans Jonas*, The Gnostic Religion, Boston, 1963, p. 177.

44 There are relatively few surviving accounts of these disputes, but those that do survive give us an idea of their intensity. One example is found in Olivelle's edition of Ānandānubhava's *Nyāyaratnadīpāvali* (found in Renunciation in Hinduism: A Medieval Debate, volume one, Vienna, 1986, pp. 98–99) where he accuses an opponent of supporting a contrary view with fraudulent verses the opponent composed himself: *yas tu mandamatih mukhyayatidveṣāt kāṃcit kathaṃ ślokāṃś ca 'prāpte kaliyuge' ityādīn hārītadattātreyādivacanatvenodāharati sma so 'timūḍhah svaviraciteṣu doṣaṃ na paśyati ... prasiddhāśramanindāyām apy udīritapramāṇavirodhaṃ kathaṃ sa śocyo laṭakaḥ karṇāṭabaṭur na paśyati.* 'A fool motivated by excessive hatred of the principal type of renouncer, has cited some story or other and some verses claiming they are statements of Hārīta, Dattātreya, etc. which begin 'When the Kaliyuga arrives ...' This man is a complete fool who does not see the flaw in these verses he composed himself! How can this miserable cad, this twerp from Karṇātaka, not see that he contradicts oft-quoted authorities when he castigates a well-known *āśrama*?'

45 *Bṛhaspatismṛti, Saṃskārakāṇḍa* 1.13: *vedārthopanibaddhatvāt prādhānyaṃ hi manoh smṛtam* |
manvarthaviparītā tu yā smṛtiḥ sā na śasyate ||

46 In this he was preceded by the neglected *James H. Nelson*, see *J.D.M. Derrett*, J.H. Nelson: a forgotten administrator-historian of India, in: Essays in Classical and Modern Hindu Law, 2, Leiden, 1977, pp. 404–423.

47 In an even more recent statement of his views, in a 1992 address to the American Philosophical Society, *Rocher* has said, 'The composers of the *dharmaśāstras* compiled treatises on *dharma*, on anything they considered worthy of being recorded as dharma with some people, somewhere. They gathered that information in books, in the language of the learned, Sanskrit.'

48 See *Richard W. Lariviere*, A Sanskrit *Jayapattra* from Eighteenth Century Mithilā, in: Studies in *Dharmaśāstra*, Calcutta, 1984, pp. 49–80.

3415 Cactus Wren Way
Austin, TX 78746
USA
E-mail: rwl@uts.cc.utexas.edu

ALBRECHT WEZLER

DHARMA IN THE VEDA AND THE DHARMAŚĀSTRAS*

In his introduction to a symposium on the 'sacramental' dimension of religious traditions, Gerhard Oberhammer (1999, 17) states that *dharma* has to be regarded 'as "sacrament" in the sense intended here – hermeneutics of religion – i.e. as an event mediating transcendence to salvation.' His characterization of *dharma* 'as the performance of ritual prescriptions that are revealed in the Veda' makes it clear that he refers to what is defined as *codanālakṣaṇo 'rthaḥ* in *MS* 1.1.2, as 'something beneficial, the characteristics of which are the Vedic prescriptions.'[1] How then is this definition related to other concepts of Hindu *dharma*? Let us take, for example, the one Hacker (1965, 93–106) has called 'the most concrete and precise' definition he knows, namely the one from *ĀpDhS* 1.7.20.6–8 which states: 'Dharma and adharma ... do not go around and say, "That is us." Nor do gods, Gandharvas, or ancestors declare what dharma and adharma is. Rather, what the Āryas praise, when it is practiced, that is dharma; what they condemn, that is adharma. One's behavior should conform to the behavior which is unanimously accepted in all countries by Āryas who are well mannered, matured, self-disciplined, and free from greed and falsehood.'[2]

Admittedly, Hacker speaks also of '*the relation*' *dharma* has '*to the Veda*.' He states further that 'what is directly demanded in the Veda is absolutely binding' and 'it leads to an otherworldly salvation.' When he adds, however, that 'the Veda is the grandest source of dharma' (Hacker, 1965, 98), then it is immediately clear, that it is not – or not only – the Veda as the palladium of instructions concerning sacrifice which he has in mind here. Sacrifice, he notes later, was recognized 'as an automatic medium for the attainment of this- and otherworldly goals.' He has likewise the Veda as the grandest source of *dharma* in mind when he concludes:

*The original article in German entitled *Über den sakramentalen Charakter des Dharma nachsinnend*, was published in Oberhammer 1999, pp. 63–113. It was translated into English by Robert Fulton and Oliver Freiberger and revised for this volume by Patrick Olivelle.

> Dharma, the contents of which refers to the castes and life stages, encompasses the entire sphere of morality, culture, law, and custom and, put into practice, effects otherworldly salvation. It is derivable neither from a philosophical principle, nor a religious origin. Rather, it is detectable merely by empirical means, be it from the Veda, or from the consensus of the Good, with regard to the geographical location.[3]

When Indologists speak about Hindu *dharma*, they have either the sacrificial instructions of the Saṃhitās and Brāhmaṇas – or the Śrautasūtras – in mind, or the *varṇāśrama-dharma* of the Dharmaśāstra texts or both at the same time, though not necessarily giving both the same attention. When I first read Hacker's well-known essay on 'Dharma im Hinduismus,' I already wondered if in fact one was dealing here with two different subjects: with the Vedic *dharma* that covers the great ceremonial sacrifices, on the one hand, and with the *varṇāśrama-dharma*, on the other. What bothered me, *inter alia*, was the remark that *dharma* was to be 'detectable merely by empirical means, be it from the Veda, or from the consensus of the Good' (Hacker, 1965, 100). Hacker characterizes the 'Hindu concept of dharma' as 'radically empirical,'[4] without the necessary addendum that for the community whose views Hacker quotes the Veda is an eternal transcendental entity – in contrast to the other 'sources of Dharma.' Moreover, he does not address the issue that in one case 'instructions' and 'prescriptions' are explicitly expressed in the Vedic texts, while in the other case the behavior of a specific group of people is taken as a model from which 'instructions' can be secondarily deduced.

This question bothers me even today, and it appears the time has come to raise it publicly in other and more definitive terms. Are the Vedic *dharma* and the *dharma* of the Dharmaśāstra – conceptually distinguished in this manner – simply two parts, sides, or aspects of a single, ultimately uniform Hindu *dharma*? Or are they, at least in their origin, two completely different and originally separate strands of ancient Indian culture? And is the comprehensive – possibly also uniform – concept of *dharma*, therefore, secondary?[5]

VEDIC AND DHARMAŚĀSTRIC DHARMA

When we consider the subject-matter of the Vedic *dharma* on the one hand, and that of the Dharmaśāstric *dharma* on the other, what stands out starkly is their radical difference. The Dharmaśāstras certainly address ceremonial Vedic sacrifices, but they do so only in connection with the duties and rights of specific classes (*varṇa*) or certain acts of expiation (*prāyaścitta*), that is, only indirectly and, as it were, casually. There are no 'instructions' for the performance of such sacrifices. Sacrificial acts described in them belong to the sphere of Gṛhya-rituals or the 'non-solemn rites' (Gonda, 1980). The Śrauta-ritual, on the contrary, at most shows certain indirect connections to the actual subject of Dharmaśāstra. Conversely, phrases or chapters are to be found in the Saṃhitās and Brāhmaṇas that shed light on law, morals, and customs of the time, as well as on household rites (Gonda, 1980, 1f). For the Mīmāṃsakas and their followers, however, who consider the regulations and prohibitions concerning the Śrauta-sacrifice as the most important constituent of the Saṃhitās and Brāhmaṇas, these phrases are merely a supplement that is usually assigned to the category of *arthavāda*.

One may ask: do the Indians themselves make a distinction between these two kinds of *dharma*? Let us take the first phrase of *ĀpDhS*: *athātaḥ sāmayācārikān dharmān vyākhyāsyāmaḥ*, 'Now, therefore, we will declare the acts productive of merit which form part of the customs of daily life, as they have been settled by the agreement (of those who know the law).'[6] The two initial particles (*atha* and *ataḥ*) signal here, as elsewhere in Vedic and early post-Vedic texts, a new subject of instruction different from the preceding one. Bühler was right to stick to the explanation of the secondary noun *sāmayācārika*[7] given by the commentator Haradatta (between 1100 and 1300 AD), namely *samayamūlā ācārāḥ* [=] *samayācārās* [,] *teṣu bhavāḥ* (Cf. Pāṇini 4.3.53) *sāmayācārikāḥ* / (*evaṃbhūtān dharmān iti* /),[8] although it might be worth considering if *samaya* means 'agreement that exists or appears in practice' rather than 'accord' or 'convention.'[9] Whether the usage of the plural *dharmān* is relevant for our question is somewhat doubtful, because the use of the plural is not unique to Dharmaśāstras; it is, in fact, encountered frequently also in older Vedic texts. Nevertheless, it is worth considering.[10]

Suppose, then, that the attribute *sāmayācārika* serves to distinguish the *dharmāḥ* that Āpastamba is going to elucidate from others. Then again the lack of this or an equivalent definition in *GautDhS* and *BaudhDhS* requires an explanation. The explanation certainly cannot be the claim that Gautama is simply older than Āpastamba – possibly even the oldest Dharmasūtra of all, according to the common view.[11] The argument that Gautama has not yet realized the necessity of such a specification (unlike Āpastamba, the author of the younger work) is not very convincing, especially in view of the fact that the even younger *BaudhDhS* is also silent on this point. Gautama (8.11), furthermore, is familiar with the expression *sāmayācārika*,[12] apparently even with the same meaning; but he does not employ it in the opening of his work. It is advisable, therefore, not to view *sāmayācārika* in *ĀpDhS* 1.1.1.1 as an attribute *necessary* to distinguish Āpastamba's *dharma* or to conclude from it the existence of another concept of *dharma*. The addition apparently only makes explicit what is expressed in the other sources as a subject of teaching by the word *dharma* only. What, however, does *dharma* mean there? It means undisputedly what I call '*dharma* of the Dharmaśāstra.' For the second *sūtra GautDhS* 1.2 (*tadvidāṃ ca smṛtiśīle*) – further examined below – the subject of which, namely, *dharmamūlam*, has to be complemented from 1.1, shows with sufficient certainty that this is precisely the content of the term *dharma* in *GautDhS* 1.1 *vedo dharmamūlam*. Similarly, it can be concluded from *BaudhDhS* 1.1.1.3 (*smārto dvitīyaḥ*) that *dharma* in *BaudhDhS* 1.1.1.1[13] *upadiṣṭo dharmaḥ prativedam*, is by no means the Vedic *dharma*[14] but nothing else than the '*dharma* of the Dharmaśāstra.' Gautama and Baudhāyana thus also have a definite and clear idea of what is labeled *dharma* (by them and in general) and what they want to deal with. This *dharma*, notwithstanding – or, should I say, even because of – the claimed relationship to the Veda, is different from 'Vedic *dharma*'! Both *GautDhS* and *BaudhDhS* – the latter is especially explicit on this[15] – have the hierarchization of the sources of Dharma in common, a feature that appears to be absent in *ĀpDhS*. I say 'appears,' because I doubt that one has to understand *ĀpDhS* 1.1.1.3 as containing a hierarchy. In other words, I doubt that because 'the Veda as a source' 'appears only in the second position,' it has to be considered merely a second-rate 'source of Dharma,' as Hacker (1965, 98) believes. The order of certain terms may signal a hierarchy, but not necessarily. The order of the *sūtras* 1.1.1.1–1.1.1.3 in Āpastamba,[16] moreover, remains comprehensible even if one assumes that the Vedas – naturally, as it were – are considered to be of higher authority than the 'agreement of *dharma* experts;' the *dharma-jña-samaya* may indeed be mentioned first only because it refers (as an explanation?) to the definition of *dharmas as sāmayācārika* in the first *sūtra*.[17]

To sum up, in can be stated that what the authors of the oldest *Dharmasūtras* regarded as '*dharma*' is exclusively what the Indologist knows as the contents of the Dharmaśāstra texts. Equally noteworthy, however, is the fact that the authors of the *Dharmasūtras* – apart from Āpastamba – speak of this matter as if a misunderstanding would be impossible or, at least, not seriously to be feared. They appear to presume that their addressees – listeners or readers – had an equally definite and clear idea of the subject labeled '*dharma*'! I do not here allude to the – also Indian – insight that one should define the terms one uses, but rather to the fact that while the subject-matter of the Śāstra is clearly specified, the understanding of the term specifying that subject is taken for granted. This appears so obvious to me[18] that I would dare to propose[19] that the Mīmāṃsā in a certain sense usurped the concept of *dharma* – in order to label *dharma* as Vedic – only secondarily. In other words, I assume that the Mīmāṃsā was stimulated to apply this term to the content of the Vedic prescriptions only by the Dharmaśāstra,[20] even though it had already been a well-known term in the sacrificial context, there denoting the cosmos-sustaining and life-preserving power (Horsch, 1967).

DHARMA AND SOCIAL NORMS

The claim that the Vedic *dharma* and the *dharma* of the Dharmaśāstra originally constitute two completely separate strands is supported by the thesis of Richard Lariviere, a thesis that is – even though broader – closely related to mine and that can explain the distinction between the two forms of *dharma*. Lariviere (1997, 97–110) states that 'the *dharmaśāstra* literature represents a peculiarly Indian record of local social norms and traditional standards of behavior,' that 'it represents in very definite terms the law of the land,' and 'that the whole of the *dharma* corpus can be viewed as a record of custom.' This nature of *dharmaśāstra*, however, 'is obfuscated by the fact that the idiom of all the *dharma* literature is one of eternality and timelessness ... and by the fact that *dharma* literature clings to the claim that all its provisions can be traced directly or indirectly to the Veda, the very root of dharma' (Lariviere, 1997, 98). Although Lariviere seeks to limit his observations to *vyavahāra*, that is, the portion of *Dharmaśāstra* dealing with legal procedure,[21] he notes his belief that 'the general notion of the ascendancy of custom and the efforts to include rather than exclude local practice within the realm of *dharma* apply equally as well to *ācāra* and *prāyaścitta*' (Lariviere, 1997, 97, fn. 1). Except for a certain reservation regarding the 'acts of atonement,' the actual Vedic origins of which Gampert (1939) has explored already (and which are apparently more complex than the other divisions of the *dharma* of the Dharmaśāstra), I agree completely with my American friend and colleague. Concerning the *ācāra* portion of the Dharmaśāstra, the assumption clearly suggests itself that it is nothing other than a codification of traditional 'customs and conventions.' There are certain arguments which Lariviere puts forth to corroborate his thesis; for example, the tradition of Dharmaśāstra itself acknowledges that 'the ultimate source of *dharma* in a legal sense was custom' (Lariviere, 1997, 102) – we could say, with Hacker, through clear statements about the empirical character of *dharma* – and that certain regulations demonstrate that 'the brāhmaṇa author explained rather than dictated custom' (Lariviere, 103). I consider these arguments as altogether so convincing, that it is my assumption that this new perspective, this new explanatory model will become widely accepted in Indology. It will, in other words, initiate a paradigm shift.

DHARMAPRAMĀṆA IN THE DHARMAŚĀSTRAS

This explanatory model is, however, not completely new and the paradigm shift is thus overdue. Already Derrett (1968, 158) stated that 'the śāstra incorporated numerous customs, inevitably, since it was itself the fruit of customs systematized, compared, and summarily set down.' He further noted that 'the fact is recognized by Kāṇe, Sen Gupta and others, also in judicial decisions' (Derrett, 1968, 158, fn. 3). Indeed, already N.S. Sen-Gupta (1953, 13) made the following claim: 'Custom then was necessarily the preeminent factor in developing and determining the law to be administered. In course of time then, customs which were studied by the scholars of the community assembled in pariṣads tended to crystallize into definite rules which were embodied in the manuals of law of these schools. These manuals became the Dharmasūtras of the particular schools.' And already a little earlier, Kane (1973, III: 874) had declared that 'the smṛtis themselves embodied the practices of the people current in their days, as Manu 1.107 declares, "in this work dharma has been fully stated as well as the good and evil qualities of (human) actions and the ancient customs and usages of the four varṇas". Derrett,[22] as this citation shows, is directly indebted to Kane; he also adopts the reference to this verse of the *Manusmṛti*. As evidence for his own formulation that the Dharmaśāstra 'was itself the fruit of customs,' the verse is, however, not sufficient.[23] Nevertheless, Derrett's general assumption is probably right.

Lariviere, however, can be claimed to have taken further these ideas about the character and origin of Dharmaśāstra in light of his fundamental insight into the relationship between Dharmaśāstra and the realm of custom and convention.

I feel confident that this new explanatory model will prevail because of the fact that *ĀpDhS* 1.7.20.6 and 7 – which is also cited by Lariviere (1997, 102) – clearly state the empirical character not only of the *vyavahāra*, but also of *dharma* as such. I see a further argument of self-disclosure, not mentioned by Lariviere, in the word *smṛti*, as it is used at least in one passage in the Dharmaśāstras.

In his commentary on *BaudhDhS* 1.1.1.3 (*smārto dvitīyaḥ*), Govindasvāmin (later than 15th century) claims that 'the word *smṛti* is secondarily used for a text which indicates memory/remembered issues' (*tadabhivyañjako granthaḥ smṛtiśabdenopacaryate*). Directly before that, he used the definition from *Yogasūtra* 1.11 for the elucidation of the meaning of *smṛti*. Bühler (1965, 143) agrees with Govindasvāmin, saying that he is 'no doubt right in doing so;' in fact, one could refer to *BaudhDhS* 1.1.2. and 2.2.4.17 where Gautama is mentioned. If we follow Bühler,[24] we could then legitimately assume an older age for the *GautDhS*, given that the *BaudhDh* is aware of at least one Smṛti-text. I hesitate, however, to embrace Bühler's assessment of Govindasvāmin's explication, for the following reasons:

A. The *BaudhDhS* is, according to the tradition, a Sūtra and not a Smṛti. It cannot be simply assumed that in this passage, the word *smṛti* necessarily alludes to a text or a class of texts, even though this usage became very common in later times. We cannot get around the question as to the date when this term assumed this meaning.

B. *BaudhDhS* 1.1.1.3 itself would be a poor witness because of its lack of clarity.

C. Gautama himself already mentions *smṛti* among the 'sources of Dharma,' viz. in the *sūtra* (1.)1.3 *tadvidāṃ smṛtiśīle* I have quoted above and to which I will return.[26] The genitive attribute that would have to be explained by *vedavidāṃ*, obviously relates to both elements of the compound – at least, I don't see anything supporting the assumption that it determines only the second element. But what should the 'smṛti[text]/smṛti[texts] of the Vedic experts' be? Texts which are to be distinguished from smṛti texts of other groups? Is not Bühler's (1965, 175) translation of *smṛti* as 'tradition' much more plausible since it is more natural? This translation and thus the view that 'tradition' is one of the sources of *dharma*, is also widely accepted (Lingat, 1973, 9).

In other words, I believe that the meaning of *smṛti* in this passage is still relatively close to the meaning resulting from its derivation.[26] It can perhaps be detected tentatively by considering the question of how a/the '*smṛti*' was originally distinguished from a/the '*śruti*.' In all probability, these two terms may have formed a pair of opposites or a complementary relationship from the very beginning. Individuals or a certain group of individuals remember what they have experienced personally. What is 'heard,' however, are, in general, sounds, especially articulated sounds, thus messages spoken by another person. Consequently, *śruti*[27] could denote – certainly not all, but rather only – specific messages that are heard. These could be messages that are received in a specific way – in the shape of holy formulas taught by the father or the teacher – so that they are learnt and memorized through repetition, in order to then reproduce them and hand them down verbatim. *Smṛti*, on the other hand, could likewise refer to specific personal memories, i.e. those concerning family, clan, tribe, and township. In other words, this includes various customs and conventions, including legal ones, and the events of times past.

Thus the difference between the textual categories finally known as Śruti and Smṛti would become understandable, as would the evaluation of both, their unequal degree of authority. The things you hear or learn[28] from a person of authority have a more imperative character than those that are remembered (by yourself) and thus remain 'mere' memory. Such memory – perhaps originally individual, but then above all collective – is, moreover, as the *PW* (s.v. *smṛti*) says, 'a tradition which is regarded as authoritative.' This is, however, not necessarily (i.e. from the very beginning) 'such a work,' a 'law book,' to quote the *PW* again. I suppose that the 'memory' in the first place comprises issues which can, sure enough, be verbalized secondarily. The developing descriptions, however, need not be fixed texts which, due to their status, would have to be protected and preserved in their exact wording. Certainly, the tendency to develop and establish such texts cannot be denied, particularly in the context of ancient Indian culture. It is still, however, quite a good – perhaps even a long – way to the formation of a text or a work, a way which – considering our sources – can sure enough be visualized only by means of imagination. In any case, it seems plausible to assume at least various steps of development from living custom, that is, existing social order, to the corresponding *dharma* prescription as part of a text or work.

GautDhS 1.2 testifies to the more ancient concept of *smṛti* ('a lore which is regarded as authoritative') sketched above, which, let me emphasize, constitutes a/the Indian equivalent of 'tradition.' We find this concept also in the oldest reference, according to *PW*, in *LāṭyŚS*

6.1.6.13 (*tisr̥sv ācāryāḥ smr̥teḥ*),[29] in which a further aspect appears: the supplemental character of *smr̥ti* in relationship to *śruti* – an idea which in later times evolved, *inter alia*, into the theological concept of the *paribr̥ṃhaṇa* function of certain *smr̥ti* works.[30]

What then is the meaning of *śīla*, mentioned by Gautama in the third place (which obviously means: as a third rank source)? According to Hara (1986), the meaning is "simply 'nature' (*svabhāva*) or habitual character." With reference to *GautDhS* 1.2, one might reasonably take the meaning "habitual behavior that reveals one's character" as a basis. Thus "habit" should be understood as "(good) conduct which roots in certain (positive) qualities of one's character and which has become a natural behavior in daily life through frequent and constant repetition – possibly practiced, however, only by rote or unconsciously."

Semantically, the term *śīla* is thus not very different[31] from the term *vr̥tta* in *ĀpDhS* 1.7.20.8 and to a great extent identical with the term *ācāra*, which in turn often replaces it in the younger works of the Dharmaśāstra whenever the "sources" are mentioned (Lingat, 1973, 14). Bühler had already assumed a clear textual agreement among the Dharmasūtras and the older Smr̥tis regarding the "sources of dharma".[32] He correctly translates the term *āgama* in *BaudhDhS* 1.1.1.4 (*tr̥tīyaś*) [sc. *dharmaḥ*] *śiṣṭāgamaḥ*) as "practice". This meaning could perhaps be specified as "traditional knowledge which manifests itself in praxis"[33], surmising a similar semantic development as with *śīla*.

Having examined more closely the Dharmasūtras and the terms they use, we can thus conclude that we face a somewhat complex picture; but their statements on the "sources of dharma" have indeed a common denominator, namely, as Lariviere says, 'custom.' Consequently, the resulting *dharma* is different from the Vedic *dharma*, which is regarded as an orally fixed instruction for specific religious activities – at least, in the perspective of those Indians who lived at a somewhat historical distance from it. The philologist, however, recognizes that the 'Veda' likewise – or at least parts of it – also consisted originally of statements or descriptions of actions, even though they were subsequently subjected to esoteric interpretation.

While investigating early Dharmaśāstra texts with regard to statements about the character and origin of their teachings, for an interpretative analysis, it is necessary to consider the metaphor 'root' mentioned in *GautDhS* 1.2 and elsewhere.[34] The normal rendering as 'source' is not totally satisfactory because it merely replaces one metaphor with another without demonstrating that the semantic content of the former has been precisely defined. The metaphor 'source' is, furthermore, just as little exactly defined, and it induces scholars to stick to vague metaphors when dealing with *dharma*, too.[35]

Mūla is to be found several times in the Dharmasūtras in its primary meaning of 'root' (as the organ of a plant which deals with fastening and nutrition). We find it, for example, in the compound 'root of a tree,' which, however, means 'foot of the tree;'[36] and it is frequently used particularly in the compound *mūlaphala*, which implies vegetarianism.[37] In addition, *mūla* is used metaphorically, meaning 'cause,' for example in *ĀpDhS* 1.8.23.3 where the removal of (the) consequences of previous faults (*doṣāṇāṃ vinirghātaḥ*) is denoted as *yogamūlaḥ* (*ĀpDhS* 1.8.23.5). Despite the differences in type, this compound reminds us of *dharmamūla* in *GautDhS* 1.1, or Manu 2.6. Another example is *ĀpDhS* 1.8.23.2 where the *ātman* (=*paramātman*) is called 'the cause (of the genesis of all bodies).'[38] Thus there are good reasons to understand *mūla* as 'cause' also in passages that speak about the *mūla* of *dharma*. What follows, however, is the question what kind of 'cause' the authors had in mind. It seems that there is only one answer to this question: it is the cause of the *knowledge* of *dharma*, the knowledge of 'this is *dharma*, and this is *adharma*.' The evidence of this cognitive relation is to be found not so much in the (later) commentaries but in *VasDhS* 1.5 which replaces *mūla* with *pramāṇa* and thus specifies the meaning.[39] Certainly, *pramāṇa* in such sentences does not mean 'means of clear perception' but rather 'authority as the relevant instance.' When, however, the status of a relevant 'authority' with respect to *dharma* is granted to something, this is not only considered to have the absolute 'authority to decide;' in addition, it is regarded as possessing the concrete knowledge which justifies this authority, a knowledge that can be, as it were, inquired from it. In other words, to be an 'authority' in the present case implies that it also acts as means of relevant cognition.

The authors might have given preference to this metaphor instead of using a simple and precise term because they may have wished to express the full dependency of the subjects they treat on these 'roots' in a meaningful and handy way. In my view, however, it is absolutely possible, even probable, that there is still more to this metaphor. Presumably, it also alludes to the procedural character of finding out from these 'roots' what *dharma* is – with regard to the particular case as well as in general, and with regard to frequent inquiry and consultation about *dharma* in the continuum of time. Thus, the metaphor might allude to the fundamental persistence of the inquiry into the realm of *dharma* even beyond the lifetime of the authors; a pattern also for future times. Precisely because of this, it is inappropriate to blame the commentators for having a historically and philologically unsustainable view when they claim that the statements on the 'roots' of *dharma* are also universal instructions which contain the method for its detection regarding possible later requirements. *Dharma* is not already perceived in its totality; in principle it is expandable, but only, at least theoretically, by making use of the legitimate 'causes' of its detection. On the other hand, it would be misleading to think that the disclosure of the sources of one's knowledge of *dharma* in its various ramifications was meant to be taken historically. The authors obviously did not intend to give an account of how their knowledge of *dharma* developed historically, but rather wanted to legitimize this knowledge by mentioning its foundation(s), that is, the sources from which it was extracted. The philologist is, of course, at liberty to draw historical conclusions from such statements, also with reference to the role of the *ācāra* in the development of Dharmaśāstra texts.

ĀCĀRA IN THE GṚHYASŪTRAS

Considering the meaning of custom and convention in the context of the origin of early Dharmaśāstra texts, one has to take into account the fact – and this is not mentioned by Lariviere – that we have evidence for the word *ācāra* already in the Gṛhyasūtras. Gonda (1980) mentions this a few times. He distinguishes two meanings: (1) 'good conduct': 'that is to say not only in religious and ritual respects, but also in what we would call moral and social respects, spheres of human conduct and activity between which in ancient India no hard and fast line was drawn,' and (2) 'custom(ary practice), traditional usage' (Gonda, 1980, 80). Already the *PW* adds to its first entry – 'behavior, mode of acting, manner, conduct; good behavior; tradition, custom, convention, observance' – the observation in brackets: 'the meanings merge in a way that makes a clear distinction impossible.' The step from the simple to the concise meaning is easy to follow, as there are numerous parallels: a behavior is a good behavior when it is in accordance with tradition, with custom and convention, i.e. with the respective model of behavior. Following Hacker's (1965, 103) differentiation of '*dharma* before its realization' and '*dharma* in its realization,' we can differentiate *ācāra* before its realization – the authoritative, ideal model of behavior[40] – and *ācāra* in its actual and practical realization. Good conduct is thus realization of custom – in Gonda's sense – and this conduct, the recollected tradition, is itself again a model and example for others.

Only few of the numerous passages in the Gṛhyasūtras that Gonda refers to will be taken up here. On the one hand, there are those passages describing the *ācāra* either of a particular group of people – not surprisingly the *śiṣṭas*[41] or larger and smaller geographical units (*janapada, grāma*)[42] – or generally as an 'authority' in accordance with which one has to act when other sources of knowledge fail.[43] Here, *ācāra* is the definitive and decisive means of cognition (*pramāṇa*).[44] On the other hand, we have *ĀpGS* 1.1 *atha karmāṇy ācārād yāni gṛhyante*, on which Gonda (1980, 4) comments that it was 'no doubt right in stating that the knowledge of the domestic rites is described from customary practice.' He had already cited the same *sūtra* in his earlier book (Gonda, 1977, 554) as follows: *atha karmāṇy ācārādyāni gṛhyante*. His translation shows that at that time, he had parsed the text incorrectly: 'Now are considered those rites which are (based on) customary conduct (or established usage) and so on.' It is not clearly recognizable whether he has noticed this fault and corrected it in his more recent work, where he remarks after referring to *ĀpGS* 1.1:

> One could, or should, supplement[45] this statement by observing that in manuals[46] this practice was supposed to be recognized – and this presupposed that it was old, traditional, related to a social group or locality and followed as a matter of obligation – hallowed by dharma (in śruti or smṛti), codified and to the best of their compilers' knowledge systematized by the authorities of the Vedic schools. (Gonda, 1980, 4)

It appears to me that in spite of his undeniably great wealth of knowledge, confusion is enhanced rather than clarity. The position of the cited *sūtra* in the very beginning of *ĀpGS* suggests the assumption that its author had the entire work in mind: 'now [those] rites [are dealt with], which are [cognitively] comprehended from the *ācāra*.' It would be possible, however, that he had in mind only a specific part, the 1. *paṭala*, for instance. Oldenberg (1892, 251) annotates this in his translation of the *ĀpGS*: 'I, 1-11. The Paribhāshās of the Pākayajñas.' He thus takes the statement of *ĀpGS* 1.1 as referring to the Sūtra in total. Indeed, his assumption is obviously confirmed by *ĀpGS* 3.7.23:[47] *karmāṇi . . . ācārād yāni gṛhyante* serves as a paraphrase of the term *gṛhyakarmāṇi*, i.e. of the contents of this *Gṛhyasūtra* as a whole. Therefore, one may approvingly take note of Haradatta's explication of *ĀpGS* 1.1: *dviprakārāṇi karmāṇi śrutilakṣaṇāny ācāralakṣaṇāni ca / tatra śrutilakṣaṇāni vyākhyātāni* [namely in the Śrautasūtra]/*athedānīṃ yāni karmāṇi vivāhaprabhṛtīny ācārāt* [=] *prayogād gṛhyante* [=] *jñāyante, na pratyakṣaśrutes,*[48] *tāni vyākhyāsyāmaḥ /*.

There is, however, no parallel or analogy to *ĀpGS* 1.1[49] in other texts of the same class, and it would certainly not be legitimate to apply what is said about Āpastamba to all of the Gṛhyasūtras. Even Gonda most likely does not do this; but rather he wants to say that the philologist may extend the statement of *ĀpGS* 1.1 to a more general historical reality. Although he does not give any reasons, it cannot be denied that this generalization, given the *laukika* character of household rites, does in fact appear legitimate. Nevertheless, it has to be pointed out that an empirical verification is not possible, and that, as already mentioned, *ācāra* has another function and rank according to the other Gṛhyasūtras.

In considering the Dharmasūtras and Smṛtis, one is tempted to complain about the lack of a statement as clear as *ĀpGS* 1.1. Yet such a complaint is not entirely valid, because there are passages that correspond to it, such as the aforementioned passage *ĀpDhS* 1.7.20.6-8 and other statements in Dharmaśāstra texts Hacker refers to in order to support his thesis on the radically empirical nature of *dharma*. The knowledge of domestic rites, as well as that of the *dharma*, are extracted from specific segments of actual human behavior. In this perspective, *dharma* is a realized ideal and not an ideal concept in multifaceted conflict with reality. The agreement between Gṛhyasūtras and Dharmasūtras (Lingat, 1973, 18, 74) – also on this point – leads to the assumption that the latter follow the example of the former regarding the revelation of their source(s).[50] We may raise the question as to why the sources are revealed, first of all, with respect to *ĀpGS*. At the same time we need to consider the possibility that the reference to the *ācāra* might contain an element of mystification, that is, a deliberately misleading justification. What is more important, however, is that both genres of text are explicitly based on one (or a corresponding) *ācāra*, either partially or entirely. Gṛhyasūtras as well as Dharmasūtras are verbalizations of certain regional or tribal-specific aspects of traditional social 'practice' of the Āryas. Although historically consecutive, they surely have factual points of contact. These verbalizations are textual 'coagulations' of the late Vedic period that were apparently regarded by the authors as fundamentally different from older parts of the tradition.

DISTINCTION BETWEEN VEDIC AND DHARMAŚĀSTRIC NOTIONS OF DHARMA

The *dharma* of the Dharmaśāstra, thus, is distinct from the Vedic *dharma* by its nature because it is, in its essential parts, a record or codification of custom and convention. This codification intends to overcome contingency – it has this effect, in any case. On the other hand, it hampered further development of the tradition, or at least complicated its consideration considerably. India would thus confirm the observation made in many other cultures that early law texts are not to be regarded as creations of law, but rather as records of an existing, traditionally applied law (records that include, of course, editorial and other changes, beginnings of systematization, and the like). This codification, that is, the genesis of the oldest texts of Dharmaśāstra literature, has certainly to be regarded as a rather long historical process; from a historical–philological point of view, the same could justifiably apply also to the single works (in any case, to many of them).

In this regard, the view Lariviere rightly puts forth against Derrett is revealing, namely that this process has continued to take place, as in the case of the *Devalasmṛti*, probably in the time of Muslim conquests of the North West of India,[51] although under changed conditions and not always necessarily according to the recording of *ācāra*.[52]

Methodologically speaking, however, I consider it very important in this context to expound the problems of the notion of 'text'. This is not because of the expansion of the notion by textual linguists or because of its almost complete dissolving by deconstructionists, but rather because the consideration of textual genesis – and textual history – in India advises caution in using the term 'text'. Thus in the present case, one may consider the possibility that certain 'legal phrases' which constitute the contents of the Dharmaśāstra, originated initially without any connection to other similar or dissimilar phrases as elements of 'tradition' (*smṛti*). In other words, the textualization might have begun with single elements of custom and legal tradition. The penchant of Indologists, however, to conclude from single elements that a text or even an entire literature must have existed, needs critical examination. This assumption would explain, among other things, that and why we find passages concerning 'law' already in older Vedic texts.

However the processes of codification[53] of *ācāra* may have developed in detail, there is no doubt that Lariviere is correct in saying that 'there certainly was "distortion or sanitizing in the brāhmaṇas" recording of custom.' With regard to this, he refers to 'the utter absence of any temporal reference and the fog of the fictional Vedic source' which clearly show 'that they are doctoring the record' (Lariviere, 1997, 102). When it comes to the mixed-caste theory, however, then 'this sort of explanation is where brāhmaṇa authors become inventive and paint the data with their unique perspective.'[54] It also seems to me that he has already mentioned the vital keywords of the analysis of these processes when he further says that 'it was the object of the recorders of these customs to integrate these practices into the brahmanical/vedic *Weltanschauung* the promotion of which was the basic motive for their recording the customs in the first place' (Lariviere, 1997,104).

BRĀHMAṆICAL APPROPRIATION OF LOCAL NORMS

However, while attempting to regard the development of the early Dharmaśāstra texts as a 'Vedification' and at the same time 'Brahmanification' of traditional custom and convention, it is necessary to have a closer look particularly at the motives. Furthermore, it has to be considered whether these descriptive categories are sufficient, or if others will have to be added.

Vedification means in the first place the development of the *vedamūlatva* concept. 'The Veda is the root of *dharma*,' *GautDhS* 1.1 states. As I have already mentioned, however, Gautama's statement is not about the genesis or even the historical origin of the *dharma* he intends to present, but rather about the (or a) source of its knowledge. Further the sūtra that immediately follows *tadvidāṃ ca smṛtiśīle* (*GautDhS* 1.2) shows this very clearly. This *sūtra*, in which, as already pointed out, the term of *dharmamūlam* is implied, thus has to be translated as 'and tradition as well as practice of those who know it (that is, the Veda), [are the root of *dharma*].' It is Gautama's intention – as it is the intention of the authors of other Dharmasūtras and Smṛtis – to make clear in the very beginning, in the introduction of their works, where the knowledge of *dharma* is extracted from.

Although the *GautDhS*, by mentioning the origins of the knowledge of *dharma*, states at the same time its relative authority, the revelation of the foundation/s of knowledge remains noteworthy in several respects. Even more important for the question at hand, however, is the fact that the second *sūtra* excludes the possibility that *dharma* means Vedic *dharma*. It is not the Vedic *dharma* which is said to be known from the Veda – a statement that would just be completely banal without the addition of 'only' – but the *dharma* of the Dharmaśāstra! Since I have not investigated into this in detail, I cannot claim that this is the meaning of the *bahuvrīhi* compound *vedamūla* in all cases. However, I consider the assumption legitimate that it is at least the more original meaning, the one the later radicalization of the term by Kumārila is based upon, as it was pointed out by Halbfass (1988, 328). Heesterman observes correctly that this 'classical claim that the entire *dharma* was based on the *Veda*, or already contained in it', is 'a pious axiom that vanishes into thin air as soon as one attempts to demonstrate the alleged close relationship between the two.'[55] However, *Manusmṛti* 2.7 already claims that 'the entire dharma, as it was declared by Manu for someone respectively (i.e. the single classes), is taught in the Veda.'[56] Should we thus assume that it originated only after Kumārila and then entered into the Manusmṛti? Or should we not rather suspect that the radicalization, the transformation of the *vedamūlatva* thesis into an all-embracing dictum, had already begun before Kumārila?

No one, to my knowledge, has denied the fact that there are certain 'connections' between the Veda and the Dharmaśāstra, as regards content (Heesterman, 1978, 85f). The concept of the four classes and many other points concerning the particular life forms, to be sure, are striking examples among others – except, however, for the system of life stages (see Olivelle, 1993). It would thus be incorrect to characterize the statement that the *dharma*, or better, a part of the *dharma* is detected from the Veda, as false. The question arises, however, whether Gautama and his colleagues were thinking of particular connections at all, or if they rather wanted to drive at a general but vague notion of the knowledge of *dharma* as being founded on the Veda. Ultimately, they might have wanted to accomplish such a form of legitimacy that any serious challenge – by a worldly ruler, for example – would appear to be impossible. Thus Gautama's statement is to be understood not necessarily in the sense that the *dharma* was to be found in the Veda in the form of clearly formulated 'law phrases'; on the contrary, this is definitely the least probable assumption.

It becomes apparent that it is not at all easy to expose the old and not yet radicalized *vedamūlatva* claim as pure fiction and to strengthen this undoubtedly legitimate suspicion.

Vedification is clearly visible, however, in the above-mentioned *GautDhS* 1.2 *tadvidāṃ ca smṛtiśīle*. In this *sūtra*, tradition and practice of those who know the Veda are mentioned together as the second source of the knowledge of *dharma*. And that the expression *vedavid* refers only to a group within the Brahmin community rather than to a group Brahmins $+x$, requires no explicit explanation. In addition to Vedification, we thus also observe Brahmanification, or rather the connection to that part of Brahmin community which is particularly, or exclusively, devoted to the preservation of the tradition of the Veda. The realm of tradition and practice from which a valid *dharma* may be derived is limited to 'those who know the Veda,' that is, to those Brahmins who really follow their class obligation of studying the Veda. This restriction clearly goes beyond attempts, testified to elsewhere, to determine the group authoritative for *dharma*, such as *ĀpDhS* 1.7.20.6–8 where the Āryas are referred to or *BaudhDhS* 1.1.1.4 which mentions the *śiṣṭas* – who are comparable to the *āptas* in epistemology. Thus, in the *GautDhS*, Vedification becomes manifest in a significant narrowing of the group of persons whose behavior is regarded as exemplary.

Without wanting to anticipate the clearly necessary comparative examination of the apparently complex idea of this group of persons in the older Dharmaśāstra texts, one may yet assume that Gautama's view is either a radicalization or a different, originally idiosyncratic, approach that then widely prevailed. The second of the definitions of the term *śiṣṭa*, as handed down in *BaudhDhS* 1.1.1.6,[57] reads, for example, '(those are called) Śiṣṭas who, in accordance with the sacred law, have studied the Veda together with its appendages...' (Bühler, 1965, 143). Furthermore, one may say that historically, Gautama is not trustworthy. The prima facie likelihood and especially the particular observations like those noted by Lariviere strongly support the assumption that in reality it was a wider circle of Āryas that carried those customs and legal practices which coagulated into texts as Dharmasūtras and Smṛtis. However, it can scarcely be denied that the Brahmins played a prominent role in this process, i.e. as collectors and preservers of the tradition and as the subject of the respective observation of reality.

Admittedly, 'coagulated into texts' is a mistaken image, since these texts were produced, of course. In fact, they were produced – how could it be otherwise in ancient India? – by Brahmins belonging to various Vedic schools. These Brahmins naturally pursued various personal interests by composing the texts, such as the establishment and the preservation of their own primacy within society, an effective help in protecting their own privileges, and in the more or less subtle disputes with the Kṣatriyas,[58] and the like. However, it was another aspect of Vedification that was decisive and fundamental for this concept of *dharma* within the perspective of history of religions. The idea of sacrifices as being constitutive for salvation, was transferred (or extended) to the *dharma* of the Dharmaśāstra – a process which can be called sacramentalization. Vasiṣṭha, for example, states: 'He who knows and follows the (sacred law is called) a righteous man; he becomes most worthy of praise in this world and after death gains heaven.'[59] At the end of the *GautDhS* (28.52), moreover, it is said that 'he who knows the sacred law obtains heavenly bliss, more than (other) righteous men, on account of his knowledge of, and his adherence to it.'[60]

I have had to go a long way back to answer the question which *dharma* can in fact be regarded as 'an event mediating transcendence to salvation' – that is to say, that (and why) this definition of 'sacrament' is applicable also to the *dharma* of the Dharmaśāstra. It holds good also for these prescriptions that 'its accomplishment affects salvation,' and that, once they are discovered, 'their authority is by no means provable nor can it be questioned.' This *dharma*, too, 'becomes a mythification of transcendence,' the 'mythical presence' of which becomes 'spatio-temporally visible through the mediation' of correct behavior in everyday life.[61] According to Hacker (1965, 103),

> Dharma is a concrete, positive and soteriologically relevant *model of conduct* that has already existed before its realization in some way and has waited to be practiced (or, a collection of such models). Dharma *in practice* then is the act corresponding to this model; *adharma* is the act contradicting it. Finally, the *dharma* substance exists also *after the practical act* as the realized model of conduct. Then it is some sort of an act coagulated to a transcendental active substance, the substance of the done act.

And this substance causes 'ascent' (*abhyudaya*), just as the performance of the Śrauta-sacrifice does, due to the transference of the ideas developed with regard to these, to the *dharma* of the Dharmaśāstra.[62]

CONCLUSION

It is characteristic of human memory, especially in traditional societies, that diachronic changes in custom and convention are not perceived; at most only regional differences are. Thus custom and convention appear as universal and timeless. The question 'why?,' if raised at all, is rejected by parents or elders with the assertion: 'It has always been this way, it has always been done this way.' The idea that the *dharma* of the Dharmaśāstra was an eternal, unchangeable 'law' – which is historically not correct also for successive times – probably did not arise only by transference from Vedic *dharma*. Rather, it was probably connected already with the word *dharma(n)*, which is common to both spheres, that of the Veda and that of the contents of the Dharmaśāstra.

I am, however, not so much thinking of word formation, but rather of the meanings of the word, that Horsch (1967) has examined. Both 'dhárman in the ritual sense' and 'dhárman in the socio-ethical sense' – the sacrifice as the power supporting the cosmos and sustaining life and the 'law' men must act upon' – elude human reshaping (Horsch, 1967, 39, 41). Furthermore, they are eternal and never-changing; they are a given, an unchangeable order of being and life. Man is called upon to act in accordance with it in order to be sound and eventually to attain salvation. And this appeal to man might be regarded as another feature common to both spheres, existing from the very beginning.

Even scholarship has difficulties in determining the purpose of certain customs and conventions. Therefore, the consideration suggests itself whether for the ancient Indians also the *dharma* of Dharmaśāstra was in its essence *adṛṣṭārtha*, an action the motive of which is not perceivable within the realm of the visible world. It is Baudhāyana (*BaudhDhS* 1.7.20.2–4; cf. Hacker, 1967, 96f) who states in unmistakable words that the *dharma* of the Dharmaśāstra is recognizable by its *adṛṣṭārtha*, that is, *adṛṣṭārtha* is thus a general characteristic of it. I must admit however, that I am not completely certain on this point, and I wonder if we are facing yet another element of the transference of ideas from the Vedic *dharma* to the *dharma* of the Dharmaśāstra. Unfortunately, the sources do not provide good evidences for either alternative and the Brahmans, moreover, carried out the Vedification so cleverly – unless it was done unconsciously – that time and again one has difficulties to see through their game.

The question, furthermore, concerning the motives for the integration of custom and convention into the brahmanical/Vedic *weltanschauung*, as Lariviere points out, is anything but simple. According to him, just the promotion of this *weltanschauung* was 'the basic motive for their recording the customs in the first place' (Lariviere, 1997, 104). It is certainly correct to assume that there is a bundle of motives underlying it – and this is not simply a makeshift solution facing the impossibility to decide between various solutions due to lack of evidence.

But is it possible at all to assess these motives? Admittedly, it is not completely clear to me what Lariviere actually means by 'promotion.' If 'promotion' is understood as 'advertisement', then it appears necessary to specify that it consists of an almost revolutionary extension or even shift in the options for salvation, basically analogous to the shift in value between the *śrauta* and *gṛhya* sacrifices (see Smith, 1989, 193f). Only by acting in accordance with *dharma* – an action, sure enough, that does not serve a 'visible goal' – one can reach the 'ascent,' i.e. one can 'attain highest salvation, just as the theist through the veneration of God, and the monist through the realization of the One' (Hacker, 1965, 104). One is tempted to regard this 'dharma piety,' or 'dharmism,' to use Hacker's words, as a democratization regarding the access to salvation.

Dharma underwent an upvaluation, as it now applies to the four classes and realized by them in daily action, and not to the Śrauta sacrifice anymore, which was affordable only to a small group of wealthier people. I assume, in other words, that the Vedification and the sacramentalization of the *dharma* of the Dharmaśāstra is related to the decline of Vedic ceremonial sacrifice, and that among the motives – for example, the ideology of the responsibility for the welfare of living beings (*GautDhS* 8.1) – are also certain interests of the Brahmans. These interests comprise, for example, the wish to ensure for themselves the possibility for 'ascent' without sacrifice and to establish income potential beyond the function as sacrificial priest, for example, as experts in all *dharma*-related questions, or as acting officials in judicature, and the like.

One could go further here, I think, with an approach based in the sociology of religion. For Hacker's (1965, 105) proposal of interpretation, which is based purely in a history of religions approach, that 'the concept of Ārya-Dharma' appears to be 'brought to clear consciousness at first in the debate with Buddhism,' and that 'consequently the reference to the Veda is emphasized again and again,' does not fully satisfy. The challenges the Brahmins attempted to meet by developing the concept of Ārya-Dharma include, in my view, also the changes caused by the development of Vedic religion itself. In addition, it is advisable to place Buddhism in the wider and also older historical context of the early ascetic movements. The Vedification and sacramentalization of the *dharma* might thus be considered also as propagation of an inner-worldly way to salvation that is accessible to every *gṛhastha* and can be pursued in the acts of everyday life.

NOTES

[1] Cited from E. Frauwallner, *Materialien zur ältesten Erkenntnislehre der Karmamīmāṃsā*, Vienna: 1968, p. 17.
[2] *na dharmādharmau carata āvaṃ sva iti / na devagandharvā na pitara ity ācakṣate 'yaṃ dharmo 'yam adharma iti //6// yat tv āryāḥ kriyamāṇaṃ praśaṃsanti sa dharmo yad garhante so 'dharmaḥ //7// sarvajanapadeṣv ekāntasamāhitam āryāṇāṃ vṛttaṃ samyagvinītānāṃ vṛddhānām ātmavatām alolupānām adāmbhikānāṃ vṛttasādṛśyaṃ-bhajeta //8//*. I take *vṛttasādṛśyaṃ* to be an adverb ('in a/the manner, that [there is] a semblance in behavior'), and surmise that therein lies the perception that the behavior of one person can never be identical with that of another person, nor with a behavior model, but can only comply in a sense of semblance.
[3] Hacker (1965, 100). What is meant here, of course, is the Āryāvarta he had mentioned earlier (p. 98).
[4] Hacker (1965, 99). Hacker's designation of Hindu dharma as 'radically empirical' caused an effect within Indology; cf., for example, H. Scharfe, *The State in Indian Tradition*, Leiden, 1989, p. 220, fn. 125, or H.-J. Klimkeit, *Der politische Hinduismus. Indische Denker zwischen religiöser Reform und politischem Erwachen*, Wiesbaden 1981, p. 56f.
[5] Certainly, once this concept would have been in existence, it would allow us to state with Hacker (1965, 96) that 'besides the actual ethics, dharma [encompasses] the entire external cultic, ceremonial side of religion' with, furthermore, 'the entire realm of civil law, criminal law, and government issues' belonging to it as well as 'the rites of expiation and penance.'
[6] Quoted from Bühler (1965, 1).
[7] Further evidence are *ĀpDhS* 1.2.7.31 and *GautDhS* (1.)8.11 (on this, see below, note 12).
[8] Doubt may arise, however, regarding the derivation of the secondary noun, since *sāmayācārika* is mentioned in the gaṇa (211) of *Pāṇini* 5.4.34 (*vinayādibhyaṣ ṭhak*), and since according to the Pāṇinīyas, the suffix *ṭhak* (=±*iká* or ±*ká*) is added *svārthe*, i.e. without changing the meaning of the primary noun. (Compare also Cārudeva Śāstrī, *Vyākaraṇacandrodaya*, dvitīyakhaṇḍa, Delhi, 1970, p. 498, where *GautDhS* 1.8.11 is cited as evidence for the assertion of *samayācāra eva sāmayācārika*). Certainly, the question arises whether *sāmayācārika* belongs to the old stock of this gaṇa. Already the Vṛtti to *Cāndravyākaraṇa* 4.4.17 shows that this is not the case, which is also confirmed by R. Birwé, *Der Gaṇapāṭha zu den Adhyāyas IV und V der Grammatik Pāṇinis. Versuch einer Rekonstruktion*, Wiesbaden (1961, 411), whose comparative table shows that the word appears for the first time in the Kāśikā in this gaṇa. Regarding *samayācāra*, cf. R. (Baroda) 2.1.19 (apparently with the attribute *laukika*), where several commentators explain *dharma*; cf. *The Rāmāyaṇa of Vālmīki. An Epic of India*. Vol. II: Ayodhyākāṇḍa. Introduction and Translation by Sheldon J. Pollok, Princeton, 1986, p. 328.
[9] Haradatta's view (put forward in his commentary on *BaudhDhS* 1.1.1.2) that 'the *samaya* of the experts of *dharma* such as Manu, et al.' is meant (*dharmajñā ye manvādayas teṣāṃ samayaḥ pramāṇaṃ dharmādharmayoḥ*) is an anachronism. Haradatta reflects his contemporary circumstances; see also below, note 14. Even in *ĀpDhS* 1.1.1.2 (*dharmajñasamayaḥ pramāṇam*, see also below, note 16), I don't consider it cogent to presume that *samaya* means 'accord (attained through discussion/debate).' The situation is different, however, in the *Mahābhārata* 6.1.26: *tatas te samayaṃ cakruḥ kurupāṇḍavasomakāḥ / dharmāṃś ca sthāpayām āsur yuddhānāṃ bharatarṣabha //*.
[10] Regarding the usage of the plural, see also Halbfass (1988, 314f, in chapter 17, entitled '*Dharma* in Self-Understanding of Traditional Hinduism'). In my view, the

plural in general expresses only the inner diversity and multifariousness of the entirety of *dharma* – in accordance with the use of the singular for some of its parts (for example, *strīdharmaḥ*, *rājadharmaḥ*, etc.) – but not various co-existing 'religions.' The final remark of this paragraph is directed against Hacker, who does not at all address the fact that the original text has a plural.

11 R.P. Kangle has argued against this view, though, in my view, not entirely convincing; see his article '*The Relative Age of the Gautamadharmasūtra* ' in '*Mélanges d'Indianisme à la memoire de Louis Renou*, Paris 1968, pp. 415–425; also Gampert, 1939, 266f. ('Anhang zu den Quellen') has another opinion concerning the relative chronology of the Dharmasūtras. For references to earlier works, see Lingat 1973, 22, fn. 3.

12 *sāmyācārikeṣv abhivinītaḥ*, Bühler (1879, 215; see now Olivelle 1999, xxv ff.) translates: '(And) who is well versed in the duties of the daily life settled by the agreement (of those who know the law)'. The *sūtra* forms part of the characterization of the Brahman, on whom (together with the king) all life and prosperity as well as the maintenance of order within society depends, according to 8.1 ff.

13 As far as I know, the riddle *BaudhDhS* 1.1.1.2 proposes, is not yet solved. For, how should the genitive be understood if the phrase *tasyānuvyākhyāsyāmaḥ* is correct at all? The postposition is not connected with this case and a partitive genitive does not make sense.

14 In connection with *BaudhDhS* 1.1.1.4 (*tṛtīyaś śiṣṭāgamaḥ*) *sūtra* 1.1.1.3 shows that the *dharma* which 'is instructed in each single Veda' is to be taken first. In addition, it shows that the ordinal numbers point to a hierarchy regarding the authority of the 'sources of dharma' and, respectively, of the means of detecting *dharma*.

15 Because of the use of ordinal numbers 'second' and 'third,' which, being scarcely redundant, seem to be very significant.

16 These read: *athātaḥ sāmayācārikān dharmān vyākhyāsyāmaḥ* //1// *dharmjñasamayaḥ pramāṇam* //2// *vedāś ca* //3//.

17 The absence Hacker mentions in the same sentence (l.c.) with reference to *ĀpDhS* 1.7.20.6–8 and *Manu* 2.1, is in itself ambiguous. My argument, however, does leave untouched Hacker's (1965, p. 98) supposition 'that these passages, which deal only with the custom or consensus of the Good . . . as the source of dharma, are very old. They arose in a time when people did not yet face the Veda as a closed, authoritative text corpus, but rather lived *in* the Veda, when the Veda was still *evolving*.'

18 I see a strong support in the point H. Bechert made recently, that *dhamma* in Pali texts, *inter alia*, has the meaning 'the law decreed by the Buddha,' 'regulatory prescriptions' (see his '*Die Gesetze des buddhistischen Sangha als indisches Rechtssystem* ' in *Recht, Staat und Verwaltung im klassischen Indien*, ed. B. Kölver, München 1997, pp. 53–64, especially 59ff).

19 Notwithstanding *ChU* 2.23.1 and *Vārttika* 11 to *Pāṇini* 4.3.120 (*Mahābhāṣya* II 319.4f.) respectively *Pāṇini* 4.2.46! For *ChU* 2.23.1, see P. Olivelle, '*Dharmaskandhāḥ* and *brahmasaṃsthaḥ*: A study on *Chāndogya-Upaniṣad* 2.23.1,' in *Journal of the American Oriental Society* 116(1996), 205–219.

20 This must have occurred before Patañjali, the Mahābhāṣyakāra, as he knows the opinion that 'the tradition of the *Ṛṣis* (*ṛṣisaṃpradāya*) is *dharma*' (I 9.16; cf. V. Svāmināthan, *Bhartṛhariviracitā Mahābhāṣyaṭīkā*, Vol. I, Vārānasī, 1965, p. 40; and, further, *Mahābhārata* [Poona], 12.110. 12a [*śrutir dharma iti hy eke*]), and he explains the expression *dharmaniyama* by extracting examples from the *loka* and the *veda* (I. 8.10ff).

21 For example, it is systematically separated from *ācāra* and *prāyaścitta* in the *Yājñavalkya Smṛti*. The classification is not mentioned by P.V. Kane, when he speaks about the 'various divisions of *dharma*' (*History of Dharmaśāstra*, Vol. II, Part I. Sec. Ed., Poona 1974, p. 2f).

[22] We can probably suspect A.S. Altekar as the one Derrett refers to as 'others.' See, *State and Government in India*, 3rd ed., Benares 1958, p. 12f.; and Lingat 1973, 178.
[23] I demonstrate this in my appendix to the original German version of this paper, 'Anhang zu *Manusmṛti* 1.107'.
[24] 1879, 'Introduction' p. LIII. See also P.V. Kane, *History of Dharmaśāstra*, Vol. I, revised and enlarged, Poona 1968, p. 33f.
[25] I want to mention also L. Rocher, 'The Introduction of the Gautamadharmasūtra', *Adyar Library Bulletin* XXXIX (1976): 90–100. I believe that Rocher's interpretation is altogether flawed, but this would have to be demonstrated in a separate article.
[26] See *Pāṇini* 3.3.94 and with it the *Kāśikā* (*'bhāve' 'akartari ca kārake' iti vartate*), which, by the way, also deals with *śruti*, denoting '(sense of) hearing' (*śrūyate 'nayeti*).
[27] See also Wackernagel-Debrunner, *Altindische Grammatik*, Bd. II, 2, Göttingen 1954, p. 636. The rendering of *śruti* by 'heard' is not new. It is often encountered in the secondary literature, but there it is not clear (see Gonda, 1977, 663) whether the Vedic *ṛṣis*' way of gaining this wisdom is referred to (see, for example, V.S. Apte, *The Practical Sanskrit-English Dictionary*, Revised and enlarged Ed., Kyoto 1978, s.v. *veda*) or the method of transmission. The former, however, is – above all, if not exceptionally so – connected with the notion of a visual perception (see also Pāṇini 4.2.7: *dṛṣṭaṃ sāma*, as well as Heesterman 1978, 82: 'the catchword is vision...'). Medhātithi's explication (on Manu 2.10: *yatra śrūyate dharmānuśāsanaḥ śabdaḥ sa śrutiḥ / yatra smaryate sā smṛtiḥ / tac ca samācāre 'py astīty ataḥ so 'pi smṛtir eva /...*) is, of course, not important for the genesis of terms, but rather for the history of their reception. See also A. Ludwig, *Der Ṛgveda*, Bd. III, Prag 1878, pp. 21–24.
[28] See *śruta* n. 'what is heard, learnt, handed down; scholarship, knowledge' (*Petersburger Wörterbuch*).
[29] The commentor Agnisvāmin says on this: *tisṛṣv ṛkṣv ācāryā gānaṃ manyante prayoge / kasmāt / smṛteḥ, eva hy ācāryaiḥ gītaṃ / smṛvtir ūhagītiḥ, smṛtitas tu paraṃ pramāṇaṃ / yady evam ācāryā manyante atha pūrvavidhānaṃ kasya / ucyate / sthavirasya gautamasyedaṃ matam... /* ('tradition' has more weight than individual opinion!).
[30] A precise examination of the various forms, developments, and receptions of this idea is, as far as I know, still lacking. See also below, note 57.
[31] On *śīla-vṛtta*, see also Hara 1986, 36f, fn. 6.
[32] Bühler (1879, 143), footnote to the fourth *sūtra*. Bühler moreover bases this on Govindasvāmin, who explains: *śiṣṭair āgamyata iti śiṣṭāgamaḥ / śiṣṭair ācarita ity arthaḥ /*.
[33] See *Petersburger Wörterbuch* s.v. *āgama* g).
[34] See, for example, *Manu* 2.6 and 2.11.
[35] See, for example, B. R. Lingat 1973, 5: 'the various sources from which it,' i.e. the *dharma*, 'proceeds'! Similarly vague is, e.g., the expression 'rests upon'.
[36] Cf. *ĀpDhS* 1.10.29.1 as well as *BaudhDhS* 2.10.18.25.
[37] See S. A. Srinivasan, *Studies in the Rāma Story. On the irretrievable loss of Vālmīki's original and the operation of the received text as seen in some versions of the Vālin-Sugrīva episode*, Wiesbaden 1984, p. 59ff.
[38] See *ĀpDhS* 1.11.32.24: The male ancestors are one's own *mūla*. On *mūla* = 'result, consequence' cf. P. Thieme, *Kleine Schriften II*, hrsg. von R. Söhnen-Thieme, Stuttgart 1995, p. 1074ff.
[39] See the expression *lakṣaṇa* in Manu 2.12 that Medhātithi glosses by *nimitta*, *jñāpaka*, while Sarvajñanārāyaṇa, Nandana, and Rāghavānanda say *pramāṇa*, and Kullūka explains as *dharmapramāṇa*.

[40] Hacker (1965) states that rendering *dharma* as 'norm,' 'law' or 'obligation' was 'far too abstract.' The same is true for *ācāra*.

[41] See *GobhGS* 3.3.29 and 38.

[42] See *ĀśvGS* 1.7.1 (here, however, with the final element *dharma*, respectively) and *PārGS* 1.8.11 (*grāmavacana*). Passages of this type have already been examined, also by Lariviere, but always regarding the Śāstra's reference to social reality or the consideration of local wedding customs, respectively. Apart from that, it seems noteworthy to me that a few (at least three) *janapadas* are referred to, which implies that the text claims a validity of specific customs for a larger region – however this unity might have been defined, whether geographically, politically, or ethnically. This is also true for *ĀpDhS* 1.7.20.8 (see above fn. 5), where *sarvajanapadeṣu* (*ekānta-samāhitam*) is mentioned. One could certainly ask how large this region actually is, but it is the author's reference to a wider geographical scope which is decisive.

[43] See *MānGS* 1.46, *VārāhaGS* 8.6 (Cf. P. Rolland, *Un rituel domestique védique. Le Vārāhagṛhyasūtra*, Aix-en-Provence 1971, p. 100f.), and *KāṭhGS* 9.8 (where the commentators Devapāla and Ādityadarśana are apparently wrong in taking *ācāreṇa* as a reference to the *ācārādhyāya*). Cf. also *GobhGS* 3.3.29.

[44] See *BaudhGS* 1.1.25 where, conditioned by context, *ācāra* is taken narrowly as *saṃsthā, kriyāsantati*. Gonda's translation and presentation of *sūtra* 1.1.28 (o. c. [fn. 72], p. 80), is highly misleading.

[45] This could point to °*ādyāni*, which then would have been misunderstood.

[46] Apparently, this alludes not only to the Gṛhyasūtras but also to the Dharmasūtras.

[47] *pārvaṇenāto 'nyāni karmāṇi vyākhyātāny ācārād yāni gṛhyante* //.

[48] Certainly, his expression makes it clear that Haradatta follows the – radical – Mīmāṃsā-thesis (cf. below, note 55) that also the 'practice' (or a certain 'practice') is based on testimonies of the *śruti* – but on those testimonies that were not preserved by the tradition in its time. The basis and precondition for this thesis is the knowledge of the loss of single parts of the Vedic tradition.

[49] This Gṛhyasūtra does not contain *mantras*. These are collected in a separate Mantrapāṭha (ed. M. Winternitz, Oxford, 1897).

[50] Certainly, one has to consider in this context also *TaittU* 1.11, where in the case of doubt concerning sacrifice (*karman*) or (correct) behavior (*vṛtta*), the teacher recommends to act in accordance with specifically qualified Brahmans (*ye tatra brāhmaṇāḥ... syuḥ / yathā te tatra varteran/ tathā tatra vartethāḥ/*).

[51] See Lariviere (1997, 105). See also, for example, Derrett (1968, 135).

[52] What was the idea the authors of these texts had of what they were doing? To what extent and whereby did they find themselves authorized to formulate *dharma*? Were they aware of the fact that they were actually creating law? Would they have referred to Kumārila, that is, his view (see Hacker, 1965, 100f.), that 'whatever thought arises to someone who knows the Veda by heart, is a Vedic thought'?

[53] I agree with Lariviere's implicit assumption that the codification took place in various regions and time periods, although it certainly does not imply that there were no interconnection whatsoever. Lingat (1973, 73f.) attempts to draw a possible picture of this process.

[54] Lariviere (1997, 103). In this case the theorization is rather easily recognizable, whereas elsewhere one has to rely on mere assumptions quite often.

[55] 'Ritual, Offenbarung und Achsenzeit', in: *Kulturen der Achsenzeit*, pt. 2, ed. W. Schluchter. Frankfurt/M., p. 235. See also Heesterman (1978, 81). This essay would be the starting point for an attempt to examine critically the development of the *vedamūlatva* idea. My own thoughts presented here concern an earlier time, as it were, the pre-history of this idea; hence my rather casual reference to Heesterman. This is true analogically with regard to another article by Heesterman relevant for

the present context: 'Power and Authority in Indian Tradition,' in: R.J. Moore (ed.), *Tradition and Politics in South Asia*, New Delhi 1979, pp. 60–85; an expanded version of this article is published in *The Inner Conflict of Tradition* (Chicago: University of Chicago Press, 1985) pp. 141–157.

[56] On this see, A. Wezler, 'Manu's Omniscience: On the Interpretation of Manu II, 7', in *Indology and Law: Studies in Honour of Professor Duncan M. Derrett*, ed. by G.D. Sontheimer and P.K. Aithal, pp. 79–105 (Heidelberg 1982) and Heesterman, 1978, 85f.

[57] *dharmeṇādhigato yeṣāṃ vedas saparibr̥ṃhaṇaḥ/śiṣṭās tadanumānajñāḥ śrutipratyakṣahetavaḥ* // See *Manu* 12.109 as well as *VasDhS* 6.43.

[58] In this regard, the passage *BĀU* 1.4.14 is particularly significant as even the Kṣatriyas are subject to *dharma* as the highest ordering principle.

[59] Namely 1.3: *praśasyatamo bhavati loke pretya ca svargalokaṃ samaśnute.*

[60] Translation from Bühler (1879). *dharmiṇāṃ viśeṣeṇa svargaṃ lokaṃ dharmvid āpnoti jñānābhiniveśābhyām.*

[61] All citations from Oberhammer (1999).

[62] 'Causing salvation' becomes virtually the textual definition of the term *dharma* ; cf., for example, Cakradhara, *Nyāyamañjarīgranthibhaṅga* (ed. Nagin J. Shah, Ahmedabad 1972, p. 147); *NM* (ed. K. S. Varadacharya, bhāg 2, Mysore 1983, p. 109: *sa eva ca dharmaḥ*) – *śreyaskarasya dharmatvāt tadanuṣṭhānāc ca śreyo 'vāpteḥ.*

ABBREVIATIONS

ĀpDh	Āpastamba Dharmasūtra
ĀpGS	Āpastamba Gr̥hyasūtra
ĀśvGS	Āśvalāyana Gr̥hyasūtra
BĀU	Br̥hadāraṇyaka Upaniṣad
BaudhDhs	Baudhāyana Dharmasūtra
BaudhGS	Baudhāyana Gr̥hyasūtra
GautDhS	Gautama Dharmasūtra
GobhGS	Gobhila Gr̥hyasūtra
KāṭhGS	Kāṭhaka Gr̥hyasūtra
LāṭyŚS	Lāṭyāyana Śrautasūtra
MānGS	Mānava Gr̥hyasūtra
MS	(Pūrva) Mīmāṃsāsūtra
PārGS	Pāraskara Gr̥hyasūtra
PW	Petersburg Wörterbuch
R	Rāmāyaṇa
TaittU	Taittirīya Upaniṣad
VārāhaGS	Vārāha Gr̥hyasūtra
VasDhS	Vasiṣṭha Dharmasūtra

REFERENCES

Bühler, G. (1879). *The Sacred Laws of the Āryas*, Pt. I *Sacred Books of the East*. Vol. II. (repr. 1965). Delhi: Motilal Banarsidass.

Derrett, J.D.M. (1968). *Religion, Law and the State in India.* London: Faber and Faber.

Gampert, W. (1939). *Die Sühnezeremonien in der altindischen Rechtsliteratur*. Prag: Orientalisches Institut.

Gonda, J. (1977). *The Ritual Sūtras*. Wiesbaden: Harrassowitz.

Gonda, J. (1980). *Vedic Ritual. The Non-Solemn Rites*. Leiden: Brill.

Hacker, P. (1965). 'Dharma in Hinduismus', *Zeitschrift für Missionswissenschaft und Religionswissenschaft* **49**, 93–106.

Halbfass, W. (1988). *India and Europe: An Essay in Understanding*. Albany, NY: State University of New York Press.

Hara, M. (1986). 'A Note on the Sanskrit Word *śīla*', *Adyar Library Bulletin* **50**, 21–45.

Heesterman, J. (1978). 'Veda and Dharma', in W.D.O' Flaherty and J.D.M. Derrett (eds.), *The Concept of Duty in South Asia* (pp. ***). New Delhi: Vikas.

Horsch, P. (1967). 'Vom Schöpfungmythos zum Weltgesetz', *Asiatische Studien* **22**, 31–61. Translated in this volume.

Kane, P.V. (1973). *History of Dharmaśāstra*, Vol. III, 2nd ed. Poona: Bhandarkar Oriental Research Institute (the first edition was published in 1946).

Lariviere, R. (1997). 'Dharmaśāstra, Custom, 'Real Law' and 'Apocryphal' Smṛtis' In [B. Kölver (ed.)] *Recht, Staat und Verwaltung im klassischen Indien*, (pp. 97–110). Munich: Oldenbourg. Reprinted in this volume.

Lingat, R. (1993). *The Classical Law of India*. Berkeley: University of California Press.

Oberhammer, G. (1999). 'Raum-zeitliche Vermittlung der Transzendenz zum Heil. Zur sakramentalen Dimension religiöser Tradition', In [G. Oberhammer and M. Schmücker (eds.)] *Raum-zeitliche Vermittlung der Transzendenz: Zur "sakramentalen" Dimension religiöser Tradition*. Vienna: Österreichische Akademie der Wissenschaften.

Oldenberg, H. (1892). *The Gṛhya-sūtras: Rules of Domestic Ceremonies*. Pt. II: Gobhila, Hiraṇyakeśin, Āpastamba. *Sacred Books of the East*, Vol. XXX (Reprint 1964). Delhi: Motilal Banarsidass.

Olivelle, P. (1993). *The Āśrama System. The History and Hermeneutics of a Religious Institution*. New York: Oxford University Press.

Sen-Gupta, N.S. (1953). *Evolution of Ancient Indian Law* (University of Calcutta Tagore Law Lectures, 1950). London: Probsthain.

Smith, B.K. (1989). *Reflections on Resemblance, Ritual and Religion*. New York: Oxford University Press.

Tichy, E. (1995). *Die Nomina agentis auf –tar- im Vedischen*. Heidelberg: Winter.

Albrecht Wezler
Berhnard Ihnen Strasse 18
D-21465 Reinbek
Germany

JOHN BROCKINGTON

THE CONCEPT OF *DHARMA* IN THE RĀMĀYAṆA

The concept of *dharma* is an extremely broad one and it has often, therefore, been subject to a degree of misunderstanding, or at least inadequate understanding.[1] In particular, there has been a tendency to read back into earlier periods the modern understanding of the term, which is heavily coloured by its use as an equivalent to 'religion'; even the apparently more precise *sanātana dharma* to denote 'Hinduism' contributes to this misunderstanding, since in the Sanskrit epics, where the phrase first occurs, it refers to tradition, especially family customs. Even among Indologists there has been a tendency to impose a universal cosmological interpretation on the term. An examination of its meaning in different periods and milieux by contextual study of its actual use in specific texts or by specific groups is therefore timely.

In an article first published 25 years ago, in which I examined shifts in the way that Rāma is perceived, as the *Rāmāyaṇa* developed into the text that we are familiar with, I commented about the phrase that I used as its title, *rāmo dharmabhṛtāṃ varaḥ*, that:

> From an original meaning which one might paraphrase as 'a pillar of the establishment', with the emphasis on *dharma* as the correct social order, there was a shift to *dharma* as 'righteousness, moral values (only)', to 'Righteous Rāma'; but in a *kṣatriya* context an emphasis on *dharma* as the correct social order, even political stability, is entirely natural.[2]

On this occasion I will survey the 1100 or so occurrences in the *Rāmāyaṇa* of the term *dharma* and closely related terms in order to establish how far this pattern holds good in general and, more particularly, how the particular nuances in its meaning change with the changing attitudes of the transmitters of the text over the centuries. For this purpose, I shall make use of the broad division into stages of this process of growth that I identified in my *Righteous Rāma*.[3] This in itself brings out an important point by showing that the concept as such is much more frequent in the second stage of growth than the first. While the majority of the occurrences of *dharma* denote broadly morality or propriety, there is a significant emphasis also on caste, family or personal duties and on an element of necessity, as well as on the duties of a king (*rājadharma*). Particularly interesting are the passages where the term is used in what we might regard as two different senses.

I shall concentrate on the *Rāmāyaṇa* but I will inevitably include comparisons and contrasts with the *Mahābhārata*. After all, whereas several modern scholars regard the *Mahābhārata* as an exploration of the problems involved in establishing the nature of *dharma*, they regard the *Rāmāyaṇa* as an affirmation of the centrality of *dharma* to all right endeavour, for, although the *Rāmāyaṇa* does not have anything corresponding to Bhīma's lengthy discourses on *rājadharma, āpaddharma* and *mokṣadharma*, it is centred on the figure of Rāma himself.

James Fitzgerald has been arguing recently that the *Mahābhārata* reveals a significant transition in the use of the term *dharma* and that this transition corresponds to the historical shift from the ritual ethics of deeds to the newer *yoga*-oriented ethics of refining one's self.[4] It is certainly true that older senses of *dharma* are linked with the concept of actions and Fitzgerald adds to that the ideas of such actions being normative or not and of such actions being beneficial – or injurious, if *adharma* – for their doer in the afterlife; it is thus similar to the concept of *karma*, which has of course undergone a similar evolution. When *dharma* refers mainly to the outcome of these 'good deeds', it can appropriately be translated as 'merit'. But the term also suggests benefits to others and this aspect is especially prominent in the *dharma* of kings, *rājadharma*. Equally, though, the ritual forms of *dharma* were dependent on the expertise and good will of brāhmans, who had a vested interest in asserting their position within society and so in promoting the concept of *varṇadharma*.

However, the middle of the first millennium B.C. saw the emergence alongside the older Vedic values – and gradually superseding them – of the new religious perspectives which cluster around *yoga* and displace the earlier emphasis on priestly and collective rituals with an emphasis on cultivating some kind of saving knowledge that brings liberation from the cycle of death and rebirth. James Fitzgerald's argument is that the tensions inherent in this shift were brought to a head during the Mauryan period, especially in the '*dharma* campaign' of the emperor Aśoka and in particular around the issues of violence and non-violence (*ahiṃsā*). In his view this is the fundamental source of the ambivalence about *dharma* in the *Mahābhārata*.

For me, this presents a cogent view of the underlying concerns of the *Mahābhārata's* redactors and helps to make sense of much that has in the past been unclear about that epic. It seems to me also to be true that the *Rāmāyaṇa* shows a broadly similar pattern of development, though not as obviously as the *Mahābhārata*, because of its rather different focus. So this is basically the position that I shall be adopting in the rest of this article. However, this is not the only view that has been put forward and there is one other that I would like to mention specifically, because it is made by a major scholar and has at least an element of truth in it.

Bimal Matilal has argued,[5] primarily on the basis of Vālin's accusations against Rāma (4.18), that the virtues expounded in the *Rāmāyaṇa* are purely formalistic – they depend simply on fulfilling a formal promise or a formal duty – and that the term *dharma* is to be seen as equivalent to these formalistic principles. This seems to me to be an unduly restrictive view of the nature of *dharma* in the text. Admittedly, there are many passages where *dharma* appears simply as one member of the *trivarga* – for example, Rāma declares that it must be following *kāma* rather than *artha* and *dharma* that destroyed Daśaratha (2.47.9 and 13) and many more instances can be adduced (1.5.4c, 2.94.53-54, 3.39.8a, 48.8-12, 4.24.8-19, 37.20-22, 5.49.27-28 and 6.51.9-12) – but even in these the meaning of *dharma* is often wider than this might suggest. But a broader view of the narrative shows it as exploring – in a more positive way certainly than the *Mahābhārata* – the ramifications of the concept of *dharma* and as making both Daśaratha and Rāma at critical points place *dharma* in the sense of the wider good above personal interests.

Before returning to the broader picture of the plot and characters as a whole, let me turn first to a brief grammatical comment and then to a survey of the senses in which *dharma* is used within the text. Within the *Rāmāyaṇa* almost invariably *dharma* follows the thematic *-a* declension, but the more archaic consonant stem *dharman* does occur just occasionally in compounds: *bhavantaḥ śrutadharmāṇaḥ* at 1.8.14a, *kaikeyyās tyaktadharmaṇaḥ* at 2.60.5d, *kṣatradharmaṇy abhirato* at 2.110.26c, and *saṃyuktaḥ kāladharmaṇā* at 6.80.8d. However, in the first three instances the large number of variant readings must cast considerable doubt on their being genuinely archaic rather than archaising (in the fourth, there is much higher agreement, when the N variant *mahatā kāladharmaṇā* of 6.1785*1 post. is taken into account).

It is of course difficult to find straightforward equivalents in English for *dharma* and in any case, the attempt to do so all too easily suggests distinct meanings for the word rather than simply the foregrounding of one aspect of its total meaning. More specific senses on the whole attach to the various compound words formed with *dharma*: from the usual meaning of 'injustice' for *adharma* (and also for *vaidharmya* attested only from the fourth stage, at 2.729*3 and possibly elsewhere) to 'local custom' for *deśadharma* (at 3.8.23d). Although *adharma* does seem usually to signify 'injustice', it can more generally mean 'wrong', as when the Devas and Asuras are aligned with *dharma* and *adharma* at 6.26.11cd-12. However, for the time being I will set aside these compound words, in order to concentrate on the main body of the material.

Around two-thirds of occurrences, then, have the sense of either 'propriety' or 'morality' – the fact that I found it impossible reliably to distinguish these is a good illustration of the point that I have just made – but the proportion is probably somewhat inflated by the fact that this was my default category, to which were assigned all instances that did not obviously belong elsewhere;[6] they are much commoner in the second stage of growth of the text than elsewhere, but this ties in with the increasing ethical as well as aesthetic concerns of that stage and is seen also with most senses of *dharma*. The next most frequent sense in the first stage – but a long way behind in frequency – is that of sacrificial or other religious activity, which then becomes particularly common in the third stage; the other senses that are commoner in the first stage than in the second are those of 'merit' or moral conduct and of law or norms. However, the second most frequent sense overall in the text is that of caste or personal duty, if we include the compounds *kṣatradharma*, *rājadharma* and *svadharma*, and this is more than three times as frequent in the second stage as the first.

Other senses roughly in order of their frequency within the text as a whole are: tradition or custom, norms, necessity and legality; there are also an appreciable number of instances of its linking with *artha* and *kāma*, or just with *artha*, in implicit reference to the *trivarga*, the schema of the three purposes of a properly ordered life. There are also just a very few instances of *dharma* being personified: some five times as a synonym for Yama, the god of death (1.26.15a, 55.1a, 2.41.22b, 6.21.22b and 33.14a) – and another five times in the form Dharmarāja (2.58.23d,33c, 7.18.5b,23a and 22.26b) – and three times as 'Morality' personified (3.35.13a, 6.113.32a and 7.91.15b); one of the latter is where Rāma himself is characterised as 'Dharma personified' (*rāmo vigrahavān dharmaḥ*,[7] 3.35.13a) by Mārīca at the climax of his praise of Rāma, when he is trying vainly to dissuade

Rāvaṇa from his plan to abduct Sītā. However, to keep the balance straight, we must also note the relatively frequent use of the instrumental case or an adverbial form of *dharma* (*dharmeṇa* and *dharmataḥ*) to mean nothing more than 'duly, in proper fashion', especially in the third stage; this is much commoner than the other use of these two forms to mean 'legally, by rights'.

I will next examine these various senses a little more closely. The most frequent sense then is the one that I characterised as 'propriety' or 'morality', where the aspect of 'propriety' is at least as prominent as that of 'morality', if not more so. An example of this is Saumitri's advice to her son Lakṣmaṇa as the trio go off to exile: 'It's a universal principle among good people that the younger should be subject to the will of the elder, and the custom of this family has always been to give alms, to undergo initiation for sacrifice, and to lay down their lives in battle' (*eṣa loke satāṃ dharmo yaj jyeṣṭhavaśago bhavet* || *idaṃ hi vṛttam ucitam kulasyāsya sanātanam* | *dānaṃ dīkṣā ca yajñeṣu tanutyāgo mṛdheṣu ca* || 2.35.6c-7d). Here it is deference to elders which is *dharma* and family custom which is characterised as *sanātana* (more on this adjective below). Other instances that I have classified here inevitably have other overtones as well – to give just one example, Mārīca declares to Rāvaṇa: 'Therefore in all situations rulers are to be honoured and respected; but you, not acknowledging propriety, have fallen into a mere delusion' (3.38.13), where this disregard of propriety is also a rejection of traditional values.

The sense of sacrificial or other religious activity shows an interesting distribution, since those instances where the activity is clearly sacrificial in fact belong mainly to the third stage of growth – the one most heavily influenced by brāhmanical values – and instances in the first or second stages (it is commoner in fact in the first stage) are mostly to the religious activities of the hermits or ascetics (for example at 2.44.20 and 48.15) and, although they are not normally spelled out, we may assume that they comprise various types of ascetic practice. Indeed, this aspect tends to merge with the next that I identified – that of 'merit', the gaining of moral credit by specific activities. A particularly interesting example of this is where Bharata exclaims about Rāma in exile: 'He, for whom accumulating merit by sacrifices duly performed is proper, now pursues merit that is produced by bodily privation (*yasya yajñair yathadiṣṭair yukto dharmasya saṃcayaḥ* | *śarīrakleśasaṃbhūtaṃ sa dharmaṃ parimārgate* || 2.93.33). This contrasts the traditional behaviour appropriate to a *kṣatriya* of sponsoring sacrifice with the ascetic practices of the sages in the forest which are, however, directed to *dharma* not *mokṣa* (a concept which is absent from the *Rāmāyaṇa*).

Not surprisingly the aspect of *dharma* as caste, family or personal duty is most frequent in the *Ayodhyākāṇḍa*, in which the events surrounding Rāma's banishment are narrated, and both there and elsewhere mainly in passages belonging to the second stage of growth of the text. For example, Rāma goes to the forest 'to maintain his integrity' (*vanaṃ gate dharmapare rāme ramayatāṃ vare* 2.55.1ab; cf. 2.88.27c[l.v.], which uses *kuladharma*); elsewhere we find Rāma in similar fashion referring to himself as grounded in his ancestral duties, *dharme pitṛpaitāmahe sthitam,* at 4.18.39cd. This aspect is given greater precision in the compounds *kṣatradharma, rājadharma* and *svadharma* which account for the majority of instances of this sense (although it should be noted that *kṣatradharma* is most frequent in the third stage of growth); [8] there is also one instance of the uncompounded form *kṣātra dharma* when Jābāli declares that he rejects the warrior code of conduct and characterises it as *adharma* combined with *dharma* (at 2.101.20ab – *kṣātra dharma* also occurs at 2.14*2 and 6.23). A particularly good example of this usage comes soon after, when Bharata, appealing to Rāma to return and become king, says 'Please show regard for the duties of kings, which are in line with our family tradition, Kākutstha, and accede to your mother's and my entreaty' (2.104.10), employing as it does the terms *rājadharma* and *kuladharma.*

The stereotyped pāda *sa hi dharmaḥ sanātanaḥ* (2.16.52d, 21.10d and 27.30d, also found four times in the *Mahābhārata*) or *eṣa dharmaḥ sanātanaḥ* (1.24.16b, 3.3.24b, 5.1.100b, 2 App.11.4 post., and commonly in the *Mahābhārata*), despite occurring only from the second stage onwards, is best translated 'this is the eternal tradition/the immemorial custom', since it is used mainly of social duty and especially in the *Rāmāyaṇa* of filial obedience. Examples of the shorter form, *dharmaḥ sanātanaḥ,* are when Rāma reproves Vālin for abandoning it by taking Sugrīva's wife (4.18.18d) and when Mālyavān, in conflict with Viṣṇu, declares that he does not acknowledge the eternal *kṣatriya* tradition (*kṣatradharmaṃ sanātanam* 7.8.3b). It is perhaps relevant to add at this point that the adjective *sanātana* 'perpetual, immemorial' shows an increase in frequency from the first to the third stages of growth (3 occurrences in the first stage, 10 in the second and 11 in the shorter third stage).

The other aspects that I identified – norms, necessity and legality – are all relatively infrequent and to quite an extent interrelated. An example of the sense of 'norms' or 'laws' is a description of Rāvaṇa, among other mostly positive attributes, as an 'uprooter of laws and fondler of other men's wives' (*ucchettāraṃ ca dharmāṇāṃ paradārābhimarśanam* 3.30.12ab), where the use of the plural helps to confirm this sense as dominant rather than a more general one of 'morality'. Others include Tārā seeking to excuse Sugrīva's neglect of Rāma's cause and indulgence in sexual dalliance by reference to *dehadharma,* the demands of our body or perhaps bodily urges (4.34.9a), and Hanumān responding to Svayaṃprabhā's welcome by speaking of *ātithyadharma,* the norms of hospitality (4.51.16a).[9]

The aspect of 'necessity' or perhaps better 'inevitability' is seen almost exclusively in the compound *kāladharma,* 'the law of time' as the Princeton translators render it, alternatively 'the decree of fate' or the 'inevitability of death', used as a euphemism for death, which occurs seven times; indeed, on one further occasion the first member of the compound is *maraṇa,* 'dying', when the Rākṣasa Khara boasts that he could subject a personified Death to the rule of mortality (*mṛtyuṃ maraṇadharmeṇa saṃkruddho yojayāmy aham* 3.22.20cd; cf. 6.928*4). This compound usually occurs in the *Mahābhārata* in the more archaic form *kāladharman,* which has led Vassilkov to regard the concept as relatively early, while also suggesting that to 'yield to the Law of Time' denotes dying peacefully of old age, rather than a violent death in battle.[10] However, only one of the *Rāmāyaṇa* occurrences (that at 6.80.8d) has the consonantal stem form and, while its use for death in the fullness of time is broadly true of the *Rāmāyaṇa* (but not of *maraṇadharma* cited above, nor of *kāladharman* at 6.80.8d), five out of the seven occurrences in fact belong to the third stage of growth (possibly because the matter-of-fact *kṣatriya* approach to death had by then been replaced by brāhman squeamishness) and thus tend to invalidate Vassilkov's dating in relation to the *Rāmāyaṇa.*[11]

There are a very limited number of instances of *dharma* in the sense of 'legality', even though this is quite a common usage in classical Sanskrit (indeed, from the time of the *dharmaśāstras* onwards). The impending marriage of Rāma and Lakṣmaṇa to Sītā and Urmilā respectively is declared by Viśvāmitra to be a *dharmasaṃbandha,* 'a lawful union' (1.71.3a). Mantharā talks to Kaikeyī about Bharata's rightful claim to the kingdom (2.8.23). There are a couple of instances of the instrumental, *dharmeṇa,* being used to mean 'legally, by rights': a heavenly voice declares to Janaka when he finds Sītā in the furrow that the baby is legally his (2.110.30d) and Aṅgada castigates

Sugrīva's appropriation of his brother Vālin's wife, who is legally or by rights his mother (4.54.3c). Similarly, but only from the third stage of growth, there are some four instances of the adverbial form, *dharmataḥ,* used in this sense: Viśvāmitra asserts that the wonder-cow Śabalā is legally his (1.52.9f) and Kumbhīnasī abducted by Madhu and Rambhā raped by Rāvaṇa are declared to be legally too closely related to their violators for sexual relations to be allowable (7.25.25d, 26.21c,23c).

With regard to the three aims of life, one of the fullest passages is that where Rāma outlines to Sugrīva the proper behaviour of a king, first in terms of his adherence to *dharma, artha* and *kāma* and his apportioning them suitably, then by a warning against putting *kāma* first, and finally by stating that a king who kills his enemies and supports his allies gains merit (*dharma*) and enjoys the fruits of the *trivarga* (4.37.20-22). Not only does this passage contain one of just two actual occurrences of the term *trivarga* in the text (the other is at 1.6.5b) but it also links the three aims with activities by a king. In general, it can be said that use of the term *dharma* in such contexts still points to the older pattern of *dharma* as normative and beneficial actions.

Up to this point I have been offering interpretations from outside for the meaning of *dharma* but from time to time we do find definitions of the term *dharma* being offered within the text itself. These include *dharma* being summed up as filial obedience, the equivalence of *dharma* and *satya,* 'truth', and once that the highest *dharma* is absence of cruelty. Let me amplify each of these a little. Perhaps the clearest statement about one's duty consisting of obedience to one's parents is Rāma's declaration to Sītā: 'this is duty, my shapely wife, obedience to father and mother, and so, if I disregarded their command, I couldn't bear to live' (2.27.29, cf. his similar sentiments to his mother in App.I.11), to which – as so often – a contrast is provided by Lakṣmaṇa's outburst just before, at 2.20, when he threatens violently to overturn their father's command. Interestingly, a little earlier still in the narrative, Rāma has preceded a similar declaration, that one should not render a father's, mother's or brāhman's command vain (2.18.34), with a statement that *dharma* is supreme in the world and *satya* 'truth' is founded on *dharma* (2.18.33). We also find statements to the effect that *satya* is founded on *dharma,* for example at 2.101.12cd + 13, where Rāma declares that truth is the highest *dharma* in the world, truth is the lord of the world, and everything is rooted in truth; such statements tend to belong to later stages of growth of the text and, for example, in the fourth stage, Kaikeyī turns the equivalence of truth and *dharma* to her own ends at 2.234*1-3 (where 1post. reverses 2.18.33b). Perhaps significantly, the statement about the highest *dharma* being absence of cruelty (*ānṛśaṃsyaṃ paro dharmaḥ* 5.36.34c), which forms part of the message that Sītā gives to Hanumān to take back to Rāma, does not actually use the term *ahiṃsā* but a similar one. It is, however, the nearest parallel in the text of the *Rāmāyaṇa* to *Mahābhārata* affirmations of *ahiṃsā* as the highest moral value, occurring especially of course in the *Śāntiparvan*, where the term *ahiṃsā* occurs 38 times.[12] In contrast, the term *ahiṃsā* only occurs twice in the text of the *Rāmāyaṇa* (5.29.3a and 6.23.31c), as does the related adjective *ahiṃsaka* (2.101.31c[l.v.] and 7.33.18c[l.v].) ; the first of these is where Hanumān rather inconsistently describes Daśaratha as having been not only devoted to non-violence and compassionate but also as truly valiant (*ahiṃsāratir akṣudro ghṛṇī satyaparākramaḥ* 5.29.3ab).

Hanumān's conversation with Sītā, from which my last examples came, also includes Hanumān's assertion that Rāma is the guardian both of the living world and of his own family, both of his own conduct and of *dharma*, and of the four-class system in the world (*rakṣitā jīvalokasya svajanasya ca rakṣitā | rakṣitā svasya vṛttasya dharmasya ca paraṃtapaḥ || rāmo bhāmini lokasya cāturvarṇyasya rakṣitā |* 5.33.10-11ab). This expansion of a central incident during the second stage of growth provides a good indication of what were regarded as being the constituents of *dharma* by that period. However, whereas in the first two stages references to the four *varṇas* are almost all incidental (2.15.11, 76.30b, 98.57, 5.33.11, 6.113.29), showing that little significance was yet attached to the topic, in the third stage the sage Nārada bewails the decline of *dharma* in successive *yugas* as the other *varṇas* usurp the privileges of brāhmans (7.65.8-26, cf. 7.67.10). Besides Nārada's dirge, the third stage also includes the lengthy Viśvāmitra episode (1.31-64, cf. Mbh. 1.165), which centres on the antagonism between the brāhman Vasiṣṭha and the *kṣatriya* Viśvāmitra, particularly over the wonder-cow Śabalā. Superficially this story points to the separateness and mutual distinctiveness of the *varṇas* but its ramifications paint a somewhat different picture when looked at in detail.[13]

Next I will provide just a couple of examples of passages where more than one aspect of *dharma* is present. The first is Bharata's woeful response to Rāma (2.95.1cd-2): *kiṃ me dharmād vihīnasya rājadharmaḥ kariṣyati || śāśvato 'yaṃ sadā dharmaḥ sthito 'smāsu nararṣabha* | *jyeṣṭhaputre sthite rājan na kanīyān bhaven nṛpaḥ* || which I would translate 'What will a king's duties do for me, bereft of merit as I am ? This perpetual tradition has always been established among us that, while the oldest brother is alive, a younger should not become king', using 'duties', 'merit' and 'tradition' to translate *dharma*. The second is a more extended passage from the *Uttarakāṇḍa,* when in Rāma's subsequent rule the untoward death of a brāhman boy leads to the discovery of a *śūdra* practicing asceticism – an example of the hardening of caste exclusivism by the third stage – and a passage of five *ślokas* within Nārada's dirge has *dharma* used in a compound with *satya* 'truth', with the meaning of caste duties, with reference to the norms of the *yugas,* in the negative as 'injustice' and as 'merit'/ 'moral credit' (7.65.16-21).

The commonest compound words incorporating *dharma* are *dharmātman* and *dharmajña*, both of which are general terms of commendation broadly translatable as 'right-minded' and with no more specific denotation; they are distinguished from the other compound words in being more frequent in the first stage of growth than the second, as well as by their greater frequency overall (*dharmātman* occurs 68 times in the first stage, 47 times in the second and 66 times in the third, while *dharmajña* occurs 45 times in the first stage, 35 times in the second and 29 times in the third). Third in frequency – but a long way behind the first two – is *dharmacārin,* which by contrast is more specific in meaning; in addition, more than half its occurrences refer to women (14 out of 24 occurrences) and a third are instances of a stereotyped expression – these two categories overlap. The senses in which *dharmacārin* is used are those of hermit or ascetic, or at least to describe those following that life style, of practising virtue (not necessarily very distinct from the preceding sense), of a wife (especially in the two occurrences of *sahadharmacāriṇī*, which might perhaps be translated 'lawful companion' and has obvious links with *dharmapatnī*, itself found five times in the text), and once to mean 'law-abiding' (4.17.33d). The stereotyped expression is *tāpasī dharmacāriṇī* in its feminine form, occurring seven times and used for example both of the ascetic tribal woman Śabarī and of Sītā while in the forest, and in the masculine form *tāpasā dharmacāriṇaḥ,* used three times of various groups of ascetics (in addition once in the dual and once in the singular) ; this *pāda* is so standardised that it seems to me that both halves are simply denoting ascetics rather than *dharmacārin* having any very specific sense and that this is the case in other instances too. Even if the term is descriptive rather than denotative, that just underlines the point made earlier about these ascetics, who are more hermits than renouncers, following *dharma,* not *mokṣa.*

The distribution of certain other *dharma* compounds provides a measure of interest, as well as the precise nuances of their meaning. Thus, *dharmanitya,* 'contant in duty', occurs only five times in the text but more frequently in the fourth stage; *dharmapatnī,* 'lawful wife', already referred to, occurs four times in the first stage to once in the second; *dharmavatsala* and *dharmavid* occur more frequently in the second stage than the first (and *dharmavid* more frequently in the third stage than in the first and second stages together); *dharmaśīla,* 'well-behaved/law-abiding', is markedly more frequent in the first stage than the second or third (8, 3 and 1 occurrences respectively) ; and, for reasons that I cannot yet provide an explanation for, just over half the occurrences of *dharmasaṃhita,* 'consistent with morality', are in the *Kiṣkindhākāṇḍa* (8 out of 15) and half of those are in the two *sargas,* 4.17-18, containing Vālin's reproach against Rāma for unethical behaviour and Rāma's reply.

Of the various adjectives, *dhārmika* is much the most common, mainly because of its frequency in the *Bālakāṇḍa* (33 occurrences there and another 8 in the *Uttarakāṇḍa,* against 12 in the first stage of growth and 14 in the second; it is also frequent in the fourth stage). The next most frequent is the superlative form *dharmiṣṭha,* occurring 6 times in the first stage of growth, 4 times in the second and 12 times in the third. The only one not to follow the pattern of highest frequency in the third stage is *dharmya* (occurring 8, 3 and 4 times in the first, second and third stages). The last, *dharmin,* is so infrequent (once in the second stage and three times in the third) as to be of no real account, any more than is *vaidharmaka,* 'immoral' (only at 7.72.17d in the text).

Let me now return to the basic narrative. A key term in understanding the plot of the *Rāmāyaṇa* is 'fidelity': Daśaratha is faithful to his vow to Kaikeyī, Rāma faithfully performs his filial duty, Bharata refuses to usurp his older brother's rights, Lakṣmaṇa loyally serves Rāma and Sītā in their exile, Sītā accompanies her husband to a life of hardship and, after her abduction, resists all Rāvaṇa's threats and blandishments, and Rāma undergoes great perils to rescue her. This seems to me a better way to understand some of these episodes than Matilal's formal promises and formal duties. Admittedly, when Daśaratha sees it as his duty to keep his promise to Kaikeyī, he fails to see that he is thereby infringing his duty to give his people the best ruler and is being unjust to his rightful heir, Rāma. But equally, in the third stage of growth of the text, when Rāma banishes Sītā in order to allay the suspicions of the people about her virtue while in Rāvaṇa's hands, he subordinates his personal happiness to his idea of duty.

Rāma is portrayed as a model of piety at all times. He makes no protest when told of his father's unexpected decree and even goes so far as to advise that messengers be sent to recall Bharata. He shows no rancour towards those who have caused his banishment and attributes his own purity of motive to others, refusing to suspect either Bharata or subsequently Vibhīṣaṇa when others find their approach alarming. Nevertheless, though true to his pledged word down to the last detail (as shown, for example, by his refusal to leave the forest and pass the rainy season in Kiṣkindhā), he can be devious when he wishes to avoid a public display of emotion. He evades the citizens of Ayodhyā who attempt to follow him into exile, and the method of Sītā's banishment in the third stage is positively deceitful. Indeed, although it is in the third stage that the concept of 'righteous Rāma' is most stressed, this does not seem to extend to the personal level.

In the early stages Rāma is viewed as the perfect *kṣatriya*; indeed, it is when he declares that he will live in the forest like an ascetic in the manner more usually associated with brāhmans, that his role as the perfect *kṣatriya* comes most to the fore. When the sages in the forest complain of harassment by the Rākṣasas, Rāma immediately agrees to protect them. By the second stage, however, qualms about the morality of his position have crept in. Sītā is made to put forward a limited version of the doctrine of non-violence (*ahiṃsā*), although she does not use the term; she argues that he should not attack the Rākṣasas without direct provocation and thus forces Rāma to justify his action by asserting his duty both to protect the sages and to fulfil his pledged word (3.8-9). An interesting sub-unit within this passage is the story alluded to at 3.8.14, where Indra leaves a sword with an ascetic 'to thwart his asceticism' and thus causes his downfall by stirring up in him thoughts of violence. There is also an interesting contrast with the subsequent episode where Sītā mourning Rāma, killed as she thinks in the battle, describes him as possessing all virtues, including *ahiṃsā* (6.23.31) – the second of the two occurrences of the word in the text.

Rāma's championing of Sugrīva and killing of Vālin provide further evidence of this conflict of opposing ideals. Although Sugrīva is presented within the text as the wronged brother and is unhesitatingly accepted as such by Rāma, the rights and wrongs of the matter are by no means clear-cut. Much of that does not concern us now but for Rāma to interfere as he does in the duel between Sugrīva and Vālin is deceitful – shooting Vālin as he does from concealment, while Vālin and Sugrīva are engaged in a duel – and it constitutes a clear breach of the conventions of warfare, as the dying Vālin points out in a second-stage insertion. To justify himself, Rāma claims the duty of punishing Vālin's crimes as Bharata's agent and then lamely adds that anyway Vālin is only an animal and therefore fair game (4.17-18). The point is that the original authors were more concerned with telling a story which extolled Rāma's martial qualities and it was only later redactors who became worried by moral scruples. This is equally the reason for Rāma's apparent sudden change of attitude after the siege of Laṅkā, when he coldly spurns Sītā, until her virtue has been exonerated by the so-called fire-ordeal (6.102-4).

A superficially different procedure – but one that has clear parallels in the *Mahābhārata* – is that of one character being set up to question *dharma* and so providing the opportunity for another to affirm it – the well-known 'straw man' technique. For example, sarga 70 of the *Yuddhakāṇḍa,* again belonging to the second stage (and not attested in the *Rāmopākhyāna*), in the wake of the apparent killing of Sītā, contains Lakṣmaṇa's angry tirade on the inefficacy of *dharma* and the value of *artha,* here basically prosperity or wealth, but then Lakṣmaṇa regularly acts as a foil to Rāma, either to heighten Rāma's virtues by contrast or to afford Rāma an opportunity to expound the correct values; incidentally, some of the proverbial matter at 6.70.31-32, 34 and 37-38 is paralleled in Mbh. 12.8.16 and 18-21.[14] In rather similar fashion, at 2.100 (again from the second stage and not attested in the *Rāmopākhyāna*), the brāhman Jābāli argues on generally materialistic grounds of expediency and self-interest for Rāma's immediate return from exile and so gives the opportunity for Rāma in the next *sarga* angrily to rebuff him and Vasiṣīha in the next *sarga* again to add further refutation from an orthodox standpoint. This can easily be understood as a none too subtle attack on heterodox beliefs and in fact considerable parts of Jābāli's speech and Rāma's reply are proverbial or at least traditional in character.

The recurrent epithets linked with Rāma's name mirror this development of the text as a whole. The commonest – and distributed fairly evenly throughout the stages – is *rāmasyākliṭakarmaṇaḥ* 'of ever-zealous Rāma' (23 times in the text); this adjective is virtually specific to Rāma in the *Rāmāyaṇa* but in the *Mahābhārata* characterises both Kṛṣṇa and Arjuna. Next most frequent are the simple patronymic *rāmo daśarathatmajaḥ* (with 26 occurrences) and *rāghavasya mahātmanaḥ* 'of noble Rāma' (with 29 occurrences). 'The truly brave Rāma', *rāmaḥ satyaparākramaḥ,* occurs 16 times, while *rāmo dharmabhṛtāṃ varaḥ* or *śreṣṭhaḥ,* 'Rāma, the best of upholders of tradition', occurs a dozen times. Although *dharmabhṛtāṃ varaḥ* is exclusive to Rāma, its odd-*pāda* alternant *dharmabhṛtāṃ śreṣtha* is used of Daśaratha at 2.21.23c and by Rāma to Bharata at 2.97.18c – significantly as he seeks to persuade Bharata to return to Ayodhyā to take up the kingship and for the same reason addresses him by the dynastic title Rāghava (2.97.18c + 19b) – as well as occurring in *rāmo dharmabhṛtām śreṣṭhaḥ* at 5.56.17c (also 1.123*4pr.). These last two epithets stress the *kṣatriya* values, firstly of truth and valour, secondly of upholding tradition, which form the basis of the original story, although it is worth noting that the first of them is most frequent in the second stage, no doubt in part because of the emphasis in some passages on justifying Rāma's actions in moral terms, and that *dharmabhṛt* is not uncommon in the first and second stages (8 and 10 occurrences) but oddly is absent from the third stage. Rāma is projected as the conqueror of foes or strangers in several pādas (such as *rāmaḥ parapuraṃjayaḥ*) but the relative lack of stereotyping suggests that this martial aspect was not particularly important in the poets' understanding of Rāma's character. But the shift by the later stages to a devotional attitude towards Rāma is reflected in several new formulaic pādas. Incidentally, it is among those first appearing in later stages that parallels to the forms preferred in later literature, from Kālidāsa to Tulsīdās, are to be found.

I have endeavoured to make clear the way in which the understanding both of *dharma* and of the story itself develops over time, but in the process I have tended to jump from one stage to another, so let me now sum up my conclusions from this survey. One of the basic points established is that the concept of *dharma* is on the whole more frequent in the second stage of growth of the *Rāmāyaṇa* than it is in the first. Another obvious one is that the particular nuances in its meaning change with the changing attitudes of the transmitters of the text over the centuries. The older pattern of *dharma* being associated with the concept of actions that James Fitzgerald identifies in the *Mahābhārata* is on the whole that found in the *Rāmāyaṇa* and indeed there is very little allusion to the newer values of *ahiṃsā* and the like. While the majority of the occurrences of *dharma* denote broadly propriety or morality, there is a significant emphasis also on caste, family or personal duties and on an element of necessity, as well as on the duties of a king (*rājadharma*). In the first stage of growth, the heroic basis of the story is most evident, the religious pattern is markedly nearer to the Vedic than to the Purāṇic, with relatively little interest in religious matters being shown by the early redactors, and *dharma* is seen very much in terms of the *kṣatriya* concern to maintain the status quo. With the second stage of growth, alongside a certain shift from the heroic to the aesthetic, somewhat more emphasis is placed on religious matters (though still on the whole with a popular approach), and *dharma* is understood increasingly in terms of ethical behaviour.

The ethical polarisation already becoming apparent in these developments of the second stage, though coming from within the plot itself, leads naturally to a stress on Rāma's activity on behalf of *dharma* and his defeat of evil in the person of Rāvaṇa. This receives its fullest development within the *Rāmāyaṇa* in the *Uttarakāṇḍa*, belonging to the third stage of growth, where Rāvaṇa's genealogy and past exploits are so presented as to turn him into an adversary of the gods; Rāma's defeat of him is thereby given the same cosmic significance as Indra's defeat of Namuci and Viṣṇu's of Bali. Yet even here the primary emphasis is on action, for the understanding of *dharma* is not just something abstract and impersonal, but the inner struggle is always at the least hinted at. The *Rāmāyaṇa* is far more than merely a morality tale, in which Rāma epitomises kingly virtues and Sītā those of womanhood; it can indeed be read on many different levels.

NOTES

[1] An earlier, more general version of this article was presented to the Senior Seminar, School of Theology and Religious Studies, University of Leeds, 10th December 2002. Previous studies of *dharma* in the *Rāmāyaṇa* are surprisingly few. The main book-length treatment is Benjamin Khan, *The Concept of Dharma in Valmiki Ramayana*, Delhi, 1965. Even some articles which appear from their titles to offer relevant material (for example, W. Ruben, 'Über die ethische Idealgestalt des Rāma', *Studia Indologica: Festschrift für Willibald Kirfel*, ed. Otto Spies, Bonn, 1955, pp. 277–295, or rather more recently Nirmala Nayak, 'Man and the moral order in the Valmiki Ramayana', *Man in India* 66, 1986, pp. 259–264), fail adequately to do so.

[2] '*Rāmo dharmabhṛtāṃ varaḥ*', reprinted from *Indologica Taurinensia* 5, 1977, pp. 55–68, in *Epic Threads: John Brockington on the Sanskrit Epics*, ed. Greg Bailey and Mary Brockington, Oxford University Press, New Delhi, 2000, pp. 250–264, quoting pp. 250–251. The *pāda* occurs at 2.21.12b, 31.24b, 33.12b, 3.5.6b, 6.7b,8b, 4.38.1b, 6.99.35b, 102.5b,9d and 106.10d (also 2.1619*3post.).

[3] *Righteous Rāma: the evolution of an epic*, Delhi, 1984.

[4] He has done so principally in the introduction to the *Śāntiparvan* in his *The Mahābhārata, volume 7: 11, The Book of the Women, 12, The Book of the Peace,* tr., ed. and annotated by James L. Fitzgerald, Chicago University press, Chicago, 2004. I am grateful to him for an advance copy of his typescript.

[5] 'Rāma's Moral Decisions', *ALB* 44–45, 1980–1981, pp. 344–351. My remarks here follow my comments in *The Sanskrit Epics*, Leiden, 1998, p. 453.

[6] A further comment on procedure is in order: there was a small proportion of instances which could equally well be assigned to more than one category and these have been counted in each category (rather than an artificially exact half being credited).

[7] Despite this being its sole occurrence in the *Vālmīki Rāmāyaṇa*, this phrase has been seized by later tradition as a typical one, as illustrated by the title of Calambur Sivaramamurti's collection of essays, *Rāmo vigrahavān dharmaḥ: Rama, embodiment of righteousness,* Kanak Publications, New Delhi, 1981.

[8] For the record, *kṣatradharma* occurs once in the first stage, 3 times in the second and 8 times in the third, *rājadharma* occurs twice in the first stage and 5 times in the second, and *svadharma* occurs once in the first stage, 7 times in the second and 5 times in the third.

[9] The sense of a specific code of laws seems to be particularly late but it occurs for example in *dharmapāṭhaka*, 'lawyer, law-teacher', at 7 App.8.309 and 426(iic).

[10] Yaroslav Vassilkov, '*Kālavāda* (the doctrine of Cyclical Time) in the Mahābhārata and the concept of Heroic Didactics', *Composing a Tradition: Concepts, Techniques and Relationships* (Proceedings of the First Dubrovnik International Conference on the Sanskrit Epics and Purāṇas), ed. Mary Brockington and Peter Schreiner, Zagreb, 1999, pp. 17–33, especially p. 26.

[11] For the record, it should be noted that in *kāladharmaviśeṣavid* at 4.28.6d the first two members are in a dvandva relationship, not tatpuruṣa, and so the form is not relevant here.

[12] There is, however, at least one example from the fourth stage of growth, for several N manuscripts substitute for part of Sītā's homily this piece of advice to Rāma: *ahiṃsāniratah saumya bhava dharmaparāyaṇaḥ* (3.135*1, replacing 3.8.28).

[13] See further at *The Sanskrit Epics,* Leiden, 1998, p. 426 §1. Other third-stage references to the four *varṇas* are found at 1.1.75,79, 6.16-17, 12.12,17cd, 24.15 and 25.5. More generally on this topic see my 'Concepts of Race in the Mahābhārata and Rāmāyaṇa', *The Concept of Race in South Asia*, ed. Peter Robb, Delhi, 1995, pp. 97–108.

[14] For some discussion of this *sarga* see Benjamin Khan, *The Concept of Dharma in Valmiki Ramayana,* Delhi, 1965, pp. 60–67.

JAMES L. FITZGERALD

DHARMA AND ITS TRANSLATION IN THE *MAHĀBHĀRATA*

The word *dharma* signifies a concept that is one of the most central and important topics of thought and debate in the *Mahābhārata* (MBh). But it has also proved to be the single most difficult and vexing term I have encountered in my ongoing translation of the *Śāntiparvan* of the MBh.[1] The concept is complex and often under contestation in the MBh, explicitly and implicitly. And the usage of the word in the epic is varied and elusive, as seems often to be the case with highly important words in a language. This essay offers distillations of the understandings of the concept and the word *dharma* I arrived at as I struggled to grasp fully what was being said in instance after instance in the *Śāntiparvan* read against the background of the epic as a whole.[2] It also presents and discusses the translational strategies I employed in the first half of the *Śāntiparvan* and will employ in revising the second half of that book of the MBh.

Before moving into the straightforward presentation of my understanding of the concept and my patterns of translating it, I would like to make a few limited observations that I think are pertinent to the study and discussion of *dharma* in the MBh. I start by invoking the apt advice of the *Āpastamba Dharmasūtra*: "*Dharma* and *adharma* do not go about saying 'Here we are!' Nor do the Gods, Gandharvas, or Ancestors tell us 'This is *dharma*,' 'This is *adharma*.'"[3] The same holds true for the words as well as the entities which the words represent: We are seldom given direct, explicit indications of exactly what a word means and how it means what it means. Some philosophers do occasionally tell us this or that about *dharma* or the word *dharma* in the MBh and elsewhere, but I think it is a mistake to treat those direct, often self-conscious, and sometimes sophisticated and intellectually very interesting, statements unreflectively as direct presentations of the "true meaning" of the word. Less self-conscious, less sophisticated, perhaps ultimately less intellectually interesting uses of the word are, at least initially, equally important for charting such a word and the idea or ideas it represents. And these uses are the more frequent ones. Most of the time in the MBh we are left to observe the word *dharma* used in the rough and tumble of practical discourse and we must try to discern the scope and operation of the word in this usage.

The single biggest problem in coming to terms with *dharma* in the *Mahābhārata* is the tremendous abundance of instances of it, and then the many different modes of variation within and among those different instances of the word. The word *dharma* occurs in a number of different contexts and applications in the epic and these various pragmatic situations give the word an initially indistinct range of nuances and colorings. Many passages in the *Mahābhārata* often present the value and importance of *dharma* as taken for granted, but it is not easy to abstract a common, taken-for-granted element from all these passages. Also, the *Mahābhārata* does not always speak with one voice about the particular behavior or behaviors that actually have the status of *dharma,* and sometimes what particular actions or behaviors constitute *dharma* are said to be unknown. A number of didactic passages in the text take it upon themselves to spell out in detail the variety of behaviors that are *dharma* for different people, an action that, besides its explicit messages, implies that someone felt some kind of need to put these matters straight. Many other passages see the word *dharma* invoked when characters in the epic debate among themselves whether some behavior is *dharma* or not, or debate the evaluation of actions done in the past, or pit one claim of *dharma* against another, or set one character to persuading another, or others, that some behavior is or is not *dharma*. The word is also used to praise (or, if its opposite, *adharma*, occurs, to criticize) some agent's motives, ethical sensibilities, or the general quality of his or her life and accumulated deeds. And while the basic attitude toward *dharma* may be one of respect, or even reverence, that attitude is not shared by all the epic's characters. Not even all the supposed 'good guys' in the *Mahābhārata* assume that *dharma* is the most important and valuable kind of action: Draupadī and Bhīmasena and even Kṛṣṇa Vāsudeva call its fundamental value into question at different times, all asserting that this-worldly self-interest [*artha*] is sometimes more important. And not only is *dharma* frequently said in the *Mahābhārata* to be very subtle (*sūkṣma*) and difficult to know, whole sections of the text develop the point that often what appears to be *dharma* is actually *adharma*, and vice-versa. This last point bears both upon the epistemological question of how humans can have reliable knowledge of *dharma* and upon the axiological point that different values sometimes conflict and must be ranked. And it bears too upon the issue of hypocrisy, of true virtue as opposed to apparent virtue, and of inner virtue as opposed to outer virtue. The word *dharma* points to something that someone holds to be religiously right and good; some voices in the *Mahābhārata* claim to know definitely what that, or those things, are; but often characters in the *Mahābhārata* exhibit uncertainty about the content of what is claimed to be *dharma* and ambivalence toward the idea itself.

Finally, I want to acknowledge that a very significant portion of what I have come to understand about *dharma* has been fundamentally informed by and agrees with what was very well stated in Paul Hacker's 1965 article "Dharma im Hinduisms;"[4] similar credit goes to Wilhelm Halbfass' essay "Dharma in the Self-Understanding of Traditional Hinduism."[5] In particular I agree with Halbfass' emphasizing that the word *dharma* is not a descendent of Vedic *ṛta* and does not refer to some kind of free-standing, overarching cosmic natural law. I see little or no basis in the *Mahābhārata* justifying this wide-spread understanding of *dharma*; various passages which some may see referring to such a natural-law use of *dharma* are, in my judgment, to be explained otherwise.

In his grief after the war, poor Dhṛtarāṣṭra said to Vidura at MBh 11.5.1, "Recount for me at length the whole path of understanding (*buddhimārga*) so I can traverse with understanding the unfathomable mystery of Law (*dharmagahana*)."[6] Exactly what *dharma* means here is not clear, but it is clear Dhṛtarāṣṭra saw the knowledge of *dharma* as something difficult and murky, a *gahana* (which also means "thicket" and "cave"). It is with some trepidation that I put myself in Vidura's place here and offer some sort of *buddhimārga*; it is my own response to what I too once felt to be a bewildering *dharmagahana*.[7]

THE UNITY OF THE SPECIFICALLY ETHICAL WORD *DHARMA*[8]

The specifically ethical word *dharma* is a single word, though I see it used in three distinct ways (please see Table I). Common to all its uses is the unified idea "What is 'transcendently' good or right to do or be." By using the word "transcendently" I mean to indicate that the goodness or rightness involved here refers to the unseen realm, the realm of life's awesome mysteries, the stratum of human experience and imagination which is often valorized with the sense of holiness, in this case the life beyond death. The word *dharma* under consideration here always refers to some kind of human goodness that connects the

TABLE I
Overview of the word *Dharma* in the MBh

	Dharma: Basic unity of the word – What is "transcendently" good or right to do or be		
	I	II	III
Three senses evident in MBh	Normative *action* that is beneficial to its agent after death Good action appropriate to specific kinds of people	Abstract quality of correctness, rightness, goodness, or justice	Universally good character attributes, habits, dispositions
Anchoring translation and main supplements	Law Merit	Right Just	Virtue Piety

man or woman of *dharma* to good circumstances of one kind or another (whether good *lokas*, a fortunate *saṃsāra*, or the beatitude of *mokṣa*)[9] in the future, specifically after death. This religious dimension is essential to the word and must always be registered in any translation of it. One of the ways I try to accomplish that in my translation is by the practice, now archaic in standard English, of using hieratic capital letters for the basic words translating *dharma*. The other major way of trying to communicate this sense is by choosing English words that do, or at least can, convey some of this religious charge.

THE THREE SENSES OF THE WORD *DHARMA*

The single word *dharma* has three distinct meanings; that is, there are three varieties of the word which express the idea of 'transcendently good action or being' in three different forms: First there is what I call the 'Basic Theme of *dharma*,' where the word signifies "*Normative action* (*karman*) *that is beneficial to its agent after death*." (This usage refers to actions such as performing sacrificial rites, studying the Veda, generating offspring, offering hospitality to guests, honoring one's parents and seniors, bathing at venerable "crossings" [*tīrthas*] between this world and the celestial world, fighting in battles, observing fasts, speaking the truth, and the like. Because the king had an overarching obligation to ensure the overall welfare of his subjects both materially [his concern with *artha*, the prosperity of the realm and its inhabitants] and in connection to the unseeable future [their accumulations of *dharma*], his *dharma* included a series of activities – the administration of justice, the conduct of foreign policy, the management of his ministers and officials, the building and maintaining of various elements of regional and local infrastructure, and so on.) Second, there is a more abstract and specialized usage that occurs in contexts in which the ethical *quality* alone of something done is in question or under discussion, and where the word signifies "the abstract *quality* of the correctness, rightness, goodness, or justice" of some action – its being normative or not. The third usage is another specialized development from the Basic Theme, one in which the word refers not to any *karman*, but to the inner attributes (*guṇas*) of a person, to his or her character, his or her enduring attitudes (dispositions to certain actions) and habits (particular patterns of action). (The attitudes and habits included in this sense of the word are such virtues as generosity, kindness, honesty, being long-suffering, humility, and so on. These virtues enter the general topic of *dharma* as "common, or general, *dharma*," that is, obligations of *dharma* that are incumbent upon everyone, regardless of their particular nature [*sāmānya*- or *sādhāraṇa-dharma* as opposed to 'one's proper' or *sva-dharma*]; see below in the "Dharma *signifies specific forms of action*" on p. 678 section). I anchor the translation of the Basic Theme of *dharma* with 'Law,' 'Lawful Deed(s),' supplemented often with 'Merit' and 'Meritorious, Lawful Deed(s).' I use 'Virtue,' supplemented, rarely, with 'Piety,' for the third usage. These two uses of *dharma*, the first and the third, are very distinct from each other, and the third one, *dharma* as Virtue, seems to become more frequent in those parts of the MBh that seem later for other reasons (I refer here primarily to the texts of the *Mokṣadharmaparvan*).[10] Of course this variation of the word becomes a major sense of it in the Vālmīki *Rāmāyaṇa*. The second use of *dharma*, the abstract sense of Rightness, occurs a couple of times in the Eleventh and Twelfth Books and I translate it with 'Right' (and 'Wrong,' for corresponding cases of *adharma*).

THE BASIC THEME OF *DHARMA*

The 'Basic Theme of *dharma*' is quite complicated and I am going to summarize it in terms of three layers of its meaningfulness: The central idea it expresses, the full continuum of the reality intended (that is, comprehended or embraced) by that idea, and the concrete forms of behavior to which this continuum ultimately points. Table II lays out a translational continuum for the 'Basic Theme' that runs parallel to the first two of these layers. (I need to note here for the record the word *adharma*, which corresponds to some usages of *dharma* as its exact opposite, as 'action that violates the norms and which harms its agent after death;' I will not mention *adharma* in most of what follows, but it is usually implied, *mutatis mutandis*.)

The idea: "Normative action (karman) that is beneficial to its agent after death"

First of all, in the Basic Theme the word refers to action, behavior, work. *Dharma* is a species of *karman*, it is a kind of deed, a deed done most concretely in a body in space and time that is publicly observable. But for many in ancient India all *karmāṇi*, all actions, have an unseen analog that accompanies the action's agent and operates in his or her future. So the word *dharma* refers to a publicly observable deed and it also refers to the unseen analog that really exists and necessarily must have effects in the future; that is to a person's 'good karma.' This unseen form of *karman* is the basis for *dharma's* being beneficial to its agent in life after death. The word can refer to either kind of *karman*, or to both kinds simultaneously, without distinction.

The full continuum of dharma

(See Table II, row 1.) The two dimensions of *karman* just distinguished are two structural aspects of the idea of *dharma* by virtue of *dharma's* being a species of *karman*. Next, because *dharma* is *'normative'* action, the idea gets enlarged in a somewhat different way. *Dharma* is not simply a deed done and the concomitant *puṇyakarman*, it is also the command that enjoins the deed (a rule, an injunction, a command, a norm, a law, a custom [*vidhi*, *śāstra*, *śāsana*, *etc*.]). And beyond that, it is the compulsion felt within the prospective agent to conform to such commands (it can be one's duty, one's responsibility, an obligation, a debt, etc. [*kārya*, *ṛṇa*]) So the word *dharma*, because it is *normative action*, embraces the whole continuum beginning with a deed commanded or recommended by some authoritative voice outside the agent, moving next to the deed accepted as an obligation or means by the prospective agent, moving next to the deed done fulfilling the

TABLE II
The translational continuum of the 'Basic Theme of *Dharma*' (Sense I in Table I)

	Dharma			
The word's actual 'referential continuum'	External command	Internal obligation	Deed, work	Continued existence of the deed as 'karma'
Sanskrit synonyms	*Vidhi, śāsana*	*kārya, ṛṇa*	*karman, kṛta*	*sukṛta, puṇyakarman*
Nuanced translations in highly determinate contexts	Rule, command, norm, law, custom	Obligation, responsibility, duty, task, job, office, debt	Action, deed, work	'Merit,' good deeds, good karma
Translations of typical complex uses of the word	(a) Law, (the) Laws (b) Lawful, Meritorious Deed(s)			(the) Merit (of a particular deed); a person's accumulation of Merit
Translation of comprehensive, collective uses of the word	The Laws, the Law, Law, the Good Law			

command, to, finally, the good karma that accrues to the agent from actually doing the deed. And of course *dharma*, as action prescribed by the norm-setting elite of society, is "good" action (*puṇya*) and its consequences are beneficial to its agent on the other side of death.

A given occurrence of the word *dharma* either intends the whole continuum simultaneously or is focused upon a particular segment of the continuum that may be salient in a particular discourse context: The command, or the sense of obligation, or the deed, or the good karma. In a given discourse context one or another aspect of this continuum may be the salient feature of meaning, and the proper translation of the word in that context needs to express the relevant sense of *dharma*. Most frequently, though, *dharma* refers synthetically to the whole undivided continuum and I use the word Law, capitalized, to translate that predominant use of the word. 'Merit,' capitalized, is sometimes a more appropriate translation of the Basic Theme. Sometimes I use some variant of the phrase Lawful, Meritorious Deed.

The concrete referents of dharma

As I have just argued, in the Basic Theme *dharma* always refers to some form or element of *karman* and predicates of said action the brahminic qualities of being normative and transcendently beneficial. There are two basic ways the actions that are said to be *dharma* are indicated: individually and collectively.

Dharma *signifies specific forms of action*

Frequently the *dharma* referred to is one specific, concrete, deed or work enjoined for some particular sort of people – the idea of *svadharma*. There are as many such *dharmas* as there are particular kinds of people and the noun is frequently used in the plural to refer to these enjoined actions or forms of action.

In the Basic Theme of *dharma* in the *Mahābhārata* the particular kind of laws and obligations that the word refers to are specific, concrete actions that are restricted to certain kinds of people (such as *yāgas*, which only the twice born may perform) or are peculiar to different kinds of people (such as the characteristic *vṛttis* of the four different *varṇas*). A very large class of the deeds or activities that are *dharma* vary according to the different kinds of people, and the words *dharma* and *dharmas* (the plural is not at all unusual) refer to some work or pattern of behavior that is supposed to be characteristic of a given class of persons: There is *varṇadharma*, *āśramadharma*, *strīdharma*, *yatidharma*, *rājadharma*, *etc.*[11] Everyone has a *svadharma*, a proper *dharma*, a pattern of life incumbent upon him or her that will ensure his or her welfare after death. But though ancient Indian *karman* is highly individualistic, one's *svadharma* is not individual or personal: It varies according to one's sex, one's *varṇa*, and one's *āśrama*, etc. The point here that is relevant to my discussion is that it fits tightly into the Basic Theme of *dharma* as I have sketched it out above. In this theme *dharma* fundamentally refers to objective deeds (conceived of as the complex continuum I outlined) and we see that one of the main forms of the content of *dharma* is a large, highly differentiated collection of specific, concrete forms of behavior.

Dharma *signifies collective aggregations of actions*

But on the other hand, the word is sometimes used in the singular in very broad, comprehensive, relatively indeterminate ways, basically the *sanātana dharma*.[12] The single most frequent use of *dharma* in the MBh is as a broad, comprehensive designation of a collection of some or all the of the specific *dharmas*.

These facts give us the necessary guidance to understand the frequent use of *dharma* in vague, highly generalized, indeterminate ways. It has been customary in the past for some to interpret such usage as referring to *dharma* as a fundamentally unified, cosmic principle that itself causes the orderliness of the universe. Following Halbfass, I have to say there is no evidence in the MBh for such an independent causal principle of order in the universe. When the word *dharma* is used in vague, comprehensive unitary ways it is a collective noun referring to the loose aggregation of all the particular *dharmas*. There are a few instances where this collectivity may appear to be spoken of as an entity having some kind of internal unity, as when we occasionally encounter phrases such as "*kṛtsna dharma*"[13] and references to *dharma* being 'four-footed' originally and losing one of its *pādas yuga* by *yuga*. But such expressions do not necessarily imply organic unity, and never have I seen any agency of any kind attributed to such a *dharma*. The notion of the shrinking of *dharma* foot by foot or quarter by quarter across the *yugas* implies a unity, but it is obviously a partitive idea, implying the unity of aggregation. And while the notion of the exhaustion of *dharma* that appears in the *Gītā* involves a more complex image that is not obviously partitive, it does not really challenge the interpretation of *dharma* as an aggregation of *dharmas*.

As Wilhelm Halbfass writes, "... even in the later [post-Vedic and post MBh] use of the concept, when the singular prevailed, a plurality of precisely established "rules" remained a determining and constitutive factor of *dharma*."[14]

So the basic word *dharma* may vary in its reference from pointing to some single, specific "Law," to some more general set of "Laws," all the way to all the "Laws" considered as a single comprehensive aggregation. Consequently my translation 'Law' will vary in the same way among 'Law,' 'Laws,' and 'the Law' and 'the Good Law,' and I leave readers to the specific indications of each passage to determine what level of aggregation may be intended.

THE TRANSLATION TACTICS FOR THE THREE VARIETIES OF *DHARMA* IN THE MBH

I will conclude by indicating a few considerations apropos the translations of this word and its three forms of use. One of the main considerations for all three is that the English word used be one that is capable of hieratic elevation; that is, the English word must be able to convey, or at least intimate, the transcendent element of the word *dharma*. The English word must be able to stand on the same pedestal *dharma* does. Thus, for example, 'Good Deeds' is not a candidate to replace the semantically less suitable 'Merit.'

The three major usage patterns

I translate each of the three different uses of *dharma* with a different basic translation or 'anchor word,' which is intended to render the word accurately and also create an identity for that usage in the memory of readers. But the anchor word is not always the most apt translation, so I have a limited set of formulas for supplementing the translation. For the third *dharma* usage I use 'Virtue' as the anchor and supplement that a couple of times with Piety; for the second I use Right. There are only one or two occurrences of this usage in the 11th and 12th Books, and 'Right' is right for them; but I believe that 'Just' would be an appropriate variant of this usage in the story of Āṇi Māṇḍavya in the *Ādi Parvan*. There is no need to discuss the translation of these two usages now.

The three degrees of specificity of the Basic Theme

But the Basic Theme of *dharma* is much more complex than these two specialized derivative usages. There are three distinct levels of generality at which this sense of the word is applied: (1) Relatively well delimited occurrences where the word refers to only one segment of the continuum; (2) occurrences where the word is referring to a particular species of action and, in labeling it '*dharma*,' the text is ascribing to that action the whole complex continuum of the ideas of "normative, transcendently beneficial action." Finally, (3) there are many highly indeterminate passages where the word occurs and the most that can be said about *dharma* in them is that it seems to refer to the entire collectivity of specific *dharma* practices which is of great benefit to everyone. Rows 3–5 of Table II make these distinctions and indicate specifically how I handle them. The most general type of application of the word I render unvaryingly with 'Law' or 'the Law.' The aggregative usage I anchor with 'Law,' and I supplement that frequently with 'Merit.' Finally, there are the more sharply defined contexts where the word is best translated as 'rule,' 'good deed,' 'duty,' etc. When a given passage allows me to determine that the word *dharma* is being used in a such way that clearly emphasizes one segment of the entire continuum of the Basic Theme, I then translate the word in these more specific and nuanced ways. In fact, there are not many instances in the first half of Book 12 where the highly nuanced translation of *dharma* is right; there are more of these opportunities in earlier Parvans of the MBh. The great majority of occurrences of *dharma* as the Basic Theme in the *Śānti* are of the very general, comprehensive, relatively indeterminate sort.

The Pros and Cons of 'Merit' and 'Law'

'Law' and 'Merit' are unsatisfactory compromises for translating the Basic Theme of *dharma*, but for now I see nothing better than these two words.

'Merit'. Merit has the virtue of indicating something that adheres to an agent as a result of his or her own actions and influences his or her future beneficially. It suffers from being a rather abstract term, when we want a more substantive term to refer to enduring bundles of energy that act causally upon physical substances in the world. Also, as Hacker emphasized, the word Merit often implies judgment by some judging subject and fails to indicate the mechanical nature of

dharma as good *karman*.[15] But English 'Merit' does not necessarily entail an approving agent, and other advantages of 'Merit' are that it has been established in this sense by prior translational tradition and it lends itself to being a hieratic technical term that aptly suggests the accrual of transcendent benefits to a person.

'Law.' The basic suitability of 'Law' as a translation of *dharma* derives from the fact that one of the most important and consistent elements in the word's use is the normative element, the recommendation or assignment of behavior to an agent, whether negatively as a restriction excluding other forms of behavior, or positively as encouragement to do this or that. The pre-eminence of the normative element is shown in the fact that *adharma* contrasts with *dharma* at exactly this point.

'Law' is unsatisfactory because, while 'law,' like *dharma*, is a predicate of deeds and behavior, the word cannot really signify by itself a deed or an action. Nor does it communicate the positive element of *dharma*, the fact that *dharma* is a means to ensure a good *loka* ('heaven') or *yoni* (a 'womb' where one begins his or her next life) after death. Especially in contemporary American English, where the primary denotations of 'law' are civil and criminal codes enacted by elected legislators and enforced by the police ('the Law') and bureaucracies of 'lawyers'; where 'law' implies punishment rather than benefit; especially in such a context the word law has some difficulty conveying the sense of *dharma* as a religious form of action. But the English word law, at least for now, transcends this contemporary emphasis on individual behavior conceived as transactions in a contractually legitimated, mercantile society. The language still knows such phrases as 'the Law of God,' 'laws of nature,' and 'common law,' which all point to different world-views and different kinds of legitimation than those prevalent in America today. That is the word 'law' has not yet been completely demythologized and it can, I think, be forced to carry *some* of the religious charge of Sanskrit *dharma*.

So in sum, 'Law' is a passable translation of *dharma* because it covers the first two critically important segments of the continuum of the Basic Theme; it does emphasize the restriction of behavior; and it is capable of moving easily from more specific to more comprehensive collective senses. It is not at all capable of expressing the third and fourth segments of the continuum, *karman* and *puṇyakarman*. The latter of these two terms is covered with 'Merit,' and when the third is called for the translation 'Law' has to be supplemented with 'deed' or 'action.' Finally, 'Law' is still capable of intimating some of the religious charge of *dharma*.

NOTES

[1] Fitzgerald (2004). This book, volume 7 in the planned 10 volume series begun by J.A.B. van Buitenen, contains the *Rājadharmaparvan* and the *Āpaddhar-maparvan* from the *Śāntiparvan*. The *Mokṣadharmaparvan* is now in preparation and will be published as volume 8 of the series.

[2] My initial approach to the word *dharma* (and other difficult ideas of the text such as *āśrama, tejas, tapas*, etc.) was merely to transcribe the words instead of translating them. I came to regard this policy as seriously mistaken for the *Mahābhārata* project, at which time I began explicitly studying the use and occurrence of these words in the epic. In the case of *dharma* I carried out an analysis of a number of passages in which *dharma* played a pivotal role. I cannot present the analysis of those passages at this time, but they stand behind the synthesis presented in this essay.

[3] *Āpastamba Dharmasūtra* 1.20.6: *na dharmādharmau carata āvaṃ sva iti / na dev-agandharvā na pitara ity ācakṣate 'yaṃ dharmo 'yam adharma iti* (quoted from Olivelle, 2000). Readers will note, however, that my translation is more in line with Bühler's than Olivelle's "The Righteous (*dharma*) and the Unrighteous (*adharma*) do not go around saying, 'Here we are!'."

[4] Hacker (1965).

[5] Halbfass (1988).

[6] MBh 1.1.5.1: *yad idam dharmagahanaṃ buddhyā samanugamyate / etad vistaraśaḥ sarvaṃ buddhimārgaṃ praśaṃsa me //* (This and all other quotations from the MBh are taken from John Smith's electronic text.)

[7] On a later occasion I will supplement this highly abstract essay with a fuller discussion of concrete passages and the judgments of other translators and scholars on the interpretation of *dharma* in them.

[8] Of course nothing I say here relates to the word *dharma* with the meaning of "characteristic." I am directing myself only to *dharma* as a specifically ethical word. The other word *dharma*, while not exactly rare in the MBh, is not frequent and stands apart from the ethical usage. It occurs a couple of times in the first half of the 12th Book in the epithet of death *kāladharma*, and I think the authors experience it as separate from the ethical *dharma* and play with the likeness of the words.

[9] In the *Mahābhārata* there is a recurring juxtaposition of "this world" and "the next world" (*iha paratra ca* and the like). In the epic the afterlife is typically thought of as life in heaven (or hell); much less commonly, though not rarely, it is life again in this world by rebirth.

[10] I have laid out some of the basic reasons for such a judgment of 'Higher Criticism' in the introduction to my forthcoming translation of the first half of the *Śāntiparvan* (see Fitzgerald, 2004).

[11] So, to name only some of the most common or interesting expressions that occur, we have *kṣātra dharma* and the equivalent expressions *kṣatradharma, kṣatriyasya dharma*, and *kṣatriyāṇāṃ dharma* (the *dharma* of members of the second "Order" of society, that of *kṣatriyas*, the warriors and rulers); *rājadharma* and *rājñāṃ dharma* (the *dharma* of rulers and kings) and the plural *rājadharmāḥ* (the *dharmas* of the king); *brāhmaṇasya* and *brāhmaṇānāṃ dharma* (the *dharma* of brahmins), *vaiśya-dharma, śūdradharma*; *gārhastya dharma* and *gṛhasthadharma* (the *dharma* for heads of households), *yatidharma* (the *dharma* of ascetics), *ṛṣidharma* (and *ārṣa dharma*, the

dharma of seers), and *strīdharma* (the *dharma* for women). Interestingly, it virtually never occurs that *dharma* is qualified with a proper name: *bharatadharma* and *bharatānāṃ dharma* (referring to the Bharata family) do not occur, while *bhāratadharma* and *bhāratānāṃ dharma* (*Bhārata* is synonymous with Bharata in such contexts) each occur once; *kurudharma* occurs once and *kaurava* (Kuru is the name of a descendent of King Bharata who also became an eponymous ancestor of the protagonists of the *Mahābhārata*, the "Kauravas") or *kauravāṇāṃ dharma* (these last three terms all refer to the descendents of Kuru Bhārata; that is, again, the Bharatas) occurs once or twice (5.29.29 is ambiguous). I have observed no other instances of *dharma* qualified by the name of a tribe or people, nor by the name of an individual.

In addition to these uses, where the word *dharma* is qualified by different kinds of people, there are occurrences of *dharma* where it is qualified by a word designating some particular goal or a set of activities that form part of some particular goal-oriented context of activity. Examples of this are the words *nītidharma* (the *dharmas*, "rules, or guidelines," of practical administration or governance), *yuddhadharma* (the *dharmas*, "laws or rules" for fighting and war), *dānadharma* (the *dharmas*, "rules, norms, or guidelines" for making gifts and grants), and *mokṣadharma* (the *dharmas*, "norms" for gaining *mokṣa*, 'Absolute Freedom').

[12] As, for example, in the epithet *dharmarāja* shared by Yudhiṣṭhira and Yama, the Lord of Death. Or when Dhṛtarāṣṭra laments his fate in the wake of the war, saying "Nor would I listen to the advice that Bhīṣma gave, which was always consistent with Law (*dharmayuktaṃ prabhāṣitam*). Or when, a little further in the text, at 11.8.39, where Vyāsa, trying to encourage the despondent Dhṛtarāṣṭra, says, "While you, sir, are dedicated to Law (reading *dharmaparaḥ* for *karmaparaḥ*, which is a typographical error, as I explain at length in a note to my translation of the passage) and are preeminent in understanding – knowing that creatures go and come back again – you do not have your wits about you."

Sometimes the usage is even more general, referring to the entire category of *dharmas* all together, simultaneously, as, frequently with expressions describing people who "support all the *dharmas*," (*sarvadharmabhṛt*) or "know (all) the *dharmas*" ([*sarva*]*dharmajña*, [*sarva*]*dharmavid*, [*sarva*]*dharmaviśārada*). The basic specificity of the Basic Theme of *dharma* presented earlier, and the frequent use of plural forms of *dharma*, (the natural corollary of that specificity) are the primary reasons that I insist upon calling these more general uses of *dharma* "aggregative." As Wilhelm Halbfass notes, there is a frequent tendency, even among Indologists and Sanskritists, to impose "a universal cosmological interpretation of *dharma*," upon these old texts, one that "presupposes that the concept of *dharma* involves universal cosmic laws." But, as Halbfass writes there, "... the idea of an objective natural order effective in the world, specifically in inanimate things, i.e., of something like a natural law, has little importance for the ancient and traditional usage of *dharma*." The use of *dharma* in the kind of compound words I mentioned above is *aggregative*; it does not refer to some cosmic entity that is "*Dharma*," not even when the word occurs outside of such compounds and in the singular.

[13] As at MBh 12.7.37, 32.4, 53.23.

[14] "Dharma in the Self-Understanding of Traditional Hinduism:" 315.

[15] A point duly emphasized by Hacker (1965, pp. 103–104).

REFERENCES

Fitzgerald, J.L. (editor, translator, annotator). (2004). The *Mahâbhârata: Book 11: The Book of the Women, Book 12: The Book of Peace, Part 1*. Chicago: University of Chicago Press.

Hacker, P. (1965). Dharma im *Hinduismus. Zeitschrift für Missionswissenschaft und Religionswissenschaft* **49**, 93–106.

Halbfass, W. (1988). Dharma in the self-understanding of traditional Hinduism. Chapter seventeen of his India and Europe: *An Essay in Understanding*. (pp. 310–333) Albany: State University of New York Press. A revised, enlarged, and updated translation of *Indien und Europa*: *Perspektiven ihrer geistigen Begegnung*. Basel: Schwabe & Co. (1981).

Olivelle, P. (editor and translator). (2000). *Dharmasūtras*: *The Law Codes of Āpastamba, Gautama, Baudhāyana, and Vasiṣṭha*. Delhi: Motilal Banarsidass.

Smith, J.D. 1999–2001. *Electronic Text of the* Mahābhārata (with the appendices and the star passages). Cambridge: http://bombay.oriental.cam.ac.uk/john/mahabharata/statement.html.

Department of Religious Studies
University of Tennessee
Knoxville, TN 37996-0450
USA
E-mail: glfitzgerald@comcast.net

ASHOK AKLUJKAR

CAN THE GRAMMARIANS' *DHARMA* BE A *DHARMA* FOR ALL?*

N.B.: The present article draws its evidence mainly from Patañjali's Vyākaraṇa-mahābhāṣya and Bhartṛhari's Trikāṇḍī. It situates that evidence, its analysis and its implications in the larger context (a) of the sociolinguistics of ancient India and (b) of the assumptions and predilections of current Indology. Readers interested only in knowing what Patañjali and Bhartṛhari have to say on *dharma* should move from §1.1 to §§2.2–3.11 and from §§5.1–5.2 to §§6.1–6.10. I attempt to explain the probable thinking behind the little-discussed *dharmābhivyakti* view in §§3.7–3.9.

BACKGROUND, WHICH CAN ALSO BE VIEWED AS RAMIFICATIONS

§1.1.

It is generally known to students of the Sanskrit grammatical tradition that the authors belonging to the most influential tradition of Sanskrit grammar (Vyākaraṇa),[1] namely that of Pāṇini, show concern with the notion of *dharma*, distinctively and organically,[2] when they wish to establish the usefulness of Pāṇini's work, the Aṣṭādhyāyī, and thereby of the discipline of Vyākaraṇa. The position of the Pāṇinian authors in this regard can briefly be stated thus: "One can use Aṣṭādhyāyī-derivable expressions as well as expressions

* My thanks to professors Akihiko Akamatsu, Muneo Tokunaga, Hideyo Ogawa and Toru Yagi for making available to me several books that I needed to make my references precise after I began to finalize in Kyoto the draft of this paper that I had brought from Vancouver. Professor Patrick Olivelle attended promptly to my request to be the 'second pair of eyes' for the semifinal version and helped in identifying instances of oversight, obscure phrasing and unnecessary elaboration. I am grateful to him and to Professor Albrecht Wezler who later helped similarly.

I have not italicized in the following pages common Sanskrit names of branches of literature and the titles of texts; the latter are italicized only in the 'References' section at the end.

that appear related but cannot be said to have the backing of the Aṣṭādhyāyī."[3] In fact, there are persons who do exactly that. Communication, which is the chief function of language, takes place with either kind of expression. Is there then any difference *in the way* in which it takes place? Some theoreticians would be inclined to say the following: In the case of those who are accustomed to grammatical expressions, the meanings of ungrammatical expressions are understood through a recollection of the corresponding grammatical expressions. In the case of those who are used to ungrammatical expressions, comprehension is similarly intervened but in the reverse direction. When they hear grammatical expressions, their memory is triggered in the direction of related ungrammatical expressions. We, Pāṇinīyas, however, are of the view that in the case of both groups, if communication takes place, it takes place with equal directness.[4] However, although there is no difference in directness, whether a sentence contains grammatical forms or ungrammatical forms, that is, although the practical efficacy is the same, it is better to use grammatical forms because one can gain[5] *dharma* by using them.

§1.2.

The preceding statement, despite its brevity, has the potential to indicate how the grammarians' position touches upon matters, such as linguistic cognition, that interest philosophers and matters such as religio-spiritual merit that engage the minds of students of religion. Some historians of Indian society, religion, culture etc., on the other hand, may see in the statement another piece of evidence to the effect that ancient Indian thinkers could almost never think secularly – that considerations such as *dharma* (and *adharma*) that would determine one's existence in another world or one's ability to escape this word for ever were always around the corner in the thinking of most theoreticians of ancient India. Why – the historians are likely to ask – could the grammarians not think like modern linguists and be simple observers of the various linguistic phenomena, eschewing value judgments? Why this privileging of one linguistic form over another and that too without advancing some kind of secular worldly benefit as the primary reason? Could the grammarians not have made a case for their branch of knowledge, say, for example, by pointing out that the speakers of standard languages find easier or wider acceptance in influential social groups and get better jobs? If the representatives of a science in which ancient India is thought to have excelled all other parts of the world could not keep apart the descriptive and the prescriptive, mixed the 'is' with the 'ought' and listed something otherworldly or spiritual as the basis of the 'ought,' can we realistically expect any unalloyed objectivity or true rationality from the traditional Indian thinkers?

§1.3.

Upon coming to know the nature of the grammarians' recommendation, several historians working in the present academic climate may get on a different but equally negative tangent. In the discouragement to use un-Pāṇinian forms, which to a great extent are the same as non-Sanskritic forms, they may see a disparagement of the Prakrit and Apabhraṃśa forms used by the general populace and thus an attempt to control society on the part of Brahmins.[6] The more charitable among them may not go so far as seeing a linguistic conspiracy, dictatorship or exploitation of the credulous masses in the grammarians' position. They may stop at observations such as the following: "The attempts to stick to a particular form of Sanskrit led to the death of the language as a truly living language. Such attempts came in the way of genuinely inspired literary creation in the later centuries and resulted in a convention-bound literature meant largely to excite the brains of a small minority. Pāṇini's grammar, however impressive it may be in its technique and coverage, proved to be a stranglehold for Sanskrit. It became an invitation to waddle in stagnant waters."

§1.4.

The volume edited in 1996 by Houben and the volumes of well-known histories of Sanskrit literature contain several pieces of evidence suggesting that there was considerable vitality and variety in the Sanskrit tradition. The regrettable aspect of some of the histories is that their authors, under the influence of the 19th and 20th century Western ideas of literature and language use, do not realize that they have missed this evidence and do not try to explore the phenomenon of loss or reduction of creativity on the larger background of the changed political and economic circumstances, primarily in the second millenium A.D. But one can, if one wishes, use the material painstakingly collected by them, to determine the extent of verve and free spirit present in classical Sanskrit literature.

The charge that rationality, truly secular theorization etc. do not exist in the pre-modern Indian tradition is by now an old canard. It is more a matter of failure to recognize that one and the same phenomenon (or what is essentially the same phenomenon) can take place in different contexts and consequently with different idioms in the cultures we have than of any real absence (cf. the scrutiny by Bimal Krishna Matilal, Karl H. Potter, J.N. Mohanty etc. of the view that there is no genuine philosophy, as distinct from religious or spiritual thinking, in India; see, for example, the passage translated in §2.3 below). In exploring such issues, one needs to bear in mind also the possibility that some cultures might have realized the limitations of a particular approach (or what is essentially the same approach) at an early time in their history and consequently not spoken of it frequently or as something universally useful. In particular, I find the thesis in Bronkhorst (1999, 2001), namely that rationality originated only once in human history and that the rational component in early Indian thought is a result of India's contact with the Greeks, quite untenable.

In the case of the other issues to which §§1.2–1.3 refer, the following sections will only indirectly respond. Anyone reading them should be able to decide, with a little reflection, which of the historians' conclusions, charges, etc. should be accepted or should be accepted as stated.

SCOPE AND APPROACH OF THIS PAPER

§2.1.

It may be asked if what I have stated in §1.1 above was the position of *all* the grammarians in the Sanskrit tradition whose works are available to us. As is to be expected given the cultural and regional diversity of India and the loss of ancient texts that has occurred, we do not know with certainty in each case. The statements of the position that have come down to us are not many. Even fewer among them contain new details. The earliest ones are found in Patañjali's Vyākaraṇa-mahābhāṣya (not later than second century B.C.) and Bhartṛhari's Trikāṇḍī (not later than early fifth century A.D.). Only the latter has an extensive discussion, and that too mainly because it gets into the related epistemological issues. The commentators of Patañjali, of course, elaborate upon his statements, but the elaborations do not essentially go beyond the indirect comment that is available in the Trikāṇḍī.

An overview of Pāṇinian grammar and the other traditional or pre-modern grammars of Sanskrit is given in Aklujkar (2004a, forthcoming). Most of the grammars in the latter category, which also happen to be later in their surviving forms, can be thought of as recasts of the Aṣṭādhyāyī (or its similar predecessors) guided by this or that pragmatic or sectarian consideration. Their coverage of word forms and closeness to the Vedic tradition differ, reflecting the needs of the times, the communities in which and for which they were composed and the composer's intention (whether pedagogical or purely scholarly). But their overall perception of why and how grammars should be composed remains the same. True, most of them do not overtly speak of the relation between grammar and *dharma*. Further, the Jain and Buddhist grammars, having been composed in times when the policy of not accepting the Veda as an infallible authority had been formulated in some Jain and Buddhist circles, had no particular need to make their determination of acceptable usage dependent on the Veda. Consequently, in their treatment, *dharma* was not as closely tied to forms closer to the Vedic tradition as in the Brahmanical treatment. One may also detect in them a slightly greater emphasis on meaning or import than on accurate pronunciation. But the absence of statements explicitly stating that grammars help one in preserving the Āgamas and are thus instrumental in *dharma* acquisition need not imply that the connection between grammars and *dharma* was rejected or was not implicitly maintained in practice. Recent research has been increasingly (and rightly) indicating that in *dharma* praxis and management the Jains and the Buddhists were far closer to the Vedic or Brahmanical tradition than has so far been realized by the scholarly community at large. In many areas, they had parallel norms and procedures, if not exactly the same. It is, therefore, possible that no explicit statement on the relationship between grammaticality and *dharma* was made because it was not deemed necessary – that it was a commonly accepted relationship in the contemporary Indian intellectual culture. Besides, it is not the case that the importance of proper pronounciation and preservation of the Āgamas has not been articulated in the two surviving Śramaṇa traditions. The Jain practice, in particular, of attaching *dharma-lābha* to the copying of Āgama texts (and to knowledge preservation in general through the copying of manuscripts) makes it likely that a value beyond mere practicality was seen in keeping alive the tradition of acceptable word forms. The Buddhist notion of *ārṣa* speech similarly suggests commitment to perserving acceptable word forms.[7] A tradition of referring to the Tīrthaṃkaras or Jinas as *ṛṣis* and to Ardhamāgadhī, the Jain canonical language, as *ārṣa* is found also among the Jains. Thus, as far as the perception that some linguistic forms are related to *dharma* is concerned, one does not need to confine it to the Aṣṭādhyāyī-derivable forms as distinct from the forms that were considered proper in other grammars.

§2.2.

Subsequent to the preceding explanation of why this paper restricts itself mainly to two sources, I would like to specify how I will refer to those sources.

I use 'P' and 'MB' as abbreviations in referring to Patañjali's work and 'BH,' 'TK,' 'TK V' and 'MBT' as abbreviations in referring to Bhartṛhari's works. 'TK' stands for 'Trikāṇḍī,' 'TK V' for 'Trikāṇḍī Vṛtti'and 'MBT' for 'Mahābhāṣya-ṭīkā'. The last, BH's commentary on the MB, carries the historically inaccurate title 'Mahābhāṣya-dīpikā' in the more commonly cited editions.

The title more commonly used at present for the TK is 'Vākyapadīya'. In my view, the original situation was like this:

Book 1: Āgama-samuccaya or Brahma-kāṇḍa
Book 2: Vākyapadīya or Vākya-kāṇḍa
Book 3: Prakīrṇa(ka) or Pada-kāṇḍa, divided into chapters called samuddeśas

'Trikāṇḍī' may not have been the title used by the author. Its attestation is not older than that of 'Vākyapadīya' as a title for the second book or for the first two books. It is to be preferred mainly because it does not go against the evidence establishing that in the earlier times 'Vākyapadīya' did not refer to all three books taken collectively.

The available ancient commentaries of the TK, tentatively understood as a text consisting of kārikās only, not as a composite of kārikā and Vṛtti, are:

Book 1:
(a) Vṛtti, authored by BH, according to a well-attested tradition which has as yet not been proven to be wrong despite the attempts of certain modern researchers. Even if one were to ascribe only the kārikās to BH and take the Vṛtti as someone else's work, the temporal distance, as research is increasingly establishing, between the two texts would be very short – at the most a student of BH would be eligible for the credit of

Vṛtti authorship. There would be no grounds for reading a significant transformation in thought, including the follow-up of P's statements by BH.
(b) ṭīkā, called Paddhati or Sphuṭākṣarā, by Vṛṣabha, Vṛṣabha-deva or Śrī-vṛṣabha on both the kārikās and Vṛtti.
Book 2:
(a) Vṛtti, authored by BH; see above.
(b) ṭīkā, possibly called Vākya-pradīpa by its author, who really seems to be Helā-rāja, despite the attribution of the work to Puṇya-rāja in some manuscripts and published editions. This offers an explanation only of the kārikās. Its surviving form is probably an abridgement made from a damaged original.
Book 3:
ṭīkā, called Prakīrṇa(ka)-prakāśa, explaining only the kārikās, authored by Helā-rāja, in which two gaps are filled by words taken from the work of Phulla-rāja, who may be the same person as Puṇya-rāja.

I follow Wilhelm Rau's enumeration of the TK kārikās. The numbers for the same kārikās in other published editions are not likely to be off by more than two or three numbers.

Where my readings are different from those in the published editions, they should be understood as coming from my TK edition under preparation.

§2.3.

Below, I will not attempt a comprehensive philological or historical-semantic study of the use of the word *dharma* in the writings of P and BH.[8] As far as I can determine, the range of this use is covered by three meanings:

(a) 'what an individual person is expected to do' or 'what the *śāstra* or *āgama* advises one to do,'
(b) 'a positive and unseen, that is, non-mundane effect generated by sticking to a norm' and
(c) 'an attribute, property or quality.'[9]
None of these is distinctive to grammar.

One encounters the third usage particularly frequently, which is not unexpected, given the nature of the major concerns of the works. A grammarian needs to refer to qualities frequently, since he must appeal to notions such as adjectives and adverbs on many occasions. Similarly, a philosopher's discussion can hardly proceed without notions such as substance and quality or qualificand and qualifier. For our present purpose, however, it is meanings (a) and (b) that are especially relevant.

In two passages, I suspect that meaning (a), taken in a collective sense, that is, as a set of all *śāstra* or *āgama* prescriptions, can be read. This meaning is close to at least one aspect of the current Western notion of religion. The passages, in Kielhorn's edition, are:

MB p. I.9 lines 15–17: *dīrgha-sattrāṇi vārṣaśatikāni vārṣasahasrikāṇi ca. na cādyatve kaścid api vyavaharati. kevalam ṛṣi-saṃpradāyo dharma iti kṛtvā yājñikāḥ śāstreṇānuvidadhate.* "The long sacrificial sessions (mentioned in the Vārttika) are the ones which extend to hundreds of years or thousands of years. No one performs (them) nowadays. Only because whatever (*saṁ*) the seers have given is *dharma*, the ritualists follow (it) up with instruction."

MB p. I.1 lines 18–19: *āgamaḥ khalv api. brāhmaṇena niṣkāraṇo dharmaḥ ṣaḍaṅgo vedo 'dhyeyo jñeya iti.* "Moreover, the inherited (authoritative) teaching is that a Brahmin should study (and) come to know the Veda with its six ancillary (texts), which is a causeless (or motiveless) *dharma*."

A detailed consideration of this issue, which will need much space, must await another occasion. The translators and commentators have explained the passages variously. The syntax of the second passage is not clear. The translations I have given are at least not less plausible than the ones available in print. They should suffice to indicate how *dharma* could have the sense 'a complex formed by teachings meant to direct human behavior in a certain way out of concern with the after-life – a sense close to that of 'religion'.

§2.4.

Meanings specified under (a) and (b) above, are closely related. One may interpret their relationship in one of the following two ways: (i) Because the *śāstra* or *āgama* knows that a certain effect is good for human beings, it advises the way it does. (ii) Because the *śāstra* advises something, one's following of that advice must produce a positive effect for oneself.

Pursuing the consideration of either relationship logically leads to two fundamental problems of religion and philosophy: (i) From where is scriptural or person-centered authority derived? How can one defend one's acceptance of that authority logically? (ii) What are the limits of rationality? How can one delimit reliance on faith?

That BH was aware of the problems to which *dharma* understood in sense (a) or sense (b) leads is revealed well by the following passage, which also seems to be historically precious, as I have not come across its content elsewhere in the Sanskrit literature I have managed to read. TK V 1.172, Subramania Iyer edition pp. 224–225, runs thus:

tatra kecid ācāryā manyante. na prakṛtyā kiṃcit karma duṣṭam aduṣṭaṃ vā. śāstrānuṣṭhānād eva, na tu kevalād, dharmābhivyaktiḥ. śāstrātikramāc ca pratyavāya-yogaḥ. yeṣām eva hi brāhmaṇa-vadhādīnāṃ viṣayāntare pātakatvaṃ, teṣām eva viṣayāntare prakṛṣṭābhyudaya-hetutvaṃ śāstreṇa vidhīyata iti.

anye tu manyante. bhāva-śaktim eva pratiniyata-viṣayāṃ śāstram anuvadati. ko hi śāstrasya, krīḍata iva kāraṇasya, puruṣānugrahopaghātābhyām arthaḥ. śāstra-sva-bhāvābhyupagamād dravya-sva-bhāvābhyupagama eva yuktataro dṛśyate. tathā hi. dṛṣṭārthāsu cikitsādiṣu smṛtiṣu viṣauṣadhādīnām [/ °ṣadhyādīnām] evārtha-kriyāsu sāmarthyam upalabhyate, na smṛti-śāstrāṇām. tasmāc chāstra-sva-bhāva iva pakṣān-tare, dravyādi-sva-bhāvo 'yaṃ na śāstreṇa parāṇudyate.

"There (in the context of Śruti and Smṛti and the latter's determination of what is conducive to human good and what is not), some teachers hold (the following) view: no action is flawed or unflawed in itself. Only from doing what the *śāstra* (scriptural teaching) is, not from doing alone, results *dharma* manifestation (see §3.7) and from going beyond the *śāstra*, the association with impediments (to one's elevation). Take, for example, actions such as the slaying of a Brahmin. In one context, they produce (or are said to produce) ruinous sin; in another, they are (or are spoken of as) bases for excellent elevation. It is *śāstra* which brings both (power to lead to ruinous sin and power to lead to excellent elevation) about.

"Other (teachers), however, hold (the following) view: The *śāstra* only confirms the powers of things as they are contextually constrained. What would the *śāstra* have to gain by favoring and damaging human beings as if it were a cause sporting about (a force using human beings merely as playthings)? It seems more logical to accept (in this matter) specific natures of substances than a specific nature of the *śāstra*. To elaborate: in the case of Smṛtis with attested outcomes, e.g. medicine, it is the capability only of (substances), such as poisons and herbs, with respective to (various) purposive actions that one notices, not (the capability) of Smṛtis, which are *śāstras* (in the present context). Therefore, just as in the other (i.e., the first) view the nature of *śāstra* is not nudged away, the nature of substance etc. present (in our view) is not nudged away (i.e., is not opened to compromise or allowed to be questioned) by *śāstra*."

The message implicit in this passage is that excessive credulousness should not be allowed, healthy circumspection should be maintained, and the bond with what actual experience indicates should not be severed. It is noteworthy that the position appearing in the second place is left uncontroverted.

§2.5.

A contextually affected case of the meaning (c), 'attribute, property, quality,' for example, would be the notion of *puruṣa-dharma*. Here, when *dharma* unites with *puruṣa* as the first member of the compound, it continues to express the specified common meaning as can be seen from the occurrences of the compound in TK V 1.30 and TK V 1.130 (cf. Vṛṣabha's explanations at both occurrences). But it comes close to playing a technical role especially suitable for grammar when BH's commentators use it to speak of the mental state, mood or stance of a speaker or hearer that can be related to the category of the form which he or she uses or to which he or she is subjected.

Puṇya-rāja/Helā-rāja 2.77–2.83: *śāstrasya tu śabdārtha-puruṣa-dharmeṣv adhikāraḥ … puruṣa-dharmā vaktṛtva-pratipattṛtva-prabhṛtayaḥ. tatra vaktṛ-dharmā ābādhāsūyā-saṃmati-kopa-kutsana-bhartsanādayaś ceti. pratipattṛ-dharmās tu kutsyamānatva-prabhṛtaya eva.*

"The *śāstra* (of grammar) is concerned with words, meanings and attributes of human beings … Attributes of human beings are 'being a speaker,' 'being a hearer' etc. The attributes of the speaker, further (*ca*), are (mental stances like) affliction, envy, agreement, anger, censure, scolding etc. The attributes of the hearer are the same (*eva*) 'being censured' etc. (i.e., the suitable counter parts from what has been listed for the speaker)."

Helā-rāja 3.9.105, where *prayoktṛ-dharmaḥ śabdārthe śabdair evānuṣajyate* ("The attribute of the speaker is attached to word meaning by the words themselves") is the kārikā wording: *adhyāropyate prayoktṛ-dharmaḥ prayojyasya śabdasyābhidheye śabdenaiva. tasmin hi prayukte gamyate sa dharmaḥ prayoktarīti gamyamānatvād ābādhādivad yuktaṃ śabda-saṃskāra-nimittatvam asya. puruṣa-dharmeṣv api hi śāstram adhikṛtam iti vicāritaṃ vākyapadīye.*

"By the word itself, the attribute of the speaker is superimposed on (or is transferred to) what the word to be employed expresses, for after that (word) is used we come to know that the particular attribute exists in the speaker. It is fitting that this (attribute) should be a cause in deriving the word because it is like affliction etc. in being something that is figured out. That the *śāstra* (of grammar) is concerned with the attributes of human beings was taken into consideration (by me) in the Vākyapadīya (= the preceding part or second book of the TK)."

Passages such as these are relevant to philosophy of language, philosophy of grammar, epistemological and ontological issues approached linguistically, and psychology of emotions and literary sentiments. They inform us about the wider relationships and consequences of what we understand from words. However, in studying them in the context of our present topic, we should note that the *puruṣa-dharmas* or qualities of persons of which they speak are not the grammarian's concern at the same level as *dharma* is in defending the enterprise of grammar. They concern the grammarian to the extent the derivation of grammatical forms is determined or explained by attributing, at least temporarily, qualities such as a censuring mood or entertaining of hope to the speaker of a sentence. Thus, they are internal to the derivation of the object language and do not pertain to the non-mundane effect etc. of the derived forms, with which we are at present concerned.

THE EVIDENCE FROM P AND BH

§3.1.

The passages in the MB and TK which are directly relevant to the focus of this essay, because they make *dharma* a concern of the grammarian through the notion of grammaticality, are the following:

MB: Kielhorn's edition p. I.2 line 18 – p. 3 line 5; p. I.8 line 3 – p. 11 line 14.

TK: 1.11–14, 1.25d, 1.27–43, 1.144–147, 1.155–158, 1.171–183; 3.3.30, 3.13.21[10]

These are, mostly, not difficult to understand in terms of translation (understanding the reasoning contained in them precisely may not be so easy). Besides being worded in a relatively simple language, they are generally well-preserved. A few textual problems do arise in the major section in the first book of the TK (verses 1.28–42 and the V thereto) in which BH addresses the issue primarily. But these problems pertain to indirectly relevant statements such as the ones pointing out the instability and limited validity of inference as a means of knowing (*pramāṇa*). They do not make the main lines of argumentation, summarized in §3.3 below, obscure. The text of the corresponding statements in BH's MBT has not faired as well, but it too is fairly understandable as to its general import. Given this state of affairs, I will not, in what follows, cite all the relevant passages from P or BH and explain them individually. My mention here of the publications in European languages in which the passages and their translations can be found should suffice: for P, such publications would be Abhyankar-Shukla (1969, 1975), Joshi-Roodbergen (1986), and for BH, they would be Biardeau (1964), Subramania Iyer (1964, 1965), Deshpande (1993a, b), Bronkhorst (1987), Houben (1995).

§3.2.

As can be inferred from §3.1, P's direct statements on the topic with which we are concerned are few.[11] They are found only in the opening chapter (*āhnika*) of his work. When the lines he devotes to issues of interpretation, examples, analogies and incidental exchanges with the assumed interlocutor are set aside, only three statements that can justifiably be said to express his own view (albeit historically derived from the Vārttikas) remain:

(a) *samānāyām artha-gatau śabdena cāpaśabdena ca, dharma-niyamaḥ kriyate, śabdenaivārtho 'bhidheyaḥ, nāpaśabdeneti. evam kṛiyamāṇam abhyudayakāri bhavati iti.* "Although the access to meaning through a grammatical word and that which deviates from such a word is alike, a *dharma* restriction is instituted (by the *śāstra*) that one should express meaning only through the grammatical word, not through that which deviates from such a word. (The communication) which is done thus, leads to elevation (i.e., brings benefit to the speaker; more on *abhyudaya* in §3.6 and §3.9 below)."

(b) *śāstrapūrvakaṃ yaḥ śabdān prayuṅkte so 'bhyudayena yujyate.* "He who uses words backed by (preparation in) the *śāstra* comes to be associated with elevation (i.e., brings benefit to himself)."

(c) *atha vā punar astu jñāne dharmaḥ* "Or, let there again be (the position that) *dharma* exists in (i.e., is to be located in, is to be understood as resulting from) knowledge (of the grammatical words)."

In the last, P, in effect, reverts to an earlier part of his work in which the question of whether one should view *dharma* as resulting from knowing (*jñāna*) grammatical words or from the use (*prayoga*) of such words is discussed. He removes the objections to the former view and takes leave of the discussion. He can thus be understood as presenting himself to be in favor of the *jñāna* view and differing from the Vārttikakāra's *śāstra-pūrvaka prayoga* view, but it still remains unclear if he differs from the Vārttikakāra only in the matter of wording or in substance. The *jñāna* meant here, unlike the *jñāna* in some other fields, could come from just being born in a family or community that speaks grammatically; it may not need any special effort that would deserve the reward that *dharma* is. One's interpretation thus may hinge on whether one is willing to accept grammar-independent use of Sanskrit, close to the Aṣṭādhyāyī-derivable Sanskrit, in P's time. However, the type of arguments with which P defends the *jñāne dharmaḥ* view and, indirectly, the evidence we have for the state of Sanskrit in his time indicate that even in the *jñāne dharmaḥ* view considerable discrimination, implying existence of special effort, is involved.[12] Thus, P's final position would be one that essentially integrates the *jñāne* view and the *śāstra-pūrvake prayoge* view, suggesting that, although there is a difference in wording, there is no benefit under either without special effort: '*Dharma* results from knowing (the grammatical words) or from the use (of such words) that is preceded by the (user's) knowledge of the *śāstra*.' This is also how his direct and indirect commentators have understood him.[13]

§3.3.

P's colloquially worded assertions do not get into larger philosophical issues. Even if one were to assume that P was aware of these issues, it would be unfair to expect him to engage in a largely philosophical discussion, given what his immediate concern and his anticipated readership obviously were. The situation in the case of BH is different. An outline of how he defends the linkage of *dharma* with grammar would be as follows:[14]

'One cannot establish an item's capability to generate *dharma* through perception and inference alone. Ultimately, *āgama* 'inherited knowledge,' which can be expressed in specific words or in the behavior of certain spiritual elite (*śiṣṭas*),[15] must be accepted as the arbiter in non-mundane matters. Some teachers claim to have 'seen,' that is, to have thought or realized, something extraordinary entirely with their own effort; some are credited by others with that sort of achievement. However, the achievement, being extraordinary, must have some extraordinary cause – something that is not present in or is not attainable by most worldly personalities. It must presuppose a preparation to transcend average human limitations to such an extent as is not successfully undertaken by a majority of ordinary people. Now, how is it determined that preparation X will succeed and not preparation Y? The determination must be based on some past experience, that is, some inherited knowledge. (If it is deprived of such a basis or test, the attribution of seerhood etc. to someone will simply be a matter of personal preference or belief, worthy of no rational inquiry as is presupposed in the present discussion. There will be no means to ensure that something extraordinary has in fact been achieved.) This being the situation, the proposition that some linguistic usage leads to *dharma* (and, by implication, some does not) should not come across as outlandish, as long as the usage in question is recommended or exemplified by individuals who are thought to have cognitively or spiritually elevated themselves by following the practices approved by *āgama* (regardless of whether these individuals make a claim of elevation and regardless of whether average human beings can personally ascertain that they are elevated). The needed recommendations and attestations do, indeed, come from such individuals (as earlier authors or texts show). An ordinary person following them will benefit in terms of *abhyudaya* (elevation) and later, perhaps, even in terms of *brahma-prāpti* 'attainment of the ultimate reality.'

§3.4.

The following propositions are clearly at the core of what BH is saying.

(a) A *sādhu śabda* or grammatical expression is something supported by *āgama* or testimony. In consonance with this, the same source advises us not to saturate our lives with those expressions which deviate from the *sādhu śabda*.

(b) Both evaluations in the *āgama* are prompted by a consideration of what is good for the acquisition of *dharma* and thereby for spiritual progress.

(c) A *śiṣṭa* is the adviser, explicitly or implicitly through his practice, regarding what is *sādhu* and, by implication, what is *asādhu*. He is also a repository, in words or in behavior, of testimony.

These details, among possibly others, should immediately make a philosophical mind wonder if BH situates the discussion of the usefulness of his discipline in a larger epistemological context. As the above outline indicates, he in fact does, especially by getting into the question of whether the validity of perception and inference is limited.

To a mind conversant with the specific concepts of Indian culture, the details should further issue an invitation to wonder if BH has related his immediate and particular concern with concepts such as Smṛti, *ṛṣi*, Śruti and Veda that are applicable beyond grammar. Again, as the above outline indicates through its reference to *śiṣṭa* and *āgama*, this second set of anticipated relationships is also to be found in BH's writings. He explicitly speaks of Vyākaraṇa as a Smṛti, just as he speaks of it as an *āgama*. He further makes statements to the effect that the *munis* or sages of the Pāṇinian tradition, namely Pāṇini, the Vārttika author(s) and P were *śiṣṭas*. The Smṛti-*āgama*-*śiṣṭa* complex of concepts is logically related to the *ṛṣi*-Śruti-Veda complex. BH does not fail to make use of the latter as well.

§3.5.

Now, a few more specific clarifications, largely of philological and historical nature, are in order. It has been hinted, especially in §§2.2–3, that in the present context *dharma* must mean some kind of positive effect created by the user of the language with which P and BH were concerned; it must mean a good quality acquired by the user for himself (or herself) at least for a certain time. Can we throw any more light on this *dharma*?

In the present context, *dharma* is spoken of as directly leading to some kind of elevation and, indirectly, to attainment of *brahman* or spiritual liberation (*mokṣa*). It clearly then has the ability, probably dependent on how much of it is acquired and for how long, to affect one's surroundings and one's own personality or being. It seems to be a force or an unseen item resembling energy or potency that is conducive to one's welfare, particularly spiritual welfare. It is physical in nature but not in the sense in which an inert object is physical. It is not someone's count in favor of a person or a credit bestowed by one person (even if that person be God) on another person. It is a force like the one denoted by *karman* and *adṛṣṭa* that can affect what it comes into contact with without needing an agent's initiative or permission to affect, although the agent, through the freewill aspect of his personality, may direct the course of how it will affect. The latter possibility suggests that the nature of the agent's interest – whether that interest has self as the basis or is devoid of selfish considerations – may determine how *dharma* affects, for the agent's interest is also another form of energy or potency.

If one is careful not to lose awareness of the preceding considerations, one may translate *dharma* with 'religious merit' or 'religio-spiritual merit' in the present context.[16] Further clarification in this regard will indirectly come from what I observe in the next few sections.

§3.6.

The elevation (*abhyudaya*) spoken of as a consequence of *dharma* may either be a general term inclusive of *brahma*-attainment or may refer to a kind of benefit (or benefit-complex) that is other than *brahma*-attainment.[17] The latter is more likely to be the case for the following reasons:

(a) The earlier Upaniṣadic tradition distinguishes between *preyas* and *śreyas*. The association of *abhyudaya* with the former and of *brahma-prāpti* with the latter seems justifiable. An inherited distinction is not likely to be lost in the grammarians' conception of the good effects of *dharma*.

(b) P talks of spiritual union in passages that are different from the passages in which he refers to *abhyudaya*. His idiom in those passages is varied, whereas in the passages specified above the employment of *abhyudaya* remains constant.[18]

(c) BH's statements (TK V 1.14–22, 1.144–147, 1.159–170) move from the *abhyudaya* notion to the *brahma-prāpti* notion (sometimes the latter is denoted by other words). The sequence in them suggests that, in worldly terms, *brahma-prāpti* would be a· higher achievement.

(d) The later Indian philosophical tradition distinguishes between *abhyudaya* and *niḥśreyasa*. In this pairing of terms, *niḥśreyasa* would be a synonym for BH's *brahma-prāpti*. Vr̥ṣabha, the earliest commentator of BH whose work is available to us, utilizes the '*abhyudaya : niḥśreyasa*' distinction in explaining BH's thinking in TK V 1.5.

The word *abhyudaya*, understood as denoting a lower-level benefit of grammatical usage, can be rendered with 'rise in the world, going ahead in terms of what is usually valued in the world' or, to be short, with 'worldly benefit.' It should be noted, however, that this benefit has a range and that the world implicit in its employment is not this world only. In fact, it may principally stand for any world that is better than our own.[19] It is also worth noting that nowhere in the explanations of *abhyudaya* do the commentators of P or BH make such observations as we would in stating the benefits of proper speech or excellent writing habits. Remarks like 'one gets better employment opportunities if one speaks like a university graduate' or 'one impresses people favorably if one can communicate in the standard dialect' are not found. Ancient Indians were certainly aware of the benefits of what we may call cultured speech, display of good compositional skills etc. But those benefits are not mentioned in the context of *abhyudaya* at least as far as the currently available statements in the tradition of P and BH are concerned.[20]

§3.7.

Up to this point in the discussion, I have assumed, for the sake of simplicity of presentation, that *dharma* is something acquired or generated in the view of our authors. It is now time to note that the words actually used by BH express manifestation or revelation. They are forms of the roots *abhi* + *vi* + *añj* or *āvis* + *bhū*, very commonly employed in Sanskrit to speak of appearing, coming to the view, as distinct from being newly brought into existence. The following passages bear this out:

MBT (Abhyankar-Limaye edition) p. 1: *ye ca śabdā anāmnātā apūrvasyābhivyaktau vyāpriyante ...* "And those words, which (though) not in traditional transmission, are employed in the manifestation of a rite's potency ... "

MBT p. 8: ***dharma-prayojano veti*** *mīmāṃsaka-darśanam. avasthita eva dharmaḥ. sa tv agnihotrādibhir abhivyajyate. tat-preritas tu phalado bhavati. yathā svāmī bhṛtyaiḥ sevāyāṃ preryate phalaṃ prati ...* [21] "(The MB's explanation of *dharma-niyama* with the phrase) *dharma-prayojano vā* refers to the view of the Mīmāṃsakas (which goes as follows): *dharma* is already in place.[22] It is only manifested (made operational) by such (rites) as the *agni-hotra*. Set in motion by them, it bestows the fruit, just as, in service, a master is moved by the servants (through the excellence of their service etc.) toward a reward."

TK V 1.14: *sādhu-prayogāc cābhivyakta-dharma-viśeṣaḥ ...* "And (the person) in whom a distinction (i.e., excellence) of *dharma* appears, as a result of (his) employment of grammatical expressions (preceded by the knowledge of grammar) ..."

TK V 1.25d: *tatra sādhor yaḥ saṃbandho 'rthena sa ... dharmābhivyaktāv aṅgatvaṃ pratipadyate.* "There (in the context of signification or communication), the relationship which a grammatical expression has with (its) meaning ... becomes a part in manifesting (i.e., activating) *dharma*."

TK V 1.144: ... *āvirbhūte dharma-viśeṣe niyato 'bhyudayaḥ*. "When a distinction (i.e., excellence) of *dharma* appears, worldly elevation is certain."

Vṛṣabha on TK V 1.12 (in addition to his glosses on the TK V passages specified earlier): *abhyudaya-hetutvād iti dharmābhivyakteḥ* "(The expression) *abhyudaya-hetutvāt* stands for *dharmābhivyakteḥ* 'because of the manifestation of *dharma*.'"

The implication, as the second MBT passage quoted above confirms, is that *dharma* is something that already or always exists. All that a particular human action or mode of behavior does is to activate it – bring it to the forefront or bring it into action.

The problem with such a predication regarding *dharma* is that scholars have been unable to make much sense of it. The difficulty in making a satisfactory sense is, in turn, due to the fact that we do not find sustained discussions of the *dharmābhivyakti* view in the commonly studied Sanskrit texts. The most comprehensive collection of the references to the view known to date would be Kataoka (2000), augmented by some of the references I have specified above which escaped Kataoka's attention.[23] No reference, unfortunately, gets into the logic of the view.

It may seem that an exception to the assertion I just made is furnished by *yathā svāmī bhr̥tyaiḥ sevāyāṃ preryate phalaṃ prati* on MBT p. 8 and *kārye kāraṇopacārād agni-hotrābhivyaṅgyo 'gni-hotram iti* in Siṃha-sūri-gaṇin's commentary on Malla-vādin's Dvādaśāra-naya-cakra (Muni Jambū-vijaya's edition, p. 141, lines 7–9).[24] However, the former contains only an explanatory analogy, and the latter appeals to metaphorical usage to explain what the meaning of a sentence like *agni-hotraṃ juhuyāt svarga-kāmaḥ* under the *abhi-vyakti* view would be. Both have the air of warding off objections. They do not amount to an explanation of how the view was arrived at in the first place.

Similarly, two references in Uddyotakara and one reference in Siṃha-sūri-gaṇin (passages 3a, 3d and 6a in Kataoka, 2000) amount only to suggesting two preventive observations:

(a) The *abhivyakti* view does not suffer from the same difficulty as the creationist view of *dharma* or *apūrva* would. The latter faces a hurdle in the fact that a ritual act is performed at time t but its result is said to occur at time $t + n$, even when n does not follow t immediately.[25]

(b) There is a way in which the *abhivyakti* view can accommodate the fact that performers of recommended acts get different results – that a philosopher's acceptance of *dharma* manifestation need not imply that every one is rewarded the same way.

§3.8.

Since, thus, we have no real ancient guidance on what the rationale behind the *dharmābhivyakti* view was, we have no alternative but to speculate about it within the frame formed by the other specifics of

BH's thought. We may not be able to determine the precise nature of the rationale but we may be able to sketch the world view it presupposes.

It is knowledge (probably backed by restraint and concentration), speech (of a particular sort) and actions (incorporating a certain discipline in the form of fixed sequence, accurate pronunciation of scripture passages etc.) that are said to bring *dharma* to a stage in which it becomes manifest. *Dharma* meant here then must ultimately be in the same medium as these modes of human liveliness are. Otherwise, it would be impossible for them to connect with it and affect it so that it takes a specific form leading to a reward for the actor. Now, knowledge, speech and actions are manifestations of energy or the life-force (*cit*, *citi*, *caitanya*, *prāṇa*, sentience, consciousness). *Dharma* too then should belong to the energy arena or sphere.[26]

In §3.5 above, we arrived at the same hypothesis on the basis of independent considerations. This should bolster our confidence in our approach. So also Kumārila's thesis (cf. Yoshimizu 2000: 154–157) that *apūrva,* which is *dharma* revealed by a properly performed ritual act, has *ātman* (which is identical with *brahman*, the universal sentience) as its seat.

Further, given the other things that have been said about *dharma*, it should be a positive energy or force, one that can be productive and, if properly handled, add to what is already there and lead to prosperity in that sense.

If such a *dharma* is said to be always there like a potential waiting to be used, the theoretical model which goes with it and which I am trying to reconstruct must contain a source of information about it (i.e., about *dharma*) right from the beginning of the cosmos. The information source's primary role must be to advise us on how to dip into the potential called *dharma* and ensure the furtherance and prosperity of cosmic creation. This guess is confirmed by what BH says about the Veda. It is evident from his remarks in passages such as TK V 1.5 that in his view the premier *śāstra* and/or *āgama* is the Veda, which is (or which, in theory, must be thought of as something) as old as creation itself. Further, this Veda, in the form in which it has come down to us, is (or is, in theory, to be thought of as) a composition of the seers who witnessed the *dharma* or *dharmas/dharmans* (existing beneficial or detrimental properties of things that ordinary people do not see; the non-mundane extensions of the objects that constitute the physical world) directly – who were *sākṣāt-kṛta-dharmāṇaḥ* (Aklujkar, 1991, 2004b, forthcoming).

In the present state of our knowledge, the preceding seems to be the best way to make sense of the *dharmābhivyakti* view. I am aware that in sketching this way I have taken recourse to concepts such as 'energy,' 'force,' 'non-mundane extension' and 'model,' to which the Sanskrit philosophers do not give direct expression and to concepts such as 'make operational,' 'set in motion,' and 'move,' which are not raised to the level of technical or philosophical terms. except, perhaps, in isolation in a system or two. I am also aware that the outline involves some metaphorical usage ('medium,' 'connect,' 'arena,' 'sphere') and occasionally may sound like sectarian mystic talk. However, it is not difficult to see that, even in the absence of a word like 'model,' most traditions of philosophy in Sanskrit are exercises in model building. Also, metaphorical language cannot be avoided at all levels of rigorous logical thinking, especially when one is dealing with cosmogony. As for the possible impression of 'sectarian mystic talk,' we should not allow it to be formed simply because entities like *dharma* and Veda are mentioned. Although these entities figure in religio-spiritual discussions, it behooves us to explore them for the function they serve in the world of philosophers who otherwise appear to be as much given to logic, reasoning, rationality etc., as we or the philosophers from any other tradition.

The *dharma* to which the preceding sketch points is the force for sustenance and regularity of the cosmos, implicit in *brahman*, the first cause, itself and a kin of what *ṛta* etc. of the Vedic ideology convey. It is probably also viewed as apportioned in or distributed over the objects of the world when the world comes into being. A particular recommended action is said to activate it and to deliver through it a particular outcome to the actor.[27] It is, however, also possible to use the word *dharma* secondarily to speak of the entities that are conceptually related to this central or original *dharma*. In these secondary usages, *dharma* would refer to the recommendation in a Vedic text, the action urged by the recommendation, the individual impelling force the action creates, or the end result the action produces.[28]

As the process of spiritual liberation is also basically a revelation process (a phenomenon of 'going back to the roots' by taking off the obscuring layers), constantly accomplished *dharmābhivyakti* can lead to *brahma-prāpti*.

Not doing the recommended actions primarily creates an impediment (*pratyavāya*) in the operation of the universe. As a result of non-observance, activations cease or become less frequent, and the course of the universe is halted or does not go on to the desirable extent. The non-observer becomes a culprit to the common cause. For that reason, his or her failure to help in the full realization of *dharma* and cosmic continuity may be thought of as demerit or sin, but the failure is primarily thought in terms of obstacle creation, unless the intended actor deliberately decides to work against the common good – misuses his or her freewill.

§3.9.

We are now back to the role of intention briefly touched upon in §3.5. We noted above that a distinction is made between *abhyudaya* and *brahma-prāpti*. The former is said to be a worldly attainment, although not confined to the earthly world or the present world of ours. However, in certain passages there is also the suggestion that the cause of *abhyudaya*, namely the manifestation of *dharma*, can be instrumental toward spiritual liberation.[29]

A conceptual link or parallelism between *dharma* manifestation and spiritual liberation as revelation was mentioned above in §3.8. But such a link does not amount to an explanation of the mechanism. How should we account for this double role of *dharma*? What are the stages or steps between the initial manifestation(s) and the final manifestation (*mokṣa* or *nirvāṇa*)?

My efforts to find an answer to this question in the writings of BH or his commentators have so far not been entirely successful. One reason for my inability to advance toward an answer has been that the relevant segments of BH's texts seem to have suffered damage in transmission. The key notion of *śabda-pūrva yoga*, literally meaning 'discipline or contact (or union) preceded by (grammatical) expression(s),' which probably did not need elucidation in his time, has few, if any, leads left in the later tradition. The attempts to elucidate the notion that are found in Subramania Iyer (1964a), and Bronkhorst (1996) are helpful but not adequate.[30]

On the background of the preceding admission, I would put forward two mutually non-exclusive answers as possibilities:

(a) As in the tradition of Śaṃkara's Vedānta, BH could have thought of *dharma*, in the sense of *puṇya* or practice of *śama*, *dama* etc., as performing a cleansing role and gradually preparing the mind for the ultimate redeeming insight.

(b) If *dharma* is a potency or power, and selfish engagement with oneself, being a series or set of thoughts, is also a potency or power, the latter could be coming in the way of the former and restricting its usefulness. Thus, *dharma*, prevented from realizing its full spread, could lead to *abhyudaya*, the worldly kind of benefit whose range may include improvement in the quality of one's mind or change in one's worldly personality. When, on the other hand, *dharma* does not have to share the mind's stage with selfish interest, it may occupy the whole being of the agent, transforming that being thoroughly from within.

§3.10.

Subsequent to the clarification that the talk of *dharma* acquisition or generation should be replaced by the talk of *dharma* manifestation, I should alert my readers about the use of "grammatical" in the rendering of *sādhu śabda* (or of *śabda* when it is contrasted with *apaśabda* or *apabhraṃśa*). I have followed and will follow my predecessors in the field in retaining the renderings such as "grammatical" or "proper." These are justifiable in the sense that *sādhu śabdas* are grammar-approved, directly or indirectly, and generally receive social endorsement, just as grammar-approved usage is acceptable and respectable in our own times. However, it is important to note that the capability for *dharma* manifestation that is ascribed to *sādhu śabdas* is time-sensitive and is not ascribed to them *primarily* because they are found in grammars, in the usage of the grammarians or in the usage of the social elite. The ultimate judges of the presence or absence of the capability are the *śiṣṭas*, and the *śiṣṭas* are not given this judgeship only or mainly because they always or almost always speak grammatically or because they can determine the 'standard' dialect because of their knowledge of the dialects. The main basis for their being entrusted with the judgeship is their spiritual standing, more specifically, their ability to determine the beneficial and harmful qualities of things and actions at the non-mundane level. The determination they carry out (or are said to have carried out) can change according to the time in which it is made. Thus, although, as we will see, the '*sādhu* : *asādhu*' distinction has an important role to play in social management, in particular, in managing the linguistic aspect of social life, the distinction is more a Dharma-śāstra notion than a linguistic notion. Its acceptance may prevent the pre-modern Indian grammarians from becoming the exact equivalents of our linguists, but that should not bother us as long as we do not hold that everything more recent is necessarily better than its predecessor or if we notice that linguists too, especially as practitioners of sociolinguistics or as authors of grammars, engage in finding out which expression elicits a favorable reaction and which does not, but leave things there, suggesting at the most that a person looking for worldly advancement or social acceptance should stay with what elicits favorable reaction. Must we think of it as a deficiency in the ancient Indian grammarians that they try to provide a reason, not just a purpose, for knowing and using *sādhu śabdas*? Must we think negatively of their integration of the linguistic phenomenon of acceptability with what takes place, is recommended or is required in certain other areas of life? Could at least economy in the theory of social management, if not the virtue of displaying a broader or holistic vision of the human condition, not be counted in their favor?

§3.11.

P and BH refer to the opposites of *sādhu śabda* with the terms *apaśabda* and *apabhraṃśa*. Do both terms mean exactly the same thing? As one would expect, there is a difference of meaning; *apaśabda* was a term with a wider meaning. Any slip in pronunciation etc. could make a word *apaśabda*, regardless of whether that slip led to a variant form gaining currency.[31] On the other hand, *apabhraṃśa* seems to be reserved for deviants and variants that came to stay. It connotes greater distance from the assumed standard (=what *we* may call Sanskrit). In accordance with its component *bhraś/bhraṃś* signifying a 'falling off,' 'slipping,' it refers to a vertical development, while *apaśabda* has no such historical dimension, that is, it includes a vertical as well as a horizontal deviation. This determination of meaning difference is confirmed by the later usage of *apabhraṃśa* to refer to new dialects and languages that emerged from an earlier source.[32]

SOCIOLINGUISTICS OF THE GRAMMARIANS' DHARMA

§4.1.

The preceding collection and explication of the evidence found in the works of P and BH should enable us to proceed toward a study of how the evidence has been used. In the present context, the most germane use is the one made in reconstructing the sociolinguistic history of India. Our examination of that use will not only answer the charges and apprehensions in §1.3, it will pave the way for a proper exploration of the larger relationships in the intellectual history of India.

My good friend Professor Madhav M. Deshpande (henceforth 'D' in abbreviation) has discussed the MB and TK-MBT statements about grammaticality, *śiṣṭa* etc. in a number of publications. He has been, over the last three decades, the most prominent scholar, forming almost a one-member class, in the area of sociolinguistics of early India. No other scholar, as far as I know, has given so much attention to the role played by Pāṇinian grammar in India's religious and social history. While I have learned much from his sustained work and while I agree with him on many other issues in the study of Sanskrit and Pāṇinian grammar, I think that we need a different reconstruction of the sociolinguistic and cultural history of India from the one he has given or presupposed.

D (1979a: 7–11) says: "By the time of Kātyāyana (about 300 B.C.) and Patañjali (about 100 B.C.), ... even Brahmins have begun using Prakrits as their first languages, while Sanskrit is retained in the ritual and scholastic contexts. Kātyāyana concedes that one can indeed communicate in a Prakrit language as well as in Sanskrit, but he insists that only the use of Sanskrit leads to religious merit (*dharma*). ... in terms of their social office and historical traditions, they [= the Brahmins] emotionally identified with the 'preserved' Sanskrit language ... Another significant factor involved in this Brahmanical view is that Buddhism and Jainism were not only opposed to Vedic religion, but they were also opposed to the Sanskrit language in an attempt to undermine the authority of the Brahmins and to align themselves with the non-Brahmanical masses. ... Only on this hypothesis can we fully understand why Kātyāyana claims that only the use of Sanskrit leads to *Dharma*, while the 'subnormal' languages lead to *Adharma*."[33]

A part of the preceding is confirmed by D 1993a: 25: "From even a casual reading of the Mahābhāṣya, a fact clearly emerges, namely that there was a fierce competition between Sanskrit and Prakrit, and that in this competition the Prakrit had already surpassed Sanskrit as the language of the world (*loka*). Under these circumstances, the Sanskrit grammarians defended Sanskrit as the language of *dharma*, rather than as a language of worldly communication."

§4.2.

I will point out on another occasion that the following suppositions of D, *as far as he makes them with respect to the period with which we are concerned*, are questionable or stand in need of significant qualification: (a) Buddhism and Jainism were opposed to Vedic religion. (b) Buddhism and Jainism were opposed to Sanskrit. (c) Buddhism and Jainism were attempting to undermine the authority of the Brahmins and to align themselves with the non-Brahmanical masses.

To come to the rest of D's assertions, is it really likely that Brahmins would use Prakrit languages and still look upon them as substandard? This crucial question seems to have occurred to D, since he (1979a: 9) remarks: "Though even Brahmins used these substandard languages, they did not, at this stage, identify themselves with these languages." He sees the Brahmins as 'emotionally' identifying themselves with Sanskrit. If this emotional identification is understood as comprising (a) special affection for Sanskrit as a language of Brahmanical religious texts, (b) insistence on using only Sanskrit as an accompaniment of ritual activity, (c) interest in preserving Sanskrit's purity and (d) cultivating Sanskrit for various fields, I would go along with D's reconstruction. However, if it is to include dislike of Prakrit languages and literatures and of certain individuals and communities simply because they spoke Prakrit (note 33), then I differ from him.

One also needs to ask the following questions in this regard: Could a community, spread over a large area at a time in which offering mutual support was not easy, have maintained emotional attachment to a language for a long period? If Sanskrit was no longer the community's mother tongue and was primarily learned as a father tongue or school language, is an emotional bond to it likely without an exceptionally high degree of indoctrination? Do we have any clear evidence of such an indoctrination? Would sustained indoctrination not have required a heavy commitment of resources? Are Brahmins likely to have commanded those resources during most of the period concerned, if not throughout?[34] Are there examples in ancient world history of a language having been sustained over three to five centuries (note 34) and over a large area mainly for emotional reasons against economic and practical odds? Would it not be more reasonable to assume that Sanskrit enjoyed in the period concerned considerable state support as a language which a significant number in the populace spoke in various dialects, which most people of (north) India understood (and probably liked) and which was found most convenient for official business and cultural communication?

§4.3.

More cogently, the evidence mentioned by D does not add up to prove that the Brahmins looked down upon the Prakrits in the time of (Kātyāyana and) P and thought of *Prakrit* expressions as leading to *adharma* or religio-spiritual demerit.

When P speaks of *apabhraṃśas*, his statements are phrased in terms of individual words and speech sounds (*helayo, gāvī, goṇī, gotā, gopotalikā, ḷtaka*). Even a juxtaposition of Sanskrit and any other Indo-Aryan *language* is not found in those statements, let alone an explicit contrasting or comparison *as languages*. There is no suggestion in the contexts that it is languages which are in P's purview. If his intent was to speak of distinctions in languages, should there not be employment of terms like *bhāṣā* and *vāc* at least once? Also, given the fact that he considered expressions in the non-Sanskrit forms of Indo-Aryan to be developments coming out of Sanskrit, is it not more probable that he would view the non-Sanskrit Indo-Aryan languages as forming a continuum with Sanskrit rather than as truly separate entities – that, in the passages used as evidence by D, P (and Kātyāyana) were not thinking of related but different *languages*?[35]

§4.4.

D (1979: 10) informs us that the very words cited as *apabhraṃśas* of *go* are 'found in the Jaina Ardha-māgadhī texts' and 'some' can 'be traced in the Pāli canon.' He refers to Gandhi (1927: Intro. p. 72) and Pischel (1965: 6) [=Jha, 1965: 6; Jha, 1981: 6] as his sources for this information. However, Gandhi records occurrences of only *gāvī* and *goṇī*, with *goṇa* as a variant, from Ardha-māgadhī literature. Pischel's remark, in Jha's translation, reads: "Of these [forms cited by P], in Prākṛit, the most usual form is *gāvī*; of JM [=Jaina Māhārāṣṭrī]. *goṇī*, the masculine is *goṇo* (§393)." Thus, Gandhi and Pischel have nothing to say on the remaining words. As far as their guidance to us goes, only about half of the *apabhraṃśas* cited by P are relatable to known or imaginable Prakrit languages. Nor do Gandhi and Pischel bring Pāli into the realm of attestation.[36] Further, the most telling feature of Prakrit proper, namely the loss of intervocalic consonants, is missing in the forms (as Bhandarkar, 1877 noted). A form like *gopotalikā* even comes across like a linguistic item resulting from compounding typical of (what we call) Sanskrit. As P has given them to us, the forms in question look more like variants in dialects close to Sanskrit. The occurrence of some of them in the Prakrits is more likely to be a case of fossil preservation or deliberate retention in the process of creating partly artificial and widely intelligible languages that could be used in texts that would form the canon.[37]

§4.5.

Two further facts supportive of the view that *adharma* was not associated with the use of Prakrit languages in the mind of P are these:

(a) The notion of *apaśabda*, which is very closely related to that of *apabhraṃśa*, is not confined in its applicability to Prakrit or Prakrit-like words (§3.11). P's successors have cited even such Sanskrit words as *nyāṅkava* and *naiyaṅkava* as lacking the capacity to generate or reveal merit in certain times[38] and thus being amenable to the label *apaśabda*, albeit in a temporally restricted way.

(b) P's discussion does not conclude by saying that the so-called Prakrit words necessarily produce *adharma*. The '*yarvāṇas-tarvāṇaḥ*' passage (MB p. I.11) does not find anything wrong with the use of 'prakritisms' in ordinary life as D (1979a: 8) himself notes.[39] The *apabhraṃśas* or so-called Prakrit words *gāvī* etc. were also likely to have been used in ordinary life.

§4.6.

In short, unless we decide to impute our perspective to the past and to impose our current terminology on authors who did not use it, Kātyāyana and P cannot be said to have declared Prakrit languages as such substandard. They did declare some words that would be pāli-isms and, perhaps, prakritisms according to our terminology to be substandard, but they viewed these as parts of the same continuum as Sanskrit, and their declaration was made with an eye on non-mundane results, not as a social judgment. What was really looked down upon was the absence of potential for *dharma*, not linguistic features in themselves, and this absence was seen in some Sanskrit words as it was seen in what *we* identify as non-Sanskrit words in the family of languages to which Sanskrit belongs. The main criterion for (*sādhu*) *śabdatva* or *apaśabdatva* was theological or spiritual in nature, if one may use a terminology alien to the thinking of Indian authors.

P'S AND BH'S UNDERSTANDING OF *ŚIṢṬA*

§5.1.

The preceding discussion brings us to the question of who the proper informant of *dharma*-worthiness of linguistic usage should be – on whose authority we should accept a particular expression to be capable of producing religio-spiritual merit. This question is briefly addressed by P in his discussion of an aphorism of Pāṇini with some short sentences that have more an air of asserting well-known truths than of providing a step-by-step justification. BH's treatment of the same issue, on the other hand, is scattered through the available parts of the MBT and TK as far as the identification of the informant (*as śiṣṭa*) goes. As to the explanation of why the choice must be the *śiṣṭa*, however, it is concentrated in fairly continuous sections in the first book of the TK. My presentation in §3.3–11 above, being based on these sections, specifies them.

The difference in P's treatment and BH's treatment is due largely to the fact that P was commenting on someone else's largely non-philosophical work and had to follow the order of that work, whereas BH was writing an independent work, the first part of which was to be specifically devoted to stating the philosophical or theoretical underpinnings of the Pāṇinian tradition; he had the freedom to introduce ideas not falling in the area of a specific grammar (ideas over and above those which emerged in *prakriyā*, grammatical derivation) wherever he wanted and to any length that was necessary.

The difference could also be due to the time difference between P and BH. The relevant socio-religious ideas could have evolved further in the centuries that passed after the time of P and before the birth of BH. However, given the similarity of central parts of P's and BH's statements with a statement in Baudhāyana-dharma-sūtra 1.1.1.4–5, it is unlikely that a major change of *essence* took place.[40]

§5.2.

Patañjali's remarks are prompted by Pāṇini 6.3.109 (*pr̥ṣodarādīni yathopadiṣṭam*), a *sūtra* which adds a set of forms to the acceptable usage derived from Pāṇini's other rules. The *sūtra*, however, does this without specifying any grammatical or semantic features that would limit the set's members. The natural concern then is to ensure that the set does not become uncontrollably open-ended. This concern, furthermore, is to be addressed by taking into consideration the fact that the sūtra makes an oblique reference to an agent or a group of agents of the activity of *upadeśa* 'instruction, teaching.' P's remarks thus, appropriately, seek to identify the individuals, an acceptance by whom or a matching with whose usage would make a form, underived by Pāṇini's other rules, eligible for inclusion in the *pṛṣodarādi* group and thereby for inclusion in acceptable usage.

These individuals are the *śiṣṭas*. They are to be looked upon as arbiters or sources of guidance in those cases for which the Aṣṭādhyāyī does not offer guidance or does not offer precise guidance. That this is P's intention is evinced by his employment of *anya* 'other, additional' in *anyān api* (*śabdān*) *jānāti* appearing toward the end of his comment.

P's linguistic *śiṣṭas* resemble the *śiṣṭas* mentioned in other traditional branches of knowledge in India in that their status is not derived only from having a thoroughly imbibed body of knowledge. They are expected to maintain a particular kind of behavior and to live in a community that facilitates the maintenance of that behavior (*nivāsataś cācārataś ca*). They are not exempt from the requirements that the judges of *dharma* must meet according to the Dharmaśāstras and Smṛtis. It, therefore, makes sense to hold that they would be viewed as embodying something over and above what is found in books containing traditionally handed down instruction and that their testimony, as of the *śiṣṭas* serving as guides for other activities of life, would be invoked as complementation of the Smṛti – as constituting an unwritten Smṛti (*aśabda-nibandhanā*) as distinct from *śabdavatī*; cf. TK V 1.158). The distinction P makes between the Vaiyākaraṇas, who learn standard usage from texts such as the Aṣṭādhyāyī, and the *śiṣṭas*, who do not study or are not studying the Aṣṭādhyāyī[41] but who employ expressions derived by the Aṣṭādhyāyī, indirectly supports such a reading of his statement. His *śiṣṭas*, then, are primarily those who meet certain spiritual and behavioral requirements and who have internalized the Aṣṭādhyāyī usage and usage close to the Aṣṭādhyāyī usage to such an extent that they can be said to have an instinct for what would agree with that usage and what would not. Given P's obviously high regard for the Aṣṭādhyāyī (and the Vārttikas associated with it), we may speak of the Aṣṭādhyāyī usage as what he viewed as 'standard' usage.

§5.3.

D (1993a: 31) is right in suggesting that, for the age in which P lived, Pāṇinian Sanskrit should not be identified with *śiṣṭa* Sanskrit. However, I cannot go along with him when he suggests that *śiṣṭa* Sanskrit had a status comparable to what a modern linguist may view as the standard dialect, or when he leaves the impression that, up to P's time, efforts were made to test the outputs of the Aṣṭādhyāyī against the usage in one specific (*śiṣṭa*) Sanskrit dialect and to modify and interpret the Aṣṭādhyāyī in such a way as to make the outputs agree with the usage in that dialect. The efforts actually seem to be eclectic and functional in their orientation, as befits the conditions of the time and the approach revealed in the Aṣṭādhyāyī itself (although, as in the Aṣṭādhyāyī, the efforts led to impressive coverage and sophistication of technique). While P viewed the Aṣṭādhyāyī as a grammar concerned only with the *śiṣṭa* usage (cf. MB 1.3.1.19) and as a means of identifying the *śiṣṭas* (MB 6.3.109), he did not view the Aṣṭādhyāyī as a grammar to be modified, *generally and exclusively,* in light of *contemporary śiṣṭa* Sanskrit. One can attribute such a procedure to modern linguists, but it would be alien to P's thinking[42] and almost impossible to implement in his time. In his view, the usage of the *śiṣṭas* was to be compared, and perhaps they were to be asked if they would use a particular form in those cases in which the guidance available in the Aṣṭādhyāyī was insufficient (e.g., in the case of the *pṛṣodarādi* for which 'taught/uttered/employed by whom' is not specified). Also, in extending the coverage of the Aṣṭādhyāyī through the inclusion of new items (in *ākṛti-gaṇas* etc.), agreement with *śiṣṭa* usage and view was probably to be sought. But the procedure was not one of comparing the contemporary *śiṣṭa* dialect with the Aṣṭādhyāyī-derived dialect and making changes in the body or interpretation of Aṣṭādhyāyī rules only in the light of differences that might emerge. Rather, P, like his Vārttikakāra predecessors, proceeded on a case-by-case basis, with the cases being taken from a variety of (what we would call) dialects. The *śiṣṭas* as persons are more central to his perspective than their generalized or categorized speech as such. Also, the decisions the *śiṣṭas* are expected to make are based on a consideration of potential for *dharma*, not on a consideration of social acceptability etc. as a modern sociolinguist or a native speaker professor specializing in the study of a language would make.[43]

§5.4.

What does the preceding reconsideration of evidence indicate that would have a bearing on the possibilities entertained in §1.3?

There is no evidence of a negative attitude toward languages like Pāli and Ardha-māgadhī or toward Prakrit languages in the broad sense ('non-Sanskritic but relatable to Sanskrit') in the works of the early Sanskrit grammarians. Consequently, the Brahmins or, more broadly, the followers of the Vedic tradition, cannot be said to have looked down upon the Jains and Buddhists on that score (although they may have other reasons for not liking the Jains and Buddhists).[44]

The Aṣṭādhyāyī does not seem to have been used as any kind of rigid or coercive control, and there appear to be no grounds that would allow us to infer that it became an instrument in stifling creativity. The manner in which it was allowed to exercise control was different, but the extent to which it exercised control does not appear to be significantly or categorically different from what our standard grammars and dictionaries do.

GRAMMARIANS AND THE LARGER INDIAN CONCERN WITH DHARMA

§6.1.

P's and BH's *sādhu śabdas*, in their 'historical' perspective, primarily belong to the same stream as the one which went back to the language of the Veda. The Veda language was, in turn, a reflection or the most direct descendent imaginable of the ultimate reality or the speech principle. The stream was changing, and it was considered desirable that it should not change or that it should not change too much.[45] The means employed to control the change do not seem to be essentially different or more severe than we would see employed in our times. Just as, along with standard grammars and dictionaries, we may appeal to an Oxford University professor's usage or the usage of a good local speaker, P and BH appeal to the *śiṣṭas* (sometimes even to the Oxford professors of their times, namely the Āryāvarta *śiṣṭas*) and smart charioteers, in addition to grammars like the Aṣṭādhyāyī (and whatever lexicons existed in their times).

Just as, despite giving an impression to the contrary from time to time, our linguists do not compare the output of an entire grammar with the usage of an entire group or community, the grammarians of the P-BH family tested only certain usages or output possibilities by asking or studying a few members of the community.[46] They presupposed the existence of a standard form of language just as the modern linguists do in recording the peculiarities of local dialects, although their language notion was muted and the dialect notion does not seem to have existed in their conceptual universe.

Another similarity that is not so easy to notice is that there is probably an anticipation of our language family view and an acknowledgement of the necessity to restrict the investigation to kindred languages in what we find in the works of P and BH. The former does not cite as *apabhraṃśas* words which could not be related to Sanskrit. The latter tells us that *śabdena vācyam*, "one should express oneself with grammatical words," should not be interpreted to mean *drāmilakena bhavati vaktavyam*, "One should express oneself with Drāviḍa words" (TK V 1.153–154). There very likely was an awareness on their part of the linguistic variety to be taken into account for the '*śabda* : *apaśabda*' distinction. Even to imagine that P and BH were smugly absorbed in their little Vedic universe and did not give a hoot about what happened outside of it, they would have to know where the outside began (apart from the fact that their works furnish no evidence of looking down upon the rest of humanity).

§6.2.

Are we coming to a point where we could say "The more things looked different initially, the more similar they are turning out to be at the end of our analysis"? Not quite. The important difference of manner in which the interface between grammar-derived language and linguistic diversity (here, including historical change) is handled remains. A modern grammarian or linguist is unlikely to invoke the notion of *dharma* as something capable of affecting an important concern of his or her discipline. We have our differences regarding whether grammar should be taught in our schools. But it is extremely unlikely that either party to the debate would take the position that it should be taught because it would increase our students' prospects of gaining religio-spiritual merit. What does the difference tell us about how the intellectuals of ancient India, particularly the Brahmins, thought?

Were the Brahmins trying to control society by raising the phantom of *dharma*? If so, were they doing this for selfish communal reasons or did they have some sort of big-hearted or farsighted philosophy of social management behind it? In particular, were they playing up Sanskrit by invoking the consideration of *dharma* because they could no longer make a case for it as a language having popular support (and, without its widespread use their livelihood would be threatened) or because that was one of the ways in which they could ensure that the Jains and the Buddhists did not get an upperhand through their popular Prakrit languages?

As I have demonstrated above, there is neither textual evidence nor probability in favor of the latter. Whatever other battles the Brahmins and other followers of the Vedic path might have fought with the so-called heretics, linguistic battles are not a part of them. And, if at all any tension was felt, it has led to the adoption of an inclusivistic 'continuum' strategy on the part Brahmins which makes it unlikely that in the preceding period anything that would leave a bitter divisive memory took place.

§6.3.

In the following, I will try to demonstrate that the Sanskrit grammarians' engagement with *dharma* is of a piece with what we see elsewhere in Brahmanical social theory and practice. The similarity between P's or BH's understanding of a *śiṣṭa* and the Dharma-śāstra understanding of the same is not merely a case of an interesting borrowing or historical coincidence. The grammarians' use of concepts such as Smṛti and *āgama*, which, in turn, lead to Śruti (or Veda) and *ṛṣi*, already suggests that some deeper or organic relationship may be at work. It may be rewarding to ascertain if such indeed is the case.

§6.4.

Ultimately, what the grammarians claim is not that one gains *dharma* through grammatical usage simply because the usage is grammatical – because one succeeds in imitating someone whose usage happens to be deemed correct, faithful to the authorities or respectable. The usage must be backed or preceded by a knowledge of the *śāstra* behind it (note 13). This requires special effort, staying away from at least some of the pleasures that attract common men. In other words, it presupposes restraint of the senses and concentration of the mind to the extent one is capable of such things.[47] Acceptance of a similar mode of living, in which *saṃyama, dhyāna* and allied features have some place, is elsewhere said in ancient Indian literature to make one a better person.

§6.5.

In most other strands of Indian thinking, (e.g., Vedānta), it is not claimed that a life of restraint and concentration will, by itself, lead to final release from the cycle of life and death, that is, to *mokṣa* or *nirvāṇa*. While its importance is acknowledged through the emphasis placed on it or through the frequent mention made of it, its limitation is also acknowledged. It is presented primarily as a tool, one that cleanses the mind and makes it capable of seeing or realizing the higher truth, just as the wiping of a dusty mirror restores its ability to reflect objects. The life of restraint and concentration that is presupposed in the grammarians' championing of the cause of grammatical usage also initially leads only to *abhyudaya*. (§3.9)

§6.6.

There is a propensity in Brahmanical thinking to turn every act into some kind of *yoga* or *yajña*. It sees much scope for turning even the ordinary socially expected acts into acts of spiritual cultivation or worship (the latter taken in a larger, metaphorical sense). What is deemed necessary for this to occur is change in the way in which one approaches the acts. The pure physicality or socio-biological necessity of acts should be accompanied by an informed mind that is aware of the need to sacrifice – to give up a little bit of one's selfish interest and to expand thereby. The grammarians' *dharma*-through-grammar thinking could be but one part of the larger intellectual landscape that resists division between the religio-spiritual and the secular. Like the other manifestations of *dharma*, this manifestation too does not need a particular time or place to practice.

§6.7.

While it places a great store by the observance of ways that would eventually lead to a cleaner or purer mind (just as it places a great store by the observance of duties suitable to each social class and rank), Brahmanism associates no guilt or sin with what people must do naturally or biologically. It is not a crime to refuse to be elevated as we can deduce, among other indications, from the saying: *āhāra-nidrā-bhaya-maithunaṃ ca samānam etat paśubhir narāṇām / pravṛttir eṣā bhūtānāṃ. nirvṛttis tu mahā-phalā //* "Eating, sleep, fear, sexual intercourse – human beings share these with animals. These (acts and states) are what living beings naturally turn to. But turning away from them brings great benefits." In consonance with this is the fact that while the grammarian recommends grammatical usage, he does not say that one incurs sin or demerit through non-grammatical usage. P's discussion does not end in a statement asserting that words like *gāvī*, coming in the place of *go*, produce *adharma* (§4.5).[48] The term used, at least by the earlier authors, while speaking, in their preferred version of the '*dharma* through grammaticality' thesis, in the case of persons who fail to practice the grammar *yoga* is *pratyavāya* 'hindrance,' not *pāpa*. Given the context that the other related ideas (§§3.7–9, §§6.4–6) form, *pratyavāya* may mean that, through a constant use of *apabhraṃśas*, one develops a mind that comes in the way of realizing higher truths – one makes one's mind dense, as it were, and creates an obstacle for oneself.

§6.8.

śiṣṭa and Smṛti were notions of pivotal importance to early Brahmanic social management. To use our contemporary idiom, implicit in the former is the principle that decisions affecting a large number of individuals in the society be made by individuals who are informed or learned enough and who have the potential to arrive at judgments unaffected by vested interests. Such a potential does not generally arise naturally or all of a sudden, simply because the individual is assigned to a task requiring separation of selfish motives. It must be preceded by a long period of training or trying (and even then not all individuals will succeed in developing it). It is a matter of individual effort plus social facilitating. (The society must accord the requisite protection and physical facilities to the group from which the knowledgeable and dispassionate individuals are expected to come). It does not materialize only through constant preaching or mere intellectual understanding of what is expected. The prospects for its realization to any significant extent realistically exist only if the individual goes, or is made to go, through a particular life-style in which non-attachment is practiced to the highest possible degree and an attitude of reaching for mastery in a particular field with no worldly gain in sight it is inculcated. P's words, also echoed in the words of Dharma-śāstra texts, are quite unambiguous: *etasminn ārya-nivāse ye brāhmaṇāḥ kumbhī-dhānyā alolupā agṛhyamāṇa-kāraṇāḥ kiṃcid antareṇa kasyāścit vidyāyāḥ pāragāḥ, tatra-bhavantaḥ śiṣṭāḥ*. "The honorable *śiṣṭas* are those Brahmins who in this dwelling place of the Āryas do not possess more than a potful of grain, who are not greedy, who have no motivating factors that can be discerned (and) who have reached the end of some branch of knowledge for no (ordinarily found) reason." One may, then, read in the grammarians' prescription, just as in the comparable prescriptions of the Dharma-śāstrakāras, a realistic awareness of the need to practice socially useful virtues for a long time and in as many activities as possible before they become second natures of the individuals to whom positions of great responsibility are to be offered to create a civil (*ārya*) society.

§6.9.

The other principle implicitly recognized in the *śiṣṭa* notion, particularly as it is articulated by BH, is that the normal, average, natural or 'god-given' human capabilities of cognition can be enhanced. What is required for such an enhancement is not essentially different from what is required to develop a specialist's skills.[49] A jeweller's son can acquire, through constant guidance and practice, the ability to see the distinctions and defects of precious stone which common people cannot see (assuming that the son did not possess such an ability innately.) With enough self-application and focused guidance, a person who had no musical ear can learn to distinguish as etherial and subtle a thing as musical notes. The possibility, therefore, that a life dedicated to a particular pursuit and a particular way of living should enable a person to come to know those properties of things which escape an average man can logically be entertained.

§6.10.

The relationship between the *śiṣṭas* and Smṛtis is close. The former preserve and/or compose the latter. Sometimes the latter are not actually composed but can be inferred from how the former behave. *śiṣṭas* become the embodiment of Smṛtis, and Smṛtis become the non-personal representatives of the *śiṣṭas*. The great convenience the Smṛtis offer is that, under certain constraints, they can be changed to suit the times. They are the vehicles for accommodating change and managing the dynamic aspect of societies in such a way as not to cause great upheavals. The grammarians avail themselves of a similar strategy when they make the *dharma*-generating capabilities of linguistic expressions relative to the times in which they were or are used (§4.7).

§6.11.

To return to the question in §6.2 which I left unanswered, it seems unlikely that with so many signs of agreement with what we notice elsewhere in the Brahmanical ideas on the management of individual and social life, the Sanskrit grammarians' invoking of *dharma* could be an improvised, spur-of-the-moment response to the danger posed to Brahmin or Vedic dominance by the rise of Jainism and Buddhism (assuming for the moment that the nature of Brahmin dominance was what many modern historians take it to be and that the Brahmins really perceived a danger). Nor has it been proved that the points of agreement appear in Brahmanical thinking only after the rise of Jainism and Buddhism, so that the whole complex of the Brahmanical ideas to which I have referred, not just the grammarians' complex, could be considered a strategy for survival.

The point I am making is not that there could not have been cunning, selfish or sectarian Brahmins. Obviously, like any other community, the Brahmins must have had their share of ideal Brahmins, not-so-ideal Brahmins, those Brahmins who could not rise beyond the level of the most ordinary persons and those Brahmins who were outright bigots. My point rather is that, until we have good evidence to stand on, we should not think only in terms of self-serving strategies on the part of groups of characters populating ancient Indian history. Being hardnosed about the evidence or reading between the lines of the evidence are procedures that a good historian should always practice, but these procedures should not be applied only to one group or tradition or by going beyond the contextually supportable meanings of the words in our evidence. The Pāṇinians' conception of the relationship between grammar and *dharma* is not as outlandish or self-servingly brahmanical as it may seem at first. The conception fits quite well the other features of the dominant mode of ancient Indian intellectual life. This mode is different. It is quite out of fashion in our own times. But it cannot be inferior just for those reasons. It has not been proved that it lacks validity, and it may in fact be the case that we can learn something valuable from it.

NOTES

[1] Since Vyākaraṇa is fairly co-extensive with what we understand by 'grammar' in our times, I will use 'grammar' as its English equivalent, without worrying about the differences of detail and cultural associations (such as acceptance as Smrti, which will be noticed in the following pages). In keeping with this, I will use 'grammarian' as a synonym of Vaiyākaraṇa. It may be suggested that the first letters of 'grammar' and 'grammarian' be capitalized, on the pattern of 'Vedānta,' "Naiyāyika" etc., to indicate that works and authors of a particular tradition or school are intented. However, since in this essay the context can enable the reader to distinguish the general noun usage from the singular noun usage, I have not followed the path of capitalization except at sentence beginning.

[2] I add the qualification 'organically' to exclude the occurrences of *dharma* in grammatical examples and in discussions of a general nature in which what is being

said does not have any direct or specific bearing on what is expected of the grammarian.

[3] Here, the grammarian is not concerned with sentences which the hearer would not recognize as belonging to any language that he can understand. The number of words ungrammatical or unfamiliar to the hearer is presumed to be manageable. Also, their nature is presumed to be such as would come close to that of the words the hearer knows.

[4] Deshpande 1979a: 12–18 contains the following statement: "Bhartṛ-hari ... believes that a 'substandard' (*apabhraṃśa*) word is one which lacks the proper grammatical process, ... and that such words signify their meaning only by reminding one of the proper Sanskrit word. He finally concedes that through centuries of 'incorrect' usage by the 'deficient' speakers, these 'substandard' expressions acquire direct significance. This is a grudging admission."

A more nuanced statement on the matter is needed. I cannot find any words in the relevant passages of BH, specified at the beginning of §3.1 below, suggesting that he reluctantly agrees to attribute capability of direct signification to 'substandard' speech. (One may read regret in the passages that an age of pristine purity has gone by or the wish that people would be more diligent, although even to do so the usual meanings of words must be stretched). In fact, in TK 3.3.30, BH speaks of those who would attribute only indirect signification to 'substandard' speech with *kaiścit*, which indicates that he distances himself from the view. Also, the view would go against his theses of unitary sentence and sentence meaning, since having a two-step linguistic communication implies segmentation. Where a triggering of memory is invoked, one would expect BH to take the position that the sentence heard has simply failed in its intended mission and an ontologically different sentence had to carry out that mission. In his view, the first sentence may lead to this different sentence, directly or through other sentences comprising the recollection process and it may even be very similar to the second sentence, but it does not incorporate the second sentence or its distinctive part (the recollected grammatical or ungrammatical expression, depending on whether the hearer is used to grammatical speech). He would say that if one were to think of the sentence as something whose parts can be replaced when it is in the process of delivering its meaning, that would be a theory which is not borne out when we analyze linguistic communication comprehensively and properly. Furthermore, all the statements to the effect that only *sādhu śabdas* (approximately synonymous with our :'proper word,' 'standard speech' or 'grammatical expression') are direct signifiers (*vācaka*) are made in the narrow context of Pāṇinian grammar or with respect to those who are accustomed to the language derived by grammars such as Pāṇini's. Note also the implication of TK 2.326-339 and the V thereto.

[5] I have used 'gain' and will stick to that expression and its synonyms for the sake of convenience. See, however, §3.7 for an important corrective.

[6] Some readers may think that historians will probably not argue along the lines I have indicated. The discussion I will carry out below of a set of implications drawn in writing a sociolinguistic history of India should establish that an argument with the indicated sequence is not improbable at this time when much writing on India's history reveals more about the historians than history. (Some of the authors, especially the ones writing about history in newspapers and pamphlets, do not even deserve the designation 'historian.' This is all the more true in the case of politically motivated websites.) The rightly respectable scholar whose conclusions I scrutinize in §§ 4.1–6 does not take his logic so far as I have indicated, but it is not unlikely that some less careful and/or doctrinaire historian will turn his suggestion that Brahmins were attaching *dharma* to Sanskrit to preserve that language into an assertion to the effect that Brahmins kept tight control over Sanskrit to ensure that other social groups could not wield the power that comes with knowledge. In fact, the assertion

has already been made more than once. It has, as far as I can recall, just not been linked to the position of the Pāliinian authors that we are discussing.

[7] The word *ārṣa* here has its literal sense 'coming from the *ṛṣi*' adjusted to mean 'coming from the Buddha(s).' References to the Buddha as a *ṛṣi* are found in the Buddhist tradition.

[8] Even when we confine ourselves to *dharma* as something resulting from the use of grammatical expressions (and possibly *adharma* as a consequence of the employment of ungrammatical expressions) or, in a more general way, *dharma* as resulting from proper action (and *adharma* as resulting from improper action), it would be a risky method to try to determine what P and BH have to say about *dharma* only on the basis of occurrences of *dharma* (and *adharma*) in their works. Other words such as *adṛṣta, pratyavāya, pātakatva, abhyudaya, anugraha* and *upaghāta* must also be taken into account if our overall philological study is not to be misled.

[9] The words like *adharma* then have corresponding contrary senses. For simplicity and brevity of statement, I will avoid referring to these contraries wherever I can in the following pages. They should be understood as implied, if the context is suitable.

[10] In all these cases, the corresponding MBT and TK V parts are to be understood as included. The same applies to the commentaries of Vṛṣabha and Helā-rāja. That some of the specified TK kārikā and V parts deal with indirectly related matters is to be overlooked. TK V 2.59 (*loke 'py arthena prayukteṣu śabdeṣu śāstreṇa dharma-niyama-mātram eva kriyate)*, which could be added to the list, is but an echo of a statement found in the MB.

[11] An indirectly relevant but important statement, P on Pāṇini 6.3.109, is discussed below in §§5.1–4.

[12] (a) P's use of the word *niyama-pūrvam* under Varttika 9, where the *śāstra-pūrvaka-prayoga* alternative is discussed, primarily applies to the analogy 'study of *Veda-śabdas*,' but it strengthens the possibility that he had a similar association in mind with the item to which the analogy was being applied.

(b) Cf. TK 1.176 (*asva-goṇyādayaḥ* ....) and the V thereto; also the verse *śabdārtha-saṃbandha-nimitta-tattvaṃ* ... quoted in TK V 1.12.

[13] Cf. TK V 1.155: *jñāne śāstra-pūrvake vā prayoge 'bhyudayaḥ* ... Vṛṣabha TK V 1.6: ... *jñānataḥ prayogato vā* ... Vṛṣabha TK V 1.14: ... *prayogād jñanad va* ....

[14] This outline is in effect a summary of the passages specified in §3.1, particularly of TK 1.28–42, and, to some extent, of TK 1.148–152.

[15] BH's multi-layered understanding of *āgama* is discussed in Aklujkar 1989.

[16] (a) These translations are in fact common even in the context of the grammarians' *dharma* as a perusal of the books of Joshi-Roodbergen,Deshpande etc. will bear out.

(b) *adharma* should, correspondingly, be understood as standing for the opposite of *dharma* or for the absence of *dharma* (and its effects).

[17] It can be misleading to speak of *brahma*-attainment as a benefit or even to use 'attainment,' *prāpti* etc. in conveying the concept. It has been stated in many Indian sources that, in discussing *mokṣa, nirvāṇa* etc., the talk of attainment, movement etc. is only metaphorical. One must indulge in it and give the impression of progress from point *p*-1 to point *p*-2, because one cannot otherwise convey the goal associated with *mokṣa* etc. Further, anything like *brahma*-attainment comes as a benefit when all concern with benefits (or lack of them) on the part of the attainer has ceased.

[18] P p. I.3 line 22: *mahatā devena naḥ sāmyaṃ yathā syād ity adhyeyaṃ vyākaraṇaṃ.* "So that we will be the same as the Great God, we should study grammar."

Page I.4 lines 7–8: *vāṅ no vivṛṇuyād ātmānam ity adhyeyaṃ vyākaraṇam.* "So that the (Goddess) Speech should reveal herself to us, we should study grammar."

Page I.4 lines 14–17: ***atra sakhāyaḥ sakhyāni jānate.*** *sāyujyāni jānate. kutaḥ.* ***bhadraiṣāṃ lakṣmīr nihitādhi vāci.*** *eṣāṃ vāci bhadrā lakṣmīr nihitā bhavati.* "The meaning of the phrase *sakhyāni jānate* in the Vedic line *atrā sakhāyaḥ sakhyāni jānate*

("Here companions come to know companionship" is) 'they come to know that they are connected (at the source).' How so? (the other line in the same Vedic passage, namely *bhadraiṣāṃ lakṣmīr nihitādhi vāci* gives the reason.) The auspicious Excellence is placed (i.e., is to be found) in the speech of these (persons)."

Page I.5 lines 3–4; *satya-devāḥ syāmety adhyeyaṃ vyākaraṇam*. "So that we should be Truth-gods, we should study grammar."

[19] Cf. Vṛṣabha on Vṛtti 1.5: ***yathābhyudayasya*** *iti svargasya*. "The word *abhyudaya* in the V pharse *yathābhyudayasya* stands for 'a better other world, heaven.,"

[20] (a) Deshpande 1993: 99–100, referring to Palsule's translation of the MBT line *śabdāḥ smaryante abhyudayāya* as "(Correct) words are taught for worldly prosperity in the Smṛtis," remarks: "I would suggest that we not render the word *abhyudaya* by 'worldly prosperity.' Such a rendering brings in the contrast between the notions of *abhyudaya* 'worldly prosperity' versus *niḥśreyasa* 'spiritual prosperity' as seen in the works of Śaṅkara, such as the introduction to his Gīta-bhāṣya. This is a very late contrast and is intended neither in Bhartṛ-hari's work, nor in the works of Kātyāyana and Patañjali." Here, D does not tell us how the word *abhyudaya* should be rendered. As my discussion above shows, the *abhyudaya : niḥśreyasa*' contrast is unlikely to be very late. I agree with D, however, that 'worldly prosperity' does not capture the range of *abhyudaya*.

(b) Akamatsu 2000: 246, like D, puts forward the view that BH did not see a categorical separation between *abhyudaya* and *brahma-prāpti* (or *niḥśreyasa*) — that, for BH, *abhyudaya* was a stage on the way to *brahma-prāpti*. My response to this can be inferred from §§3.8–9.

[21] This sentence is echoed in Vṛṣabha on V 1.25d: *avasthita eva dharma-padārthaḥ, kevalaṃ jñānena prayogeṇa cābhivyajyate*. "The *dharma* entity is already there. It is only manifested by knowledge and use (of grammatical expressions)."

[22] The *eva* of the original, which usually signals emphasis or exclusion and is commonly rendered with words such as 'definitely, to be sure' or 'only, alone,' is best rendered in the present context with 'already.' Besides implying exclusion of newness or adventitious association, it captures the suggestion of being well-rooted or being firm that *ava* in *avasthita* has.

[23] Kataoka's important article became accessible to me through the kindness of Professors Ogawa and Tokunaga and Ms. Yoshie Kobayashi. As can be seen from what I write below, my approach to solving the issue is significantly different from his. In my view, it would have been better if he had left out the passages 3b, 3c and 6b, which he studies on pp. 170–171 and 175–176. His perception (p. 175, p. 177) that the structure behind the *abhivyakti* view could be parallel to the structure '*sāmānya : viśeṣa : vyakti*' seems problematic to me.

[24] In the rest of the present section, my bibliographic particulars should be understood as identical with the ones in Kataoka, 2000. The only exception to this would be the BH texts.

[25] Vṛṣabha on TK 1.30, p. 85, speaks of the same problem in another but parallel context: *na tāvad arthānāṃ abhyudaya-niṣpadana-śaktiḥ pratyakṣa-gamyā, tasyāḥ pratyakṣāgamyatvāt. kāryam api cāsyāḥ kālāntare, ity anumeyatāpi nāsti*. "To be sure, the ability of things to bring about elevation is not a matter of perception, for (the sheer or obvious fact) that it is not perceptible. Its effect also takes place at another time. Therefore, it is not a matter of inference either."

[26] (a) Such a linking would be compatible with BH's acceptance of the view that *mantras* can affect physical reality. There is unlikely to be a total separation in his world view of *dharma* as a physical force on the one hand and thoughts, sounds and actions as physical but non-inert entities on the other.

(b) For the view ascribed to BH in (a), see: TK V 1.33: *mantrauṣadhi-rasādibhir yogyeṣv api dravyeṣu dāhādikaṃ pratibadhyate*. "Even in the case of things that are amenable (to burning etc.), the actions such as burning are not allowed to take place through the employment of *mantra*, herbal extracts etc." Also, TK V 1.174: ... *mantrauṣadhādiṣu ca doṣa-pratīkāra-sāmarthyaṃ* ..., and TK 2.323 and its V.

27 Cf. *tat-preritas tu phalado bhavati* in the MBT passage cited above and the passages 3a, 3d and 6a from Uddyotakara and Siṃha-sūri-gaṇin cited in Kataoka, 2000: 170–171.

28 (a) A suggestion of my remark here is that the passage from Jayanta-bhaṭṭa's Nyāya-mañjarī, which has been used to determine the relative priority of the *abhivyakti* view vis-à-vis the *nirvartyatā* ('production, new creation') view should not have been used for that purpose. First of all, Jayanta does not use any form of *abhi + vi + añj*. Secondly, he gives us only the meanings different thinkers have assigned to *dharma* in the context of individual ritual acts. His intention is not to divide the Mīmāṃsakas into *abhivyakti-vādins* and *nirvartyatā-vādins* but to argue that certain referents of *dharma* are unjustifiable or problematic.
(b) It follows from (a) that the Nyāya-mañjarī passage should not be used to guess the relative chronology of Śabara and BH either.

29 Note TK V 1.14–22: *sādhu-prayogāc cābhivyakta-dharma-viśeṣo mahāntaṃ śabdātmānam abhisaṃbhavan* .... "(The spiritual aspirant) in whom an excellence of dharma is manifested due to grammatical usage, becoming one with the Great Śabdātman ..."

Note also, *tad-abhyāsāt* in TK V 1.144–147 which can grammatically stand only for *dharma-viśeṣābhyāsāt* or *abhyudayābhyāsāt*. As the latter depends on *dharma*-manifestation, it would, in effect, come to mean essentially the same thing as *dharma-viśeṣābhyāsāt*. Cf. Vṛṣabha: *evaṃ svargāṅgatām ākhyāya mokṣāṅgatām āha* ***tadabhyāsāc ceti****. punaḥ punaḥ prayogeṇa dharmābhyāsāt*. "Thus, having stated that *dharma* contributes to (the attainment/realization) of a better/heavenly world, (the V author or BH) says *tad-abhyāsāt*. (What he means by this expression is) because of the constant application of oneself to *dharma* through the employment (of grammatical expressions) again and again."

30 As I am not aware of any evidence in P's MB that would enable us to determine if he would have favored the *dharmābhivyakti* view or the *dharma-nirvartyatā* view, I have left him out of consideration in §§3.7–9.

31 P. I.4 lines 19–20: *āhitāgnir apaśabdaṃ prayujya prāyaścittīyaṃ sārasvatīm iṣṭim nirvapet*. "A person who has taken the vow to maintain the sacred fire (*āhitāgni*) should offer a relatively less elaborate rite (*iṣṭi*), having Sarasvatī as its deity and meant as a means of expiation, if he employs an ungrammatical expression." The *apaśabda* meant here must be a Vedic or *sādhu* Sanskrit word that was mispronounced.

32 In a passage repeated three times (p. I.2, 5, 10), P calls *gāvī* etc. *apabhraṃśas*. On p. 5, if the reading found in the present editions is genuine, he speaks of the same as *apaśabda*.

33 In the part I have not quoted at this point, D asserts that the Brahmin evaluation of Prakrit languages was so negative that it led even to a negative evaluation (a) of the speakers of Prakrits, (b) of the scriptures written in Prakrits and (c) of the religions practiced by the speakers of Prakrits.

34 The period presumed here starts from Pāṇni (not later than 5–4th century B.C.). It is not confined to the time of Puṣya-mitra Śuṅga (not later than 2nd century B.C.), who could be presumed to have provided sufficient resources to Brahmanism and Sanskrit. In the case of other powerful rulers of India belonging to the B.C. centuries we do not have even prima facie evidence of strong support to Brahmanism at the expense of Buddhism etc. In the case of Puṣya-mitra too, as far as I could determine, there is no evidence of any particular support for Sanskrit. The currently dominant

scholarly view, accepted by D too, is that the first Sanskrit inscriptions come from the early centuries of the Christian era, that is, long after Puṣya-mitra's rule.

[35] If my point is granted, 'coming out of Sanskrit' in this sentence should be replaced by 'existing or situated within a language continuum called Sanskrit.' Similarly, the qualification 'what *we* call' should be understood before 'non-Sanskrit,' 'Indo-Aryan' and 'Sanskrit.' Since the transcendence of duality, implicit in what I take to be P's way of looking at his contemporary linguistic situation, can be convyed only by using the products of duality, we must continue to use here designations such as 'Sanskrit' and 'Indo-Aryan.'

[36] Pischel refers to Pāli in the same section only for *āṇapayati, vāṭṭati, vaḍḍhati* and *supati* cited in the MB (following Kielhorn in the case of the last three forms). It is Bhandarkar (1877) who, on the basis of the *go*-variants and the forms cited just now, (rightly) concludes that P shows an awareness of a language like Pāli. It is worth noting that Bhandarkar, Kielhorn and Pischel do not assert that the language *is* Pāli. Nor does Bhandarkar attribute an awareness of Prakrits to P. An explicit statement to that effect is missing in Pischel too, although one may read such a statement in his attribution of *gāvī, goṇa* (the masculine counterpart of *goṇī*) and *āṇapayati* to Prakrit (not specifically to Ardha-māgadhī), Jaina Māhārāṣṭrī and the language of Aśoka's inscriptions, respectively.

[37] In Aklujkar, 2003, I point out that the process of creating a semi-natural canonical language through grafting seems to have taken place in the case of Sanskrit, Ardha-māgadhī and Pāli.

[38] Cf. BH, MBT, Abhyankar-Limaye 1967: 41–42 = Bronkhorst 1987: 34, 101, 139, Abhyankar-Limaye 1967: 108 = Palsule 1985: 12, 35, 126–127; Vṛṣabha on TK V 1.43 p. 100, TK V 1:171 p. 223; D 1993b:99.

[39] Cf. *na mlecchitavyaṃ yajñādau.* "One should not speak like a *Mleccha* in sacrificial worship etc.," appearing in a quotation found in Sāhitya-mīmāṃsā prakaraṇa 6, Trivandrum Sanskrit Series edition p. 94.

[40] D (1993b: 113–114) seeks to establish that BH's understanding of *śiṣṭa* was substantially different from that of P. I am not convinced that such indeed is the case. BH clearly thought of P (and Kātyāyana and Pāṇini) as *śiṣṭas*. His list of *śiṣṭas* would, therefore, be probably longer than P's. His interest in the *śiṣṭa* notion is more sustained and wider than P's. To this extent, I agree with D. However, I do not think that this implies a substantial or essential difference in BH's notion of *śiṣṭa* from that of P. One can argue for less mythification in P only if one plays down the presence of *daivānugraha* 'divine favor' that he has used in reference to the *śiṣṭas*. I see such down-playing taking place in D's discussion, without his being aware of it.

[41] D 1993b: 97 has 'who has never studied' as the translation of *anadhīyānam*, but D 1993: 28 has the correct translation 'who is not studying.'

[42] As indicated in §4.3 and as I will point out in a later study, P probably did not think in terms of dialects. Given his awareness of the Aṣṭādhyāyī's concern with Chandas, Bhāṣā etc., he is unlikely to have viewed the purpose of the Aṣṭādhyāyī as derivation of a single dialect.

[43] Related to what I have discussed so far is the question of whether P was viewed by the later Pāṇinīyas as being the last author in (the surviving part of) their tradition who had direct access to standard Sanskrit or to Sanskrit as a truly living language for the purpose of testing or expanding the coverage of the "Aṣṭādhyāyī" — whether they considered P to be the last accessible linguistic *śiṣṭa* for Sanskrit. I have dealt with this question in Aklujkar, 2004b, forthcoming.

[44] The reasons and the extent of the dislike, if any, remain unspecified for the early period. Because practically any guess would be as good as any other guess, a historian should proceed cautiously.

45 Let us leave the reasons out for the present, just as I have left out the possibility of there being differences in P's perspective and BH's perspective for convenience in taking the discussion ahead.
46 The grammarians of Sanskrit in P's or BH's time clearly did not have as many means and facilities as modern linguists. Therefore, even if they had thought of ambitious projects like the one I mention here, they would not been able to carry them out.
47 In TK V 1.5, *dāna* 'charity,' *tapas* 'austerities' and *brahmacarya* 'celibacy' are said to be the means of *abhyudaya*. The self-sacrifice which characterizes all these must have been associated with the other cause of *abhyudaya* with which we are dealing here, namely, cultivating grammatical speech. One could make the same deduction from the inclusion of the study of grammar in the best of austerities and *svādhyāyas* 'Vedic learning' in TK V 1.11.
48 On p. I.11, P shows three ways in which one can account for the fact that testimony does not associate *adharma* with *apaśabda-jñāna* while associating *dharma* with *śabda-jñāna*. The first way here is very much like the position taken in the *āhāra-nidrā* ... verse I have quoted in §6.7. The natural actions of coughing, laughing and scratching are said not to lead to any deficiency just as they do not lead to *abhyudaya* (cf. TK V 1.27: *aśiṣṭāpratiṣiddhāni ca hikkita-śvasita-kaṇḍūyitādīni* "Coughing, (heavy?) breathing, scratching etc. are neither recommended nor prohibited."). Then, moving from knowing *apaśabdas* to using *apaśabdas*, he unhesitatingly states that their use leads to *adharma* only in a sacrificial context (*yājne karmaṇi*).
49 That the skills which come with better technology or devices external to the individual are not meant here is implied by the context. We are concerned here with a human's cognitive development, not just with ability to operate machines etc.

REFERENCES

Abhyankar, K.V. (ed.) (1967). *Mahābhāṣya-dīpikā of Bhartṛ-hari*. Other editor: Viṣṇu Prabhākar Limaye. Poona: Bhandarkar Oriental Research Institute.

Abhyankar, K.V. (1969). *Patañjali's Vyākaraṇa-mahābhāṣya (Navāhnikīi); with English Translation and Notes*. Other author: Jayadev Mohanlal Shukla. [Poona Cultural Research and Publication Dept. of Sanskrit Vidya Parisamstha]. Vasudev Shastri Abhyankar Publication Series, serial no. 15.

Abhyankar, K.V. (1975). *Patañjali's Vyākaraṇa-mahābhāṣya ühnikas 1-3 with English Translation and Notes*. Other author: Jayadev Mohanlal Shukla. Pune: Bhandarkar Oriental Research Institute. Research Unit Publications, no. 1.

Akamatsu, A. (2000). *Abhyudaya* and *niḥśreyasa* in Bhartṛ-hari. In Mayeda 2000, pp. 235–247.

Aklujkar, A. (1989). Prāmāṇya in the philosophy of the grammarians. In A. Kumar, et al. (eds), *Studies in Indology: Professor Rasik Vihari Joshi Felicitation Volume* (pp.15–28). New Delhi: Shree Publishing House.

Aklujkar, A. (1991). Bhartṛhari's concept of the Veda. In J. Bronkhorst (ed.), *Panels of the VIIth World Sanskrit Conference*. Vol. IV–V (pp. 1-18). Leiden: E.J. Brill.

Aklujkar, A. (1996). The Early History of Sanskrit as Supreme Language. In Houben 1996a, pp. 69–85.

Aklujkar, A. (2003). A different sociolinguistics for Brahmins, Buddhists and Jains. In BhuDev Sharma (ed.), *Contemporary Views on Indian Civilization*. (pp. 54–69). India and USA: World Association for Vedic Studies.

Aklujkar, A. (2004a, forthcoming). Traditions of language study in South Asia. In *Language in South Asia*, being edited for Cambridge University Press by Professors Braj B. Kachru and S. Sridhar.

Aklujkar, A. (2004b, forthcoming). Where do *lakṣaṇaika-cakṣuṣka* and *lakṣyaika-cakṣuṣka* apply? *Bulletin of the Deccan College Post-Graduate Research Institute.* Professor A.R. Kelkar Felicitation Volume.

Aklujkar, A. (2004c, forthcoming). Veda revelation according to Bhartṛ-hari. In *Proceedings of the International Seminar on Language, Thought and Reality in Bhartṛ-hari.* Being edited by Professor V.N. Jha for Motilal Banarsidass, Delhi.

Bhandarkar, R.G. (1877). *Wilson Philological Lectures (on Sanskrit and the Derived Languages).* Poona: Bhandarkar Oriental Research Institute. 1929. *The Collected Works of R.G. Bhandarkar, vol. IV.* Reprint 1: Poona: Bhandarkar Oriental Research Institute. 1974. Reprint 2: New Delhi : Asian Educational Services, 1991.

Biardeau, M. (1964). (ed, tr.). *Vākyapadīya Brahmakāṇḍa avec la Vṛtti de Hari-vṛṣabha.* Paris: Éditions E. de Boccard. Publications de l'Institut de Civilisation Indienne. Série IN-8ß. Fascicule 24.

Bronkhorst, J. (1987). (ed., tr.) *Mahābhāṣya-dīpikā [= MBT]. Āhnika I.* Pune: Bhandarkar Oriental Research Institute, Post-Graduate and Research Department Series n°. 28, Fascicule IV.

Bronkhorst, J. (1996). Studies on Bhartṛ-hari 7: Grammar as the door to liberation. *Annals of the Bhandarkar Oriental Research Institute*, **76**, 97–106.

Bronkhorst, J. (1999). Why is there Philosophy in India? *1998 [Sixth] Gonda Lecture.* Amsterdam: Royal Netherlands Academy of Arts and Sciences.

Bronkhorst, J. (2001). Pourquoi la philosophie existe-te-elle en Inde? In J. Bronkhorst (ed.), *La Rationalité en Asie. Rationality in Asia.* Originally published in *Etudes de Lettres* 2001/3.

Deshpande, M.M. (1993a). *Sanskrit & Prakrit: Sociolinguistic Issues.* Delhi: Motilal Banarsidass.

Deshpande, M.M. (1993b). The changing notion of *śiṣṭa* from Patañjali to Bhartṛ-hari. *Asiatische Studien / Études Asiatiques* **37.1**, 95–115. Reprinted with the same pagination in the book *Bhartṛ-hari: Philosopher and Grammarian. Proceedings of the First International Conference on Bhartṛ-hari.* Edited by Saroja Bhate and Johannes Bronkhorst. Delhi: Motilal Banarsidass, 1994.

Gandhi, L.B. (ed.) (1927). *Apabhraṃśa-kāvya-trayī [by Jina-datta-sūri].* Baroda: Gaekwad's Oriental Series no. 37. Reprinted by the same publisher in 1967.

Helā-rāja. See Subramania Iyer (1963) and (1973).

Houben, J.E.M. (1995).*The Saṃbandha-samuddeśa (Chapter on Relation) and Bhartṛ-hari's Philosophy of Language. A Study of Bhartṛ-hari's Saṃbandha-samuddeśa in the Context of the Vākyapadīya, with a Translation of Helā-rāja's Commentary Prakīrṇa-prakāśa.* Groningen: Egbert Forsten. Gonda Indological Studies, volume II.

Houben, J.E.M. (1996a). (ed.) *Ideology and Status of Sanskrit: Contributions to the History of the Sanskrit Language.* Leiden, New York, Köln: E.J. Brill.

Houben, J.E.M. (1996b). Sociolinguistic attitudes reflected in the work of Bhartṛ-hari and some later grammarians. In Houben, 1996a, pp. 157–193.

Jha, S. See Pischel.

Joshi, S.D. (1986). *Patañjali's Vyākaraṇa-mahābhāṣya Paspaśāhnika. Introduction, Text, Translation and Notes.* Other author: J.A.F. Roodbergen. Pune: University of Poona. Publications of the Centre of Advanced Study in Sanskrit, class C, no. 15.

Kahrs, E.G. (1992). What is a *tad-bhava* word? *Indo-Iranian Journal,* **35**, 225–249.

Kataoka, K. (2000). Reconstructing the *Dharma-abhivyakti-vāda.* In S. Mayeda, 2000, pp. 170–177.

Mayeda, Sengaku. 2000. (ed.) *The Way to Liberation.*, Delhi: Manohar. Vol. 1 of Indological Studies in Japan and vol. 3 of Japanese Studies on South Asia.

Palsule, G.B. (1985). (ed., tr.) *Mahābhāṣya-dīpikā. Āhnika III*. Pune: Bhandarkar Oriental Research Institute, Post-Graduate and Research Department Series n°. 22, Fascicule I.

Pischel, R. (1900). *Die Grammatik der Prākrit Sprachen*. Strassburg: Verlag von Karl J. Trübner. Grundriss der Indo-Arischen Philologie und Altertumskunde (Encyclopedia of Indo-Aryan Research), Begründet von G. Bühler, fortgesetz von F. Kielhorn. I. Band, 8. Heft. Reprint 1977: Tokyo: Meicho-Fukyū-kai. English translation 1965. *Comparative Grammar of the Prakrit. Languages* by Subhadra Jha. Delhi: Motilal Banarsidass. A second revised edition of this translation was published by the same publisher in 1981. A reprint, probably of the second revised edition, by the same publisher is reported to have appeared in 1999.

Puṇya-rāja. See Subramania Iyer (1983).

Rau, W. (1977). *Bhartṛ-hari's Vākyapadīya. Die Mūla-kārikās nach den Handschriften herausgegeben und mit einem Pāda-Index versehen*. Wiesbaden: Kommissionsverlag Franz Steiner GMBH. Abhandlungen für die Kunde des Morgenlandes (Monograph Series of the Deutsche Morgenländische Gesellschaft) no. XLII, 4.

Subramania Iyer, K.A. (1963). *Vākyapadīya of Bhartṛ-hari with the Commentary of Helā-rāja. Kāṇḍa III, Part 1 [Samudeśas 1–7]*. Poona: Deccan College. Deccan College Monograph Series. No. 21.

Subramania Iyer, K.A. (1964a). Bhartṛ-hari on Vyākaraṇa as a Means of Attaining Mokṣa. *Adyar Library Bulletin* 28.112–131. [Reprinted in *Proceedings of the Twenty-sixth International Congress of Orientalists* (pp. 238–245). New Delhi, January 4–10, 1964. Vol. III, part I, Poona, 1969.

Subramania Iyer, K.A. (1964b). Bhartṛ-hari on Apabhraṃśa. *Vishveshvarananda Indological Journal*, **2**, 242–46.

Subramania Iyer, K.A. (1965). *The Vākyapadīya of Bhartṛ-hari with the Vṛtti. Chapter I, English Translation,* Poona: Deccan College Building Centenary & Silver Jubilee Series 26.

Subramania Iyer, K.A. (1966). *Vākyapadīya of Bhartṛ-hari with the Vṛtti and the Paddhati of Vṛṣabha-deva*. Poona: Deccan College Postgraduate and Research Institute. Deccan College Monograph Series 32.

Subramania Iyer, K.A. (1973). *Vākyapadīya of Bhartṛ-hari with the Prakīrṇaka-prakāśā of Helā-rāja. Kāṇḍa III, Part II [Samudeśas 8–14]*. Poona: Deccan College. [Continuation of Deccan College Monograph Series no. 21?].

Subramania Iyer, K.A. (1983). *The Vākyapadīya of Bhartṛ-hari, Kāṇḍa II with the Commentary of Puṇya-rāja and the Ancient Vṛtti*. Delhi, etc: Motilal Banarsidass.

Vṛṣabha: *Paddhati* or *Sphuṭākṣarā*. See Subramania Iyer (1966).

Yoshimizu, K. 2000. Change of view on *apūrva* from *Śabara-svāmin* to *Kumārila*. In Mayeda, 2000, pp. 149–165.

ABBREVIATION

D	Deshpande, Madhav M.
MB	*Vyākaraṇa-Mahābhāṣya*. See P.
MBT	*Mahābhāṣya-ṭīkā,* published under the title *Mahābhāṣya-dīpikā*. See Abhyankar-Limaye 1967, Bronkhorst 1987, Palsule 1985.

P Patañjali. *Vyākaraṇa-mahābhāṣya*. Ed. F. Kielhorn. 1980–1985. Revised third ed. K.V. Abhyankar. Pune: Bhandarkar Oriental Research Institute.

TK *Trikāṇḍī*. See Rau, Subramania Iyer.

V *Vṛtti*. See Subramania Iyer (1966) and (1983).

Department of Asian Studies,
University of British Columbia,
Vancouver, B.C.
Canada V6T 1Z2
E-mail: aklujkar@interchange.ubc.ca

JOHANNES BRONKHORST

SOME USES OF DHARMA IN CLASSICAL INDIAN PHILOSOPHY

The word *dharma* is used in a variety of meanings. In philosophical parlance it is mainly used in two totally different ways, which one might call the Buddhist and the Brahmanical way. This article will briefly present the way in which the Buddhists came to use the term (usually in the plural), then sketch the development which the Brahmanical concept of dharma (singular) underwent in the hands of the adherents of the Vaiśeṣika philosophy.

With regard to Buddhism we can be brief.[1] The word *dharma* here came to be used for the items collected in lists in what is known by the name Abhidharma. These lists may originally have contained no more than items considered important to be memorized, often mental states. For our present purposes all that counts is that when at last one of the Buddhist schools decided to put order into the inherited teachings, it promoted the items thus collected, the dharmas, to the status of being the ultimate, and only, constituents of all that exists.

This revision, which amounted to a philosophical revolution, apparently took place in the north-west of the Indian subcontinent, at some time during the centuries preceding the common era, and the outcome was primarily preserved in the texts of the Sarvāstivāda school of Abhidharma. This intellectual revolution did more than just turn dharmas into elements of existence. It imposed a thoroughly atomistic vision on common sense reality, thus reducing the latter to non-existence. All complex entities – which includes virtually everything that we are familiar with from experience – were stated to be non-existent, precisely because they were nothing beyond their constituent elements. The impetus to this radical rejection of common sense reality must have come from the Buddhist doctrine according to which no person exists. What we believe is a person is made up of numerous mental and physical states, precisely the things known as dharmas.[2] That is to say, the person does not exist, but the elements that constitute it do. Or more explicitly: the person does not exist because it is complex; its ultimate constituent elements on the other hand do exist. The same reasoning was applied to other things that have constituent elements.

It will be clear that this kind of logic inevitably leads to the conclusion that only dharmas exist, and that these dharmas cannot themselves harbour constitutive elements. That is to say, the dharmas are irreducible and are for that reason the ultimate constituents of the things that make up phenomenal reality. Strictly speaking the dharmas are the only things that exist, for the objects of phenomenal reality, being made up of more elementary constituents, do not.

Seen in this way, the ontological position of the Buddhist dharmas can easily be defined: they are the only things that really exist. The Sarvāstivādins had more to say about their dharmas, to be sure. Their thoroughly atomistic approach led them to another postulate: the dharmas are momentary. They also made an effort to enumerate all dharmas in an exhaustive list and to categorize them. They went to the extent of deviating from traditional forms of categorization and introducing a new system, called Pañcavastuka, which far more comprehensively summarized all the dharmas in five categories.[3] Nor did they hesitate to introduce newly invented dharmas which they felt were required to arrive at a coherent vision of the world. All this led them into sometimes frighteningly complex arguments, which have the unfortunate tendency of obscuring from view the overall vision that is hidden behind it.

This particular understanding of the dharmas as elements of existence, the only things that really exist, characterizes later developments in Buddhist thought, even in philosophical developments (such as the Madhyamaka philosophy) that came to reject the existence of the dharmas. The position of these latter, called *dharmanairātmya* "non-reality of the dharmas", amounts to a radical denial of all that exists, a position in which even the last remaining anchors in reality, i.e. the dharmas, are removed. In an important way the denial of the dharmas was a continuation of the original denial of empirical reality that characterized the postulation of dharmas as the only existing entities. The denial of composite objects and personalities justified, all by itself, statements of the kind that no Buddha exists or has ever existed, which we find, for example, in the Buddhist Prajñāpāramitā literature. Denying the existence of the dharmas hardly sounds radical in a Buddhism that has already denied the existence of its founder.

Within the Brahmanical philosophies the word dharma is not used as in Buddhism. Fundamentally dharma is here something like 'merit'.

As such there is nothing noteworthy in the concept of dharma in the Brahmanical philosophical systems. Some of these – first of all the Vaiśeṣika – tried to specify the concept. This led to the developments which will be outlined here.

Dharma occupies a prominent position in the *Vaiśeṣika Sūtra*. This text begins with the announcement that dharma will be explained (*athāto dharmaṃ vyākhyāsyāmaḥ*). This suggests that dharma plays a fundamental role in this school of thought. However, when we consider this philosophy in its classical form, we find that dharma is not so fundamental after all.

The classical doctrine of Vaiśeṣika finds expression in Praśasta's *Padārthadharmasaṅgraha*, also known by the name *Praśastapādabhāṣya*. This text divides all that exists into six categories, called 'substance' (*dravya*), 'quality' (*guṇa*), 'activity' (*karman*), 'universal' (*sāmānya*), 'specificity' (*viśeṣa*) and 'inherence' (*samavāya*) respectively. It states that knowledge of the essence of these categories, through the similarities and differences between them, is the cause of the highest good.[4] Dharma and its opposite and companion adharma are classified among the qualities; they are qualities that can only reside in a single substance, 'soul' (*ātman*), not in other substances.

Dharma and adharma are not the only qualities that can reside only in the soul. The text provides a complete list of such qualities: knowledge (*buddhi*), pleasure (*sukha*), pain (*duḥkha*), desire (*icchā*), repulsion (*dveṣa*), effort (*prayatna*), dharma and adharma;[5] subliminal impressions (*saṃskāra*) might be included in this list, even though other aspects of saṃskāra allow it to reside in other substances as well. Together, these qualities of the soul account for the psychological functioning of a person. Knowledge, which is experience, causes pleasure or pain; these give rise to desire and repulsion, respectively. Desire and repulsion bring about effort (*prayatna*), which in its turn brings about bodily activities aiming to reestablish or avoid the sources of pleasure and pain, respectively. This leads to new experiences, etc. etc. A further effect of these activities is the production of dharma and adharma, which determine one's future state. Correct knowledge, which is primarily knowledge of the Vaiśeṣika philosophy, will free a person from passion, as a result of which in the end no more dharma and adharma will be produced and liberation from rebirth will be obtained.[6] Dharma and adharma obviously play some kind of intermediary role in all this. Dharma in particular can help a person some way in the direction of final liberation, but not all the way, for all the remaining dharma has to be consumed before liberation can take place. That is to say: the soul quality called dharma is an important causal factor with respect to liberation,[7] but it would not be justified to say that dharma, or knowledge of dharma, brings it about. Yet this is what the *Vaiśeṣika Sūtra* appears to say, as we will see below. For the *Padārthadharmasaṅgraha*, as we have seen, the cause of the highest good, i.e. of liberation, is knowledge of the Vaiśeṣika categories. It is true that this knowledge has to follow a number of preparatory conditions, which are described in some detail in the text; this does not change the fact that the clinching element is knowledge.

There is one passage in the *Padārthadharmasaṅgraha* which appears to use the word *dharma* in a way that differs from its classical usage. This passage reads:[8]

(1) *dravyaguṇakarmasāmānyaviśeṣasamavāyānāṃ ṣaṇṇāṃ padārthānāṃ sādharmyavaidharmyābhyāṃ tattvajñānaṃ niḥśreyasahetuḥ / tac ceśvaracodanābhivyaktād dharmād eva* / (WI p. 1 Section 2)
Knowledge of the essence of the six categories – viz. substance (*dravya*), quality (*guṇa*), activity (*karman*), universal (*sāmānya*), specificity (*viśeṣa*) and inherence (*samavāya*) – , by way of the similarity and dissimilarity [between them], is the cause of the highest good. That [knowledge comes about] as a result of dharma that is manifested through the injunctions of the Lord."

The last part of this passage is not free from difficulties. If we assume that here, too, *dharma* designates the quality of the soul described above, how then are we supposed to understand that liberating knowledge can only result from dharma which is manifested through the injunctions of the Lord? What could it mean that this specific quality of the soul is manifested through the injunctions of the Lord? Does God utter injunctions to the effect that dharma that is already present in a soul must manifest itself? The *Padārthadharmasaṅgraha* contains no hint suggesting that any such manifestations of dharma ever take place. And the early commentators do not provide help either.

There is however an obvious answer to these questions, if only we are willing to look outside the Vaiśeṣika system. *Mīmāṃsā-sūtra* 1.1.2 defines dharma as follows: *codanālakṣaṇo 'rtho dharmaḥ*. Frauwallner (1968: 17) translates this: "Der Dharmaḥ ist etwas Nützliches, dessen Kennzeichen die (vedischen) Weisungen sind." In other words: dharma is *characterized* by *codanā* in the *Mīmāṃsā Sūtra*, just as it is *manifested* by *codanā* in the *Padārthadharmasaṅgraha*. This strongly suggests that Praśasta here uses the term *dharma* as it was used in Mīmāṃsā, and not as he uses it everywhere else in his *Padārthadharmasaṅgraha*. That is to say, *dharma* in this passage of the *Padārthadharmasaṅgraha* does not refer to the classical Vaiśeṣika idea of dharma, a quality of the soul, but to the Mīmāṃsā idea of dharma. It is true that Praśasta adds one word to mark his difference from the Mīmāṃsā position. He prefixes the word *īśvara* 'God' to *codanā*, thus indicating that he, unlike the Mīmāṃsakas, looks upon Vedic injunctions as coming from God. This by itself is not surprising, because Praśasta appears to have been one of the first, if not the first, to introduce the notion of a creator God into the Vaiśeṣika system.[9]

This different use of the term *dharma* in one single passage of the *Padārthadharmasaṅgraha* suggests that the new Vaiśeṣika understanding of dharma as a quality of the soul replaced an earlier one, within the Vaiśeṣika school itself, that was close to, or identical with, the Mīmāṃsā idea of dharma. The present passage would then preserve a trace of this earlier usage.

Various considerations confirm the view that the classical Vaiśeṣika understanding of dharma as a quality of the soul represents a change of doctrine within the school that had taken place at some time before Praśasta but after its earliest beginnings. Consider the following:

(a) The way in which the *Padārthadharmasaṅgraha* presents the qualities, and dharma in particular, allows us to conclude that much had changed between the time of the *Vaiśeṣika Sūtra* (since the surviving text has undergone various modifications, the expression "time of the *Vaiśeṣika Sūtra*" is imprecise) and that of Praśasta. The *Padārthadharmasaṅgraha* initially cites *Vaiśeṣika-sūtra* 1.1.5, which enumerates seventeen qualities.[10] Dharma and adharma do not figure among these. The *Padārthadharmasaṅgraha* then adds seven more qualities (which cover dharma and adharma, see below), which it claims are covered in the sūtra by the particle ca. It seems safe to conclude that the *Vaiśeṣika Sūtra* known to Praśasta did not yet include dharma among the qualities. The same is true of all its surviving versions.

(b) The *Padārthadharmasaṅgraha* says that it enumerates seven additional qualities, but in fact it enumerates only six items: heaviness (*gurutva*), fluidity (*dravatva*), viscosity (*sneha*), *saṃskāra* (no single translation is possible; see Kapani (1992–1993: I: 277) ff.), 'the unseen' (*adṛṣṭa*) and sound (*śabda*).[11] The solution to this riddle lies in the fact that the single item *adṛṣṭa* stands for the two qualities dharma and adharma, as is clear from other passages in the same book: the enumeration of qualities of the soul, for example, does include *dharma* and *adharma* rather than *adṛṣṭa*[12] and *dharma* and *adharma* are sometimes used to refer back to *adṛṣṭa*[13]. *Adṛṣṭa* is a term that occurs a number of times in the *Vaiśeṣika Sūtra*, primarily in the fifth chapter, most often to explain physical processes: "adṛṣṭa moves objects in ordeals and magnetic processes; it causes extraordinary movements of earth and water, the circulation of water in trees, the upward flaming of fire, the horizontal blowing of wind or air, the initial movements of atoms and 'minds' (*manas*, in the process of forming new organisms)" (Halbfass, 1991: 311). Halbfass (1991: 312 f.) further points out that the *Vaiśeṣika Sūtra* nowhere states that adṛṣṭa and dharma / adharma are identical, nor that they are different. He draws attention to the fact that the *Nyāya Bhāṣya* of Vātsyāyana knows dharma and adharma as being inherent in the soul, but does not use the term *adṛṣṭa* as a synonym for these two. This term is here rather used with reference to a theory that is rejected and that maintains that there is adṛṣṭa in the material atoms (*aṇu*), as well as in the 'mind' (*manas*),[14] and that gives them the kinetic impulse needed for the formation of bodies and so on. Also the commentator Vyomaśiva on the *Padārthadharmasaṅgraha* is acquainted with, and rejects, the theory that adṛṣṭa resides in atoms and not in the soul. Halbfass (1991: 315) assumes that adṛṣṭa "may primarily have been a gapfiller in the causal explication of the universe".[15] We may conclude that the classical notions of dharma and adharma as qualities of the soul absorbed the notion of adṛṣṭa which was initially different from these two.

It is clear from the above that the *Vaiśeṣika Sūtra* as known to Praśasta, just like the versions known to us today, did not count dharma and adharma among the qualities. And yet dharma plays a central role in the first three sūtras of this text,[16] which read as follows (for an interpretation, see below):

(i) *athāto dharmaṃ vyākhyāsyāmaḥ*
(ii) *yato 'bhyudayaniḥśreyasasiddhiḥ sa dharmaḥ*
(iii) *tadvacanād āmnāyasya prāmāṇyam*[17]

Sūtra (i) announces that dharma will be explained, presumably in the remainder of the *Vaiśeṣika Sūtra*; sūtra (ii) adds that on the basis of dharma one reaches *abhyudaya* and *niḥśreyasa* (to be understood as residence in Brahmaloka and liberation respectively, according to the commentator Candrānanda); while sūtra (iii) appears to state that the Veda is authoritative because it teaches dharma.[18] The dharma taught by the Veda is not, of course, the quality of the soul accepted by later Vaiśeṣikas. It must be something very similar to the dharma which the Mīmāṃsakas believed was taught in the Veda. And indeed, if we assume that Praśasta's characterization of dharma as *īśvaracodanābhivyakta* 'manifested by the injunctions of the Lord' continues an earlier Vaiśeṣika tradition, we can conclude that early Vaiśeṣika shared in most essential respects its notion of dharma with ritual Mīmāṃsā.[19]

This does not necessarily entail that all occurrences of the word *dharma* in the *Vaiśeṣika Sūtra* have to be interpreted as in Mīmāṃsā. One should never forget that the *Vaiśeṣika Sūtra* is not the unitary composition of one single individual. Already before the time of Praśasta, this text had undergone numerous modifications. There is, for example, reason to think that sūtras had been added and that their original order had been changed.[20] It is not therefore impossible that the new meaning of *dharma* manifests itself already in some parts of the *Vaiśeṣika Sūtra* as we know it. At some places (VS(C) 4.2.5: *dharmaviśeṣāt*; 6.2.18: *icchādveṣapūrvikā dharmādharmayoḥ pravṛttiḥ*) one has indeed the impression that *dharma*, already in the surviving *Vaiśeṣika Sūtra*, is used in its classical sense, referring to a quality of the soul. This merely suggests that the new meaning of *dharma*, its understanding as a quality of the soul, had been introduced into Vaiśeṣika already before Praśasta. Unfortunately no evidence is known to me that would allow us to determine with more precision exactly when this change may have taken place.

How is the term *dharma* used in Mīmāṃsā? We have already seen that dharma is "characterized by injunctions (*codanā*)" (*Mīmāṃsāsūtra* 1.1.2). Beyond this, the *Mīmāṃsā Bhāṣya* of Śabara, the classical text for this school of Vedic interpretation, says remarkably little about it. Indeed, while introducing sūtra 1.1.2 Śabara states that experts have varying opinions as to what is dharma.[21] Sūtra 1.1.2 (*codanālakṣaṇo 'rtho dharmaḥ*; see above) is meant to resolve this issue. Dharma is what one gets to know through Vedic revelation, which consists in injunctions. What do we learn through these injunctions? Primarily what activities – sacrificial activities – lead to heaven. The intermediary between a sacrifice and heaven (which is reached long after the termination of the sacrifice) is represented by the mysterious apūrva, which guarantees the connection between the two. Dharma, apūrva and codanā are closely connected, and in one passage Śabara states in so many words that one speaks about codanā to indicate apūrva.[22] Elsewhere he identifies dharma with 'the Agnihotra etc.', i.e., with ritual activity.[23] A passage in Jayanta Bhaṭṭa's *Nyāyamañjarī* observes that the old Mīmāṃsakas identify dharma with apūrva which is without substratum (*nirādhāra*) and is produced by ritual activity, whereas the followers of Śabara identify it with ritual activity itself.[24] Yoshimizu (2000: 163 n. 27) – drawing attention to a passage in the Śābara Bhāṣya on sūtra 2.1.1 where dharma and apūrva are identified – points out that Śabara, measured by Jayanta's criteria, is an 'old Mīmāṃsaka" rather than a "follower of Śabara". An analysis of Śabara's observations, on the other hand, seems to suggest that he may think of apūrva as having a special connection with or even as inhering in the human soul.[25]

Halbfass (1991: 302, 334 n. 46), who draws attention to the abovementioned passage of the *Nyāyamañjarī*, also refers to some passages in other works where *apūrva* is supposedly a synonym of *dharma*. Not all these passages do however provide evidence for the presumed identification of dharma and apūrva in early Mīmāṃsā. Neither of the two passages from Bhartṛhari's *Vākyapadīya* which he refers to makes this identification. The first one (Vkp 3.7.34) does use the word *apūrva*, but does not mention *dharma*; the second (Vkp 3.8.37) uses neither of these two terms. The commentator Phullarāja on the first of these two verses[26] explains that, according to some, apūrva is identical with dharma / adharma and with adṛṣṭa.[27] The identification of dharma / adharma with adṛṣṭa suggests that Phullarāja does not here introduce us to "an old Mīmāṃsā theory of apūrva", but to the classical Vaiśeṣika doctrine of dharma / adharma, with as added peculiarity that now apūrva is said to be the same as the Vaiśeṣika qualities of the soul known by those names.

Uddyotakara's *Nyāya Vārttika* on *Nyāya-sūtra* 1.1.7, too, uses the term *apūrva* as a synonym of *dharma* and *adharma*.[28] As in the case of Phullarāja, this suggests that we are here confronted with a new interpretation of apūrva, which identifies it with the new Vaiśeṣika qualities of the soul called *dharma* and *adharma*. However, Uddyotakara is acquainted with a position which looks upon apūrva, and dharma and adharma, as being eternal. This eternal apūrva is supposedly manifested by people:[29] "Although apūrva is [one and] eternal, [only] the person who makes [it] manifest has [its] fruit. And ritual act is [done] for the sake of manifestation. And because it is [done] for manifestation, ritual act is not left unperformed. [For] it is seen that whatever is manifested gives its fruit only to the one who manifests it." Kei Kataoka (2000) has recently argued that the notion of dharma as an eternal entity that is made manifest as a result of sacrificial activity was current among certain Mīmāṃsakas, and was at least sometimes identified with apūrva. Such a notion appears to be attributed to the Mīmāṃsakas by authors as diverse as Bharthari (commentary on the *Mahābhāṣya*),[30] the author of the *Vṛtti* on Bhartṛhari's *Vākyapadīya*,[31] Siṃhasūri the commentator of Mallavādin's *Dvādaśāra-Nayacakra*[32] and of course Uddyotakara. Also the chapter on Mīmāṃsā in Bhavya's *Madhyamakahṛdaya* mentions apūrva and describes it as "to be manifested by [ritual] action".[33] His auto-commentary *Tarkajvālā*, moreover, identifies apūrva with dharma.[34] Kataoka concludes from all this evidence that the theory which he calls *dharma-abhivyakti-vāda* must go back to the latter half of the 6th century.

It seems, then, that early Mīmāṃsā had rather hazy ideas about the precise nature of dharma. Later on, at least in part under the influence of classical Vaiśeṣika , it tried in various ways to give a more precise meaning to this originally imprecise term.

We have seen that the ontological concerns of the Vaiśeṣika school of thought made them specify what exactly dharma is. In doing so, they ended up with a notion of dharma as a quality of the soul, a notion which, as a result of this transformation, had moved a long way from the Mīmāṃsā understanding of this term which they started from. Mīmāṃsakas after Śabara were not uninterested in the new qualities dharma and adharma. It appears, indeed, that Brahmanical thinkers of the time felt pressed to specify what kind of thing dharma really is. Where earlier thinkers of the Vaiśeṣika and Mīmāṃsā schools used the term *dharma* in a rather general sense – expressing something perhaps not too dissimilar to English 'virtue, merit, appropriateness' – later thinkers of these two schools felt obliged to specify its precise ontological status. In the case of Vaiśeṣika this is not surprising, for ontology has been a central concern of this school, perhaps from the beginning; the presence of an important element in its philosophy (*dharma* is mentioned in its first sūtra) whose ontological status was less than clear posed a challenge which the school had to come to grips with. Mīmāṃsā was perhaps under less pressure; yet it did not escape from the ontological concerns of its fellow philosophers.

By way of conclusion some few words can be said about the other classical schools of Brahmanical philosophy. Sāṃkhya – which here includes the so-called Yoga philosophy – underwent a strong influence of Vaiśeṣika in matters psychological, but its efforts to precisely define what kind of thing dharma was did not lead to noteworthy results. Dharma and adharma are explained as parts of buddhi, one of the evolutes of primary matter (*pradhāna*); the constraints of the system hardly allowed for another possibility. The Yuktidīpikā, for example, describes dharma as follows:[35] "The disposition which is part of [the constituent called] sattva, and which resides in the buddhi as a result of carrying out acts that have been prescribed in the Veda and in the sacred tradition, is called *dharma*." The so-called Vedānta philosophy presents itself as a better form of Mīmāṃsā, but one which, unlike ritual Mīmāṃsā, does not study dharma but Brahma. *Brahma-sūtra* 1.1.1 reads *athāto brahmajijñāsā*, which is an adaptation of *Mīmāṃsā-sūtra* 1.1.1 *athāto dharmajijñāsā*. The Śārīraka Mīmāṃsā – later also called Uttara-Mīmāṃsā – builds in an essential way on ritual Mīmāṃsā, to which it has left the study of dharma; it can now concentrate on Brahma. Dharma does not therefore play as crucial a role in it.

APPENDIX

The following passage occurs, as we have seen, in the Padārthadharmasaṅgraha:

(1) *dravyaguṇakarmasāmānyaviśeṣasamavāyānāṃ ṣaṇṇāṃ padārthānāṃ sādharmyavaidharmyābhyāṃ tattvajñānaṃ niḥśreyasahetuḥ / tac ceśvaracodanābhivyaktād dharmād eva* / (WI p. 1 Section 2)

It is not possible to seriously discuss this passage without taking into consideration passage (2), which is a sūtra in one of the surviving versions of the *Vaiśeṣika Sūtra*:

(2) *dharmaviśeṣaprasūtād dravyaguṇakarmasāmānyaviśeṣasamavāyānāṃ padārthānāṃ sādharmyavaidharmyābhyāṃ tattvajñānān niḥśreyasam* (VS(Ś) 1.1.4)

This is sūtra 1.1.4 in the version of the *Vaiśeṣika Sūtra* commented upon by Śaṅkara Miśra. It does not occur in the other surviving versions of this text.[36] We will refer to it as "the fourth sūtra".

The similarity between (1) and (2) is undeniable, and we have to accept that the two did not come into existence independently of each other. The question is: Which one influenced, and therefore preceded, the other?

Erich Frauwallner (1984: 39) argued that 'the fourth sūtra' (2) was composed under the influence of *Padārthadharmasaṅgraha* passage (1). He further argued that 'the fourth sūtra' (2) is indispensible after the three sūtras that precede it, and must therefore be accepted as belonging in their company, in spite of the fact that it has only been preserved in the version commented upon by Śaṅkara Miśra. These four initial sūtras, Frauwallner argued, must have been composed after the original character of Vaiśeṣika had been modified around the time of Praśasta. The original beginning of the *Vaiśeṣika Sūtra* was different, and Frauwallner makes an attempt to reconstruct it.

Frauwallner's arguments that original Vaiśeṣika was not interested in concepts like liberation and that such ideas, along with the idea of a creator God, did not enter the system until around the time of Praśasta, have found little favour among more recent scholars. Halbfass (1986, 1992: 69 f.) has described Frauwallner's thesis about the "original beginning" of the *Vaiśeṣika Sūtra* as "challenging, but not convincing". Houben (1994) criticizes Frauwallner's position according to which originally Vaiśeṣika was a pure philosophy of nature without interest in liberation. This implies that the beginning of the *Vaiśeṣika Sūtra* may have been as it is today, already before the time of Praśasta.

This raises the question whether 'the fourth sūtra' may be older than Praśasta. This question is to be distinguished from the other one as to whether "the fourth sūtra" is inseparable from the three initial sūtras of the *Vaiśeṣika Sūtra*. If it is inseparable from those three, the 'fourth sūtra' must be as old as the other ones, and therefore older than Praśasta. But it may conceivably be older than Praśasta without being inseparable from the three initial sūtras. It may conceivably have existed as part of a commentary, or as a sūtra that was added long after the first three but still before Praśasta. The question as to how old the 'fourth sūtra' is must therefore be considered on its own, independently of speculations about its connection with other sūtras.

Isaacson (1995a: 234) is of the opinion that "... there is no good reason to regard the sūtra as old". In another publication (1995b: 757 n. 22) he criticizes Frauwallner: "Frauwallner's keen philological instinct may perhaps have erred ... It is precisely the absence of the expected enumeration of categories which is likely to be original here.

Indeed an enumeration of six categories would be suspect, for I think it very likely that in the *earliest* period of composition of sūtras the classical list of padārthas had not yet been settled on." This last argument may be valid, and would show that the "fourth sūtra" cannot have belonged to the earliest period of composition of sūtras. This does not however help us all that much, for passages that existed before Praśasta do not for that reason necessarily belong to the earliest period of Vaiśeṣika. There is indeed some reason to think that Praśasta, if he knew passage (2) at all, did not recognize it as a sūtra, this because Praśasta normally clearly indicates that he considers something a sūtra.[37] He might then have cited it to justify (1). This does not exclude the possibility that (2) had once been a sūtra that, because of its length, came to be looked upon as part of a commentary.[38] We here find ourselves in the midst of speculations from among which the available evidence does not allow us to make a sensible choice.

Let us look somewhat more closely at passages (1) and (2). Both agree that knowledge of the essence of the Vaiśeṣika categories is the cause of the highest good. Both agree that this knowledge results from dharma. According to the *Padārthadharmasaṅgraha* this dharma is "manifested by the injunctions of the Lord" (Jha, 1915/1982: 16). The "fourth sūtra" (2) merely states that this dharma is special (*dharmaviśeṣa*).

An important difference between the two passages is that the former recognizes a creator God where the latter does not. It is known that the notion of a creator God entered Vaiśeṣika rather late (Bronkhorst, 1996). However, if one accepts the obvious, viz., that passages (1) and (2) are not independent of each other, it will be difficult to conclude from this that the 'fourth sūtra' (2) was composed under the influence of passage (1). As far as our knowledge of the development of Vaiśeṣika goes, the idea of a creator God was accepted by all subsequent texts of the school, certainly by all those that based themselves on the *Padārthadharmasaṅgraha*. It is hard to believe that the author of the 'fourth sūtra' – assuming that he composed this sūtra under the influence of the *Padārthadharmasaṅgraha* – could leave out God and simply speak of a special dharma (*dharmaviśeṣa*). Influence in the opposite direction – the passage in the *Padārthadharmasaṅgraha* was composed under the influence of the 'fourth sūtra' (2) – avoids this difficulty.

This position is confronted with one difficulty. We had occasion to observe that the word *dharma* in passage (1) is closer to Mīmāṃsā and early Vaiśeṣika usage than to the classical Vaiśeṣika use of this term. The "fourth sūtra" (2), on the other hand, would seem to use the term in a way which agrees with classical Vaiśeṣika . The compound dharmaviśeṣa occurs several times in the *Padārthadharmasaṅgraha*,[39] but does not appear to be used in Mīmāṃsā.[40] Is this proof that the 'fourth sūtra' must be more recent than passage (1)?

It is not. We saw that passage (1) uses the word *dharma* archaically and is therefore something of an anachronism in the *Padārthadharmasaṅgraha*. We concluded from it that the classical meaning of *dharma* may have been introduced into Vaiśeṣika before Praśasta. The classical use of *dharma* in the 'fourth sūtra' does not therefore prove anything regarding its age.

If, then, we are forced to choose between these two possibilities: either the *Padārthadharmasaṅgraha* passage (1) influenced the "fourth sūtra" (2), or vice-versa, we may have to consider the second possibility as the more likely. The 'fourth sūtra' may be older than the *Padārthadharmasaṅgraha*, and Praśasta may have known it, even if not as a sūtra. It is true that we may not be forced to make such a choice. The similarity between these two passages might be due to the fact that both were influenced by an earlier common source. Either way, it seems unlikely that the "fourth sūtra" was composed under the influence of passage (1).

NOTES

1 The section on Buddhist dharmas heavily draws upon Bronkhorst (2000a).
2 Cp. Gethin's understanding of dharma as "an instance of one of the fundamental physical or mental events that interact to produce the world as we experience it" (Wijeratne & Gethin, 2002: xix).
3 See Frauwallner (1963/1995).
4 The passage (WI p. 1 Section 2) is cited below.
5 WI p. 16 Section 80: tasya (=*ātmanaḥ*) *guṇāḥ buddhisukhaduḥkhecchādveṣaprayatnadharmādharmasaṃskārasaṃkhyāparimāṇapṛthaktvasaṃyogavibhāgāḥ*. The remaining qualities of this list can also occur in other substances.
6 Bronkhorst (2000b: Section 4, Section 6)
7 Cp. WI p. 63 Section 308: *kartuḥ priyahitamokṣahetuḥ [dharmaḥ]*.
8 Some editions omit *ṣaṇṇāṃ* others read *sādharmyavaidharmyatattvajñānaṃ*; some again have °*nodanā*° for °*codanā*°.
9 Bronkhorst (1996).
10 WI p. 1 Section 5: *guṇāś ca rūparasagandhasparśasaṃkhyāparimāṇapṛthaktvasaṃyogavibhāgaparatvāparatvabuddhisukhaduḥkhecchādveṣaprayatnāś ceti kaṇṭhoktāḥ saptadaśa*. (Some editions omit the first ca, one omits °saṃkhyā°, another one iti.) Compare this with VS(C) 1.1.5: *rūparasagandhasparśāḥ saṅkhyāḥ parimāṇāni pṛthaktvaṃ saṃyogavibhāgau paratvāparatve buddhayaḥ sukhaduḥkhe icchādveṣau prayatnaś ca guṇāḥ*.

[11] WI p. 1–2 Section 5: *caśabdasamuccitāś ca gurutvadravatvasnehasaṃskārādṛṣṭaśabdāḥ saptaivety caturviṃśatir guṇāḥ.* (Variants: one edition reads *tu* for *ca*, one omits *saptaiva* and reads *eva* for *evaṃ*, some read *caturviṃśatiguṇāḥ.*)
[12] See note 3, above.
[13] E.g. WI p. 43 Section 228: ... *adṛṣṭāc ca*; Section 231: ... *tat sarvaṃ saṃskāradharmābhyāṃ bhavati* / ... *tat sarvam adharmasaṃskārābhyāṃ bhavati* /
[14] The *Mīmāṃsākoṣa* (IV p. 2241) cites a passage from Prabhākara's *Bṛhatī* according to which some consider dharma a quality of the buddhi, others a quality of the self (p. 26: *dharmaṃ kecit buddhiguṇaṃ manyante kecit ātmaguṇam*). On p. 2249 it cites a line from Pārthasārathi Miśra's *Śāstradīpikā* according to which dharma and adharma are fluctuations (?*vṛtti*) of the internal organ (1.1.5.5, p. 114 l. 3: *dharmādharmayoḥ antaḥkaraṇavṛttitvāt*).
[15] For at least some Buddhist thinkers *acintya* appears to have played a similar role; see Kritzer (2002).
[16] VS 1.1.1–3. These sūtras figure in all surviving versions of the *Vaiśeṣika Sūtra*, i.e., the ones commented upon by Candrānanda, Bhaṭṭa Vādīndra and Śaṅkara Miśra respectively, as well as the two further recensions discovered and edited by Isaacson (1995a: 216, 270). About the question whether originally a fourth sūtra, now only preserved in the version commented upon by Śaṅkara Miśra, concluded this set, see the appendix.
[17] VS(C) 1.1.3 has *āmnāyaprāmāṇyam.*
[18] The expression *tadvacanāt* has been interpreted to mean:
(i) because Hiraṇyagarbha has uttered it (Candrānanda)
(ii) because it teaches *svarga* and *apavarga* (Bhaṭṭa Vādīndra)
(iii) because God has uttered it (Bhaṭṭa Vādīndra, Śaṅkara Miśra)
(iv) because it teaches *dharma* (Bhaṭṭa Vādīndra, Śaṅkara Miśra)
(v) because it teaches the self (Bhaṭṭa Vādīndra)
There can hardly be any doubt that (iv) is by far the most natural understanding of this expression in its context. It leads to the following interpretation of the sūtra: "The Veda is authoritative because it teaches dharma."
[19] Thakur (1961: 3) suggests that *dharma* at the beginning of the *Vaiśeṣika Sutra* means *padārthadharma*, "'property' or 'attribute' of the different categories" (Houben, 1994: 732 n. 27). This seems unlikely.
[20] See Bronkhorst (1993a, 1994).
[21] Frauwallner (1968: 16): *dharmaṃ prati hi vipratipannā bahuvidaḥ / kecid anyaṃ dharmam āhuḥ, kecid anyam /*
[22] Śabara's *Bhāṣya* on *Mīmāṃsā-sūtra* 2.1.5 (Ānandāśrama edition p. 358): *codanety apūrvaṃ brūmaḥ.* Cited in Biardeau (1964: 92 n. 1). See further Yoshimizu (2000: 161 n. 16), on the interpretation of this sentence.
[23] Śabara on *Mīmāṃsā-sūtra* 1.1.5; Frauwallner (1968: 24): *autpattikaḥ śabdasyārthena saṃbandhas tasya* ***agnihotrādilakṣaṇasya dharmasya*** *nimittaṃ pratyakṣādibhir anavagatasya.*
[24] Jayanta Bhaṭṭa, *Nyāyamañjarī* (ed. Śukla I p. 255 l. 3–4; ed. Varadacharya I p. 664 l. 6–7): *vṛddhamīmāṃsakāḥ yāgādikarmanirvartyam apūrvaṃ nāma dharmam abhivadanti, yāgādikarmaiva śābarā bruvate.* Further p. 255 l. 8–9 / p. 664 l. 15–16: *svargayāgāntarālavartinaś ca sthirasya* ***nirādhāras****yāpūrvasya niḥpramāṇakatvāt jarajjaiminīyapravādo 'py apeśalaḥ.* The first of these two positions finds expression in Mādhava's *Jaiminīyanyāyamālāvistara* (2.1.1: *apūrvasyaiva dharmatvāt*). Cp. Yoshimizu, 2000: 163 n. 27.
[25] Bronkhorst (2000b: Section 13). I am not sure that the passage from Śabara's *Bhāṣya* (on sūtra 7.1.7) referred to by Yoshimizu (2000: 151) is in contradiction with this idea.

[26]Helārāja's commentary on this and the following stanzas is not available, as indicated by the editor Subramania Iyer (1963: 261 n. 31).
[27]Subramania Iyer (1963: 261 l. 12) (on Vkp 3.7.34): *apūrvaṃ dharmādharmākhyam adṛṣṭasaṃjñakaṃ kecid evaṃrūpaṃ taṃ sāmarthyalakṣaṇaṃ bhāvam āhuḥ.*
[28]NV on 1.1.7, p. 175 l. 2–3: *asiddham apūrvasyānityatvam / na prāyaṇānupapatteḥ / yadi dharmādharmau nityau bhavataḥ kasya prakṣayāt prāyaṇam iti /* etc.
[29]NV on 1.1.7, p. 175 l. 9–10: *nityam apy apūrvaṃ yo 'bhivyanakti tasya phalam, abhivyaktyarthā kriyeti, ato na kriyālopa iti / yena yad abhivyajyate tasyaiva tat phaladātṛ bhavatīti dṛṣṭam /*. Tr. Kataoka (2000: 170).
[30]Bronkhorst, 1987: 25 l. 24–27: *dharmaprayojano vā iti mīmāṃsakadarśanam / avasthita eva dharmaḥ / sa tv agnihotrādibhir abhivyajyate / tatpreritas tu phalado bhavati / yathā svāmī bhṛtyaiḥ sevāyāṃ preryate phalaṃ praty evam ayaṃ niyamo dharmasya phalanirvṛttiṃ prati prayojaka iti /*. Cf. Bronkhorst, 1989: 112 [383] ff.; Kataoka, 2000: 168.
[31]Iyer, 1966: 224 l. 5–6 (on verse 1.136 = Vkp 1.172): *tatra kecid ācāryā manyante: ... / śāstrānuṣṭhānāt tu kevalād dharmābhivyaktiḥ / ...* Kataoka (2000: 167–168).
[32]DNC I p. 140 l. 25: ... *parasparaviśiṣṭābhir yajñasaṃsthābhir agniṣṭomādibhir iṣṭibhiś cābhivyaktavyā apūrvā api ...*; as emended in Kataoka (2000: 174). DNC I p. 141 l. 8: ... *dharmaḥ kriyābhivyaṅgya[ḥ]* ... Kataoka (2000: 176).
[33]Bhavya, *Madhyamakahṛdaya* 9.10: *apūrvo 'pi kriyāvyaṅgyaḥ kriyā mokṣe 'pi sādhanam / somapānādikā vidvān nirjayed antakaṃ yayā //* "Moreover, apūrva is to be manifested by [ritual] action, and ritual action such as drinking soma etc. are the means to [attain] liberation (*mokṣa*). By means of such [ritual action] a knowing person may overcome death." Cp. Kawasaki (1977: 10–11); Lindtner (1997: 96–97, 1999: 254–255, 2001: 93).
[34]See Kawasaki (1977: 10 n. 9).
[35]YD p. 191 l. 33–35: *tatra śrutismṛtivihitānāṃ karmaṇām anuṣṭhānād buddhyavasthaḥ sattvāvayava āśayabhūto dharma ity ucyate.* Cp. Bronkhorst (2000b: 56).
[36]The Trivandrum manuscript edited by Isaacson (1995a: 270, 1995b: 757) has *sādhanāny asya dravyaguṇakarmāṇi.*
[37]Bronkhorst (1993a: 83 f).
[38]Cp. Bronkhorst (1993b: 164 f).
[39]WI p. 131, s.v. *dharma-viśeṣāt, dharma-viśeṣa-sahitebhyaḥ.*
[40] Cp. *Mīmāṃsākoṣa* IV pp. 2241 s.v. *dharma* etc.

REFERENCES

Biardeau, M. (1964). *Théorie de la connaissance et philosophie de la parole dans le brahmanisme classique*, Le monde d'outre-mer, passé et présent, premiére série, études XXIII. Paris – La Haye: Mouton.

Bronkhorst, J. (ed., tr.)(1987). *Mahābhāṣyadīpikā of Bhartṛhari. Fascicule IV: Āhnika 1*, Post-Graduate and Research Department Series, 28. Poona: Bhandarkar Oriental Research Institute.

Bronkhorst, J. (1989). 'Studies on Bhartṛhari, 2: Bhartṛhari and Mīmāṃsā.' *Studien zur Indologie und Iranistik* **15**, 101–117. (Reprinted in: R.C. Dwivedi (ed.), *Studies in Mīmāṃsā. Dr. Mandan Mishra Felicitation Volume*, (pp. 371–388). Delhi: Motilal Banarsidass, 1994.)

Bronkhorst, J. (1993a). Studies on Bhartṛhari, 5: Bhartṛhari and Vaiśeṣika. In *Proceedings of the First International Conference on Bhartṛhari* (University of Poona, January 6–8, 1992). *Asiatische Studien / Études Asiatiques* **47**(1), 75–94

(Reprinted in: Bhartṛhari (Philosopher and Grammarian) *Proceedings of the First International Conference on Bhartṛhari* (*University of Poona, January 6–8, 1992*) pp. 75–94). Saroja Bhate &Johannes Bronkhorst. (eds.) Delhi: Motilal Banarsidass. 1994.)

Bronkhorst, J. (1993b): The Vaiśeṣika vākya and bhāṣya. Annals of the Bhandarkar Oriental Research Institute 72–73 [for the years 1991 and 1992 (Amtamahotsava (1917–1992) Volume)], 1993, pp. 145–169.

Bronkhorst, J. (1994). Once again Vaiśeṣika sūtra 3.1.13. *Asiatische Studien / Études Asiatiques* **48**(2), 665–681.

Bronkhorst, J. (1996): God's arrival in the Vaiśeṣika system. *Journal of Indian Philosophy* **24**(3), 281–294.

Bronkhorst, J. (2000a): 'Die buddhistische Lehre.' In Von Heinz Bechert et al. (eds.), *Der Buddhismus I. Der indische Buddhismus und seine Verzweigungen* (pp. 23–212). Die Religionen der Menschheit, Vol. 24,1. Stuttgart: W. Kohlhammer.

Bronkhorst, J. (2000b). *Karma and Teleology. A problem and its solutions in Indian philosophy*, Studia Philologica Buddhica, Monograph Series, 15. Tokyo: International Institute for Buddhist Studies, International College for Advanced Buddhist Studies.

Frauwallner, E. (1963/1995): Pañcaskandhaka and Pañcavastuka. = Frauwallner, 1995: pp. 135–147.

Frauwallner, E. (1968).: *Materialien zur ältesten Erkenntnislehre der Karmamīmāṃsā*. Wien: Hermann Böhlaus. (ÖAW, philosophisch-historische Klasse, Sitzungsberichte, 259. Bd., 2. Abhandlung; Veröffentlichungen der Kommission für Sprachen und Kulturen Südasiens, Heft 6).

Frauwallner, E. (1984). Ernst Steinkellner (ed.) *Nachgelassene Werke. I: Aufsätze, Beiträge, Skizzen*. Wien: Verlag der Österreichischen Akademie der Wissenschaften (ÖAW, philosophisch-historische Klasse, Sizungsberichte, 438. Bd.; Veröffentlichungen der Kommission für Sprachen und Kulturen Südasiens, Heft 19).

Frauwallner, E. (1995). *Studies in Abhidharma Literature and the Origins of Buddhist Philosophical Systems* (Translated from the German by Sophie Francis Kidd, under the supervision of Ernst Steinkellner). Albany: State University of New York Press.

Halbfass, W. (1986). Review of Frauwallner, 1984. *Journal of the Amerian Oriental Society* **106**, 857–858.

Halbfass, W. (1991). *Tradition and Reflection. Explorations in Indian thought*. Albany: State University of New York Press.

Halbfass, W. (1992): *On Being and What There Is. Classical Vaiśeṣika and the history of Indian ontology*. Albany: State University of New York Press.

Houben, J. E.M. (1994): 'Liberation and natural philosophy in early Vaiśeṣika: some methodological problems.' *Asiatische Studien / Études Asiatiques* **48**(2), 711–748.

Isaacson, H. (1995a). Materials for the Study of the Vaiśeṣika System. Unpublished doctoral thesis, Leiden University.

Isaacson, H. (1995b).: Notes on the manuscripts transmission of the Vaiśeṣika sūtra and its earliest commentaries.' *Asiatische Studien / Études Asiatiques* **48**(2), 749–779.

Iyer, K. A. Subramania (ed.)(1966). *Vākyapadīya of Bhartṛhari, with the Vṛtti and the Paddhati of Vṛṣabhadeva. Kāṇḍa I*, Deccan College Monograph Series, 32. Poona: Deccan College.)

Jayanta Bhaṭṭa. Nyāyamañjarī. (1) Edited with notes by Pt. Surya Nārāyana Śukla. Part I. Varanasi: Chowkhamba Sanskrit Series Office. 1971. (Kashi Sanskrit Series, 106; Nyāya Section No. 15.) (2) Edited, with Ṭippaṇī-Nyāyasaurabha by the editor K. S. Varadacharya. Vol. I. Mysore: Oriental Research Institute. (Oriental Research Institute Series, 116.)

Jha, Gaṅgānātha (tr.) (1915/1982). *Padārthadharmasaṅgraha of Praśastapāda, with the Nyāyakandalī of Śrīdhara* Translated into English, Chaukhambha Oriental Studies, 4. (Reprint: Chaukhambha Orientalia, Varanasi, Delhi, 1982)

Kapani, Lakshmi (1992–1993). *La notion de saṃskāra*. 2 Vols. Paris: Diffusion de Boccard. (Collège de France, Publications de l'Institut de Civilisation Indienne, fascicule 59.)

Kataoka, K. (2000): 'Reconstructing the dharma-abhivyakti-vāda in the Mīmāṃsā tradition.' In Sengaku Mayeda (ed.), *The Way to Liberation. Indological Studies in Japan*, Vol. I. (pp. 167–169). New Delhi: Manohar. (Japanese Studies on South Asia No. 3.).

Kawasaki, Shinjō (1977): 'The Mīmāṃsā chapter of Bhavya's Madhyamaka-hṛdaya-kārikā: text and translation. (1) Pūrva-pakṣa.' Institute of Philosophy, The University of Tsukuba, Studies 1976. pp. 1–16.

Kritzer, R. (2002). "Unthinkable matters: The term acintya in the Abhidharmakośabhāṣya.' *Early Buddhism and Abhidharma Thought: In Honor of Doctor Hajime Sakurabe on His Seventy-seventh Birthday* (pp. 65–86) Kyoto: Heirakuji Shoten.

Lindtner, C. (1997). 'Bhavya on Mīmāṃsā.' Studia Indologiczne (Oriental Institute, Warsaw University) 4 (Aspects of Buddhism, Proceedings of the International Seminar on Buddhist Studies, Liw, 25 June 1994), pp. 91–123.

Lindtner, C. (1999). 'Bhavya on Mīmāṃsā. Mīmāṃsātattvanirayāvatāraḥ, with English translation.' Adyar Library Bulletin 1999, pp. 245–302.

Lindtner, C. (ed.) (2001). *Madhyamakahdayam of Bhavya*. Adyar, Chennai: The Adyar Library and Research Centre, The Theosophical Society.

Śaṅkara Miśra Upaskāra (commentary on the Vaiśeṣika Sūtra). In Ḍhuṇḍirāja Śāstrī (ed.), *Vaiśeṣikadarśane maharṣipravara-Praśastadevācāryaviracitaṃ Praśastapādabhāṣyam, vidvaccūḍāmaṇi-śrī-Śaṅkara-Miśra-vinirmitaḥ Upaskāraś ca*. Kāsī Sanskrit Series, 3, Kāśī: Caukhambāsaṃskṛtapustakālaya.

Sinha, Nandalal (tr.)(1911/1986). The Vaiśeṣika Sūtras of Kaṇāda, with the commentary of Śakara Miśra. Delhi: S. N. Publications, (Reprint, 1986).

Subramania Iyer, K.A. (ed.)(1963): *Vākyapadya of Bharthari with the commentary of Helārāja. Kāṇḍa III, Part 1*, Deccan College Monograph Series, 21. Poona: Deccan College.

Thakur, Anantalal (ed.)(1957). *Vaiśeṣikadarana of Kaṇāda, with an anonymous commentary*. Darbhanga: Mithila Institute of Post-Graduate Studies and Research in Sanskrit Learning.

Thakur, Anantalal (1961): 'Introduction.' See VS(C).

Vaiśeṣika Sūtra. (1) Edited, with the commentary of Candrānanda, by Muni Jambuvijaya. Baroda: Oriental Institute. 1961. (Gaekwad's Oriental Series,136.) (2a) Edited, with an anonymous commentary, by Anantalal Thakur. Darbhanga: Mithila Institute. 1957. (2b) Edited, with the commentary of Bhaṭṭa Vādndra, by Anantalal Thakur. Darbhanga: Kāmeśvarasiṃha-Darabhaṅgā-Saṃskṛta-Viśvavidyālaya. 1985. (3) Edited, with a translation of the sūtras, of the commentary of Śakara Miśra and of extracts from the gloss of Jayanārāyaṇa, by Nandalal Sinha. Delhi: S.N.Publications. 1986. The three numbers that specify a sūtra refer to these three editions respectively. Where only one number is given, the reference is to the first of these three.

Wijeratne, R.P., & Gethin, R. (tr.) (2002). *Summary of the Topics of Abhidhamma (Abhidhammatthasaṅgaha) by Anuruddha – Exposition of the Topics of Abhidhamma* (Abhidhammatthavibhāvinī) *by Sumagala, being a commentary to Anuruddha's Summary of the Topics of Abhidhamma*, Sacred Books of the Buddhists, 50. Oxford: Pali Text Society.

Yoshimizu, K. (2000). 'Change of view on apūrva from Śabarasvāmin to Kumārila. In Sengaku Mayeda (ed.), *The Way to Liberation. Indological Studies in Japan*,

Vol. I. (pp. 149–165) (New Delhi: Manohar. 2000. (Japanese Studies on South Asia No. 3.)

ABBREVIATIONS

DNC Dvādaśāra Nayacakra of Mallavādin. Edited, with the commentary Nyāyāgamānusārṇi of Siṃhasūri Gaṇi Vādi Kṣamāśramaṇa, by Muni Jambūvijayajī, 3 parts, Bhavnagar: Sri Jain Ātmanand Sabha, 1966, 1976, 1988.

GOS Gaekwad's Oriental Series, Baroda

NV Nyāya Vārttika de Uddyotakara, in the following edition: Nyāyadarśanam with Vātsyāyana's Bhāṣya, Uddyotakara's Vārttika, Vācaspati Miśra's Tātparyaṭīkā & Viśvanātha's Vṛtti. Chapter I, section I critically edited with notes by Taranatha Nyaya-Tarkatirtha and chapters I-ii – V by Amarendramohan Tarkatirtha, with an introduction by Narendra Chandra Vedantatirtha. Calcutta: Metropolitan Printing & Publishing House, 1936.

ÖAW Österreichische Akademie der Wissenschaften, Wien

Vkp Bhartṛhari, Vākyapadīya, ed. W. Rau, Wiesbaden 1977

VS Vaiśeṣika Sūtra

VS(C) Vaiśeṣikasūtra of Kaṇāda, with the Commentary of Candrānanda, critically edited by Muni Śrī Jambuvijayaji, second edition, Baroda: Oriental Research Institute, 1982 (GOS 136)

VS(Ś) Vaiśeṣṣika Sūtra in the version commented upon by Śaṅkara Miśra; for an edition see Sinha, 1911/1986.

WI Word Index to the Praśastapādabhāṣya: A complete word index to the printed editions of the Praśastapādabhāṣya, by Johannes Bronkhorst & Yves Ramseier, Delhi: Motilal Banarsidass, 1994

YD Yuktidpīkā, ed. in Albrecht Wezler and Shujun Motegi, Yuktidpīkā: The most significant commentary on the Sāṃkhyakārikā, Vol. I, Stuttgart: Franz Steiner, 1998 (Alt- und Neu-Indische Studien, 44)

Faculté des Lettres
Section de langues et civilisations orientales
Université de Lausanne
BFSH 2
CH-1015 Lausanne
Switzerland
E-mail:Johannes.Bronkhorst@orient.unil.ch

FRANCIS X. CLOONEY, S.J.

PRAGMATISM AND ANTI-ESSENTIALISM IN THE CONSTRUCTION OF DHARMA IN *MĪMĀṂSĀ SŪTRAS* 7.1.1–12

1

Dharma is treated in distinct ways at various points in the *Mīmāṃsā Sūtras* of Jaimini.[1] First, there is the well known and reasonably well studied definition of dharma in 1.1.2: *codanālakṣaṇārtho dharmaḥ*, 'dharma is that artha (purpose, referent) distinguished by codanā (injunctive verbal force).' There are also related discussions in the expositions of dharma in Śabara's *Bhāṣya*, Kumārila's *Ślokavārtika*, Prabhākara's *Bṛhatī*, and later commentaries on 1.1.2 and all of 1.1, the so-called *Tarka Pāda*. Second, there is also the consideration of authority and tradition in 1.3 of the *Sūtras*, similarly elaborated by Śabara, Kumārila, Prabhākara, and later theorists. There, the social and linguistic dimensions of dharma as an explicitly and implicitly mapped reality are spelled out. Third, dharma is a word and concept deeply imbedded in the sacrificially oriented bulk of the *Sūtras* that comes after 1.3, the approximately 2500 sūtras pertaining to the details of sacrificial performance and the harmonization of the pertinent brāhmaṇa and mantra texts. Dharma is most often discussed and argued, and therefore understood, in the negotiation of sacrificial details. As authorized detail, dharma occurs when particular actions, material substances, and agents are located properly in relation to one another in an integral and smooth performance authorized and generated by the relevant texts.

Fourth, there are also a few intermediate adhikaraṇas dedicated to theorizing about the nature of sacrifice (*yajña*) and its verbal dimensions, in order to identify the rules by which practice and the language of practice are properly ordered. In such adhikaraṇas, where terms stand on the edge between practice and theory, 'dharma' is explored as a reality that is practical and conceptual, intelligible and to be enacted. Here we find an integral, original theorizing about dharma, and the pathway from a consideration of dharmas – sacrificial details – to a consideration of Dharma as the larger reality of Mīmāṃsā philosophy and social theory. One such intermediate adhikaraṇa is 2.1.9–12, dedicated to the notion of dharmamātra karma, 'action that is solely dharmic.'[2] In an essay on that adhikaraṇa,[3] I argued that Jaimini consistently gives priority to action (*karma*) over things (*dravya*), except in specific and explicit cases where the action is secondary, as preparatory of some thing to be used in sacrifice. Dharmamātra karma is action valuable in itself because it contributes directly to the completing of a particular sacrifice, and not simply through preparing some thing to be used in a sacrifice. Such action is dharmic because it is in a sense 'effective in itself,' without reliance on mediate visible effects, for example by the use of affected substances.

In this essay I investigate another intermediate adhikaraṇa, 7.1.1–12. This adhikaraṇa is dedicated primarily to analyzing and defending the notion of the transfer of details (atideśa) from a model sacrifice (*prakṛti*) to a derivative sacrifice (*vikṛti*). Though the adhikaraṇa is not primarily focused on dharma, dharma as detail plays a central role in it, and we are afforded an interesting reading of how dharma/Dharma is understood, constructed, and managed in the course of ordinary Mīmāṃsā reflection. This essay therefore aims at putting in place another small piece in the large mosaic of Mīmāṃsā notions of dharma.

I first give an overview of 7.1.1–12 by translating the sūtras and analyzing them very briefly. Then I discuss the use of dharma in the adhikaraṇa and *Bhāṣya* reading of it. Thereafter, I analyze the major topic of the adhikaraṇa, the discussion of atideśa in the twelve sūtras, particularly with reference to the exposition in Pārthasārathi Miśra's *Sāstradīpikā*. I then connect atideśa to dharma, in order to sum up what we learn of dharma here. Finally, I suggest the path back to the wider discussion of dharma by reference to a key discussion in adhikaraṇa 1.1.2.

2

Here first is my translation of the 7.1.1–12:[4]

1. śrutipramāṇatvāc cheṣaṇāṃ mukhyabhede yathādhikāraṃ bhāvaḥ syāt

s: When on explicit textual authority there is a dividing of a primary sacrifice, the accessory details recur (in newly differentiated sacrifices) only as warranted. (An archetypal sacrifice [*prakṛti*] generates derivative sacrifices [*vikṛti*] in part different, in part the same as the archetype. Details recur, but not entirely.)

2. utpattyarthavibhāgād vā sattvavad aikadharmyaṃ syāt
   p: No. In the original setting, the details are not differentiated from the (authorizing) purpose and so, as with existence, (in the newly differentiated sacrifices) there is a unity of details. (All details should carry over from the archetype to the derivative sacrifices.)
3. codanāśeṣabhāvād vā tadbhedād vyavatiṣṭheran utpatter guṇabhūtatvāt
   s: No. Because accessory details exist due to injunctive verbal force, they are sorted out according to a dividing of that force; for the original setting is secondary. (Some authorizing injunction must be recognized as explicitly or implicitly in force, for the details to carry over.)
4. sattve lakṣaṇasaṃyogāt sārvatrikaṃ pritīyeta
   s: Because (every existent) is connected by definition to existence, (that it exists) should be presumed to obtain in every case. (Individual instances all share characteristics generic to the idea of the thing at issue.)
5. avibhāgāt tu naivaṃ syāt
   p: No. Because (the details) are undivided (in the original setting), (they cannot be differentiated) thus. (There are no grounds for differentiating details.)
6. dvyarthatvaṃ ca vipratiṣiddham
   p: Moreover, a duality of intent (in the original setting, treating different details differently) is prohibited. (A statement cannot include two intents, each allocating different details differently; a single intent governs all the details.)
7. utpattau vidhyabhāvād vā codanāyāṃ pravṛttiḥ syāt tataśca karmabhedaḥ syāt
   s: No. Because there is no (differentiated) prescriptive statement in the original setting, their actualization should occur only when there is injunctive verbal force, on the basis of which there is a dividing of actions. (The order that we find in

the archetypal sacrifice applies there, but lacks the injunctive force to apply automatically elsewhere.)

8. yadi vā 'pyabhidhānavat sāmānyāt sarvadharmaḥ syāt
p: No. If it is like a name (that is applicable to many instances), then due to commonality the same character (applies to all). (The characterization of the archetypal sacrifice carries over to the derivative sacrifices, in the way that a name serves to indicate multiple instances of the same thing.)

9. arthasya tvavibhaktatvāt tathā syād abhidhāneṣu pūrvavattvāt prayogasya karmaṇaḥ śabdabhāvyatvād vibhāgāc cheṣāṇām apravṛttiḥ syāt
s: Because an object is undivided (from its name), it should be thus regarding names; for usage has an antecedent. Because an action is brought into being through word, when separated (from that word) accessory details would not occur. (There are two uses of language: names describe what already exists, while a word with injunctive verbal force brings into existence what it describes.)

10. smṛtir iti cet
p: Suppose we simply remember (the details from the archetypal sacrifice to the derivative one)?

11. na pūrvavattvāt
s: No, since (remembering) pertains to what has an antecedent. (By contrast, the apūrva by definition has no antecedent.)

12. arthasya śabdabhāvyatvāt prakaraṇanibandhanāc śabdād eva anyatra bhāvaḥ syāt
s: Because a sacrificial element is brought into being through word, it is only by word, connected with a context, that (such elements) can be introduced elsewhere. (As a new purpose is introduced, generating a new sacrifice, so too only if generated there do details carry over to a new context.)

The adhikaraṇa distinguishes ordinary experience and its norms from Vedic practice, separating the ordinary extensions of knowledge by comparison and analogy from the new realities (sacrifices and their component parts) generated by Vedic injunctive verbal force. New sacrifices and their needed details are generated by explicit and implicit verbal force which bring them into existence. Sacrifices are events, not essences. Likewise, dharmas occur; they are constructed and are not essences.

3

Turning to the meaning of dharma in 7.1.1–12, we notice first that Jaimini uses 'dharma' only twice, in sūtras 2 and 8. In 7.1.1, it is śeṣa and not 'dharma' that indicates a sacrificial accessory or detail. That a sacrifice 'has a unity of details' (*aikadharmya*) indicates (according to the pūrvapakṣin) that a derivative sacrifice is characterized by the same accessory details as the one upon which it is modeled. 'All the dharmas' (*sarvadharmāḥ*, 7.1.8) similarly indicates that a new, derivative sacrifice has all the details that had belonged to the sacrifice on which it was modeled, and that once properly placed, such details are its dharmas.

In the pūrvapakṣin's view, accessory details can be extended from the archetypal to the new sacrifice, because the new and old are as it were instances of the same genus of 'sacrifice,' or even of a particular species of sacrifice, and so naturally bear common features such as 'existence.' A sacrifice derived from the Darśapūrṇamāsa, for instance, belongs to its genus and shares its essential features, simply by being what it is. The siddhāntin's objection rests ultimately on a distinction between essence and event, with a preference for the latter; sacrifices are constructed, they occur as events, and so are never merely 'there.' In turn this is rooted in the distinction between the injunctive verbal force (*codanā*) and prescriptive statement (*vidhi*). The prescriptive statement stipulates how a particular sacrifice is to be performed, while the injunctive verbal force brings that sacrifice into existence. The prescriptive statement does not in itself possess the injunctive verbal force that generates an actual sacrificial performance, even if normally the injunctive verbal force and the prescriptive statement go together, as what is prescribed is what actually happens. The actual nature of a primary sacrifice does not lie in the prescriptive statements about it. One cannot merely infer from the form or name of one sacrifice what another is to look like, even if the latter is known to be derived from the former. Rather, the verbal display of details – the prescriptive statement mentioning the means (*karaṇa*) and the manner of performance (*itikartavyatā, ithaṃbhāva*)[5] – must be actualized by the injunctive verbal force.

Although Śabara adheres to Jaimini's basic intent, he uses 'dharma' more frequently. Notably, he replaces śeṣa with 'dharma,' so that "dharma" indicates the details of sacrifices, things, acts, sequences and relations, all the elements serving a subordinate purpose in a sacrifice. For Śabara, a dharma is any subordinate element generated by verbal force. Most simply, dharmas are sacrificial details: the details of the Darśapūrṇamāsa sacrifice are borrowed by the Aindrāgna, etc. (7.1.1);[6] the offering material, deity, mantra used at a sacrifice (which in essence is the offering of some offering material to a deity while a mantra is enunciated; 7.1.5);[7] the fore-sacrifices; the gold pieces offered at the fore-sacrifices (7.1.6);[8] *rāśṭabhṛta* offerings to the gandharvas and apsarasas at a marriage sacrifice (7.1.12).[9] These examples mark dharmas as elements found in the sacrificial context, the array of posited acts, words, things authoritatively introduced into the sacrificial realm, to make a sacrifice possible. The sacrifice subsists, as it were, in the details accompanying it, and these details are its dharmas. To sacrifice properly is to implement dharma, but it is also to make use of myriad details, all in their proper dharmic order.

A detail's presence and place are negotiable, moveable or not, depending on specific contextual factors; when authorized and present, a detail becomes a dharma. Accordingly, the siddhāntin holds that dharmas are applicable in derivative sacrifices only if generated by injunctive verbal force. Like sacrifices, dharmas depend on generative, effective language, and do not occur based merely on a conceptual grasp of what they would be, if real. In general, qualities are to be assessed – introduced or left out – not with reference to the thing to which they are most obviously connected, but to that for the sake of which they are introduced. The coloring of cloth is meant to please the men and women who wear the dyed clothing, not to please the cloth that is dyed. Similarly, dharmas are introduced with respect to the effective purpose of a particular sacrifice – its reality as something new (apūrva), an event – and not merely in accord with some previously prescribed sacrifice (7.1.7).[10]

The pūrvapakṣin and siddhāntin argue analogies between ordinary experiences and the functioning of dharma and knowledge about dharma. Some characteristics belong to one individual and not to another, even if both are of the same genus. The clothing and land of Devadatta are not the land and clothing of Yajñadatta, and only by stipulation would one assert such a commonality (7.1.1).[11] One cannot merely generalize from one individual to another. One can feed Devadatta his favorite food, but one has to stipulate, and not merely assume, that the same food should be given to Yajñadatta (7.1.12).[12]

In sūtras 7.1.3 (where 'sattvavat' occurs) and 7.1.8 (where 'abhidhānavat' occurs), Śabara's pūrvapakṣin (proposing the analogies 'as with existence' and 'like a name') and siddhāntin (rejecting them) also debate more philosophical analogies. Both discuss dharmas and the original and later sacrifices to which they belong by way of analogies with conceptual forms and instances of it. Thus, what applies to 'cow' applies to actual cows. When one is instructed, '"Touch the cow" with one's foot,' the idea of 'cow' cannot be touched with one's foot, so it is some particular existent cow that must be touched (7.1.2).[13] 'Cow' is qualitatively different from particular cows, but the word 'cow' names every particular cow. This is why what is said with reference to 'cow' is legitimately and quickly extended to all cows. Similarly, the pūrvapakṣin suggests, dharmas are qualities of one sacrifice that can be applied to another sacrifice similar to the first. So too, just as 'tawniness' is a qualification of some particular calf, so too 'Darśapūrṇamāsa' is a qualification of 'sacrifice,' even if 'tawny' and 'Darśapūrṇamāsa' are not entirely analogous qualifications. (7.1.3).[14]

The siddhāntin objects that dharmas do not relate immediately to 'sacrifice' and are bound to particular sacrifices not in their essences, but as particular events. That is, the dharmas pertain to some particular sacrifice as novel, apūrva (7.1.4), and cannot be assumed to apply even to a similar case elsewhere.[15] Even proper generalizations need to be taken cautiously: barley is preferred by Vāhīkas (Panjabis), and one can assume that everyone in the Vāhīka land is a Vāhīka and also fond of barley. For dharmas to be similarly generalizable, either 'sacrifice' or 'apūrva' would have to be like names applicable to the array of individual sacrifices and apūrvas. But this is not the case, since they are not essences but individual events (7.1.8–9).[16] Sacrificial details are introduced not by way of generalized analogies, but only as stipulated textually, and only then do details become dharmas. It is appropriate to feed Yajñadatta with food pleasing to Devadatta only if someone has stipulated that this is to be done, and not merely because one assumes that food pleasing to the one will also please the other (7.1.12).[17] So too, the transfer of dharmas must be stipulated.

In the *Tantraratna*, Pārthasārathi Miśra adds a few other illuminating examples from ordinary life, where descriptive features are possibly like dharmas. For instance, one can identify Devadatta's house by its individual features – its doorway, flowers, garden; so too, dharmas characterize the sacrifice to which they belong (7.1.3).[18] When one is instructed to purchase for sacrificial purposes a tawny, one year old calf, the qualifications 'tawny' and 'one year old' together prompt the act of buying a calf of this certain color and age.

Neither the color nor age is sufficient to determine which calf is to be bought. Similarly, it is the Darśapūrṇamāsa sacrifice as a particular event with particular characteristics (dharmas) that is enacted, not 'sacrifice in itself' (7.1.3).[19]

The siddhāntin's reading of such examples aims to assert that only specific, individual instances can be handled in action, never the generic idea of something, be it a calf or a sacrifice. By extension, knowledge of what something is may not be a reliable guide to determining what something else, derived from the first thing, may actually be. Śabara, marking the path for later Mīmāṃsā theorists, thus resists the ordinary and habitual ways of viewing things and qualities, since these do not illustrate properly how a sacrifice or a dharma is to be thought of. Any particular sacrifice or any particular dharma is an event, a construction, and not an essence. Observable analogies based on generalization and knowledge of essences – this is like that, it looks like that, what that was this will be, or the features of the one apply to the other – do not work reliably with respect to sacrifices and their dharmas.

Analogies are considered, restricted, and often discarded – but this process is instructive, indicating how a dharma is not an ordinary quality of something, liable to conceptualization and prediction. There can be only a limited similarity between instances drawn from ordinary experience and the extension of dharmas from one sacrifice to another. A dharma – a thing, character, quality or sacrifice – is an event, new in each case, never a reality constituted merely by copying from some precedent reality. No shared 'natural reality' or 'natural observation' is useful in explaining Vedic knowledge and Vedic practice. 'Vedic reality,' which does matter, occurs on a linguistic and practical level where word has the power to construct the reality to which it refers. Vedic words make ordinary things, qualities, actions, and persons into dharmic realities.

4

The preceding comments on the verbal construction of dharmas quickly lead us to the topic of the adhikaraṇa, atideśa. This is the allocation of accessory details (śeṣa, dharma) from one sacrifice to a similar one by an allocation for which there is only implicit authority. The siddhānta insists that the archetypal sacrifice is itself an instance, a single enacted sacrifice, not an ideal form with common features automatically carried over from derivative sacrifices. The borrowing of details (dharmas) is possible, but it requires at least implicit authorization. To understand this clearly, however, we must take up more specifically the issue of atideśa.

According to a tradition enunciated as early as Śabara's *Bhāṣya*, though not signaled by Jaimini, 7.1.1–12 inaugurates a second major section of the *Sūtras*. By the standard reading, Ādhyāyas 1–6 deal with sacrifices and the related texts having to do with the specific ordering of sacrifices and the details of their performance. This explicitly detailed arrangement of details is traditionally termed simply upadeśa, perhaps 'direct instruction.' As distinct, Ādhyāyas 7–12 deal with the allocation of details – acts, things, order – needed for sacrifices that are not fully described in any Vedic texts but which are modeled on fully described sacrifices. Ādhyāyas 7–8 do so directly, and Ādhyāyas 9–12 focus on the many cases where the borrowing is limited or prohibited. If derivative sacrifices lack a complete set of details, one must introduce details borrowed from an archetypal sacrifice into the derivative context. In the latter context, they are again dharmic. This extended borrowing or allocation is known as atideśa.

The first adhikaraṇa, 7.1.1–12, has as its core issue whether there is the need and possibility for atideśa as an 'instruction-beyond' an original setting – neither as direct instruction (upadeśa) nor by common analogy.[20] The key concern, unsurprisingly, pertains to the authority for allocating details, since the superfluous or unwarranted introduction of details is a disvalue in Mīmāṃsā. At issue too are the epistemological warrants for atideśa, the limited inferences that can be made on the basis of texts and contexts. Details must be introduced, but only as enacted in obedience to injunctive verbal force.

The philosophical problem, already introduced in the preceding section, is that of generalization: is an archetypal sacrifice more like a genus or an individual? If the former is true, then characteristic features may be presumed to carry over to derivative forms, even if no text explicitly directs this; if the latter, stronger justification is required for extending the details from one sacrifice to another. Here again, we can think of ordinary and largely valid generalizations commonly made, such as rightly generalize from one instance to another. Similarly, derivative sacrifices may be like their archetypes, and the details thought to carry over automatically. Or so the pūrvapakṣin argues. The meaning and significance of a given sacrifice are internal to it; the act of sacrifice, the means, and the manner of performance are parts of a coherent whole, and they can be presumed to carry over to new, derivative sacrificial contexts. Accordingly, the transfer of details is unproblematic, such details are automatically reconstituted as dharmas in the new context, and an inquiry into th rules and limits of atideśa is unnecessary.

Rejecting this view, the siddhāntin insists that things, acts, qualities, etc., are integral when they are rightly related to a performance with respect to its finality and are verbally authorized. The materials, such as rice, are accessories useful toward the accomplishment of the result (*phalabhāvanā*) by way of actualizing the apūrva. The completion of the sacrifice in its details effects the apūrva, and this in turn eventuates in the result. All the subordinate actions are part of the event of a given sacrificial event, not merely in a conceptual relationship with one another. Due to this focus on outcome instead of essences, there is an analogy of action, not of essence. Similar actions, properly warranted, lead to similar results. One moves from sacrifice as concept and one particular sacrifice, to another sacrifice. There can be no generic particular transition, and so some authorizing verbal guidance is required to activate the necessary supporting factors that enable the whole to come into existence. When ordinary things are introduced, the inferences that work in ordinary life are not adequate to the task of locating these things properly as dharmas. The event of a successful, fruitful sacrifice is not a phenomenon drawn from ordinary experience, and neither are its component parts, either in an original or derived sacrifice, known from ordinary experience. Instruction from a Vedic text is required. Finding such warranty when none is explicitly given is the task underlying the study of atideśa in Ādhyāyas 7 and 8.

Distinctive to Śabara's reading of the adhikaraṇa is his view that atideśa is based in the dependence of dharmas on apūrva, not on sacrifice or the abstract act, 'to-sacrifice.' Śabara emphasizes dharmas' potency, future-oriented dynamism toward the result of the sacrifice – and thus toward the apūrva actually eventuating in that result. Dharma is action-oriented because it is connected with the novelty, the apūrva, of a sacrifice. The appeal to the notion of apūrva gives priority to sacrifice as process and act, over any reification of it, and hearkens to the energy and vitality of the injunctive verbal force over against conceptual, essentialist extensions of one sacrifice to others.

If there is an internal efficacy to the relation of the act of sacrifice, the means and manner in which it is actualized, this act, means, and manner are integrally related without reference to apūrva, and so cannot be separated out. The pūrvapakṣin suggests that since the act of sacrifice, means and manner all contribute to the effecting of the phala (henceforth, result), they are not to be separated from one another; where the act of sacrifice is present, all its means and manner – the dharmas – are present.

In rejecting the view that coherence is internal to a sacrifice in its essence, the siddhāntin reinforces the view that the coherence of any particular sacrifice, and thus the cohesion of its parts, lies outside itself, in the result and the mediating apūrva. This is in turn dependent on the verbal generation of its cohesion as an event irreducible to a merely known, extendable essence prescribed in the prescriptive statement. Thus, the subordinate factors are ordered not to one another, nor to the particular sacrifice or its derivative sacrifices as conceptual wholes, but rather toward the completion of the apūrva and result for which the sacrifice is performed. The means and mode are intelligibly related according to their finality, so that one can assess when they – and the dharmas they entail – are to change.

Dharmas can be transferred, and the transfer needs to be justified. Accordingly, Ādhyāyas 7 and 8 take up the task of finding verbal authorization for the introduction of things, related actions, or words, even when some evident or implied analogies from one sacrifice to another seem to justify adequately a transfer of details. In 7.1.13–16, for instance, a question is posed regarding the derivation of the Śyena and Iṣu sacrifices from the Jyotiṣṭoma. In describing the Iṣu, after just a few details are given, it is said, 'The rest is like the Śyena' (*samānam itarat śyenena*). According to the pūrvapakṣa, this phrase means that the Iṣu, like the Śyena, receives its missing dharmas from the Jyotiṣṭoma. According to the siddhānta, the 'rest' most easily refers to what is unique to the Śyena; the Iṣu borrows from the Śyena what is unique to the Śyena. An already established transfer – from the Jyotiṣṭoma to the Śyena – has less force than the subsequent, newly and verbally mandated transfer from the Śyena to the Iṣu. Some details of the Śyena then become dharmic again in the Iṣu. Similarly, the following adhikaraṇas take up other problematic instances. 7.3.1–4 considers how the name 'agnihotram' authorizes extending details from the daily agnihotram to the monthly one; 7.4.1–12 considers oblique references and omissions on the basis of which the borrowing of procedures must and can be presumed.[21] One might say that Ādhyāyas 7 and 8 offer case studies in the practice of transferring details from sacrifice to another. It may be, in fact, that it is only in such specific acts of exegesis that one really understands what dharma means for the Mīmāṃsā scholars.

5

We have thus finished examining the meaning and use of dharma in 7.1.1–12, and the teaching on atideśa in the same adhikaraṇa. We can now combine our reflection on dharma with our reflection on atideśa to generalize what we have learned. From the discussion of dharma, we glimpse a framework for reflection on dharma in very specific ways. While the means of knowledge – the explicit meaning of texts and their inferred meaning, context, 'need,' and so on – are familiar and explained in various Mīmāṃsā manuals, in 7.1.1–12 we see the means of valid knowledge operating in practice in a specific Mīmāṃsā context, where the allocation of dharmas is at stake. From the discussion of atideśa, we gain insight into the practical logic underlying sacrifice construction and modification. Together, the reflections on dharma and atideśa show us how there developed, from Śabara on, an understanding of dharma as a quality or characteristic of a sacrifice. 'Dharma' has to do with acts, things, the order of actions; as ordinary, they are not in themselves of Vedic relevance, but they can be reconstituted as dharmas by the authority of explicit and implicit texts. 'What is dharma?' is subordinate to 'Where is the dharma?' and 'By what rule can this dharma be introduced elsewhere?' Reasoning about natural properties and ordinary analogies are not adequate to the task of making sure that the right elements are introduced in new, derivative sacrificial contexts. Ordinary imagination and ordinary judgment do not work because a dharma is not to be envisaged as an ordinary object in the world. Dharma is a matter of a non-visual – non-generalizable, non-inferable – verbal construction, and the dharmic lies in the proper ordering of things and acts, defended according to proper exegesis. These things receive 'dharma' as a second name, affording deeper significance to whatever might be their ordinary names.

6

To sketch the way toward a more general and probably more familiar understanding of dharma, I turn finally and briefly to the differently demanding philosophical reflections on dharma near the beginning of the Sūtras, to view both the move toward theorization and also the Mīmāṃsā ambivalence about it. For instance, let us consider the discussion occurring at the important second sūtra (1.1.2): *codanālakṣaṇo 'rtho dharmaḥ*: '*dharmah*' is the artha distinguished by injunctive verbal force.'[22] A key question comes to the fore: Is dharma solely about sacrificial action or is it also rooted in what certain things are and how they are to be valued? This question is of primary concern, but answering it requires reflection on how one learns about dharma from the Veda, so another question is also asked in the commentaries on 1.1.2: How is dharma to be known? Perhaps we can say that 'What is dharma?' and 'How is dharma known?' are in fact two ways of asking the same question, since dharmas exist only as constituted by the very texts that inform us about those dharmas.

We begin with a few comments on the Prābhākara position, since the writings of Prabhākara and his commentator Śālikanātha Miśra conceptually (if not chronologically) constitute the older of the Mīmāṃsā schools. Both Prabhākara and Śālikanātha Miśra insist that the referent of dharma in the Vedic context and according to Vedic authority is nothing but action; what is not action must be construed as action-related. They reject the turn to essences suggested by the notion that dharma is simply what is real or good, instead staying closer to the act-generating and act-specific power of the Vedic, and thus closer to the notion that dharma is a reality actualized by an authorizing Vedic word. As emphasized by Śālikanātha Miśra in the *Śāstrapariccheda Section* of the *Prakaraṇapañcikā*[23] (a section directly related to 1.1.2) at issue is the basic nature of language, language-learning, and vocabulary. These are learned by observing usage in practice. Only thereafter, and by secondary construal, can broader and more general meanings be known. The Veda does not inform us directly or merely about things and values; rather, it teaches action-related meanings that are not otherwise knowable.

Arguing the alternative Bhāṭṭa position in the *Śāstradīpikā* at 1.1.2, Pārthasārathi Miśra does not dispute that the Veda is the privileged source of knowledge about dharma, or that dharma has primarily to do with action. He too wishes to secure the meaning of dharma within the realm of Vedic reference, but in doing so he seems to defend a broader, content-based reference. For the sake of argument, he agrees with the Prābhākaras that words' meanings (inside and outside the sacrificial context) are known first in relation to action. But established realities too are made known by the Veda, and knowledge of these is not merely for the sake of action. Many words in the Veda refer to existing things that are to be known, most famously the imperishable self. Pārthasārathi Miśra accordingly charges that the Prābhākara view undercuts the Vedic authorization for statements such as 'Indeed, this self is indestructible' (*avināśī vā are ayamātmā*),[24] because it is neither directly instigatory of action nor in any obvious way supportive of action.[25] Straightforward knowledge about things is communicated in the Veda; understanding of dharma cannot be separated from the wide informative dimension of the Veda, and so the questions related to the 'where' and 'how' of dharma, enunciated in 7.1 and elsewhere, are now accompanied also by questions of nature and essence.

The Prābhākaras and Bhāṭṭas are not radically opposed, and their differences on the epistemology and ontology of dharma are subtle. What is at stake is made somewhat clearer when the commentators introduce as problematic the Śyena sacrifice. In 7.1.13–16, the frame of reference was neutral, as the Śyena was treated simply with respect to the dharmas of the Jyotiṣṭoma and the Iṣu. In 1.1.2, however, it is characterized as a malevolent sacrifice. A major portion of the commentaries on 1.1.2 is given over to ruling out the Śyena as a legitimate dharmic sacrifice. Instigatory verbal force – 'Let the one doing harm perform the Śyena'[26] – apparently legitimates performance of the Śyena as a dharmic act. But that verbal force is judged ineffective here by a consensus view that the Śyena, as malevolent, ought not to be performed. The question is why.

It would be easiest simply to say that sacrifices intending harm are wrong; but then dharma would be in part dependent on some external criteria as to what is right and wrong.[27] Prabhākara and Śālikanātha[28] therefore want instead to rule out the Śyena while yet avoiding an assessment of dharma according to standards of value and morals that would determine dharma and adharma by judgments of virtue. Their approach is to indicate a more basic and apt distinction that remains within the internal realm of the sacrifice (*kratvartha*).

By their view, anything announced as to be done in the Veda is established in two steps: something is established (*upadeya*) as potentially doable, and only thereafter can it actually be enjoined (*vidheya*). Obligation to an action to be performed (*kārya*) necessarily presumes a content – a material basis, an *upadāna* – already established and thus able to 'become' dharmic as a sacrificial act. The Śyena is indeed expressed as an action to be performed, but there is no properly established action liable to become one that must be performed, and so its establishment as something to be performed is never merely a settled matter, to be taken for granted.[29] The blocking of the command legitimating the Śyena is explained in technical sacrificial terms as the matter remains under the aegis of the sacrificial perspective (*kratvartha*), internal to the world of the Veda as word and practice. There is no generalized appeal to the moral or the true, and dharma is not generalized as essence or value.

From the Bhāṭṭa viewpoint, the Śyena is not performed because one can judge that it is wrong to perform a sacrifice intended harm for one's enemies. The Veda is attuned to moral values – Dharma on a larger scale – so even discourse about dharma as sacrificial performance has a substantive and evaluative dimension in fact distinct from directives regarding action. Thus, the issue of the allocation of dharmas as details is now linked to a judgment about what is or is not morally acceptable. Because the Śyena is wrong, it is not dharmic even if apparently enjoined. Dharma henceforth is in part at least a matter of what is right and wrong. Despite these externalist implications, however, Pārthasārathi too exegetes the meaning of 1.1.2 on primarily internal grounds. He asks why the sūtra reads *codanālakṣaṇo 'rtho dharmaḥ* instead of a briefer *codanālakṣaṇo dharmaḥ*. That is, what is the point of complicating the appeal to the injunctive verbal force by adding that it is an artha that is subject to that force? The solution is not vākyabheda, as if there are in the sentence two sentences, 'What is to be done is Vedārtha' and 'Artha is dharma.' Rather, there is a single claim, 'that artha which is enjoined is dharma.' Only an artha, in some way a good, can be enjoined, and only an enjoined artha can be dharma. If upādāna bore the weight of the necessary distinction for the Prābhākaras, here artha serves that purpose. As highlighted, artha implies the rightness of the intended goal, measured in part by a wider ethical consensus about the impropriety of performing sacrifices in hopes of destroying one's enemies. Dharma is a kind of artha, knowable in part as a reality irreducible to action and not exempt from moral judgment. What things are and how they are to be valued come to the fore as keys to the meaning of dharma. Dharma thus begins to be something to be known, assessed, accepted on a general basis. More general theorizing about dharma now finds an entrée into Mīmāṃsā, particularly in its Bhāṭṭa school.

More could be said on the intricate debates at 1.1.2, and these remarks offer only a preliminary indication. I have introduced the matter simply to sketch the path from the reflection on dharma evident in 7.1.1–12 toward a broader history of dharma in the Mīmāṃsā system. For 1.1.2 is conceptually later than 7.1.1–12, as well as freer of considerations of dharma as detail. Were one to assume that 1.1.2 was argued before 7.1 was settled, there would have been no strong reason to carry on the debate we have seen at 7.1, except perhaps for completeness – even sacrifices never to be performed, such as the Śyena and Iṣu, should be properly understood. But the debate, and specifically the Prābhākara position at 1.1.2, makes rather more sense after and not before 7.1. 1.1.2 suggests a move toward abstraction and essentialization, and thus another step in the Mīmāṃsā intellectual history.

7

In 7.1 things, actions, and persons properly aligned with one another contribute to the completion of an archetypal sacrifice and so, as authorized verbally, gain the status of dharmas. Dharmas can be transferred to other sacrifices, only if those latter sacrifices too are generated by injunctive verbal force, and not merely thought to be similar to the archetypal sacrifice. This propriety, constitutive of dharma, is generated by action-instigating Vedic instructions, and not by other kinds of knowledge, nor even by extrapolations from settled examples of Vedic sacrificial practice. Dharma is not something to be known; it is rather an enactment to be heard in the Veda, and judiciously implemented. Every dharma arrives by way of an event, established in a particular case, by explicit Vedic instructions (upadeśa), or by carefully extended Vedic instructions (atideśa). We find a complication of the matter at 1.1.2, where dharma is defined as a topic for regular inquiry.

The Bhāṭṭa position in particular seems to open the door slightly to the reconstruction of dharma as a kind of knowable essence. Dharma is nearer to being what is good (excluding the Śyena), more reliably referential to true realities (including even an imperishable self). Such complications mark inevitable further questions in Mīmāṃsā's intellectual history, as dharma is redefined, only partly in keeping with earlier and more ritually imbedded determinations. We understand the history of the idea of dharma more clearly if we move not from a high ideal of dharma down to dharma as detail, but rather from dharma as a verbally enacted feature of sacrificial performance to the later understanding of dharma as value and essence.

NOTES

[1] See Clooney (1985, 1990).
[2] See Clooney (1985).

[3] See Clooney (1989).
[4] I have tried to adhere to a more literal translation, while yet paying due respect to the commentarial tradition beginning with Śabara. 'P' and 's' indicate *pūrvapakṣa* and *siddhānta sūtras*. The subsequent parenthetical remarks are my own elucidations.
[5] In general, the means (*karaṇa*) refers to the deity, mantra, and offering; the manner (*itikartavyatā*) refers to the host of other details.
[6] P. 1229; Sanskrit, p. 374.
[7] P. 1235; Sanskrit, p. 383.
[8] P. 1235; Sanskrit, p. 383.
[9] P. 1239; Sanskrit, p. 386.
[10] P. 1236; Sanskrit, p. 384.
[11] P. 1230; Sanskrit, p. 376.
[12] P. 1239; Sanskrit, p. 386.
[13] P. 1231; Sanskrit, p. 377.
[14] P. 1234; Sanskrit, p. 381.
[15] P. 1234; Sanskrit, p. 383.
[16] P. 1237; Sanskrit, p. 385, and p. 1238, Sanskrit, p. 285.
[17] P. 1239; Sanskrit, p. 386.
[18] P. 681.
[19] P. 683.
[20] For brevity, in describing the issues at stake with reference to atideśa I follow the exposition offered by Pārthasārathi Miśra in his *Sāstradīpikā*, in supplement to Śabara's exposition.
[21] See Clooney (1990, pp. 71–77).
[22] Here too I use the *Sāstradīpikā* for a relatively succinct summation of the issues involved, and also the *Bṛhatī* of Prabhākara, and the *Sāstraparicheda* section of the *Prakaraṇa Pañcikā*.
[23] See the *Sāstraparicheda*, pp. 235–243, particularly 240–241.
[24] *Bṛhadāraṇyaka Upaniṣad* 4.5.14.
[25] Tr. p. 17; Skt. p. 16.
[26] *Śyenena abhicaran yajeta*, as cited in Śabara *Bhāṣya*, Skt. p. 22; identified by Jha as *Sadviṃśa Brāhmaṇa* 8.1–2; tr. p. 7.
[27] See Clooney (2003).
[28] Following the *Bṛhatī* with *Ṛjuvimalā* on 1.1.2.
[29] On upadāna and upadeya, see Yoshimizu.

REFERENCES

Clooney, F.X. (1985). Dharmamātra Karma: a re-evaluation of the Pūrva Mīmāṃsā Sūtras 2.1.9–12 with Śābara Bhāṣya. *Journal of Oriental Research, Madras,* 157–168.

Clooney, F.X. (1989). The Concept of Dharma in the *Mīmāṃsā Sūtras* of Jaimini. *Kuppuswami Sastri Birth Centenary Commemoration*, Vol. II (pp. 175–187). Madras: Kuppuswami Sastri Research Institute.

Clooney, F.X. (1990). *Thinking Ritually: Rediscovering the Pūrva Mīmāṃsā of Jaimini.* Vienna: Publications of the de Nobili Research Library 17.

Clooney, F.X. (2003). Pain but not harm: some classical resources toward a hindu just war theory. In P. Robinson (ed.), *Just War in a Comparative Perspective.* London: Ashgate Publishing Ltd.

Jaimini (1976). In K.V. Abhyankar & G.A. Joshi (eds.), *Mīmāṃsādarśanam*. 7 Volumes. Ānandrāśramasaṃskṛtagranthāvaliḥ, 17. Pune.

Jha, G. (1942). *Pūrva Mīmāṃsā in its Sources*. Varanasi: Banaras Hindu University.

Miśra, Pārthasārathi. (1930–1979). In G. Kaviraja (ed.), *Tantraratna*. Saraswati Bhāvanā Texts, No. 31. 5 Vols. Varanasi: Vidya Vilas Press.

Miśrà, Pārthasārathi. (1940). *Śāstradīpikā* (*Tarkapāda*). *Tr. by D. Venkatramiah. Baroda: Gaekward's Oriental Series 89.*

Miśra, Prabhākara. (1934–1967). *Bṛhatī with the Ṛjuvimalāpañcikā of Śālikanātha Miśra*, Vol. 1. Varanasi: Vidya Vilas Press.

Miśra, Ś. (1961). *Prakaraṇa Pañcikā with Nyāyasiddhi*. Banaras Hindu University Darśana Series N. 4. Banaras: Banaras Hindu University.

Miśra, P. (1988). *Śāstradīpikā with the Yuktisnehaprapūraṇī of Rāmakṛṣṇa* (*I.1*) *and the Mayūkhamālikā of Somanātha* (*I.2–XII*). *Krishnadas Sanskrit Series 103. Varanasi: Krishnadas Academy.*

Śabara (1933–1936). *The Śābara Bhāṣya*. Tr. by Ganganatha Jha. 3 Vols. Baroda: Gaekward's Oriental Series 66, 70, 73.

Yoshimizu, K. (1994). Bādari & Prabhākara. In R.C. Dwivedi (ed.), *Studies in Mīmāṃsā*. Dr. Mandan Miśra Felicitation Volume. (pp. 389–413). Delhi: Motilal Banarsidass.

Yoshimizu, K. (1997). *Der 'Organismus' des Urheberlosen Veda*. Vienna: Publications of the de Nobili Research Library 25.

Department of Theology
Boston College
140 Commonwealth Avenue
Chestnut Hill, MA 02467
USA
E-mail: clooney@bc.edu

SHELDON POLLOCK

THE MEANING OF *DHARMA* AND THE RELATIONSHIP OF THE TWO MĪMĀṂSĀS: APPAYYA DĪKṢITA'S 'DISCOURSE ON THE REFUTATION OF A UNIFIED KNOWLEDGE SYSTEM OF PŪRVAMĪMĀṂSĀ AND UTTARAMĪMĀṂSĀ'

Among Sanskrit intellectuals active in the last centuries prior to the consolidation of colonialism and the introduction into South Asia of radically different knowledge systems, the most remarkable in southern India, for the breadth of his learning and his striking innovation in multiple disciplines, was Appayya Dīkṣita.[1] His literary activity fell in the last half of the 16th century, possibly extending into the early 17th. But astonishingly little hard information about his life is available, despite the fact that scores of works attributed to him are extant.[2] What is known more or less for certain can fit on a single printed page (and that page has recently been written, in the introduction to a new edition and translation of one of Appayya's linguistic treatises).[3] Both the breadth of his learning and the quality of his innovation are fully on display in two works, one truly grand, the other more modest, that deserve to be far better known than they are. The first is the *Caturmatasārasaṃgraha*, 'Compendium of Essential Tenets of the Four Schools', a monumental review of the four major Vedānta systems of Appayya's time, and, so far as I am aware, the only such systematic account ever produced in the premodern period (it is the Humvee to the Kia of Mādhava's doxographical epitomes in the *Sarvadarśanasaṃgraha*). These remarkable verse compositions (except in the case of the second, which is in prose) set out in accordance with the topics of the *Brahmasūtra* (BS) text the major tenets of Dvaita (in the *Nyāyamuktāvalī*), Viśiṣṭādvaita (*Naya mayūkhamālikā*), Śaivādvaita (*Nayamaṇimālā*), and Advaita (*Nayamañjari*), in what is probably an evaluative sequence.[4] The second is the work under consideration here, the *Pūrvottaramīmāṃsāvādanakṣatramālā*, 'The Milky Way of Discourses on Mīmāṃsā and Vedānta.' We might better capture the spirit if not the letter of the title by translating it 'Collected Essays in the Prior and Posterior Analytics', or perhaps instead, with a nod to Gadamer rather than Aristotle, '. . . in Philosophical and Theological Hermeneutics'.

'Essays', however, I mean quite seriously: the genre here is a new one, presenting a series of independent studies (a set of twenty-seven) of particular and often very abstruse topics in the two systems.[5]

The relationship between Pūrvamīmāṃsā and Uttaramīmāṃsā flagged in Appayya's title is the object of a long-standing debate in many Vedānta schools.[6] Both knowledge systems ground themselves on the authority of the Veda, and employ many of the same exegetical principles to make sense of the Vedic textual corpus. Yet their semantics and pragmatics, so to speak – what they understood the texts to mean and how they proceeded to act upon that understanding – appeared to many traditional thinkers to be radically incommensurable, and finding a way to reconcile them was a serious challenge. Indeed, their problematic relationship is embodied in the very nomenclature that links them, in the differentiation itself of a 'posterior' from a 'prior' *darśana*, like that of a 'new' from an 'old' testament. Viewed more historically, the nomenclature seems likely to have emerged out of the dispute that hinges on this relationship and that forms the central problem of Appayya's essay translated here.

Whatever may be the earlier history of the terminology (and I am unaware that it has ever been clearly traced), we find it distinctly if still inchoately articulated in the text that forms the *pūrvapakṣa* of Appayya's account, namely the *Śrībhāṣya* of Rāmānuja (11–12th century). Rāmānuja's summary of the purpose of the first *sūtra* of the BS (the *jijñāsāsūtra*) runs as follows: 'Since the fruit of works known through the *prior part* of the Mīmāṃsā (*mīmāṃsāpūrvabhāga*) is limited and non-permanent, and since the fruit of the knowledge of *brahma* – which knowledge is to be reached through the *latter part* (*uparitanabhāga*) of the Mīmāṃsā – is unlimited and permanent; for this reason *brahma* "is to be known", after the knowledge of works has previously taken place'.[7] It may not be without some further significance to determining this terminological history that in the summary contained in Bodhayana's *vṛtti* (early centuries C.E.?) reproduced by Rāmānuja there is no mention of 'prior' and 'latter'. But that does not mean that the problem of the relationship of the two knowledge systems was not already on the table. Indeed, what the Vṛttikāra insists on is precisely the unity (*aikaśāstrya*), as Rāmānuja puts it: 'He [Bodhayana] will declare later on "This *śārīraka*-doctrine is integrated (*saṃhitam*)[8] with Jaimini's doctrine so as to make up 16 *adhyāya*s" – that is, the Treatise of Twelve Chapters, or the *Mīmāṃsāsūtra*s (MS) of Jaimini, and the Treatise of Four

Chapters, or the BS of Vyāsa Bādarāyaṇa, should be taken together as constituting a single work of Sixteen Chapters; 'this proves the two to constitute one body of doctrine'.[9]

Whereas Rāmānuja provides a range of reasons in his commentary on BS 1.1.1 why the 'latter part' of Mīmāṃsā requires the 'earlier', he nowhere seems to base this on the notion that the definition and nature of *dharma*, the subject of the major thesis (*pratijñā*) of the Pūrvamīmāṃsā ('Now, then, the inquiry into *dharma*', *athāto dharmajijñāsā*), comprise not only its declared topic, *karma*, but also *brahma*, whose definition and nature form the subject of the major thesis of the Uttaramīmāṃsā ('Now, then, the inquiry into *brahma*', *athāto brahmajijñāsā*). Arguing out this theorem appears to have been the contribution of Rāmānuja's great commentator of the early 14th century, Sudarśanasūri in his *Śrutaprakāśikā*. It is that commentator whom Appayya has squarely in his sights when defining the limits of the term *dharma* and critiquing the doctrine of the unified knowledge systems.[10] There can be no doubt whatever about Appayya's conclusion itself: 'Therefore, given that contradiction between the two systems – with respect to primary meanings and end-results – ever rears its head, even the rumor that they form a single knowledge system can gain no standing in the thoughts of the learned' (*saṃgrahaśloka* 13 infra). What is unclear, to me at least, is whether this should be taken as representing Appayya's personal view, given the complexities that remain to be disentangled. Not least of these is the fact that Śrīkaṇṭha, the founder of the Śaivādvaita Vedānta system to which Appayya apparently subscribed, declares explicitly 'We do not hold that the two systems, the analysis of *dharma* and the analysis of *brahma*, are completely different; on the contrary, we hold that they form a single knowledge system'.[11] One thing beyond dispute, however, is that Appayya's rejection of the theory should not taken as intended to undermine the validity of Vedānta itself. As he declares in his commentary on Śrīkaṇṭhaśivācārya's text, what refuting the unity of the two systems is meant in fact to provide is scope for the commencement of the BS.[12]

Whatever his own views may have been on the points of intersection and separation in the two knowledge systems, Appayya's work is a valuable index of Pūrvamīmāṃsā thinking on the problem of the scope of *dharma*, the system's very keyword. Indeed, the way the essay frames the term's meaning is crucial. Here and there throughout the history of Mīmāṃsā an anxiety is almost palpable concerning the potential expansion of *dharma*'s semantic field, about its slippage or spread or appropriation. The present collection of essays is eloquent testimony to how very real the possibility of this extension was – an extension that, in the view of Mīmāṃsā, was wholly unwarranted. To one of the preeminent thinkers of the early-modern period in Indian intellectual history, *dharma* meant first and foremost what it meant for the Mīmāṃsā system from the beginning: ritual action based on transcendentally authoritative texts, the Veda. And it is hard not to see his *Vādanakṣatramālā* as yet another attempt in the long history of attempts by Mīmāṃsā to maintain its monopoly over this primeval definition against actual historical encroachments.

Rather than dismissing the development as 'encroachment', however, we do better to link this to what the Egyptologist Jan Assmann has called 'subversive inversion', a process of transvaluation of semantic and conceptual goods across socio-religious boundaries found in many times and places. It is richly illustrated in Indian history, especially by Buddhists in their appropriation of *vaidika* categories and concepts – preeminent among them *dharma* itself.[13] The most remarkable attempt in Sanskrit intellectual history to arrest this process of subversion by delimiting in the strictest possible terms what does and does not count as *dharma* and to defend the proposition that its sole source is the Veda is offered by Kumārila in his *Tantravārttika* on MS 1.3. There he observes that, like spoiled children who hate their parents, the Buddhists refuse, out of shame and resentment at any competing foundational claim, to acknowledge that every metaphysical truth in their system – anything concerning *dharma* – must be derived from the Veda.[14]

We do not have to go outside the *vaidika* world, broadly viewed, to find evidence of this process of extension as well as of Mīmāṃsā angst. A well-known example is in fact the term *veda* itself, which forms the textual reference point of the system. Despite Mīmāṃsā's constantly reiterated restrictions on the category (the *vidhi, arthavāda, mantra*, and *nāmadheya* of the *Ṛk*, *Yajus*, and *Sāma saṃhitas*), 'Veda' too was a category ever at risk of illegitimate expansion. Think only of Jayantabhaṭṭa's elaborate defense (in the fourth chapter of the *Nyāyamañjarī*) of the *Artharvaveda* as a fourth (or as he says, actually the first) Veda, or of the *Mahābhārata's* famous claim to constitute a 'fifth Veda', or of the tendency of the Upanishadic corpus toward almost infinite expansion. One final related point may be made here. Mīmāṃsā itself was a prime source for terms and categories that either through inversion or extension became keywords in Indian culture at large. The very idea of *smṛti*, for instance, or so I have suggested, originated with Mīmāṃsā – as a Vedic text no longer extant, no longer actually still being 'heard' (*śruti*) in its original wording during recitation, but existing only as a 'memory' (*smṛti*) of the original, and in new wording – and migrated thence to the wider intellectual universe, again despite Mīmāṃsā's attempt to delimit the genre. Precisely the same thing could be demonstrated for other expressions and ideas, such as that core component of *dharma*, *puruṣārtha* itself.[15]

Much remains to be explored in reference to Appayya's project in the *Nakṣatramālā*, both within the general context of early-modern Indian intellectual practices and discursive styles, and specifically in the *Auseinandersetzung* with Viśiṣṭādvaita, to say nothing of the detailed problems that confront us in just making sense of the text. The present essay has been ripped somewhat untimely from the womb so as to provide to this collection of reflections on the history of the concept of *dharma* one important local attempt to make sense of the term and its limits near the end of the creative period of Sanskrit intellectual history. It is especially valuable for us to encounter the actual arguments of those for whom *dharma* was a living reality, and who themselves struggled to understand its nature and the claims it made upon them. In my effort to make these arguments heard I have striven to provide a translation as readable and usable as possible, though the text is one that does not always yield its meaning readily, or offer easy solutions to its stylistic complexity.[16]

The Discourse on the Refutation of a Unified Knowledge System of Pūrvamīmāṃsā and Uttaramīmāṃsā (*appayyadīkṣitānāṃ pūrvottaramīmāṃsāvādanakṣatramālāntarbhāvy- aikaśāstryanirākaraṇavādaḥ*)

[235] Accordingly, insofar as *brahma* has been proved [in the previous discourse][17] to exist as the ultimate referent of all language, it must of necessity also be the referent of the word *dharma*, which is used to refer to ritual action's (*karma*) being a means to otherworldly good (*alaukikaśreyaḥ*). Moreover, *brahma* must be directly expressed by the word *dharma* by reason of the semantic relation just noted. This is so because Mīmāṃsakas argue that the meaning of the word *dharma*, insofar as it is held to be used in reference to a thing's being a means of securing the good as understood from the Veda, must refer to class categories, properties, and substances no less than to ritual actions. [Thus Kumārila:] 'It will be established that class categories, properties, and substances are *dharma*. Even though these are perceptible

entities [whereas *dharma* is imperceptible], it is not in their sensory form that they are *dharma*. Their being means of securing the good is cognized from the Veda alone [and not from perception]; and it is in that form that they are *dharma*, and so beyond the realm of the senses'.[18] Thus, the word *dharma* used in the [first] *sūtra* [of the Pūrvamīmāṃsā system], 'Now, then, the inquiry into *dharma*' [MS 1.1.1] must comprise *brahma*, and *brahma* must therefore also be an object of the examination of *dharma* that Jaimini [the author of the MS] in that *sūtra* states as his main thesis (*pratijñā*) to undertake. To examine whether or not this is in fact the case is the reason for initiating the following discourse.

Our opponents, who argue that *brahma* is the object of the examination of *dharma*, attempt to prove this by the following syllogism:

[*pūrvapakṣa*] *brahma* – its true nature, the sources of knowledge about it, the means of attaining it, and the end-results of doing so – is an object of Jaimini's proposed examination, because *brahma* is a means of attaining otherworldly good, just like ritual action itself.

The long qualification beginning 'its true nature' is meant to preclude the possibility of the above inference being [vitiated by the fallacy of] proving what has already been proved, since *brahma*, in its character of being a deity in general (since it is included as such in the 'offerings to the constellations' [*nakṣatreṣṭi*] and other similar rites), would already have to be [1] an object of Jaimini's examination of whether or not the deity is predominant or subordinate [in its relation to the act of sacrifice]; or, in that same character, [2] an object of his examination of the question whether or not deities have the right to engage in ritual action. [236] This is the first position in the debate.

[*siddhānta*] Now the second position. Were *brahma* the object of Jaimini's proposed examination of *dharma*, one would have expected the examination of *brahma* to occur at the beginning of his work, but we do not find that to be the case. Nor is it possible to suppose that the great sage wanted to undertake an examination of *brahma* but was somehow impeded from doing so, or simply forgot. This is a sage who analyzed the whole field of ritual action – its true nature, the sources of knowledge about it, the means of attaining it, and the end-results of doing so – in the *Treatise of Twelve Chapters* [i.e., the MS], and who, noticing that certain interpretive principles used in that text were not explicitly given in *sūtra* form, produced the *Saṃkarṣaṇakāṇḍa* as a supplement to the *Treatise* in order to gather these principles together. How then are we to suppose that he either was impeded from examining, or just plain forgot to examine *brahma*? Nor can it be claimed that the analysis of the true nature of *brahma*, the sources of knowledge about it, the means of attaining it, and the end-results of doing so was accomplished by the same principles used to examine ritual action, and for this reason no separate examination of *brahma* had to be provided. That the interpretive principles used for the analysis of sentences concerned with *brahma* are distinct from those used for sentences concerned with *dharma* is proved by the fact that the latter were systematized in the *Treatise of Four Chapters* [i.e., the BS]. Nor is it possible to believe that the stated thesis of examining *brahma* can be brought to fruition only on the assumption that the *Treatise of Twelve Chapters* and the *Treatise of Four Chapters* form a single knowledge system. There is no valid reason to believe that they do form one system: they have different authors (*vaktṛ*); their introductions containing the statement of their major theses (*pratijñopakrama*) concern the examination of *dharma* on the one hand and *brahma* on the other, and they were undertaken to frame analytic principles regarding positive and negative objectives that are mutually distinct. [237] Hence, the inference given above is blocked. [This can be shown by a counter-syllogism:] *brahma* [an already existent thing] is not expressed [by the word *dharma*] as something to be accomplished [i.e., an action] is so expressed, because it is something different from ritual action, just as a pot [is not expressed, being different from ritual action.]

[*pūrvapakṣa*] Now the third position. My inference is not blocked, because it is possible for the theses [of the MS and the BS][19] to be brought to fruition only by the supposition that [Mīmāṃsā and Vedānta] form a single knowledge system. And there are factors lending support to such a supposition, such as the fact that both works are commentaries on a single text, namely the Veda. Nor does the fact of their having different authors militate against this supposition: the exegeses of Vāmana and Jayāditya, for example, even though the authors are different, form a single knowledge system, insofar as they are a commentary on a single work, namely [Pāṇini's] grammar. Nor do their introductions containing the statement of their major theses regarding *dharma* on the one hand and *brahma* on the other block my inference: the word *dharma* refers equally to *karma* and *brahma*, and when the thesis of the *Treatise of Twelve Chapters*, which is [thus] common (*sāmānya*) to the *Treatise of Four Chapters*, has been dealt with, it stands to reason that thereafter, after the examination of *karma*, we should have a reference to the sub-thesis (*avāntarapratijñā*), that is: 'Now, then, the inquiry into *brahma*', just as we have [the reference to another sub-thesis in the continuation of the MS], 'Now, then, the inquiry into what is subsidiary' [MS 3.1.1]. Nor is the inference blocked by the argument that [the two systems] frame analytical principles that are mutually distinct. That there should be a distinction in analytical principles (*nyāya*) in accordance with [differences in the] objects to be analyzed makes perfectly good sense. We find in the *Treatise of Twelve Chapters* itself that distinct analytical principles are framed in accordance with the objects to be analyzed, such as the division of ritual action [MS 2], the relationship of dominant and subsidiary elements in a rite [MS 3], and so forth. Thus, my inference is not blocked, whereas yours is ineffectual.

[*siddhānta*] Now the fourth position. I do not mean, by saying that the principles are 'distinct', merely that they are different. I mean that they are contradictory. [238] And this contradiction is a matter of common knowledge, given that, in the *Treatise of Four Chapters*, we find that Jaimini's doctrines are generally presented as the prima facie view to be refuted. These are two knowledge systems, initiated by two different authors relying on two contradictory doctrines, and it is impossible therefore to suppose that they were produced as a single system by these same two men in unanimity. As for the word *dharma*, it is used in counterpoint to *brahma* as referring to sacrifice and other ritual action in the *sūtra* 'Jaimini [thinks] for the same reasons that *dharma* [is what brings about the fruits of actions]' [BS 3.2.40],[20] which is contained in the topic 'From him [i.e., the Lord, there comes] the fruit [of works]; for [that only] is possible' [BS 3.2.38]. Moreover, the great sage Āpastamba uses the word *dharma* only in the sense of action to be performed such as sacrifice, when he says, '*Dharma* and *adharma* do not wander about saying "Here we are!" Nor do the gods and *gandharvas* or the ancestors proclaim "This is *dharma*, that is *adharma*".[21] Rather, it is what the *āryas* commend to see performed that is *dharma*, and what they condemn is *adharma*' [ĀDS 1.7.6]. In accordance with his view, therefore, the word [*dharma*] contained in the *sūtra* on the inquiry into *dharma* must be admitted to refer to sacrifice and other such action to be performed. And so it is unreasonable to suppose that the two *sūtras*, one on the inquiry into *dharma* and the other on the inquiry into *brahma*, can be distinguished as referring to a thesis that is common to both systems [MS 1.1.1] and to one meant to be a sub-thesis

[BS 1.1.1] (*sādhāraṇāvāntarapratijñāparatvavibhāga*). Therefore, your inference is blocked, and mine is not ineffectual, because anything that, under a given description, cannot be *performed* can have no connection, under that description, with being taken in the sense of the word *dharma*, since this denotes actions that are to be performed.

[*pūrvapakṣa*] Now the fifth position. It is not proved that the doctrines of Jaimini and Vyāsa stand in contradiction with each other. In some places in the *Treatise of Four Chapters* Jaimini's doctrine is not in fact presented as the prima facie view to be refuted. With respect to the topic dealing with human goals (*puruṣārtha*) [239], the prima facie *sūtra* containing a repudiation of *brahma*, 'On account of [the Self] standing in a supplementary relation [to ritual action], [the statements as to the fruits of the knowledge of the Self] must be narrative portions (*arthavādas*) [in praise of action], thus Jaimini believes' [BS 3.4.2] is a restatement, not of Jaimini's own position, but rather of a position that he[22] includes as a supplement (*abhyuccayavāda*) [and that does not therefore necessarily reflect his own views]. And that is why, in such *sūtra*s as 'To the highest [*brahma*] [the souls are led], so Jaimini believes, owing to this being the principal sense [of the word *brahma*]' [BS 4.3.12], we find a restatement of a position as belonging to Jaimini that proceeds precisely by way of recognizing *brahma*.[23] Similarly, the *sūtra* 'Jaimini [considers that scriptural passages mentioning those stages of life in which celibacy is obligatory contain] a reference only to those stages; they are not injunctions; for [other scriptural passages] forbid [those stages]' [BS 3.4.18] restates a repudiation of ascetic renunciation merely provided as a supplement by Jaimini; it is not a restatement of his own settled view. Accordingly, in the *sūtra* 'But of him who has become that [i.e., entered onto a higher life-stage] there is no becoming not that [i.e., descending to a lower stage], according to Jaimini also. . .' [BS 3.4.40], it is shown that Jaimini also disapproves of any deviation from renunciation once a person has renounced. Thus elsewhere as well, in each individual case [apparent] contradiction may be resolved through interpretation. Moreover, the use of the word *dharma* to refer uniquely to something to be performed (*anuṣṭheyāsādhāraṇya*) is also unproved. We find it used to refer generally to the Blessed One (*bhagavatsādhāraṇyokteḥ*) in the *Mahābhārata*:

> The sages who know the Veda and the people who know the transcendent Self say that Krishna, the great one, is the eternal *dharma* [MBh. 3.86.22 crit. ed.].

Thus, because [1] real contradiction between the two knowledge systems does not exist; or, [2] even if contradiction were thought somehow to be present, an actual refusal to recognize *brahma* is not expressed in any *sūtra* in the *Treatise of Twelve Chapters* ; and [3] because the word *dharma* is common to the topics of both systems [*karma* and *brahma*] – for all these reasons, there are no grounds for refusing to accept that they form a single system even though the authors are different. Thus, your inference is indeed ineffectual, insofar as something not performed can very well be an object of Jaimini's proposed examination, since the word *dharma* is found used in reference to such things.

[240] [*siddhānta*] Now the sixth position. The statement that there is no contradiction is unproved. There is an undeniable contradiction between accepting *brahma* or renunciation and rejecting them. Moreover, one cannot maintain that the *sūtra* that presents Jaimini's acceptance of both *brahma* and renunciation is an indictor that this acceptance of the two constitutes his real settled view. For this situation can be accounted for differently: Jaimini's thought is being represented as self-contradictory and introduced in the *Brahmasūtra* with the intention of showing its unacceptability for that reason, according to the interpretive principal enunciated in the topic 'On Sāṃkhya': 'And moreover [the Sāṃkhya doctrine] is objectionable on account of its contradictions' [BS 2.2.10].

It is also illogical to state that, while granting that Jaimini and Bādarāyaṇa may stand in contradiction with each other over certain either/or issues (*aikāntyādiṣu*) such as the acceptance or rejection of *brahma*, still, insofar as the rejection of *brahma* and so on is never actually *enunciated* in any single *sūtra* in the *Treatise of Twelve Chapters*, that treatise does not therefore stand in contradiction with the *Treatise of Four Chapters* and so can reasonably be said to form a single knowledge system with it. The reason this argument is illogical is because it does not prove that the principal aims [of the two *śāstras*] do not stand in contradiction with each other.

(1) For example, when Jaimini proposes a description of the means of knowing *dharma* in the *sūtra* 'An investigation of the conditions [of knowing] it' (MS 1.1.3), the description of these means offered in his first chapter is already in contradiction [with the BS]. To explain: One *pūrvapakṣa sūtra* reads 'Since the purpose of the Veda lies in the enjoining of actions, those parts of the Veda that do not serve that purpose are purposeless; and with regard to those parts the Veda must be said to be non-eternal [unreliable]' [MS 1.2.1].[24] This means

that scripture in its entirety, if it is to culminate in something purposeful, must of necessity have some action as its purpose. Those portions of scripture not having that purpose – that is, portions whose purpose is not action insofar as they are not concerned with action-sentences (an action-sentence is something like 'He who desires prosperity should sacrifice a white animal dedicated to the Wind Deity') – are said to be 'purposeless', that is, without any function. [241] Therefore, it is claimed [in the prima facie view] that the whole range of sentences that do not have action as their purpose have no validity. On the basis of this *sūtra* thus understood the MS goes on to raise a doubt about the validity of the narrative portions of the Vedas. The *siddhānta sūtra* on this topic reads 'Since [these narrative portions] form single discursive units with commandments, [they can acquire validity] through the purpose of commending [the actions that actually are the object of commandments]' [MS 1.2.7]. This *sūtra* means that narrative portions concerned with already-accomplished entities can have a purpose by way of the function of commending commandments [that is, substantiating their credibility, value, etc.], since these portions form discursive units with commandment sentences. On the basis of this *sūtra* thus understood, the validity of such portions of the Vedas is established in the topic 'On the *arthavāda*' [MS 1.2.1-18] insofar as these do form single discursive units with commandments. And this position is corroborated in the topic 'On the *audumbara* post' [MS 1.2.19-25]) by referring back to the matter raised in 'On the *arthavāda*' when it is said, 'But the fact of such sentences being taken along with other sentences has already been explained [i.e., the narrative passages are to be taken along with other injunctive passages]' [MS 1.2.22]. Now, if the proposed inquiry into *dharma* were meant to be inclusive of an inquiry into *brahma*, then the proposed description of the means of knowing *dharma* given in the *sūtra* 'An investigation of the conditions [of knowing] it' would be inclusive of a description of the means of knowing *brahma*. And if that were in fact the case, then, given the doubt about the purposelessness of non-action matters, this [purposelessness] would have to have been refuted [in the MS] by the following sort of division: that the validity of some would be established by their being considered supplementary to commandments regarding acts like sacrifice that are means to ends, and the validity of others, by their promulgating entities such as *brahma* that are ends in themselves. There are additional substantive contradictions raised elsewhere in the epistemology chapter that would have to have been reconciled.

(2) Likewise, a topic in the eighth chapter [beginning] 'When there is [apparent] conflict [between commandments], the procedure should be determined by the sacrificial substance, since the act as such bears upon the substance' [MS 8.1.32-34] is introduced in order to ascertain that the procedure to be followed in the case of the cake offering to the god Indra should be that of the rite of cake offerings to the Fire god, given the identity of sacrificial substances; rather than the procedure of other rites relating to Indra using other substances, given the identity of the deity in question. Here the reasoning approved by Jaimini is that 'deity' is a secondary element, since it is merely a verbal referent. Yet this view stands in contradiction with the view of Vyāsa [242]. In Vyāsa's system, in the topic 'On the deity' [BS 1.3.26 ff.], it is maintained that the deities are actually present in the sacrificial space and are to be considered predominant elements since they are consumers of the oblation.

(3) Another example: In a topic in the second chapter, 'Commandment, however, is an undertaking' [MS 2.1.5],[25] Jaimini has maintained that ritual action produces its end-results by means of a 'transcendental potency', *apūrva*. That position is contradicted by Vyāsa's as expressed in the topic 'From him [i.e., the Lord, there comes] the fruit [of works]; for [that only] is possible' [BS 3.2.38]. There he argues that it is [not *apūrva* but] the supreme Lord who bestows the end-results when his grace is gained by ritual action and worship. What we have therefore is a contradiction between the two knowledge systems themselves [and not just between their authors].

(4) There is also a contradiction between them occasioned by the repudiation of *brahma* and renunciation. To explain: There are discourses [in the BS] concerning *brahma*, such as 'That art Thou', which make known the identity of *brahma* and the individual soul. Now, by the Mīmāṃsā rule 'Because it forms a single discursive unit with a commandment' [MS 1.2.7], whereby a discourse unrelated to action is held to be supplementary to a commandment [of action], these discourses are said to be supplementary to a commandment to perform worship. Acts of worship, for their part, by another Mīmāṃsā interpretive principle (on 'sprinkling' [MS 2.1.9-12]), become supplementary to sacrificial rites insofar as they purify a ritual substance, namely, the agent himself who is engaged in the rite. [This is so for the following reason:] An agent pure and simple (*kārtṛmātra*) is something common [to both ritual action and] worldly action, since worldly action is possible even if the Self is held to be identical to the body.[26] [Nevertheless] the Self referred to as an element to be

purified by worship in those Vedānta [i.e., Upanishadic] passages that are not found in the context of any specific ritual activity, such as 'One should worship the Self', must have an existence separate from the body: this is presupposed by the commandment to sacrifice as well as by the Self's being said to be an enjoyer of heavenly rewards. This Self is thus necessarily connected with ritual acts; and thus, by way of both [the syntactical association of the Self-as-agent with the act to be performed] and the scriptural passage 'One that is performed with knowledge...' [CU 1.1.10], it makes sense to connect these [acts of worship] with ritual acts.[27]

It will not do to object that acts of worship of the Self cannot be supplementary to a sacrificial rite because *brahma* [=the Self] is proved to transcend the individual soul in view of the scripture that ascribes to *brahma* qualities such as absolute purity that are unimaginable in the individual soul [243]. For Jaimini established a hard and fast rule that all non-action discourses must be taken as supplementary to commandments, and only by violating this rule in the topic 'On coherence' [BS 1.1.4 ff.] could the [passages of the] Vedānta pretend to acquire validity independent of action. And it is, after all, only when this putative validity is established with respect to *brahma* and its qualities – by means of indications of general purport such as [congruence with] an introductory passage (*upakrama*) – that *brahma* can even be proved to transcend the individual soul through qualities such as absolute purity. But according to the view of Jaimini, the mention of such qualities is only supplementary to ritual commandments: the description of them has in fact the purpose of commending the individual soul, and it is this that provides for the coherence of the discourse as a whole. Who would dispute this? We find in various *mantra*s and narrative passages of the Veda commendatory descriptions of unimaginable qualities of one entity or another that is connected with the ritual, as in the following: 'Do not scratch the heaven with your index finger, nor harm the atmosphere with your middle, O origin of the earth'; 'Let your smoke ascend to the heaven, your flame to the atmosphere; fill the earth with your ash, *svāhā*'; 'The seasons are devoid of sin'; 'This universe was water'.[28]

Moreover, when *brahma* has been repudiated, the means of attaining *brahma*, namely renunciation, has likewise been repudiated. And this is why Mīmāṃsakas commonly hold that renunciation is nothing but a ruse for self-advancement[29] on the part of those disqualified from participating in ritual action, blind people, for example, or cripples. It is therefore incorrect to hold that there is no contradiction between these two knowledge systems.

(5) It is also incorrect to hold that the word *dharma* ultimately expresses the same thing as the word *brahma*. It is perfectly reasonable to assume that the purpose of the *Mahābhārata* sentence you cited earlier – 'They say Krishna, the great one, is the eternal *dharma*' – is commendation, just like the sentence 'Rāma is *dharma* incarnate'. Therefore my inference is not blocked, [244] and yours is indeed ineffectual.

[*pūrvapakṣa*] Now the seventh position. My inference is not blocked for the following reasons: (1) It is possible to avoid the contradiction revealed in the description of the means of knowing [*dharma*] found in the first chapter of the *Mīmāṃsāsūtra* in the following way: In the Pūrvamīmāṃsā, it is true that the premises of validity and the doubt about the lack of validity of non-action passages (on the grounds that they would be purposeless) would seem to apply equally to discourses concerning *brahma*. But whereas Jaimini enunciated an argument for validity with respect to narrative portions that are supplementary[30] to commandments of ritual action – namely, that they have their purposefulness precisely through such supplementation – he hid his intention with regard to the discourses on *brahma*, and did not openly broach the argument for validity [that he really did believe, namely] that these have intrinsic (*svata eva*) validity, irrespective of their supplementing commandments of ritual action, because their object is *brahma*, which in itself is the supreme human goal.

(2) It is possible to avoid the contradiction cited for the topic in the eighth chapter. In the settled view of this topic, 'When there is conflict...' [MS 8.1.32], the argument is not that the deity is a subsidiary element, because then there would be no difference between a substance's being a subsidiary element and a deity's being such. Rather, the fundamental argument (*mūlayukti*) of the passage is indicated by the rest of the *sūtra*, 'since the act as such bears upon the substance': The identity in the sacrificial substances is decisive because what we see pertaining to these substances is the ritual act itself, which has the form of the offering of such substances: It is the substance and not the deity that we actually see being offered up.[31]

(3) It is possible to avoid the contradiction in the topic 'Commandment, however, is an undertaking' [MS 2.1.5]. Here it is only said that there exists an instrumentality of ritual action. It is not maintained that *apūrva* and *apūrva* alone is the instrument while dismissing the role of the Lord's grace.

(4) It is possible to avoid the doubts about, among other things, the repudiation of *brahma*. The rule 'Because it forms a single discursive unit with a commandment' [MS 1.2.7] is concerned with establishing the authoritativeness only of narrative discourses like 'The Wind is the swiftest...' [245] and so on, by their supplementation of commandments; it is not concerned with discourses dealing with *brahma*.

(5) Last, it is unreasonable to assume that the statement in the *Bhārata* has merely the purpose of commendation. According to the *Bhārata*, the word *dharma* expresses merely a means to other-worldly good, and so it can be used equally to refer to *brahma*. The assumption that the accurate use of *dharma* requires additional modifiers such as the fact of being something commanded or performable, so that its primary expressive power should exclude *brahma*, lacks explanatory parsimony, and is thereby vitiated. Therefore, my inference is not blocked, whereas yours is ineffectual.

[*siddhānta*] Now the eighth position. First of all, your resolution of the contradiction [between the MS and] the matter in the first chapter [of the BS] is incorrect. It is ridiculous to assume that Jaimini, after having resolved doubts about the authoritativeness of some discourses not concerned with action, should have 'hidden his intention' with respect to other similar discourses [i.e., those of the Upaniṣads], given that the general thesis (*sāmānyapratijñāna*) [regarding authoritative knowledge about *dharma*] and doubt about lack of authoritative knowledge applies equally to both. Jaimini established the authoritativeness with regard to *dharma* of the Veda in all its four parts – commandments, narrative portions, *mantra*s, and proper names – and in their specific modalities (*saprakāram*) [by directly commanding, by commending, and so on], and went on to establish the authoritativeness of Vedic texts remembered (*smṛti*) and of the practices of those learned in the Veda to the degree necessary there [in MS 1]. Now, how are we to believe that the same man proposed an analysis of the means of knowing *dharma*, in common with [in your view] an analysis of the means of knowing *brahma*, and raised certain doubts about the authoritativeness [of some discourses on *dharma*] because of their apparent purposelessness – something common also to those narrative portions of the Vedānta section that are concerned with *brahma* – but only resolved the doubts about the narrative portions that are supplementary to action, and not those related to the narrative portions of the Vedānta that are concerned with *brahma*? Why would anyone who understands the principles of interpretation (*nyāyavid*) place trust in such empty speculation? [246].

Furthermore, the thesis of examining *dharma* and the thesis of examining the means of knowledge about it apply [according to your view] to both ritual action as well as to *brahma* and the worship of *brahma* equally. Now, in the topic 'On narrative portions' [MS 1.2.1-18], one of the *sūtra*s that state the prima facie view reads 'Because of the purposelessness [that would be entailed] of other [enjoined actions]' [MS 1.2.4].[32] The target of this *sūtra* is not only those passages that narrate the end-results of commandments for ritual action (such as 'By means of the final oblation one attains all desires') but also those passages that narrate the end-results of commandments for worship, since the objection, the 'purposelessness of other [enjoined actions]', applies equally to both. Thus:

[1] If the narrative of the end-result of the 'Prajāpati Wisdom' [CU 8.7.1] – 'He attains all worlds *and* all desires who understands in accordance with a knowledge of this Self' – were meant to be taken literally, then the worship of the '*brahma* consisting of bliss' would be pointless, since that is described in scripture as merely for the purpose of attaining all desires ('He enjoys all desire' [TU 2.1.1]); the worship of the 'subtle' (*dahara*) [CU 8.1.1 ff.] would be equally pointless, since it is described in scripture as merely for the purpose of attaining all worlds ('Those [worshippers] become able to wander at will through all worlds').

[2] If by the aforementioned acts of worship one attained not only all worlds and all desires but also liberation, then the 'Wisdom of the Honey' [CU 3.1] whose end-result is the attainment of liberation along with pure pleasure of the sort enjoyed by the Vasus, Rudras, Ādityas, Maruts, and Sādhyas; the 'Upakosala Wisdom' [CU 4.10], whose end-result is liberation preceded by the attainment of the three worlds (the Gārhapatya and so on); the 'Akṣara Wisdom' [BAU 3.8.7 ff.] and all others whose end-result is liberation pure and simple, without the addition of one or another enjoyment contingent on the attainment of a particular world – all these would be pointless.

[3] Now consider the person authorized to perform worship but who is completely indifferent to the enjoyment of objects and wishes only to attain the bliss of *brahma*. For him the end-result is not the attainment of a particular world or the enjoyments found there – on the contrary, these are held to be merely obstacles to the attainment of the results he really wants. [247] Thus, since the 'Akṣara Wisdom' and others are prescribed in scripture as affording the desired results immediately and without obstacle, others such as the 'Honey Wisdom' that are not so described would be pointless.

[4] If the end-result of all forms of *brahma* wisdom – whether enhanced by greater or lesser degrees of [acts of] the *dharma* of social orders and life stages; whether endowed with greater or lesser excellences; or unregulated by length of time, that is, whether undertaken at no regulated time or throughout one's entire life – were unqualified liberation, then those forms of *brahma* wisdom that are described as superior in regard to excellence, act, or time, would be pointless.

[5] If the narrative portions concerning the end-result of wisdom (such as '[The man of wisdom] becomes spotless and goes to a highest state of perfection' [MU 3.1.3]) were meant to be taken literally, then liberation too would be obtained as the end-result of this commandment. If this were so, then two other statements on the attainment of all desires ('For all desires the new and full moon sacrifice...'; 'For all desires the *jyotiṣṭoma*...') would likewise have to comprise liberation. And thus since one could obtain liberation from performing the new and full moon offerings just once, or the *jyotiṣṭoma* sacrifice just once, then all acts of worship of *brahma* meant to be performed throughout one's life, along with all [acts of the *dharma*] of social orders and life stages, would become pointless.

Since the *sūtra* on 'the purposelessness of other [enjoined actions]' would have this kind of broad application, a rejoinder that applies equally to all [such passages on both *karma* and *brahma*] would have to have been enunciated in a *sūtra* [by Jaimini]. What we find however is that the *sūtra*s offering this rejoinder, MS 1.2.16 and 17 ('The mention of "all" refers to the fact of the man being entitled [to perform all acts and obtain all their rewards]; The result being accomplished by means of actions, the difference in the results could be due to the magnitude of the actions'), apply only to narrative portions concerning commandments of ritual action. In the case of the first of these two *sūtra*s, the word 'knowledge' is carried over from the previous *sūtra* (1.2.15, 'It is praise of knowledge'): We are to understand that in the discourse on the final ladle offering, mention of the 'complete attainment of desires' is merely for the purpose of commending the rite, and is not intended literally to be enunciating the end-result, and also because the final ladle offering is a ritual purification of fire [248] and is enjoined independent of any end-result. The 'complete attainment of desires' mentioned for the sake of praise is concerned with the question of qualification: Only after the final ladle offering has been made and the sacred fire has been fully 'accomplished' does a man become qualified for sacrificial rites with their full range of end-results. The accomplishment of such results is contingent on the performance of the full-ladle offering, and so the complete attainment of results is mentioned as the result of the full-ladle offering, for the purpose of praising it.

One might object that, by reference to the end-results of ritual acts accomplished with fire, the full-ladle offering itself should not be praised as the means for the attainment of all desires, because there are things that in fact are not attained by acts accomplished with fire, such as the ability to fly or the acquisition of heavenly virgins. But the matter is expressed this way because the reference to 'all' in the statement about the full-ladle offering is contingent on a contextual proviso: its scope is limited to the domain of end-results provided for in the command statements of ritual acts. We see such limitation by context or other factor at work in such [everyday] statements as 'He has eaten all the rice.'

This aspect of commendation, however, cannot be posited in the case of statements that communicate actual end-results like 'He enjoys all desires', just as is the case with the narrative of the Evening Session [cf. MS 4.3.17].

The second *sūtra* [MS 1.2.17] obviates the doubt that, insofar as heaven is achieved by the *agnihotra* ritual, all other rites like the [full and new moon] sacrifice, the *soma* sacrifice, and so on are pointless; and it does so by stating that a multiplicity of ritual acts produces a multiplicity of end-results, on the analogy with farming. Now, the doubt raised here applies equally to the section concerning worship, but we do not find that doubt to be obviated in the section containing the system's settled views. For in the section [on worship] the principle of a multiplicity of end-results in consequence of a multiplicity of ritual acts does not even apply. The *sūtra* expressing the prima facie view, 'Thus because of the absence of any end-result' [MS 1.2.3], enunciates that the stated result does not occur, and this would be a cause of its invalidity. This putative invalidity is common to the narrative portion concerning end-results found in the ritual section (such as 'His face shines who has this wisdom') [249] and the narrative portion concerning end-results found in the *brahma* section (such as 'Anyone who knows this will become handsome and famous') [CU 3.13.8], but it is only with reference to the former that a *sūtra* obviating the doubt is found: 'There is commendation of wisdom' [MS 1.2.15]. The wise man's face is said to shine thus only from his understanding the meaning of the Brāhmaṇa passage on the Gargatrirātra, not, as in the case of a woman's face, by reason of natural beauty. Thus the wisdom is being commended. But this mode of obviating [the doubt regarding the end-result of worship] cannot apply to the statement 'Anyone who knows this will become handsome and famous', since these two states, being handsome and famous, are held to be the actual end-result of attaining the 'Light Wisdom' [CU 3.13.7 ff.]. In short, *sūtra*s such as 'Because of the purposelessness of other [enjoined actions]' [MS 1.2.4] must inevitably be held to apply equally to narratives about the end-results of the various commandments for worship, yet we find that various *sūtra*s on the system's settled views have been composed that apply only to narratives about the end-results of the commandments for ritual action. So who would not find it a ridiculous attempt at a way out to claim that in one place Jaimini revealed his rebuttal and in another hid his true intentions?

So [Jaimini] believes that the acts of worship of the Self must be supplementary to ritual acts, and the narratives about their end-results are not to be taken literally, any more than the narrative 'Not hearing any evil report of oneself' [regarding the end-result of making one's ladle of *palāśa* wood, MS 4.3.1] is to be taken literally. It is in view of this that the doubt about the 'purposeless of other [enjoined actions]' and the arguments obviating this doubt are not raised in connection with them. And that is why there is the prevailing attitude of the followers of Jaimini that 'the Vedānta [i.e., the Upaniṣads] is the wasteland of the Veda', that is, they hold it is without substance insofar as there is nothing therein [relating to action] to deliberate over. And that is why your resolution of the contradiction [of Uttaramīmāṃsā] with the matter of the first chapter [of the Pūrvamīmāṃsā] is completely without merit.

The same holds true for your resolution of the contradiction with the topic in the eighth chapter. You argue as follows: Although all that is seen is the oblation, the sacrifice is something meant to conciliate the deity, and it is the deity, once its grace is won, that bestows the end-result, so the deity must be the predominant element; hence, [250] the similarity of deities trumps any similarity of oblations. It is precisely to dispel this doubt that the following *sūtra* is offered: 'The scriptural reference to the deity is as a subsidiary element' [MS 8.1.34]. Nor can one respond that this can be construed as referring to a supplementary position [*abhyuccaya*, that is, one that Jaimini himself does not actually hold but only reports]. For in the ninth chapter Jaimini makes the following argument. He offers the prima facie view first with this *sūtra*: 'Or, it is the deity that motivates, since the feeding of a guest is for the sake of a guest' [MS 9.1.6], which is to say: hospitality consists of paying worship to a guest, and since it is intended to please the guest, the guest must be the predominant element in the act; in the same way, a sacrifice consists of paying worship to a god, and since it is intended to please the deity, the deity must be the predominant element in the act – it is the deity, being thereby pleased, that bestows the end-result. This prima facie view Jaimini answers with the following *sūtra*: 'No, rather, it is the act of sacrifice itself that is predominant, since it is the act that follows from scripture; the scriptural reference to the deity is as a subsidiary element' [MS 9.1.9], which is to say: the predominant element in a sacrifice is not the deity, since it is sacrifice itself that, by way of a 'transcendental potency', *apūrva*, generates the end-result, not the deity pleased by the oblation. Rather, the deity is referred to as something subordinate to the sacrifice, since it is the reference point for the [offered] substance. After enunciating this settled view Jaimini shows the disanalogy of hospitality to sacrifice in the following *sūtra*: 'With respect to a guest, it is he who is predominant in [the act of hospitality]; but this is not so in a ritual act, because [in hospitality] it is the pleasing of the guest that is predominant [and this is not the case with a deity in a ritual act]' [MS 9.1.10], which is to say: in hospitality the pleasing of a guest is required, that is, one is required to act in such a way that the guest is pleased, and so it makes sense that the guest should be predominant there; but in a sacrificial act, no pleasing is required, that is, one is not required to perform the act in such a way that the deity is pleased, and so the deity is not the predominant element in a sacrifice. Hereby Jaimini has refuted the predominance of the deity in the sacrifice unequivocally.

Hereby fails your resolution of the contradiction with the topic 'Commandment, however, is an undertaking' [MS 2.1.5] [251]. For it can be ascertained that, having clearly refuted the predominance of the deity, Jaimini too must hold the position adopted by all commentators on the topic 'Commandment, however...' namely that *apūrva* alone is the instrument [by which ritual produces its end-results, not the grace of the Lord].

Also incorrect is the resolution of the contradiction of the repudiation of *brahma* and the means of attaining it, namely renunciation. Jaimini holds that the discourses concerning *brahma* communicate the nature of the individual soul, which is the object of acts of worship supplementary to ritual in the form of purifications of the agent [of the sacrifice]. Given this belief, there is no longer any proof at all for the existence of *brahma* [since the discourses on it are now shown to refer to something else], and accordingly it is impossible to avoid the conclusion that both the two [*brahma* and renunciation] are indeed repudiated.

It is for this reason that [Kumārila,] the author of the *Vārttika*, in the topic 'On narrative portions' [MS 1.2.1 ff.], after corroborating the view that narrative portions such as 'Wind is the swiftest...' are supplementary to commandments, states: 'Hereby is explained the non-deontic character (*nairākāṅkṣya*) of the Upaniṣads too.'[33] But the fact that, in the topic 'On grammar' [MS 1.3.24 ff.], the author of the *Vārttika*, after citing certain discourses on the commandments and end-results of acts of worship of the supreme Self, asserts that these [Upaniṣads] function as the means of achieving a state of flourishing and final bliss independently [and not supplementary to commandments of sacrificial rites],[34] is something he has done entirely as a result of his own anxiety about repudiating *brahma* and renunciation; it is not in accordance with the doctrine of the author of the (Mīmāṃsā) *sūtra*s, since we have shown that the *sūtra*s of Jaimini and those of Vyāsa stand in clear contradiction with each other.

You also make the argument that, in order to avoid the charge of lack of explanatory parsimony with regard to accurate usage, we must necessarily accept that the word *dharma* is used equally to refer to *brahma* [as well as ritual actions], and that therefore there is no reason to suppose that the statement of the *Bhārata* [where *dharma* is used in reference to Krishna] must have the purpose of commendation [instead of being meant literally]. This can be answered as follows: True enough, there is no reason to *suppose* it is meant as mere commendation – for this is something actually *proved* from the context itself, which after all is a commendation of Krishna. That [context] does not sustain the argument that the word *dharma* expresses simply a means of other-worldly good [and not specifically sacrificial action] [252]. Were that the case, then the word *dharma* would refer equally to individual souls, which are means of other-worldly good insofar as they are agents, and to a host of other things insofar as they are causes – and then in what way would it be praising the Blessed One to say that the word *dharma* refers to him? Therefore we must accept that the word *dharma* signifies simply ritual acts such as sacrifice if we are to preserve the prevailing and natural meaning (*svārasyaprasiddhyartham*) of the passage cited from the *Bhārata*. And it would then indeed be praise of him to say that the Blessed One, having descended to earth in order to preserve *dharma*, is himself *dharma* incarnate.

Or let us accept, for the sake of argument, that the word *dharma* [in the *Bhārata* passage] somehow can refer to *brahma* as well. Even so, the word *dharma* mentioned in the [very first] *sūtra*, on the 'inquiry into *dharma*' – just like the word *dharma* in the *sūtra* 'Jaimini [thinks] for the same reasons that *dharma* [is what brings about the fruits of action]' [BS 3.2.40] – has to be taken to exclude *brahma*. This is so because the *dharma* proposed as the object of examination is said to be something defined by Vedic commandment (in the *sūtra* '*Dharma* is a good defined by Vedic commandment' [MS 1.1.2]). The word 'commandment' (*codanā*) is derived from a verbal root (*cud*) that means 'impel' [*Dhātupāṭha* 10.53] and so it must enunciate a statement that prompts action. Therefore a commandment is a direct source of knowledge about *dharma*, whereas a statement providing information about already-existent entities that is transmitted in connection with this or that commandment can be a source of knowledge about it only insofar as it forms a unified discourse with such a commandment, by way of offering commendation or other [supplementary information about the act in question]. The end-result enunciated in narrative portions (on the Evening Session and the like) is to be taken literally only insofar as these form a unified discourse with a principal commandment, because this end-result is required by the commandment in question. By contrast, the end-result enunciated with respect to acts of worship of the Self, which are only subordinate elements of ritual acts since they are purifications of the agent, cannot be taken literally because that end-result is not required by a commandment. It is precisely with this in mind that Jaimini did not bother to answer criticisms [about such acts of worship] such as that deriving from [the prima facie view expressed in the *sūtra*] 'Because of the purposelessness of other [enjoined actions]' [MS 1.2.4].

The blessed Bādarāyaṇa, however, [253] observed that Jaimini believed that *dharma* takes the form of sacrifice, produces an end-result that is only a state of flourishing, something both perishable and non-ultimate, and thereby constitutes the meaning of the entire Veda. And he observed further that Jaimini had no understanding of the fact that *brahma* is proved to exist by the entire Vedānta [the Upaniṣads], whose central idea is communicated by its introductory passages and similar [aspects of discourse] (*upakramādi*); that the end-result of acts of worship of *brahma* was final liberation, the eternal and ultimate human goal; and that ritual action was only contributory to this means. And he thought that, lest the world go completely astray by focusing on Jaimini's system, he would confer a benefit on the world by composing the knowledge system that starts 'Now, then, the inquiry into *brahma*.' Accordingly, there is indeed a very great contradiction between the two knowledge systems of Jaimini and Bādarāyaṇa. Since they cannot form a single knowledge system your inference is blocked, whereas mine is not ineffectual, and this for the following reason: Jaimini proposed as his object of analysis only action such as sacrifice,[35] whose end-results are both perishable and non-ultimate; therefore, whatever is other than sacrifice cannot be for him an object of analysis in this system.[36] You cannot object, on the grounds that we do find [in the MS] analysis as to essential nature, physical dimensions, and the like, of things such as the sacrificial post, the oblation fire, milk-pail, and so on that are strictly speaking 'other than sacrifice', that *brahma* too, accordingly, could be an object of analysis. For what is meant by the word 'ritual action' is the object of an act aimed at an end-result that is perishable and non-ultimate. Nor can you charge that the inferential reason [namely, that *brahma* is included in 'whatever is other than sacrifice'] is unproved given that *brahma* is in fact connected with the sacrifice, insofar as it is a deity. The deity may be the addressee of the spent oblation, but it is only the word that refers to the deity that is the object of an act – i.e., of the effort made to pronounce the word – and therefore the deity itself is not the actual object of the act.

Thereby is also laid to rest the following doubt [raised by our opponents] [254]: Although the *dharma* that Jaimini aims to analyze is concerned with action, and so cannot in any direct way be connected with *brahma*, it cannot be denied that [Jaimini's notion of *dharma*] must also be concerned with acts of worship [of the Self], and accordingly it must have a connection with *brahma* since *brahma* is both the end-result and the object of those acts; and therefore by somehow dismissing the contradiction, on the grounds [of its being subsumed under] the common thesis [MS 1.1.1] [the BS] can be said to form a unified system [with the MS]. For we have already stated that the word *dharma* is concerned only with action whose end-result – as an examination of the totality of the *Later Sūtras* (*uttarasūtrajāta*) themselves shows – consists of a state of flourishing, something both perishable and non-ultimate. For there is a Vedic usage of the word *dharma* in this sense of mere action:

Other than *dharma* and *adharma*, other than this, what is done and not done, other than what is both past and future – speak to me of what there is of this sort that you have insight into.

This *mantra* from the *Kaṭhavallī* [KU 2.14] is concerned with three things, agent, end, and means, that are different from the action constituting the means of producing perishable and non-ultimate end-results, the end-results themselves produced by those means, and the actor active with such means. Both sides agree on this [interpretation].[37] But in the *sūtra* 'And there is question and explanation relative to three things only [not to the *pradhāna*]' [BS 1.4.6], the *mantra* has been explained by our opponents in the following manner to obtain the aforementioned three entities:

'*Dharma*' refers to sacrifice and the like whose end-result is a state of flourishing; 'other than it', i.e., 'a *means* that is different from sacrifice.' '*Adharma*' refers to what is other than *dharma*, i.e., what is achieved by *dharma*, namely a state of flourishing (heaven and the like); 'other than it', i.e., an *end* different from heaven. 'Than this' refers to the agent of the sacrifice who is present to our awareness, that is, the human person who is inclined toward end-results in the sphere of transmigration; 'other than this', i.e., an *agent* different from this person. 'What there is of this sort', the triad of agent and so on, 'that you have insight into.' 'What is done and not done... what is both past and future' are qualifications of all three, *dharma*, [*adharma*, and 'this']: 'done and not done', that is, the whole mass of things undertaken but not completed; 'speak of' some triad different from this familiar triad of means, [end, and agent] that is past, present, and future.

Another interpretation of the passage [they offer] is as follows:

'Other than *dharma* and *adharma*' is a question about what is not a *means* of normal good and evil; 'other than this, what is done and not done, [255] other than what is both past and future' is a question about an eternal *end* different from the non-eternal ends that have a past, present, and future. The question about the *agent* is included in the question about the end, since the agent is eternal and already implied by the end.

Now, the first interpretation is flawed because the construction is awkward for the following reasons: interpreting the word *adharma*, which is commonly used in the sense of evil, as the end-result (heaven and so on) of *dharma*; interpreting 'than this', which can be understood as an adjective to 'done and not done', separately as referring to the agent himself; taking 'what is done and not done', which can be understood as the substantive construing with the adjective 'than this', as an adjective referring to all [three], *dharma* and so on; interpreting 'what is both past and future', which can be understood independently because of their construing with the word 'other' that is used separately in the clause, as an adjective referring to all [three], *dharma* and so on.

The second interpretation is flawed because the question about the agent is not really made available: If you agree that the agent is comprised in the second question on the grounds that the agent is (a) eternal and (b) already-implied, an agent different from the agent of the end-results of sacrifice and the like is not made available, since (a) the agent of the end-results of sacrifice is also eternal and so can be included within the comprehensive concept of being other than something past, present, and future; and (b) it is already-implied insofar as it is the entity qualified by heaven and the like, just as the liberated being is qualified by the manifestation of absolute purity and so on.

Thus the opponents' constructions are unacceptable; ignoring them we offer another, correct interpretation: By the first quarter-verse is posited a *means* different from both the one that has end-results that are perishable and non-ultimate but unaffected by any powerful adversity, and from the one that has end-results that are so affected. By the second quarter-verse is posited an *agent* different from agent of sacrifice, which is denounced in another *mantra*: 'These are unsteady boats, these sacrifices, [256] in which is found the eighteen-fold action, and which fools welcome as the ultimate good – only to progress to old age and death forever more' [MU. 1.2.7]. (Here the interpretation of 'what is done and not done' is [as a *bahuvrīhi* compound]: one whose deeds are 'not done', i.e., as good as undone.) By the third quarter-verse is posited an *end* different from such ends as heaven; the two 'ands' construing with 'past' and 'future' are meant to include the present, which has the form of both past and future.

Since the set of three questions is composed eloquently by the three quarter-verses in order, with respect to an instrument, agent, and their end-results such as are different from those made known by. . .[38] why do they torture it for the sake of a construction that produces just this meaning?[39]

Thus, on both sides there is no dispute about the fact that in the *mantra* the word *dharma* is concerned solely with action whose end-result is perishable and non-ultimate.

Furthermore, even though we find this sort of usage [throughout the Vedas and in the MS], it would be a mistake, in view of later idiom (*agrimavyavahāra*), to assume that Jaimini's usage alone is concerned with [ritual action], that no other such concept of *dharma* exists [elsewhere].[40] For we find, in a *sūtra* of Kaṇāda ('Now, then, we shall explain *dharma*' [VS 1.1.1]), that the word *dharma* is posited as an object of examination, and that the *sūtra*s that follow are concerned with *dharma* [as we understand it] if only slightly: For though in the beginning no consideration is paid to the type of performance concerned with sacrifice and the like, in the first section of the sixth chapter consideration is paid to the *dharma* of giving and receiving [257], and in the second section to some extent[41] the *dharma* of the four life-stages is considered synoptically.

Therefore it is proved that the thesis of examining *dharma* is rightly considered not to comprise an examination of *brahma*. Here follows a summary of the two views:[42]

1. 'For a thing to be *dharma* there must be a relation to a class property, substance, or attribute, and this can pertain equally[43] to *brahma*: Acts of worship of *brahma* are undoubtedly *dharma*.
2. 'The thesis of considering *dharma* directly envisions this.[44] *Brahma* would have to be considered[45] like heaven or as [some other] end-result of action.'
3. Those who have insisted thusly that the two Mimamsa systems form a single knowledge system must be enlightened so as to remove any such hope.
4. If the thesis of the Prior System, through its various discourses, is supposed to touch on *brahma* the way it is conceived of by you [Viśiṣṭādvaitins] as an object of its inquiry,[46] then there must be such inquiries, and why are they not present? Surely, at all events, any contradiction [in the MS with *brahma*] would have to have been removed.
5. The word 'command' contained in the definitional *sūtra* [MS 1.1.2, *codanālakṣaṇo 'rtho dharmaḥ*] means an 'injunction' prompting action. It necessarily implies[47] that discourse not concerned with action is purposeless – implies, that is, the prima facie view[48] of the interpretive principle of 'narrative portions.'
6. The purposelessness of narrative portions is obviated by their being held to be supplementary to commandments. Does that commandment pertain to the discourses of [Upanishadic] scripture? Surely even in your eyes that is equally present in them.
7. If it does not pertain to these [scriptural discourses],[49] then Jaimini would have had to compose an explicit *sūtra* to the effect that they are ends in themselves. On what grounds could one assume that [although he did not] such must have been his 'hidden intention'? [258] Only a dimwit would do so.
8. How far are we asked to believe that this hidden intention of the great seer extends? Such arguments as those based on 'The purposelessness of other [enjoined actions]' [MS 1.2.4] and on the end-results of commandments[50] should apply equally to your [Upanishadic texts as well]. Or why, when the definition [of *dharma*] was being set out [by Jaimini in MS 1] to establish the entire and perfect[51] source of knowledge of *dharma* that applied equally to *smṛti* and custom[52] – why didn't[53] the Vedānta portion similarly follow the way of *smṛti*?[54]
9. Who would put any trust in your boast that the two form the work of a single system...[55]

10. In the eighth and ninth chapters Jaimini says that the deity is a subordinate property of the sacrifice, whereas Bādarāyaṇa says it is predominant in itself. What resolution of this conflict can present itself here?[56]
11. And no resolution is possible for the disagreement that exists between the one who holds that *apūrva* alone is the instrument of the sacrifice, and the other, the Lord's grace.
12. Therefore, in the Prior System, the *dharma* under analysis is the object of a person's willed action (*kāmikārya*) and has end-results that are perishable and determinate. And with respect to this *dharma* the sage Jaimini holds that the Veda in its entirety is the source of valid knowledge. The Blessed One of the Lotus Eyes himself composed [new] *sūtra*s for the knowledge of *brahma*, in order to make known to those devoted solely to ritual action that the view of their teacher was detrimental (*ahitam*).
13. Therefore, given that contradiction between the two systems – with respect to primary meanings and end-results – ever rears its head, even the rumor that they form a single knowledge system can gain no standing in the thoughts of the learned.

NOTES

1 I am grateful to Ethan Kroll and Samuel Wright (Chicago) for their suggestions, and especially to Lawrence McCrea (Harvard) for his careful critique of an earlier version of the translation.

2 The traditional number of his texts is the sacral 108. The *New Catalogus Catalogorum* lists 62. The Srimad Appayya Deekshitendra Granthavali Prakashan Samiti, Hyderabad, which has been issuing volumes intermittently since 1971, is planning to publish what I count as 41 texts in 15 volumes.

3 Gerow (2001: i).

4 A new edition – and in the case of the *Nyāyamuktāvalī*, the editio princeps (on the basis of a manuscript held by the Oriental Research Institute, Mysore, one of only two, it seems, that exist) – was published by the Samiti in 2001.

5 We are only beginning to understand the innovations of late precolonial Sanskrit scholarship. For a sympathetic account of Appayya's literary science, see Bronner (2002, 2003).

6 See for example Clooney (1993).

7 *Śrībhāṣya*, p. 21. The translation is that of Thibaut slightly modified, p. 5 (italics added); he gives 'earlier' for *pūrva*, but I find no suggestion in the original of temporal antecedence; Rāmānuja seems to have in mind, rather, an almost spatial relationship between two parts of a single text.

8 Vedāntadeśika remarks on this: 'Their being called *saṃhita* implies that "unified system" means not only that they constitute a single knowledge-discipline (*vidyāsthāna*) but that they constitute a single text (*prabandha*)' (*Tattvaṭīkā*, p. 39).

9 Trans. Thibaut (emended). Appayya has the Viśiṣṭādvaita *siddhāntin* cite precisely this passage of the *Śrībhāṣya* to clinch the argument for system unity (*Caturma-*

tasārasaṃgraha Nayamayūkamālikā, p. 122). *The siddhāntin* also notes that in the traditional list of fourteen *vidyāsthāna*s, the term 'mīmāṃsā' must comprise both *pūrva* and *uttara*, since otherwise the number would have been fifteen (p. 123).

10 See *Śrutaprakāśikā* (in *Śrībhāṣya*) pp. 24 ff.

11 *na vayaṃ dharmabrahmavicārarūpayoḥ śāstrayor atyantabhedavādinaḥ kiṃ tv ekatvavādinaḥ*, and he goes on to say, of the text stretching from the first *sūtra* of the MS to the last of the BS, *etāvatparyantam ekam eva śāstram* (*Brahmasūtrabhāṣya* of Śrīkaṇṭhaśivācārya, p. 49).

12 *tasmād dharmavicāraśāstreṇa brahmavicārasya siddhyabhāvāt tadartham idaṃ śāstram ārambhanīyam* (*Maṇidīpikā* on *Brahmasūtrabhāṣya* of Śrīkaṇṭhaśivācārya, p. 27).

13 See Assmann (1997). The case of the early Buddhists is discussed in Pollock (2004).

14 *vedamūlatvaṃ punas te tulyakakṣamūlākṣamayaiva lajjayā ca mātāpitṛdveṣiduṣṭaputravan nābhyupagacchanti* (*Tantravārttika*, p. 113.21; cf. p. 81.17 ff.) Kumārila's text engaged the energies of commentators for much of the following millennium; the last great contributors to this conversation, the seventeenth-century Varanasi scholars Śaṅkara Bhaṭṭa, Dinakara Bhaṭṭa, and Khaṇḍadeva, are discussed in my forthcoming edition of the *Bhāṭṭadinakara*.

15 On *dharma* see my 1990 article, on *smṛti*, 1997; an essay on *puruṣārtha* is planned.

16 Appayya's work was published only once, from Srirangam in 1912, on the basis of two palm leaf manuscripts in private collections and 'Mss. at the Mysore Government Oriental Manuscripts Library' (p. 9). In addition to this printed edition, I have been able to consult two manuscripts of the work, one from the Adyar Library and Research Centre (referred to here as 'Adyar'; this appears to be a transcript of one of the manuscripts originally used for the edition, since they share some errors) and one from the British Library (referred to as BL). It has proven impossible, however, to get access to any of the more than a dozen other manuscripts that exist and that undoubtedly would help clarify lingering uncertainties in the constitution of the text. A number of the arguments that are set forth at great length in the *Vādanakṣatramālā* are briefly adumbrated in *Nayamayūkamālikā* (*Caturmatasārasaṃgraha*, pp. 120 ff.), as well as in Appayya's commentary on Śrīkaṇṭha's *Brahmasūtrabhāṣya*, the *Maṇidīpikā* (see especially pp. 48 ff.) and these occasionally shed light on the present text.

17 Brackets contain translator's additions; parenthesis, by contrast, indicate material contained in the text but subordinated typographically in the interests of clarity.

18 *Ślokavārttika Codanāsūtra*, 13–14. Only vs. 14 is actually cited by Appayya; I add the preceding vs. for obvious contextual reasons.

19 Or perhaps the thesis of just the former, or less likely, of just the latter.

20 The translation of Thibaut is generally followed here and throughout.

21 The text reads *dharmaḥ*, and omits the *na* at the beginning of the citation.

22 Read *tadīyasya* for the *madīyasya* of the printed edition (so BL, and, it seems, Adyar; see below, *tadīyasiddhāntasya*).

23 In the *Maṇidipikā* (p. 49) a different argument based on this *sūtra* is offered: 'Although in such *sūtra*s Jaimini is presented as the *pūrvapakṣin*, the very fact that Jaimini did not include these prima facie views in the *śāstra* devoted to the analysis of *dharma* shows that it makes perfectly good sense to hold that the *śāstra* devoted to the analysis of *brahma* was composed as part of a single knowledge system with the other.' This is essentially the same as the view advanced below, 'even if contradiction. . .' (the fifth position).

24 Here as occasionally elsewhere the translation of Jha is followed.

25 Understood traditionally to mean '*apūrva* exists, however, [given that] action [is enjoined].'

26 *dehātmabhāvenāpi [laukikakriyopappateḥ]*; Adyar, *dehātmabhāvenārtham api* (corrupt); BL unclear, but apparently: *dehātmabhāve 'pi*. The passage is obscure to me. Presumably the *upāsanā* produces a *saṃskāra* in the *ātman* without perceptibly changing it, just as the *prokṣaṇa* does for the rice. The Mīmāṃsā *nyāya* of *prokaṣṇa* is usually invoked to identify an *apūrvavidhi* (an act we would never do except for the fact a Vedic injunction tells us to), which does not seem relevant here.

27 I owe my understanding of this complex passage to discussions with L. McCrea. Upanishadic passages are generally given in the translation of Olivelle.

28 The citations (not always exact) are, respectively, TS1.3.5.1; KS 3.3. and 6.6.; AB 4.25; TA 10.22.1.

29 *kathaṃcid gatyupanyāsaḥ*. Or perhaps, less cynically, 'a suggested course of action.'

30 Reading *kriyāvidhiśeṣa-* (as two lines below) for *kriyāviśeṣa-* of the printed text and for Adyar's *kriyāvidhiviśeṣa-* (BL has a large lacuna here). The printed text would give: 'narrative portions belonging to particular ritual acts.'

31 And this, implicitly, has no bearing on the actual presence of the deity at the sacrifice (I read *tadupāsyatvāt* for *tadupākhyatvāt*).

32 If texts that do not enjoin actions but simply describe existent things, such as results, were to remain true and authoritative about matters of *dharma*, then texts that describe such things as attaining all desires by a single rite would render all other rites meaningless. Such texts are therefore not to be taken literally but must be interpreted as subservient to other ritual action.

33 Presumably referring to *Tantravārttika* on MS 1.2.7 (especially p. 13 ff.), though I do not find mention of the Upaniṣads here nor this exact quote.

34 Presumably referring to *Tantravārttika*, p. 227.

35 We should probably read with Adyar *yāgādikarmaiva* (for the printed *yāgādikam eva*).

36 In what follows the printed text shows a lacuna through haplography; Adyar (folio 129) has the correct reading: *na ca karmānyate 'pi... iti tadvad brahmaṇo 'pi kiṃ na syād iti vācyam. kṣayiṣnusātiśayaphalodeśyakānuṣṭhāne viṣayasya [*read: *-anuṣṭhānaviṣayasya] karmaśabdena vivakṣitatvāt. na ca brahmaṇo 'pi devatātvena...*

37 It is not clear to whom the 'both sides' refers, since Mīmāṃsā is unlikely to be one of them.

38 The printed ed. and BL (*anyatra dharmam anunā*) as well as Adyar (*anyatra dharmam anumānā*) all seem to be corrupt, but a reasonable conjecture eludes me.

39 This is a *saṃgrahaśloka* of Appayya.

40 Ed. *bhrāntikṛtā kalpayitum*. BL: *bhrāntikṛtam api kalpayitum*; Adyar: [*prayogādarśane...*] *bhrāntikṛtam avikalpayitum*. I am uncertain whether I have grasped the true meaning of the sentence.

41 Ed. *kiyān api cintitaḥ saṃgrahataḥ;* BL: *kiyān saṃgṛhītaḥ*; Adyar: *kriyāt saṃgṛhītaḥ* (corrupt).

42 The verses show a number of text-critical problems, and their real meaning is not always clear to me.

43 I read *samam eva* with BL, Adyar (Ed. *samavetam*).

44 BL: *tatsākṣātkṛtigocaraṃ... -pratijñānam*; Ed., Adyar: *tatsākṣādgocared... -pratijñānam* (Adyar *pratikriyā*).

45 Ed. *vicāryaḥ*; BL, Adyar: *vicārya* [Adyar omits *vā*, hypometric]. Conjecture *vicāryaṃ* (cf. vs. 4b)?

46 In place of the printed text (which gives *tat tad vaco hi*) I read with Adyar *tattadvacobhi[ḥ]*.

47 Literally, 'does not abandon' (*nojjhati*).

48 Adyar *pūrvapakṣiṇam* (for *pūrvapakṣatām*).

49 BL *ca tāni* (for *tato hi*).

[50] Adyar and BL *vidhiphaloktyādi* (for *viphalatoktyādi*).
[51] Adyar and BL *anagham* (for *-manasam*).
[52] Adyar and BL *smṛtyācārādivad vā* (Ed. *smṛtyācārādi tadvat*).
[53] Adyar and BL *na* (for *nu*).
[54] Ed. and Adyar *smṛtipaṭham* (BL *smṛtiphalam*). I am unsure of *pāda*s bcd here.
[55] *Pāda*s ab are dark to me: 'When the matter cannot be hidden, [as?] when the syllable OM itself is clearly mispronounced'?
[56] The Adyar ms. has a lacuna here to the end of the chapter.

REFERENCES

Primary Sources

Pūrvottaramīmāṃsāvādanakṣatramālā of Appayya Dīkṣita. Edited by T.K. Balasubrahmanya Aiyar Srirangam: Srivanivilasamudrayantralay, 1912; Adyar Lib. ms. 9.K.10/61683; Eggeling [Catalogue of the Sanskrit manuscripts in the Library of the India Office] 1894, v.1 pt. 4, p. 763, entry 2387.

Brahmasūtrabhāṣya of Śrīkaṇṭhaśivācārya, with the commentary *Śivārkamaṇidipikā* of Appayya Dīkṣita. Edited by Vrajavallabha Dviveda. Varanasi: Jangamavadimatha, 1986.

Caturmatasārasaṃgraha of Appayya Dīkṣita. Edited by Pullela Sri Ramachandrudu and Kambhampati Sitaramanjaneyulu. Hyderabad: Srimad Appayya Deeskshitendra Granthavali Prakashana Samiti, 2001.

Ślokavārttika of Kumārila. Edited by Swami Dwarikadas Sastri. Varanasi: Tara Publications, 1978.

Śrībhāṣya of Rāmānujācārya with the *Śrutaprakāśikā* of Śudarśana. Mysore: Vedantadesikaviharasabha, 1960.

Tantravārttika of Kumārila, in *Mīmāṃsādarśanam*. Edited by K.V. Abhyankar and G. Joshi. Pune: Anandashrama Press, 1970–76.

Tattvaṭīkā of Vedāntadeśika. Edited by Uttamur Viraraghavacharya. N.p., n.p., 1974. Ubhayavedantagranthamala.

Secondary Sources

Assmann, J. (1997). *Moses the Egyptian: The Memory of Egypt in Western Monotheism*. Cambridge, MA: Harvard University Press.

Bronner, Y. (2002). 'What is New and What is *navya*: Sanskrit Poetics on the Eve of Colonialism', *Journal of Indian Philosophy* **30**(5): 441–462.

Bronner, Y. (ms.). 'Is *Moonlight* the *Joy of the Water Lily*? Appayya Dīkṣita's *Kuvalayānanda* and its Remaking of Jayadeva's *Candrāloka*', Paper presented at the World Sanskrit Congress, Helsinki, 2003.

Clooney, F. (1993). *Theology after Vedānta. An Experiment in Comparative Theology*. Albany: State University of New York Press.

Gerow, E. (ed. and trans.) (2001). *The Vṛttivārttika, or Commentary on the Functions of Words*. New Haven: American Oriental Society. American Oriental Series 87.

Pollock, S. (1990). 'From Discourse of Ritual to Discourse of Power in Sanskrit Culture', *Journal of Ritual Studies* **4.2** (1990): 291–320.

Pollock, S. (1997). 'Tradition' as 'Revelation': Śruti, Smṛti, and the Sanskrit Discourse of Power', In S. Lienhard and I. Piovano (eds.), *Lex et Litterae: Essays on Ancient Indian Law and Literature in Honour of Oscar Botto* (pp. 395–417). Turin: Edizioni dell'Orso. (A corrected reprint will appear in Federico Squarcini, ed.

Boundaries, Dynamics and Construction of Traditions in South Asia. Florence: Florence U. Press.)
Pollock, S. (2004). 'Axialism and Empire', In J. Arnason (ed.), *Axial Civilizations and World History*. Leiden: Brill.
Pollock, S. (ms). 'The *Bhāṭṭadinakara* of Dinakara Bhaṭṭa, 1.3. Edited for the first time, with an Introduction'.

APPAYYADĪKṢITĀNĀṂ PŪRVOTTARAMĪMĀṂSĀVĀDA-NAKṢATRAMĀLĀNTARBHĀVYAIKAŚĀSTRYANIRĀKARAṆAVĀDAḤ*

[235] evaṃ sakalaśabdavācyatvena siddhaṃ brahma alaukikaśreyaḥsādhanatvapravṛttinimittakakarmavācidharmaśabdavācyam api bhavati; sākṣād api uktapravṛttinimittasaṃbandhena tad vācyaṃ bhavitum arhati 'śreyaḥsādhanatā hy eṣāṃ nityaṃ vedāt pratīyate / tādrūpyeṇa ca dharmatvaṃ tasmān nendriyagocaraḥ' iti vedāvagamyaśreyaḥsādhanatākatvapravṛttinimittakatayā abhyupagatasya dharmaśabdasya karmavat jātiguṇadravyāṇy api artha iti mīmāṃsakair uktatvāt; tena 'athāto dharmajijñāsā' iti sūtragatadharmaśabdagṛhītatayā brahmaṇo 'pi jaiminīyadharmavicārapratijñāviṣayatvam asti na vā iti vicārārthaṃ kathāntaraṃ prastūyate –

tadastitvavādināṃ pareṣām idam anumānam – brahma svarūpapramāṇasādhanaphalaiḥ saha jaiminīyavicārapratijñāviṣayaḥ, alaukikaśreyaḥsādhanatvāt, karmavat; brahmaṇo 'pi nakṣatreṣṭyādiṣu devatātvenānvayāt jaiminīye yāgeṣu devatāprādhānyatadabhāvavicāre devatāsāmānyātmanā viṣayatvam asti, devatānāṃ karmādhikāranadhikaravicare ca tadātmanā viṣayatvam astīti si [236] ddhasādhanavāraṇāya svarūpapramāṇasādhanaphalaiḥ saha – iti viśeṣaṇam – iti prathamā kakṣyā.

atha dvitīyā

brahmaṇo jaiminīyadharmavicārapratijñāviṣayatāyām agre tadvicāreṇa bhāvyam, na tv asau tatra dṛśyate; na ca tam api cikīrṣato maharṣeḥ vighnaḥ kaścit utprekṣituṃ śakyate; nāpi vismaraṇam, yo hi dvādaśalakṣaṇyāṃ svarūpapramāṇasādhanaphalaiḥ saha karmajātaṃ nirṇīya tatrāsūtritān kāṃścit tadupayuktān nyāyān ālakṣya tatsaṃgrahārthaṃ dvādaśalakṣaṇīśeṣaṃ saṃkārṣaṇakāṇḍam akārṣīt, tasya maharṣeḥ brahmavicāre vighnaṃ vismaraṇaṃ vā katham ut-

*In preparing the Romanized Sanskrit text the printing conventions of the original Vani Vilas edition have been followed.

prekṣāmahe; na ca karmavicāropayuktanyāyair eva brahmaṇo 'pi svarūpapramāṇasādhanaphalanirṇayaḥ sidhyatīty abhipretya pṛthak tadvicāro na kṛta iti śakyaṃ vaktum, karmaparavākyārthanirṇāyakanyāyebhyo vilakṣaṇānām eva brahmaparavākyārthanirṇāyakanyāyānāṃ caturlakṣaṇyāṃ grathanadarśanāt; na ca dvādaśalakṣaṇīcaturlakṣaṇyoḥ aikaśāstryābhyupagamena brahmavicārapratijñānirvāhaḥ kalpayituṃ śakyaḥ, bhinnavaktṛkayoḥ dharmabrahmavicārapratijñopakramayoḥ parasparavilakṣaṇasādhyāsādhyārthanirṇāyakanyāyagrathanapravṛttayoḥ tayor aikaśāstryakalpane pramāṇā [237] bhāvāt; ato bādhitam idam anumānam iti – brahma noktaṃ sādhyavat, karmānyatvāt ghaṭavat – iti.

atha tṛtīyā kakṣyā

na bādhitaṃ madanumānam, aikaśāstryakalpanena pratijñānirvāhopapatteḥ; na ca tatkalpakābhāvaḥ, vedarūpaikagranthavyākhyātvasya tatkalpakatvāt; na ca vaktṛbhedaḥ tatkalpanābādhakaḥ, vaktṛbhede 'pi vyākaraṇarūpaikaprabandhavyākhyānatvena vāmanajayādityavṛttyoḥ aikaśāstryadarśanāt; nāpi dharmabrahmavicārapratijñopakramau tadbādhakau, dharmaśabdena karmabrahmasādhāraṇena dvādaśalakṣaṇīcaturlakṣaṇīsādhāraṇapratijñāyāṃ vṛttāyāṃ karmavicārānantaram 'athāto brahmajijñāsā' ity asya 'athātaḥ śeṣalakṣaṇam' itivat avāntarapratijñāparatvopapatteḥ; na ca parasparavilakṣaṇanyāyagrathanaṃ tadbādhakam, nirṇeyārthānusāreṇa nyāyavailakṣaṇyopapatteḥ; dvādaśalakṣaṇyām api karmabhedaśeṣaśeṣibhāvādinirṇeyārthānusāreṇa vilakṣaṇanyāyayagrathanadarśanāt; ato na bādhitaṃ madanumānam, tvadanumānaṃ tu aprayojakam – iti.

atha ca caturthī kakṣyā

nyāyānām iha vailakṣaṇyaṃ bhedamātraṃ na vivakṣitam, kiṃ tu [238] virodhaḥ; prasiddho hi virodhaḥ; caturlakṣaṇyāṃ jaiminimatasya prāyaḥ pūrvapakṣīkaraṇadarśanāt; na hi parasparaviruddhamatadvayāvalambanena dvābhyāṃ pravartitaṃ śāstradvayaṃ tābhyām aikamatyena ekaśāstratayā kṛtam iti kalpayituṃ śakyam; dharmaśabdaś ca brahmapratikoṭitayā yāgādikarmaparatvena 'phalam ata upapatteḥ' ity adhikaraṇe 'dharme jaiminir ata eva' iti sūtre prayuktaḥ; āpastambena ca maharṣiṇā 'dharmādharmau carata āvāṃ svaḥ iti na devagandharvā na pitara ity ācakṣate ayaṃ dharmo 'yaṃ dharma iti yat tv āryāḥ kriyamāṇaṃ praśaṃsanti sa dharmaḥ yad garhante so 'dharmaḥ' iti anuṣṭheyayāgādāv eva dharmaśabdaḥ prayuktaḥ; atas tadanusāreṇa dharmajijñāsāsūtragatasyāpi tasya yāgādyanuṣṭheyaparatvaṃ vācyam iti dharmabrahmajijñāsāsūtrayoḥ sādhāraṇāvāntarapratijñāparatvavibhāgakalpanam api na yuktam; tasmāt bādhitaṃ tvadanumānam, madanumānaṃ ca nāprayojakam, yat yena rūpeṇa nānuṣṭheyaṃ tasya tena rūpeṇa anuṣṭheyapara-dharmaśabdagrāhyatvāyogāt iti

atha pañcamī

asiddho 'yaṃ jaiminīyavaiyāsikamatayoḥ virodhaḥ, caturlakṣaṇyāṃ kvacid api jaiminīyamatasya pūrvapakṣīkaraṇābhāvāt; yat tu [239] puruṣārthādhikaraṇe 'śeṣatvāt puruṣārthavādo yathānyeṣv iti jaiminiḥ' iti brahmāpalāpaparaṃ pūrvapakṣasūtram, na tat jaiminyabhimatasya pakṣasya anuvādakam, kiṃ tu madīyasyābhyuccaya-vādasya; ata eva 'paraṃ jaiminir mukhyatvāt' ityādisūtreṣu brahmābhyupagamenaiva pravṛttasya pakṣasya jaiminīya-tvenānuvādaḥ; evaṃ 'parāmarśaṃ jaiminir acodanā cāpavadati hi' iti sūtraṃ saṃnyāsāpalāpasya jaimininā abhyuccayavādatvena upa-nyastasyaivānuvādakam, na tu tadīyasiddhāntasya; ata eva 'tad-bhūtasya tu nātadbhāvo jaiminer api niyamātadrūpābhāvebhyaḥ' iti sūtre saṃnyastavataḥ saṃnyāsāt pracyutiḥ jaiminer api na saṃmatā ity uktam; evam anyatrāpi tatra tatra virodhaparihāra unneyaḥ; dharmaśabdasya anuṣṭheyāsādhāranyam api asiddham, 'ye ca vedavido viprā ye cādhyātmavido janāḥ / te vadanti mahātmānaṃ kṛṣṇaṃ dharmaṃ sanātanam' iti mahābhārate bhagavatsā-dhāraṇyokteḥ; ato virodhābhāvāt kathaṃcit virodhasadbhāve 'pi brahmānabhyupagamādeḥ dvādaśalakṣaṇyām asūtritatvāt dharma-śabdasādhāraṇyāc ca kartṛbhede 'pi aikaśāstryāṅgīkāre na kācit anu-papattiḥ; tvadanumānaṃ tu aprayojakam eva, ananuṣṭheyasyāpi dharmaśabdagṛhītatvena jaiminīyavicārapratijñāviṣayatvopapatteḥ iti.

[240] atha ṣaṣṭhī kakṣyā

yad uktaṃ virodho nāstīti, tad asiddham, brahmasaṃnyāsābhyupa-gamānabhyupagamābhyāṃ virodhasyāpratyākhyeyatvāt, yat tu jaimineḥ tadubhayābhyupagamapradarśakaṃ sūtram, tat tadabhyu-pagama eva tasya siddhānta ity asya jñāpakam iti na avadhārayituṃ śakyam, 'vipratiṣedhāc cāsamañjasam' iti sāṃkhyādhikara-noktanyāyena jaiminimatasya parasparaviruddhatayā anupādeyatvodghāṭanaparatvena anyathāsiddheḥ; yac coktaṃ brahmānabhyupagamatadabhyupagamaikāntyādiṣu jaiminibādarāyaṇayoḥ virodhasadbhāve 'pi brahmānabhyupagamādeḥ dvādaśalakṣaṇyām asūtritatvāt aviruddhāyās tasyāḥ caturlakṣaṇyā saha aikaśāstryam upapadyata iti, tad apy ayuktam, aviruddhārthatvāsiddheḥ; tathā hi 'tasya nimittaparīṣṭiḥ' iti dharmapramāṇanirūpaṇaṃ pratijñāya prathamādhyāyena yat tatra pramāṇanirūpaṇaṃ kṛtam, tat tāvad viruddham; tatra hi 'āmnāyasya kriyārthatvād ānarthakyam atadarthānāṃ tasmād anityam ucyate' iti sūtreṇa – āmnāyasya kṛtsnasyāpi prayojanaparyavasānāya kriyārthatvāvaśyaṃbhāvāt atadarthānām 'vāyavyaṃ śvetam ālabheta bhūtikāmaḥ' ityādikriyāvākyānapekṣitatayā kriyārthatvarahitānām ānarthakyaṃ niṣprayojana [241] tvam, tasmāt akriyārthavākyajātam apramāṇam ucyate – ity etadarthakena vedeṣv arthavādānāṃ aprāmāṇyam āśaṅkya, 'vidhinā tv ekavākyatvāt stutyarthena vidhīnāṃ syuḥ' iti sūtreṇa – siddharthavādānāṃ vidhivākyena ekavākyatvāt vidhīnāṃ stutirūpeṇārthena saprayojanāḥ syuḥ– ity etadarthakena teṣāṃ vidhyekavākyatayā prāmāṇyam upapāditam arthavādādhikaraṇe; audumbarādhikaraṇe 'pi – 'uktaṃ tu vākyaśeṣatvam' iti arthavādādhikaraṇoktārthasmāraṇena tad dṛḍhīkṛtam; dharmavicārapratijñāyā brahmavicārasādhāraṇye hi 'tasya nimittaparīṣṭiḥ' iti dharmapramāṇanirūpaṇapratijñāpi brahmapramāṇanirūpaṇasādhāraṇī syāt; tathā sati akriyārthānām ānarthakyaśaṅkāyāṃ keṣāṃcid akriyārthānāṃ phalasādhanayāgādividhiśeṣatvena keṣāṃcit svataḥphalabhūtabrahmapratipādakatvena ca prāmāṇyam upapadyata iti vibhajya pariharaṇīyam; evam anyatrāpi pramāṇādhyāyārthavirodho 'nusaṃdheyaḥ; tathā 'vipratipattau haviṣā niyamyeta karmaṇas tadupākhyatvāt' ity āṣṭamikādhikaraṇe aindrapuroḍāśeṣu haviḥsāmānyāt āgneyavidhyantaḥ, na tu devatāsāmānyāt aindravidhyanta iti nirṇayārthe pravṛtte – devatāyāḥ śabdena uddeśyamātrarūpatvena siguṇatvāt iti yuktiḥ jaiminyabhimatā; tad api mataṃ vaiyā [242] sikamataviruddham – vaiyāsikatantre devatādhikaraṇe devatānāṃ yāgadeśe saṃnidhānasya havirbhoktṛtvena prādhānyasya ca samarthitatvāt; tathā 'codanā punar ārambhaḥ' iti dvaitīyīkādhikaraṇe karmaṇām apūrvadvārā phalasādhanatvaṃ jaimininā samarthitam, tad api 'phalam ata upapatteḥ' iti vaiyāsikādhikaraṇena viruddham; tatra karmopāsanaprasāditasya parameśvarasya phalapradatvasamarthanāt; tasmāt śāstrayor eva virodho 'sti; brahmasaṃnyāsāpalāpaprayukto 'pi tayor asti virodhaḥ; tathā hi – 'tat tvam asi' ityādibrahmaviṣayāṇi vākyāni jīvaṃ brahma bodhayantīti 'vidhinā tv ekavākyatvāt' – iti akriyārthānāṃ vidhiśeṣatvoktyā teṣām upāsanāvidhiśeṣatvam uktaṃ bhavati; tadupāsanāś ca kratūpayuktakartṛrūpadravyasaṃskāratvāt prokṣaṇādinyāyena kratuśeṣatāṃ bhajante; kartṛmātrasya laukikakriyāsādhāraṇye 'pi dehātmabhāvenāpi laukikakriyopapatteḥ; 'ātmānam upāsīta' ityādiṣu anārabhyādhīteṣu vedānteṣu upāsanāsaṃskāryatvenānūditasya ātmanaḥ svargādibhoktṛyāgādividhyākṣiptadehātiriktātmarūpatvena avyabhicaritakratusaṃbandhitayā taddvārā vākyapramāṇena 'yad eva vidyayā karoti' iti śrutipramāṇena ca tāsāṃ kratusaṃbandhopapatteḥ; na ca apahatapāpmatvādijīvāsaṃ [243] bhāvitaguṇāmnānena brahmaṇo jīvād adhikatvasiddheḥ tadupāsanānāṃ na kratuśeṣatvaprasaktir iti vācyam, akriyārthānāṃ vidhiśeṣatvaniyamasya jaiminyabhimatasya samanvayādhikaraṇena bhaṅgaṃ kṛtvā vedāntānāṃ svātantryeṇa upakramāditātparyaliṅgena ca brahmatadguṇeṣu prāmāṇye vyavasthāpite khalu apahatapāpmatvādiguṇaiḥ jīvādhikaṃ brahma sidhyet, jaiminidṛṣṭyā teṣāṃ vidhiśeṣatve tathābhūtaguṇavarṇanasya jīva eva stutyarthatvenānvayaṃ ko vārayet; dṛśyate hi kratvanvayitattadvastvasaṃbhāvitaguṇavarṇanaṃ tattanmantrārthavādeṣu – yathā 'divam agreṇa mā lekhīr antarikṣaṃ madhyena mā hiṃsīḥ pṛthivyā saṃbhava', 'dyāṃ te dhūmo gacchatu antarikṣam arciḥ pṛthivīṃ bhasmanā pṛṇasva svāhā', 'apahatapāpmāno vā ṛtavaḥ', 'āpo vā idaṃ sarvam' ityādiṣu; evaṃ brahmāpalāpe sati tatprāptyupāyaḥ saṃnyāso 'pi apalapito bhavati; ata eva karmānadhikāriṇām andhapaṅgvādīnāṃ kathaṃcit gatyupanyāsaḥ saṃnyāsa iti mīmāṃsakapravādaḥ; tasmāt śāstrayor virodho nāstīti ayuktam; dharmaśabdasya brahmasādhāraṇyavacanam api ayuktam, 'te vadanti mahātmānaṃ kṛṣṇaṃ dharmaṃ sanātanam' iti bhāratavacanasya 'dharmo vigrahavān rāmaḥ' itivat stutyarthatvenāpi upapatteḥ; tasmāt madanumānaṃ na bādhi [244] tam, tvadanumānaṃ tu aprayojakam iti.

atha saptamī

na tāvat bādhitaṃ madanumānam, pūrvatantre prāmāṇyapratijñāyā akriyārthānām ānarthakyenāprāmāṇyaśaṅkāyāś ca brahmaparavākyasādhāraṇye 'pi, kriyāviśeṣārthavādeṣu vidhiśeṣatvena sārthakatayā prāmāṇyaprakāram uktvā, brahmaparavākyeṣu svataḥ puruṣārthabrahmaviṣayatayā kriyāvidhiśeṣatvam anapekṣya svata eva prāmāṇyam iti tatprāmāṇyaprakāram anudghātya, tadviṣaye gūḍhābhisaṃdhir āsīt jaiminir iti prathamādhyāyodghāṭitavirodhaparihārasaṃbhavāt; 'vipratipattau haviṣā niyamyeta' ity āṣṭamikādhikaraṇasiddhānte devatāyā guṇatvaṃ na yuktiḥ, dravyasyāpi guṇatvāviśeṣāt; kiṃ tu 'karmaṇas tadupākhyatvāt' iti sūtraśeṣoktā – havistyāgarūpasya yāgakarmaṇo haviḥṣu upalabhyamānatvāt haviḥsāmānyaṃ balīyaḥ, havir hi tyajamānam upalabhyate, na devateti eṣaiva mūlayuktiḥ – ity āṣṭamikādhikaraṇavirodhaparihāralābhāt; 'codanā punar ārambhaḥ' ity adhikaraṇe karmaṇāṃ dvārasadbhāvamātram uktam, na tv īśvaraprasādapratyākhyānena apūrvam eva dvāram iti samarthitam iti tadvirodhaparihāralābhāt; 'vidhinā tv ekavākyatvāt' ity atra vāyukṣe [245] piṣṭhādivākyānām eva vidhiśeṣatvena prāmāṇyam uktam, na brahmaparavākyānām iti; ata eva brahmāpalāpādiśaṅkāparihāralābhāt bhāratavacanānusāreṇa dharmaśabdasya alaukikaśreyaḥsādhanamātravācitayā brahmasādhāraṇyasaṃbhave tatpravṛttinimitte vihitatvānuṣṭheyatvādiviśeṣaṇānupraveśena brahmavyāvṛttaśaktikalpanasya gauravaparāhatatayā bhāratavacanasyastutyarthatvakalpanānupapatteḥ; tasmāt na bādhitaṃ madanumānam, tvadanumānaṃ tu aprayojakam eveti.

athāṣṭamī kakṣyā

prathamādhyāyārthavirodhasamādhānaṃ tāvat ayuktam, 'sāmānyapratijñānāprāmāṇyaśaṅkayoḥ sādhāraṇye, keṣucid akriyārtheṣu aprāmāṇyaśaṅkāṃ parihṛtya keṣucit gūḍhābhisaṃdhir āsīt iti kalpanasyāpahāsyatvāt; yaḥ khalu vidhyarthavādamantranāmadheyātmakavedasya dharmaprāmāṇyaṃ saprakāram upapādya smṛtyācārayor api tatra saṃbhavat prāmāṇyam upapādayāmāsa, sa kathaṃ jaiminiḥ brahmapramāṇavicārasādhāraṇyena dharmapramāṇavicāraṃ pratijñāya brahmaparavedāntabhāgarūpārthavādasādhāraṇyena ānarthakyād aprāmāṇyaśaṅkām udbhāvya kriyāśeṣārthavādamātre parihāram āha, na tu brahmaviṣayavedāntarūpārthavādeṣu – iti katham idam asāram utprekṣaṇaṃ nyāyavidaḥ [246] śraddadhīran; kiṃ ca dharmavicārapratijñāyās tatpramāṇa-vicārapratijñāyāś ca karmabrahmatadupāsanādisādhāraṇye 'anyānarthakyāt' iti arthavādādhikaraṇapūrvapakṣasūtrasya 'pūrṇāhutyā sarvān kāmān avāpnoti' ity ādikarmavidhiphalārthavādavat upāsanāvidhiphalārthavādā api viṣayā bhaveyuḥ, tulyaṃ hi teṣv api anyānarthakyacodyam – yadi 'sarvāṃś ca lokān āpnoti sarvāṃś ca kāmān yas tam ātmānam anuvidya vijānāti' iti prajāpatividyāphalārthavādo 'pi vivakṣitārthaḥ syāt, tarhi 'so' śnute sarvān kāmān' iti kevalaṃ sarvakāmāvāptyarthatvena śrutānandamaya-brahmopāsanā, 'teṣāṃ sarveṣu lokeṣu kāmacāro bhavati' iti kevalaṃ sarvalokāvāptyarthatvena śrutā daharopāsanā ca vyarthā syāt; yadi uktopāsanābhiḥ sarvalokakāmāvāptisahitā muktiḥ, tarhi vasurudrādityamarutsādhyatattulyabhogamātraprāptisahitamuktiphalā madhuvidyā gārhapatyādilokatrayaprāptipūrvakamuktiphalopakosalavidyā lokaviśeṣaprāptitatratyabhogarahitakevalamuktiphalākṣarādividyā ca anarthikā syāt; yadi sakalaviṣayabhogaviraktaṃ brahmānandaikaprepsum upāsanādhikāriṇaṃ prati lokaviśe-ṣaprāptiḥ tatratyabhogaś ca na phalam, kiṃ tu svepsitaphalaprāptau antarāyamātram iti iṣyate, tadā nirantarāyāvilambitepsitaphala [247] prāpakatvena akṣarādividyāḥ śrutā iti atathābhūtā madhuvidyādayo 'narthikāḥ syuḥ; yadi aniyatakālārambhatvena yāvajjīvikatvena ca aniyatakālaparimāṇāḥ nyūnādhikaguṇāḥ nyūnādhikavarṇāśramadharmānugṛhītāś ca sarvā api brahmavidyā aviśiṣṭamuktiphalāḥ, tadā guṇataḥ karmataḥ kālato vā adhikā anarthikāḥ syuḥ; yadi 'nirañjanaḥ paramaṃ sāmyam upaiti' ityādayo vidyāphalārthavādā vivakṣitārthāḥ syuḥ, tadā mukter api vaidhaphalatvaprāptau 'sarvebhyaḥ kāmebhyo darśapūrṇamāsau', 'sarvebhyaḥ kāmebhyo jyotiṣṭomaḥ' iti sārvakāmyavākyayoḥ tatsaṃgrāhakatvam api syād iti sakṛtprayuktābhyāṃ darśapūrṇamāsābhyāṃ sakṛtprayuktena jyotiṣṭomena vā muktisiddheḥ sakalavarṇāśramasāhityena yāvajjīvam anuṣṭheyāḥ sarvā api brahmopāsanāḥ anarthikāḥ syuḥ – ity evam anyānarthakyasūtrasya sarvaviṣayatve ca sarvasādhāraṇena parihāreṇa sūtritena bhavitavyam; karmavidhyarthavādamātraviṣayatvam eva ca parihārasūtrāṇāṃ dṛśyate 'sarvatvam ādhikārikam', 'phalasya karmaniṣpatteḥ teṣāṃ lokavat parimāṇataḥ phalaviśeṣaḥ syāt' iti; tatra ādyasūtreṇa 'vidya praśaṃsā' iti pūrvasūtrataḥ praśaṃsāpadānuvṛttiyuktena pūrṇāhutivākye yat kāmasarvatvam, tat praśaṃsāmātram, na tu sākṣāt phalam, agnisaṃskārasya [248] ca pūrṇāhuteḥ phalānapekṣatvāt, praśaṃsārtham upādīyamānakāmasarvatvam ādhikārikam, pūrṇāhutyanantaram agnisiddhau satyām eva hi nānāphaleṣu karmasu adhikriyate puruṣaḥ; teṣāṃ phalānāṃ siddhiḥ pūrṇāhutyadhīneti tat phalasarvatvaṃ pūrṇāhutiphalatvena praśaṃsārtham upādīyate; na ca agnisādhyakarmaphalagrahaṇena sarvakāmāvāptisādhanatayā pūrṇāhutiḥ praśaṃsituṃ na śakyate, ākāśagāmyamarakanyālābhādeḥ agnisādhyakarmaphalatvābhāvād iti śaṅkyam, yataḥ pūrṇāhutivākye sarvatvam adhikārāpekṣam – yāvat phalajātaṃ karmavidhivākyeṣv adhikṛtam, tāvaty eva saṃkucitavṛtti, sarvaudano 'nena bhuktaḥ – ityādau prakaraṇādinā saṃkocadarśanāt ity ayam artha ucyate; na ca itthaṃ praśaṃsārthatvam 'so 'śnute sarvān kāmān' ityādiṣu rātrisatrārthavādavat phalasamarpakeṣu aṅgīkartuṃ śakyam; dvitīyasūtreṇa agnihotrataḥ svargasiddheḥ iṣṭisomādyānarthakyam – ityādiśaṅkāparihārāya kṛṣinyāyena karmabhūyastvāt phalabhūyastvam ucyate; tatra śaṅkā tāvat upāsanābhāge 'pi samānā; tatparihāraḥ siddhāntabhāge na dṛśyate; na hi tatra karmabhūyastvāt phalabhūyastvanyāyaḥ pravartate; 'tathā phalābhāvāt' iti sūtroktam ucyamānaphalābhāvarūpam aprāmāṇyakāraṇam 'śobhate 'sya mukhaṃ ya evaṃ veda' [249] ityādikarmakāṇḍagataphalārthavādasya 'cakṣuṣyaḥ śruto bhavati' ityādibrahmakāṇḍagataphalārthavādasya ca sādhāraṇam, karmakāṇḍagatārthavāda eva parihārasūtraṃ dṛśyate; 'vidyā-praśaṃsā' iti viduṣo mukham evaṃ gargatrirātrabrāhmaṇārthavedanenaiva śobhate, na vanitāmukhaval lāvaṇyena iti vidyā praśasyata iti; nāyaṃ parihāraḥ 'cakṣuṣyaḥ śruto bhavati' ity atra pravartate, cakṣuṣyatvaśrutatvayoḥ jyotirvidyāphalatvābhyupagamāt; evam anyānarthakyādisūtrāṇām avarjanīye tattadupāsanāvidhiphalārthavādasādhāraṇye tattatsiddhāntasūtrāṇāṃ karmavidhiphalārthavādaviṣayāṇām eva grathane 'pi, jaimineḥ kvacit parihārodghāṭanaṃ kvacid abhisaṃdhinigūhanam ity evaṃ gatyāśrayaṇaṃ kasya nāpahāsyam; tasmāt ātmopāsanānāṃ kratuśeṣatvātapāpaślokaśravaṇādivat tatphalārthavādā avivakṣitārthāḥ ity abhipretya anyānarthakyaśaṅkā tatparihāraś ca teṣu na pravartitāḥ; ata eva vedoṣarā vedāntā iti vicāraṇīyābhāvāt asāratvābhiprāyojaiminīyānāṃ pravāda iti prathamādhyāyārthavirodhasamādhānaṃ tāvad ayuktam eva; tathaiva āṣṭamikādhikaraṇavirodhasamādhānam api; tatra hi – haviṣo dṛśyamānatve 'pi yāgasyadevatārādhanarūpatvāt devataiva prasannā phaladātrī pradhānabhūtā; ataḥ [250] tatsāmānyaṃ haviḥsāmānyāt balīya iti śaṅkānirākaraṇārthaṃ sūtram – 'guṇatvena devatāśrutiḥ' iti; na caitad abhyuccayaparatvena yojayituṃ śakyam, navamādhyāye jaimininā 'devatā vā prayojayed atithivad bhojanasya tadarthatvāt' iti sūtreṇa yathā atithipūjātmakam ātithyam atithiprītyarthaṃ sat atithipradhānam – evaṃ devapūjātmakaṃ yajanam api devatāprītyarthaṃ sad eva devatāpradhānam, saiva ca prītā devatā phaladātrīti pūrvapakṣaṃ kṛtvā 'api vā śabdapūrvatvāt yajñakarma pradhānaṃ syāt guṇatvena devatāśrutiḥ' iti sūtreṇa na devatāpradhānaṃ yajanam; tad eva apūrvadvārā phalajanakam; na tu haviṣā prītā devatā; tasyās tu dravyoddeśyatayā yāgopasarjanatvenaiva śrutir iti siddhāntam abhidhāya, 'atithau tatpradhānatvam abhāvaḥ karmaṇi syāt tasya prītipradhānatvāt' iti sūtreṇa ātithyavaiṣamyaṃ yajane darśitam – ātithyam atithiprītividhānam – yathā atithiḥ prīyate tathā kartavyatayā vihitam iti tad atithipradhānaṃ yujyate, karmaṇi tu nāsti prītividhānam – yathā devatā prīyate tathā karma kartavyam iti; ato na devatāpradhānaṃ yajanam iti kaṇṭhata eva devatāprādhānyasya nirākṛtatvāt; etena 'codanā punar ārambhaḥ' ity adhikaraṇavi [251] rodhasamādhānam api nirastam, jaimininā devatāprādhānye spaṣṭaṃ nirākṛte 'codanā punar ārambhaḥ' ityadhikaraṇe vyākhyātṛbhiḥ vyavahṛtam apūrvam eva dvāraṃ jaiminer api abhimatam iti avadhāraṇāt; brahmatatprāptyarthasaṃnyāsāpalāpavirodhasamādhānam api ayuktam, brahmaviṣayavākyānāṃ kartṛsaṃskārarūpakarmāṅgopāsanāviṣayajīvātmasvarūpasamarpakatvam abhyupagacchataḥ jaimineḥ mate brahmaṇi pramāṇābhāvenaiva taddvayāpalāpasiddher anivāryatvāt; ata eva arthavādādhikaraṇe vārtikakāraiḥ 'vāyur vai kṣepiṣṭhā' ityādyarthavādānāṃ vidhiśeṣatvasamarthanānantaram uktam – etena upaniṣadām api nairākāṅkṣyaṃ vyākhyātam iti; yat tu vārtikakāraiḥ vyākaraṇādhikaraṇe paramātmopāsanāvidhitatphalavacanāny udāhṛtya tāsāṃ svātantryeṇa abhyudayaniḥśreyasasādhanatvam uktam, tat sarvadhā brahmāpalāpabhīrūṇāṃ teṣām eva manīṣikayā pravṛttam, na tu sūtrakārābhimatatayā, jaiminīyavaiyāsikasūtrāṇāṃ sphuṭavirodhasya darśitatvāt; yat tu pravṛttinimittagauravaparihārārthaṃ dharmaśabdasya brahmasādhāraṇyāvaśyaṃbhāvāt bhāratavacanasya stutyarthatvaṃ na kalpyata iti; tatredam uttaram – addhā tasya stutyarthatvaṃ na kalpyam, kiṃ tu kṛṣṇastutiprakaraṇād eva siddham; tat dharmaśabdasya alaukikaśreyaḥsādhanamātravācitāyāṃ na nirva [252] hati; tadā hi anuṣṭhātṛtvena alaukikaśreyaḥsādhanānāṃ jīvātmanāṃ nimittatvena tathābhūtānām anyeṣāṃ ca bahūnāṃ dharmaśabdaḥ sādhāraṇa iti tadvācyatvoktyā bhagavataḥ kā stutir labhyate; tasmād udāhṛtabhāratavacanasvārasyaprasiddhyartham eva dharmaśabdasya yāgādikarmamātravācitvam aṅgīkartavyam – dharmasaṃsthāpanārtham avatīrṇo bhagavān sākṣāt svayam eva dharmaḥ ity uktyā stuto bhavati; astu vā yathākathaṃcit dharmaśabdasya brahmaṇy api vṛttiḥ; tathāpi dharmajijñāsāsūtroktaḥ dharmaśabdaḥ 'dharmaṃ jaiminir ata eva' iti sūtragata iva brahmavyāvṛtta eva grāhyaḥ, 'codanālakṣaṇo 'rtho dharmaḥ' iti vicāryatvena pratijñātasya dharmasya codanālakṣaṇatvokteḥ; 'cudapreraṇe' iti dhātoḥ niṣpanno hi codanāśabdaḥ pravartakavacanam ācaṣṭe; tasmāt codanā dharme sākṣāt pramāṇam; tattaccodanāsaṃnidhyāmnātāni siddhārthabodhakāni vacanāni stutyādidvārā tattaccodanaikavākyatayā tatra pramāṇāni; pradhānavidhyekavākyeṣv eva rātrisatrādyarthavādeṣu śrūyamāṇaṃ phalaṃ vidhyapekṣitatvāt vivakṣitam; kartṛsaṃskāratvena karmāṅgeṣu ātmopāsaneṣu śrūyamāṇaṃ tu phalaṃ vidhyanapekṣitatvāt na vivakṣitam ityabhiprāyeṇaiva na teṣu jaimininā anyānarthakyādidoṣaparihārāś cintitāḥ; bhagavān bādarā [253] yaṇas tu kṣayiṣṇusātiśayābhyudayaphalaṃ yāgādirūpaṃ dharmam eva sakalavedārthaṃ manvānaḥ jaiminiḥ upakramādyavagamitamahātātpāryasakalavedāntapramāṇakaṃ brahma nityaniratiśayapuruṣārtharūpamuktiphalāni tadupāsanāni karmaṇāṃ tatsādhanasahakāribhāvaṃ ca nājñāsīt – ity etad ālocya jaiminīyaparyālocanena loko mā momuhat iti lokānugrahāya 'athāto brahmajijñāsā' ityādiśāstraṃ praṇināya – iti asty eva jaiminīyabādarāyaṇīyayoḥ śāstrayoḥ mahān virodhaḥ; ataḥ tayor aikaśāstryāsaṃbhavāt bādhitaṃ tvadanumānam, madanumānaṃ tu nāprayojakam, kṣayiṣṇusātiśayaphalaṃ yāgādikam eva vicāryatvena pratijñātavataḥ tantre tadanyasya vicāryatvāyogāt; na ca karmānyatve 'pi yūpāhavanīyagodohanādīnāṃ svarūpapramāṇādibhir vicāro dṛṣṭa iti tadvat brahmaṇo 'pi devatātvena yāgādyanvayasadbhāvāt hetvasiddhiḥ, devatāyāḥ tyajyamānadravyoddeśyatve 'pi tadvācakaśabdasyaiva uccāraṇārthakṛtirūpānuṣṭhānaviṣayatvena tasyāḥ tadviṣa yatvābhāvāt; etena jaiminīye vicāryaparasya dharmaśabdasya karmaparatvena sākṣāt brahmāsparśitve 'pi upāsanarūpakarmaparatvasyāpratyākheyatayā tadviṣayaphalarūpabrahmasparśitvam avarjanīyam iti pratijñāsādhāraṇyāt yathākathaṃcit virodham avadhūya aikaśāstryaṃ [254] samarthanīyam ity api śaṅkā nirastā, dharmaśabdasya uttarasūtrajātaparyālocanayā kṣayiṣṇusātiśayābhyudayaphalakarmamātraparatvasya uktatvāt; asti hi dharmaśabdasya tathābhūtakarmamātre 'pi vaidikaḥ prayogaḥ – 'anyatra dharmād anyatrādharmād anyatrāsmāt kṛtākṛtāt / anyatra bhūtāc ca bhavyāc ca yat tat paśyasi tad vada' iti; ayaṃ kaṭhavallīmantraḥ kṣayiṣṇusātiśayaphalasādhanakarmatatsādhyaphalatatsādhakakartṛvilakṣaṇasādhanasādhyasādhakatrayapara iti matadvaye 'pi samānam; 'trayāṇām eva caivam upanyāsaḥ praśnaś ca' iti sūtre paraiḥ uktatrayalābhārtham ittham ayaṃ mantro vyākhyātaḥ – dharmo 'bhyudayaphalakayāgādiḥ, tato 'nyatra tadvilakṣaṇaṃ sādhanam, adharmo dharmād itaraḥ tatsādhyaḥ svargādir abhyudayaḥ, tato 'nyatra tadvilakṣaṇaṃ sādhyam asmāt, buddhisaṃnihitāt yāgādisādhakāt sāṃsārikaphalapraṇavāt puruṣād anyatra tadvilakṣaṇaṃ sādhakaṃ ca – iti yat tat sādhanāditrayaṃ paśyasi, kṛtākṛtāt bhūtāc ca bhavyāc ceti dharmādīnāṃ trayāṇām api viśeṣaṇam, kṛtākṛtaṃ prārabdhāparisamāptaṃ yat prakāram ucyate, tena bhūtabhaviṣyadvartamānātmakāt prasiddhasādhanādeḥ vilakṣaṇaṃ sādhanāditrayaṃ vada ity uktaṃ bhavati; yad vā anyatra dharmād anyatrādharmāt – iti prasiddhapuṇyapāpayor asādhanapraśnaḥ, anyatrāsmāt kṛtākṛtāt [255] bhūtāc ca bhavyāc ceti bhūtabhaviṣyadvartamānātmakānityasādhyetaranityasādhyapraśnaḥ, sādhakapraśnasya tu sādhyapraśna evāntarbhāvaḥ, sādhakasyāpi nityatvāt; sādhyakoṭitvāc ceti; tatra adharmaśabdasya pāpe prasiddhasya dharmaphalasvargādiphalatvena, asmāt ity asya kṛtākṛtaviśeṣaṇabhāvena pratīyamānasya vibhidya svayam eva sādhakatvena, kṛtākṛtād ity asya asmāt ity etadviśeṣyabhāvena pratīyamānasya dharmādisarvaviśeṣaṇatvena, bhūtāc ca bhavyāc ca ity anayoḥ pṛthak anyatraśabdayogāt svātantryeṇa pratīyamānayoḥ dharmādisarvaviśeṣaṇatvena ca yojanā kliṣṭeti prathamaprakāre doṣaḥ; dvitīyaprakāre sādhakapraśnālābho doṣaḥ, nityatvena prāpyakoṭitvena ca dvitīyapraśnasaṃgrahītatvābhyupagame yāgādiphalasādhakavilakṣaṇasādhakālābhaḥ yāgādiphalasādhakasyāpi nityatvena bhūtabhaviṣyadvartamānānyatvarūpasaṃgrāhakakroḍīkṛtatvāt, apahatapāpmatvādyāvirbhāvaviśiṣṭatvena muktasyeva svargādiviśiṣṭatvena prāpyatvāc ca; tasmāt anupapannā parakīyā yojaneti, tām upekṣya asmābhiḥ anyā ṛjvī yojanā darśitā, prathamapādena yat balavadaniṣṭānanubandhikṣayiṣṇusātiśayaphalam, yac ca tadanubandhi tathābhūtaphalam, tadubhayavilakṣaṇaṃ sādhanam upanyastam, dvitīyapādena 'plavā hy ete 'dṛḍhā yajñarūpā aṣṭādaśoktam avaraṃ [256] yeṣu karma/etac chreyo ye 'bhinandanti mūḍhā jarāmṛtyū te punar evāpiyanti' – ityādimantrāntaranindítayāgādisādhakavilakṣaṇaḥ sādhaka upanyastaḥ; tatra kṛtākṛtāt ity asya kṛtam apy akṛtam akṛtaprāyaṃ yasya tasmād iti vyākhyā, tṛtīyapādena svargādisādhyavilakṣaṇaṃ sādhyam upanyastam, tatra cakārābhyāṃ bhūtabhavyānvitābhyāṃ bhūtabhavyobhayākārasya vartamānasya saṃgrahaḥ, evam –

anyatradharmamanunā prathitetareṣu
praśnatraye karaṇasādhakatatphaleṣu /
pādatrayeṇa suvace kramaśo nibaddhe
kliśanti taṃ kim iti tatparayojanārtham //

iti matadvaye 'pi tatra dharmaśabdaḥ kṣayiṣṇusātiśayaphalakarmamātrapara iti nirvivādam; kiṃ ca tathāvidhaprayogadarśane 'pi agrimavyavahārānusāreṇa tāvanmātraparatvaṃ jaiminīyaprayogasya tāvān eva dharmo nānyo 'stīti bhrāntikṛtā kalpayituṃ śakyam; dṛṣṭaṃ hi 'athāto dharmaṃ vyākhyāsyāmaḥ' iti kaṇādasūtre vicāryaparasya dharmaśabdasya agrimasūtrānusāreṇa kiṃciddharmaparatvam; agre hi yāgādyanuṣṭhānaprakāro na cintitaḥ; kiṃ tu ṣaṣṭhādhyāye prathamāhnike dānapra [257] tigrahadharmaś cintitaḥ, dvitīyāhnikena cāturāśramyadharmaḥ kiyān api cintitaḥ saṃgrahataḥ; tasmāt yuktaṃ dharmavicārapratijñānasya na brahmavicārasādhāraṇyam iti siddham. atrāyaṃ matadvayasaṃkṣepaḥ –

jātidravyaguṇānvayi dharmatvaṃ brahmaṇo 'pi samavetam /
tadupāsanakriyāyā niḥsaṃdehaṃ ca dharmatvam //1//

tat sākṣād gocarayed dharmavicārapratijñānam /
svargādivad vicāryaḥ kriyāphalatvena vā brahma //2//
ity aikaśāstryam ubhayor mīmāṃsāśāstrayor yad āsthiṣata /
tatrāśām apanetuṃ teṣāṃ pratibodhanaṃ kriyate //3//
bhavadabhimatarūpaṃ brahma tattadvaco hi
spṛśati yadi vicāryaṃ pūrvatantrapratijñā /
kim iti na bhavitavyaṃ tadvicārais tad āstām
nanu pariharaṇīyaṃ sarvadhā tadviruddham //4//
lakṣasūtragatacodanāpadaṃ prerakaṃ vidhipadaṃ hi nojjhati /
akriyārthavacasām anarthatām arthavādanayapūrvapakṣatām //5//
arthavādavacasām anarthatā paryahāri vidhiśeṣabhāvataḥ //
tat kim āgamavacāṃsi na spṛśec codanaṃ tava samaṃ hi teṣv api //
na spṛśed yadi tato hi jaiminiḥ sa svayaṃphalaparāṇi sūtrayet /
[258] atra gūḍham abhisaṃdhim alpadhīr asya kalpayati kena hetunā //7//
itthaṃ gūḍhābhisaṃdhiḥ kiyati tu viṣaye kalpanīyo maharṣer
anyānarthakyayuktyādy api hi viphalatoktyādisādhāraṇaṃ te /
kṛtsnaṃ dharmapramāṇaṃ kalayitum anasaṃ lakṣaṇe tanyamāne
smṛtyācārādi tadvat smṛtipatham agamat kiṃ nu vedāntabhāgaḥ //8//
atra nirbharam aśakyasaṃvare prasphuṭe praṇava eva visvare /
śraddadhīta ka iveha tāvakīm aikamatyakṛtikatthanāṃ tayoḥ //9//
aṣṭame ca navame ca devatām adhvareṣu guṇam āha jaiminiḥ/
svapradhānam atha bādarāyaṇas tatra vā parihṛtiḥ krameta kā //10//
dvāraṃ yāgādīnāṃ yad apūrvaṃ devatāprasāda iti /
vaiṣamyaṃ tatrāpi pravartate naiva parihṛtiḥ kāpi //11//
tasmāt pūrvatra tantre kṣayaniyataphalaḥ kāmikāryo vicāryo
dharmas tatraiva vedaṃ sakalam api munir jaiminir mānam ūce /
etat karmaikaniṣṭhair gurukṛtam ahitaṃ tanmataṃ bodhayiṣyan
brahmajñānāya sūtrāṇy akuruta bhagavān puṇḍarīkākṣa eva //12//
iti tantrayor virodhe pradhānabhūtārthaphalasamālambe /
jāgrati na dhīṣu viduṣāṃ labhate padam aikaśāstryavārtāpi //13//

ABBREVIATIONS

AB	*Aitareya Brāhmaṇa*
ĀDS	*Āpastamba Dharma Sūtra*
BAU	*Bṛhad Āraṇyaka Upaniṣad*
BS	*Brahma Sūtras*
CU	*Chāndogya Upaniṣad*
KS	*Kāṭhaka Saṃhitā*
KU	*Kaṭha Upaniṣad*
MS	*Mīmāṃsā Sūtras*
MU	*Muṇḍaka Upaniṣad*

TA	*Taittirīya Āraṇyaka*
TS	*Taittirīya Saṃhitā*
TU	*Taittirīya Upaniṣad*
VS	*Vaiśeṣika Sūtra*s

Department of South Asian Languages and Civilizations
Foster Hall
1130 East 59th Street
Chicago, IL 60637
USA
E-mail: s-pollock@uchicago.edu

DONALD R. DAVIS, JR.

DHARMA IN PRACTICE: ĀCĀRA AND AUTHORITY IN MEDIEVAL DHARMAŚĀSTRA

That *dharma* in the Dharmaśāstra was derived in a historical sense not from the Vedic literature but from 'custom' has long been accepted.[1] In the clearest exposition of this thesis, Lariviere writes, "the whole of the *dharma* corpus can be viewed as a record of custom" (1997: 98, also included in the present volume).[2] An important distinction must be preserved here between *dharma* and Dharmaśāstra, for the former is a concept and an idea, while the latter is a series of textual reflections on that concept. It is Dharmaśāstra that derives its substance primarily from what Lariviere and others call 'custom.' For *dharma*, by contrast, 'custom' is only one of its sources. 'Custom' is an ambiguous translation for the Sanskrit term *ācāra*, one of the three principal sources of *dharma*, along with *śruti* and *smṛti*, i.e. the Vedas and Dharmaśāstra texts themselves.

The uncertainty about the denotation of 'custom' stems from a vacillation between custom as norm and custom as behavior (see, e.g., Lariviere, 1997: 104; Wezler, 1999: 84–88)[3] and from a lack of critical reflection on the possible differences between custom and customary law. Both Lariviere and Wezler presuppose the nature of custom without due reflection on the ambiguities of the term. The purpose of this paper is to extend their arguments by examining the nature of *ācāra* itself and its relation to the authority of *dharma*.

The ambiguity of custom in English is deeply embedded in Anglo-American jurisprudence in which custom, also called the Common Law, has, from the times of Blackstone and his predecessors, been considered the truly great source of law's authority, in contradistinction to the modern legislations of parliaments.[4] From legal circles 'custom' entered colonial discussions of social, religious, and legal problems engendered in the encounter between Britain and its new colonies, especially India (Vollenhoven, 1927; Jain, 1963; Bhattacharya, 1996; Chakravarty-Kaul, 1996: 187–198). Social anthropologists are the latest group to continue to expand, evolve, and criticize the idea of 'custom,' again as part of a process of cultural and intellectual encounter (Moore, 1978, 1986; Renteln and Dundes, 1994). Over the last 50 years or so, however, an impressive literature has accumulated on the historical and linguistic problems involved in using the term 'custom' in comparative legal and religious studies.[5] Geertz provides a summary criticism, "The mischief done by the word 'custom' in anthropology, where it reduced thought to habit, is perhaps only exceeded by that which it has done in legal history, where it reduced thought to practice" (1983: 208). It is precisely this extrication of thought and agency from the understanding of *ācāra* that leads me to question the suitability of 'custom' as a transparent English equivalent. If the Sanskrit term *ācāra* is to be related to the concept of *dharma*, to the point of being the very foundation of *dharma* in the Dharmaśāstra (Wezler, 1999), then we must be clear about what is meant by calling *ācāra* 'custom.'

In this essay, I will contend that *ācāra* refers to norms or standards consciously and deliberately established by the elites of a given group.[6] Both as one of the three traditional divisions of Dharmaśāstra (*vyavahāra* and *prāyaścitta* being the other two) and as a generic term for local and regional laws (Davis, 1999: 191ff.), *ācāra* refers to norms, expressed in the form of rules. As Ganganatha Jha writes in his exposition of the Mīmāṃsā understanding of the relationship of *ācāra* and *dharma*, "we are to accept as Dharma only those actions of good men which they do as Dharma; that is to say, any and every act done by good men is not to be regarded as Dharma; when they do an act, thinking it to be Dharma, then alone is that act to be regarded as Dharma" (Jha, 1916: 68).[7] In other words, there is an agentive process, typically in the form of consensus or legislation, whereby a certain behavior is accorded the status of *ācāra* and thereby becomes a norm, a rule, a law. *Ācāra* has attached to it a sense of behaving according to a certain set of well-known standards (cf. Wezler, 1999: 84). There may be many behaviors common to a particular group or region, but only when such a behavior has been authorized somehow can it be called *ācāra*, a standard or law. Medieval Dharmaśāstra commentaries are full of glosses and synonyms for *ācāra* that indicate both its nature as a norm and its conceptualization as practical and practiced *dharma*.

Ācāra, therefore, is *dharma* in practice, the practical, 'real' life of *dharma* that acts as a normative precedent for future action,[8] even though in practice it may sometimes differ from place to place and time to time.[9] If *dharma*'s authority rests primarily on three sources, then it makes sense to examine the relationship of these sources to each other and to *dharma* itself. Elaborating on the medieval Dharmaśāstra presentations of the sources of *dharma*, I would argue that in general the authority of *dharma* derives both: (1) historically – from the currency and political significance of *ācāra* and (2) academically or theologically – from the ideologically powerful connection of *ācāra* with *śruti* and *smṛti*. The first source of authority operates both within and outside of the theological and jurisprudential discourses of Dharmaśāstra, i.e. in the realm of praxis as well, while the second is restricted primarily to this academic branch of learning. However, to the extent that experts in Dharmaśāstra, mostly or exclusively Brahmins, had political and cultural influence, the ideological connection of *ācāra* with Vedic tradition shaped and informed the historical importance of *ācāra* as *dharma* in practice. On the whole, I am concerned here primarily with the theological connections of *ācāra* and *dharma*, although I believe the historical connections impinge on the theology and vice-versa. This essay will, therefore, attempt to illuminate the authority of *dharma* as presented in medieval Dharmaśāstra texts with particular attention to *ācāra* as the least studied of the three classic sources.

THE AUTHORITY OF THE PERSON IN DHARMAŚĀSTRA AND MĪMĀṂSĀ

The first step in understanding the authority of *dharma* in the religio-legal discourses of medieval Dharmaśāstra takes off from the fact that the most important school for the exegesis of both the Vedas and Dharmaśāstra, the Pūrva-Mīmāṃsā,[10] recognized one of the principal sources of knowledge and authority in matters relating to *dharma* to be human beings who know the Veda (*vedavid*). To be clear, the Vedas as *scripture* are the starting point for all Mīmāṃsā, but it is also clear from the tradition as a whole that the Vedas have power and authority only insofar as it is known, understood, and followed by human beings. Part of this grounding of authority in human beings relates to *dharma*'s foundation in reason, as well as on the Veda. Halbfass elaborates:

> Essentially, *dharma* is that which can only be learned from the Veda and justified through the Veda; there are no other means for knowing it, and no other sources for legitimizing it: to be sure, this 'rooting in the Veda' (*vedamūlatva*) should itself be secured by reason and argumentation (*yukti*, *nyāya*). The *dharma* is *vedamūla*; yet the insight that this is so is considered as *nyāyamūla*, as being based upon reason. (1988: 325–326, cf. Medhātithi on Manu 2.6 in Jha, 1999: V.1: 58)

The medieval *Sarasvatīvilāsa* is somewhat more explicit when it makes *nyāya* (reason, logic, common sense, etc.) into a kind of natural supplement to the Veda "*vidheyasya darśanasya kathamaṃśapūrakatvena pramāṇakoṭiniveṣāt* [because it enters into the category of authority (*pramāṇa*) by supplying (completing) the 'how-portion' in regard to the performance of what is enjoined]" (Shama Shastry, 1927: 13).[11] *Dharma*'s basis in *nyāya* begins to shift the locus of authority away from texts to the people who know the texts and their accompanying ritual and legal traditions.

Medieval Mīmāṃsā texts corroborate the idea that authority also rests in the human person who knows the Vedic texts and traditions. The point is clearly made in commentaries to the 3rd section of the 1st chapter of the *Pūrva-Mīmāṃsā Sūtras* (PMS) of Jaimini. The first *sūtra* establishes the position of the *pūrvapakṣa*, i.e. the interlocutor or straw man, against which the author establishes his opinion through syllogisms. This wrong opinion reads: "*dharmasya śabdamūlatvād aśabdam anapekṣaṃ syāt* [Because the basis of *dharma* is the Veda, that which is not part of the Veda should be considered unrequired (as *dharma*)]" (PMS 1.3.1, see Jha, 1916: 55). The *siddhānta*, or established teaching, of Jaimini, however, states: "*api vā kartrsāmānyāt pramāṇam anumānaṃ syāt* [On the contrary, the presumption (of a Vedic text) should be the proof (of the authority of *smṛti* and *ācāra*) because the agents are identical]" (PMS 1.3.2, see Jha, 1916: 56). In this case, the *pūrvapakṣa* suggests that human beings are only obliged to do things that are explicitly stated in the Vedas; in everything else, they can do as they please. However, Jaimini, in the voice of the *siddhānta*, refutes this claim. Jha sums up the medieval commentarial interpretations of the *sūtra* as follows:

> Because the agents or persons who compiled the Smṛtis are the same that performed actions laid down in the Veda; that is to say, we know that during their lives, Manu, Yājñavalkya and other writers on Smṛti, acted fully in accordance with the injunctions laid down in the Veda; and for persons who were such strict followers of the Veda in conduct, it is not possible that they should have made assertions except in accordance with direct Vedic injunctions known to them; therefore, we conclude that the Smṛti is authoritative (Jha, 1916: 57).

This argument opened the conceptual floodgates for the Mīmāṃsā tradition because it was extended also to the conventional standards and practices (*ācāra*) of these same "agents" (*kartṛ*) who followed the Vedas.[12] Such a view allowed medieval Dharmaśāstra commentators such as Medhātithi to incorporate *ācāra* under the same heading, and, therefore, the same status, as *smṛti* itself.[13]

Another aspect of the Mīmāṃsaka argument here merits a slight elaboration. The Mīmāṃsakas acknowledge that the authority of Dharmaśāstra texts (*smṛti*) and local laws (*ācāra*) derives not directly from the *extant* Vedas, the contents of which overlap very little with Dharmaśāstra texts and local laws, but indirectly from people who respect and know the Vedas. Moreover, and here the argument stretches somewhat, the Mīmāṃsakas developed the doctrine that in a case where a rule of *smṛti* or *ācāra* cannot be derived from a Vedic text, we should infer or presume (*anumāna*) the existence of a lost Vedic text to which the accepted rule of *smṛti* or *ācāra* corresponds.[14] The key point here is not the doubtful historical validity of this 'lost Veda' doctrine, but the hermeneutical gymnastics performed by the Mīmaṃsakas to permit or recognize, in the first place, the authority of humanly constructed norms and to connect that authority, in the second place, with the authority of the Veda.

With this recognition of the authority of certain human pronouncements about religious and legal life, we return to the argument described earlier in which Lariviere, Wezler, and others have asserted that Dharmaśāstra's real origins lie in 'custom,' i.e. *ācāra*. Although the Mīmāṃsakas would likely not characterize Dharmaśāstra's origins in this way, it seems possible to read Mīmāṃsā as permitting such a view provided that what we might call 'the lost Veda corollary' is also understood as part of the characterization, an important corollary in that it allows the Mīmāṃsakas to claim that all sources of *dharma* are ultimately based on the Vedas, whether extant or 'lost.' As a result, one way of extending the historical thesis of Lariviere and Wezler is to suggest that even Hindu theology accords considerable importance and authority to standards and observances proclaimed and promulgated by humans. The authority of the person provides Dharmaśāstra with an apparatus of change and adaptability, one that can meet the challenges of historical developments while preserving an orthodox theological view of the 'roots' of *dharma* as uniformly Vedic.

THE PRODUCTIVE TAUTOLOGY OF DHARMA AND ĀCĀRA

One striking aspect of the authority of *dharma* in medieval Dharmaśāstra (one that characterizes many earlier and later conceptions as well) is its tautological nature. The tautology works like this: *dharma* is constituted and promulgated by those who already possess authority, but those authorities must be people who follow and know *dharma*. This sociologically constructed tautology with the *śiṣṭas*, the educated elites, as the living focal point was both hermeneutically and socially efficacious in classical and medieval India. Hermeneutically, the tautology provided theological justification for a diversity of injunctions, rules, and laws while still according importance to *dharma* by permitting convention to define it only partially. Socially, the tautology allowed the authority for *dharma* to rest with the leaders of a community who determined the *ācāra* for their group. Moreover, it provides us with a more plausible way to understand what Indians meant by *ācāra* and similar words in legal and religious contexts.

An interesting instance of this tautology at work in medieval Dharmaśāstra concerns the so-called 'bad customs' (*durācāra*) or 'special customs' (*anācāra*, lit. 'not-customs') of particular groups or regions. The relationship of *dharma* to these deviant standards of conduct – deviant, at least, from an outsider's perspective – says a great deal about the importance of *ācāra* in a general way to the substantive content of *dharma* in practice.

A tension between pan-Indian and regional standards of conduct acutely appears in Dharmaśāstra texts. Scholars have sometimes characterized the conflict as being between a transcendent *dharma*, on the one hand, and 'customary' rules, such as *ācāra*, *deśācāra*, *kulācāra*, etc.(not to mention the synonymous, and on this view rather paradoxical terms *deśadharma*, *kuladharma*, etc.) on the other hand (e.g. Lingat, 1973: 176ff.). I think this characterization creates a dichotomy where there should be a continuity. Pitting *dharma* and *ācāra* against each other fails to account for the connections between the two described in *dharma* texts. A look at *anācāra* in a late medieval Dharmaśāstra text known as the *Laghudharmaprakāśikā* (LDhP, Tamburān 1906) helps us see the connections of *dharma* and *ācāra*. The date of the LDhP, also called *Śāṅkarasmṛti*, is unknown but is probably no earlier than the 16th century AD. Its provenance, however, is certain – Kerala. In fact, the text calls itself the rules for the people of Kerala (*kēraḷavāsi*).[15] The LDhP is one of at least three texts which records the 64 *anācāras* of Kerala and Kerala Brahmins (see Parpola, 2001).

Whereas *anācāra* would usually refer to standards of behavior that deviate from the norm, in the LDhP, it refers to a set of standards for religious, political, moral, and legal behavior which were intended to be normative only for Kerala people, especially Kerala Brahmins, to whom most of the rules apply. In other words, despite its negative prefix, *anācāra* is a positive label for prescribed norms, not prohibited ones. The *an-* here is restrictive, not prohibitive, at least from the point of view of those who accept these rules. I have not seen *anācāra* used in this way anywhere else, although Derrett (1977: 55) has made a cryptic reference to what he calls the 'marginal *anācāra* literature' and to a text called *Anācāranirṇaya*, which I have not been able to locate.

More relevant, however, is Wezler's discussion (1985) of *durācāra* in the *Gīrvāṇapadamañjarī* and *Gīrvāṇavāṅmañjarī* from Bengal.[16] Both of these texts use *durācāra* to refer to accepted norms that were restricted to a particular region. So, we are told that Brahmins in Andhra ride horses, Brahmins in Karnataka eat without bathing first, and that women in the Dravida and Kerala regions do not cover their breasts. The list includes several standard regional norms that were mentioned as early as *Baudhāyanadharmasūtra* 1.2.1-6 (Olivelle, 1999: 133) as well as others. The point here is that this label *durācāra* for certain regionally sanctioned practices comes from outside of the region where they are authoritative, i.e. *not* from the perspective of those who accept the restricted standards. From an internal or insider's point of view, what is *durācāra* to an outsider means positive prescriptions dictating authoritatively sanctioned behavior in many areas of life.

The interesting fact about *anācāra* and the Kerala case, as opposed now to *durācāra*, is that the insiders *themselves* are calling their standards *anācāra*, specifically recognizing that they deviated from standards elsewhere. Such a recognition of separateness reveals a consciousness of Kerala as a separate cultural entity which deviates in certain ways from pan-Indian norms, here implicitly deemed *ācāra*, not *dharma*. Moreover, nowhere in these discussions of *durācāra* and *anācāra* are these terms said to be *adharma*, a fact which would seem to support the interpretation of the terms as sources of *dharma* in a restricted context.

A few brief examples will clarify exactly what kinds of standards we are talking about. In general, the list of 64 *anācāra*s in the LDP includes rules for bathing, eating, clothing, study, occupation, *antyeṣṭi* funerary rites, ritual, inheritance, and marriage. The first rule states, for example, "*varjayet dantakaṣṭhāni* [Do not clean your teeth with sticks]." This contradicts the standard rule in *Yājñvalkyasmṛti* and elsewhere to use a twig for cleaning one's teeth. Another rule prohibits bathing before sunrise, which conflicts again with rules found in *Yājñavalkya-*, *Manu-*, and *Viṣṇu-smṛti*, among others. We also find a rule restricting marriage and, by implication, inheritance to the eldest son "*jyeṣṭhabhrātā gṛhī bhavet* [(only) the eldest son shall become a householder]" – a practice prevalent among Namputiri Brahmins. There are also rules for non-Brahmins as well. Kṣatriyas, for instance, are enjoined to follow matrilineal inheritance, called *marumakkattāyam* in Kerala. Saṃnyāsins, we are told, should not look at women. These short examples demonstrate the brevity of the rules as well as their diversity.

The list of these rules is introduced as follows (LDhP 12.4.1-2):

athāto 'nupravakṣyāmi nṛṇām kēraḷavāsinām
anācārān samāsena bhārggaveṇa pradarśitān

anyatrācāraṇābhāvād anācārān bhṛgūdvahaḥ
yān ācaṣṭa catuḥśaṣṭim ākhyāsye tatra tān api

[Now, therefore, I shall declare *anācāra*s for the people who dwell in Kerala as they have been fully put forth by Bhārgava. Among those (previously stated rules), I shall explain these 64 *anācāra*s as well which the offspring of Bhṛgu has made known because they are not followed elsewhere.]

The verses make clear that the rules applied only to the "people who dwell in Kerala." Twice the rules are called *anācāra* because, as the text says, "they are not followed elsewhere" and are, therefore, restricted only to people in Kerala. The question then is how do we make sense of these rules in the context of *dharma?*

Based on these opening lines, we might be led to think that everything people did in Kerala was *anācāra*, while what people in other regions did was *ācāra*. In fact, I think this is not the case. *Anācāra* only refers to this specific list of special rules for people in Kerala, while *ācāra* remains a general term in the LDhP and in Kerala generally for other standards of conduct approved and accepted by the Kerala community and, presumably, shared by other regions as well. Although *dharma* is not mentioned specifically, I think it must be understood that both the *anācāra*s and *ācāra*s were *dharma*s for the people of Kerala, especially considering the frequent reference to *dharma* in earlier portions of the LDhP. The nature of and relationship between the three terms becomes clearer, however, because of this unusual use of *anācāra* in a positive sense.

Note how the LDhP says that these *anācāra*s were '*proclaimed* by Bhārgava.' From this, we learn that *anācāra*s and, by inference, *ācāra*s as well were proclaimed or pronounced by people with power and authority. They were not just random patterns of behavior, but rather authorized standards of conduct. The link between *anācāra*,

ācāra, and *dharma* was the *śiṣṭas*, the *ṛṣis*, the elites who proclaimed them. The rules for morality, ritual, politics, law, etc. lived in the persons who held the power to dictate those rules, and these persons struggled not only with traditional Dharmaśāstra texts but also with regional standards, in this case called *anācāras*, to determine what appropriate conduct should be in given circumstances. The tautology of *ācāra* and *dharma* neatly operates in the LDhP such that even *ācāras* that explicitly deviate from standards elsewhere are given the force of *dharma* because they have been proclaimed by a sage.

The LDhP is a clear case, admittedly unusual, in which it is explicitly recognized that a specific set of regional standards are more important than pan-Indian standards, and yet both were *dharmas*, albeit with different provenances. In the LDhP, these regional standards constituted *dharma*, not vice-versa. Given the understanding described above of Dharmaśāstra as grounded in such standards, the case of the LDhP may be unusual only in that it explicitly states that it is based on the standards of a particular region.

There is no conflict between *dharma* and *ācāra*, because each is said to constitute the other in the circular manner I have described. *Ancāra* refers to a specific part of one 'little tradition,' yet even the grammatical construction of the term implies the existence of a larger tradition of *ācāra* which in turn provided the building blocks for *dharma* and the texts which describe *dharma*. Historically, the provenance of various *ācāras* was likely restricted to particular places, but, theologically, *ācāra*'s scope was held to be more or less universal if properly constituted as the sanctioned practices of the 'good.' In the end, in order to understand *dharma*, we must deconstruct it by understanding its constituent parts, namely the regional standards of India. In so doing, we see how the tautological relationship of *dharma* and *ācāra* produced a thriving religious and legal culture that balanced the elements of tradition and change necessary to any successful system of religion and law.

COMMON GLOSSES FOR ĀCĀRA IN MEDIEVAL DHARMAŚĀSTRA

The variety of medieval commentarial glosses on *ācāra*[17] provides us with another means of assessing *ācāra*'s relationship to *dharma*. The range of meanings and synonyms given for *ācāra* in these commentaries again shows that the authority for this source of *dharma* rests in the fact that it was held to be a normative model and a practical performance of *dharma* itself. In general, the glosses suggest that *ācāra* was thought to be something passed down over time, but also something that had to be accepted conventionally in the current moment. It was both the recognition of a past tradition and the creation of a future tradition that emanated from the good character and learning of those who preserved and proclaimed *ācāra*.

Several glosses equate *ācāra* with 'convention,' including *samaya* (convention), *āgama* (tradition), *vyavahāra* (daily business), and *lokasaṃgraha* (accepted by the people). The *Ujjvalā* of Haradatta explains the difficult term *sāmayācārikān* in *Āpastambadharmasūtra* 1.1 as follows, "*samayamūlā ācārāḥ samayācārāḥ teṣu bhavāḥ sāmayācārikāḥ evaṃbhūtān dharmān iti* [standards that are based on conventions are called conventional standards; something which has the nature of those (standards) is called conventionally standardized, and (he is speaking of) *dharmas* of that nature]" (Joshi, 1988: 60). The explicit connection of *ācāra* with *samaya* would also link *ācāra* with the important title of law known as the 'non-observance of conventions' (*samayānapākarma*) in which the authority is given for various corporate groups to create their own rules and laws which should be enforced by the king or by the groups' own power. *Samaya* as a gloss clearly imparts a normative significance to *ācāra*.

The other glosses of *ācāra* as 'convention' yield slightly different nuances to the semantic scope of the term. *Āgama* typically means what is passed down through a lineage of teachers (*paraṃparā*) and is found first as a synonym for *ācāra* in *Baudhāyanadharmasūtra* 1.1.4 ("*tṛtīyaḥ śiṣṭāgamaḥ* [the third (source of *dharma*) is the traditions of cultured people]") in which the expected *ācāra* is replace by *āgama*. The principal medieval commentary on this *sūtra* unambiguously equates the two with an etymology of the compound term *śiṣṭāgama*: "*śiṣṭaiḥ āgamyate iti śiṣṭāgamaḥ | śiṣṭācarita ity arthaḥ* [what is handed down by cultured people is the traditions of cultured people; the meaning is what is observed in practice by cultured people]" (*Baudhāyanavivaraṇam*, quoted in Joshi, 1988: 52). But *ācāra* is not merely that which is handed down in a traditional manner or through a specific teaching lineage, but also what is common and accepted in the present moment. For instance, *vyavahāra* 'daily business' as a gloss is not meant to suggest random activities one might engage in throughout the day, but rather routinized ways of interacting in common situations, especially in commerce, that often develop through contracts and repeated negotiations.[18] It connotes standardized ways of interaction that have developed through frequent encounters. The gloss *lokasaṃgraha* 'accepted by the people' most pointedly demonstrates that some Dharmaśāstra authors (e.g. Vṛddhagautama, cited in Joshi, 1988: 50) viewed *ācāra* as something deriving directly from a collective consent of the populace. In this context, one is also reminded of the antonyms *lokavidviṣṭa* and *lokavikruṣṭa* 'despised by the people' which describe instances in which *dharma* is set aside because it contravenes the conventions of the people. The precise limits and nature of such collective consent or dissent are not well explicated, but the general impulse is clearly to mark as *dharma* those standards of conduct that were current among at least some significant portion of the populace.

The other class of glosses for *ācāra* frame *ācāra* as an embodiment of or performance of *dharma*, including *śīla* and *anuṣṭhāna*. These glosses view *ācāra* as something that one follows based on both innate and learned dispositions of personal character. *Śīla*, for example, connotes the composite habits, propensities, and perspectives that one has developed genetically and, possibly, through education, and, therefore, may be understood as 'character' in general sense. In glossing *Gautamadharmasūtra* (GDh) 1.2 (*tadvidāṃ ca smṛtiśilē* [as well as the traditions and character of those who know them, i.e. the Vedas]), the commentator Maskarin states, "*ācārātmatuṣṭī api śila evāntarbhūte iti na pṛthag upanyaste* [standards of conduct and what is pleasing to oneself are both part of character and, thus, are not separately mentioned]" (Joshi, 1988: 43). In this conception, *śila* as a gloss for *ācāra* suggests that the latter is a kind of internal embodiment of the Vedic corpus (*śruti*) and its traditions (*smṛti*). In addition, *ācāra* as character is most likely the underlying form for the derivative term *ācārya*, or teacher, "one who possesses good character."[19]

By far the most common gloss for *ācāra* in all of medieval Dharmaśāstra is *anuṣṭhāna*, and I will end this discussion of the glosses for *ācāra* by investigating the meaning of this term, especially in relation to *dharma*. The closest English equivalent for *anuṣṭhāna* is probably 'performance,' because it connotes both an activity and a model on which that activity is based. Etymologically, *anuṣṭhāna* is a nominal form derived from the verb root *sthā* "to stand, to be fixed on, etc. 'with the verbal prefix *anu*' along, after, with, etc." The presence of the prefix *anu* suggests more than mere practice, but rather a performance or practice 'in accordance' with some rule or standard. The implicit standard here must be *śruti* and *smṛti* to which all *ācāra* is related and with which all *ācāra* is said to conform (see, e.g. GDh 11.20-1). *Anuṣṭhāna* is generally more particular in meaning than *ācāra* in that it refers to the proper performance of a previously enjoined action and not to rule-bound actions in general that carry normative weight. It is, therefore, the particular performance of *dharma* in a practical context. *Ācāra*, by contrast, refers to the whole collection of such standardized practices that conform to the *śruti* and *smṛti* and that supplement the injunctions of these sources of *dharma*. *Anuṣṭhāna* as a gloss imparts to *ācāra* a sense that it is something one must learn because it is based upon prior paradigms of conduct that have normative significance.

These two groups of synonymous/explanatory terms show the conceptualization of *ācāra* as practiced *dharma*. The issue of *dharma*'s authority seems inextricably related to the question of *dharma*'s practicability. If *dharma* is not put into practice or cannot be, then the question of its authority is moot. On the other hand, if *ācāra* represents the putting of *dharma* into practice, as I have argued, then *dharma*'s authority rests in great measure on the dissemination and understanding of *ācāra*. Ultimately, all *ācāra* is *dharma* and, in fact, constitutes the practical embodiment and performance of *dharma*.

CONCLUSIONS

In his introduction to the critical edition of the *Mānavadharmaśāstra* (forthcoming), Patrick Olivelle argues that Dharmaśāstra texts, like all *śāstra*s, "represent a meta-discourse; they deal with reality but always once removed ... *Śāstra*s exercised control over practice not directly but through the mediation of experts." Olivelle's characterization is most appropriate and persuasive, but it also begs the question of what the primary discourse of *dharma* was in medieval India. If Dharmaśāstra is a 'meta-discourse' that derives its content from *ācāra*, then it would follow that *ācāra* must be the primary discourse, i.e. *dharma* in practice. Dharmaśāstra texts contemplate and systematize *ācāra* without replacing the ongoing value of extra-śāstric *ācāra* to the evolving practical, day-to-day negotiations over the proper course of *dharma*.

The manner of textual expression used in Dharmaśāstra – a timeless, unchanging, injunctive idiom – often makes it difficult to trace developments of thought about *dharma* or other topics. The connection of *dharma* with *ācāra* was certainly not new to the medieval texts. However, *ācāra*'s significance as a source of *dharma* does appear to grow over time within the Dharmaśāstra corpus (Kane, 1946: 869–879; Altekar, 1952: 43). We find greater elaboration and detail about the nature of *ācāra*; we find *ācāra* being linked with related terms such as *caritra* and *maryādā* used in other historical sources to refer to local laws and standards (see Davis, 1999, 2002); and we also find a growing number of sources that suggest the true supremacy of *ācāra* over *smṛti* or even *dharma* itself, especially in judicial contexts.

For instance, in the medieval *Bālakrīḍā* commentary, Viśvarūpa states, "*yathaivāryāvartanivāsiśiṣṭavyavahārasthitis tathāiva smṛtyartho 'nusartavyo na tadviparyayeṇa* [The meaning of *smṛti* should be understood so as to conform with the established standards of those who dwell in Āryāvarta and not the other way around]" (Ganapati Sastri, 1921–1922). In this case, I would argue that the term *vyavahārasthiti* should be understood as a synonym for *ācāra*. Viśvarūpa modifies the absolute precedence accorded to *smṛti* by declaring *ācāra* to be an interpretive matrix within which *smṛti* must be understood and applied.

Even *dharma* gives way to *ācāra* in certain contexts as attested in the *Kātyāyanasmṛti*, cited in the medieval *Smṛticandrikā* and *Parāśaramādhavīya*: "*yad yad ācaryate yena dharmyaṃ vādharmyam eva vā | deśasyācaraṇān nityaṃ caritraṃ tad prakīrtitam* [Whatever is practiced (as a rule), whether it conforms to *dharma* or not, is called *caritra* because it has been perpetually observed (as an authoritative practice) in the locality]" (Joshi, 1937: 103).[20] Again, I would argue that *caritra* in this verse is synonymous with *ācāra*, though the former seems to be found generally in discussions of judicial procedure in Dharmaśāstra texts (Lingat, 1962). The text here, as Kane points out, "is principally concerned with the decision of legal disputes on the basis of the customs of countries and families, but his rules also have a general application" (1946: 862). In other words, the context is a legal dispute and not a general consideration of *dharma*, but this passage nevertheless inverts the basic hierarchy of the sources of *dharma* in the special context of judicial procedures (*vyavahāra*) – a move that pushes *dharma*, and implicitly *śruti* and *smṛti* as well, to a subordinate position in this important practical context. It is unlikely that the text intends to subvert the primacy of the Vedas and *śāstras* as the principal sources of *dharma*, but the inversion is intriguing as a possible circumscription of the power of these texts in favor of *ācāra*.[21] Overall, therefore, *ācāra*'s significance as a source of *dharma* and as a source of law and legal procedure in its own right expands in medieval texts.

On the basis of this expanded importance of *ācāra*, the main purpose of this essay has been to argue that *ācāra* and its relationship to *dharma* cannot be fully understood if relegated to the unhelpful category of 'custom.' The idea that *ācāra* lacks specific content and corresponds to the vague notions of 'custom' that float around legal theory circles must be reconsidered in the light of the precise manner of expression and the clearly defined content of *ācāra* as it is discussed in the texts. In this way, *ācāra* constitutes perhaps the most significant source of *dharma* in medieval Dharmaśāstra. At the same time, the authority of *ācāra* itself derives in a tautological manner from the authority accorded to knowledgeable (*śiṣṭa*) and good (*sat*) people whose character is made impeccable and trustworthy by virtue of their Vedic study and education in the *śāstra*s. The productive tautology described here lent both stability and adaptability to the religio-legal thought and institutions of medieval India. It would thus be perilous to understand *dharma* and its authority without at the same time seeing its intimate connection to *ācāra*.

NOTES

[1] A convenient summary of such acceptance by scholars such as Kane, Sen Gupta, Lingat, Derrett, Lariviere can be found in Wezler, 1999: 74 (also included in the present volume).

[2] For a similar assertion, less well articulated, see Mandlik 1880 [1982]: "The next source of Dharmaśāstra which I have now to consider is that of usage or custom. In regard to this branch of law, I am inclined to hold that this has always been the main source of the Āryan law from the earliest times; and that our Smṛtis and Purāṇas, so far as they relate to Dharmaśāstra, have been merely the records of customs that existed in those days" (xliii).

[3] The ambiguities in Wezler's original German version parallel, but not do not precisely coincide, with those in the English version (included in the present volume). The distinctions between *Sitte*, *Brauch*, *Wandel*, *Verhalten*, and '*Praxis*', all used by Wezler, do not ameliorate the contradictions entailed in describing custom as both norm and behavior. In my view, *ācāra* is closest to *Brauch* and '*Praxis*' as used by Wezler because both of these terms carry normative weight.

[4] Blackstone (1765–1769[1979]), following Hale (1713[2002]), elaborates his definition of 'customs' as unwritten laws that have been gradually codified in written form (I, 63–64) in a way that suggests that their authority and 'binding power' is not exclusively derived from ill-defined 'long usage' and 'universal reception.' He writes:

But here a very natural, and very material, question arises: how are these customs or maxims too be known, and by whom is their validity to be determined ? The answer is, by the judges in the several courts of justice. They are the depositary of the laws; the living oracles, who must decide in all cases of doubt, and who are bound by an oath to decide according to the law of the land. (I, 69)

One should also mention for this period the influential notion of custom in David Hume's work, notably *An Enquiry Concerning Human Understanding*, in which he claims that custom, in the sense of repeated experience, is at the root of all knowledge and is the very basis of epistemology as a whole (1748 [1999]: 121–122), a radically different idea of custom as part of individual, not collective experience.

[5] The most comprehensive review is found in the collected articles in Renteln and Dundes, 1994. See also Dickenson, 1929; Simpson, 1973; Pospisil, 1974; Geertz, 1983; Watson, 1984; Moore, 1986; Correas, 1994; Glenn, 1997.

[6] Here I am specifically disagreeing with Wezler (present volume, f.n. 40) where he declares, "Hacker states that rendering *dharma* as 'norm,' 'law,' or 'obligation' was 'far too abstract.' The same is true for *ācāra*."

[7] See also Kumārila's *Tantravārttika* (Jha, 1983: 184), and Haradatta's commentary on *Āpastambadharmasūtra* 1.1.1: "*na hi brūmaḥ samayamātraṃ pramāṇam iti | kiṃ tarhi | dharmajñā ye manvādayas teṣāṃ samayaḥ pramāṇaṃ dharmādharmayoḥ* [We are not saying that just any convention is a means of knowing (*dharma*). What is then? The conventions of those who know dharma such as Manu and others are the means of knowing *dharma* and *adharma*]" (Joshi, 1988: 60).

[8] Wezler states, "we can differentiate *ācāra* before its realization – the authoritative, ideal model of behavior –, and *ācāra* in its actual and practical realization. Good conduct is thus realization of custom – in Gonda's sense – and this conduct, the recollected tradition, is itself again a model and example for others" (1999: 84–85). This would seem to contradict his own footnote to this passage (cited above in f.n. 6) which empties *ācāra* of any normative content on the grounds of over-abstraction. With my reservations about the term 'custom' aside, my argument broadly agrees with his main text, but not with his footnote.

[9] Classic examples of such spatial and temporal variability of *dharma/ācāra* include Mādhava's defense of cross-cousin marriage in South India, the *Baudhāyanasūtra*'s list of five authorized regional practices (1.2.1-6), the *kalivarjya*s, and *āpaddharma*. From the perspective of Mīmāṃsā, i.e. from a theological point of view, all true *ācāra* has universal applicability and authority and cannot legitimately have authority in one geographic area and not another (Jha, 1916: 84). Medieval Dharmaśāstra seems more ambiguous about the potential variability of *ācāra*, although it, too, emphasizes the consonance of Vedic injunctions and *ācāra* rules.

[10] On the intimate connection between Dharmaśāstra and Mīmāṃsā, see Kane, 1962: 5, 1152ff. and Sarkar, 1909.

[11] The same passage also records the following opinion, "*tāsāṃ smṛtīnāṃ nyāyamūlakatve 'pi nyāyasya vedamūlakatvāt tatsmṛtīnām api vedatulyatvam iti kecit* [Even though the these *smṛtis* are rooted in reason, because reason is rooted in the Vedas, even the *smṛtis* (of the Vedas) are said to be equal to the Vedas]."

[12] See Jha, 1916: 79ff. for the full explanation of the famous Holākādhikaraṇa on the general authority of local 'customs' (*ācāra*). See also *Tantravārttika* (Jha, 1983: 244ff.).

[13] Medhātithi on Manu 2.10 (Jha, 1920–1939: Vol. 1: 70): "*śiṣṭasamācārād api dharmasya kartavyatāvagatiḥ | so 'pi smṛtir eva | tataś ca yatra kasmai cit kāryāya smṛter upādānaṃ tatra sadācāro 'pi grahītavyaḥ* [The understanding of the necessary duties of *dharma* arises from the collective standards of cultured people. Thus, these, too, are called *smṛti* (codified tradition). As a result, in whatever context and in whichever matter *smṛti* is mentioned, there the *ācāra* of good people also should be understood]" (my translation).

[14] See *Tantravārttika* (Jha, 1983: 111ff.).
[15] The traditional boundaries of Kerala are not significantly different from the borders of the modern state by the same name. The *Kēraḷotpatti*, for example, defines the Malayāla or Kērala land as the area from Gokarṇam(near modern Mangalore) to Kanyākumārī at the southern tip of India, bounded by the Western Ghats throughout.
[16] Although these two texts are not Dharmaśāstra texts, their use of the term *durācāra* resembles that in LDhP and, therefore, provides an instructive point of comparison. See also Deshpande, 1993 for further remarks on the linguistic features of the Sanskrit in the *Gīrvāṇapadamañjarī and Gīrvāṇavāṅmañjarī*.
[17] The discussion below is based on a review of the collected commentaries contained in the well-known encyclopedia of Dharmaśāstra texts, the *Dharmakośa* in the *Vārṇāśramadharmakāṇḍa* (Joshi, 1988), specifically the section on *dharmapramāṇavicāra*. This excellent compendium provides a convenient synoptic overview of the Dharmaśāstra debates and arguments concerning the sources of *dharma*, including *ācāra*. A thorough review in English of the relationship of "custom and Dharmaśāstra works" can be found in Kane, 1946: 3, 856–884.
[18] See Medhātithi's *Manubhāṣya* on *Mānavadharmaśāstra* 2.6 quoted in Joshi, 1988: 98.
[19] The opposite derivation is also possible, but in either case, the connection of the two terms seems indisputable.
[20] For a similar verse, see Pitāmaha cited in Joshi, 1937: 105. See also the discussion in Lingat, 1973: 176ff.
[21] In this regard, one should also mention *rājaśāsana*, the edict of the king, also listed in the context of judicial procedures as higher than even *ācāra*. See *Nāradasmṛti* 1.10 "The four feet of legal procedure are *dharma*, legal procedure, custom, and the king's decree; each latter one overrules the former" (Lariviere, 1989). These four 'feet' (*pāda*) should be understood as modes of judicial proof and decision-making.

REFERENCES

Altekar, A.S. (1952). *Sources of Hindu Dharma in its Socio-Religious Aspects*. Sain Das Foundation Lectures. Sholapur, Institute of Public Administration.

Bhattacharya, N. (1996). Remaking Custom: The Discourse & Practice of Colonial Codification. In R. Champakalakshmi and S. Gopal (eds), *Tradition, Dissent, and Ideology: Essays in Honor of Romila Thapar*. Delhi: OUP.

Blackstone, W. (1765–1769 [1979]). *Commentaries on the Laws of England: A Facsimile of the First Edition of 1765–1769*. 4 Vols. Chicago: University of California Press.

Chakravarty-Kaul, M. (1996). *Common Lands and Customary Law: Institutional Change in North India over the Past Two Centuries*. Delhi: OUP.

Correas, O. (1994). La teoría general del derecho frente al derecho indígena. *Crítica Juridica* **14**, 15–31.

Davis, Jr. D.R. (1999). Recovering the indigenous legal traditions of India: classical Hindu law in practice in late medieval Kerala. *Journal of Indian Philosophy* **27**(3), 159–213.

Davis, Jr. D.R. (2002). *Dharma, Maryāda*, and law in early British Malabar: remarks on words for 'law' in the Tellicherry records. *Studien zur Indologie und Iranistik* **23**, 51–70.

Derrett, J.D.M. (1977). The development of the concept of property in India c. A.D. 800–1800. *Essays in Classical and Modern Hindu Law*. Vol. 2. Leiden: Brill. [orig. pub. 1962].

Deshpande, M.M. (1993). *Sanskrit and Prakrit: Sociolinguistic Issues*. Delhi: Motilal Banarsidass.

Dickinson, J. (1929). The law behind the law. 29 *Columbia Law Review* 113–146, 285–319.

Ganapati Sastri, T. (ed.) (1921–1922 [1982]). The *Yājñavalkyasmṛti with the commentary Bālakrīḍā of Viśvarūpāchārya*. Delhi: Munishiram Manoharlal.

Geertz, C. (1983). Local knowledge: fact and law in comparative perspective. rpt. in *Local Knowledge*. New York: Basic Books.

Glenn, H.P. (1997). The capture, reconstruction, and marginalization of 'custom.' *American Journal of Comparative Law* **45**, 613.

Halbfass, W. (1988). *India and Europe: An Essay in Philosophical Understanding*. Albany: SUNY Press.

Hale, M. (1713 [2002]). In Charles M. Gray (ed.), *The History of the Common Law in England*. Chicago: University of Clifornia Press.

Hume, D. (1748 [1999]). In L. Tom (ed.), *An Enquiry Concerning Human Understanding*. Beauchamp. Oxford: Oxford UP.

Jain, M.P. (1963). Custom as a source of law in India. *Jaipur Law Journal* **3**, 96–130. [rpt. in Renteln and Dundes 1994].

Jha, G. (1916). *The Pūrva Mimāṃsā Sūtras of Jaimini: Chapters I–III*. trans. with an original commentary. Allahabad: The Pāṇini Office, Bhuvaneśwarī Āśrama.

Jha, G. (trans.) (1983). *Tantravārttika of Kumārila Bhaṭṭa: a commentary on Śabara's bhāṣya on the Pūrvamīmāṃsāsūtras of Jamini*. Delhi: Sri Satguru, 1983 [orig. pub. 1924].

Jha, G. (ed. and trans.) (1920–1939 [1999]). *Manusmṛti with the 'Manubhāṣya' of Medhātithi*. 10 Vols. Delhi: Motilal Banarsidass.

Joshi, L.S. (ed.) (1937). *Dharmakośa*. Vol 1. Pt. 1. Vyavahārakāṇḍa. Wai: Prājña-Pāṭha-Śālā-Maṇḍala.

Joshi, L.S. (ed.) (1988). *Dharmakośa*. Vol. 5. Pt. 1. Varṇāsramadharmakāṇḍa. Wai: Prājña-Pāṭha-Śālā-Maṇḍala.

Kane, P.V. (1930–1962). *History of Dharmaśastra*. 5 Vols. Poona: BORI. [Vol. 3 pub. 1946; Vol. 5 pub. 1962].

Lariviere, R.W. (1997). Dharmaśāstra, Custom, 'Real Law,' and 'Apocryphal' Smṛtis, *Recht, Staat, und Verwaltung im klassischen Indien*. ed. Bernhard Kölver. Munich: R. Oldenbourg [also in the present volume].

Lariviere, R.W. (1989). *Nāradasmṛti: A Critical Edition. 2* Vols. Philadelphia: South Asian Regional Studies, University of Pennsylvania.

Lingat, R. (1973). *The Classical Law of India*. trans. J.D.M. Derrett. Berkeley: University of California Press.

Lingat, R. (1962). Les Quatre Pieds due Procés. *Journal Asiatique* **250**, 489–503.

Mandlik, Vishwanath Narayan 1880 [1982]. *Vyavahara Mayukha or Hindu Law*. New Delhi: Asian Publication Services.

Moore, S.F. (1978). *Law as Process*. London: Routledge.

Moore, S.F. (1986). *Social Facts and Fabrications: 'Customary' law on Kilimanjaro, 1880–1980*. Cambridge: Cambridge UP.

Olivelle, P. (trans.) (1999). *Dharmasūtras: The Law Codes of Ancient India*. Oxford: Oxford UP.

Olivelle, P. (forthcoming). *Mānavadharmaśāstra*. crit. ed. and trans. New York: Oxford UP.

Parpola, M. (2001). *Kerala Brahmins in Transition. A Study of a Namputiri Family*. Studia Orientalia 91. Helsinki: Finnish Oriental Society.
Pospisil, L. (1974). *The Anthropology of Law: A Comparative Theory*. New Haven: HRAF Press.
Renteln, A.D. and Dundes, A. (eds) (1994). *Folk Law: Essays in the Theory and Practice of* Lex Non Scripta. 2 Vols. Madison: University of Wisconsin Press.
Sarkar, K.L. (1909). *The Mimansa Rule of Interpretation as applied to Hindu Law*. Calcutta: Thacker, Spink.
Shama Shastry, R. (ed.) (1927). *Sarasvatīvilāsa*. Vyavahārakāṇḍa. Mysore: Gov't Branch Press.
Simpson, A.W.B. (1973). The common law and legal theory. In Simpson, A.W.B. (ed.) *Oxford Essays in Jurisprudence*. 2nd Series. Oxford: OUP.
Tamburān, K.K. (ed.) (1906). *Śāṅkarasmṛti (Laghudharmaprakāśikā)*. Tṛśśivapērūr: Bhāratavilāsaṃ.
Vollenhoven, C.V. (1927). Aspects of the controversy on customary law in India. *The Asiatic Review* **23**, 113–128 [rpt. in Renteln and Dundes 1994].
Watson, A. (1984). An approach to customary law. *University of Illinois Law Review* 561–576.
Wezler, A. (1985). Dharma und Deśadharma. In H. Kulke, et al. (eds), *Regionale Tradition in Südasien*. Beiträge zur Südasienforschung. Bd. 104. Wiesbaden: Franz Steiner Verlag, 1–22.
Wezler, A. (1999). Über den sakramentalen Charakter des *Dharma*. In G. Oberhammer & M. Schmücker (eds.), *Raum-zeitliche Vermittlung der Transzendenz: Zur 'sakramentalen' Dimension religöser Tradition*. Wien: Der Österreichischen Akademie der Wissenschaften [also translated into English in the present volume].

Department of Languages & Cultures of Asia
University of Wisconsin
1244 Van Hise, 1220 Linden Dr
Madison, WI 53706
USA
E-mail: drdavis@wisc.edu

DOMINIK WUJASTYK

MEDICINE AND DHARMA

CONFLICTING MAGISTERIA

Dharmaśāstra, the science of law and righteousness, provides frameworks within which society can be regulated and individuals can live their lives virtuously. To some extent, this goal overlaps with the objectives of traditional medicine, ayurveda, which also lays down rules and recommendations for living a long, healthy and good life. As the *Carakasaṃhitā* says,

> Ayurveda is defined as the science wherein are explained the good and bad life, happy and painful, what is good or bad for it, its regulation and itself.[1]

Whenever two magisteria (I borrow the term from Gould) overlap like this, one can expect conflict to arise sooner or later.[2] Examining such infringements and boundary conditions can clarify the essential qualities and values of each side. I shall present some cases of conflict between dharma and medicine in order to begin an exploration of the essential features of these two spheres of regulation and their relationship.

K. V. Mūssatŭ

K. V. Mūssatŭ ("KVM") was born in 1888 near Guruvāyūr in Kerala, the son of an ayurvedic physician. He received a traditional *gurukula* education in Sanskrit under the famous scholar Punnaśśeri Nampi and later played a prominent role in the literary movements of his time, including the promotion of modern Sanskrit compositions and the translation of Sanskrit works into Malayalam. In his autobiography, published in 1966, he described his traditional education in detail. Once, during *Raghuvaṃśa* lessons, KVM had to sleep in a rice storehouse, which echoed frighteningly to the sound of birds in the early part of the night:

So I spent a couple of nights without much sleep, and after three days a slight fever started. The fever did not let up on the fourth day, and the teacher sent someone to take me home.
What happened when I arrived at home is matter for another story. My grandmother and aunt ruled, according to ritual principles, that having been in the public ferry boat I was ritually polluted, and hence I could not enter the house without a complete bath (hair included). My father (who was after all a doctor) ruled, according to medical principles, that in that case I had better stay in the rice storehouse, because a person who has fever cannot be made to bathe. So there was something of a tug of war between them. Finally the medical judgement won. It took seven or eight days for the fever to pass, and during that period any household member who touched me would have to take a bath.[3]

Several interesting points are raised by this short story. It is noteworthy that it is the women – KVM's grandmother and aunt – who exercise the ritual authority, the application of dharma, in the family. Marjatta Parpola, for example, has cited personal narratives and interviews showing how a general picture of female social subjugation in Kerala is qualified in certain circumstances where the women of a household wield considerable power, for example over matters of food, and sometimes also the management of the economy of the household, and supervising the work connected with harvesting and handling of paddy.[4] The present example is a case in point. It may also have been particularly the women of the household who would have borne the practical burden of frequent and bothersome ritual washing, since it would have been they who had to touch KVM in the course of feeding and nursing him.

Then, in the 'tug-of-war' between dharma and medicine, it is medicine that wins. This may be influenced by the fact that the medical magisterium is applied by a senior male. On the other hand, there is an unexpressed logic to the choice: uncontrolled illness may lead to death, in which case ritual purity will be impossible. But if the illness is controlled, then the ritual purity may be re-established later through penances etc. Health is logically prior to ritual, and this is a point made explicitly within the medical tradition itself. As the *Carakasaṃhitā* has it, for example,

Health is the ultimate root of righteousness, wealth, happiness and liberation. Diseases carry it away as well as happiness and life.[5]

The erudite eleventh-century commentator Cakrapāṇi emphasises this dependency of dharma and the other life-goals on health:

Therefore health is the primary cause as far as the four goals of life are concerned. It is said that it is impossible for someone who has been caught by a disease to do anything at all about the aims of man... The removal of health by diseases is one and the same thing as not achieving one's goals.[6]

In this and several other passages, the *Carakasaṃhitā* and its commentators stress the fact that the purpose of medicine is to aid the achievement of the canonical goals of life. Both the *Carakasaṃhitā* and Cakrapāṇi refer in this passage to the *four* goals of life, i.e., they include *mokṣa* or liberation. This is a prominent passage in the medical literature, but it is also untypical, in fact unique. Elsewhere, the early medical authors always refer to the *trivarga* or three goals as the norm.[7]

Meat and Medicine

From the earliest period, Ayurveda used meat in its recipes and medicines as a matter of course. For example, when the ancient author Caraka recommends the appropriate regimen for autumn, he cites a whole list of bird and animal meats which may be eaten:

> The meats of the common quail, the grey partridge, the antelope, sheep, serow,[8] deer, hare, rice, together with barley and wheat may be taken during this season [of autumn].[9]

This is just one of many such passages. In fact, there seems to be almost no limit to the animal products which can be used in medical and related conditions. When describing treatments for impotence, for example, Caraka recommends eating the meat of several cocks fried in the semen of a crocodile.[10] Elsewhere, in a list of miscellaneous therapies recommended for a patient suffering from insanity, bloodletting is included, before which, "the patient may be fed to fullness with fat meat."[11] And in yet another, more dramatic recommendation, the ancient author Suśruta recommends that if a patient does not stop bleeding after phlebotomy,

> ... one may make the patient drink the blood of Indian antelope, blackbuck, sheep, hare and boar.[12]

Even the most habitual meat-eater might flinch at being offered such a cocktail. Nevertheless, this therapy is recommended by one of the most authoritative texts of Ayurveda without explanation or apology, as if it were the most normal thing in the world. This is the standard position for medical authors up to the late first millennium CE.

Since the time of the earliest *dharmaśāstra*s, we have evidence that meat has been legally allowed for brahmans and others as long as it was prepared and eaten according to the vedic rules referred to, for example, in chapter 5 of Manu's laws.[13] Manu's rules about meat are rather tangled. The text begins by stating that meat may, indeed must, be eaten when consecrated by vedic rites. But it is a terrible sin to eat it in any non-religious context. But later verses mix contradictory views. At one place, meat-eating – apparently even in ritual contexts – produces the worst possible karma:

Wise people say that meat is 'meat' (*māṃsaḥ*) because 'he' (*saḥ*) whom I eat in this world will eat 'me' (*māṃ*) in the next world.[14]

In the very next verse, eating meat is said to be little more than the way of the world:

There is nothing wrong with eating meat, nor in wine, nor sex. This how creatures live an active life. But abstention brings great fruit.[15]

This may be confusing, until one looks past the translation, and sees that the last verse uses the words *pravṛtti* and *nivṛtti*: "This is the *pravṛtti* of creatures, but *nivṛtti* brings great fruit." Manu's attitude to eating meat is schizophrenic because it is a key example of an underlying tension that exists throughout *dharmaśāstra* between the pursuit of dharma, virtuous living, and the pursuit of *mokṣa*, liberation from (social) life altogether. *Pravṛtti* 'outward activity' is the ideology of worldly virtue and religion, leading to happiness in heaven after death. *Nivṛtti* 'turning back' is the ideology of ceasing to act intentionally in the world, thereby minimizing karma, and ultimately finding permanent blissful release from all future life, including the happy but finite heavenly life.[16]

As vegetarianism and the doctrine of *ahiṃsā* gained popularity in early India, the practice of using meat in medical recipes started to raise questions. In the early ninth century, the Jain author Ugrāditya, whose work survives in manuscripts in Mysore, wrote a special medical treatise in which the ayurvedic pharmacopoeia is stripped of all meat products in accordance with Jain doctrine.[17] Ugrāditya also delivered a long and carefully-reasoned lecture on vegetarianism to an assembly of learned scholars at the court of king Nṛpatuṅgavallabha (i.e., the Rāṣṭrakūṭa Amoghavarṣa I, fl. ca. 814–880).[18] If we can assume that Ugrāditya was not alone in his views, then we can say that by the ninth century Jain physicians were exerting their influence to persuade intellectuals and rulers that the use of meat in medicine was unnecessary and wrong.

But it was not until the third quarter of the eleventh century that a response to this change emerged within the orthodox brahman community of medical practitioners and scholars. The Bengali author Cakrapāṇi Datta, whom we met above, was a scholar of towering ability. He was a member of a family of senior cooks and physicians. Cakrapāṇi's father, Nārāyaṇa, was a minister (*mantrin*) of king Nayapāla of Bengal (1038–1055), and superindendent of the king's kitchens, an important role for physicians.[19] His brother, Bhānu, was also a court physician. Cakrapāṇi belonged to the Lodhravalī branch of the Datta lineage, one of the eight most distinguished Vaidya families of Bengal. Extraordinarily, Cakrapāṇi's family is not extinct, and descendants still exist among the inhabitants of Shillong in Meghālaya.[20]

Cakrapāṇi's surviving commentaries on the medical classics are magisterial in breadth and detailed knowledge. And embedded unexpectedly in one of these, he has left us a short disquisition on the morality of the use of meat in ayurveda.

Cakrapāṇi is commenting on a statement in the *Carakasaṃhitā* that is part of a longer description of the behaviour that qualifies as good conduct (*sadvṛtta*), and which should be followed by anyone wishing to remain healthy. Amongst other things, one should adhere to a number of virtues, including kindness or compassion:

> And finally, one should have a commitment to celibate studentship, knowledge, generosity, friendliness, compassion, joy, detachment, and calm.[21]

At first, one might think such a recommendation uncontroversial. But Cakrapāṇi grasps the opportunity to present a short but important argument about the therapeutic use of the flesh of animals in medicine. How can a physician remain dedicated to the ideals of universal compassion and yet recommend to the patient the consumption of meat? Cakrapāṇi says:

> Compassion means not behaving antagonistically towards creatures, treating them as one does oneself.
>
> But surely it must be contradictory to say that one should put compassion first? The author of this discipline himself rejects the meat of creatures that are soiled, pierced, or have died by themselves. He thereby teaches that the fresh meat of animals like deer in the prime of their life should be used. So obviously he is teaching cruelty, which is the opposite of compassion.
>
> This is not so. Out of passion, people eat the meat of living beings, which implies cruelty. This already being the case, the professor of medicine points out that for a certain ailment meat may be beneficial for one person but not for another. But he does not legislate for the eating of meat, or for cruelty.
>
> Similarly, just because he points out the benefit of wine in the regimen of healthy and ill persons, it does not make him a proponent of wine-drinking.
>
> And so, in the chapter on disease, on royal consumption etc., meat is taught. So also in passages like the regimen for the autumn season, which goes "quails, partridges..."[22] The point of this verse is to indicate that the meat of quails etc. is beneficial. It is not legislating for cruelty.
>
> Thus, both sick and healthy people do indeed reap the consequences of cruelty.

Similarly, scriptures say, "one performing magic should sacrifice an eagle".[23] It declares the rule which is purely a way of achieving the goal of the magic, for those who want magic, because it requires an eagle. In performing the magic with that eagle, unrighteousness does indeed arise.
But here is the difference: If a man cannot live without using meat which has been obtained through cruelty, then he is being cruel. Then, because the vedic statement that "one must always protect oneself" has been made a law, cruelty of that kind does not cause sin. But if there existed some alternative way of maintaining life, then that cruelty, being just for the sake of nourishment, would indeed be a cause of sin. Moreover, this is how it is with the cruelty demanded by ayurveda. And that cruelty is said to be for the purpose of the humours. *For the rules of ayurveda do not teach the achievement of righteousness. Rather, they teach the achievement of health.* Because of the statement,
The purpose of this science is stated to be action that balances the bodily elements.[24]

First, we see that Cakrapāṇi argues somewhat sophistically that the masters of ayurveda do not actually recommend meat: they merely say that meat can be good for you in certain circumstances. In a society where meat is already part of the diet of some people, cruelty is already established. Even some traditional commentators on dharma agree that someone who eats meat as part of the application āyurveda is, like someone who is maintaining their physical wellbeing, following acceptable legal procedures.[25] But Cakrapāṇi goes further, arguing the more detailed point that the responsibility for eating meat, and thereby participating in the implied cruelty of butchery, is the patient's, not the doctor's. This argument, we may recall, arises out of a discussion of *maitrī*, 'friendship' and *kāruṇya*, 'kindness', concepts particularly developed within Buddhism.[26] And Cakrapāṇi was writing, after all, as a member of a royal court known over many generations for its support of Buddhism. He may even have met the great Buddhist rector of Vikramaśīla monastery, Dīpāṅkara Śrījñāna, better known as Atīśa.[27]

Whatever his motivations, Cakrapāṇi Datta has finally arrived at very much the same conclusion as Stephen Jay Gould. Using Gould's terms, dharma and ayurveda are non-intersecting magisteria. The goal of medicine, according to Cakrapāṇi, is to achieve health, not to achieve righteousness. Science and religion have different goals.

THE PURPOSE OF MEDICINE

What, finally, is the purpose of medicine? Vāgbhaṭa answers this question at the start of his classic seventh-century work, *The Heart of Medicine*, as follows:

A long life is the means of achieving righteousness, wealth, and happiness. Someone who wants this should pay the closest attention to the teachings of medical science.[28]

This characterisation of the goal of medicine, coming as it does at the start of the first chapter of the most widely studied ayurvedic text, routinely memorised by medical students, entered profoundly into the consciousness of all traditional physicians. The verse was still being cited verbatim a thousand years after its composition,[29] and is known by heart by many ayurvedic physicians today. This, then, is the formal rationale given for the science of medicine: it enables one to live a long life, and a long life is necessary to achieve the three canonical goals of life, the *trivarga*, righteousness (*dharma*), wealth (*artha*), and happiness (*kāma*).[30]

This idea was first formulated in the ayurvedic tradition in the *Carakasaṃhitā*, as we saw above.[31] In another passage, after describing how the suppression of natural urges may lead to illness, the *Carakasaṃhitā* notes that a man whose word is good, because he has no sin of mind, speech or body, is happy and enjoys righteousness, wealth and happiness now and in the future.[32] This is the standard view of the medical authors throughout the tradition. "Ayurveda promotes dharma by counteracting the disease that afflicts one", says the *Āyurvedasaukhya.*[33]

But the *Carakasaṃhitā* is prepared to go even further, and promote the science of medicine over the Vedas themselves

Knowledge of that longevity [i.e., ayurveda] is of the greatest merit in the opinion of those who know the Vedas. It will be stated since it is good for humans in this world and the next.[34]

This is a strong claim indeed. Medical science is being promoted above the other Vedas on the grounds of utility: while religious knowledge may help in the world to come, medical knowledge helps in that world and also in this. It is twice as useful.

Cakrapāṇi expands the discussion for us:

So why is the best knowledge that defined by ayurveda, and why is it respected by those who know the Vedas? . . . Because the others, i.e., the Rig Veda etc., mainly teach only what is good for the next world. So they have merit. But this ayurveda is the most meritorious since it will explain what is good for human beings both in this world and the next, i.e., the longevity that leads to health and to dharma. So it is of absolutely the highest merit, and is therefore respected by those who know the Veda. . . . One must understand that ayurveda is of the highest merit because it delivers life. It is superior to all else because it delivers life, which is in actual fact the means for achieving the fourfold goals. And it is said, "There is no gift more special than the gift of life".[35]

Note that Cakrapāṇi has shifted his ground subtly. His claim that longevity "leads to health and to dharma" expands his previous statement in the discussion of cruelty, where he said that ayurveda led to health but not to dharma. Here, as elsewhere, the more common point is put: ayurveda leads to health and health leads to dharma.

Cakrapāṇi refers above to the gift of life. Elsewhere too, he is concerned to show that life is the highest value for living beings. Even in the face of terrible suffering, he says, people do not actually wish to end their lives, but only the suffering inherent in it:

For all living beings, life is naturally something cherished unconditionally... Someone afflicted by excessive suffering may want to give up their life. But in fact, their life is dear to them and they do not want to abandon it in itself, but because there is no other way to destroy the suffering which they so much want to get rid of.[36]

And the *Carakasaṃhitā* too makes the point that without life, all other goals cannot be achieved. In articulating a uniquely medical threesome of goals, the will for life (*prāṇaiṣaṇā*), for prosperity (*dhanaiṣaṇā*), and for the world beyond (*paralokaiṣaṇā*), Caraka places the will for life first:

Of these three, he should first and foremost develop the will for life. Why? Because when life is lost, everything is lost. A healthy person can safeguard it by following a healthy regimen; a sick person by paying proper attention to relieving disorders. Both these measures have already been discussed, and will be discussed further. And so a person who behaves in the manner prescribed will live to a ripe old age because he has safeguarded his life. This concludes the explanation of the first ambition.[37]

Cakrapāṇi points out that Caraka's whole discussion of these three goals of life – which differ from the *trivarga* – applies only to the person who is an engaged participant in the experience of life (*bhogārthipuruṣa*), not to someone seeking ultimate liberation (*mokṣārthipuruṣa*).[38]

The physicians of pre-modern India, then, recognised a healthy life as being of fundamental, even primary importance, since without it no other goal of life would be possible. In various ways and with different arguments, they subordinated the quest for dharma to the quest for health. This subordination was, at least sometimes, also carried through into actuality in social life.

NOTES

* Abbreviations used in this paper: Ah. = *Aṣṭāṅgahṛdayasaṃhitā* (*Kuṃṭe* et al., 1995), Ca. = *Carakasaṃhitā* (Ācārya, 1981), Su. = *Suśrutasaṃhitā* (Ācārya, 1992), HIML = Meulenbeld 2002. All translations are my own unless otherwise stated.

[1] Ca.1.1.41 (Ācārya, 1981, 8) *hitāhitaṃ sukhaṃ duḥkham āyus tasya hitāhitam / mānaṃ ca tac ca yatroktam āyurvedaḥ sa ucyate //*. Ca.sū.30.23–26 provide a more detailed statement of similar concepts.

[2] Gould (2001) presents the idea that there are two 'Magisteria' or realms of debate and discussion, one for science and one for religion. These two Magisteria do not, and should not be made to, intersect. Religion and science, in Gould's argument, address entirely different concerns, and there is no need, or strictly no possibility, for them to be in conflict.

[3] Mūsatū (1996), translated by Wood (1985, 67f.). The vaidyas T. C. Parameswaran Moosathu (fl.1846–1918) and Pachu Moothathu (d.1855?) described by Mooss (1938, 1949a, b) are probably K. V. Mūssatū's uncle and ancestor.

[4] Parpola (2000, ch. 9, esp. 211–4) "Women of the family: Respect and Subjugation".

[5] Ca.sū.1.15cd–16ab (Ācārya 1981, 48): *dharmārthakāmamokṣāṇām ārogyaṃ mūlam uttamam / rogās tasyāpahartāraḥ śreyasaḥ jīvitasya ca /*.

[6] Cakrapāṇi *ad* Ca.sū.1.15cd–18ab (Ācārya 1981, 6): ... *tenārogyam caturvarge pradhānaṃ kāraṇaṃ, rogagṛhītasya kvacid api puruṣārthe 'samarthatvād ity uktam / ... idam eva ca rogāṇām ārogyāpaharaṇaṃ yad anarthalābhaḥ*.

[7] E.g., "*dharmārthakāma*": Ca.sū.7.30, 11.46, 12.13, 30.29, Ca.śā.4.37(3), 4.37(6), Su.sū.2.8, 10.8 (plus *yaśas*), Su.śā.10.53 (plus *prajā*). "*Trivarga*": Ca.sū.11.25, 11.47, 30.24, Ca.si.12.35; Ah.sū.2.30.

[8] See Prater (1993), plate 61, p. 262.

[9] Ca.sū.6.43 (Ācārya 1981, 6): *lāvān kapiñjalān eṇān urabhrāñ charabhān śaśān / śālīn sayavagodhūmān sevyān āhur ghanātyaye //*.

[10] Ca.ci.2.1.48 (Ācārya 1981, 392): *na nā svapiti rātriṣu nityastabdhena śephasā / tṛptaḥ kukkuṭamāṃsānāṃ bhṛṣṭānāṃ nakraretasi //*.

[11] Ah.utt.6.46 (Kuṃṭe et al., 1995, 800): *vidhyec chirāṃ yathoktāṃ vā tṛptaṃ medyāmiṣasya vā / nivāte śāyayed evaṃ mucyate mativibhramāt //*.

[12] Su.sū.14.36 (Ācārya 1992, 66) *athātipravṛtte ... eṇahariṇorabhraśaśamahiṣavarāhāṇāṃ vā rudhiraṃ, kṣīrayūṣarasaiḥ susnigdhaiś cāśnīyāt, upadravāṃś ca yathāsvam-upacaret.*

[13] *Mānavadharmaśāstra* 5.26–56 Mandlik 1886, i.602–621; tr.Doniger and Smith 1991, 102–104).

[14] *Mānavadharmaśāstra* 5.55 (Mandlik 1886, i.619): *māṃ sa bhakṣayitāmutra yasya māṃsam ihādmy aham / etan māṃsasya māṃsatvaṃ pravadanti manīṣiṇaḥ //*.

[15] *Mānavadharmaśāstra* 5.56 (Mandlik 1886, i.620): *na māṃsabhakṣaṇe doṣo na madye na ca maithune / pravṛttir eṣā bhūtānāṃ nivṛttis tu mahāphalā //*.

[16] This distinction has been discussed by Bailey (1985). Also cf. Zimmermann (1999, 190f).

[17] Edited by Pārśvanātha Śāstri (1940). Cf. HIML, IIa. 151–55.

[18] This assembly may well have included one of the greatest Indian mathematicians, Mahāvīra. The lecture survives as the *Hitāhitādhyāya* chapter of his *Kalyāṇakāraka* (pārśvanātha, Śāstri, 1940, 714–748). It ends: *itihāsa saṃdarbha /*
khyātaḥ śrīNṛpatuṃgavallabhamahārājādhirājasthitaḥ /
prodyadbhūrisabhāṃtare bahuvidhaprakhyātavidvajjane //
māṃsāśiprakareṃdratākhilabhiṣagvidyāvidām agrato /
māṃse niṣphalatāṃ nirūpya nitarāṃ jaineṃdravaidyasthitam // ity aśeṣaviśeṣaviśiṣṭa-duṣṭapiśitāśivaidyaśāstreṣu māṃsanirākaraṇārtham ugrādityācāryair nṛpatuṃgavallabheṃdrasabhāyām udghoṣitaṃ prakaraṇam /.

[19] The king's physician traditionally played a critical role in supervising the kitchens and safeguarding the king's food from poisoners (cf. Wujastyk, 2003, 132).

[20] Cf. HIML IIa, 92f.

[21] Ca.sū.8.29 (Ācārya, 1981, 61): *brahmacarya-jñāna-dāna-**maitrī**-kāruṇya-harṣopekṣā-praśama-paraś ca syād iti.*
[22] See footnote 9.
[23] Houben (1999) discusses the ethical issues surrounding the killing of animals in Vedic rituals, and provides a valuable survey of the existing literature on vegetarianism, *ahiṃsā* and related topics. Limiting his exploration to the consideration of particular philosophical schools of thought, he does not examine the arguments from the medical tradition. The book in which this study appears contains further important explorations of violence in the Indian tradition (Houben & van Kooij, 1999).
[24] Cakrapāṇi *ad* Ca.sū.8.29 (Ācārya, 1981, 61): *maitrī sarvabhūteṣvātmanīvāpratikūlā pravṛttiḥ / nanu maitrīparaḥ syād iti viruddham etat, yenā śāstrakāra evāyaṃ digdhaviddhasvayaṃmṛtādimāṃsaparityāgena vayasthatvādiguṇayuktānāṃ mṛgādīnāṃ sadyaskaṃ māṃsaṃ sevyatvenopadiśan sākṣān maitrīvidurddhāṃ hiṃsām evāha; naivaṃ, rāgata eva prāṇināṃ hiṃsāpūrvakamāṃsabhakṣaṇe prāpte 'yam āyurvedopadeṣṭā māṃsaysa kvacidroge kasyaciddhitatvaṃ kvaciccāhitatvam upadiśati, na tu māṃsabhakṣaṇa dm hiṃsāṃ vā vidadhāti; na hy ayaṃ madirāyā api svasthavṛtte rogivṛtte vā hitatvam upadiśan madirāpānaṃ pratyupadeṣṭā bhavati; evaṃ ca rogādhikāre rājayakṣmādau māṃsopadeśas tathā śaradṛtucaryādau "lāvān kapiñjalān" (Ca.sū.6.43 (Ācārya 1981, 48)) ity ādigrantho āvādimāṃsahitatvopadeśārtho na hiṃsāvidhāyakaḥ; tena rogiṇaḥ svasthāś ca hiṃsāphalabhājo bhavanty eva; yathā "śyenenābhicaran yajeta" ity atrābhicārasya kāmata eva prāptatvācchyenasyābhicārasādhanatvamātram eva vidhir brūte, tena śyenenābhicārakaraṇe 'dharmo bhavaty eva; ayaṃ tv atra viśeṣaḥ – yadi hiṃsopārjitamāṃsopayogaṃ vinā puruṣo na jīvati, ato hiṃsāṃ karoti, tadā "sarvatrātmānaṃ gopāyīta" iti vedavacanavihitatvāt tathāvidhahiṃsā na pratyavāyahetuḥ, jīvanopāyāntarasaṃbhave tu puṣṭyādiprayojanā hiṃsā pratyavāyahetur eva; kiṃ ca bhavatu vāyurvedavihitā hiṃsā, tathā 'pi hiṃsā doṣārtham ucyate; na hy āyurvedavidhayo dharmasādhanam evopadiśanti, kiṃ tarhy ārogyasādhanaṃ*
dhātusāmyakriyā coktā tantrasyāsya prayojanam // (Ca.sū.1.53 (Ācārya, 1981, 14)) ity ukteḥ // 29 //.
The passage is also discussed by Zimmermann (1999, 192–4), although with a different emphasis.
[25] Medhātithi on *Mānavadharmaśāstra* 5.56 (Mandlik 1886, i.620): *alpasvalpā pravṛttir eṣā śāstrīyā bhūtānāṃ śarīrasthitihetvarthā pravṛttiḥ tathācāyurvedakṛt /.*
[26] See further the remarks on these terms in HIML, IIa. 608.
[27] Atīśa negotiated a peace settlement between Cakrapāṇi's patron Nayapāla and the Kalacuri king, Karṇa (Majumdar, 1957, 27). The extent and meaning of Buddhist influence in classical Indian medicine is an important topic still in need of further research. See, e.g., HIML, IIa.110–11, 602–12.
[28] Ah.sū.2 (Kuṃṭe et al. 1995, 4): *āyuḥ kāmayamānena dharmārthasukhasādhanam / āyurvedopadeśeṣu vidheyaḥ paramādaraḥ.*
[29] It is cited at the start (v.1.10) of the *Āyurvedasaukhya*, the sixteenth-century medical encyclopedia commissioned by Emperor Akbar's finance minister, Ṭoḍaramalla Dash and Kashyap 1980–1992,2.53f.; cf. Wujastyk forthcoming).
[30] Cf. Roşu (1978).
[31] See note 5.
[32] Ca.sū.7.30 (Ācārya, 1981, 50): *puṇyaśabdo vipāpatvān manovākkāyakarmaṇām // dharmārthakāmān puruṣaḥ sukhī bhuṅkte cinoti ca.*
[33] *āyurvedasyāpannarukpratikriyayā dharmasādhanatvam* (Vaidya, 1948, 11).
[34] Ca.sū.1.43 (Ācārya, 1981, 9): *tasyāyuṣaḥ puṇyatamo vedo vedavidāṃ mataḥ / vakṣyate yan manuṣyāṇāṃ lokayor ubhayor hitam //.*
[35] Cakrapāṇi *ad* Ca.sū.1.43 (Ācārya, 1981, 9): *yad anye ṛgvedādayaḥ prāyaḥ paralokahitam evārthaṃ vadanti tena puṇyāḥ, puṇyatamaś cāyam āyurvedo yad yasmān manuṣyāṇām ubhayor api lokayor yad dhitam āyur ārogyasādhanaṃ dharmasādhanaṃ*

ca tad vakṣyate, tenātiśayena puṇyatamas tathā vedavidāṃ ca pūjita iti / ... *jīvitapradātṛtvād āyurvedasya puṇyatamatvaṃ boddhavyaṃ, yataś caturvargasādhanībhūtajīvitapradam eva sarvottamaṃ bhavati* / *ucyate ca "na hi jīvitadānād dhi dānam anyad viśiṣyate" (Ca.ci.1.4.61 (Ācārya, 1981,390) iti* /.

[36] Cakrapāṇi *ad* Ca.sū.1.15cd–18ab (Ācārya, 1981, 6): ... *yato jīvitaṃ svarūpeṇaiva sarvaprāṇināṃ nirupādhyupādeyaṃ;* ... *yat tv atyantaduḥkhagṛhītasya jīvitaṃ jihāsitaṃ, tatra duḥkhasyātyantajihāsitasyānyathā hātum aśakyatvāt priyam api jīvitaṃ tyaktum icchati na svarūpeṇa* /.

[37] Ca.sū.11.4 (Ācārya, 1981, 68): *āsāṃ tu khalv eṣaṇānāṃ prāṇaiṣaṇāṃ tāvat pūrvataram āpadyeta kasmāt prāṇaparityāge hi sarvatyāgaḥ tasyānupālanaṃ–svasthasya svasthavṛttānuvṛttiḥ āturasya vikārapraśamane'pramādaḥ tadubhayam etaduktaṃ vakṣyate ca tad yathoktam anuvartamānaḥ prāṇānupālanād dīrgham āyur avāpnotīti prathamaiṣaṇā vyākhyātā bhavati.* A full translation of the whole passage about these three goals is given in Wujastyk (2003, 22–8). Cf. the valuable discussions in Rosu (1978, 259f.) and Dasgupta (1969, 2.415).

[38] Cakrapāṇi *ad* Ca.sū.11.3 (Ācārya, 1981, 67): *iheti bhogārthipuruṣādhikāre, yato mokṣārthipuruṣaṃ prati dhanaiṣaṇā sarvathaivānupayuktā.* Tr.: "By saying "here" [Caraka] means that this is applicable to the person whose goal is the enjoyment of experience, since a desire for wealth is completely inappropriate for someone whose goal is liberation".

REFERENCES

Ācārya, J.T. (ed.) 1981. *Carakasaṃhitā, śrīcakrapāṇidattaviracitayā āyurvedadīpikāvyākhyayā saṃvalitā*. 4th ed. New Delhi: Munshiram Manoharlal.

Ācārya, J.T. (ed.) 1992. *Suśrutasaṃhitā, śrīḍalhaṇācāryaviracitayā nibandhasaṃgrahākhyavyākhyayā nidānasthānasya śrīgayadāsācāryaviracitayā nyāyacandrikākhyapañjikāvyākhyayā ca samullasitā ... Ācāryopāhvena trivikramātmajena yādavaśarmaṇā ... saṃśodhitā*. 5th ed. Vārāṇasī, Delhi: Caukhambhā Oriyanṭāliyā.

Bailey, G. (1985). *Materials for the Study of Ancient Indian Ideologies: Pravṛtti and Nivṛtti*, Vol. XIX of *Collana di Letture diretta da Oscar Botto*. Torino: Indologica Taurinensia.

Dasgupta, S. (1969). *A History of Indian Philosophy*. Cambridge: Cambridge University Press. 5th reprint of 1922 edition.

Dash, B. & Kashyap, L. (1980–1992). *[The Āyurveda Saukhyaṃ of the Ṭoḍarānanda]*, Ṭoḍarānanda-Āyurveda Saukhyam Series. New Delhi: Concept Publishing Company. 8 Vols., each with a different title.

Doniger, W. & Smith, B.K. 1991, *The Laws of Manu: with an Introduction and Notes*. London: Penguin Books.

Gould, S.J. (2001). *Rocks of Ages: Science and Religion in the Fullness of Life*. London: Jonathan Cape.

Houben, J.E.M. (1999). To Kill or not to Kill the Sacrificial Animal (*Yajña-paśu*)? Arguments and Perspectives in Brahminical Ethical Philosophy. In Houben and Van Kooij, (1999) Chapt. 5, pp. 105–183.

Houben, J.E.M. and van Kooij, K.R. (eds.) (1999). *Violence, Non-violence and the Rationalization of Violence in South Asian Cultural History*. Leiden: Brill.

Kuṃte, A.M., Navare, K. and Parādkar, H. (eds) (1995). *Aṣṭāṅgahṛdayam, śrīmadvāgbhaṭaviracitam, śrīmadaruṇadattaviracitayā 'sarvāṅgasundarākhyā' vyākhyayā hemādripraṇītayā 'āyurvedarasāyanāhvayā' ṭīkayā ca samullasitam*, No.4 in Kṛṣṇadāsa Āyurveda Sīrīja. Vārāṇasī: Krishnadas Academy (Reprint).

Majumdar, R.C. (1957). *The Struggle for Empire, The History and Culture of the Indian People*. 4th ed. Bombay: Bharatiya Vidya Bhavan. 4th edn. 1989.

Mandlik, V.N. (1886). *Mánava-dharma Sástra (Institutes of Manu) with the Commentaries of Medhátithi, Sarvajñanarayana, Kúllúka, Raghavananda, Nandana, and Rámachandra, and an Appendix by the Honorable Rao Sahib Vishvanáth Náráyan Mandlik*, Vol. 2. Bombay: Ganpat Krishnaji's press.
Meulenbeld, G.J. (1999–2002). *A History of Indian Medical Literature*. Groningen: E. Forsten. 5v.
Mooss, N.S.V. (1938). Vachaspathy T.C. Parameswaran Moosathu. In *The All India Ayurvẹdic Directory*, Vol. 2. (40 p.). Kottayam: The Vaidya Sarathy Press.
Mooss, N.S.V. (1949a). Pachu Moothathu. In *The All India Ayurvedic Directory*, Vol. 5. (p. 279). Kottayam: The Vaidya Sarathy Press.
Mooss, N.S.V. (1949b). T.C. Parameswaran Moosathu. In *The All India Ayurvedic Directory*, Vol. 5. (p. 280). Kottayam: The Vaidya Sarathy Press.
Mūsatū, K.V. (1966). *Ātmakathā ["Autobiography"]*. Kottayam: National Book Stall.
Parpola, M. (2000). *Kerala Brahmins in Transition: a Study of a Nampūtiri Family*, Vol. 91 of Stud. Orientalia. Helsinki: Finnish Oriental Society.
Pārśvanātha Śāstrī, V. (ed.) (1940). *Ugrādityācāryakṛta Kalyāṇakāraka (Rāṣṭrabhāṣānuvādasahita)*, Vol. 129 of *Sakhārāma Nemacaṃda Graṃthamālā*. Sọlāpura: Seṭha Goviṃdajī Rāvajī Dośī.
Prater, S.H. (1993). *The Book of Indian Animals*. Bombay, Delhi, etc.: Oxford University Press, 4th impression of 3rd corrected 1980 edition.
Roşu, A. (1978). Études āyurvédiques: le *trivarga* dans l'āyurveda. *Indologica Taurinensia* **6**, 255–260.
Vaidya, P.L. (ed.) (1948). *Ṭoḍarānandam: śrīmadakavarasāhipradhānāmātyaśrī-Ṭoḍaramallap reraṇayā Vārāṇaseyavidvatprakāṇḍaiḥ saṃbhūya viracitam tasyāyaṃ Sargasaukhyam, Avatārasaukhyam iti Saukhyadvayātmakaḥ Prathamaḥ Khaṇḍaḥ ... VaidyopāhvaśrīParaśurāmaśarmabhiḥ Saṃpāditam*, Vol. 5 of *The Ganga Oriental Series*. Bīkanera: Anup Sanskrit Library.
Wood, A.E. (1985). *Knowledge Before Printing and After: the Indian Tradition in Changing Kerala*. Delhi: Oxford University Press.
Wujastyk, D. (2003). *The Roots of Āyurveda: Selections from Sanskrit Medical Writings*. 3rd ed. London, New York, etc.: Penguin Group.
Wujastyk, D. (forthcoming), Change and Creativity in Early Modern Indian Medical Thought. *Journal of Indian Philosophy*.
Zimmermann, F. (1999). *The Jungle and the Aroma of Meats: an Ecological Theme in Hindu Medicine*, No.4 in Indian Medical Tradition. Delhi: Motilal Banarsidass. First published Berkeley, University of California Press, 1987.

The Wellcome Trust Centre for the History of Medicine at UCL
24 Eversholt Street
London NWI 1AD
UK
E-mail: ucgadkw@ucl.ac.uk

FRANK J. KOROM

THE BENGALI DHARMARĀJ IN TEXT AND CONTEXT: SOME PARALLELS

In explanation the text had only internal relations, a structure; in interpretation it has now a significance, that is, an accomplishment in the subject's own discourse. By means of its structure the text had only a semiological dimension; by means of the actualization, it now has a semantic dimension (Ricoeur, 1971: 146).

INTRODUCTION

In a pair of earlier articles (cf. Korom, 1997a, b) I explored the identity of the Bengali Dharmarāj from an ethnographic perspective; that is, how people who worship him understand his true nature. I concluded by suggesting that Dharmarāj worship on the ground in rural West Bengal is a pluralistic set of traditions bearing family resemblances in the sense adumbrated by Wittgenstein (1976). I further concluded that contemporary Dharmarāj traditions bear very little resemblance to the medieval textual tradition that initially bolstered his elevated position in the Bengali pantheon. However, the 'ethnographic' Dharmarāj and the 'textual' Dharmarāj are interrelated insofar as the texts suggest some provocative parallels that help shed light on our contemporary understanding of the deity.

The texts to which I refer are known as *Maṅgalkābya*s, poetic narratives comprised of couplets and triplets. *Maṅgalkābya* forms the bulk of medieval Bengali poetry (Zbavitel, 1976: 156), and as such has been an area of much inquiry (cf. Sen, 1911, 1975; Bhaṭṭācārja, 1975; Bandyopādhyāẏ, 1980). Here, I highlight only those aspects of the literature that lend support to the notion of a text/context interface. As a distinct sub-genre – for it belongs to the larger branch of literature known as *pāñcālikā* (Sen, 1960: 60) – Bengali *Maṅgalkābya*s differ considerably from the Sanskrit *kāvyam* literature in that the latter is more formalized than the former (Robinson, 1980: 2). If any comparison is to be drawn between a body of Sanskrit literature and *Maṅgalkābya*, it would have to be the *purāṇa*s (cf. Rocher, 1986).

Thematically and structurally the two share many things, such as an emphasis on creation accounts, the mythology of the primary deity of the text, length, and narrative style. The authors of the Bengali texts seem to have consciously borrowed the classical model and utilized many motifs and stories from the Sanskrit texts in their attempts to indigenize the form by presenting and praising autochthonous deities. In fact, many *Maṅgalkābya*s are referred to as vernacular *purāṇ*s. But here the comparison ends. As William L. Smith writes: "These surface similarities are, however, deceptive; in their conception of the divine order, their portrayal of the relationship between god and man, as well as their caste and sexual bias, the *maṅgals* not only differ from the *purāṇa*s but are in many respects their antithesis" (1982: 69). *Maṅgalkābya*s present a unique and interesting view of Bengali religion and culture that often takes very specific theological turns not found elsewhere in India (Dimock, 1976; Smith, 1982). They also lend to the formation of a distinct Bengali regional tradition (cf. Chakrabarti, 2001).

Since one of the main functions of the *Maṅgalkābya*s is panegyric, each text praises and develops one specific deity in the Bengali pantheon. Dharmarāj (King of Dharma), also known as Dharma *ṭhākur*, or simply Dharma, stands out in this pantheon not only because of his significant role in the genre as creator (cf. Kilpatrick, 1977; Smith, 1982), but also because ethnographic evidence (Mahapatra, 1972: 60; Bhaṭṭācārja, 1975: 653; Sen, 1975: 153; Dasgupta, 1946: 279–280) suggests that the *Dharmamaṅgal*, in its various recensions, was still being performed in honor of the deity during specific ritual occasions as late as the 1960s. Not only that, out of all the texts in the sub-genre, the *Dharmamaṅgal* corpus is somewhat distinct from the other *maṅgal* texts because due to its massive length, martial imagery, royal patronage, and thematic content, it most resembles what we might call 'epic'. This observation has not gone completely unnoticed by Bengali literary scholars (e.g., Bandyopādhyāẏ, 1980: 352). Western authorities, on the other hand, tend to see the whole sub-genre as 'homogeneous' and 'epic-like' (Zbavitel, 1976: 156), based mostly on their massive length (Sen, 1960: 19). But length cannot be the only criterion for determining if a piece of literature or performance is epic or not (Blackburn and Flueckiger, 1989: 2–5). At any rate, the *Dharmamaṅgal*s are clearly distinct from other *Maṅgalkābya*s in content and style, while generally adhering to the basic structure of the typical *maṅgal* outlined by Dušan Zbavitel (1976: 159).

Numerous poetic versions of the *Dharmamaṅgal* have come down to us in various stages of completion and in manuscript form. From Mayur Bhatt's twelfth-century (? cf. Sen, 1911: 47–48) version to the early eighteenth-century work written by Ghanaram Cakrabarti, there is a considerable amount of structural (Bhaṭṭācārja, 1975: 629) and narrative consistency, even though each author emphasizes or elaborates certain portions of the story.[1] Mayur Bhatt's version (cf. Mayūrbhaṭṭa, 1381BS), for example, is more ritually oriented by focusing on the story of Ramai Pandit, the person believed to be the author of the *Śūnya Purāṇ* (Empty *Purāṇ*; cf. Ramāī Paṇḍit, 1977) – one of the religious movement's liturgical texts – and performer of the first *pūjā* (worship service) for the deity Dharmarāj. On the other hand, Ghanaram's narrative develops the story of the hero Lausen, Dharmarāj's crusader on earth.

Ghanaram's text is normatively perceived to be the most popular version because it is considered the most poetic and complete.[2] But Sandra Robinson has pointed out that certain versions are more closely associated with specific sites of worship usually located near an author's place of birth (1980: 4). This is the case with Ghanaram, who is more associated with the northern Rarh (roughly equivalent to modern-day Burdwan, Bankura and Birbhum districts) area of West Bengal, since we know from his signature verse that he was born in the village of Krishnapur, located in Burdwan District (Sen, 1975: 188). Further, because the medieval authors were often writing under royal patronage and singing for the court, popular renditions performed by singers utilizing local versions must have flourished among the broader audiences at ritual sites and elsewhere, for there are intertextual references in the texts which suggest this. Each may thus have been used as separate bases of recitation during ritual events. This contrasts to the *Śūnya Purāṇ* and the *Dharmapūjā Bidhān* (cf. Bandyopādhyāy, 1323BS), the two liturgical texts associated with the deity that were more widespread due to their ritual authority (Robinson, 1980: 18). Even today, the *Dharmapūjā Bidhān* is used, or at least invoked, in some form or another to perform Dharma rituals at many sites.

During the early stages of my research I attempted to locate the recitative traditions so well documented in the literature cited above, but gradually came to realize that the oral performance of *Dharmamaṅgals* was in decline. As I travelled to many sites of Dharmarāj temples in West Bengal, I kept expecting to find the recitative or singing tradition intact. But at each site, a ritual specialist or learned resident would send me somewhere else in search of the elusive 'performed' *Dharmamaṅgal.* Except for locating a single singer who sang one *pālā* (section) of the text concerning the hero Lausen's sacrifice of his body for Dharmarāj's boon, my attempts turned up very little evidence to suggest that the oral performance of the *Dharmamaṅgal* played a central role in the contemporary worship of Dharmarāj. What I found instead were numerous village-based systems of vibrant and complex ritual activities in honor of the deity that evoked the medieval corpus of texts in subtle ways without direct reference to it. These initial observations implied that the text/context interface within the conceptual galaxy of Dharmarāj worship would take shape quite differently from other Hindu recitative traditions on both the local (Blackburn, 1988) and transregional (Lutgendorf, 1991) level. In other words, the Dharmarāj tradition(s), as we know it/them today, raise(s) a different set of issues related to textuality because the 'text' is not situated in the center of performative ritual acts. Rather, the text functions in an imaginative way as a source of 'scriptural allusions' (cf. Briggs, 1988), themes, images, and prescriptions related to the modern-day context of religious performance. But how does one tackle such a subtle and difficult problem that defies easy answers?

Since earlier comparative studies had already been done (Mitra, 1972; Robinson, 1980), I ultimately ended up studying the annual event in a small, all-Hindu village named Goalpara in Birbhum District, West Bengal.[3] Dharma's worship as practiced in Goalpara has been mentioned in the literature (Mitra, 1972; Bhattacharya, 1986; Rohner and Chaki-Sircar, 1988: 108–111), but has not been studied in depth. I chose the village not because the observance is well known outside of the immediate area, but because it has a special meaning for the community in question. The phenomenon in Goalpara holds the distinction of being the first village in the district to celebrate the observance each year. As such, it serves as a model for other adjacent villages that celebrate their own local forms of the *pūjā* a month after the Goalpara event. Yet even though it has obvious local relevance and importance, the Goalpara Dharmarāj *pūjā* remains relatively obscure to outsiders. It is not, for example, mentioned in the virtually exhaustive four volumes of *Paścimbaṅger Saṅgskṛiti* (Ghoṣ, 1976), nor does it find mention in government census data on Bengali festivals (cf. Mitra, 1968). By choosing a small, relatively unknown site, I was able to explore in depth this community's belief system related to Dharmarāj, highlighting verbal and non-verbal aspects of religious phenomena that emphasize the deity's personal relationship with the residents of Goalpara. To a certain extent, every village that worships Dharmarāj has its own corpus of narrative about the deity (cf. Mitra, 1972: 123–133). But I have never observed a level of ethos and sense of pride taken in Dharmarāj's worship as great as Goalpara's at other sites in the region.

Even though oral accounts of personal belief and worship are quintessential factors in the study of localized forms of religious expression, very little has been published about such narratives in English. Peacock (1984) has pointed out how life stories, or portions thereof, reflect the religious beliefs of the individual and his or her community. Personal experience narratives and memorates (cf. Honko, 1964; Langellier, 1989; Korom, 2000) further provide us with rich and detailed accounts of how individuals create a sense of place and community, as Barbara Johnstone has suggested (1990: 5). It is in such narratives that we find one level of correspondence between text and context. There are others as well, which will be taken up below. In the remainder of this essay, I move away from the microstudy model of one very small community to reflect on the theoretical implications of my material. A key issue that emerges is the relationship between text and context.

TEXTUALITY AND THE STUDY OF DHARMARĀJ[4]

In the introductory section, I have been alluding to the fact that the medieval *Dharmamaṅgal* corpus serves as background for the study of the modern context in which the Dharmarāj *pūjā* is performed. But it must be emphasized that the textual tradition plays a seemingly minor role in understanding Dharmarāj and his worship in Goalpara. This is not to say, however, that the texts are irrelevant. On the contrary, it would be useful to see the relationship between the *Dharmamaṅgal* texts and the *pūjā* as a dialectical one. The former *in*forms and the latter *per*forms. In other words, although certain ritual practices emerged in Goalpara and elsewhere independent of textual prescriptions, many of the contemporary actions of participants build on a foundation of practices and beliefs that were already embedded in the texts themselves. These features suggest that the *Dharmamaṅgal*s cannot be divorced totally from the modern-day context. Although the average participant is not aware of the relationship between the actualized performance and the idealized texts, the latter have been responsible for the historical shaping of the tradition. The texts therefore provide us with insights into contemporary beliefs and ritual performances by filling in the 'blank spots' (Ingarden, 1973) otherwise unattainable from the performances themselves. From a pragmatic perspective, the texts serve an indexical function, pointing to past understandings that have subconsciously and historically influenced present-day events.

The issue of textuality is thus a necessary consideration for understanding the broader context of Dharma worship. William Hanks has defined textuality as "the quality of coherence or connectivity that characterizes text" (1989: 96). He goes on to say that connectivity is "dependent upon the inherent properties of the textual artifact, the interpretive activities of a community of readers/viewers or a combination of the two" (ibid.). But because the community of viewers does not have a great knowledge of the textual tradition, the relationship between the text and performance is ambiguous and problematic at best in Goalpara. Hanks admits that such a relationship can create a problem of disjunction, but rectifies the discrepancy by saying that "it is the fit between the sign form and some larger context that determines its [i.e., the text] ultimate coherence" (ibid.).[5] The ultimate coherence to which he refers is grounded in social action (Hanks, 1989: 103); that is, the implicit ways that the medieval texts serve as sub-texts for the annual event in modern times. This idea ties in nicely with Goalpara residents' understanding of their ritual activities as a coherent whole, rather than a random arrangement of practices, as some critics have argued.

Making a quantitative leap from medieval text to modern context can lead to speculative interpretation on the part of the researcher, but Alf Hiltebeitel (1991) has shown that much of what we label 'folk' or 'popular' Hinduism cannot be appreciated fully without resorting to textual data to complement ethnographic fieldwork.[6] One must be cautious, however, of giving priority to texts, for it is tempting to trace all modern practices on the local level back to a Vedic precedent (cf. Korom, 1990: 17). Potential misunderstandings may indeed arise when an overemphasis is placed on text. Yet attempting to understand the context of worship without reference to scripture is equally problematic. Understanding the interaction of the *Dharmamaṅgal* texts with a specific galaxy of local beliefs and practices thus requires situating the written sources in meaningful social action. Let us then move on to explore some of the ways that *Dharmamaṅgal*s can be used to inform the context of religious performance.

THE TEXT/CONTEXT INTERFACE

Although some practices are mirrored in the textual tradition, it would be pointless to suggest that the text precedes the ritual or vice versa, for one would only end up arguing the unsolvable problem of the relationship between the chicken and the egg. Making any assertion related to this controversy would only result in engaging in the myth/ritual debate, which is not my intention here. It would be more productive simply to point out the possible connections that might exist between textual and contextual features of the Dharmarāj phenomenon in order to suggest aspects of 'connectivity.'[7] To this end, I will extract some themes that we find in both the medieval sources and the modern context.

In the *Dharmamaṅgal* of Ghanaram, we find many passages that describe the context of the *gājan* (thunder), or annual worship of Dharmarāj. Many of the passages provide us with accounts about the general atmosphere of the event. The following passage, for example, describes the event in much the same way as we know it today; that is, as an occasion accompanied by much music and song (Cakrabartti, 1962: 33):

kata padya bādya bāje ādyer gājane
In Adya's (=Dharmarāj) *gājan* there was much recitation, music and song.

This passage, and others like it (cf. Cakrabartti, 1962: 62; also below), suggests that the annual rituals for the deity have always been occasions for musical and verbal performances of various sorts. Such performances ranged from intertextual references concerning the recitation of still other *Maṅgalkābya* texts to the ritual use of the *Dharmapūjā Bidhān* (Cakrabartti, 1962: 90) and riddling contests (Cakrabartti, 1962: 303–312). As mentioned above, the tradition of reciting key portions of the narrative still exists today in some villages of West Bengal, but is being increasingly replaced by other forms of music and ritual activity. Unlike the recitation of the narrative, however, the liturgical use of the *Dharmapūjā Bidhān* still exists in Goalpara and a number of other locations. The famous riddling contest between the hero Lausen and Suriksha, his female captor, described by Ghanaram in the *Golāhāṭ Pālā* of his text is not, to my knowledge, performed today. Some have suggested, however, that the riddling section of the text serves as a model for present-day verbal duels performed annually during the rite elsewhere in Bengal (e.g., Sen, 1975: 146).

Aside from references suggesting the use of folklore genres, a number of other themes and activities can be gleaned from the texts to aid our understanding of the modern performance event. These are: ritual practices, austerities, and the use of liturgical texts in the performance of the rite; the mentioning of the names of Dharmarāj's multiforms (i.e., the seven Ray brothers); Dharmarāj's form, both iconic and human; personal encounters; and the deity's relationship to low castes. I will now review each of these categories to point out the *Dharmamaṅgal* literature's essential role as background for understanding contemporary beliefs and practices.

1. *Ritual Allusions*: Many of the literary works related to Dharmarāj suggest numerous ritual dimensions of present-day activities. The most notable incident in this category is the hero Lausen's mother's *tapas* (austerity) described in the *Śāle Bhar Pālā* of Ghanaram's text (cf. Cakrabarttī, 1962: 91–114) because it encapsulates many other recurring references to ritual acts performed in the contemporary event. In this chapter, the barren queen Ranjabati makes a vow to perform ritual austerities for Dharmarāj at a place called Campai in Bankura District (Sen, 1911: 30) by impaling herself on a spiked plank. She does this in exchange for the boon of giving birth to the hero Lausen. To this end, Ranjabati sets out from her palace by boat, accompanied by her maid Shamula and a party of devotees and pilgrims. After arriving at the forested site, she hires Dalits of the Hari caste to clear the area prior to her austerities. A pandit named Ramai[8] builds a sacrificial fire, another feature we find in the modern context, and urges the queen to begin the worship service. I pick up the narrative at this point, since the section makes many references that pertain to the following discussion (Cakrabarttī, 1962: 93–97):

2. Yelling "Victory to Dharma!" they all respond with the drums.
1. The pandit says "Oh queen, why delay any longer?
2. Bathing in the waters of the river, worship."
1. In order to show approval, Shamula, along with all of the pilgrims,
2. All took canes in their hands and began to dance.
1. The musicians danced, immersed in their drum playing.
2. Coming to Campai's *ghāṭ*, they rolled on the ground.
1. First, putting a bit of the meritorious water on her head,
2. She enters the water with the pilgrims at the auspicious moment.

1. Then they bathed, performed ablutions and offered the boat,
2. Completing the Vedic and Tantric chants,
1. Everyone meditating on Dharma with a pure mind,
2. Ranja raises her hands and says "Let me be with son."
1. Wearing clean white clothes, they all got out onto the riverbank.
2. Various musicians and bands play and dance with canes in their hands.
1. While dancing, they make the victorious sounds of Dharma.
2. Coming near the deity's residence, they roll on the earth.
1. Playing intensely on the drum, the drummers stop.
2. [And] receiving the auspicious moment, they all sat in meditation.
1. The beautiful woman Ranjabati with all the pilgrims,
2. Began the *dharmapūjā* in the desire for a son.
1. A copper plate was decorated with basil, sesame and *kuś* grass.
2. Thinking of the "ultimate man" (= Dharma) and taking a vow,
1. With a book in hand, the pandit explains the rules of the rite.
2. The seats were purified in order to drive out ghosts.
1. Worshipping Ganesh and all of the other gods and goddesses, Ranjabati
2. Worships the "Lord of the World" in desire for a son.
1. According to prescription, she gives many offerings in worship.
2. Clarified butter lamps and incense; incense darkens the area.
1. Sun-dried rice, sugar, rice pudding and bananas
2. In large amounts. A huge fully-blossomed lotus garland.
1. A moon[like] garland of *c̃āpā* flowers smeared with sandalwood.
2. They worship rooted in devotion [and] in utter joy.
1. The flowers go to the heavens as an offering.
2. They are unflinching in their efforts to satisfy Dharma.
1. Some raise their arms in the air standing on one foot,
2. Along with the pilgrims shouting "Victory to Dharma,"
1. Some are burning incense over their heads.
2. Even so, the cruel-hearted Lord is not compassionate.
1. The blazing fire burns with extremely violent heat.
2. Without moving their lips, they perform chants with their tongues.
1. Lighting incense in the very special desire,
2. The twice-born Ghanaram recites the *Śridharmamaṅgal*.
1. "Oh friend of the childless Dharma, be merciful."
2. The unfortunate Ranja begs for the gift of a son.

1 + 2. Holding her hands folded above her, with feet together on the ground, she lowers her head.

1. There where the sacrificial pit was blazing with fire,
2. Ranjabati says "Lord fulfill my desire."

1. The golden doll, in the middle of the five products of the cow,
2. Rolled around in it.
1. Trumpets, hand cymbals, drums were being played intensely by the band.
2. Ranjabati worships and Shamula yells "Victory!"
1. The fire glimmers and incense floats up.
2. In that, Ranjabati rolls around in the worship of Dharma.
1. "My brother's sharp words rent my breast asunder.
2. In contempt, he said that I was barren for twelve years.
1. I am worthless and afflicted, but let me be successful in having a child.
2. The face of a child will save me from the hell of the childless.
1. Let my name as a barren woman be destroyed in India.
2. Let all of the heretics' heads be struck by thunderbolts."

. . .

1. With every difficult austerity,
2. Yoga, sacrifice, worship, recitation,
3. The auspicious day nears.
1. Bathing, worship, music, dance.
2. On the tenth day, thorns of the *gāmār* tree,
3. They yelled "Victory, Victory!" at the river.
1. The pandit along with his manual,
2. Invoked the *gāmār* tree,
3. Worshipping Ganesh and all of the other deities.
1. Welcoming the tree,
2. The pilgrims grab it.
3. He tied threads on all of their hands.
1. The blacksmith, the *gāmār* thorns,
2. Neatly arranged them in the room,
3. The mendicants laid the thorns in it.
1. "Victory, victory Nirañjan (=Dharma)!"
2. Many devotees, yelling this,
3. The great festival of the *gājan* passes.
1. Others at the *ghāṭ*,
2. The mendicants performing much worship,
3. They go to Campai *ghāṭ* with pomp and splendor.
1. Decorating the platform with plantains,
2. A cleaver is placed on the platform,
3. Dharma came onto the road and possessed them.
1. Completing the incense worship,
2. They concentrate on the deity Dharma.
3. The nine jewels of the female ascetic shine.
1. In joy, on a standard-sized platform,
2. Accompanied by recitation, music, song, and dance,

3. She passed the night in sacrifices.
1. In the morning, the horizon becomes visible,
2. When the sun appears.
3. Having plucked flowers in auspicious desire,
1. Having bathed and worshipped Dharma,
2. Having immersed [her] mind in the Brahma *mantra*,
3. Having arranged the platform, [she] got up [on the spiked plank].
1. Piercing the plank on the sacred platform,
2. [She] drives the moon-arrow-shaped blade,
3. The gruesome looking sharp-edged razor.
1. The queen desires a child.
2. Folding her cupped hands,
3. Having performed meditation as an offering to the sun.
1. Merciless should never be,
2. The Lord, the "Savior of the Sinful."
3. "[This] sinful one salutes at your feet."
1. Saying [this, she] girds [her] loins,
2. [And] closing [her] two eyes,
3. She jumps over it (= the plank) with a thud.
1. [There was] deafening drumming and cries of victory.
2. Shamula embraced her.
3. She stood up fearlessly once again.
1. Whichever devotees, including [her] entourage [were there],
2. In this way again and again,
3. [She] jumped over, [but] still no mercy.
1. Then Ranja says "Sister,
2. Fate (= Dharma) has not been pleased.
3. Let [me] renounce this body by jumping onto the spike."
1. Then Shamula says,
2. "Your mental wish shall be fulfilled.
3. The divine master of illusion will show himself to you.
1. Fruitless is the goal of everyday life,
2. [When] being a householder without a son.
3. Do not have any fear in mind.
1. Even if you die on the plank."

. . .

1. When Shamula spoke these words to Ranja,
2. The pandit says, "This is sound indeed.
1. The Lord will fall into trouble due to the murder of a woman.
2. Then [even] his father cannot deceive his devotees.
1. As [you] enter this austerity, even so [you] will attain fruit."
2. The queen answers, "[Oh] Lord! If so [it will be] the greatest auspiciousness."

1. The queen tells the group of devotees, "Everyone go home.
2. I will renounce this body at Campai, throwing [myself] onto the plank.
1. Convey my innumerable salutations to [my] husband."
2. The poor Ranjabati died throwing [herself] onto the spike.

The above passage, more than any other, brings together many metareferences found scattered throughout the *Dharmamaṅgal* literature by concisely alluding to a number of features that we encounter in the Dharmarāj rituals of Goalpara and elsewhere in West Bengal. The most obvious connection is the relationship between fertility and Ranjabati's sacrifice on the spiked plank. Although Ghanaram's text does not explicitly refer to the spiked plank as *bāṇeśvar* (arrow lord), the term used in Goalpara, he does mention an arrow (*bāṇ*) in the passage. Given the relationship between fertility (cf. Maity, 1971) and the ritual usage of the *bāṇeśvar*s in the contemporary *pūjā* context, we can be fairly certain that the connection between the textual and contextual objects is sound. Further, the specific use of thorns from the *gāmār* tree (*Gmelina arborea*) described in the passage is prevalent in other Dharmarāj rituals observed in West Bengal (Robinson, 1980: 410). In Goalpara, the type of thorn used is not from the *gāmār* tree, but the *kā̃ṭā khelā* (thorn play) – including dancing with and rolling on thorns – implicitly suggests the symbolism of impalement so graphically described in the above passage.[9] The notion of 'rolling around' for the deity as described in the text, can also be seen during the thorn play. But more generally, the theme of rolling or lying on the ground finds its parallel in prostrations done in the presence of the deity on several occasions during the annual service.

We find other thematic associations as well. Ranjabati's preparatory bathing and subsequent baths during the course of the ritual described above, for example, remind us strongly of the preparatory bath taken in the Ganges by *bhaktyā*s (devotees) as well as the constant bathing activities that are performed during the course of the annual event. The extensive use of drumming and music also suggest the central role played by the *ḍhākī* drummers while the continuous 'shouts of victory' in the passage parallel the *nām ḍāk* (name call) performed on numerous occasions during the contemporary event. In both text and context, Dharmarāj is being called to enter into the assembly of worshippers not only to view the proceedings, but also to fulfill vows (*mānasik*) taken by participants. Lastly, the use of canes, dance, incense, flower plucking at sunrise, sacrificial fire pits, and invoking the hosts of deities in the text also find their modern counterparts in Goalpara (cf. Korom, 1999).

One could argue that many of the latter features such as incense burning, flower offerings, fire sacrifices and deity invocation are part and parcel of general worship in Hinduism. This may be true, but the unique constellation of these ingredients taken together with the symbolism of thorns and spiked planks suggest the continuation of a set of practices that have been perpetuated in some cases, elaborated in others, and attenuated in still others over a long span of time.[10] The ways that these various ritual activities are brought together in different places in West Bengal suggest the distinct nature of the event in each local context, but also imply interrelations. In this sense, it would be wise to admit that the rituals, as actualized in different places, are obviously not isolated events, for they all stem from a common core of practices and beliefs related to the deity Dharmarāj. But as mentioned above, it is useful to view the Dharmarāj traditions as pluralistic, since each village localizes aspects of the broader tradition by giving it specific meaning through expression in oral narrative, religious belief, and ritual praxis. How this is done varies from place to place.

A fine example is the way in which Dharmarāj is identified and perceived in his local forms. In Goalpara, Dharmarāj has seven names and forms. *Dharmamaṅgal*s provide us some information on these forms, as I suggest below, but local innovation has led to the amalgamation of regional folk deities in a way that makes sense to the residents of this particular place. In this sense, the interpretive process leading to a local 'composite' image of Dharmarāj is not so far removed from the way nineteenth and twentieth century scholars created the image of the object of their study (cf. Korom, 1997a). But whereas scholars drew on fragmented textual sources available to them to create an overall picture of the deity, local pandits and worshippers utilized contextual sources within the realm of their immediate experiences to interpret the multiforms of Dharmarāj as one deity. A brief review of Dharmarāj's multiforms in Goalpara will be useful at this juncture.

2. *Dharmarāj's multiforms*: The names of some of the seven Ray brothers are found in textual references.[11] Although the references refer mostly to the brothers named Bankura Ray, Chand Ray, Kalo Ray, and Photik Ray in locations other than Goalpara, it is in this village that the oral tradition connects and equates the deities as being multiforms of one deity. The idea of connectivity is not unique to Goalpara (cf. Bhaṭṭācārja, 1975: 632–633), but it is the only village I

know of that coherently brings together seven local forms. On the textual side, Manikram Ganguli's *Dharmamaṅgal* is perhaps the most explicit text mentioning numerous forms of Dharmarāj as one deity. Along with a number of other appellations, his text includes references to names we are now familiar with from Goalpara: Bankura Ray, Kalu Ray and Buṛo Ray (Bhaṭṭācārja, 1975: 626). Taken together, such references, though scattered, suggest the broad diversity and local variation of the composite Dharmarāj traditions of West Bengal. In the case of the names of the deity, the texts provide recurring references to deities that have individual identities in local contexts, but become equated on the textual level. However, in the Goalpara tradition, the deities are brought into relationship with the overarching figure of Dharmarāj on the local level as well. Some residents hold the opinion that these deities once had individual identities and were gradually incorporated into the overall image of Dharmarāj. Although the evidence is too scanty to make the claim outright, it might be the case that the *Dharmamaṅgal*s facilitated the process of unifying local heroes and deities in the figure of Dharmarāj (cf. also Blackburn, 1985). Dharmarāj's form itself, as described in the texts, also partially parallels the way Dharmarāj is represented as an aniconic and nonanthropomorphic figure in the contemporary context.

3. *Dharmarāj's form*: In the opening *Gītārambha* section of Ghanaram's text, the creation (*śṛiṣṭi*) of the universe is described (cf also Caṭṭopādhyāẏ, 1338BS). Dharmarāj is here equated with Brahma, the creator, and his formlessness (*nirañjan*) is emphasized constantly (Cakrabarttī, 1962: 11):

3. In the Dharma assembly knowledge can be understood.
1. There is one Brahma that is eternal,
2. Formless, without color.
3. Beyond qualities, the ultimate cause, full of emptiness.
. . .
3. There is one Brahma, Gosai (=Dharma).
1. Nirañjan is full of emptiness.
. . .
1. Who can explain the essence?
. . .
3. The Doer's form is incomparable.

References to formlessness such as these abound both in the narratives and liturgical texts concerning Dharmarāj. And even though the texts do not explicitly state that Dharma is to be worshipped in the form of a stone, as he is throughout rural West Bengal, it is possible that the deity's formless nature led to the custom of representing Dharmarāj in nonanthropomorphic form. A note of caution is necessary, however, since it is just as possible that the worship of Dharmarāj as a stone existed before any of the texts were written in his honor. This is especially viable in light of the fact that rock representations of deities are quite ancient (Das, 1983: 679–768). Whatever the case may be, Dharmarāj's empty form (*śūnya mūrti*) has been overemphasized in the historical reconstruction of the deity, for he is often depicted in both oral and written tradition as a human during his many appearances on earth. In order to accomplish the task of creation, for example, Dharma must manifest himself so that he may create the universe (Cakrabartti, 1962: 11):

3. [He] made manifest the seed of the universe in his body.
. . .
2. Totally born of one body,
3. The beauty of his figure split the darkness.

Elsewhere in the text, he is described as a Brahman mendicant who comes to earth 'in rapture' for the sake of his devotees (Cakrabartti, 1962: 33):[12]

1. Manifesting himself as an incomparable sannyasi,
2. The charm of his body was like a freshly washed flower.
1. A white umbrella over his head, a book of scriptures under his arm,
2. A bright mark on his forehead; his head covered with matted hair.
1. Clouds formed around him with the luster of lightning.
2. His clothes were bright red, his seat a lion's skin.

Dharmarāj's appearance in human form is a motif that often occurs in the texts and is also to be found in oral sources (cf. Korom, 2000).

It thus seems that Dharmarāj must manifest himself so that human beings can comprehend and worship him. As the passage cited above continues, Dharma appears on a road to a number of worshippers during his *gājan* (Chakrabartti, 1962: 33):

1. Charmingly decorated with *mandār*, jasmine, *ṣuthī* and magnolia flowers;

2. In the aroma of incense he says to the king, "Oh father!
1. All devotees are receptacles of the Lord's mercy."
2. Having performed *dharmapūjā*, they are walking on the path [when] they meet him.
1. A cane in his hand, a fan around his neck, a Dharma mark on his forehead;
2. His head decorated with the jasmine offered to the lotus feet of the Lord Dharma
1. Seeing the world-charming form of Gosai (=Dharma),
2. They all moved aside and performed obeisance.

In his human form, Dharma also speaks to devotees. For example, after Ranjabati's sacrifice, she is lying dead on the spike. Dharmarāj appears in the 'garb of a mendicant' (*sannyāsīr beśe*) and brings her back to life by lifting her off of the plank and applying vermilion paste to her wound. The use of vermilion to heal wounds acquired during the performance of austerities is present in other locations in West Bengal such as Beliator (Bankura District) and Kamarpara(Birbhum District), where piercing of the flesh is performed by *bhaktyā*s during the annual observance. Such practices are not performed in Goalpara, but vermilion is applied repeatedly to the *bāṇeśvar* during the rite. The paste is then transferred to the heads of devotees. In any case, Dharmarāj does not reveal himself to Ranjabati. Rather, he tests her devotion by questioning his own worship in the following dialogue (Cakrabartti, 1962: 103):

1. "Longing for Dharma, I
2. settled at Campai,
3. For a long time in the company of mendicants."
1. "Still then [there] was no mercy?
2. The infatuation for Dharma [is] terrible!
3. Why do [you] make trouble for nothing?
1. Serve other gods and goddesses!
2. [That] service will be fruitful.
3. Who the hell gave [you] such advice?
1. Why so much mortification for him,
2. Who has no rules,
3. Without qualities, formless?"
1. The queen answers, "Save Dharma,
2. I do not consider others [as] Lord."
3. [Feeling] blessed at this, the merciful one said,

1. "I am Dharma, the 'Master of Illusion.'
2. [Oh] child, ask for a boon."

Not being convinced that he is Dharmarāj, Ranjabati asks the mendicant for a miracle as proof, much in the same way that people in Goalpara cite miracles as proof of the deity's active (*jāgrata*) presence in the mundane world. Dharmarāj then makes a dead margosa tree blossom with fruits and flowers. She becomes convinced and he suddenly disappears. Ultimately, Ranjabati's encounter with Dharmarāj results in her attainment of the boon. We notice here the use of miracles as proof of Dharmarāj's worldly involvement in both oral stories (cf. Korom, 2000) from Goalpara and textual narratives.[13] Dharmarāj's sudden incursion into human affairs and equally sudden disappearance is a theme that we find in both written and oral traditions, and it plays an important role in the closure of a published synopsis of Goalpara's master narrative (Mitra, 1972: 126–127):

That's a story from a long time ago. A herdsman used to take one barber's cow to the bank of the Kopai river to graze. There, Dharma *ṭhākur*, taking the guise of a human, used to play with him. Grabbing the herdsman, he used to dunk him in the water and lift him [again]. Taking responsibility for watching over the cows, he used to send him off to eat. One day the master asks him, "whose care have you placed the cows in and come?" The herdsman explained, and the barber wanted to make the acquaintance of that man. At asking about an introduction, the man said, "I am Dharmarāj. Tell your master to worship me!" After relating that conversation, the barber expresses his weakness and utter poverty. At this, Dharmarāj says, "Don't worry about this, I'll make my own arrangements for worship services and drummers. In this region, however many *dharmapūjās* there may be, I want mine to be before them all." Saying this, *ṭhākur* took the dress of a Brahman and himself began to go from one Bayen (low-caste drummers) house to the next. Gradually the Bayens started to become willing. Going to Shiyan-Shukhbazaar village as a Brahman, he appeared on the day of *mukta snān* (liberation bath) and makes his request known that the Bayens of that place should come and play. The Brahman himself took a few drummers and returned. Entering the village and coming to a small pond, he said, "You all wait, I'll wash my face and hands and come." But *ṭhākur* never returned...

Dharmarāj's unpredictable coming and going, as well as his dialogues, tests, and miracles are all themes that we find in oral narratives. It is interesting to note that one of Dharmarāj's appellations in the textual tradition is *bhakter adhīn*, which can be translated loosely as "[he who is] dependent on his devotees." Dharmarāj must make these occasional forays into the human realm for his own sake as much as for the sake of his devotees. After all, the justification for the literary narratives is to establish the worship of Dharma on earth. This textual clue corresponds rather nicely with Robinson's well-taken point that devotees must, in a sense, create Dharmarāj by giving form to the formless one.[14] The theme of absence and presence is most apparent in the visitations made by Dharmarāj that are found in the Goalpara master narrative and the memorates discussed below.

4. *Personal encounters*: In an earlier discussion of personal experience narratives, I drew parallels between the oral tradition of recounting encounters with Dharmarāj and textual accounts (Korom, 2000). I recount one such narrative here to point out the strong thematic connection that textual personal experience narratives share with oral sources. The following translation is a published account of the eighteenth-century poet Rajaram Das' *ātmā kāhinī* (autobiography) embedded in his *Dharmamaṅgal* composition. Like so many other conversion accounts in this genre (cf. Smith, 1980: 180), the poet is walking along a road at night when he encounters Dharmarāj (Kilpatrick, 1983: 2):

13. I was not able to see the way due to the dense darkness. I thought meaningless thoughts and sat down in the middle of the road.
14. Distress arose immediately in (my) mind so I sat down. A compassionate (*dayada*) sannyasi came face to face with me.
15. He had a golden trident in his hand that glistened. He was clad in a tiger skin. His two eyes were red.
16. When I saw the matted hair on his head, I became afraid. I had it in mind to flee, but I did not possess the strength.

. . .

21. [Dharma says]... "By my command compose the Story of Dharma."

. . .

23. When the stars fell to earth, they twinkled. In a flash of lightning, I saw the earth.
24. The one who had bathed after the rite pervaded the Cosmic Emptiness and vanished. Before one's eyes the stars rose in the sky.

. . .

26. When I no longer saw the Sannyāsī, I cried "Alas, Alas!" He had descended in the middle of a field almost as in a dream.
27. I felt much distressed and struck a blow to my head with my hand.

The poet is then afflicted with a wound (*ghā*) of the foot for neglecting to compose the song for Dharma. Once again, after the passing of an unspecified period of time, Dharma appears to the poet and tells him that if he does not compose the poem he will die from the wound. Wayne Kilpatrick (1967) has pointed out structural and thematic parallels to this narrative in the *ātmā kāhinīs* of Rupram Cakrabarti and Manikram Ganguli (cf. also Korom, 2000: 41–45). Taken together, these narratives bear some striking resemblances to the personal experience memorates told by residents of Goalpara about numinous encounters with the deity.

In virtually all of the accounts, both oral and written, the encounter occurs in the dark as the individual is engaged in the act of walking.[15] Other themes, such as a strong bolt of light accompanying the deity's appearance are implicated in the liturgical texts and oral accounts as well. Further, oral accounts similarly describe the affliction and personal suffering experienced by Rajaram Das. The fear (*bhaẏ*) brought on by a numinous encounter with Dharmarāj described by Rajaram Das, Rupram, and other writers is quite apparent in the stories told by people in Goalpara. Writers of *Dharmamaṅgal*s clearly experienced something very similar to the descriptions given to me by Goalpara residents. Yet to make any concrete connection between the oral and written sources would be highly speculative. For example, signs of Dharmarāj's presence in the form of non-human agents are, to my knowledge, missing from textual accounts of personal encounters with the deity, as is the specific location. Most of the contemporary encounters with Dharmarāj take place on or near specific sites that are vividly described in oral narratives. Because the texts are translocal, they are less clear about the location of such events, giving narrative priority to the experience of the individual. The transformational power of place, however, must be considered as an important factor in interpreting contemporary stories (cf. Korom, 1997c). Because the oral accounts have a limited circulation and serve the needs of a specific community, the stories not only describe the experiences of individuals, but also reinforce the notion of local sacred space. It seems that the writers of the texts, on the other hand, do not give priority to the place of occurrence because they are not writing for a localized audience. One last feature that I might point out before moving on with my discussion is that textual encounters usually occur in the context of Dharmarāj giving an explicit command to a poet or character in the narrative, whereas the oral accounts usually do not contain this feature. With the exception of the Goalpara master narrative cited above, the reasons for Dharmarāj's visitations are often obscure in the stories I recorded.

The relationship between written and oral accounts of encounters with the deity is not to be found in historical connections, for there is no evidence for continuity. Rather, we see strong thematic elements running through these accounts that suggest a common source of inspiration and experience. Themes, then, provide the 'connectivity' discussed by Hanks as a central feature of textuality. One last area of relatedness between text and context is the social issue of castes implicated in the worship of Dharmarāj. Thematically, it seems apparent that Dharmarāj is strongly connected to lower castes in the texts. I have already shown this to be true in Goalpara (cf. Korom, 2001), but let us explore how one *Dharmamaṅgal* writer conveys the relationship.

5. *Dharmarāj's relationship to low Castes*: One of Dharmarāj's textual appellations is "friend of the poor" (*dīnbandhu*; cf. Cakrabarttī, 1962: 115, 324). The use of this term suggests an intimate connection between low castes and the deity. Low castes, for example, tend to refer to Dharmarāj as *bābā* (father) and *bhaktyā*s, themselves being mostly from the subordinate castes, speak of entering *dharma gotra* (the Dharma lineage) at the time of initiation. Ghanaram's text refers to the kinship metaphor quite explicitly when speaking of an encounter between Lausen and a flower seller (*mālī*; Cakrabarttī, 1962: 282):

manete bujhila raẏ mālī śuddha jāti
putrabhāb chila tāẏ dharmmer sebāti
Ray considered in mind that the flower seller caste [is] a pure [one].
[They] were like sons; that's why [they were] Dharma's servants.

If low castes are considered to be sons of Dharmarāj, then it makes good sense that they should address him as *bābā*. These features, along with Dom and Lohar (blacksmith) claims to the deity, imply both a kin- and caste-based relationship connecting Dharmarāj to lower strata groups. But the relationship between the deity, his hero, and the lower castes is also portrayed as a servant/master bond. I have already mentioned, for example, the Hari caste's involvement in the clearing of the forest at Campai above, and the servile role played by the Dom warriors employed by Lausen during his military campaigns is well known from the *maṅgal* literature. Elsewhere, the relationship is described in terms of a teacher or counselor to a student, as in one case below where Lausen and his brother enter the home of a blacksmith. Ghanaram describes the meeting "[as] a wise householder [to his] revered preceptor" (*jñānbān gṛihastha jeman gurudebe*; Cakrabarttī, 1962: 315). In any case, the notion of serving (*sebā karā*) the deity, whether as a child to a parent, a servant to a master, or a student to a teacher, is clear in the text and performed in ritual context. One could further speculate that the servile relationships portrayed in the texts also reflect a patron/client relationship paralleling the agricultural and economic interdependence between Brahmans and low castes in Goalpara (cf. Korom, 2001, Rohner & Chaki-Sircar, 1988: 15–37).

Although the *Dharmamaṅgals* were mostly written by Brahmans – who often hesitated to take on the task of composing for fear of losing their high-caste status (cf. Smith, 1980: 180) – they still reflect superior/subordinate and devotional relationships between low-caste occupational groups and the hero Lausen. Since Lausen is a direct link to the deity, it is safe to say that the texts portray a god who finds a place among the lower castes. In fact, a Bengali proverb states that Dharma always finds a home in the Dom quarter. Such ideas found in oral tradition are reflected in textual compositions as well. Take, for instance, the following encounter between Lausen and his twin brother Karpur with a Tamali (betal nut seller) on the road to Gaur to meet the king (Cakrabarttī, 1962: 206–207):

henakāle dharmmaputra lāusen rajā
sarobar salile karilyā snān pūjā
At this time the king Lausen, the son of Dharma,
Bathed and performed worship in the waters of the lake.
bidāẏer biṣaẏ balite haridāse
tāmalitanaẏ tabe sabinaẏe bhāṣe
When told about their departure, Haridas,
The son of a Tamali, then said politely,
mahāśaẏ paricaẏ kara ataḥpar
ki kāje kothāke jābe kon deśe ghar
"Sir, now introduce yourself.
Where will you go [and] for what purpose? Which country [is your] home?"
. . .
śuniyā praṇati kari kaẏ juṛi
padaraje pabitra hailya mor bāṛī
Hearing, offering homage, [Haridas] said with folded hands,
"My house has turned sacred by the dust of your feet."
. . .
ki kaba mahimā tār prabhu jār dharmma
"How do I express his greatness, whose lord is Dharma?"
eta śuni lāusen ānande bibhāl
maitra bhābe tāmalitanaẏ dila kol
Hearing this, Lausen, overjoyed,
Embraced the son of the Tamali as a friend.
śuno bandhu edeśe āmār tumi sakhā

jātāẏāte eikhāne more pābe dekhā
"Listen friend, in this country, you are my mate.
At this place, you will see me as [I] come and go."

This passage clearly shows Lausen's growing affiliation with lower castes as he proceeds on his mission to establish the worship of Dharma on earth. As Lausen and his twin continue their journey toward Gaur, they meet a blacksmith along the way, and an event much like the encounter with the Tamali is described by Ghanaram (Cakrabarttī, 1962: 314–315):

suśīl sajjan satya bujhi karmmakāre
paraṁ pīrite paricaẏ dila tāre
Understanding the blacksmith [to be] humble, honest [and] truthful,
[Lausen] introduced himself to him very warmly.
. . .
dharmmer kinkar āmi lausen nām
ei mor anuj abanī anupām
I [am] Dharma's servant, Lausen [by] name.
This [is] my brother, having no second on earth.
gauṛpati meso mor jāba tār ghar
śuni karmmakār kahe kari joṛ kar
The lord of Gaur is my uncle; [we] shall go to [his] house.
Hearing, the blacksmith said with folded hands.
āmi paricaẏ kari śuna sumahattva
karmmakārkūle janma nām lāudatta
"I introduce myself. Listen [oh] magnanimous one!
Born into the lineage of blacksmiths, [my] name is Laudatta."
eta śuni mitā bali rāẏ dila kol
nata haẏe kahe datta ānande bibhol
Hearing this, Ray offered him an embrace, saying friend.
Saluting, Datta said exhilarated in joy.
. . .
joṛhāte kahe kāli jeẏo rājpure
kṛipā kari āji esa āmār mandire
With folded hands [the blacksmith] said, "Go to the king's palace tomorrow
Kindly come to my temple today."
saṅgsār saphal hok tari bhabasindhu
sen bale tumi mitā mor ma
"Let [my] mundane life be successful; let [me] cross the ocean of existence."
Sen said, "You [are] my friend, a great mate."
atithir bhābe sen gelā tār bās
svagoṣṭhī sahit bale pūrṇa abhilā
Sen went to his house as a guest.
[The blacksmith] told his clan, "My desires have been fulfilled."[16]

Such correspondences are to be expected in the vernacular texts, since they grow out of model relationships developed in classical literature, such as in Valmiki's *Rāmāyaṇa*, where the divine hero Ram encounters the outcaste Guhak during his forest sojourn.[17] This statement, however, should not necessarily suggest that the theme filtered down from the written to the oral then back to the written. It would be difficult to determine which direction the influence went, since it is also possible that the classical types were gleaned from an oral base of storytelling. It might be the case that vernacular and classical texts both share features of a more general Indic consciousness. Whatever the reality of the situation may be, it is clear that the texts share such thematic linkages. But the most interesting parallel between the textual narrative and Goalpara practice is the implication of the cow-herding Goyala (Gopa) caste who take the surname Ghosh. Unlike their north Indian counterparts, Goyalas are considered to be an 'unclean' caste (Smith, 1980: 69; Risley, 1981.1: 289–290) in Bengal, but their population is considerably large in the area once known as Rarh.

The villain of this *maṅgal*'s narrative is Ichai Ghosh, Ranjabati's brother, who is a Goyala by birth. Because Ichai was not informed of Ranjabati's marriage to the aged king Karnasen, he goes to great lengths to destroy Lausen. Ichai is thus portrayed in the texts not only as a conniving villain out to ruin Lausen, but as an enemy of Dharmarāj. Versions of the Goalpara master narrative also present Goyalas in a role opposing the deity. They are cursed by Dharmarāj, and eventually are destroyed because of their transgression. Although people in Goalpara do not make the connection between the textual villain and the master narrative, this is an interesting aspect of textuality. It is a subtle way that the text is implicated in reality. Yet even though the general tone of most of the versions of the master narrative suggests the ruination of the Goyala caste, one version presents the transgression in a positive light. We also cannot forget that the important hereditary role of *mūl deyāśī* (head devotee) in the village is held by Sudarshan Ghosh, a member of the Sadgop sub-caste, a faction considered to be relatively purer than other Goyalas because they have become agriculturalists (cf. Smith, 1980: 69). Similar transformations occur in other areas of the district, where the role of Ichai Ghosh is transformed from villain to hero in folk ballads because he is perceived to be the upholder of the Goyala caste. He is praised in legend for establishing Gopabhum (the land of milkmen), a residential and administrative unit created solely for milkmen in Burdhwan District (Smith, 1980: 69; Sarkar, 1985: 76ff; 104–105). The following couplet from a local song, for example, laments Ichai's fate on the morning of his impending battle with Lausen by advising him not to go (Ghoṣ, 1976.1: 124)

śanibār saptamī sammukhe bā
āji bane jeonā re ichāi goẏāl
In [Lausen's] presence, on the morning [of] Saturday the seventh.
Don't go into the forest today, oh Ichai Goyal!

CONCLUSION

In the above section, I have suggested that there is a dialectical relationship between text and context on some level. That is, the text resonates with aspects of the context and vice versa. It would be far too speculative to make any concrete assertions connecting text and context without much more historical evidence, but my point has been to suggest that textuality is a factor worth considering when attempting to understand and explain a localized version of the Dharmarāj phenomenon. The relationships between textual narratives and contemporary performances are thematic in nature, and do not suggest a direct link or connection in Goalpara.[18] Such thematic associations, however, enable us to appreciate more fully not only the interaction between a text far removed from a localized context, but also the intricate ways that a modern set of ritual performances draw on other traditions to create innovative vehicles for devotion. Moreover, combining fieldwork with textual scrutiny allows us to appreciate Dharmarāj's multiple personalities as creator, virtuous king, master of destiny, shapeshifter, friend of the poor, and boon giver.

NOTES

[1] For overviews of the *Dharmamaṅgal* literature (see Bhaṭṭācārja, 1975: 725–776; Sen, 1975: 135–224; Dasgupta, 1976: 259–342; Kilpatrick, 1977: 85–99; Bandyopādhyāẏ, 1980: 311–352).

[2] Ghanaram's text is certainly the longest in the *Dharmamaṅgal* corpus, and is important for both its informational content and poetic use of language. Two printed editions exist, but I have been working with the Mahāpātra edition. Unless otherwise cited, this is the text used throughout. All translations here are my own.

[3] For a general overview of the phenomenon in Birbhum (see De, 1392BS; Mitra, 1972; Ghoṣ, 1976.1: 315–322). For a description of the rituals in Goalpara (see Korom, 1999).

[4] The word textuality has taken on two distinct senses in anthropological literature; the first deals with the postmodern concern for representation in ethnographic writing, while the second defines the term in a sociolinguistic fashion. I utilize the latter here (see below), but for an engaging review and critique of the former (see Howes, 1990).

[5] Hanks (1989: 96) has also come up with a useful typology for kinds of texts necessary to understand the tradition with which I am dealing here. His types are: (1) Co-text, "designates the accompanying discourse in a single text;" (2) Meta-text, "any discourse which refers to, describes, or frames the interpretation of text;" (3) Con-text, "the broader environment to which text responds and on which it operates;" (4) Pre-text, "whatever prepares the ground for or justifies the production or

interpretation of text;" (5) Sub-text, "whatever understandings or themes form the background or tacit dimensions of a text, inferable but not explicitly stated;" and (6) After-text, "the constellation of consequences and outcomes of producing, distributing or receiving a text, whether foreseen or not." Most important for my considerations here is his notion of 'sub-text.'

[6] This is a point already made by Milton Singer. Singer states that "contextual studies ... help in essential ways to locate and specify the meaningful content of a religious system depicted by the textual studies of the historian of religion, the philosopher, and the philologist" (1961: 274).

[7] One could, for example, argue that since ritual practices are found in the texts, they must have existed prior to the writing of the text. Or conversely, that the portrayal of rites in the texts led to the establishment of the practices. Such arguments, however, give precedence to one over the other on speculative grounds only. Bell (1987) has recently pointed out that the academic discourse on theory may itself be at the root of the problem by making an artificial division between thought (i.e., myth) and action (i.e., ritual). It would be much more reasonable to assume that both texts and rites existed simultaneously as the tradition developed.

[8] We can assume that the name Ramai Pandit here refers to the tenth-century author of the *Śūnya Purāṇ* discussed in the introduction and, according to the texts, legendary founder of the Dharmarāj *pūjā* tradition. See Sen (1911: 30–37).

[9] The enactment of impalement is much clearer in other villages in West Bengal, such as in nearby Kamarpara, where a *bhaktyā* who has taken a vow lies on a human sized spiked plank and is paraded around the village for hours before he is finally brought to the local Dharmarāj temple.

[10] The mention of Ramai Paṇdit holding a manual (*paddhati*) in hand and reading the ritual rules to the worshippers suggests the liturgical use of the *Dharmapūjā Bidhān* during Goalpara's annual event. It would be difficult to say, however, to what degree the text has shaped ritual practices, since versions of the Goalpara master narrative also describe and explain which rituals must be performed. Further, most of the extremely detailed rules in the manuals are not followed today. Ghanaram, for example, mentions no less than 28 items from the manual which must be used by Ranjabati for the performance of her austerities to Dharmarāj (cf. Cakrabarttī, 1962: 90), most of which are not used in Goalpara, but might be found randomly at other sites throughout Bengal.

[11] Most of the references cluster around the figures of Bankura Ray, Chand Ray, Kalo Ray, and Photik Ray. Bankura Ray, for example, is mentioned in the *Dharmamaṅgals* of Sitaram (17th century), Prabhuram (19th century) and Manikram Ganguli, where Dharmarāj appears and equates himself with Bankura Ray, saying "For the sake of the universe (*biśver kāraṇ*) I am Bankura Ray." See Sen, 1975: 179; 199; 206 respectively. Manikram's text is also important because in it he equates most of the well-known manifestations of Dharmarāj. See Bhaṭṭācārja (1975: 626). There is no evidence to suggest that Chand Ray is a deified version of a historical figure of the same name who was murdered in East Bengal during 1593 (cf. Majumdar, 1943.2: 210), but Hridayram Sau, an 18th-century *Dharmamaṅgal* poet does mention the deity as the Dharma *ṭhākur* of Kharugram in Burdwan District. See Sen (1975: 200). Kalo Ray is well known in all of the *Dharmamaṅgal*s as the Dom general who is recruited by the hero Lausen to aid him in his military campaigns. Ghanaram, for example describes him as a servant of Yama, the god of death, "fat, hairy, with moustache, awful to look at" (*kāl moṭā lom gõp ghor darśan*). See Cakrabarttī (1962: 346). His identity is, perhaps, clearer than any of the other manifestations, and will be discussed below. Photik Ray is more obscure but is known elsewhere as *sphoṭikrāy̐* (or *sphoṭikeśvar* = crystal god). See Mitra (1972: 70, 189, 198) and the comments in Das (1983: 679). Sarkar, (1985: 120) mentions an unidentified Dharma slab made of 'transparent rock' in Tantipara, Birbhum District.

[12] Ghanaram makes this quite clear elsewhere, when he states (Cakrabarttī, 1962: 29):

nirākār gosā̃i ākār bkaktibeśe
karile ekānta bhakti pāi anāẏāse

The formless Gosvami takes corporeal form for the sake of devotion,
So that devotion can be performed with ease.

[13] Miracles occur quite frequently in the *Dharmamaṅgals*. Aside from Ranjabati's miraculous conception recounted above, the hero Lausen's resurrection of a dead boy (Cakrabarttī, 1962: 271ff) and a rogue elephant (Cakrabarttī, 1962: 340) as well as his alchemical transformation of cowrie shells to gold (Cakrabarttī, 1962: 289) with the aid of Dharmarāj can be cited. Also, Lausen's brother Karpur is miraculously born from camphor flowing from Dharma's lips as he smiles (Cakrabarttī, 1962: 131).

[14] "Dharma requires his devotees to complete him as a deity. He is activated through their interactions with him; they realize and actualize the god. They lend form to the Formless one" (Robinson, 1980: 71).

[15] This, of course, does not apply to the dream visitations described orally by villagers and in written form by Khelaram, but it is noteworthy that the dreaming occurs at night.

[16] Another blacksmith is implicated earlier on in the text, when he is asked to forge Lausen's magical sword and shield. See Cakrabarttī (1962: 167–191).

[17] Indeed, Ghanaram, like other *Dharmamaṅgal* poets, utilizes classical stories to frame and justify his own narrative. Thus we read in Ghanaram's text about Ram's encounter with the *caṇḍāl* Guhak as a framing device for Lausen's own encounter with the betal nut seller (Cakrabarttī, 1962: 206–207).

[18] The relationship between the *Dharmamaṅgal* texts and modern ritual contexts is much more concrete in villages such as Kamarpara or Baruipur, where the ritualized singing of portions of the epic actually accompany rituals being performed that enact the text. On this facet of the *pūjā* in the village of Baruipur (see Robinson, 1980: 76–175).

REFERENCES

Bandyopādhyāẏ, A. (1980). *Bāṅglā Sāhityer Itibritta*, Vol. 3. Kalikātā: Maḍārṇ Buk Ejensi.

Bandyopādhyāẏ, N. (ed.) (1323BS). *Dharmmapūjā Bidhān*. Kalikātā: Baṅgīẏa Sāhitya-pariṣat.

Bell, C. (1987). Discourse and dichotomies: The structure of ritual theory. *Religion* **17**, 95–118.

Bhattacharya, K. (1986): Bridge across castes – Dharmaraj. *Journal of the Indian Anthropological Society* **21**, 177–188.

Bhaṭṭācārja, A . (1975). *Bāṅglā Maṅgal Kābyer Itihās*. Kalikātā: Mukharji eṇḍ koṅ.

Blackburn, S.H. (1985). Death and deification: Folk cults in hinduism. *History of Religions* **24**(3), 255–274.

Blackburn, S.H. (1988). *Singing of Birth and Death: Texts in Performance*. Philadelphia: University of Pennsylvania Press.

Blackburn, S.H. & Joyce B.F. (1989). Introduction. In S.H. Blackburn et al. (eds.), *Oral Epics in India* (pp. 1–11). Berkeley: University of California Press.

Briggs, C. L. (1988). *Competence in Performance: The Creativity of Tradition in Mexicano Verbal Art*. Philadelphia: University of Pennsylvania Press.

Cakrabarttī, G. (1962). *Śrīdharmmamaṅgal*. Edited by Pīyuṣ Kānti Mahāpātra. Kalikātā: Kalikātā Biśvabidyālaẏ.

Chakrabarti, K. (2001). *Religious Process: The Purāṇas and the Making of a Regional Tradition*. New Delhi: Oxford University Press.

Caṭṭopādhyāy̌, B.K. (1338BS). Dharmamaṅgale Śriṣṭitattva o Dharmmadebatā Prācinatā. In N. Laha (ed.), *Haraprasād Saṃbarddhan Lekhāmālā* (pp. 94–111). Calcutta: Sāhitya Pariṣad.

Das, R.P. (1983). Some remarks on the bengali deity dharma: Its cult and study. *Anthropos*, **78**, 661–700.

Dasgupta, S. (1946). *Obscure Religious Cults as a Background to Bengali Literature*. 3rd ed. Calcutta: Firma KLM Private Limited, 1976 (3rd ed.).

De, M. (1989). Bīrbhūmer Dharmarāj. *Ānandabājār Patrikā* **1**(3), 38–41.

Dimock, E.C. (1976). A theology of the repulsive: some reflections on sitala and other mangals. In M. Davis (ed.), *Bengal: Studies in Literature, Society and History* (pp. 69–73). East Lansing: Asian Studies Center, Michigan State University.

Ghoṣ, B. (1976). *Paścimbaṅger Saṅgskṛiti*, Vols. 1–3. Kalikātā: Prakāś Bhaban.

Hanks, W.F. (1989). Text and textuality. *Annual Review of Anthropology* **18**, 95–127.

Hiltebeitel, A. (1991). *The Cult of Draupadī*. Vol. 2: On Hindu Ritual and the Goddess. Chicago: University of Chicago Press.

Honko, L. (1964). Memorates and the study of folk beliefs. *Journal of the Folklore Institute* , **1**(1–2), 5–19.

Howes, D. (1990). Controlling textuality: a call for a return to the senses. *Anthropologica*, **32**, 55–73.

Ingarden, R. (1973). *The Literary Work of Art: An Investigation on the Borderlines of Ontology, Logic and Theory of Literature*. Translated by G. Grabowicz. Evanston: Northwestern University Press.

Johnstone, B. (1990). *Stories, Community, and Place: Narratives from Middle America*. Bloomington: Indiana University Press.

Kilpatrick, G.W. (1967). 'Two autobiographical accounts from middle bengali literature. In E.C. Dimock (ed.), *Bengal: Literature and History* (pp. 47–66). East Lansing: Asian Studies Center, Michigan State University.

Kilpatrick, G.W. (1977). *A Bengal Cosmogony: Some Creation Myths in the Literature of the Dharma Cult with Transliterated Bengali Texts and English Translations*. M.A. Thesis. Department of South Asian Languages and Civilizations, University of Chicago.

Kilpatrick, G.W. (1983). Rajaram Das' middle bengali account of his conversion to the dharma cult. In R. Langsten (ed.), *Research on Bengal: Proceedings of the 1981 Bengal Studies Conference* (pp. 1–6). East Lansing: Asian Studies Center, Michigan State University.

Korom, F.J. (1990). Review of criminal gods and demon devotees: essays on the guardians of popular hinduism. *Karnataka Folklore Newsletter*, **2**(4), 16–17.

Korom, F.J. (1997a). Editing Dharmaraj: academic genealogies of a bengali folk deity. *Western Folklore*, **56**(1), 51–77.

Korom, F.J. (1997b). Oral exegesis: local interpretations of a bengali folk deity. *Western Folklore*, **56**(2), 153–173.

Korom, F.J. (1997c). Language, belief, and experience in bengali folk religion. In E. Franco & K. Preisendanz (eds.), *Beyond Orientalism: The Work of Wilhelm Halbfass and its Impact on Indian and Cross-Cultural Studies* (pp. 567–586). Amsterdam: Poznan Rodopi B.V.

Korom, F.J. (1999). To be happy: ritual, play, and leisure in the bengali Dharmarāj *pūjā*. *International Journal of Hindu Studies*, **3**(2), 113–164.

Korom, F.J. (2000). Close encounters of the numinous kind: personal experience narratives and memorates in Goalpara, West Bengal. *South Asia Research*, **20**(1), 19–45.

Korom, F.J. (2001). Liminality and communitas reconsidered: the politics of caste and ritual in Goalpara, West Bengal. *Acta Ethnographica Hungarica*, **46**(1–2), 105–130.

Langellier, K.M. (1989). Personal narratives: perspectives on theory and research. *Text and Performance Quarterly*, **9**(4), 243–276.
Lutgendorf, P. (1991). *The Life of a Text: Performing the Rāmcaritmānas of Tulsidas*. Berkeley: University of California Press.
Mahapatra, P.K. (1972). The Cult of Dharma Thakur, *Folklore* (Calcutta), **13**(2), 41–70.
Maity, P.K. (1971). Dharma thakur of bengal and his association with human fertility, *Folklore* (Calcutta) **12**(3), 81–94.
Majumdar, R.C. (ed.) 1943. *The History of Bengal*, Vol. 1. Dacca: The University of Dacca Press.
Mayūrbhaṭṭa (1381BS). *Dharmmamaṅgal*. Edited by Akhṣaẏkumār Kayāl Citrā Deb. Kalikātā: Ji. Bharadvāj āṇḍkoṅ.
Mitra, A. (1972). *Rāṛher Saṅgskṛiti o Dharmaṭhākur*. Kalikātā: Pharmā Ke. El. Mukhopādhyāẏ.
Mitra, Ā (ed.) (1968). *Paścimbaṅger Pūjā-Parbaṇ o Melā*. Kalikātā: Anu Pres.
Peacock, J.L. (1984). Religion and life history: an exploration in cultural psychology. In E.M. Bruner (ed.), *Text, Play, and Story: The Construction and Reconstruction of Self and Society* (pp. 94–116). Washington, D.C.: American Ethnological Society.
Ramāī Paṇḍit (1977). *Śūnyapurāṇ*. Edited by Bhaktimādhab Caṭṭopādhyāẏ. Kalikātā: Pharmā Ke. El. Em.
Ricoeur, P. (1971). What is a text? explanation and interpretation. In D. Rasmussen (ed.), *Mythic-Symbolic Language and Philosophical Anthropology* (pp. 135–152). The Hague: Martinus Nijhoff.
Risley, H.H. (1981). *The Tribes and Castes of Bengal*. Vols 1–2. Calcutta: Firma KLM Private Limited.
Robinson, S.P. (1980). *The Dharmapuja: A Study of Rites and Symbols Associated with the Bengali Deity Dharmaraj*. Ph.D. Dissertation. Department of South Asian Languages and Civilizations. University of Chicago.
Rocher, L. (1986). *The Purāṇas*. Wiesbaden: Otto Harrassowitz.
Rohner, R.P. & Manjusri C.-S. (1988). *Women and Children in a Bengali Village*. Hanover: University Press of New England.
Sarkar, R.M. (1985). *Regional Cults and Rural Traditions: An Interacting Pattern of Divinity and Humanity in Rural Bengal*. New Delhi: Inter-India Publications.
Sen, D.C. (1911). *History of Bengali Language and Literature*. Calcutta: University of Calcutta Press.
Sen, S. (1960). *History of Bengali Literature*. New Delhi: Sahitya Akademi.
Sen, S. (1975). *Bāṅglā Sāhityer Itihās*. Vol. 1. Barddhamān: Sāhitya Sabhā.
Singer, M. (1961). Text and context in the study of contemporary hinduism. *Adyar Library Bulletin*, **25**, 274–303.
Smith, W.L. (1980). *The One-Eyed Goddess. A Study of the Manasā Maṅgal*. Stockholm: Almqvist and Wiskell International.
Smith, W.L. (1982). The celestial village. the divine order in bengali myth. *Temenos*, **18**, 69–81.
Wittgenstein, L. (1976). *Philosophical Investigations*. Oxford: Basil Blackwell.
Zbavitel, D. (1976). *Bengali Literature*. Wiesbaden: Otto Harrassowitz.

Department of Religion
Boston University
745 Commonwealth Avenue
Boston, MA 02215
USA
E-mail: korom@bu.edu

JOHN TABER

THE SIGNIFICANCE OF KUMĀRILA'S PHILOSOPHY

Among the many important contributions of Wilhelm Halbfass to the study of Indian thought one must certainly count his essay "*Kumārila* on *Ahiṃsā* and Dharma." In this work, which first appeared in 1983 as a chapter in *Studies in Kumārila and Śaṅkara* and which was later reprinted under the title "Vedic Apologetics, Ritual Killing, and the Foundations of Ethics" in *Tradition and Reflection* (1991), Halbfass discusses central aspects of *Mīmāṃsā* ethics, specifically, *Kumārila's* views on the sources of our knowledge of right and wrong. This constituted a welcome and appropriate correction in *Mīmāṃsā* studies. Previous work on *Kumārilabhaṭṭa* had focussed almost exclusively on his epistemology, metaphysics, and philosophy of language; yet, certainly, ethics—more precisely, *dharma*—was the matter of greatest significance for *Kumārila,* as for *Mīmāṃsā* in general—that which his writings are ultimately dedicated to explicating and defending. All other aspects of his system can be seen as subordinate to this topic. *Mīmāṃsā* is, after all, as the first *sūtra* of the *Mīmāṃsāsūtra* announces, an "inquiry into *dharma*" (*dharmajijñāsā*). Moreover, Halbfass's study is concerned primarily with meta-ethical questions in *Mīmāṃsā*, that is, questions relating to the principles by which moral norms are justified, and this, too, called for an adjustment in our understanding of *Mīmāṃsā* and, more generally, Indian philosophy; for the view has often been expressed that the meta-ethical dimension is missing from Indian thought.

In this article I wish to reflect on the results of Halbfass's exploration of this aspect of *Kumārila's* thought from a philosophical, as opposed to a historical, perspective. That is to say, I wish to consider what significance *Kumārila's* views on the nature of *dharma* and its sources might have for us *now.* To some readers, the suggestion that *Kumārila's* thought might have any bearing on contemporary, Western philosophical concerns will initially seem implausible, since our historical situation, certainly, must be quite different from *Kumārila's* (though we do not really know what *Kumārila's* was); but I hope that what follows will bear this suggestion out.

I shall begin by summarizing the most important ideas of *Kumārila* to which Halbfass draws our attention.

In the context of discussing the *śyena* ritual, in the *Codanāsūtra* chapter of his *Ślokavārttika, Kumārila* considers the charge raised by heterodox thinkers that any killing, even that which occurs during a Vedic sacrifice, is *adharma.* This he strenuously denies. The Veda itself is the only criterion of right and wrong. What is prescribed by the Veda is right; what is prohibited is wrong (242c-243a); what is neither is neither.[1] There are no other, independent criteria.[2] We cannot *see* at the time a sacrifice is performed that such an act is not beneficial. (MS 1.1.2 defines *dharma* as "a beneficial purpose or thing [*artha*] indicated by an injunction," *codanālakṣaṇo 'rtho dharma.*[3]) Certainly, the beneficial nature of an act, which has to do, strictly, with its future effect on the agent, is not something accessible to perception (233). Nor can one reliably *infer* that, because an act causes pain to another being, it will eventually cause pain to oneself (234c-237b). Cause and effect do not always resemble one another. In general, rather, the result of a particular action, also, is whatever the Veda says it is (237c-238b). Principles such as "being helpful or agreeable" (*anugraha*) to another person or the "crying out of the heart," i.e., of one's conscience (*hṛdayakrośana*) are not reliable guides to right and wrong, either. They would not serve to tell us, e.g., that illicit sex is bad or the muttering of prayers (*japa*) good (243c-246b), and Mlecchas could use them to justify their customs as *dharma,* too (247c-248b)!

The opponent objects that certainly the Veda intends to teach in general that injury to living beings is bad.[4] Surely, its explicit condemnation in certain cases—most notably, the killing of a Brahmin—is meant to extend to others (249c-250b). But *Kumārila* denies that scripture asks us to attempt to ascertain the underlying principles of its prescriptions and prohibitions.[5] Everything depends on the details. Does a *Śūdra* go to hell by drinking liquor? No; for that is prohibited only for the higher castes. Or would a result accrue to a Brahmin or a *Kṣatriya* through the *vaiśyastoma*? No; for that rite is prescribed only for *Vaiśyas*. Would one derive any benefit by performing an *iṣṭi* on the fifth day of the month (when it is prescribed for either the new or the full moon), or the *agnihotra* (which is to be carried out at sunrise) in the middle of the day (252c-254b)?! An effect will follow only from the kind of action that scripture indicates as having the capacity to produce it (254c-255b). While, indeed, a general notion of the wrongness of injury to living creatures may be conveyed by prohibitions such as that against killing a Brahmin, it will be set aside by any specific injunction to perform a certain sacrifice that involves killing (255c-256b).

Halbfass summarizes on the basis of this and other passages from the *Ślokavārttika* and *Tantravārttika*:

> *Ahiṃsā* is not a rule which in itself alone would be "rationally" or "morally" self-evident; it is itself valid only insofar as it is scripturally enjoined. And even in this sense and on this basis, *Kumārila* does not like to present it as a universal, *prima facie* valid rule which would have to be modified by a specific clause such as the traditional *anyatra tīrthebhyaḥ*, "elsewhere than at sacred places," i.e., "if not during rituals". . . . In this as well as in other cases, "morality" is derived from "legality." The moral claims of *ahiṃsā* are rooted in scriptural prohibitions. Such heretics as the Buddhists and the Jainas, who advocate *ahiṃsā* against the Vedic ritual injunctions, owe the basis and starting point of such anti-Vedic teachings to the Veda itself. Only, they have misused or misunderstood the Veda, have falsely universalized its prohibitions and have disregarded the internal differentiation of its *dharma*. . . . (1991, pp. 95 f.)

Thus, we could say, *Kumārila* attempts to remove *dharma* from a sphere of discourse that is subject to the vicissitudes of human reasoning and feeling. The Veda is the sole, absolute authority in regard to *dharma*. If other principles are recognized alongside it—say, that of providing benefit to others—then even the absurd practices of the so-called *Saṃsāramocakas*, who claimed to help other people by torturing and killing them and thus liberating them from their bad karma, could be defended as *dharma*![6]

> *Kumārila* is aware of the possibilities of rationalizing *hiṃsā* as well as *ahiṃsā*. He knows about the temptations to justify a tradition in terms of its common familiarity (*lokaprasiddhi*), its acceptance by "important" (or numerous) people (*mahājanaparigṛhītatva*), its accordance with ancestral habits (*pitrādyanugama*). But he also knows that others can claim these same criteria, related to other "continents," areas outside India, in support of their own views. . . . To defend the Vedic *dharma*, including its animal sacrifices, just in these terms would amount to abandoning it. It has to be accepted in its own right, without relying on external, merely human and potentially relative standards. Only the Veda itself can uphold the identity of its *dharma*. Only the Vedic injunction (*codanā*) can save *dharma* from the "jaws of non-being" (*abhāvavaktra*). (1991, p. 111)

In sum, we can say that the means of true knowledge of right and wrong for *Kumārila* is not reason or conscience or any other human faculty—certainly, not perception!—but only scripture, specifically, the Veda. Right and wrong are not reducible to any more fundamental principle than that of being prescribed or prohibited by the Veda. While the *Mīmāṃsā* texts suggest that the Veda prescribes acts *because* they are conducive to one's "welfare"[7]—that is to say, the acts are not ends in themselves[8]—nevertheless, it is only the Veda that can tell us what such acts are. For all practical purposes, then, the approval or disapproval of the Veda is the only criterion of right and wrong.

The modern reader will initially find such a view unacceptable, primarily because it would appear to put an end to discourse about good and bad. We may not be confident that we can ever conclusively determine what good and bad are, but we are convinced that our humanity is somehow essentially bound up with the attempt to find out.[9] Are, indeed, human reason and feeling completely unreliable when it comes to matters of right action? Can we not learn to employ reason correctly in matters of morality; can't our intuitions and sentiments be educated and cultured? And can't we, subjecting moral judgements to criticism, correct them? Must we indeed renounce the possibility of basic, interculturally shared principles of moral evaluation, of joint reflection about norms on the level of fundamental principles? Must we resort to an incomprehensible, dictatorial source of ethical judgements, to deliverances *ex cathedra*? For such seems to be *Kumārila's* proposal.

One must bear in mind, however, that at the basis of *Kumārila's* insistence on the absolute, exclusive authority of the Veda with regard to *dharma* is the conviction that *humans simply cannot know independently what is right or wrong.* This conviction is based in turn on certain essential epistemological doctrines, first of all, a staunch empiricism. *Kumārila—Mīmāṃsā* in general—holds that all knowledge other than that gained from scripture is derived from sense perception,[10] while sense perception occurs only when a sense faculty is in actual contact with an object (MS 1.1.4; ŚV *Pratyakṣa* 18, 20). Thus, there is no human knowledge of the supersensible, of things in the future or beyond this physical world. *In particular, there is no direct human knowledge of what effect an action will have at a future time—perhaps after death—hence, of its value for the agent, i.e., whether it is ultimately conducive to heaven or prosperity.*[11] In this connection *Kumārila* explicitly denies the possibility of supernormal, yogic cognition (ŚV *Pratyakṣa* 26-32). More importantly, he denies the possibility of human omniscience. The Buddhists and Jainas appealed to the latter in grounding the authority of their own scriptures, arguing that we know that they contain true statements about the supersensible, in particular, about *dharma*, because their authors (the Buddha and the Jina, respectively) were omniscient beings. *Kumārila's* critique of this doctrine, one of the most polemical passages of his entire corpus,[12] is based on a hard-nosed empiricist denial of any human cognitive capacities other than those with which we are familiar in common experience.[13] *Kumārila*, in fact, is skeptical, even cynical, about human testimony in general. "Men are always for the most part speakers of untruth," he says at one point in this discussion (ŚV *Codanā* 144ab). No human statement can stand on its own but must always be supported by a judgement that the witness is at least in a position to know that of which she speaks (i.e., is in possession of a *mūlapramāṇa*[14]). Such a requirement, certainly, can never be met in the case of testimony about the supersensible.

How, then, can the Veda tell us about the supersensible, about *dharma*, if human testimony cannot? This is where the most well-known, indeed notorious, epistemological doctrine of *Mīmāṃsā*, the theory of the intrinsic validity of cognitions, comes in. According to this doctrine a cognition is true unless and until it is in some way shown to be false. Every cognition (and not just true ones—a common misconstrual of the theory) occurs with a sense of conviction, a sense that matters really are as it represents them as being. If it is not overturned either by a different cognition which declares matters to be in fact otherwise or by an awareness that there exists some "defect" in the circumstances that gave rise to the cognition—the object is very small or far away, the sense organ diseased, the mind distracted or tired, etc.—then it is true for us. Now the Veda conveys definite notions of what actions should and should not be done (with a view to a future result) which are not overturned in either of these two ways. Being about *dharma*, there are no other *valid* cognitions derived from other *pramāṇas* that contradict them. The statements of the Buddha or the Jina may contradict them, but, as we saw, they lack authority. And insofar as the Veda is eternal and authorless (*apauruṣeya*), there is no possibility of a defect in the source of these notions. Hence, they are valid for us in a way that no other statements about right and wrong can be.

This is one of the central ideas, if not the most central idea, of Brahmanical orthodoxy—that only an eternal, authorless statement can reliably inform us of the transcendent. It also, of course, finds application in *Vedānta* thought: only the *Vedavākya* can convey valid knowledge of the Absolute; it alone, and not any result of reasoning or any teaching originating from a person, no matter how revered or exalted, can evoke enlightenment (cf. Halbfass [1991, pp. 131-204]). This idea accounts for aspects of Indian philosophical thought to which many have pointed in distinguishing it from European philosophy, in particular its close connection with religious discourse and its lack of commitment to "pure theory"—matters upon which Halbfass reflected throughout *India and Europe* (see especially pp. 263-286). It also underlies the rejection of experience as a source of truths about ultimate reality, which, once again, Halbfass treated as an important orthodox tendency, in contrast to so-called Neo-Hindu thought (1988, pp. 378-402). Above all, however, it is important to see that this idea itself is rationally conceived and defended. It rests on a moderate skepticism, specifically, skepticism about the ability of humans to know the supersensible through their own faculties, which in turn is based on empiricism, as we saw. As a theory of epistemic justification, moreover, the theory of intrinsic validity is quite defensible—contrary to the judgement of most modern scholars.[15] It resembles in many respects recent proposals in contemporary philosophy, devised by Christian "analytic" philosophers seeking an "anti-evidentialist" theory of knowledge that can serve as the ground of the rationality of religious belief (Alston [1991]; Plantinga [1993]). In the *Mīmāṃsā* defense of the exclusive authority of the Veda in regard to *dharma*, rather, it is specifically the premise of the eternality of the Veda that is most questionable and in the end will render the argument, for most people, unacceptable.

It would seem that the most appropriate characterization of *Kumārila's* ethics, for our purposes, is "traditionalist." It is a version of the view that what is good or bad is what tradition approves or disapproves. To be sure, *Kumārila* distinguishes the Veda from mere tradition. The Veda is eternal; tradition originates from humans. Simply the fact that an action conforms to what one's forefathers did or is accepted by distinguished people is insufficient to consider it *dharma*. That would be to resort to "mere faith," for in fact everyone everywhere does what one's forefathers did. It would be like saying, "It is valid because it is what *we* do."[16] Moreover, there could be traditions of ignorance as well as of knowledge; there could be a tradition of one blind man telling the next blind man how things look.[17] Nevertheless, the modern reader cannot but feel that *Kumārila*, in defending the authority of the Veda over against the teachings of *Sāṃkhya*, Yoga, *Pāñcarātra*, *Śaivism*, and Buddhism, is simply insisting—in spite of his claim that the Veda is eternal and not a tradition—on the priority of what he considers a more honorable, ancient tradition over newer ones. The Veda is true, in other words, because it is the *authentic* tradition of the *Āryas*. The other "traditions" represent innovation and independent speculation. They derive from people whose characters and motives can be questioned. *They are false simply because they contradict what the culture as a whole has believed and done from time immemorial.* The attempt to ground this preference on the claim that the Veda is not, strictly, a tradition at all but an eternal, authorless teaching must, from the modern point of view, appear as an ingenious strategy, to be sure, but nevertheless as something which, as *Kumārila* himself says at one point in his critique of the Buddhist doctrine of omniscience, only a true believer could take seriously (ŚV *Codanā* 138-39). One must also keep in mind that when *Kumārila* says that the Veda is eternal he does not mean that it exists independently of its transmission by humans. He does not give voice to the belief of *Bhartṛhari* that the Veda, existing as *śabda* and contained in seed form in the *praṇava*, is ultimately identical with the Absolute (Aklujkar [1991, p. 5]). Rather, he means only that it has been forever handed down from one generation to the next. We know that the present generation learned it from the previous generation and the previous generation learned it from the next previous one, and we have no reason to believe that there ever was a beginning to this process (ŚV *Vākya* 365 ff.).[18]

Let us consider, then, for the purpose of reflecting philosophically on *Kumārila's* ideas in a contemporary context, that *Kumārila* holds right and wrong to be what tradition prescribes and prohibits, "tradition" being any teaching sufficiently ancient not to be identified as originating from a particular source.[19] This is perhaps the most widely held of all ethical theories, but it has rarely been philosophically defended. Philosophical ethics, rather, has always tended in the other direction, away from a traditionalist ethics toward the elucidation of "deeper" principles which can be used to question and critique tradition. Indeed, independence from tradition is often considered to be of the very essence of *philosophical* ethical reflection. *Kumārila*, therefore, is unique in offering a reasoned justification of tradition as an ethical criterion. He provides a justification, not in the sense of an explanation of why it should be the standard of right and wrong, but in the sense of why it unavoidably is. This justification, as I would reconstruct it, is essentially as follows: the norms handed down by one's culture serve as valid standards of right and wrong simply because they are ineluctable. We cannot but think in terms of them when reflecting on ethical matters; as Kant would say, they appear to us as (synthetic) a priori principles which are the conditions of any possible experience of value. And they have this ineluctable quality, because the sense of conviction with which they are originally received—when they are first taught to us—never diminishes, while all other norms are questionable. They are not negated by judgements deriving from human beings consulting their reason, conscience, sentiments, or whatever; for we know that humans are fallible in the use of these faculties. Moreover, it is not even clear that we can ever discern what one *ought* to do by means of such faculties. The judgements of tradition retain the validity with which they are originally received, we could say, because they have the appearance of impersonal objectivity. They lack the aspect of contingency that attaches to other judgements. They are, simply, "there" as seemingly timeless commands, ascribable to no individual or group of individuals but part of the common property, even the very essence, of the culture.

In order to appreciate the force of this theory we must reconsider the doctrine of intrinsic validity upon which it is ultimately grounded. According to that theory,[20] all cognitions have *prima facie* validity; they present themselves as true when they occur. A visual perception of a book on the desk in front of me does not have to be verified in turn by other cognitions in order to be valid for me. It stands on its own as a valid cognition without the support of extrinsic evidence. Such cognitions—cognitions which we are spontaneously inclined to accept as true and which have not in any way been falsified—form the foundation of all that we know.[21] Indeed, knowledge must begin somewhere, with certain cognitions the validity of which is taken for granted. The notion that we are entitled to consider a cognition true only if we have confirmed it by means of another cognition leads inevitably to a regress *ad infinitum*. Now, not only a perceptual cognition, but any cognition of one of the recognized *pramāṇas*, including testimony (*śabda*), can be valid in the suggested way. Just as I am naturally inclined to consider true a visual perception of a book in front of me unless and until it is falsified, so am I naturally inclined to consider true a cognition evoked by a statement made by another person.[22] Of course, we learn through experience to restrict our acceptance of testimony. We learn that certain people, certain circumstances, and certain subject matters are likely to render statements false. As mentioned above, *Kumārila* holds that in general in order for human testimony to be valid (for us) we must be aware that the witness is in possession of a *mūlapramāṇa*, a means of knowledge which serves as the legitimate basis of her belief—in other words, that she is at least in a position to know that of which she speaks (ŚV *Codanā* 102 ff.)

A statement that one ought or ought not do a certain thing that is received, not from a particular person or group of people, but from the culture as a whole—that is, it is not only articulated from time to time by certain individuals but is brought home in a thousand other ways by the discourse, practices, and habits of the society in which one lives—such a statement will, like any other, have initial validity for us; for, once again, we are so constituted that if we are told something definitely and unambiguously, we believe it. (Were we not constituted in this way, Thomas Reid claims, we would perish at an early age.[23]) And its validity will not be sublated, first, because no belief deriving from another source will have the power to contradict it. Any counterstatement that one should or shouldn't do something else that has an identifiable human source will be immediately questionable. How, indeed, could he (or they) ever be in a position to know what one should or should not do? What tells *them* that this or that should or should not be done (i.e., what is their *mūlapramāṇa*)? Perception? Inference (i.e., reason)? As we saw above, *Kumārila* stresses that it is not apparent how either of these is capable of apprehending any connection between a particular action and a future benefit. With slightly more sophistication, the Western empiricist tradition (Hume) tells us that these faculties can inform us only of how things *are*, not how they *ought to be*. Is it, then, known by means of sentiment or conscience? But—now contrary to the Western empiricist tradition—our sentiments tell us only what we prefer or do not prefer, not what is right or wrong. And conscience, which by contrast would seem to be concerned with right and wrong, is so inconsistent that few have ever seriously considered it a genuine faculty of knowledge.

Nor will a traditional injunction or prohibition be undermined by the consideration that it, too, must ultimately derive from humans. Perhaps eventually it will—although *Kumārila* is by no means impressed with the arguments that seek to prove that the fundamental social institution of language, for instance, is established by convention—but that would be an achievement of speculative, theoretical reason. For the time being, in everyday practice, the injunction of tradition presents itself as anonymous and impersonal. As far as we can determine, it originated from no one, at no time. It is simply given, as if it were eternal. And so it remains true—at least subjectively, for us, in everyday practice. As *Kumārila* says, one doesn't even suspect the invalidity of a Vedic injunction (ŚV *Codanā* 68 cd: *vede . . . apramāṇatvaṃ nāśaṅkām api gacchati*).[24]

In sum, the ethical judgements of tradition will be binding for us, because they have in practice the lasting appearance of truth. The interesting corollary of this thesis is that *only* traditional judgements will be binding for us; for we cannot comprehend any other way a genuine "ought" can originate. In this respect, the theory is parallel to the *Mīmāṃsā* doctrine of the eternality of the denotative power (*śakti*) of words (in fact, it can even be seen as a special case thereof, insofar as the force of an injunction can be traced to the optative ending of the verb): since the ability of words to mean things cannot be explained as originating from some cause—cannot be construed as in any way contingent—it must be eternal. As a further result, any "new" ethical notion that has force for us will in reality be a traditional one, taken down from the shelf and dusted off, as it were, after long neglect. That "there is nothing new under the sun" applies especially to ethics. For this reason *Kumārila* accuses the heterodox critics of Vedic practice of ingratitude; they refuse to acknowledge that their notions of non-violence, benefiting others, and so forth, come from the Veda itself (Halbfass [1991, p. 96]). More generally, any wholesale overthrowing of tradition in the name of "higher" ideals or "deeper" principles must be seen as an act of bad faith; for it is tradition that provides the resources, the conceptual categories and values, for the working out of those ideals and principles. The opposing of such "new" ideals to tradition has to do, for the most part, with the application of already recognized principles to new circumstances, that is, with the proper interpretation of the complex system of values that has been handed down. Ethical discourse, properly conceived, is really a hermeneutical project.

The modern philosopher who has gone farthest in developing this idea is H.G. Gadamer. Tradition, Gadamer argues, is inescapable. It forms the context in which any reflection is carried out, even that which opposes and transcends tradition. It provides the "prejudices" (Vorurteile)—the motivations and presuppositions—that are the indispensable guidelines of inquiry. "That which has been sanctioned by custom," Gadamer writes in *Truth and Method*,

> has an authority that is nameless, and our finite historical being is marked by the fact that always the authority of what has been transmitted—and not only what is clearly grounded—has power over our attitudes and behaviour.[25] All education depends on this, and even though, in the case of education, the educator loses his function when his charge comes of age and sets his own insight and decisions in place of the authority of the educator, this movement into maturity in his own life does not mean that a person becomes his own master in the sense that he becomes free of all tradition. The validity of morals, for example, is based on tradition. They are freely taken over, but by no means created by a free insight or justified by themselves. This is precisely what we call tradition: the ground of their validity. And in fact we owe to romanticism this correction of the enlightenment, that tradition has a justification that is outside the arguments of reason and in large measure determines our institutions and attitudes. (1982, p. 249)

Gadamer, of course, does not advocate clinging to tradition at all costs, as *Kumārila* sometimes seems to advocate. These observations, rather, "lead to the question whether in the hermeneutic of the human sciences the element of tradition should not be given its full value" (1982, p. 250), that is, whether we should not cease pretending to be able to achieve a detached scientific knowledge of history by divorcing ourselves from tradition and its "prejudices" and instead recognize that historical understanding takes place within the horizon of tradition itself. The point is to see tradition as constructively contributing to our understanding of both ourselves and the past, and to respect tradition as a source—perhaps indeed the only source—of values that will enable us to come to terms with new circumstances. *Kumārila's* thought, I believe, can be seen as contributing to this project by offering a convincing explanation of why traditional judgements have binding force for us. As we saw, the power of traditional beliefs according to *Kumārila* has to do simply with the epistemic status they have in the belief systems in which they occur, as defined by a proper theory of epistemic justification, viz., the theory of intrinsic validity. This explanation construes the power of traditional beliefs as epistemically legitimate and not merely the result of such factors as blind obedience or narrow-mindedness.

Another way in which *Kumārila's* philosophy might be seen as contributing to modern ethical thought is in suggesting a solution to the conundrum about whether value is objective or subjective.[26] Is value a fact that we discover about the world? Or is it something our minds impose on the world? David Hume, for example, suggested that the value we see in actions is simply a projection of our sentiments, of our likes and dislikes. The first alternative, typically championed by rationalist philosophers, accords with the fixed and definite—seemingly, necessary and universal—character of moral judgements. When we consider murder bad, for example, we consider it so for everyone everywhere. It would appear to have little to do with sentiment; for surely, even if we all enjoyed killing people, it would still be wrong. Presumably this property of moral judgements is best explained by their being based on cognitions of the real properties of things: seeing actions to be what they really are, we are compelled to judge them in certain ways. The second alternative, on the other hand, which is advocated by empiricist philosophers, accords with the fact that we do not seem to be able to isolate and identify the properties of things that make them good or bad. Value is not a discoverable aspect of reality. It is not the sort of thing that any scientific inquiry has ever unearthed. When we analyze how things really are, value disappears.

> Take any action allowed to be vicious: Wilful murder, for instance. Examine it in all its light, and see if you can find that matter of fact, or real existence, which you call *vice.* In which-ever way you take it, you find only certain passions, motives, volitions, and thoughts. There is no matter of fact in the case. The vice entirely escapes you, as long as you consider the object. (Hume [1958, p. 468])

Kumārila himself says, ". . . at that time, when killing and so forth are carried out, there is no observation of a fault" (*na hy hiṃsādyanuṣṭhāne tadānīṃ doṣadarśanam* (ŚV *Codanā* 233 cd). Therefore, the empiricist would say, value must be something our minds impose on things.

A traditionalist ethical theory such as *Kumārila's* might be able to avoid both horns of this dilemma. On the one hand, it does not consider value to be an objective aspect of reality. For value is merely what is dictated by tradition, not our cognitive faculties apprehending facts, and we may suspend judgement about how tradition ever in the first place came up with the notion that this or that action is good or bad. That is something that we cannot really conceive; no ethical theory to date, in any case, has given an adequate account of it; values just seem to endure or emerge, mysteriously. All we know according to this theory is that, for us in our present circumstances, the guiding notions of good and bad are handed down to us ready-made. On the other hand, a traditionalist ethical theory does not construe value as an expression of human subjectivity, either—of our sentiments, our predilections and aversions; for tradition transcends humans. It is invented by no one; it is merely received by each generation.

In short, a traditionalist ethics might be able to avoid the dilemma about the objectivity of value *by abstracting altogether from the issue of how judgements of value originate*, for the latter dilemma, strictly speaking, has to do only with that issue. Yet at the same time, as we saw, it can explain how ethical judgements are binding on us, i.e., how they can appear universal and necessary—at least in certain contexts. A moral belief can be binding without being grounded on a cognition of some ethical "matter of fact" or on any awareness of "the Moral Law." A belief can be binding just by appearing to have a distinctive degree of warrant—as explained by a proper theory of justification. (One need not resort to metaphysics or transcendental psychology to explain the universal and necessary character of certain beliefs, in other words; it can be explained, rather, within the framework of analytic epistemology.) An ethical judgement, therefore, can have force for us, simply because, regardless how it arose, it appears true. At the same time it can be seen how a traditionalist ethical theory can account for the fact that different ethical judgements have authority in different societies. For an ethical judgement has force insofar as it is traditional; but different judgements will be traditional in different cultures. A traditionalist ethical theory, in other words, will explain how certain ethical judgements can be authoritative—impersonally "objective" and not just expressions of preference or sentiment—in certain societies without being in the fullest sense, for all societies, universal and necessary. Such a theory will imply relativism only if the cultural resources of different societies are indeed so impoverished as to be unable to process and come to terms with radically different points of view. Although *Kumārila's* own inflexible rejection of the heterodox movements of his day is discouraging on this score, the open-mindedness of other leading thinkers of his tradition toward some of those very same movements (see below) gives us reason to hope.

My intention in this article has been only to provide the barest outline of the essential idea of an ethical theory that can be *extrapolated* from *Kumārila's* writings. Of course, much of what I have said *Kumārila* himself would reject. For he does not hold that the Veda is a "mere" tradition, no matter how ancient; rather, it is eternal. Otherwise, indeed, it would be on a par with other scriptural writings—a conclusion he would find intolerable. But most modern readers will be unable to go along with Kumārila in making such an assumption. If what *Kumārila* says is to have any relevance today—outside a small community of orthodox Brahmins in India—it seems we must reconstrue it as pertaining to a Veda that is not really eternal but only apparently so, i.e., a *tradition* that is so ancient as to *seem* eternal and anonymous, in contrast to teachings that have an identifiable, human source. If his ideas are to become viable and interesting for us in the West at all—if they are to speak to the contemporary Western philosopher, but even, I think, if they are to speak to the modern, largely Western-educated Indian—then we must for a moment suspend our concern with historical accuracy.

I have not really begun to develop the ramifications of the traditionalist ethical theory that I see in *Kumārila's* writings or defend it here; nor am I sure myself that it is ultimately tenable. I hope, however, to have aroused the reader's interest enough for him to consider it worth further investigation. To restate the central insight of the theory: When you walk into a room and see a table, your perception is valid for you until other considerations arise that contradict it. Similarly, when you are told you ought to do this or that, your idea that you ought to do it remains valid for you so long as it is not contradicted. But the things tradition tells us are never effectively contradicted. Therefore, we think, what tradition tells us is what we really should and should not do. Where, after all, do "oughts" come from? Ethics, it seems, has never been able to answer this question. (A moderate skepticism, once again, is an important component of this theory.) It is not entirely incongruous to suggest, therefore, that they in effect come from nowhere. Any valid "ought" for us is one that is already there, which is tantamount to saying that tradition delivers it. And its validity has to do precisely with the fact that it is traditional, which means that, while conveying a clear sense that something should be done, it is not ascribable to any particular source and so (at least for us in everyday practice) is not questionable.

To recommend such a theory is to go along with Gadamer's suggestion that we "give tradition its due," that is, once again begin to take tradition seriously as a source of insight into right and wrong in dealing with contemporary issues. Perhaps in distancing ourselves, since the Enlightenment, as far as possible from tradition we have not advanced toward a better, more just world at all but simply muddled the tradition of which we are inescapably a part, while ceasing altogether, in certain areas of life, to be moral.

As a postscript to this discussion I would like to revert from thinking philosophically about *Kumārila's* thought to thinking about it historically and say a word about its historical significance.

Why is *Kumārila* so conservative in his treatment of revelation? Why does he accept only the Veda as a valid guide to pious living? Why are other sources of insight into transcendental matters so firmly, even vehemently, rejected by him? Why does he ignore, not only mystical experience, but even a personal intuition of value, of right and wrong? Halbfass, too, puzzled over this problem in *Tradition and Reflection*, noting that other approaches were taken in the classical period (1991, p. 39). There was, e.g., *Bhatṛhari's* acknowledgement of all philosophies as the continuing unfoldment of *śabdatattva* and as anticipated in the Veda itself. There was Abhinavagupta's reliance on the *Śaivāgamas*,

Yāmunācārya's defense (in his *Āgamaprāmāṇya*) of the authority of the *Pāñcarātrāgamas* and *Jayantabhaṭṭa's* acknowledgement of various religious traditions on the basis of their "acceptance by great (and/or many) people" (*mahājanaparigṛhītatva;* Halbfass [1991, p. 63]). Including *Kumārila* together with *Bhartṛhari*, *Śaṅkara*, and *Prabhākara*, Halbfass asks:

> Why did they rely on the Veda, and only the Veda? Why not on any other kind of "revelation"? Why did they not simply recognize the need for "revelation," or "objective epiphany," as such and in general? Are there any truly philosophical reasons, apart from cultural, psychological, and ideological motivations? (1991, p. 39)

I believe that we can take a step toward answering this question by regarding a striking Western parallel to *Kumārila* : Thomas Hobbes. Hobbes is most commonly known as one of the founders of English empiricism and political philosophy, yet his *magnum opus* the *Leviathan* contains in its third and fourth parts a lengthy discussion of religion. There Hobbes attempts to bring Christianity up to date, so to speak, by bringing its teachings as much as possible into harmony with the emerging natural sciences, the epistemological groundwork for which he had laid in the earlier parts of the work. But he is primarily concerned, more broadly, with the problem of religious authority and the legitimacy of scriptural interpretation. He will conclude, extraordinarily enough, that only the sovereign of the commonwealth has the right to determine what is true or false in matters of doctrine and worship.[27] There is no valid, independent source of insight into the meaning of scripture. He even admits that this may in the end cause him to retract his own interpretation of Christianity.

It is in the details of the discussion that the parallels to *Kumārila* emerge. In restricting religious authority to the sovereign Hobbes adopts a thoroughgoing rationalizing attitude. Such biblical notions as spirit, angel, inspiration, Kingdom of God, heaven, and hell are radically demystified. The spirit of God (frequently mentioned in the Old Testament) is considered variously as wind or breath, insight, violent emotion, etc. Angels are "subtile" or "thin" bodies, made perhaps of air; otherwise they are mental fantasies induced by God. Hobbes insists that nowhere does the

Bible require us to believe in an incorporeal substance, which he considered as much an impossibility as Berkeley later considered corporeal substance to be. God Himself is declared incomprehensible in nature. The Kingdom of God is the society of believers in God, between whom and God the Bible records various covenants. The Kingdom of Heaven will be the society of physically resurrected believers presided over by Christ at the end of time. Hobbes denies, once again, that the Bible speaks of an incorporeal soul which might conceivably travel to a heavenly realm; orthodox Christianity, rather, maintains the resurrection *of the body.* Miracles *qua* supernatural events Hobbes grudgingly admits as possible through God's agency. But he holds that much of the time supposed miracles will have a natural explanation. It is the fact that those who witness it are unable to explain it, given the state of their scientific knowledge—that is, its psychological effect—and God's employment of it for his purposes, that makes something a miracle.[28]

None of this, of course, is exactly matched in *Kumārila.* For one thing, *Kumārila* was hardly a materialist; he argues at length for the existence of an immaterial soul. But the spirit of the discussion is identical. The *Mīmāṃsakas,* too, and *Kumārila* foremost among them, attempted to explain away the supernatural content of the Veda. All passages of a mythopoeic nature are—indeed, rather scandalously and frequently without even an honest attempt to reinterpret them, as Hobbes makes—dismissed as *arthavāda,* hence to be construed, in some way or other, figuratively.

The thrust of Hobbes's rationalizing and demystifying of scripture, however—besides bringing it more in line with our understanding of nature through physical science—is to exclude all claims of extraordinary revelation. Here the parallels to *Kumārila,* specifically, to his polemic against the visionary capacities that were alleged to be possessed by the Buddha and the Jina, are more marked. The prophecy recorded in the Old and New Testaments occurs typically not by means of any direct experience of the Divine, Hobbes observes, but by visions, voices, or dreams induced in the mind of the prophet by God. Only, it seems, in the case of Moses did God address His messenger face to face. Considering, then, that such experiences may occur from natural as well as supernatural causes, there is a special need of the use of reason and judgement in discerning genuine prophecy. Moreover, while the person to whom God speaks, as it were, in this manner may well be convinced that God spoke to him, "how the same may be understood by another, is hard, if not impossible to know." For how could it be proved?

To say that he [God] hath spoken to him in a Dream, is no more than to say he dreamed that God spake to him; which is not of force to win beleef from any man, that knows dreams are for the most part naturall. . . . To say that he hath seen a Vision, or heard a Voice, is to say that he hath dreamed between sleeping and waking: for in such manner a man doth many times naturally take his dream for a vision, as not having well observed his own slumbering. To say that he speaks by supernaturall Inspiration, is to say he finds an ardent desire to speak, or some strange opinion of himself, for which he can alledge no naturall or sufficient reason. So that though God Almighty can speak to a man, by Dreams, Visions, Voice, and Inspiration; yet he obliges no man to beleeve he hath so done to him that pretends it; who (being a man), and (which is more) may lie [sic.]. (Hobbes [1985, p. 411])

In general, therefore, we cannot trust those who claim to have direct access to God's word. Even the Bible warns repeatedly against false prophets. Any claim to prophecy must be tested by the criteria mentioned by scripture itself: accompaniment by miracles (themselves difficult to authenticate) and harmony with established doctrine. However, since miracles have ceased to occur in our day, harmony with scripture remains the sole criterion.

We have no sign left, whereby to acknowledge the pretended Revelations, or Inspirations of any private man; nor obligations to give ear to any Doctrine, farther than it is conformable to the Holy Scriptures, which since the time of our Saviour, supply the place, and sufficiently recompense the want of all other Prophecy; and from which, by wise and learned interpretation, and careful ratiocination, all rules and precepts necessary to the knowledge of our duty both to God and man, without Enthusiasme or supernaturall Inspiration, may easily be deduced. (1985, p. 414)

In the end, since the authority to interpret scripture rests with the sovereign power of a Christian commonwealth, to whom its citizens have relinquished most rights for the sake of their own survival and prosperity and whose commands they have agreed to consider law—not, as Hobbes will go on to argue, with one Vicar of Christ constituted over the universal Church, i.e., the Pope!—the legitimacy of any religious teaching is ultimately to be decided by the sovereign.

Every man therefore ought to consider who is the Sovereign Prophet, that is to say, who it is, that is Gods Viceregent on Earth; and hath next under god, the Authority of Governing Christian men; and to observe for a Rule, that Doctrine, which in the name of God, hee command to bee taught; and thereby to examine and try out the truth of those Doctrines, which pretended Prophets, with miracle, or without, shall at any time advance. . . . (1985, pp. 468 f.)

Here, of course, Hobbes differs from *Kumārila* in putting forward a particular human being as the final arbiter in religious disputes. However, that is not because he does not consider scripture as it has been handed down to us the only source of religious truth—indeed he does, though of course he does not go so far as to say that it is eternal. But Hobbes also realizes that different people will interpret scripture differently. That is where the problem of religious disagreement lies for him, for he lived in a culture in which religion and Christianity were synonymous. *Kumārila*, on the other hand, often gives the impression that he believes that once the Veda is accepted by all, things will go smoothly—an impression that his own intricately argued interpretations of Vedic passages, of course, belie.

Overall, *Kumārila* and Hobbes are in remarkable agreement about the need to eliminate the influence of "private revelation" on religious life. Both propose theories of prophecy and religious authority—coinciding in some points but diverging in others—which are suited to inhibiting innovation and promoting uniformity of belief and practice. The question remains, why? In Hobbes's case, he himself gives us the answer in the continuation of the last passage cited:

For when Christian men, take not their Christian Soveraign, for Gods Prophet; they must either take their own Dreams, for the Prophecy they mean to be governed by, and the tumour of their own hearts for the Spirit of God; or they must suffer themselves to bee lead by some strange Prince; or by some of their fellow subjects, that can bewitch them, by slander of the government, into rebellion, without other miracle to confirm their calling, then sometimes an extraordinary success [i.e., a mere coincidence], and

Impunity; and by this means destroying all laws, both divine, and humane, reduce all Order, Government, and Society, to the first Chaos of Violence, and Civil warre. (1985, p. 469)

It is well known that Hobbes wrote the *Leviathan* in response to the English Civil War, which he believed to have been caused above all by religious strife. Only by the recognition of a single sovereign who has supreme authority in matters both religious and secular, but who is established and legitimized by a covenant instituted among the citizens of the commonwealth, would peace be restored.

We know virtually nothing for certain about *Kumārila's* historical situation. We can guess, by the usual method of cross-referencing, that he lived in the seventh century. He seems to belong to the same period as *Dharmakīrti, Maṇḍana, Śaṅkara,* and *Prabhākara.* His considerable familiarity with South Indian linguistic forms and customs suggests but does not prove that he lived in the South. It seems safe to say, however, that wherever *Kumārila* might have lived in the latter half of the first millenium in India, he would have been exposed to fierce competition among religious sects that in turn fueled political strife and persecution. Certain passages in the *Tantravārttika* reflect a concern, even anxiety, about the spreading influence of non-orthodox sects;[29] some traditional sources hold *Kumārila* himself to have been an agent of persecution.[30] *Kumārila* may not have experienced the turmoil caused by religious dissension in the same form Hobbes did—civil war—but that he did experience it in some form is almost certain. The evident analogy to Hobbes that I have tried to draw, I believe, supports the explanation of *Kumārila's* extraordinary conservatism with regard to religious practice and belief as being motivated, not just by a widespread trend toward rationalism—a de-emphasis of the supernatural and a focus, instead, on logic and epistemology—in his age, but also by specific social and political circumstances.[31]

NOTES

[1] *Kumārila,* following *Śabara,* suggests that the *śyena* sacrifice, which is a means of killing one's enemy, is not prescribed categorically by the Veda but only hypothetically. As such, "by itself" (*svataḥ*), it is neither dharma nor *adharma.* Because it results in killing, however, which is prohibited elsewhere in the Veda, it is figuratively termed *adharma* by *Śabara* (265a-267b). Or else, the Veda does not enjoin the *śyena* sacrifice at all, but by *śyenenābhicaran yajeta* merely communicates the causal relationship between the *śyena* and *hiṃsā* (219c-222b).

[2] Cf. ŚV *Autpattika* 1-8.

[3] Śabara understands *artha* as "that which is conducive to welfare/prosperity (*śreyaskara*)" and also, it seems, as "the highest good" (*yaḥ puruṣaṃ niḥśreysena saṃyunakti, sa eva dharmaśabdenocyate*). *Kumārila* explains *śreyas* as "the happiness of man" (*puruṣaprīti*), *Codanā* 191a. See D'Sa (1980, pp. 49-54) for further discussion of the possible meanings of *artha.*

[4] *Mīmāṃsakas* generally recognize as a Vedic prohibition: *na hiṃsyāt sarvāṇi bhūtāni.*

[5] Specifically, by the method of *āvāpodvāpa,* "addition and subtraction" (250cd), which I understand to mean (the idea is obscure): by discerning the common element in various injunctions or prohibitions to be X, the variable elements to be A, B, C, etc. Cf. 256c-258b.

[6] The problem of the identity of the Saṃsāramocakas is discussed by Halbfass in this same essay, pp. 99-111.

[7] *Ya eva śreyaskaraḥ, sa eva dharmaśabdenocyate,* MSBh, p. 20, 4-5. *Kumārila* offers only a minimal definition of 'welfare' as human happiness, ŚV *Codanā* 191a: *śreyo hi puruṣaprītiḥ.*

[8] The *Prābhākara* interpretation of *vidhi,* however, tends in this direction. See Maitra (1978, pp. 117 ff.).

[9] The reverse side of skepticism is nihilism. By telling us that we cannot achieve anything through the exercise of our cognitive faculties, it undermines one of the most important dimensions of human existence: rational discourse. Thus, global skepticism will always be resisted. Moderate skepticism, on the other hand—the notion that we cannot achieve knowledge of everything—is simply common sense.

[10] *Pratyakṣapūrvakatvāc ca anumānopamānārthāpattīnām apy akāraṇatvam,* MSBh, p. 22, 19-20.

[11] Cf. Plato, *Theaetetus* 178a-179b. Socrates refutes the view that "knowledge is perception," which he equates with Protagoras's doctrine, "Man is the measure of all things," partly on the grounds that knowledge of what is beneficial or in the interest of a society or an individual is clearly not

perceptual, since whether a particular policy or course of action is beneficial or not pertains to *how it will turn out in the future.*

[12] The discussion of *Kumārila's* lost work, the *Bṛhaṭṭīkā*, which is much more extensive than the ŚV, is preserved in the *Tattvasaṇgraha* as the *pūrvapakṣa* of the *Atīndriyārthadarśiparīkṣā.*

[13] ŚV *Codanā* 113:

yajjātiyaiḥ pramāṇais tu yajjātīyārthadarśanam /
bhaved idānīṃ lokasya tathā kālāntare 'py abhūt / /

[14] The doctrine of the need for a *mūlapramāṇa* in the case of human testimony is developed by *Kumārila's* commentators on the basis of his mentioning of *pramāṇāntaramūlatā* at *Codanā* 71b and *mūla* at 103a. See also *Codanā* 136 and 165.

[15] See Taber (2005, pp. 38-43).

[16] Cf. TV I.3.4, p. 113:

mahājanagṛhītatvaṃ pitrādyanugamādi ca /
te 'pi dvīpāntarāpekṣaṃ vadanty eva svadarśane / /
tatra śraddhāmātram evaikaṃ vyavasthānimittaṃ sarveṣāṃ svapitṛpitāmahādicaritānuyāyitvāt.

[17] This is noted in a *pūrvapakṣa,* TV I.3.1, p. 73.

[18] Cf., however, VP(V) I.124 (Iyer edn.), where *Bhartṛhari* is also perhaps thinking of the eternality of the Veda in terms of a beginningless transmission.

[19] Buddhism and Christianity could even be considered "traditions" in this sense; for although both in fact originated with historical founders, each is typically transmitted as the "truth" without reference thereto (except insofar as the onto-theological status of their founders is a point of dogma). *Kumārila,* interestingly enough, considers at TV I.3.11 (pp. 162-166; cf. ŚV *Codanā* 119-120) attempts by the Buddhists and others to base the authority of their scriptures on their eternality. It would seem, then, that any tradition after a while begins to regard itself as eternal. Often the historical founder of a tradition comes to be viewed as an eternal, metaphysical principle. Buddhism and Jainism specifically teach that their doctrines are re-expounded by enlightened preceptors in every cosmic cycle. Against the appeal to eternality by the Buddhists *Kumārila* argues that it would contradict other fundamental Buddhist tenets, e.g., the momentariness of entities and the non-eternality of language. Moreover, in *Kumārila's* cultural sphere, at least, there is a "firm memory" of the authors of these traditions.

The reader should keep in mind that in considering *Kumārila* as upholding *tradition* as an ethical criterion I am reconstruing his statements in a manner with which he would not agree, precisely because it puts the Veda in a class together with all other scriptural writings.

[20] I discuss here only the so-called *svataḥ prāmāṇyaṃ jñaptitaḥ* doctrine, which I believe is the proper interpretation of *Kumārila's* view of validity in the *Codanāsūtra.* The *svataḥ prāmāṇyam utpattitaḥ* doctrine seems to have

originated with Umbeka's interpretation of *Kumārila* in his *Ślokavārttikavyākhyātātparyaṭīkā*. See Taber (1992).

[21] Thus, the theory is best characterized as a type of "fallible foundationalism." For recent discussions see Audi (1993) and Lehrer (1990, pp. 63 ff.).

[22] The eighteenth-century Scottish philosopher Thomas Reid refers to this tendency as "the credulity principle" (1983, pp. 95-97).

[23] Loc. cit.

[24] This should not be taken to mean, however, that they are indubitable, but that they appear to us in every way true and there is no basis for considering them false.

[25] Gadamer says elsewhere (1982, p. 241): ". . . the sheer fact of something being written down [we could also say, of being transmitted through a formal oral tradition] confers on it an authority of particular weight. It is not altogether easy to realize that what is written down can be untrue."

[26] For a recent treatment of this problem see Stroud (1989).

[27] Within certain obvious limits, of course. He cannot require that his subjects profess anything that contradicts the most basic tenets to which a Christian is committed by conscience, such as that Jesus is the Christ.

[28] Such ideas as these might be taken as support for the thesis put forward by Leo Strauss that Hobbes was really an atheist who feigned piety in order to avoid persecution. His real attitude toward religion was always that "religion must serve the State and is to be esteemed or despised according to the services or disservices rendered to the State" (1936, p. 74). I believe, however, that this view has been decisively refuted by Glover (1965) and others.

[29] Cf., e.g., TV I.3.4, p. 113, ll. 1-10.

[30] See Kaviraj (1983, pp. vi-x).

[31] I would like to thank Karin Preisendanz and Eli Franco for suggestions and corrections that led to significant improvements in this paper.

REFERENCES

Aklujkar, Ashok. (1991). "*Bhartṛhari's* Concept of the Veda." In: Madhav Deshpande (Ed.) *Panels of the Eighth World Sanskrit Conference.* Vol. 5. Leiden: E.J. Brill, pp. 1-18.

Alston, William. (1991). *Perceiving God: The Epistemology of Religious Experience.* Ithaca, New York: Cornell University Press.

Audi, Robert. (1993). "Fallibilist Foundationalism and Holistic Coherentism." In Louis Pojman (Ed.) *The Theory of Knowledge: Classic and Contemporary Readings.* Belmont, California: Wadsworth, Inc., pp. 263-279.

D'Sa, Francis X. (1980). *Śabdaprāmāṇyam in Śabara and Kumārila.* Vienna: De Nobili Research Library.

Gadamer, Hans-Georg. (1982). *Truth and Method*. New York: Crossroad Publishing.

Glover, Willis B. (1965). "God and Thomas Hobbes." In K.C. Brown (Ed.) *Hobbes Studies*. Cambridge, Massachusetts: Harvard University Press, pp. 141-168.

Halbfass, Wilhelm. (1983). *Studies in Kumārila and Śaṅkara*. Reinbek: Verlag für orientalistische Fachpublikationen.

Halbfass, Wilhelm. (1988). *India and Europe*. Albany, New York: State University of New York Press.

Halbfass, Wilhelm. (1991). *Tradition and Reflection*. Albany, New York: State University of New York Press.

Hobbes, Thomas. (1985). *Leviathan*. London: Penguin Books.

Hume, David. (1958). *A Treatise of Human Nature*. Ed. L.A. Selby-Bigge. Oxford: Clarendon Press.

Kaviraj, Gopinath. (1983). "Introduction." In: *Gaṅgānātha Jhā* (Trans.) *Kumārila Bhaṭṭa: Tantravārttika. Sri Garib Das Oriental Series*. No. 9. Delhi: Sri Satguru Publications.

Kumārilabhaṭṭa. (1978). *Ślokavārttika* (ŚV). Ed. *Svāmī Dvārikadāsa Śāstrī*. Varanasi: Tārā Publications.

Kumārilabhaṭṭa. (1981). *Tantravārttika* (TV), I.2-II.1. Ed. *Gaṇeśaśāstri Jośī*. *Ānandāśrama Sanskrit Series*. No. 91. Varanasi: *Ānandāśrama* Sanskrit Series.

Lehrer, Keith. (1990). *Theory of Knowledge*. San Francisco: Westview Press.

Maitra, Sushil Kumar. (1978). *The Ethics of the Hindus*. New Delhi: Asian Publication Services.

Plantinga, Alvin. (1993). *Warrant and Proper Function*. Oxford: Oxford University Press.

Reid, Thomas. (1983). *Inquiry into the Human Mind on the Principles of Common Sense*. In Ronald Beanblossom and Keith Lehrer (Eds.) *Thomas Reid's Inquiry and Essays*. Indianapolis: Hackett Publishing.

Śabarasvāmin. (1968). *Mīmāṃsāsūtrabhāṣya* (MSBh). In Erich Frauwallner (Ed. and Trans.) *Materialien zur ältesten Erkenntnislehre der Karmamīmāṃsā*. Vienna: Österreichische Akademie der Wissenschaften.

Strauss, Leo. (1936). *The Political Philosophy of Thomas Hobbes*. Oxford: Clarendon Press.

Stroud, Barry. (1989). "The Study of Human Nature and the Subjectivity of Value." In Grethe Peterson (Ed.) *The Tanner Lectures on Human Values*. Vol. 10. Salt Lake City: University of Utah Press, pp. 211-259.

Taber, John. (1992). "What Did Kumārilabhaṭṭa Mean By *svataḥ prāmāṇya*?" *Journal of the American Oriental Society*. 112/2, 204-221.

Taber, John. (2005). *A Hindu Critique of Buddhist Epistemology: Kumārila on Perception*. London: RoutledgeCurzon.

Department of Philosophy
University of New Mexico
Albuquerque New Mexico, U.S.A.

PAUL HACKER

DHARMA IN HINDUISM*[,1]

Hinduism is a label for the indigenous religion of India that orients itself toward the Veda, the sacred texts from the oldest Indo-Aryan period, without actually being Vedic in either its myth or ritual; the religion, that intends to cultivate and pass down the religious customs of the Āryas, but that nevertheless absorbed and created anew many things that did not belong to the original Ārya religion. The word Hinduism came into use only in the 19th century; it would be more correct historically to speak of the Ārya religion or the group of Ārya religions. The word Ārya denotes thereby a cultural community, the elite classes of which called themselves Ārya throughout the centuries. The religion of this cultural community, which spread throughout the immense area of India, is in truth a group of religions which have much in common between them, but in which there are also many differences and contrasts – highly visible diversity of myths, rituals, customs, teachings, and religious views.

Among the commonalities belonging to this group of religions is a peculiar concept denoted by the word *dharma*. I should just mention that Buddhism, which does not recognize the Veda and, therefore, cannot be considered part of Hinduism, also has a concept of *dharma*, but I cannot consider it here.

What then is *dharma* in Hinduism? I do not want to engage in etymological explanations; these are more often than not misleading. I will also set aside the question of how the Hindu concept of *dharma*

* This essay was originally published as "Dharma im Hinduismus" in *Zeitschrift für Missionswissenschaft und Religionswissenschaft* 49 (1965): 93–106, and reprinted in *Kleine Schriften: Paul Hacker*. Ed. Lambert Schmithausen. Wiesbaden: Steiner Verlag (1978): 496–509. The original page numbers are indicated in the translation at the appropriate points.

[1] I presented the content of this article in a somewhat shorter form as an inaugural lecture on the occasion of my assuming the Chair of Indology at the University of Münster.

may be differentiated from what the Vedic texts understood by *dharma*.[1a] I will first address two cases in which the Hindu notion of *dharma* came into contact with Western concepts, not in learned analysis, but rather in real life.

A few years ago an inscription of the Indian emperor Aśoka from the year 258 BC was discovered in Kandahār in Afghanistan. Inscriptions of this ruler are well known throughout India and its border regions. They are composed in a variety of languages. In the western border regions, even Aramaic has appeared as a language. The new inscription also contains Greek text and therein appears a Greek rendering of the Indic *dharma*: the word *eusébeia*.

Emperor Aśoka was an enthusiastic Buddhist but not a religious scholar. Even if his concept of *dharma* as it appears in many of his [94, 497] inscriptions was inspired by Buddhism, it nevertheless was clearly not exclusively Buddhist nor was it meant to be. Aśoka wanted to promote a *dharma* that would be acceptable to all his subjects, whether Buddhist or Hindu. He understood by *dharma*, generally stated, a right and moral conduct, the exercise of duty toward the human community.[2] One may claim that this idea of *dharma*, although upheld by lay Buddhists with a special devotion, was also not unknown in early Hinduism. For this reason we might also draw upon this Aśokan inscription in explaining the Hindu concept of *dharma*.

As stated the word *dharma* is rendered in the new inscription by *eusébeia*. Scholars of Hellenistic Greece assure us that this Greek word in Hellenistic contexts refers not only to the veneration of gods, but also to a "generally reverential attitude toward the orders of life," and that it is used "also for conduct toward relatives, between husband and wife, and even for the conduct of slaves toward their master."[3] It is this concept that the Greek speaking officials of this Indian ruler rediscovered in the Indic *dharma*. This is all the more understandable when we recall that Aśoka's understanding of *dharma* as it appears in his inscriptions includes an element of reverence, namely of the mutual esteem between humans, even though the word has in its derivation nothing to do with fear or backing off in awe, in

---

[1a] [Translator's note]: On *dharma* in the Vedic texts, see Horsch (2004), Brereton (2004), Olivelle (2004), and Wezler (2004).

[2] Compare Étienne Lamotte, *Histoire du bouddhisme indien*, Bibliothéque du Muséon 43. Louvain, 1958; pp. 249ff.

[3] W. Foerster, *Theologisches Wörterbuch zum Neuen Testament*. Vol. 7, p. 177, line 10.

contrast to the Greek *eusébeia* which is connected to *sébomai*.[3a] Aśoka's inscriptions frequently preach the duty of obedience toward one's parents and persons of respect, of friendliness and helpfulness in the interaction with all human beings.

The new inscription is of inestimable value because it brings us closer to the spirit of a central concept of Indic thought through a gloss in the principal language of the ancient Mediterranean. Such a case is extraordinarily rare. However, we should not now simply equate *dharma* and *eusébeia* with each another as exactly parallel. The gloss at least conveys the atmosphere that the Greek speaker felt when confronted with the Indic *dharma*. This was without a doubt a religious, not merely a legal, atmosphere.

The encounter with this inscription encourages us to make a leap of 2200 years forward in time to the moment when Europe and India again came into contact – this time, however, in an incomparably more intensive manner than in the Hellenistic period – in order to ask which Western term is today juxtaposed to the Indic. Today it is, to be sure, not a matter of translating from an Indic to a European language, but [95, 498] the reverse. Thanks to the Anglicized school system, educated Indians have since the 19th century learned to think in European terms, and now use, when writing in Indic languages, Indic words to express European concepts. It is therefore now a question of transposition from European to Indic, not the opposite. In this way, *dharma* appears now as an equivalent for the European word religion.

Now this translation is not so very different from that which was put forth by the Hellenistic Greeks. The Greek *eusébeia* is also, if stated simply, in many instances translatable by "religiosity" or "religion." Moreover, the modern habit of using *dharma* as a cipher for the concept "religion" is a point of entry into the meaning of *dharma*, but here too we cannot simply equate them. What is true of the juxtaposition of *dharma* and *eusébeia* is also true of *dharma* and *religion:* both concepts overlap without coinciding, and the translation developed in living contact suggests an important element of its meaning. It is an approximation that shows what especially stood out in the foreign concept: what *dharma* was to the Greeks in the third

[3a] [Translator's note]: *Sébomai* occurs ten times in the New Testament for "worship" or, as an adjective, for "devout" or "God-fearing" and implies humility and, in the Christian sense, the "fear of the Lord."

century BC, the European concept "religion" is to modern Indians.[3b] If we can assume a continuity of the Indic concept over 2200 years – and we are certainly justified in doing so – then we can make the observation that *dharma* has something in common with morality as well as with religion.

Now I want to go into the concept of *dharma* as it is presented in the specialist literature that exists in Hinduism about this idea.

In the meaning of *dharma*, what is moral becomes especially clear when Hindus speak of general or common *dharma*, *sāmānya-* or *sādhāraṇa-dharma*. There we find injunctions or prohibitions valid for all humankind such as, for example, the prohibitions of killing or violence, of theft and adultery, or the injunctions of truthfulness, friendliness, or of reverence for gods as well as for persons of respect, parents, and teachers.

However, the domain of what is moral was never as clearly emphasized in Hinduism as it was in Buddhism. On the one hand, the realm of *dharma* stretches out well beyond what is moral; on the other hand, *dharma*, in most of its contents, is not common to all humankind, but rather bound to the cultural community of Āryas and within this to specific social groups. *Dharma* is by definition *varṇāśramadharma*, that is the *dharma* of castes and life-stages. The system of castes and life-stages, itself belonging to the system of *dharma*, is the framework in which all the contents of *dharma* are enmeshed. The textbooks (Lehrtexte[3c]) of *dharma* distinguish four principal castes: Brahmins; Kṣatriyas, meaning warriors, rulers, or nobles; Vaiśyas, meaning farmers and merchants; and Śūdras, or servants, who undertake menial jobs and trades. Cross-cutting this system is that of the [96, 499] four life-stages: the *brahmacārin* or student; the *gṛhastha* or married man; the *vānaprastha* or hermit; and the *pārivrājaka* or wandering ascetic. How far real life ever corresponded to these classifications is another question. There have always been many more castes than just four; the *dharma* texts explain them as (actually illegitimate) mixings of the four castes. Whether the institution of religious education was ever observed generally seems doubtful; the fact that the textbooks present extensive prescriptions for irregularities in the observance of the system is

---

[3b] [Translator's note]: An important comparison here is the ironic paralleling of a Indic to Greek conceptual rendering with a European to Indic rendering, whereby *dharma* becomes *eusébeia* and then religion becomes *dharma*.

[3c] [Translator's note]: The German term Lehrtexte, literally "teaching-text," conveys well the sense of the Sanskrit term *śāstra* in a way that no common English word can.

revealing. However, the ideal, officially recognized *dharma* system according to the texts consists nevertheless in the framework of four castes and four orders of life. To each caste and to each order of life the texts apportioned their respective duties as their special *dharma*. The *dharma* of a Brahmin is for instance to learn the Veda, to teach and perform sacrifices for others, thus to perform sacerdotal services. The special *dharma* of a Kṣatriya is to rule; of a Vaiśya, to carry out agriculture and animal husbandry. In addition, both of the latter castes also had to learn the Veda and make sacrifices through the intermediacy of Brahmins. The Śūdras, who are, as it were, half-citizens (Beisassen) of the religious and social system of the Āryas, may not become familiar with the Veda; they have only to serve the three upper castes. For each of the special caste *dharmas*, there are then innumerable individual prescriptions of ritual and customs for the individual orders of life. There are also many variants, mostly regional, and these are accepted as legitimate in the regularly produced codifications of *dharma*.

In addition to morality proper, therefore, *dharma* also encompasses the entire external ritual, ceremonial side of religion, and everything in life is attended by such ceremonies and customs. Furthermore, the entire realm of civil law, criminal law, and statecraft – royal law – form part of *dharma*. And for offenses against the innumerable prescriptions rites of expiation and penance exist that also form part of *dharma*.

Dharma is qualified religiously not only because the specifically religious tradition belongs to it, but above all because it has a connection to salvation. This also forms part of the definition of *dharma*, just as much as the aforementioned characteristic that it is differentiated and qualified according to caste and life-stage. Salvation is something otherworldly, something that transcends this life. Accordingly, part of the nature of *dharma* is that it ought not to be done out of worldly, thisworldly motives.[4] In the 7th century AD, the great systematizer Kumārila expressed it negatively: "When good persons act according to certain rules, and no motive or goal is apparent in the realm of the observable, then this is to be [97, 500] understood as *dharma*."[5] Motives in the realm of the observable are apparent, for instance, when someone does something for self-preservation or for

---

[4] *Āpastambadharmasūtra* 1.20.1.

[5] Kumārila, *Tantravārttika*, Ānandāśramasaṃskṛtagranthāvalih. Vol. 97, p. 205, line 9ff. An English translation has been provided by Gaṅganātha Jhā, Bibliotheca Indica, Vol. 161, Calcutta 1924, Vol. 1, p. 184. [Translator's Note]: Throughout the article, Hacker's German renderings of Sanskrit have been translated into English, though Hacker himself points to other existing English translations in several places.

personal enjoyment or for the purpose of material acquisition; nothing of this sort is *dharma*. None of these motives are present when someone makes a ritual gift (usually to Brahmins), when he performs the daily oblation rites, when he participates in a religious festival, and so forth. Of course it can occur that someone does these with an added worldly motive as well, for instance, to acquire some prestige for himself, but according to the explicit rules of a Dharmasūtra his act is then simply not *dharma* and it produces no otherworldly reward, no "ascension," as they say. Worldly goods in fact follow one who fulfills *dharma* only as accessories, just as a mango tree, which is really there to produce fruit, also creates shade and fragrant blossoms. Even if no worldly goods or benefits are acquired by the fulfillment of *dharma*, the *dharma* still remains undiminished: so teaches one *dharma* text.[6]

This notion serves among other things to demarcate *dharma* from other existential goals. Hinduism or the Ārya religion classifies three or four goals of life: sexual life, acquisitive life, and the life of *dharma* that can be described approximately, if not precisely, as the religious life; above these rises the highest goal of life, the striving after liberation from transmigration, the condition of always having to be reborn. The thoughts I have laid out here thus mark off the life of *dharma* sharply from all striving for acquisition and forms of worldly life. If motives arise from these pursuits, then the act of *dharma* is "fruitless," it is *dharma* no more.

I repeat again Kumārila's negative definition: "When good persons act according to certain rules and no motive or goal is apparent in the realm of the observable, then this is to be understood as *dharma*." In this definition, something important is not yet explained: the good, lawful, righteous person, the *sādhu*. Who is a *sādhu* in the sense of this statement? The word *śiṣṭa*, which may be translated as "cultured" or "well-mannered," has a similar meaning for Kumārila and others, as well as the word *sat*, which can again be rendered by "good." For Kumārila the good or well-mannered person is one who, insofar as something is directly prescribed in the Veda, always orients himself toward the Veda. In such a person is, as it were, the substance of the Veda; he thus acts correctly and his decisions are a norm for others as well, in cases for which an existing Vedic prescription cannot be tracked down. [98, 501]

From this we see a further characteristic of *dharma* that is explicitly declared in most texts: *dharma* has a connection to the Veda, to the

[6] *Āpastambadharmasūtra* 1.20.2–4.

sacred texts from the oldest Indo-Aryan period. What is directly enjoined in the Veda is categorically obligatory. It is *dharma*, it leads to the otherworldly salvation. The Veda is the foremost source of *dharma*.

But it is not the only source. In addition to the Veda and to the texts known as *smṛti*, many texts refer to the *practice of the good* or the well-mannered or the experts as a source of *dharma*. Kumārila combines both sources of *dharma* by attributing the goodness of good people back to the Veda which he explains as follows: The good are those who orient themselves toward the Veda wherever it is possible. Other texts, however, do not give this explanation, and there are portions of texts that were probably originally independent in which the Veda is not known as a source at all[7] or appears only in second position.[8] Viewed historically, I would like to hypothesize, those sayings which speak only of the practice or consensus of the good and the expert as a source of *dharma* are very old; they may stem from a time when the Veda was not yet seen by men as a closed, authoritative textual corpus, when they rather still lived *in the Veda*, when the Veda *was still evolving*. But what is it then that qualifies certain people to be an authority for *dharma*, whether that they are an exclusive authority or that their opinion or their practice is definitive in cases for which no explicit rule is provided in the Veda?

Sometimes moral qualities are given as such qualifications: people who are free from passionate affection or antipathy, from greed and anger.[9] A geographical demarcation is common, too. There is a region of North India known as Āryāvarta, the practices of which serve as generally exemplary and normative. The agreement or consensus of the upper three castes among the Āryas is also known as a characteristic of proper *dharma*. The most striking instance of a definition of this sort is found in the *Āpastambadharmasūtra*. There it is said:

> *Dharma* and *adharma* (that is, the opposite of *dharma*) do not go around saying, "That is us." Nor do gods, Gandharvas, or ancestors declare what is *dharma* and what is *adharma*. Rather what Āryas praise when it is done, that is *dharma;* what they condemn is *adharma*. One should model one's conduct after the conduct that is unanimously approved in all countries by Āryas who are well-mannered, aged, and self-disciplined, and who are free from greed and deceit.[10] [99, 502]

---

7 *Manusmṛti* 2.1; *Āpastambadharmasūtra* 1.20.6–8.

8 *Āpastambadharmasūtra* 1.1.3.

9 *Manusmṛti* 2.1. Compare *Āpastambadharmasūtra* 2.29.13–14.

10 *Āpastambadharmasūtra* 1.20.6–8.

This is the most concrete and precise definition of the Hindu concept of *dharma* that I know. The definition is radically empirical. There is no superordinate principle from which *dharma* and *adharma* may be derivable. Only by experiential inquiry can one determine what *dharma* is: one must ask morally qualified, learned Āryas.

Since the beginning of the 20th century one sometimes hears from Hindus that Hindu philosophy in particular taught a universal principle of *dharma* and *adharma*,[11] and therefore *dharma* and *adharma* correspond directly to the moral concepts of good and evil. In this view, the principle follows from Vedānta monism and means: Do good to others because the self of others is identical with your own self. But this notion is not authentically Hindu. The pure gnostic monism of Vedānta admits of no ethical, meaning will-related, consequence at all, and never in ancient and medieval India was such a consequence derived from monism. The seemingly Hindu principle was established instead by the German philosopher Schopenhauer, and has become known in India through the intermediacy of the Schopenhauerian and Indologist Paul Deussen, where it is today taken by many Indians to be a bona fide part of ancient Hinduism.[12]

Historical Hinduism never attempted to derive the *dharma*-ness of *dharma* from a universal philosophical or religious principle. A philosophy of *dharma* exists only in rudimentary attempts; the thought of Kumārila is one such attempt, which I adduced and to which I will again return. Once again: the Hindu concept of *dharma* is radically empirical. To learn what *dharma* is, one must go to India, preferably to Āryāvarta, to the Āryas and observe what those who are aged, learned, well-mannered, and disciplined, unanimously accept as *dharma*. In order to establish or produce consensus, specific procedures are sometimes prescribed: the creation of committees that should consist of a certain number of members from different social groups.[13]

It is also remarkable that the previously cited Dharmasūtra text explicitly denies that gods declare or expound *dharma*. Nevertheless, *dharma* is religiously qualified, as stated. We must surmise that the Hindu concept of *dharma* developed at a time when the old polytheism collapsed and the new quasi-monotheisms had not yet assumed a fixed, conceptualized form. To the same time period falls

[11] Compare P.V. Kane, *History of Dharmaśāstra*. Vol. 2. Pt. 1 (Poona, 1941), p. 7.

[12] Compare my article in *Saeculum* 12 (1961), pp. 366ff., especially pp. 385f.

[13] *Manu* 12.110–112.

the origin of Buddhism and [100, 503] of the philosophical system of Sāṅkhya, and in both the existence of gods is not completely denied, but it is rejected that they collectively or individually have any determinate influence over the fate of humankind. In this same time, Brahmins offered sacrifices without thinking anymore that by the sacrifices higher beings were venerated or propitiated. The sacrifice was a means to the achievement of worldly or otherworldly goals that was effective in and of itself. And this sacrifice was a prominent part of *dharma*. The theory of sacrifice as part of the Hindu notion of *dharma* was in its beginnings also formulated at this time.

If one considers these historical connections, it is no wonder that *dharma* in Hinduism is innately impersonal. In later theistic Hindu religions the concept of *dharma* was, it is true, integrated in such a way that the highest god, mostly Viṣṇu, functioned as the origin, proclaimer, and protector of *dharma*; but Hindu *dharma* still never lost its impersonal quality and its independence from the deity. The connection to theism remained external and artificial. *Dharma* is not the will of a personal god or gods.

Let me recapitulate briefly: *Dharma*, based in its contents on the castes and life-stages, encompassing the entire realm of what is moral, ritual, legal, and customary, and effecting through its observance an otherworldly salvation, is not derivable from a philosophical principle or from a religious source, but rather only empirically ascertainable, whether from the Veda or from the consensus of the good with regard to geographical place.

However, there are unforeseen cases in which neither the Veda nor the accepted *smṛti* texts nor the practice of the good enable a decision about which conduct is *dharma* and which is not. What then should serve as the rule?

Here what applies is that in doubtful cases the good person follows what satisfies his heart, his own inner feeling, what he feels driven to. This is the principle of *ātmatuṣṭi*. Kumārila has once again connected this notion with the relationship of *dharma* to the Veda. He says:

> If a person ceaselessly directs his mind toward the Veda and his mind is purified by this, then what is satisfying to his heart is a yardstick in deciding what *dharma* is. If someone, over a long time, immerses himself in the Veda and in the knowledge of its contents, his imagination is formed in such a way that it follows the path determined by the Veda and cannot take a wrong turn. That is why it is taught: "Whatever thought occurs to one who knows the Veda by heart, this is a Vedic thought." Such a thought is Vedic because it is formed from the residue of what is Vedic. Just as everything that grows in the salt mines of Rūma and in the lustrous [101, 504] golden

soil of Meru becomes salt and gold, respectively, so it is with the inner condition of one who knows the Veda.[14]

I quote Kumārila's statement not only because it is a piece of *dharma* philosophy, but also because it is a typical expression of Hindu substantialism, and because this substantialism must be considered in any complete analysis of the concept of *dharma*. That the mind is "purified" and the imagination "formed" by engagement with the Veda is not to be understood psychologically in our sense. It is the psychology of Hindu substantialism. The Sanskrit text has the participle *saṃskṛta* and the noun *saṃskāra*. These words denote a transcendentally substantial "shaping", a "preparation." The comparison with mythical landscapes, where everything turns to gold or salt, makes it very clear that the Veda here is understood as a kind of substance, almost a fine stuff. When this stuff is in the mind of a man, all contents of the mind are automatically permeated by it. Therefore, everything that such a man thinks or does is automatically Vedic, filled with the substance of the Veda, and it is not necessary that he seek a specific Vedic source as an authority for his decisions.

The occurrence of the word *saṃskāra* in the excerpt translated above reveals what was understood by this word. *Saṃskāra* is also the name for the rites that accompany the life of a Hindu from conception to cremation and that form an important part of *dharma*. The sense and meaning of the *saṃskāras* has not been fully considered; they simply pertain to the "shaping" of Ārya life.[14a] The translation of *saṃskāra* by "sacrament" (recently for instance in: *India and the Eucharist*, Ernakulam: Lumen Institute 1964, p. 19ff.) is misleading. The essentially personal structure of a sacrament, namely that it is "effective from God" as an *opus operatum* and imparts grace, i.e. the "self-communication of God,"[14b] is lacking in the concept of *saṃskāra* which, as with *dharma* generally, is essentially *impersonal*.

In another comparison, the substantialism becomes even more dramatic. Kumārila says, "Just as a place that is inhabited by a sacred man becomes sacred through the contact with him – and then,

[14] Kumārila, *Tantravārttika*, *op. cit.*, p. 207 ln. 20ff.; an English translation in Jhā, pp. 187–188.

[14a] Compare P.V. Kane, *History of Dharmaśāstra*. Vol. 2. Pt. 1 (Poona, 1941): pp. 190ff.

[14b] Compare K. Rahner and H. Vorgrimler, *Kleines theologisches Wörterbuch* (Freiburg i. Br. 1961, Herder-Bücherei 108/109) under Sakrament, opus operatum, Gnade, Selbstmitteilung Gottes.

as we are convinced, becomes sanctifying itself – likewise the acts and the inner condition of those who are replete with *dharma* become dharmic, *dharma*-ful."[15] [102, 505]

This last explanation omits the reference to the Veda. According to this a man is good if the *dharma*-substance is in him, and then all his decisions and everything that seems proper to him and to which he is drawn is automatically dharmic, *dharma*-ful. The idea that Kumārila articulates here of a substantial, almost material, sacredness that is transmissible through contact is universal in Hinduism. Just as according to this idea sacredness adheres externally and is transmissible, so also, Kumārila intends, is it within the mind of an individual. If the *dharma*-substance is in it, then it colors all other contents of the mind or permeates them without requiring a conscious act.

A famous example of the application of the *ātmatuṣṭi* principle occurs in the drama *Śakuntalā* by the poet Kālidāsa.[16] King Duṣyanta doubts whether Śakuntalā, whom he loves, is also suitable for him according to caste so that he could take her as a wife. In the end he decides according to the principle of *ātmatuṣṭi*. He says: "In doubtful cases what is right for good people is that to which they feel drawn." He considers himself a good person. Certainly that does not mean in this case that he is an extraordinary knower of the Veda, but rather only that he is a noble Ārya and that the *dharma*-substance is in him. He feels drawn to Śakuntalā – therefore she must be suitable for him according to caste. This thought of the poet is accepted by the systematizer Kumārila. He explicitly cites the relevant verse from Kālidāsa's *Śakuntalā*.[17]

I have used the expression "*dharma*-substance" several times. It seems to me that it is in fact necessary for a complete understanding of the concept of *dharma* to note that the Hindus themselves thought of *dharma* by analogy with the category of substance. This is not presented explicitly and theoretically in the textbooks, but the reflections on *dharma* were not very well developed anyway. The category of substance generally prevailed in classical Hindu thought – in stark opposition to Buddhist thought which was a naturalistic actualism. A leading philosopher of Hinduism states explicitly that

[15] Kumārila, op. cit., p. 207; English translation, p. 189.

[16] Act I, Verse 22: *satāṃ hi sandehapadeṣu vastuṣu pramāṇam antaḥkaraṇapravṛttayaḥ*.

[17] Kumārila, op. cit., p. 207, ln. 10; English translation, p. 188.

the categories of quality and action are in essence also substances.[18] The classification of *dharma* under the category of substance was realized in fact, even if it was not reflexively enunciated.

Someone who has followed my argument critically may perhaps take exception to the fact that I sometimes speak of *dharma* as though it were a norm, prescription, or duty, and, by contrast, sometimes as though it were an event, a doing. But this inconsistency exists only in our [103, 506] habitual ways of thinking. It follows directly from the substantialism of the conception of *dharma*. We must imagine *dharma* as primarily a substance or a transcendental, immaterial thing. This substance, this immaterial thing is first of all in concrete duties, as they are passed down as fixed norms and prescriptions – indeed, these norms *are dharma*, that is, *dharma before its performance*. Because these norms already *are dharma*, however, *dharma* before its performance actually does not correspond to our concepts "norm," "rule," "law," or "duty." All of these are far too abstract. *Dharma* is rather a concrete *model of behavior* with positive significance for salvation that somehow exists already before its performance and waits for realization, or rather it is a collection of such models. Dharma *in performance* then is conduct that corresponds to this model, *adharma* conduct that deviates from it. Finally, the *dharma*-substance exists also *after performance* as the realized model of behavior. It is something like a doing that is congealed into a transcendental active ingredient, the substance of a done deed. Deed is *karman* in Sanskrit, and by this is understood not only the deed in performance, but also the transcendental residue of the deed that adheres to the doer as *dharma* or *adharma*. It is in this sense that one speaks of good or bad *karman*. *Karman*, the substance of done deeds, makes its impact according to the Hindu belief in human fate, and mainly in future existences only, in the course of the soul's transmigration. This notion gives rise to the popular way of speaking that *karman* can sometimes mean something like "fate."

The effect of the done deed happens automatically. By the power of its own internal quality, the performed *dharma* or *adharma* determines the kind, content, and course of rebirth in the next existence. Not, however, such that man is absolutely predetermined. There is always a realm of freewill in which new *karman*, new *dharma* or *adharma*, can be accumulated.

---

[18] Śaṅkara, *Brahmasūtrabhāṣya* 2.2.17.

One cannot therefore speak here of a "reward" of the good deed, nor in fact of "merit" (although such expressions are often used in translations of Indic works), because reward and merit presuppose a judging person, a rewarding God. There is no room for this, however, in the mechanism of *dharma–adharma*'s functioning. True, Hindu theism had tried in various ways to grant an influence on *karman*-events to the highest god. But just as it was difficult for the Hindu to be in a position to understand *dharma* consequently as the will of God, so also was it difficult for him to conceptualize the effects of a performed or omitted *dharma* as a reward or punishment of merit or fault. The role of the highest god in the mechanism of *dharma–adharma* causality remained that of an essentially superfluous overseer. This mechanism, in the same way as the hypertrophic substantialism, did not permit a theistic personalism to develop. Only from the substantialism of the [104, 507] conception of *dharma* in connection with the notion that *dharma* exists before, during, and after its performance can it be understood how it is that, as the texts say, *dharma* can "decrease." This can mean that the norms are no longer followed. But it can also mean that *dharma* after its performance, good *karman*, decays, as in the passage from the *Āpastamba-Dharmasūtra* to which I earlier referred. There it is said that even if worldly benefit is not acquired by an act of *dharma*, nevertheless *dharma* does not decrease. That does not mean, as one European translator (Bühler) said, that "at least the sacred duties have been fulfilled."[18a] Rather what is meant is that even if worldly benefit or gain is not obtained, nevertheless the performed *dharma* is preserved undiminished as an active ingredient, as it were, for a coming existence, so long as the model of *dharma* is unfailingly fulfilled.

I had already stated at the outset that *dharma* had a connection to salvation. But does not salvation, in the theistic religions of Hinduism, have something to do with the highest god and is not salvation in Hindu monism identical with that self-realized true self of man? How does the salvation that is achieved by action relate to the salvation that theism or monism promise?

Viewed historically, these different ideas are in fact distinct and they originally belong to different spheres. One who adhered to the

---

[18a] [Translator's Note]: The quote comes from Georg Bühler's translation (1879) in the Sacred Books of the East, 1.7.20.4 which reads in full: "But if (worldly advantages) are not produced, (then at least) the sacred duties have been fulfilled." The recent translation of Olivelle (2000) reads: "Even if he does not obtain them, at least no harm is done to the Law."

specific religion of *dharma* wanted in fact to achieve the highest salvation by means of *dharma*, just as the theist by means of the worship of god and the monist by means of a gnostic realization of total unity. There are passages in the older Hindu literature for which salvation through *dharma* is truly what is final and highest – liberation. However, a broad stream of Hindu thought running through many schools and groups united both ideas of salvation into one system of rank and established a value relation between them. There it is taught that a salvation achievable by acts of *dharma* is merely a relative and transient one. It imparts to man an existence in the divine heaven and in the best circumstance he can be reborn as the god Brahmā. But this glory is fleeting. When the substance of his accomplished *dharma* is exhausted, a man must again descend to earth, even if only after millions of years. Ultimate salvation, whether conceived theistically or monistically, is not achievable by doing *dharma*. *Dharma* does not remain the highest value in the religion. In the rank of the goals of life it is subordinated to liberation. The different schools and religions of Hinduism teach variously about the path to liberation. The concept of *dharma* overlaps therefore only partially with that of religion. There are areas of what is religious that extend beyond *dharma*, namely the teachings of the highest god, of the human soul, of the relationship of god to the world and mankind, and of ultimate salvation, as well as the practices that were to lead to eternal liberation. [105, 508] Also, apart from certain compromises and accommodations, the area of Yoga, which is certainly assigned to religion, is not connected to *dharma*. Furthermore, one does not call mythology *dharma*. If, on the other hand, *dharma* also covers areas such as civil law, criminal law and the law of the absolute monarchical government, then we would be inclined to exclude these from what is religious; but since *dharma* is always oriented toward an otherworldly salvation, these areas too are included in what is religious. That does not mean that they are related to *God*, but the fulfillment or the breach of *dharma* here also has an orientation toward salvation.

The incongruence of *dharma* and religion is first and foremost to be explained historically. There is a religiousness of *dharma*, for which *dharma* is the whole religion, and this Dharmism belongs especially to a certain period. Other areas of religion by contrast developed later or in different circles than did Dharmism. But the balancing, adapting, and harmonizing thinking that was always at work in Ārya-ness or

Hinduism led to the fact that the concept of *dharma* remained valid in all schools and groups and views and religions. Even when *dharma* was relativized, it was still always regarded as an inescapable preliminary to liberation. Most appropriately, we should perhaps describe the process of intellectual history that has occurred in this case in such a way that the theistic religions as well as monism were able to supercede the earlier periods only by incorporating the mechanism, substantialism, and impersonalism of the concept of *dharma*.

The concept of Hindu *dharma* – viewed historically, we should preferably say, the concept of Ārya *dharma* – appears to have come first into clear awareness in the disputes with Buddhism. For this reason, the orientation to the Veda was always emphasized because Buddhism differentiated itself in no clearer manner from the Ārya religion than by its rejection of the Veda. It is the self-awareness of Ārya-ness that is expressed in the concept of *dharma*, and, initially, a self-awareness of a particular period of intellectual history. Therefore, the marks of its period of origin are preserved in the concept of *dharma*. These marks include above all the fact that the connection to the gods and the teachings of the gods were secondary in religious consciousness, in contrast to rites and ceremonies which were of totally dominant importance for otherworldly salvation; they include furthermore the fact that the quasi-monotheistic and the monistic movements with their notion of salvation that transcends the ritual had not yet prevailed. Later the *dharma* texts did indeed also make compromises with these notions.

As an expression of the self-awareness of Ārya-ness, the concept of *dharma* was preserved over time, with several accommodations of more advanced ideas, [106, 509] but still little changed at its core. It was, in all its indeterminacy and in its empiricism, the unifying link of Ārya-ness, the one thing that held together the multiformity of Hindu-ness. In this function, it has stood the test of time even after the incursion of Islam.

Today, to be sure, this old concept of *dharma* can no longer fulfill this function. Although since the end of the last century it has become common to speak of the unity of Hinduism, the establishment of this unity has been attempted by means other than the old concept of *dharma*. This concept is no longer useful because it contains so much that people no longer want to adhere to today, for example, the fundamental commitment to castes, life-stages, and geographical places. Sometimes today a new meaning is being given to the word *dharma*. Into that, however, I cannot go further.[19]

ACKNOWLEDGEMENTS

My thanks to Oliver Freiberger who meticulously checked and corrected my draft translation and saved me from at least one major mis-step. Thanks also to the *Zeitschrift für Missionswissenschaft und Religionswissenschaft* for permission to publish this translation.

TRANSLATOR'S APPENDIX: BIBLIOGRAPHIC NOTE

Hacker's essay on *dharma* in Hinduism has been very influential in German Indology, but, until recently, not among English-speaking Indologists. The curious history of its punctuated influence on the field generally may be seen through the work of several notable scholars who make reference to the essay. Most recently, Wezler's 1999 (English 2004) study of *dharma* is in many respects an extension of and commentary upon Hacker's article, with particular attention the differentiation of the *dharma* of the Veda and the Dharmaśāstra. Wezler writes that "Hacker's designation of Hindu *dharma* as 'radically empirical' caused an effect within Indology" (2004, p. 649, fn 3), and points to the work of Hartmut Scharfe (1989) and Hans-Joachim Klimkeit (1981) as examples. Paul Horsch's essay (1967) appears to be something of a counterpoint or a response to Hacker's in that its description of *dharma* as a mythological and cosmological order directly conflicts with Hacker's sense of *dharma* as radically empirical. Horsch takes up the etymological and Vedic notions of *dharma* that were ignored by Hacker as uninteresting. The two articles of Hacker and Horsch seem to have served as standard references for two distinctive views

[19] Compare my article in this journal, Vol. 42 (1958), p. 1ff. [Translator's note]: The article in question, "Dharma im Neuhinduismus" has been translated by Wilhelm Halbfass in *Philology and Confrontation: Paul Hacker on Traditional and Modern Vedānta* (Hacker, 1995, 257–272).

of the semantic history of *dharma* in German Indological literature for the last 40 years.

Surprisingly, I have found no references to the articles of Hacker and Horsch in the work of three luminaries in the study of the Dharmaśāstra, Derrett, Lingat, and Rocher, despite the fact that all three read and/or published in German. It is, furthermore, regrettable that the very influential ethnosociology pioneered by McKim Marriott (1990) and articulated most effectively by several of his students never acknowledged or engaged with Hacker's arguments concerning Hindu substantialism.

It appears that Wilhelm Halbfass's *India and Europe* (1988) provided the first major bridge to English for both Hacker's and Horsch's ideas. One should also mention Clooney's important discussion of both Halbfass and Hacker (1990: 150–159). The recent special issue of the *Journal of Indian Philosophy* dedicated to *dharma* contains a translation of Horsch's article and other articles that build upon the framework outlined by Horsch (Olivelle, 2004; Brereton, 2004) as well as reflections on Hacker by Wezler (2004) and Fitzgerald (2004). The "effect" of these two articles within German Indology seems to be repeating itself in Anglophone Indology, though the reasons for the delay in taking notice of these two seminal studies of *dharma* in English works are not clear. Whatever the reasons for the delay, this presentation of Hacker's essay in English translation is intended to bring his thought-provoking formulations to a wider academic audience and to rekindle the same kind of excitement and critical reaction inspired by the essay's original publication.

REFERENCES

Brereton, J.P. (2004). '*Dhármam* in the *Ṛgveda*'. *Journal of Indian Philosophy* **32**, 449–489.

Bühler, G. (1879). *The Sacred Laws of the Âryas: As Taught in the Schools of Âpastamba, Gautama, Vâsishtha, and Baudhâyana. Sacred Books of the East*. vol. 2, Oxford: Clarendon Press.

Clooney, F.X. (1990). Thinking Ritually: Rediscovering the Pūrva Mīmāṃsā Sūtras of Jaimini. Vienna: De Nobili.

Fitzgerald, J. (2004). '*Dharma* and its Translation in the *Mahābhārata*'. *Journal of Indian Philosophy* **32**, 671–685.

Hacker, P. (1995). In W. Halbfass (ed.), *Philology and Confrontation: Paul Hacker on Traditional and Modern Vedānta*. Albany: SUNY Press.

Halbfass, W. (1988). *India and Europe: An Essay in Philosophical Understanding*. Albany: SUNY Press.

Horsch, P. (2004). 'From Creation Myth to World Law: The Early History of Dharma'. *Journal of Indian Philosophy* **32**, 423–448.
Klimkeit, H.-J. (1981). *Der politische Hinduismus: Indische Denker zwischen religöser Reform und politischem Erwachen*. Harrassowitz: Wiesbaden.
Marriott, M. ed. (1990). *India through Hindu Categories*. New Delhi: Sage.
Olivelle, P. (2004). 'The Semantic History of Dharma: The Middle and Late Vedic Periods'. *Journal of Indian Philosophy* **32**, 491–511.
Olivelle, P. (2000). *Dharmasūtras: The Law Codes of Āpastamba, Gautama, Baudhāyana, and Vasiṣṭha*. Delhi: Motilal Banarsidass.
Scharfe, H. (1989). *The State in Indian Tradition*. Brill: Leiden.
Wezler, A. (2004). '*Dharma* in the Veda and the Dharmaśāstras'. *Journal of Indian Philosophy* **32**, 629–654.

Translated by

Donald R. Davis, Jr.
Department of Languages & Cultures of Asia
University of Wisconsin
1244 Van Hise, 1220 Linden Dr
Madison, WI 53706
USA
608-890-0138
608-265-3538 (FAX)
E-mail: drdavis@wisc.edu

[illegible] [illegible]